A History of
Afro-American
Literature ～Volume I

The Long Beginning, 1746–1895

Blyden Jackson

LOUISIANA STATE UNIVERSITY PRESS *Baton Rouge and London*

98 97 96 95 94 93 92 91 90   5 4 3 2

Designer: Patricia Douglas Crowder
Typeface: Linotron 202 Goudy Old Style
Typesetter: G & S Typesetters, Inc.
Printer: Thomson-Shore, Inc.
Binder: John H. Dekker & Sons, Inc.

LIBRARY OF CONGRESS CATALOGING-IN-PUBLICATION DATA
Jackson, Blyden.
   The history of Afro-American literature.

   Bibliography: v. 1, p.
   Includes index.
   Contents: v. 1. The long beginning, 1746–1895.
   1. American literature—Afro-American authors—
History and criticism.   2. Afro-Americans—Intellectual
life.   I. Title.
PS153.N5J33   1989   810'.9'896073   88-26603
ISBN 0-8071-1511-8 (v. 1: alk. paper)

The paper in this book meets the guidelines for permanence and durability of the Committee on Production Guidelines for Book Longevity of the Council on Library Resources. ∞

This publication has been supported by the National Endowment for the Humanities, a federal agency which supports the study of such fields as history, philosophy, literature, and languages.

To my father, who taught history, and to my wife, devoted comrade of my labors on this book

Contents

Acknowledgments

Ever since I began even to think of writing this book, I have been able to count on encouragement and excellent advice from Beverly Jarrett, associate director and executive editor of Louisiana State University Press, whom I am happy to regard (properly, I am sure) as a long-standing friend of mine. To my great good fortune, the editing of the manuscript of this book was entrusted to Catherine Landry. She has provided me with every assistance I could possibly desire. On some matters of research I owe a special debt to the staff of the humanities reference division of the library of the University of North Carolina at Chapel Hill.

A History of Afro-American Literature, Volume I

Introduction

It is possible to argue that the story of black Americans and, therefore, of Afro-American literature, should be considered to extend at least as far back into the West's historic past as A.D. 1441. In that year Antam Gonçalvez, a young Portuguese sea captain—the chronicler Zurara calls him "very young"—who had managed to push his ship down to the southernmost latitude of Morocco's Atlantic coast, captured some Africans. Homeward bound, his vessel fell in with the ship of another young Portuguese, Nuño Tristão. Tristão joined with Gonçalvez in capturing additional Africans. So, Gonçalvez and Tristão disembarked in Lisbon with twelve Africans on whom they had fastened the status of slaves. These Africans, incidentally, were not blacks, but probably olive-complected Moors. Unwittingly, however, the two young captains had initiated what was to become the greatest forced migration in the annals of the human race. They had started the Atlantic slave trade.

In actual fact Gonçalvez and Tristão harbored, probably, little permanent interest in either slavery or the slave trade. Their overweening concern undoubtedly was their desire to advance their standing with Dom Enrique, Prince Henry the Navigator, whose ardent dream they shared of finding an oceanic passage to the Far East, barred from access by land to Europeans like themselves ever since the Ottoman Turks had established their hegemony in the Middle East. Prince Henry (who was no friend to blacks) died in 1460, but not his dream. In 1486 the Portuguese Bartholomeu Diaz reached the tip of Africa closest to Antarctica and rounded it. His sovereign named the promontory there the Cape of Good Hope. Twelve years later, ten months and twelve days after sailing out of Lisbon, still another Portuguese, the twenty-eight-year-old Vasco da Gama, anchored at Calcutta. Meanwhile, in 1492, the Genoan Christopher Columbus, sailing west in the employ of Spain, had "discovered" America. The age of European exploration was well on its way. In 1522, eighteen of an original 239 Europeans whose leader, the Portuguese Ferdinand Magellan, also sailing for Spain, had lost his life in the Philippines, returned home after three long years, in which 220 of their comrades, in addition to Magellan, and 4 of their 5 ships had been lost, to be able to claim that they had, by circling back to their port of embarkation, voyaged completely around the globe, the first men ever to accomplish such a feat. Other Europeans, as the decades and centuries passed, continued in the tradition of Diaz, da Gama, Columbus, and Magellan until, even at the Poles, virtually no place on this earth remained uncharted by man. In scientifically highly ingenious projects executed by Russians and, later, by Americans of European stock, twentieth-century European exploration finally burst beyond the physical confines of earth itself and penetrated daringly into realms of space beyond our planet's atmospheric reach. More than girdling the globe, it now stretches toward the stars.

But to speak of European exploration (great though it be) is, or can be, to introduce a much more complicated phenomenon, European expansionism, within which European exploration has constituted only one of at least three often complementary and even interdependent forms of enterprise. For, time and again, Europeans did not simply go places to which they had not been. Sometimes they followed their initial entry and succeeding survey—their exploration—with conquest, if not also with colonization as well. Where fairly dense populations already existed, as in India, China, and much of Africa, the intrusive Europeans tended to content themselves largely with conquest only. Even the English away from England who lived long in India, for example, never became Indians in too significant a sense, despite the Indian food, clothes, customs, and women they sometimes added to their lives. They were, as would be future countrymen of theirs sipping apéritifs in dinner jackets in the tropics, unrelentingly Britishers sojourning, decidedly in proconsular fashion, abroad. Typically, children born to them on Indian soil were sent home to England to be educated.

Vast, comparatively uninhabited territories, as in North America (not including Mexico and the American Southwest), Australia, and the islands of New Zealand, invited the colonization as well. To Europeans who came to them, these places presented what seemed almost perfectly designed opportunities for acquiring wealth and power over others, and with good reason, therefore, in such tempting situations, Europeans did not hesitate to augment and intensify their conquest with colonization. In a departure from a rule, Spaniards and Portuguese colonized quickly portions of the Western Hemisphere already heavily populated by Indians like the Aztecs, the Mayas, and the Incas. The Englishmen, however, who outraced other Europeans to a long stretch of America's Atlantic shore, found there an almost ideal set of circumstances for their colonization, as well as conquest, of a "new" land. When a hundred or so of these Englishmen arrogated unto themselves, in 1607, a settlement at Jamestown, there may not have been quite 300,000 Indians in all of the present United States east of the Mississippi and the country beyond the river's western bank. These Englishmen learned at once, of course, that they would not get rich, as some of them had, however naïvely, at least half actually believed, from picking up huge pieces of pure gold off the bare American ground and, as genuine Croesuses, returning with such easily appropriated plunder to lord it over other Englishmen in England. They came to understand that they would have to stay in America and work, sweatily for some time, or get someone similarly to work along with, or under, them (or, as they actually did, do both), if they were to make any fortune from the land that lay so open to them. But they also came to understand, clearly and most persuasively, that, although some of them had been the very dregs of society in Europe, given a sufficient supply of labor—theirs, and possibly, others'—they could prosper in America as fully as if they were, in the most direct sense, removing gold from a literal eldorado.

It ill serves, then, the muse of history or the interests of truth to speak disparagingly of the amount of sheer muscular energy contributed by such English men and women, their descendants, and other whites to the making of modern America. Even so, many of the toilers in America, especially those who were, under duress, working for others than themselves, almost from America's very birth have been black. The first of these black toilers were born, of course, in Africa. America was to them—these dark-skinned aliens brought here by the trade of which Gonçalvez and Tristão had been, more or less, the founding fathers—a foreign soil, a land to which they came without choice from lands they had shown no disposition of their own to leave. They could, and did, remember another world, vestiges of which, as was to be expected, they could not fail but bear across the ocean to their new homes as part of the identities they had already formed. What, however, would survive in America of their already existing selves—the Africa—they brought with them was undoubtedly affected by their number (or actually, rather, their relative lack of number) and by the chronology of their infusion into the populace of the developing state of America. For, while it is true that, through the agency of the Atlantic slave trade, millions of Africans born in Africa did end up as slaves in the Western Hemisphere, it is also true that, most appreciably in relative terms, very few of those millions were transported without interruption to the country we call America. Likewise, this relative few almost all came, in effect, at the same time, during the eighteenth century, particularly in its last three quarters.

The Atlantic slave trade in all that it encompassed unquestionably did last for a much longer time than merely any one century. Indeed, it continued from 1502 until well past the middle of the 1800s, when, incidentally, our Civil War was over. Estimates of the Africans it shipped on its famous Middle Passage, its route over water, have run as high as 25 million. Yet Philip Curtin, a careful scholar, sedulously weighing what seems to him the most acceptable evidence, concludes that, in sum, the Atlantic slave trade conveyed to the Americas 9,566,100 native Africans. He further concludes that, of this number, only 399,000 were brought to our part of the New World rather than to other parts of the Americas where Europeans were planting colonies.[1] He thus agrees with authoritative opinion on this subject as it stands at the present. Robert Fogel and Stanley Engerman, for example, in their *Time on the Cross*, stipulate that all of the native Africans involved as articles of merchandise in the Atlantic slave trade reached, in the aggregate, 9,500,000, essentially Curtin's figure, while also specifying that this trade, of its victims, delivered 40 percent to the Caribbean Islands, 38 percent to Brazil, 17 percent to Spanish America, and only about 6 percent (or less than 600,000) to mainland North America.[2] Speaking, hence, in figures easy to recall and sufficiently accurate for a comprehensive picture of the Atlantic slave trade not exceedingly fine in detail, about a half a million Africans over the whole period of the Atlantic slave trade were landed on our shores by ships which transported native Africans to North America straight from Africa. It may well have been, moreover, that only a small trickle of this

---

1. Philip D. Curtin, *The Atlantic Slave Trade: A Census* (Madison, Wis., 1969), 268.
2. Robert Fogel and Stanley Engerman, *Time on the Cross: The Economics of American Negro Slavery* (2 vols.; Boston, 1974), I, 15, 14. Some minute looseness with fractions accounts for these percentages adding up to one more than a hundred.

half a million, not even a thousand, or too many hundred, were thus transported before 1700. Curtin concedes that 51,000, one out of ten, of them may have been smuggled in to mainland America after 1811.[3]

In 1980 about 26.5 million Negroes did live in the United States, more than 50 each for every native African whom the Atlantic slave trade brought directly here. While the Atlantic slave trade flourished, some native Africans, it must be admitted, after being taken first to the West Indies, where, to use the language slavers would have used, they were kept a while for "seasoning," were eventually resold into this country. Even had there been as many of these "seasoned" transplants as of native Africans brought directly here—and there were not, by a difference, except in our North, no less, probably, than ten to one—the size of the present Negro population of the United States would still be so great in comparison with any original native-African base as to undoubtedly indicate (and underscore) the American nativity of the American Negro. He came to this country, however lacking in self-determination he may have been, during this country's earliest period of receiving, other than Indians, its present ethnic groups. The first census of the United States, completed in 1790, enumerated 757,208 of his kind, a number already then in excess of the half a million Negroes who we repeat it has been rather convincingly demonstrated were all of the Negroes brought here directly from Africa. According to selected national censuses subsequent to the census of 1790, there were 1,002,037 Negroes in America in 1800; 1,771,656 in 1820; 2,873,648 in 1840; and 4,441,830 in 1860. The approximately six times greater number of Negroes in America in 1980 than in 1860 is attributable to the same cause as the very existence of most of the three quarters of a million Negroes living in America when America's first census was taken, to natural increase—in other words, to the Negroes who were born, brought up, perhaps delivered of children, and certainly permitted to die in America, not to any inundation of Negroes born elsewhere, in Africa or the West Indies, and then imported here. It was always possible, it is true, on some plantation of the antebellum South (or even, it may have been, in some town of the antebellum North), to encounter a "salt-water Negro," as Negroes born in Africa were once sometimes known. But long before the last living signer of the Declaration of Independence had drawn his dying breath, it was far from probable. And all "salt-water Negroes" in America tended,

3. Curtin, *The Atlantic Slave Trade,* 268.

always and everywhere, from within a generation of the "twenty negars" landed at Jamestown in 1619 (the first Negroes to live here), to be a minority of themselves and their fellow blacks before they joined their own ancestors who had perished in Africa far across the sea.

As early as 1820, the year of the Missouri Compromise, the typical American Negro not only knew nothing from his own immediate personal experience of Africa. Neither did his parents. On virtually absolute terms an American environment has supplied all but a notably minuscule fraction (less than 1 percent) of Afro-Americans with the physical setting of their entire lives. Only the two so-called world wars of the present century have provided occasions when any contingent of these Afro-Americans larger than the population of a hamlet has resided for sufficient time in some country other than America to savor with a degree of intimacy beyond that of a tourist a non-American environment.

Yet, as overwhelmingly and intensely American as have been both the Negro American's nativity and the environment which has surrounded and almost exclusively conditioned him, America has not treated blacks as it has other Americans. The "twenty negars" (originally John Rolfe's phrase) left at Jamestown in 1619 remain shadowy figures for the historian. They were passengers against their wills on a Dutch privateer of no name in the record of its Jamestown visit. Whence came this vessel to execute its sortie into Jamestown, where it acquired the Negroes in its possession (although almost surely not from any place in Africa), and what course it set after tarrying only briefly, once it transacted its business, in the estuary of the James River and turning again, apparently, toward the open sea, are no less matters of mystery than its name. What is not so mysterious is that it did not sell the Negroes with whom it parted for cash, but bartered them for food, and what has been strongly conjectured, on the basis of quite persuasive evidence, is that these same Negroes were inducted into the life of Jamestown, not as chattel slaves, but as indentured servants—with, therefore, precisely the same status at the start of their existence in America as a notable percentage of the whites who entered America from western Europe while America was still in its embryonic phase.

Indentured servitude did not necessarily blight the life of an immigrant to early America. Such servitude was a class distinction, temporarily attached to whoever bore it, and could be far overcome. As a matter of fact, since it bonded only labor—and that for a term hardly ever exceeding five or seven years—the spectacle of an indentured servant who, somehow, did not remove his indenture would have then occasioned, in the eyes of contemporary observers, perhaps more genuine wonder than the sight of that same person free of his indenture and prospering, however auspiciously, as a respected pillar of a relatively fluid society. There came a rather long period, indeed, in the pre-Revolutionary era, which was dominated by New World old families like the Byrds of Westover and the Carters of Corotoman, when over half of the members of the lower chamber of Virginia's haughty House of Burgesses, according to the most reliable estimates, were persons once indentured. But during the same period all the members of both chambers of the Burgesses were white. The identical state (up to, and probably including, social equality) of blacks and whites in America did not weather American aversion to blacks even for a generation. By 1663 Maryland had adopted a law which established chattel slavery in that colony and made it clear that bondage for life—*durante vita,* the statute explicitly said—was Maryland's preferred prescription for every Negro. Virginia adopted a similar statute within this same decade. Also, in 1662 Virginia had legislated that "any [white] christian . . . commit[ting] Fornication [note where the capital letters are, and are not, in this quotation] with a negro man or woman" should pay double the usual fine. Only ten years later Maryland banned by law marriages between whites and blacks. Throughout colonial America, accordingly, well before the advent of the eighteenth century, two institutions, slavery and color caste, had been devised which did blight black American lives and which certainly profaned every claim of justice and equality associated with the professed idealism of American democracy.

The day of slavery in America is over. The day of color caste is not. Obviously, for a quite long time in American life, the two aided and abetted each other. Which of them in their close collaboration while slavery still existed was the greater source of indignity and discomfort for the Negro conceivably can be argued at some length. Supporting, however, the conclusion that, of the two, color caste may be the more accountable for the stigmatization of the Negro in America is the mountainous array of evidence which suggests that, entirely without a shred of help, unless in the form of memory, from formally declared slavery, color caste has, now for more than a century, preserved so largely intact enough of America's time-honored constraints upon America's Negroes as to cause many of those Negroes to feel very much as if they still were slaves. The one huge, omnipresent, obsessive nagging prepossession, therefore, of a state of mind shared by all blacks in America for over three hundred years, whatever their wealth or class or individual temperament, and wherever they have lived, has been a keen consciousness of color caste—a consciousness hardly reprehensible, and certainly not paranoid, since it has represented a reaction to a reality no one can say is only a figment of someone's imagination. It does not matter, interestingly enough, that color caste remains, as it has always been, an important factor in their lives of which only the merest handful of black Americans have ever been aware by the appellation "color caste," nor does it matter to any greater degree that white Americans have been no freer in their familiar discourse with the use of these particular two words than have American blacks. Americans of every color all have known, unerringly and well, as if they had imbibed certain rather cabalistic lore with their mothers' milk, precisely the specific customs and laws, as well as sentiments and attitudes, which have coalesced with one another to make color caste, as it were, in America, universally a highly prosperous enterprise. All of these Americans have tended readily to infer correctly, for example—however they may have differed in race, religion, social class, level of intelligence, regional location, and time of birth—the significance as American behavior of the tolerance in America for miscegenation (provided only that it involves white males and black females) and the clearly related intolerance, of orthodox Americans, for intermarriage, an intolerance classically articulated in the question with supposedly only one acceptable answer, "Would you (unless you were also black) want your daughter to marry a Negro?"

If all black Americans have tended to be bitter about color caste, no group has tended to be so bitter about it, as no group has tended to sense it more, than the black Americans who have contributed to Afro-American literature. These black Americans have written, in J. Saunders Redding's fine and fitting phrase, a "literature of necessity." Their involvement with color caste, an involvement full (for them) of anguish and a constant admixture of rage, has been the force above all else responsible for the coherence of their group expression and for the development by them of a literature which can be called both theirs and the literature of all black Americans. In their common passion they have found a common cause, the cause of racial protest (really the cause of opposition to color caste), and as they have kept *au courant* with their external world the terms of that protest (that opposition), they have manifested in common their adjustments to the changes in the political and social climate of America which have primarily determined the shape as well as the content of their literature. So they have, in effect, divided their literature into its ages, or periods. But so, also, they have established the continuities which have made their literature both racially distinctive and yet, if only because of where they were born and how they were bred, unmistakably American in all its quintessential qualities.

As much of a vade mecum, however, as is the strain of racial protest in almost all Afro-American literature, it appeared only after a moment of absence in the work of America's first black writers. Nothing of authorship by a black hand has come down to us from America's seventeenth century. At the beginning of the eighteenth century, approximately a quarter of a million "Americans" lived in America, among them, sparse as they were, blacks numbering (as we have seen) only in the hundreds. America grew marvelously, for that day, within the century. By 1800 over five million people considered themselves inhabitants of the fledgling United States. Natural increase, incidentally, played the same major role in the growth of the total population of early America as it played (and continues to play) in the growth of black America. In any case, black writers did begin to write in America by the middle of the eighteenth century. They wrote in English, using the language of by far the majority of the white Americans around them. And they wrote, also, very deliberately as faithful students of the models of literary composition in letters, pamphlets, periodicals, books, and documents of various kinds available to them for their perusal in the written exercises of the whites, so much more numerous than they, whose ways of doing things were the overriding influences in shaping the blacks' habits of conduct in their own lives. As these black writers, or their parents or parents' parents, had once been apprentices in a strange land in the learning of a strange and new language, so the writers were now apprentices in the learning of a strange and wonderful new skill. They were, indeed, in what can well be called, for black literature, the Age of Apprenticeship. Soon enough, it would be true, protest would creep into their utterance. But the utterance itself, the simple making of it in a fashion which could be labeled a success, was, at first, their sole preoccupation and their prime concern. Nothing else was, for them, with respect to what they wrote, so important. They were substantially engrossed in a process of mimesis. Even the themes they most affected, as of the perfidy of Indians or the providence of Abraham's Almighty God, were there for them to find in the previously written white literature from which they were copying the ways and means of a special kind of literacy. There would be black writers of many kinds to follow them. But there would never again be black writers so white.

One way to differentiate these first Afro-American writers from their immediate successors, although all but two of the early writers were born in the North, is to think of these early black writers as living in an America with a Jeffersonian South. Their immediate successors would come of age and practice the profession of literature in what might well be called the America of the Calhoun South. There were planters and a planters' aristocracy in the Jeffersonian South, just as there were slaves and slave unrest, including, before Jefferson's death, two of the three best-known of American slave revolts. But there was, in the Jeffersonian South, no cotton kingdom and little, if any, of the rift between the North and South which would eventually lead to a clash of arms. When Washington—like Jefferson, a Virginian—was sworn in as America's first president, Virginia was America's most populous state and would not be superseded in that regard until 1820 by New York. Philadelphia, with forty thousand inhabitants, was America's most populous town. Next to it in size, in descending order, were New York City, Boston, and Charleston. Land, its ownership or profitable sale, and ocean commerce, alike all over America, north and south, were the royal roads to wealth, prestige, and power. The Virginians had been longer on those roads than other Americans. Philadelphia, New York, and Boston in the North, and Charleston in the South, had done better from their connections with the sea than other American seaports. But no Americans differed greatly from any other Americans in their concept of the good life and how to get it because of where they lived or who they were. The codfish aristocracy of Massachusetts, the Dutch patroons of the Hudson Valley, the Pennsylvania Quaker merchants, and the landed gentry of tidewater Virginia and lowland South Carolina all believed in the efficacy for the would-be opulent of huge acquisitions, under favorable terms, of land which could be farmed or speculatively sold, or of argosies which returned to him who sent them out with their worth in gold multiplied several fold. Ubiquitously, moreover, in the American world, where such redoubtable mercantilists were uniformly the upper class, uniformly the humbler Americans, much like Jefferson's proverbial yeoman, lived on farms which were scattered clearings in the great American forest or at crossroad settlements where, perhaps, not a dozen timbered edifices huddled around a tavern. Industry in this America uniformly was handicraft, performed at workplaces in, or near, their homes by artisans or by wives and daughters providing for a family's domestic wants. Often in such a world, relations with a slave could hardly be invested with the impersonalities which might permit that slave to become too much of an abstraction on a huge estate.

Washington was still president and the South still Jeffersonian when the Connecticut Yankee Eli Whitney, tutoring in Georgia, invented the cotton gin (short for cotton-cleaning-engine: it relieved the cotton of its seed) and, thus, altogether unwittingly initiated the chain of events out of which emerged the Calhoun South. It took a while (as W. J. Cash engagingly demonstrates in *The Mind of the South*) after the invention of the gin for the Calhoun South to form.[4] A realization of the monumental increase in the marketability of cotton made possible by the gin required no time at all. But the Calhoun South, a South to be ruled by one staple crop, needed land, space for the growth and harvesting of the billions of fleecy white bolls on which a new eldorado was to be founded. Much— too much, it seemed to many—of the soil of the southern states along the Atlantic seaboard was already shorn of its fertility. Moreover, the South along the seaboard was obviously limited in its extent. The dreamers about cotton turned west toward the South beyond the barrier of the Appalachians. But they did not turn west at all on the same terms as their fellow Americans who were prospecting through the old Northwest Territory and into the upper reaches of the Louisiana Purchase. The westering southerners were committed to the raising of their one staple crop, cotton, ideally under conditions that would compel from them no moves which would hinder their consignment of all their eggs into a single basket. Their system would be in place by approximately a full generation after the invention of the gin and would impenetrate and render relatively monolithic both the old antebellum South along the coastal plain and the new antebellum South the rich bottomlands of which were the great lure for the younger sons hurrying away from their homes in the east.

Before the hegemony of this new version of the South—this, as we have called it, Calhoun South—some of the region's leaders had spoken of slavery as a wrong and an aberration which, in free America, would die a natural death. As late as 1827, indeed, of abolitionist societies in America only 24, with a membership of 1,500, were in the North, far

4. W. J. Cash, *The Mind of the South* (New York, 1941). See all of the first chapter, "Of Time and Frontiers."

less than the 130, with a membership of 6,625, which were in the South.[5] But slavery was crucial to the Calhoun South. Its defense—and, more, its extension in time and space—became, therefore, a categorical imperative and a monomania which crazed, at all too highly feverish a pitch, not only large southern slave owners but also such supposedly disinterested representatives of morality and ethics as southern educators and southern clergy. Meanwhile, slavery had ceased to be crucial at all in the North. Indeed, there it was no longer legal anywhere after 1829. The Industrial Revolution had started in England almost (albeit for no significant reason) coterminously with the American Revolution. The North, however, was to adopt and exploit this radical reformation of Western living so quickly and so ingeniously as to foreshadow, even in the infancy of America's modern industry, the American North's ultimate displacement as the empire of industrial empires of the very England where the Industrial Revolution had been born. As the North grew more sectional, it would become a citadel of manufacture. The land that opened to the northern west presented its beckoning frontier as free soil where free farmers, using machinery, as did northern factories, could (and would) raise corn, wheat, beef, and pork, as well as other products, to feed the New World and the Old. In the North, turnpikes and canals would begin to solve the problem of transportation. Then would come, along with steamboats, the railroads, on many more miles of track than in the South, which would have railroads, too, but never the equal of the tracks and trains that tied the North to the West, as to ocean ports which would carry northern goods around the globe. By 1830 the Jeffersonian South was dead, and the Calhoun South, as sectional now as the North, but decidedly not industrial in character, was on the move to consolidate its own peculiar interests and crush all dissent within its borders—if, too ominously, not elsewhere—so that no southerner who did not adulate the cotton kingdom and countenance slavery would be considered at all safe or tolerable in his southern neighbor's eyes.

By 1830, also, the first age of Afro-American literature was over. A different age was making its way in. Protest had come virtually to govern and inflame the utterance of all black writers. It was protest the major object of attack of which was slavery and the powers, far from least of them the Calhoun South, which supported slavery. The writers who

---

5. Benjamin Lundy, *Genius of Universal Emancipation*, October 13, 1827, quoted in Benjamin Quarles, *Black Abolitionists* (New York, 1969), 10.

wrote this protest, and who seemed to live it in their bones, were either persons born as slaves who had escaped the South or Negroes born in the North who nevertheless ardently supported abolition. Abolitionism, then, had captured the hearts and minds of all these writers, irrespective of their histories as persons, and so it captured their literature as well. These black abolitionists did not all (or, as a matter of fact, any) die when slavery was ended at the end of the Civil War, although they tended, by that time, all to be quite mature and beyond a second birth in their interpretations of the world and their reactions as writers to their own such interpretations. The generalization can be applied to them that they did not cease to be abolitionists in their creative urges even as they grew old. From about 1830 to about 1895 they were the prevailing force in Afro-American literature. Theirs was the second age of Afro-American literature, the Age of the Abolitionists.

But they, of course, being human, themselves eventually passed off the scene. In their last years they could not have liked the America they were leaving. Slavery was gone, but the South, still excessively Calhounian in spite of its growing northernness, had been "redeemed." To some—a clear majority of Americans for a long time—this "redemption" meant that the South had been rescued from the horrors of Reconstruction, when the bottom rail had been put on the top: venal, ignorant, baboonlike Negroes, sitting in southern legislatures or acting in the South in other positions of public trust, had almost ruined the South with their sordid misuses of local and state revenues and incredible idiocies; only the heroics of such gallant superpatriots as the hooded knights of the Ku Klux Klan had preserved white southern womanhood and Aryan culture from defilement by an inferior race; and a labor force not competent to fend for itself had been too often and too leniently permitted opportunities to get out of hand. For others—and, certainly, from a black perspective—"redemption" was a great misnomer for the travesty upon emancipation which developed in America between the military victory of the North in the Civil War and the dawn (anything but bright for Negroes) of the twentieth century.

In America, indeed, in the last third of the nineteenth century and the opening years of the twentieth, one thing was sure beyond all doubt. The times did not encourage crusaders for the Negro in the mold of a Charles Sumner or a Robert Gould Shaw. What flourished in those days was a Gilded Age and Robber Barons whose hearts beat high, not at a call to succor underdogs of whatever color, but from the scent of some public holding or private property into which they might nuzzle their greedy snouts. The North, emerging from the Civil War bigger, stronger, and more vigorous than ever, looked ahead to even huger wealth and power at the end of rugged individualism's rainbow. The section's railroads and telegraphs spanned a continent. Its might would grow exponentially, spurred by invention, capital, entrepreneurial enterprise, and modern science. Its Silas Laphams would disappear before its Carnegies, its Rockefellers, its Morgans, its Edisons, and its Fords. The problem people on its horizons were hardly Negroes, but immigrants from parts of Europe other than the British Isles, Germany, and France. Some of those immigrants, notably the Scandinavians who went to Wisconsin and Minnesota, and their siblings and cousins of Willa Cather's fiction, would farm. But most of them would land and stay in the big cities of the North, as on the east side of New York's Manhattan or in the steel mills of Pittsburgh and Cleveland. Yet the twin metaphors of the Melting Pot and of Liberty lifting her lamp beside the golden door, despite delays, would come true enough in time for them, in so doing, among other peripheral effects, underscoring the reality of color caste and the lamp it did not lift for ostensibly liberated slaves and their offspring already inside this supposed portal to unlimited opportunity.

Three amendments to the Constitution of the United States deal directly with the Negro. The Thirteenth Amendment (1865) abolishes slavery, a service not performed, as is sometimes erroneously proclaimed, by President Lincoln's Emancipation Proclamation. The Fourteenth Amendment (1868) aims at guaranteeing Negroes' civil rights. Voting is the issue covered by the Fifteenth Amendment (1870), the language of which extends to Negroes the right of franchise. But even before the adoption of any of these amendments, Sherman, from Savannah, at the end of his march to the sea and after an evening in which he and Secretary of War Edwin Stanton talked with a score of Negro leaders, had issued his famous Field Order 15 designating somewhat more than 400,000 acres of land along the coasts, and on the islands off the coasts, of South Carolina and Georgia for settlement and at least temporary possession by former slaves and their families. Sherman's order encouraged the distribution of this land in plots of forty acres and addressed a concern—the economic one, untouched by any of the "Negro" amendments—which was basic to the welfare of the freed black people. Field Order 15 is symbolic today of the economic aftermath of slavery, a true tale of woe, for the Negro. All too utterly, Field Order 15 was gradually repudiated as were (and usually not gradually), virtually everywhere, all efforts to give a people, turned loose on their own completely bare-handed, some stake with which to start new, free, independent lives. The Freedmen's Bureau, anathema to many southerners, established by Congress just before the cessation of hostilities in the Civil War, tried to ease the transition from slavery to freedom of these four million persons, a huge army, who were venturing into a fresh chapter in their lives. Before Congress permitted its expiration in 1869, the bureau played a significant role in alleviating hunger and sickness among the freedmen. It experienced, in spite of energetic effort on its part, only small success in securing for the freedmen portions of the southern land confiscated by the North during the war. It was more successful in protecting the freedmen's rights as laborers. Courts and boards it promulgated, as well as its officials in the field, prevented many abuses of contract which would have injured freedmen. And it was, to paraphrase John Hope Franklin, most successful in education.[6] At every level of schooling, it made its presence felt. Howard University is named after the bureau's first head, a Civil War general who served, early in the university's history, as the university's president. Yet, economically, the freedmen entered a competitive society about as defenseless as they could be. What amounted to an almost complete nullification of the amendments added to the Constitution for their protection would, within less than an average human lifetime, leave them equally defenseless in civil rights and in the areas of their existence which were mainly social.

Circumvention of the Fifteenth Amendment was achieved in the South through a combination of terrorism and law, the law, of course, itself unlawful and a form of terrorism. The use of physical force to intimidate and discourage would-be Negro voters in the South may be easily documented from at least the early 1870s. The withdrawal of the last federal troops from the South by President Hayes constituted an apparently clear signal to everyone that the national government would no longer provide even a pretense of safeguarding Negroes in voter registration or at the ballot box from such force, however violent. The institution of poll taxes and literacy tests, which could always be unfairly administered, insinuated a semblance of law into a massive program of Negro disfranchisement capped by the invention, in Louisiana in 1898, of the grandfather clause, a refinement of provisions already included in

6. John Hope Franklin, *Reconstruction After the Civil War* (Chicago, 1961), 38.

the constitutions of some other southern states. The clause added, as it were, the touch of a final turning of a screw to a campaign which, in effect, nullified the Fifteenth Amendment.

Attacks on the Fourteenth Amendment coincided in time with those on Negro suffrage. Segregation and discrimination very patently could rely more upon the actions of individuals and groups unsanctioned by law than the exclusion of the Negro from the electorate. Negro sociologist Bertram Doyle wrote a book on the systematic patterns of behavior used by the postbellum South in its control of Negroes without, it seems safe to say, coming close to exhausting his subject.[7] Even so, the South, expeditiously enough, by law also exerted itself to nullify the Fourteenth Amendment. For this South, the same Supreme Court which, in 1889, discovered, as trusts began to flourish, that corporations were persons, hence not to be deprived of life, liberty, or property without due process of law, in 1896, through *Plessy* v. *Ferguson*—the celebrated classic case enunciating the "separate but equal" doctrine by means of which the Court justified "black" and "white" railroad travel—stripped Negroes, despite a ringing dissent from the Kentuckian and former slaveholder John Marshall Harlan, of the very civil right, due process, it had affirmed for a class of entities no less ideational than the Court itself. Some aspects of cotton tenancy for the sharecropper, who tended to be black, and all aspects of peonage, whose victims also tended to be black, jeopardized even the Thirteenth Amendment. Were things ever worse for Negroes in America than they had become by 1900? Around this time has been called by at least one respected black historian, Rayford Logan, the Negro Nadir—nadir, of course, meaning the lowest point.

Frederick Douglass died in 1895, perhaps the most conveniently topical twelve months in all of Negro history. This greatest of black abolitionists and major figure in Afro-American literature succumbed abruptly to heart failure on a February evening in his Anacostia home. He had just dined and was expecting to go out to be honored for a second time that day. Only months later, in September, at the Cotton States Exposition in Atlanta, Booker T. Washington, greatest of black accommodationists and also a black writer, delivered the address which so completely confirmed him in the favor of white America, especially among its high and mighty, as to put him in a position of leadership for the black America of his day similar, at least in its preeminence, to that occupied

7. Bertram Doyle, *The Etiquette of Race Relations in the South* (Chicago, 1937).

by Douglass in his day. It almost seems as if the gods had dramatized, in Douglass' death and Washington's speech, even to the sequence of the two events, the epochal supersession of one order by another, its exact antithesis, on the captain's bridge for black America. Equally, moreover, if not quite so dramatically, a third age of Afro-American literature seems synchronous, as well as similar in character, with the years when Washington and his leadership so ingloriously were to typify a philosophy and a strategy in American race relations Douglass and leaders of his disposition would have rather opposed to their deaths than given any quarter. It was an age of relative atrophy for Afro-American literature. It may well be, then, sufficiently consistent with historic fact to borrow from Logan and denominate that age in Afro-American literature the Age of the Negro Nadir. It would be followed by the Age of the Harlem Renaissance and thus would extend, with no more arbitrariness than comparable arrangements of the past, from 1895 to 1920.

In surely the two most frequently repeated passages of his Atlanta speech, Washington had said, first, clearly in a message meant for southern Negroes, "Cast down your bucket where you are," and, later, in another message just as clearly meant for southern whites, "In all things purely social we [whites and blacks] can be as separate as the fingers, yet one as the hand in all things essential to mutual progress." So he had advised and warned his fellow southern Negroes to stay in the South while simultaneously assuring southern whites that southern Negroes, were they of his mind, would adjust, without a murmur, to second-class citizenship and, certainly, would engage in no attempts to gain what southern whites particularly abhorred for blacks, social equality. Jubilantly and gratefully, the white South welcomed a capitulation to its creed as thorough, as prominent, and as loftily placed as his. It had once claimed that Negroes irked by slavery were unsound of mind or were tools in the hands of agitators. Washington now was their prime exhibit of a Negro who was intelligent and reasonable. Even so, not all of Washington's black contemporaries thought, or acted, as did he. In fact, it was not difficult to find in Washington's world blacks who despised his accommodationism, most conspicuously among them, probably, the Harvard-trained W. E. B. Du Bois. For Du Bois was in the tradition of Douglass and, in words and deeds, said so repeatedly. Nor were many Negroes who may not have been as outspoken as Du Bois any less inwardly rebellious than he. In the interest of mere survival, these Negroes often renounced for themselves much that was dear to them, concentrating on preparing what they hoped would be a better future for their children as well as on conditioning their children for that future.

One measure to which this breed of rebel resorted, almost as if offering a direct answer to Washington's "Cast down your bucket where you are," took the form of departure from the South. In 1880 those of them who would sometimes be called the Exodusters had gone to Kansas. But after the exodus to Kansas (which went pathetically awry), it was the urban North most of all which called to them, drawing them, with their hopes of a new life still intact, away from the folk Negro's historic American home in the agrarian South. Their trickle north increased to something of a flood when World War I interrupted immigration from Europe at precisely the moment during which northern industry was avid for labor to help it reap the profits it foresaw from its functioning as the "arsenal of Democracy" both before and after America became, herself, a dispenser in battle of the munitions large earlier consignments of which it had sold to Germany's foes. By 1920, despite the lynchings and race riots of the "Red Summer" of 1919—with their indication to any Negro, especially if he was returning from France, that the war had not changed things in America for him—the era of Washington, who had died in 1915, was joining that of Douglass as a portion of the Negro past. There was a New Negro in literature and life. In life this New Negro surged along State Street in Chicago, along Lenox Avenue in New York City, and through Paradise Valley in Detroit. In literature he allied himself with other New Negroes in the so-called Harlem Renaissance and thereby precipitated a fourth age of Afro-American literature, the Age of the Harlem Renaissance.

The writers of the Harlem Renaissance tended not to have been born in Harlem. They gravitated there from around America. Two of them were Caribbeans, "monkey-chasers," in street Harlemese. Becoming quite a coterie in their Harlem setting, these writers unified themselves in both ideology and behavior as had no other group of Negro writers antecedent to them. Indeed, it was they, and not some scholars of the future, who first spoke of their movement as a renaissance and coined for themselves the distinguishing appellation of the "New Negro." Decidedly their "Newness" involved a criticism and rejection of Washingtonian accommodationism. It involved, also, undoubtedly to their parents' gratification, a more open resistance on their part to the dictates of American racism than had emanated from their parents. They could, and did, challenge old concepts of what Negroes were and should be.

Especially they championed the folk Negro, that humble representative of his race hitherto most distant in manner and means from America's bourgeois whites. Yet the "New" black writer indulged in his own relapses into accommodationism, or something very like it. He had white friends, with some of whom he socialized. White patronage was important to his development of an audience. And he was, with or without accommodationism, very American—very much a creature of his American time, belonging to the same Lost Generation that had jettisoned the Genteel tradition and stomached well neither Babbitry nor Puritanism, the generation of Fitzgerald, Faulkner, Hemingway, and the Thomas Wolfe who was to say he could not go home again.

The Harlem Renaissance itself was brief, beginning and ending with the 1920s. It was born and it expired within an America finally a genuine world power. Until the 1890s, America had subdued militarily and diplomatically only its own continent. But after that, in the short time before World War I, it had annexed Hawaii, made its presence felt in the Caribbean, the Philippines, and Central America, and built the Panama Canal, complete control of which it would maintain far into the twentieth century. Still, the real miracle of twentieth-century America transcended triumphs won on fields like Chateau-Thierry and Vimy Ridge. Values and virtues largely bourgeois had created a new world in America which, in terms of material progress, if nothing else, beggared any achievements of men with nature before its time. The rising skyline of New York City, so striking a sight from land or sea, was an almost perfect visual symbol and sign of the American economy in the post-Versailles world. Moreover, inside America the miracle was abundantly apparent. Sinclair Lewis' Main Street vibrated from the pressures of the automobiles that ran upon it. Everywhere in the America of that Main Street there was a cornucopia of goods made by American industry and science. Everywhere in that same America there were schools, roads, hospitals, factories, banks, stores, churches, homes, and philanthropies, in their reflection of America an indication that, truly, twentieth-century America had become a paragon of production and technological skill both for its own day and for all time before it.

This America did not enthuse all Americans. American writers, for instance, including the blacks of the Harlem Renaissance, tended to think of it as a morass of philistinism. But it had come so far from the nation to which Cornwallis surrendered at Yorktown that ecstasy over its achievements and even some conviction that it was a special ward of

Providence, especially from its rapturous apologists for its culture (not inconsiderable in number), were easily understandable. In 1920 it added an Eighteenth Amendment and a Nineteenth Amendment to its Constitution, banning alcoholic beverages with the one and permitting women to vote with the other. Unfortunately, Warren Harding, of prepossessing physical appearance and wretched performance as America's chief citizen, was the first president elected after female enfranchisement. He was not, however, a harbinger of the future. Women have been anything but a curse to American politics. Prohibition, on the other hand, mandated by the Eighteenth Amendment, was a curse. It did not stop drinking, and it did start a flouting of the law unparalleled in American history.

Consumerism in America by the 1920s exceeded, possibly, the wildest fantasies of owning things of all previous human generations. An abundance of unprecedented creature comforts had been largely responsible for sweeping innovations in life-styles at most levels of American society. Conceivably, too, a postwar psychology, releasing inhibited appetites for self-indulgence, affected American minds. In any case, a special frenetic quality characterized America of the 1920s. It was the heyday of jazz, of flappers, of bootleggers, and of buccaneering in business and the stock market. The Wall Street crash of the fall of 1929 ushered in the Great Depression, which would temper all American life throughout the 1930s. And the Great Depression, among the many things it killed, killed the Harlem Renaissance.

With the patrician Franklin D. Roosevelt leading the way, Americans fought the Depression throughout the 1930s. Roosevelt was no radical and, certainly, no Marxist. But he was able to infuse his panaceas for a hemorrhaging capitalism with doses of compassion the results of which (to the horror of many members of his own class) served well the needs of those unfortunate constituents of his whom the collapse of the American economy had harmed the most. He improvised remedies and reliefs sometimes magnificently when his program for salvation was placed against the background of the indifference to the common good and the obsequiousness to the special interests of those whom he called "malefactors of great wealth" of his immediate predecessors in the White House. He had little, if any, help from nature. Indeed, the 1930s was the period of the Okies, the destitute families streaming away to other parts of America from the plains of America just east of the Rockies whence the soil was going with the wind. Agriculture staggered in the South, also, after the depredations of the boll weevil were compounded with problems inherent in the basic structure of cotton tenancy. Nevertheless, Roosevelt's Civilian Conservation Corps, Works Progress Administration, public housing, innovations in health care and aid to the indigent, young, and old, and not least, such legislation as the Wagner Act, steadily dissipated the fear and gloom remaining in America from the bleak years of the Depression's first coming. Meanwhile, America, with many of its citizens long hardly aware of its drift, was moving toward combatant status in World War II. Although Roosevelt was an Anglophile, it was against Japan, after the spectacular provocation of Pearl Harbor, that America first launched its armies, its fleets, and its planes. Then it joined the crusade against Hitler. As it had in World War I, in World War II it sent two armies overseas, one white and one black. For that matter, it trained two armies on its own grounds in segregated camps. It followed World War II, however, with less of a rude returning of the Negro to his place than that with which it had welcomed Negroes home after World War I. Within ten years of its assault on Omaha Beach, its Supreme Court, unanimously, would rule, in the Brown decision of May 17, 1954, against segregated schools.

To reach its ruling the Court struck down *Plessy* v. *Ferguson.* Fundamentally, the Court's decision reflected changes in American life that were profound and had been long oozing, as it were, through the veins and capillaries in the viscera of America's conception of herself. Color caste had not vanished, in the early 1950s, from America. But the Calhoun South, except in isolated pockets, north and south, of virulence fed from brackish waters of the past, had lost by then all but little of its original vitality. American youth in World War II had fought around the world and come home to go—many of them—to colleges and universities where their teachers were as cosmopolitan as the returned veterans in uniform. Moreover, whatever its shortcomings, an industrial, urban-oriented America was far less hospitable to a cumbersome etiquette of race relations afflicted with ritualistic taboos—such as the South sought to defend when its agrarianism, and even its adjustments to the North of the kind lauded by Henry Grady, still seemed to require the cooperation of a Booker T. Washington—than it had been before it searched its soul during the Great Depression. Desegregation in America would not come overnight. Old ways die hard. It is true that President Eisenhower supplied no vigorous executive initiatives to help implement the Supreme

Court's call for an end to discrimination, as it carefully said, "with all deliberate speed," in public schools, and really, if only by implication, in public facilities of every kind. Still, sparks of an incipient conflagration were fanned into a flame by such events as the boycott, in the late 1950s, of buses by Negroes in Montgomery, Alabama. Civil-rights activism, patterned largely on the nonviolence of the bus boycott, although it did not altogether escape violent reactions to the demonstrations it bred, provided pressures Eisenhower had not. Then, in the administration of Lyndon Johnson, the law and the executive joined the civil-rights activists. Congress, by statute, supported the Court. Johnson swung the weight of his office behind the actions of the dismantlers of segregation. Had Booker T. Washington lived for another fifty or sixty years, he would not have known his America, or his South.

Partly, he would not have known either because of a very remarkable man. Currents which run deep in American life ultimately do account for the fact that America in the last third of the twentieth century is not, in either what it does or what it apparently feels in regard to race, Booker T. Washington's world. Yet, without the work of Charles H. Houston, a most unsung of heroes, the new day for Negroes in civil rights and personal freedoms may well not have come as early as it did. Houston, like Du Bois, was Harvard trained, although in law, not history. He had friends in the inner circles of the National Association for the Advancement of Colored People and shared the Weltanschauung of such NAACP magnates as the Spingarn brothers, James Weldon Johnson, and Walter White. Highly competent intellectually himself, and steeped in the tenets of political liberalism which owe much to the philosophy of John Locke and to Shaftesburian optimism, he had faith in the NAACP's legal strategy, the program to which the NAACP had committed itself of appealing to America's finer instincts through the good offices of reason and respect for the principles of law. A particularly energetic spirit in this program before Houston had been James Weldon Johnson, especially with his efforts, including his persistent lobbying in Washington, D.C., to secure a federal antilynching law. Johnson undoubtedly made some friends for the Negro, and himself, in Congress as he tried for passage of the law he wanted. But he did not prevail. He died, in 1938, with lynching still uncontrolled by Congress. In the meantime, however, Houston had begun the long campaign which was to culminate triumphantly in the Brown decision. Where Johnson had placed emphasis on lawmaking,

Houston concentrated his implementation of a legal strategy upon law interpretation. He recruited for his purposes a corps of brilliant advocates, one of whom, for example, Thurgood Marshall, would become an associate justice of the Supreme Court and another, James Nabrit, the president of Howard University.

Houston's plan was simple and amenable to gradual advances. He began with cases which ostensibly did not challenge *Plessy* v. *Ferguson*, the "separate but equal" doctrine. Thus, in courts in various southern and border states, he and the members of his team argued that, even in segregated schools, Negro teachers should be paid as well as white teachers of equal training and experience in white schools and that, whether in segregated schools or elsewhere, "separate but equal" should be so construed and so applied that Negro students would not receive an education qualitatively inferior to the education they would most likely receive if they were white. Litigation instituted under Houston's aegis tended, if its plaintiffs were students, to focus on professional (especially law) and graduate schools. But all of this litigation tended, also, to generate evidence which suggested that "separate" could never be "equal." And so, by the sheer impetus of the logic of its own empirical revelations—inevitably, it seemed—the legal strategy of the NAACP reached the point where, apparently, it could not avoid an unequivocal, direct challenge of *Plessy* v. *Ferguson*. Houston died in the fifty-fifth year of his life in 1950. But beyond any question, the overthrow, four years later, of *Plessy* v. *Ferguson* was primarily his accomplishment. In theory at least, he and his colleagues had integrated America. They were worthy forerunners of a Gandhian Martin Luther King.

Something of a parallel exists between Charles Houston and Richard Wright. They both dominate a certain aspect of an era. What Houston was to the civil-rights struggle of the Negro for more than two decades after the Depression Richard Wright was to Afro-American literature, if not more so. Perhaps Wright, whose early life was greatly troubled, expressed superbly the *Zeitgeist* of years when neither blacks nor whites in America could be very complacent about their presents or their futures. Powerful with words and with the images he created of blacks and black life in the American social order, he impacted tremendously on his contemporary black writers. They all tended to write well. Indeed, they may have produced what is, thus far, the golden age of Afro-American literature. Yet they all, also, more or less tended to repeat, in what they wrote,

Richard Wright. No other black writer has had nearly Wright's effect upon a group of contemporary black writers. In Afro-American literature, the years after the Harlem Renaissance are Wright's, the years of the Age of Wright, from about 1930 to the end of the 1950s.

Both Houston and Wright were integrationists. The prime intent of the legal strategy of the NAACP which Houston adopted was to further the inclusion of the Negro in the sometimes so-called mainstream of American life. It does not follow that Houston and other legal strategists worshiped everything in white America. Actually, they did not. They were reformers, as had been Douglass and the abolitionists, or a long, unbroken line of white Americans beginning with Thomas Paine in the days of the Revolution, who had not failed to find fault, here and there, with America's *status quo*. And so Wright and Houston, in their time, did find imperfections in America against which they railed. But they were not so disenchanted with either America or Western culture as a whole that they renounced all trust in them and preached, for Negroes, a quarantine from whites. Not even Wright was that extreme although, despite the disdain he acquired for Communism, he remained, from his early manhood until his death, a stalwart Marxist. Moreover, when Wright left America soon after the end of World War II to settle permanently as an expatriate in France, his gesture was that of a soul in limbo, of one who, however reluctantly, was resorting to an expedient which expressed, not a preference, but the apparently best available alternative to a genuine wish fulfillment.

Like that of Houston, Wright's truly big dream had been of an America that would work for him as it had worked for whites. Treasuring this dream as he did, abandonment of it was beyond the range of possibility forever for him. And Houston died leaving for his son an integrationist's message. However, there developed, as the civil-rights activism of the 1960s examined its own premises, something widely different from the thinking of a Houston or a Wright, an anti-integrationism associated with black militancy which postulated as its first commandment a flat rejection of the dream shared by Houston and Wright, and thus a corresponding flat rejection of all of white bourgeois America. This anti-integrationism asserted not only that white America had sinned against blacks, as against all humanity, but also that no way existed for anyone with the capacity for normal human decency to come to terms with whites and the world as whites intended it should be. In the black past, insofar as that past, stretching back to Africa, had been preserved by blacks not "co-opted" by white America, lay the lessons to be learned for Negroes to live as they should. Black was "beautiful," and a major mission—if not *the* major mission—of blacks who understood their world was to spread the truth of the worth of blackness and the abominable character of white America. By the early 1960s, partisans of such a doctrine began to appear in Afro-American literature. Their prominence seems to suggest an age following, in Afro-American literature, the Age of Wright which might well be called, in recognition of these partisans, the Age of the Black Militant.

The 1960s and the 1970s have, of course, not been simply years of civil-rights activism. In one regard they have witnessed technological and scientific progress dwarfing even the comparable progress so arresting in earlier years of the twentieth century. In another regard they have articulated additional stages in America's development as a world power. Surely some Americans have not found unpalatable in the second half of the twentieth century the concept of, upon all nations, a Pax Americana. America has fought undeclared wars in Korea and Indochina. From its Korean conflict it received, perhaps, unclear results. From its excursion into Indochina, it received, with no uncertainty, more anguish than content. The younger generation of Americans from whom, at the end of the 1960s and the beginning of the 1970s, the bodies came which were dispatched to Asia had exhibited, even before the use of American power on a relatively weak people not a clear and present danger to America, some querulousness about the America of their elders. Far from every young American, it seemed, wanted to be an organization man, or woman, and some young Americans were not content with their elders' tastes in clothes or manners or art, popular or otherwise. Differences between generations of Americans concerning American foreign policy only accentuated, then, disagreements domestic in nature, so that attitudes of America's generations toward each other became an issue, primarily divisive, of great importance in America of the 1970s. The mere presence of the nuclear bomb, inseparable from the global political polarities associated with America and Russia, did nothing to lessen tensions as the world moved toward the twenty-first century.

In Afro-American literature conceivably, as an old century moves toward its close and a new century rises upon the near horizon, a new age may be immediately in the offing, if not already here. Afro-American literature has had, with approximate dates, from its beginnings until 1830, an Age of Apprenticeship; from 1830 until 1895, an Age of Abolitionists; from 1895 until 1920, an Age of the Negro Nadir; from 1920 until 1930, an Age of the Harlem Renaissance; from 1930 until 1960, an Age of Richard Wright; and from 1960 until as an yet undetermined date, an Age of the Black Militant. What lies ahead for it remains to be seen. The subjects it has treated surely will not soon disappear. But what shapes it will take, if it does not disappear, obviously now belong to the unknown.

Part One ❧

The Age of Apprenticeship

1. The First Poets

In our present state of knowledge about Afro-American literature, we may, and probably should, mark the beginning of that literature with the following poem:

BARS FIGHT

August, 'twas the twenty-fifth,
Seventeen hundred forty-six,
The Indians did in ambush lay,
Some very valient [sic] men to slay,
Samuel Allen like a hero fout,
And though he was so brave and bold,
His face no more shall we behold.

Eleazer Hawks was killed outright,
Before he had time to fight,—
Before he did the Indians see,
Was shot and killed immediately.

Oliver Amsden he was slain,
Which caused his friends much grief and pain
Simeon Amsden they found dead
Not many rods distant from his head.

Adonijah Gillett, we do hear,
Did lose his life which was so dear.
John Sadler [sic] fled across the water,
And thus escaped the dreadful slaughter.

Eunice Allen see [sic] the Indians coming,
And hopes to save herself by running;
And had not her petticoats stopped her,
The awful creatures had not catched her,

Nor tommy hawked her on the head.
Young Samuel Allen, Oh, lack-a-day!
Was taken and carried to Canada.

Composed in 1746, the year of the stirring episode it commemorates, this poem was not published until 1893 in an article, "Negro Slavery in Old Deerfield," by George Sheldon in the *New England Magazine.* The version given here, however, comes from a later work of this same Sheldon, his precisely, but expansively, entitled *A History of Deerfield, Massachusetts: The Times When and the People by Whom It Was Settled, Unsettled and Resettled,* and there are differences between the versions.[1] The version in the *New England Magazine* is not divided into stanzas, varies slightly from our presently quoted version in punctuation and one conjunction, spells *catched* as "cotched," and has the decapitated Simeon Amsden "not many rods *off* [italics mine] from his head." Of Sheldon, incidentally, it may be noted that his paternal ancestors had lived in Deerfield virtually from the establishment of the town in the late seventeenth century, constantly increasing, it would seem, their fond attachment to Deerfield through marriages into other highly respected Deerfield families. Of "Bars Fight" it can hardly not be noted that nothing about the poem suggests the race of its reputed author. It refers only to whites and Indians and speaks of both of them only from a point of view clearly "white." Even so, "Bars Fight" is credited to a black, a sixteen-year-old girl (although sixteen-year-old girls were women in the 1700s) named Lucy Terry.

About Lucy Terry information is scant.[2] Nevertheless, what we do know of Terry tends to present her to us as a person of considerable vitality, ability, and forcefulness of character. From somewhere in West Africa a slave ship brought her to Rhode Island while she was, at most, scarcely more than an infant. Thus, by 1735, even then still a child only five years old, in Deerfield, under the approving supervision of her master, Deacon Ebenezer Wells, she was baptized in the Christian faith. Coincidentally, 1735 was the year of the Great Awakening, when a massive wave of evangelical fervor swept through the west of Massachusetts, kindled by the earnest preaching of Jonathan Edwards in Northampton,

1. George Sheldon, "Negro Slavery in Old Deerfield," *New England Magazine,* n.s., VIII (March–August, 1893), 56, and *A History of Deerfield, Massachusetts: The Times When and the People by Whom It Was Settled, Unsettled and Resettled* (2 vols.; Deerfield, Mass., 1895), II, 548–49.

2. The principal source of information here about Lucy Terry and "Bars Fight" is Sheldon, "Negro Slavery in Old Deerfield." The information that will appear in the text soon about the actual encounter which "Bars Fight" describes is taken from Sheldon, *A History of Deerfield, Massachusetts,* 545–50.

close to Deerfield. Lucy Terry married, in 1756, the free Negro Abijah Prince, a native of Wallingford, Connecticut, where he had once been the slave of the Reverend Benjamin Doolittle. Prince was twenty-four years her senior. Nevertheless, this wedding of May to November lasted thirty-six years (Prince did not die until 1792), produced six children—Cesar, Duroxa, Drucilla, Festus, Tatnai, and Abijah, Jr.—two of whom lived into the 1850s, and seems, in every way, to have been an ideal union. Somehow, also, in connection with it, Lucy Terry gained her freedom—either because her master freed her or because her husband purchased her freedom—as all of her children were born free. From 1762 the Princes lived in Vermont, first in Guilford, then in Sunderland, where Prince was one of the charterers of the town, and, again, in Guilford, where Prince died. After his death, Lucy Terry returned to Sunderland, whence, in a gesture anything but suggestive of unpalatable reminiscence, she made an annual pilgrimage on horseback over mountainous trails to her husband's grave until her own death, at the ripe old age of ninety-one, in 1821.

The twenty-six lines of irregular iambic tetrameter in "Bars Fight," if authentically Lucy Terry's, constitute the entirety of her contribution to the body of literature of her people and her country. They are about as humble as a beginning could ever be. There is no way to speak of them as if they were anything but doggerel. Yet Lucy Terry, who became, to Deerfield, after her marriage, Lucy Abijah, never Lucy Prince, was widely esteemed in Deerfield as a storyteller of parts. People—especially young people—gathered at her house to hear her practice her skill. Accountably, then, in "Bars Fight," even while her ineptitude as a poet—a poet's role, apparently, was unfamiliar to her—is all too enormously clear, her competence at narration still remains, in appreciable measure, at her command. How well, indeed, she both states with reasonable accuracy a series of occurrences in an actual historic incident and yet employs some simple, but effective, strategies for adding interest to her relation of an unsavory tale may be surely realized by making available for comparison with her poem the bare facts of the fight at the Bars.

The Bars itself was a small plateau on the outskirts of Deerfield, as well as on a bank of the Deerfield River. On August 25, 1745, a Sunday, Samuel Allen and his three children, Eunice, thirteen, Caleb, nine, and Samuel, eight; the two Amsdens, Oliver, eighteen, and Simeon, nine; two soldiers, John Saddler of Deerfield and Adonijah Gillett from a town in Connecticut; and Eleazer Hawks, Samuel Allen's brother-in-law, repaired to Stebbins' Meadow adjacent to the Bars to complete a job of haying. The presence of the soldiers attested to a state of alarm in Deerfield. Indians allied with the French were known to be rampaging along the northern English frontier. The haymakers went to work, unaware of the Indians lurking under cover in a nearby thicket. These Indians were where they were, and as they were, it might well be added, precisely because they were hoping, and expecting, the haymakers to return. Eventually the Indians did reveal themselves. They killed, in spite of a brief, spirited resistance, Samuel Allen, both Amsdens, Gillett, and Hawks. Caleb Allen, the only member of the party of whites not mentioned by Lucy Terry, escaped from the onslaught, as did John Saddler. Young Samuel Allen was captured. Actually, it had been English captives that the Indians were primarily seeking. And so, in a manner of speaking, they were largely foiled. They were foiled, too, by Eunice Allen. She survived her tomahawking by seventy-two years.

The Indians in "Bars Fight" were a detachment from a band of marauders led by the Frenchman De Vaudreuil. In their limited way, they were participating in a struggle that was to have vast consequences, the struggle for an empire in America between France and England. "Bars Fight" is not only "white." It is also English. Lucy Terry, apparently, never forgot, nor forswore, her African origin. Indeed, it is reported that no little of her fame as a storyteller derived from the stories she told of her Africa remembered. But she identified with New England, first, as it was when it was still English, still a colony of a mother country, and later, as it became when it grew and changed after America achieved a state of independent nationhood. Her oldest son, Cesar, fought with America, possibly as one of Ethan Allen's Green Mountain Boys, in the Revolutionary War. Her second son, Festus, married a white woman. Like other enterprising Americans of their time, Lucy Terry and her husband exploited land grants. They even successfully resisted, ultimately through a hearing before the Supreme Court of the United States, an attempt by one of their neighbors, a Colonel Eli Bronson, to claim as his some of the land they thought was theirs, and Terry took part, in open court and very effectively, in the oral argument offered to the attendant ears of the most powerfully placed arbiters of the law in the homeland of her adoption (Royall Tyler was one of Bronson's lawyers). She did not completely transcend color caste. Williams College refused on racial grounds to admit a son of hers, in spite of a three-hour verbal appeal, larded with quotations from the Bible and Anglo-Saxon jurisprudence, made by her to the Williams trustees. Yet her color was not, in her mind, the issue, enveloping all other issues, that color would later become in the minds of most Afro-American writers. She was a creature of her moment and milieu. As such, she was a willing apprentice in the American system of getting ahead and, certainly on the basis of her performance in "Bars Fight," a willing apprentice in the use of the language, cultural ideas, and literary forms associated with that system.

With Lucy Terry virtually unknown, until only a decade or two ago it was generally supposed that the honor of being the first Negro American writer belonged to another northern Negro slave named Jupiter Hammon.[3] Hammon was a native of America, born (before Lucy Terry) on Long Island on October 3, 1711. Like Lucy Terry, he lived a long life. Although the year of his death has not been established, it may well have been as late as 1806 and was certainly not before the late 1780s. He belonged to a succession of Lloyds, a father, his son, and his great-grandson, in order, who were important landholders in the village (now, of course, the borough) of Queens at Lloyd's Neck, Long Island. The Lloyds were also, according to Hammon, benign in their treatment of him. We have his claim, "I suppose I have had more advantages and privileges than most . . . slaves . . . have ever known and I believe more than many white people have enjoyed." And, in a deed that may have been more corroborative of his eulogy apropos the Lloyds than any merely spoken praise, he accompanied the Lloyds to Connecticut and remained steadfastly with them when they, as staunch supporters of the American cause, were exiled for years from their home during the Revolutionary War. At least one competent commentator suspects, from Hammon's assertion of how well he fared as a slave, that Hammon was a slave artisan. This commentator quite reasonably infers that any master might value a

---

3. *Cf.*, e.g., James Weldon Johnson, *Black Manhattan* (New York, 1930), 261; Vernon Loggins, *The Negro Author: His Development in America to 1900* (New York, 1931), 9; Benjamin Brawley, *Early Negro American Writers* (Chapel Hill, 1935), 8; J. Saunders Redding, *To Make a Poet Black* (Chapel Hill, 1939), 3–4; Sterling A. Brown, Arthur P. Davis, and Ulysses Lee (eds.), *The Negro Caravan: Writings by American Negroes* (New York, 1941), 274; and Margaret Just Butcher, *The Negro in American Culture* (New York, 1956), 117. A version of "Bars Fight," attributed to Terry and clearly dated, did appear in Lorenzo J. Greene, *The Negro in Colonial New England, 1620–1776* (New York, 1942), 242–43. The first recognition in our time of Lucy Terry and "Bars Fight" by representatives of the world of letters probably occurs in Arna Bontemps and Langston Hughes (eds.), *The Poetry of the Negro, 1746–1970* (New York, 1970). *Cf.* there the reference to Terry on vii and the version of "Bars Fight" on 3.

slave with a special skill above other slaves able to supply only ordinary untrained manual labor. It has also been conjectured that the Lloyds allowed Hammon the liberty of preaching to his fellow slaves.[4] Certainly, a letter exists from one G. Muirson in which Muirson, a physician, reacting to intelligence from a Lloyd that Hammon was suffering from a "gouty Rumatick Disorder," prescribed for Hammon the bleedings, boluses, roots, barks, whey, and diet which, in keeping with the medical practice of that day, Muirson would probably, for a similar complaint, not have hesitated to impose on the most socially elite of his patients.[5] Moreover, the tone of Muirson's letter is interesting. It could hardly be more solicitous had Hammon been a blood relative of the Lloyds.

Whether Hammon ever preached we truly do not know. Indeed, the little we know about his life is actually less than the little we know about the life of Lucy Terry. We do know, however, that he wrote the first poem published by an American Negro. His "An Evening Thought: Salvation by Christ with Penetential [sic] Cries" appeared as a broadside in 1760. In 1788 he issued, from Hartford, Connecticut, another broadside, "An Address to Miss Phillis Wheatly [sic], Ethiopian Poetess in Boston, who came from Africa at Eight Years of Age, and Soon Became Acquainted with the Gospel of Jesus Christ." His poem "An Essay on the Ten Virgins," printed at Hartford in 1779, seems to be lost. But two other poems of his exist, in each case in combination with a piece of prose. One of these poems, with a title decidedly ill suited to our present notions of enlightened child rearing, "A Poem for Children with Thoughts on Death," was appended to the sermon "A Winter Piece," and therewith was published at Hartford in 1782. The other of these poems, "A Dialogue, Entitled, The Kind Master and Dutiful Servant," follows another sermon, "An Evening's Improvement. Shewing, The Necessity of beholding the Lamb of God," in a publication at Hartford which is undated, although almost surely published also in the early 1780s. Hammon's most substantial single work is his last, the prose *Address to the Negroes in the State of New York*, delivered in 1784, but printed in New York in 1787.

In his small way, then, Hammon was a man of letters, a somewhat

---

4. Jupiter Hammon, *An Address to the Negroes in the State of New York* (New York, 1787), 6; Redding, *To Make a Poet Black*, 4; Loggins, *The Negro Author*, 10; William H. Robinson (ed.), *Early Black American Prose* (Dubuque, Ia., 1971), 35.

5. Muirson's letter may be read in Oscar Wegelin, *Jupiter Hammon: American Negro Poet* (New York, 1915), 8.

dedicated practitioner of the art of literature, as Lucy Terry was not. Because of its historical distinctiveness, "An Evening Thought" has attracted more attention than any of his other works. As poetry it approximates the level of quality of the poetry in "Bars Fight." It is eighty-eight lines long and affects the ballad stanza as that stanza had been corrupted in the hymns written by the Methodists whose new version of Christian piety had arisen in Hammon's own era. Perhaps more importantly, "An Evening Thought" evinces the seemingly almost absolute sovereignty exercised by Methodism over Hammon's life and thought. One can only conjecture how Hammon, a lowly slave, would have reacted to Calvinism with its aristocratic doctrine of the few and favored elect. But Methodism, through its advocacy of Christ's redeeming grace, offered salvation to everyone, no matter how mean or desperate the state on earth in which that someone had lived. In "An Evening Thought" the very term *salvation* occurs twenty-three times. A crude echolalia haunts the poem. *Jesus* occurs in it nine times; *Lord,* or *God,* fourteen; and there is repeated reference in it to the Holy Word. Perhaps Hammon was enthralled by incantation. It appears far likelier, however, that his obsessive reiteration of certain terms reflects an interest of his not so much in sound as in sense. He lived in a world which was yet to experience the impact of post–Darwinian science. Clearly, an eschatology culminating in a final divine judgment—beyond the grave, of course—whereby saints and sinners would finally receive their due and just rewards permeated at every juncture his reactions to the environment with which he daily dealt. He is consistent in all that he wrote. He addresses Phillis Wheatley to remind her of her good fortune in being brought from savagery to a Christian land and to admonish her to make the most of her possible advantages from such a providential turn in her affairs. His thoughts on death for children are thoughts on damnation and salvation. His kindly master is a Person of the Holy Trinity and is not to be mistaken as a mere human slave owner, like any one, for instance, of the Lloyds. So his dutiful servant is a wise seeker after the peace that passeth all understanding, the blissful peace of angelic immortality. Even when he lectures his fellow Negroes, slaves and free, in the state of New York, it is not so much their lot here as what their lot may be in a hereafter which is his major theme.

Hammon's Christianity, then, does incorporate into itself attitudes which bespeak his race. Thus he differs from Lucy Terry. It is as black Christian to black Christian that he lectures in verse to Phillis Wheatley.

And his prose *Address to the Negroes in the State of New York*, while essentially echoing the familiar Christian argument found, for example, in Bunyan's *Pilgrim's Progress*, does set even that kind of an argument within an ethnocentric context and charge it with an ethnocentric bias. The Negroes in the state of New York, he says, should be good Christians. That means, he concedes unabashedly, that they, if slaves, should obey their masters. The word of God, and of Paul, he finds distinct and unequivocal on this point. It also means, he insists, that all Negroes should be honest and trustworthy, should not profane (thus bowing to the Third Commandment), and should learn to read, since no Christian should lack his own immediate access to scriptural truth.

In the 1780s Hammon was, apparently, no crusader. It seems safe to assume, indeed, that he had never been. When he wrote his *Address* he had passed his seventieth birthday. In the then New York City, restricted to present-day lower Manhattan, but even under eighteenth-century conditions a close neighborhood to Queens, slaves rebelled violently in 1712 and were punished for a suspected conspiracy against whites in 1741. Nor would it be implausible to suppose that, in the century of Jefferson and Paine, Hammon may well have heard of the natural rights of man. Moreover, in the North, by the 1780s, slavery was a dying institution, although New York, which resorted to gradual emancipation, was the last of the northern states, except New Jersey, to free its slaves.[6] Yet Hammon's *Address* sounds no tocsin. In temperate agreement with the course that events, apparently, were already taking, whatever else might transpire, the *Address* did admit the probable benefit of freedom for young Negroes. Hammon, at his age, however, and in view of the privileges he had enjoyed, and was continuing to enjoy, was firmly of the opinion that emancipation would do him, personally, little, if any, good, and that, as a matter of fact, there was a greater prospect that it would do him harm. What he does emphasize in the *Address* is his conviction that Negroes, more than any other people in the world, should look ahead to heaven. Having lost more in this world, he reasons, than any other people, Negroes have, in heaven, more than all others to gain.

The printers of the *Address* prefixed it with a statement. It was, they said, "wrote in a better stile than could be expected from a slave." As a

---

6. In 1799, by legislative act, New York decreed that no male slave born on or after July 4, 1799, could be held in bondage after July 4, 1827. For female slaves the corresponding date was three years earlier.

consequence they provided, in effect, an affidavit that it was Hammon's unaided work. They had good reason to do as they did. A speculative reader, not knowing the author, would certainly attribute the *Address* to someone considerably more literate than an untutored slave. Hammon's verse was childish. His prose was not. And, if he was no tribune for his people in the cause of liberation, it is still curiously true that the veiled, subdued, and oblique criticism of a social order inherent in his assumption—apparently sincere—that all blacks should expect, compensatorily, a better afterlife than nonblacks, does constitute, at its very low level of rancor (since it seems more to bemoan than to rebuke), the first note of racial protest in American Negro literature. It is also probably true that, in this very assumption and his way of stating it, Hammon may have taken, moreover, at least another tentative step or two along a road which justifies his proclamation as the first Negro writer in an additional category. He may be, that is, however dimly and distantly, a sort of harbinger—the first we can descry—of the Negro spiritual. Admittedly, he never lived where the spirituals eventually did establish their homeland, in the agrarian South as it developed after cotton had begun to dominate the regional economy and to determine the life-style of the black folk with whom we associate the spirituals. Admittedly, also, this particular life-style—the life-style as it once was of southern blacks—significantly manifests itself in the spirituals. And yet the basic idea of the spirituals, the notion of a peculiar solace in the Christian faith for a special oppressed breed of God's children, does exist, if nowhere else in Hammon, at least in germ in his *Address*. The sober prose of the *Address* is a far cry from the moving folk poetry of the spirituals. Hammon's idiom and the idiom of the spirituals are also figuratively worlds apart. Then, too, much of the power of the spirituals resides in their imagery—in green trees abending as poor sinners stand atrembling; in a Christ on the cross and in the tomb never saying a "mumberlin" word; in the sweet chariot from heaven that does swing low to take home a black Christian who has, through monumental trials and tribulations, kept the faith. Nothing like this imagery attaches itself to the *Address*. Still, the black Christian, different from all other Christians, is there, to link Hammon with anonymous folk artists of his own race he would never see and thus to distinguish him with the honor of being the earliest discernible contributor to a strain of racial expression he could suggest but never be sufficiently an artist, or a black, as to encompass.

The full, extended title of Hammon's "An Evening Thought" relates it to Christmas Day of 1760. Only weeks later the respected and affluent Boston tailor John Wheatley, having in mind his wife's desire for a young slave girl whom she could train for her special needs, from a group of bonded Africans newly arrived in Boston Harbor purchased a little girl of almost pathetically frail physique whose bones seemed to show through both her skin and her only semblance of apparel, a piece of dirty carpet. Whether John Wheatley or his wife (who may, or may not, have actually gone herself to the Boston wharves) selected this little girl is now a matter not resolved. In any case, the tiny waif was so small and sickly in appearance that she sold for only a "trifle."[7]

The Wheatleys named their purchase Phillis and brought her into their home on fashionable King Street, only a short distance from the statehouse. There she joined John, his wife, Susannah, the eighteen-year-old Wheatley twins, Mary and Nathaniel, and the other relatively well-treated Wheatley slaves. Phillis Wheatley seems to have been eight years old in 1761, ten years younger than the twins. Apropos of this point we have a statement by Benjamin Brawley, "Phillis' poem on Whitefield published in 1770 said on the title page that the author was seventeen years old, and the formal notice of her death in 1784 said she was thirty-one."[8] It has been generally supposed, on no hard evidence, by those who have speculated on the issue of her provenience, that she came from Senegal (although, as weak and forlorn as she looked in Boston Harbor, she may have been "refuse" from a cargo of slaves first taken to the West Indies). She did, apparently, mention only one item from her African past, her recollection of her mother's morning libation to the rising sun, in itself an old African custom, yet, nevertheless, not incompatible with the probability that her people (the Fula, it has been conjectured) were Mohammedans. Some extra significance, incidentally, may be attached to a Mohammedan background for her, as it could have been a circumstance, since any Mohammedans then had access to a long tradition of literacy, which abetted the remarkable innate abilities she demonstrated in the speed of her mastery of the English tongue. Whatever she had experienced, in Africa, if not also in the West Indies, within sixteen months of her arrival in the Wheatley household, according to John Wheatley, she had "attained the English language, to which

7. Merle A. Richmond, *Bid the Vassal Soar* (Washington, D.C., 1974), 69–70.
8. Brawley, *Early Negro American Writers*, 34–35.

she was an utter stranger before, to such a degree, as to read . . . the most difficult parts" of the Bible.[9]

The Wheatleys nourished the young prodigy's precocity. She was taught grammar, a little astronomy, a little ancient history, some ancient and modern geography, the Bible, and the leading Latin classics, particularly Virgil and Ovid.[10] For a young woman of her time, therefore, she was decidedly erudite. For a slave, at any time, she was pampered. Her penchant for poetizing appeared perhaps as early as in her fourteenth year. Around the Wheatley house she performed most minimally as a domestic, on rare occasions, perhaps, lightly dusting a table or a chair. In deference to her precarious health, as well as to the impossibility of predicting when, by day or night, an inspired thought that should be noted down might occur to her, she was permitted candles, heat, pen, ink, and paper in her room (which, be it emphasized, was her room). And when, as she approached womanhood, she became increasingly a local celebrity, valued for, among her other talents, her powers as a conversationalist, she was transported to and from visits to other Boston homes in the Wheatley coach. It may be added here, however, that, if food was served during such a visit of hers, it seems to have been her custom, at her own behest, to partake of it at a table set aside from the table which accommodated the rest of the company. But she did not, apparently, restrict her diplomacy in human relations to those whom the world considered her superiors. She so comported herself with her fellow slaves in the Wheatley household, rumor asserts, that they retained a genuine fondness for her in spite of the great difference in the Wheatleys' treatment of her and them.

Phillis Wheatley's first published poem, an elegy on the death of George Whitefield, the famous English evangelist, appeared as a broadside in 1770. In 1771 she was made a communicant of the Old South Meeting House in Boston. By January, 1773, she had published three other elegies as broadsides and one poem not an elegy in the *London Magazine*. Her years of basking in the sun were upon her. She, of course, could not know how few they would be or what a contrast lay beyond them. Indeed, in 1773 she went to England, traveling with Nathaniel, one of the Wheatley twins (and on a ship, the *London*, owned by John Wheatley).

9. John Wheatley's paean occurs in a letter of his "to the Publisher" included in the prefatory material prefixed to Phillis Wheatley's sole volume of poems, *Poems on Various Subjects, Religious and Moral* (London, 1773).

10. Benjamin Brawley, *The Negro in Literature and Art in the United States* (3rd ed.; New York, 1929), 16.

Her owners' concern for her health, which, they had been advised, a sea voyage should improve, partly accounted for her trip. But in England, also, an expectant and sympathetic audience awaited her. The Wheatleys were Methodists, of the same stripe as those Methodists in England— still, in the 1770s, tolerated within the Anglican communion—among whom Selina Hastings, the countess of Huntingdon, played a highly eminent and bountiful role. Sixty clerics fostered Methodism at sixty chapels in England and Wales because the livings there were the countess' to grant. These clerics were sometimes known as the countess' chaplains. George Whitefield had been one of the countess' additional chaplains— her "missionary" chaplain whose mission field was America. The Wheatleys were her correspondents. To some extent Phillis Wheatley entered England as the countess' protégée and so, to some extent, her almost royal reception in England may be attributed to the countess' interest in her affairs.

Wheatley seems to have been in London and its vicinity, where she spent all her English sojourn, only about six weeks, arriving there just after the middle of June and leaving just before the advent of August.[11] She had come out of season, at the height of summer, when society was vacationing. Yet among the notables whom she met were the earl of Dartmouth; Lord Lincoln (otherwise, General Henry Clinton, the elder); Israel Mauduit, agent in England for Massachusetts; Benjamin Franklin; Granville Sharpe; Ladies Cavendish and Webb; Mary Palmer, Sir Joshua Reynold's sister; Alderman Kirkland; and Brook Watson, later to be lord mayor of London, who gave her a folio edition of *Paradise Lost* that is now in the Houghton Library at Harvard University. She was to have been presented at court and to have met her powerful patroness, the countess, when the countess returned to London from South Wales. But alarming news about the decline in health of her cherished mistress, Mrs. Wheatley, now chronically ill, precipitated a change in her plans and an earlier return by her to Boston than had been originally intended. Arrangements had been completed before her departure for the publication of a book of her poems. Thus, in 1773, her *Poems on Various Subjects, Religious and Moral*, both the first book of poetry and the first book of any

---

11. The usually reliable Richmond in *Bid the Vassal Soar*, 38, grants Wheatley "less than a month" in England. Richmond had not the advantage of scrutiny of the careful dating (based on a study of letters and shipping news) of her English trip in Mukhtar Ali Isani, "Phillis Wheatley in London: An Unpublished Letter to David Wooster," *American Literature*, LI (1979), 255–60.

kind by an American Negro, was printed and published overseas in England.[12]

At home in America, Mrs. Wheatley died in the spring of 1774. The Wheatley family circle, as it had been in its fairest days, was disintegrating. Its loss of cohesion, with accompanying effects detrimental to its vitality, had truly begun with the marriage of the twin Mary, Wheatley's most diligent tutor, to the Reverend John Lathrop, pastor of the Second Church of Boston, in 1771. At some point between September 13 and October 18, 1773, directly on the heels of her return from England, Wheatley was freed.[13] Moreover, America was embarking on its own divergence from England. The Boston Tea Party occurred in December, 1773. The British began their blockade of Boston Harbor on June 1, 1774. The Battle of Bunker Hill was fought in June of the next year, 1775. With open warfare all too literally at its very door, what was left of the Wheatley household vacated its premises in Boston and sought relative safety elsewhere. Phillis Wheatley now, of course, could have gone her own way. She chose, however, to remain within the Wheatley fold. So, in the four years following Mrs. Wheatley's death, she lived, under Wheatley auspices, in Boston; Providence, Rhode Island; Chelsea; and Wilmington. It was from Providence that she addressed a commendatory letter and equally commendatory poem to George Washington in the fall of 1775 after he had been appointed to lead the armies of the Continental Congress. It was from Chelsea that, at Washington's invitation, she visited him in Cambridge in the spring of 1776. But in 1778, first John Wheatley, then Mary Wheatley Lathrop, died. Nathaniel, acceding to the strength of his English ties, before his father's death had removed permanently to England, where, incidentally, he died in 1783. A month after the elder Wheatley's death, Phillis Wheatley, her old moorings vanished or vanishing, married the free Negro John Peters.

Harsh words have been used in most quarters to describe Peters. He is reported to have affected a tiewig and a cane and to have tried his hand, at one time or another, at barbering, operating a grocery, and practicing medicine and law. Part of the indictment against him alleges his inap-

12. Mukhtar Ali Isani, "The First Proposed Edition of *Poems on Various Subjects* and the Phillis Wheatley Canon," *American Literature*, L (1977), 97–103. Here Isani also marshals convincing evidence of plans to publish *Poems on Various Subjects* in America two years before it was eventually published in England.
13. Isani, "Phillis Wheatley in London," 259–60.

titude and ill preparation for any of these occupations. A not-so-hidden premise in the criticism of him is the argument that he did not know his place. On the other hand, it has been said of him that he was handsome, a good writer and public speaker, and one not reluctant to demonstrate his interest in advancing the cause of his race. Whatever he was, no visible good accrued to Wheatley from her marriage to him. She bore him three children, two of whom died before the final year of her life. She did advertise a second book of poetry that would also include some of her letters. This book was apparently never assembled and certainly never published. Her marriage had taken her outside the comfortable orbit of her previous life. In her last months of life, her circumstances became so straitened that, in order barely to subsist, she was forced to drudge as a maid of all work in a Negro boardinghouse in Boston. There she died in early December, 1784. Her third and sole surviving child, an infant in arms, died shortly after her on the same day. She and this child were buried with the same ceremony and in the same grave.

No black poet until Paul Laurence Dunbar in the 1890s was so widely known as Phillis Wheatley, and probably none should have been. She was not only much more a beneficiary of training in literacy than either Lucy Terry or Jupiter Hammon. She was also born, apparently, with more of a native endowment for poetry than either of them. Neoclassicism was the prevailing mode for writers of her time. It was a mode to which she gave a close and conscious allegiance. She was sympathetically acquainted with such Latin poets as Virgil and Ovid, exemplars of the poetic art from classical antiquity whom neoclassicists revered.[14] Milton, incidentally, clearly appealed to her, and Miltonic influences may be detected widely in her work. Even so, Pope, the arch practitioner of English neoclassicism, was her model of models. Of the thirty-nine poems in her *Poems on Various Subjects,* all but five are not only in the neoclassic heroic couplet but also in that particular form of couplet—to the full extent, apparently, of which she was capable—precisely in both the manner and spirit of Pope. Pope preeminently affected satire, often of the most virulent tone and the bitterest, most savage content. Phillis Wheatley—perhaps, it can be conjectured, because of her vulnerable position in society—was one neoclassicist who did not turn to satire. But in every other significant respect, she followed Pope and the neoclassicists religiously.

14. Wheatley read Latin. See Julian D. Mason, Jr. (ed.), *The Poems of Phillis Wheatley* (Chapel Hill, 1966), xxiv.

She invoked the muses. She wrote elegies, fourteen in her *Poems on Various Subjects*. She adopted subjects which permitted her to expatiate on abstractions, as in her "On Recollection" and "On Imagination." She indulged rather freely in personification, as became an orthodox neoclassicist, and always in that special neoclassical way which is divided by all too thin a line from abstraction, not because, in it, the process of abstraction has been too personified, but because, in it, the purported process of personification has been too abstract. She was urbane, logical, impersonal in tone (even when writing, as she did in her elegies, of people she knew), and prone to the use of poetic diction—all of these as a good neoclassicist should have been. Her poetry functioned to remind its audience of mankind's universal traits and sentiments and of the occasions in human experience which all men tend to share. Thus, it is axiomatic with her critics that she was an occasional poet, very much in keeping with her neoclassic bent.

A poem of Wheatley's typically is a short lyric at least twenty, but no more than fifty, lines in length. Her two poems of greater length, "Niobe in Distress" (an abbreviation of the title) and "Goliath in Gath," incline, however, toward narrative. "Niobe in Distress" obviously reflects her exposure to classical mythology, another evidence of her neoclassicism. Julian D. Mason has observed of her that the two strongest influences on her work were "definitely" religion and neoclassicism.[15] She was indeed, like Jupiter Hammon, intensely religious. As a trusted ward of the Wheatleys, she could hardly have been otherwise. "Goliath in Gath" reflects the world of Methodist zeal to which the Wheatleys introduced her. Of the more than one hundred poems attributed to her, those not still in manuscript which did not appear exclusively in *Poems on Various Subjects* were published either as broadsides or in magazines.

In a rather famous comment Thomas Jefferson said of Wheatley, whom he called Phillis Whately, that the "compositions published under her name are below the dignity of criticism."[16] But Jefferson's comment seems irresponsibly harsh, especially when Wheatley is compared with other American poets of her time. A couplet from her "On the Death of a Young Lady of Five Years of Age," "Her morning sun, which rose divinely bright, / Was quickly mantled with the gloom of night," well represents the level of art that is probably most likely to be found at random

15. Mason (ed.), *Poems of Wheatley*, xxiii.
16. Thomas Jefferson, *Notes on the State of Virginia* (London, 1787), 135.

in her verse. Increasing knowledge of her poetic activity tends to confirm the indications within her verse that she applied herself with some rigor and delicate sensitivity to the nuances of her craft.[17] She could, then, and did, especially when she was, in a manner of speaking, "at the top of her form," write quite respectably. One may, therefore, with J. Saunders Redding, see well how excellently she sometimes achieved by examining the following lines from her "Thoughts on the Works of Providence," which Redding uses to illustrate her right to be considered an artist of genuine worth:

> Infinite love, where'r we turn our eyes,
> Appears: this ev'ry creature's want supplies;
> This most is heard in nature's constant voice;
> This makes the morn, and this the eve, rejoice;
> This bids the fostering rains and dews descend
> To nourish all, to serve one gen'ral end,
> The good of man: yet man ungrateful pays
> But little homage, and but little praise.
> To Him whose works arrayed in mercy shine,
> What songs should rise, how constant, how divine![18]

And so it does seem that Julian Mason speaks warrantably and judiciously of Wheatley when, even while maintaining that she "wrote too many run-of-the-mill elegies which, except for their historical interest, might now just as well be lost," he also argues:

Yet, some of her poems reveal an exceptional being producing exceptional poetry. Most of her best work is in her nonoccasional poems, certainly in her more philosophic ones. In this regard it is interesting to note that various commentators have chosen different ones of her small body of poems to praise as the best . . . and almost all writers on this subject favor to some degree "An Hymn to the Morning" and "An Hymn to the Evening." One would also be amiss not to place in this company "On Virtue" and "Goliath of Gath" . . . for in certain complete poems and in parts of other poems, Phillis was able to surpass to great degree what was at once both her great asset and her great liability—a favor for and remarkable spontaneous ability to re-create the neoclassical poetic mode of Alexander Pope and his followers in diction, meter, rhyme, and syntax. In some happy instances she avoided ordinary subject matter and clichés, using instead striking, appropriate poetic figures in pleasing form which attracted both the

17. See, for example, the study of her revisions in Gregory Rigsby, "Phillis Wheatley's Craft as Reflected in Her Revised Elegies," *Journal of Negro Education*, XLVII (1978), 402–13.
18. Quoted in Redding, *To Make a Poet Black*, 12.

mind and ear. In these she was more than just an imitator, and she reflected a fortunate influence of the best neoclassicism.[19]

Like Lucy Terry and Jupiter Hammon, Phillis Wheatley under no circumstances could be candidly described as a slave to whom slavery was onerous. She was privileged, as were they. And she comes extremely near to complete avoidance of any allusion to either her race or her enslavement in the poetry she wrote. In her "To the University of Cambridge in New-England" she once refers to herself as "an Ethiop." In her "To the Right Honourable William Earl of Dartmouth, His Majesty's Principal Secretary of the State for North America, & C" she observes:

> Should you, my Lord, while you peruse my song,
> Wonder from whence my love of Freedom sprung,
> Whence flow these wishes for the common good,
> By feeling hearts alone best understood,
> I, young in life, by seeming cruel fate
> Was snatch'd from *Afric's* fancy'd happy seat:
> What pangs excruciating must molest,
> What sorrow labour in my parent's breast
> Steel'd was that soul and by no misery mov'd
> That from a father seiz'd his babe belov'd:
> Such, such my case. And can I then but pray
> Others may never feel tyrannic sway?

And in eight lines which form entirely her "On Being Brought from Africa to America," she counsels her reader:

> 'Twas mercy brought me from my *Pagan* land,
> Taught my benighted soul to understand
> That there's a God, that there's a Savior too:
> Once I redemption neither sought nor knew.
> Some view our sable race with scornful eye,
> "Their colour is a diabolic die."
> Remember, *Christians, Negroes*, black as Cain,
> May be refin'd, and join th' angelic train.

The note of open protest against racism which runs like an agonized sentinel's cry throughout the length and breadth of black American literature from the 1830s to the present simply does not occur in the poetry of Phillis Wheatley. She pays the same homage to Christianity and, presumably, to the culture of her masters as does Jupiter Hammon when

19. Mason (ed.), *Poems of Wheatley*, xii, xxi–xxii.

she speaks of Africa as a fancied happy seat and of blacks who need to be refined before they can be admitted into the angelic train. That her slavers seize African babes from fathers hardly accords with Western assumptions of propriety, where madonnas, not young Josephs, customarily are conceived of as the parents who carry infants in their arms. But rarely, if ever except this once, would an image or concept projected from Wheatley's verse represent a probable departure from convention to her white contemporaries. She was, as all her critics agree, a paragon of acculturation to the Anglo-American environment into which the Wheatleys and their ancestors had been born. Her poetry and her life were to become an important symbol of the Negro's natural rights for northern abolitionists before the Civil War as well as a source of pride in themselves to succeeding generations of black Americans until now. Opinion about her intrinsic worth as a poet obviously has varied rather widely. Direct influence from her upon the literary art of the black writers she has preceded seems negligible, if not nonexistent. Certainly, black poets after her have not been neoclassic, as she was. Nor has she contributed to later black poets anything distinctively racial, either in manner or content, which they could have incorporated into their work. No later black poet has been able to point back to her and say, for example, "I got my sense of rhythm from her and she learned it from the lore of other blacks." Nor can any such poet say, for instance, that any of his insights about special significances connected with being black are traceable to Wheatley. In her demonstration that her white contemporaries possessed no exclusive right or power to write poetry, even on terms prescribed by them, Wheatley did become, nevertheless, in effect, an icon representative of the inherent abilities of her race. To an appreciable extent, although not solely, it is as such an icon that she has survived.

2. The First Writers of Prose

Black American prose seems to begin with a fourteen-page narrative published in 1760 and entitled *A Narrative of the Uncommon Sufferings and Surprizing Deliverance of Briton Hammon, A Negro Man, Written by Himself.* The title does imply what the substance of the narrative confirms: that Hammon, like many, if not overwhelmingly most, of his Christian contemporaries, quite literally and quite firmly believed that God's eye is on the sparrow, so that absolutely nothing, great or small, happens in this universe save by the direct intervention of God's will.

Hammon must have been another privileged slave. In his *Narrative,* explicitly with his master's consent, he sails from Plymouth, Massachusetts—hardly a good day's walk in his day from his home in Marshfield—for the West Indies. His ship touches for several weeks at Jamaica. Then, at what he calls the Bay (possibly Montego), it acquires, presumably for its homeward voyage, a cargo of, again in Hammon's language, logwood. The vessel founders on a shoal off the coast of Florida. Its captain refuses to jettison some of his cargo, an expedient which his eleven fellow shipmates (one of them, Moses Newmack, a "molatto") unanimously and most insistently counsel him might well lighten the vessel sufficiently for it to clear the reef. Indians, arriving on the scene in canoes, kill everyone connected with the ship but Hammon, whom they take with them as a captive. Later, Spaniards effect Hammon's release from the Indians. He suffers subsequent long imprisonments in Havana, eventually is spirited away from Cuba on an English man-of-war, and is continuing what has become a life at sea when, during one of his periods on shore in England, he discovers that his master is in England also. Joyfully reunited with his

master, he returns to Marshfield and composes his account of his un-
intended twelve-year sojourn in foreign lands.

Writing under the spell of much the same spirit of respect and awe
toward Providence as Briton Hammon, John Marrant completed, and
published in 1785, in forty pages, and with a full title several hundred
words long, *A Narrative of the Lord's Wonderful Dealings with John Marrant, a Black*. Readers of Marrant's *Narrative* whose mental picture of the
Old South includes only the familiar scenario from the age of Calhoun,
with its demeaning superimpositions upon all black life, may be startled
at least a little both by what does not, and by what does, seem to be
everyday normality in the *Narrative's* projection of its eighteenth-century
America. Marrant was born free, apparently of free black parents, in
New York in 1745. His father died before Marrant was five years old. His
mother then came south, bringing her family of at least four children
with her, and living successively in Florida, Georgia, and South Carolina. The *Narrative* is preeminently an account of Marrant's conversion
to Christianity and its immediate sequel, which, unless Marrant is guilty
of the most arrant mendacity (or pitiable self-deception), well deserves
his characterization of it as "wonderful."

As the *Narrative* unfolds, Marrant experiences his conversion in
Charleston as a direct result of exposure to the evangelism of George
Whitefield. A boy in his fourteenth year, Marrant is living in Charleston
as a trade apprentice to a second master after having completed an apprenticeship on the violin to a first. But the only masters of whom Marrant speaks in his *Narrative*—other, of course, than Jesus—are these
masters to whom he is apprenticed. Although he is living in the South,
he never mentions slavery or slaves. Nor does this seem an affectation or
aberration on his part. He speaks of the decisions and activities of himself
and of members of his family quite without any indication that he conceived of himself, his mother, and her other children as different in any
way in social status or in their power to assert their personal prerogatives
from anyone else he mentions in his *Narrative*. His voice could be, indeed, insofar as his sense of his own freedom is concerned, the voice of a
young Benjamin Franklin or a young Daniel Boone. When, for instance,
the desire to become a trained musician becomes virtually a passion with
him, he is apprehensive only from his fear that his mother may not grant
his appeal to her for her approval to do what he wants. When, moreover,
his mother consents to his appeal, she needs to worry only about the
drain of his apprenticeship upon her purse. She pays immediately to Mar-

rant's master twenty pounds and agrees to be responsible for Marrant's subsistence throughout the term of his apprenticeship.

Marrant's *Narrative*, however, truly dwells, not upon his apprenticeships, but upon the marvels of his first months as a redeemed Christian. His conversion plunges him into an inquisitorial mood which leads him to forsake his comfortable, settled surroundings and wander into the forest, armed with the Bible and a book of Isaac Watts's hymns, where, without other food, he eventually feeds upon grass and drinks muddied water. Chance attaches him to an Indian hunter with whom, pursuing game, he spends ten weeks. Parted from the hunter, in the towns of the Cherokee nations, he faces death from an ingenious form of being roasted alive. Wondrously his prayers, begun in English but quickly converted by him into the language of the Cherokees, which he has learned from the Indian hunter, abetted by his verbal communings with Jesus that may be even more impressive to the Cherokees because they see and hear no second party in the vacant air he is addressing, so affect the Cherokees, along with his direct proselytizings of his deity to them, that, far from killing him, they make of him a special guest. Many of them, including a daughter of their king, become Christians. They share Marrant, if we can believe him, with other Indian tribes and villages in their part of the world, but only in a way which does him honor, for they let him go nowhere without an imposing retinue of their braves and even, when they finally do bring themselves to part with him, according to his report, escort him, still with his attendant retinue of their braves intact, for 160 miles through their own and their neighbors' territory to the end of their wilderness and the edge of English settlement before bidding him reluctantly adieu.

Marrant did not live a long life. He died, apparently, in 1790. From his *Narrative* we learn that he served in the British navy during the Revolution. How he felt about American independence he does not say, although he makes it clear that his choice of sides in connection with what he called the "American troubles" was more or less forced upon him. Musicians, the British thought, were in too short a supply on their fighting ships. He was a musician. So they commandeered him, through impressment, in order to gain what help they could from his musical skills in elevating the morale of their fleet. They kept him, incidentally, at sea for almost seven years, during which time, among his other experiences, he was wounded and hospitalized. Discharged from the navy, he resided for a while in London. But Marrant, it seems, was at least as devout and staunch a Methodist as either Phillis Wheatley or Jupiter Hammon. Moreover, like a goodly number of other eighteenth-century Methodists, as we have seen, he became, in effect, a small planet revolving around the mammoth sun of the countess of Huntingdon. Ordained a Methodist minister, and probably under the countess' patronage, he went as a missionary to Nova Scotia. Yet by 1789 he was chaplain to the African lodge of Masons in Boston, Massachusetts. A sermon, containing a spirited attack on slavery, delivered by him in that year to his brethren in the lodge for their Festival of St. John has survived, as has also his *Journal of John Marrant*, published in London in 1789, which is approximately twice and a half as long as his *Narrative*, but which, nevertheless, as Loggins correctly describes it, "is scarcely more than an adaptation" of the earlier work.[1]

Marrant obviously is linked to Briton Hammon by the circumstance that both wrote narratives. But the two are linked, additionally, by something else. They are both, that is, in how and what they wrote, even in Marrant's cited attack on slavery, Anglo-Americans of the eighteenth century without, culturally, it may be said in more than jest, an African bone in either of their quite African-appearing bodies. Thus, of course, they are close replicas of Jupiter Hammon, born like them (or, certainly, like Marrant) in America, and of Lucy Terry and Phillis Wheatley, not born in America, but so overwhelmingly conditioned by an American environment that, behaviorally, they might as well have been. White Christians of the eighteenth century tended notably, for instance, to believe in a providential God—in a God, that is, who could, and did, intervene (if necessary, with miracles) in mundane affairs, great or small, whenever he so desired. This God (the God, with his providential character much in evidence, it will be remembered, of Lucy Terry, Jupiter Hammon, and Phillis Wheatley) was the God, as has been here noted earlier, who "surprizingly delivered" Briton Hammon, providentially, from a cruel and evil fate, after first, undoubtedly in a test of Hammon's steadfastness in Christian doctrine, putting Hammon in jeopardy from that very fate. He was the God in praise of whom Marrant heard Whitefield preach and who accompanied Marrant, providentially, into the South Carolina forest.

As this God was not an African deity, so it was not an African design for the construction of a story which influenced either Briton Hammon

---

1. Vernon Loggins, *The Negro Author: His Development in America to 1900* (New York, 1931), 33.

or Marrant when each took care to incorporate into his narrative some reference to captivity among the Indians. Indeed, in permitting themselves to be taken and held as captives by Indians and then surviving to tell of their captivity, Hammon and Marrant found a means which could hardly have been surpassed for proving how utterly non-African they were. Very markedly, Indian captivities as narratives reflected a favorite horror of Anglo-American life in the epoch of America's beginning and were a form of literature which flourished mightily in the American colonies, where, certainly by the eighteenth century, it may well have seemed that every white American not only read but wrote them.[2] Moreover, as the God of Briton Hammon and Marrant was decidedly not an importation from Africa, neither were their Indian captivities, nor was (finally, in this vein) their interest in travel and exploration. That, too, was part of their Afro-Americanism, although it came from a syndrome of exploits and conceptualizations of history less local in its dispersion through either time or space than the set of correspondences with the real world on which the Indian captivities were based. For Americans were only part of the army of watchers and listeners in the Western world who, from the beginning of the end of the West's insularity during the days when the first whites reached places like the West Indies and Southeast Asia, had feasted, as it were, upon the accounts of faraway places and exciting, unusual deeds brought back to the West's stay-at-homes by Western wanderers around the globe. A literature of travel and exploration, by the era of Hammon and Marrant, accordingly, had impacted on the Western mind for centuries. It may never, however, have been more pervasive throughout a culture than in the eighteenth century, when its presence could be detected, not only in the actual tales of actual travel then in circulation, but also in the fictitious travel associated with such literary *tours de force* as *ingénu* satire and the *romans africains*, as well as in some of the exotica of eighteenth-century fashions in furniture, decoration, clothes, manners, and even gardening.

The hold of the literature of travel and exploration upon Marrant and Briton Hammon was anything but obsessive in its control of their imaginations. Yet it did affect their narratives. In his narrative, Marrant ventures into a wilderness, albeit that wilderness is sufficiently adjacent to his home for him to walk into it. He does find, in this wilderness, a way

---

2. *The Garland Library of Narratives of North American Indian Captivities,* in its 111 volumes, preserves 311 such narratives.

of life somewhat unlike the way of life to which his Afro-American up-
bringing has assimilated him. He travels, then, and, in confronting
scenes and human customs hitherto unknown to him, also explores. Furthermore, brief as are his references in his *Narrative* to his years at sea and
his sojourns in England and Nova Scotia, those years and those sojourns
extend his stature as a traveler. As for Briton Hammon, all of his *Narrative* is, in literal fact, a travelogue. It is exploration, also, bearing Hammon into alien scenes under different, brighter skies than those of his
dour and familiar New England, and into an area of the world where the
Catholic Spaniard, not Protestants from northern Europe, holds sway.
Hammon is as aware as any other Westerner contemporary with him of
the antipathies between Catholics and Protestants. His *Narrative* reveals
that he is and also that virtually every one of the narrow prejudices
against Catholics which the most bigoted Protestant of his time might
have been expected to entertain he found himself able uncritically to regard as his own. On this ground, and others, therefore, his *Narrative*
easily suffices to illustrate the nature and direction of his cultural af-
finities. He, and all of the earliest black American writers, are black
Anglo-Americans. Blacks preserving cultural distinctions which separate
them from other Americans and proclaim their African identities and
past emphatically they, as a group, are not.

Because Briton Hammon was a slave, it is altogether proper to allude
to his *Narrative* as a slave narrative. Perhaps it should not be. We have
already noted the lack of the restraints we might associate with slavery on
Hammon. He was, de facto, no matter what the law said of him, as free
as Marrant. Still, it is through him, not Marrant, that a tie exists between the very earliest black American writers and the one class of literary works to which inheres, if only for the reason that slavery is indispensable to it, a special, exclusive, and apparently genetic relationship
with Afro-American literature. That class is the slave narrative and,
thus, Hammon's *Narrative* belongs to a class, a genre, of which there
have been, in America, from versions hardly a paragraph in length to
bulky volumes, possibly more than six thousand examples over a period
of almost two hundred years, and a counterpart of which can no more be
found in American literature written by whites than the roots of blues
and jazz can be discovered in American music of white folk origins. Yet
an interesting anomaly obtains for Hammon's *Narrative*. Some literary
historians do not grant it pride of place as the first of all slave narratives

even though it has long been generally credited with being the first piece of prose by a black American author.

Thus, in his classic study of slave narratives, *Many Thousand Gone*, Charles H. Nichols attributes the distinction of being the first American slave narrative to *Adam Negro's Tryall*, which appeared in 1703, as does also John F. Bayliss in the introduction to the collection *Black Slave Narratives*, edited by him.[3] Adam Negro was a slave who, in 1701 in Boston, sued his master, John Saffin, a merchant and jurist, alleging that Saffin had promised to free him but was not abiding by his expressly given word. A protracted litigation ensued from Adam's suit, occupying the better part of three years and the attention of the inferior court of Massachusetts on two occasions before four additional hearings in the superior court of the same commonwealth. Adam contended that Saffin had pledged him the grant of liberty in 1694, subject only to seven years of faithful service from Adam to Saffin beyond 1694. At some point during these seven years, however, Saffin bonded Adam out to a Thomas Shepard, one of Saffin's tenants, with whom, according to Saffin, Adam conducted himself "turbulently, negligently, insolently, and outrageously," thus clearly relieving Saffin, Saffin maintained, of any obligation to manumit Adam.[4] Moreover, after the litigation between Saffin and Adam began, and as it dragged tortuously on, Saffin pleaded a fear of physical danger, if not of murder, at the hand of Adam, who, Saffin said, had boasted that he might very well wring Saffin's neck as he would the neck of a snake. Nevertheless, Saffin sat as a judge in one of the trials of Adam, which found for Saffin, to the great disgust of the famed Samuel Sewall, whose tolerance for Saffin, not great at any time (to make money Saffin gagged at nothing, not even smuggling slaves), was hardly increased when he learned that, not only had Saffin been a judge, but one of his tenants had been a juror, in the legal controversy between Saffin and Adam. In any case, Sewall was himself a judge and a man of influence to boot. He championed Adam's cause, which ultimately triumphed on appeal, and Adam, in 1703, by law became as free as Saffin.

A number of documents, legal and otherwise, accumulated around

3. Charles H. Nichols, *Many Thousand Gone: The Ex-Slaves' Account of Their Bondage and Freedom* (Bloomington, Ind., 1969), x; John F. Bayliss (ed.), *Black Slave Narratives* (New York, 1970), 9.
4. Lorenzo J. Greene, *The Negro in Colonial New England, 1620–1776* (New York, 1942), 296. Greene gives, on 296–97, an excellent account of the highly acrimonious tug-of-war between Adam and Saffin. To Greene I am principally indebted for my picture of Adam.

Adam's case. This aggregation, a genuine miscellany, fittingly termed by Frances Smith Foster both a "conglomeration" and a "potpourri of pamphlets, court records, diaries and events," in no wise achieves the character of a true autobiography written by a single, responsibly identified autobiographer. And so, if a slave narrative, especially as the designation applies to Afro-American literature, should meet the requirement, first of all, that it be an autobiography whose author is a slave or, at least, an ex-slave—a requirement which does not seem at all unreasonable—then *Adam Negro's Tryall* can never be called a slave narrative. It is about Adam. It is far from by him. Foster categorizes it, in what appears to be an excellent job of finding the right name to apply to it, as a precursor of the true slave narratives.[5] It could be the first precursor. It does not appear to be the only precursor, although it is surely the only known possible precursor composed, as it surely is, of nothing more than a rather motley array of written materials by several hands not one of which belonged to someone engaged in giving his own version of all, or part, of his own life.

Another possible precursor, it would seem, to the whole class of slave narratives is the account written down by Thomas Bluett and published in 1734 as *Some Memoirs of the Life of Job, the Son of Solomon the High Priest of Boonda in Africa; Who was a Slave about Two Years in Maryland; and afterwards being brought to England, was set free and sent to his native land in the Year 1734.* Thomas Bluett was white and a resident of Maryland when, in 1731, Job ben Solomon, as he was called in America and England, having been landed at Annapolis, Maryland, was put to work as a slave on nearby Kent Island in Chesapeake Bay. In his own country of Bondu (Bluett's Boonda), near the Senegal River but over three hundred miles from the coast of West Africa, Job was known as Ayuba Suleiman Diallo. His father, reputed to be the high priest of Bondu, was at least a man of some eminence in his homeland, where Mohammedism was the religion that prevailed. Job, on a trading mission for his father, had strayed unwisely into hostile territory within the homelands of peoples oriented toward the Gambia River, too far from Bondu for his own safety, and had been captured, sold as a slave, and brought in an English ship to Maryland. It would be down the same Gambia River, some thirty-six years later, that Kunta Kinte, Alex Haley's ancestor in

---

5. Frances Smith Foster, *Witnessing Slavery: The Development of Ante-bellum Slave Narratives* (Westport, Conn., 1979), 30, 31, 32.

Roots, would be transported out of Africa and conveyed, like Job, to Maryland, even to Annapolis.

Job not only attracted attention in Maryland because of his aristocratic bearing, his obvious unfitness for labor in fields where tobacco was being planted and grown, and his dutiful practice of the Mohammedan religion. Once it became known, in Maryland, from where in West Africa he had come and his family's position there, he benefited from the eighteenth-century rivalry between the English and the French. For, in the 1730s, the French were the leading Europeans along the Senegal. The English were the leading Europeans along the Gambia. And Bondu was in the French sphere of influence, which the British were eager to penetrate. The possible uses of Job in such a penetration were so evident that they could hardly be ignored. Thomas Bluett participated in the exchange of information, as did James Oglethorpe in the negotiations, which led to Job's delivery from slavery in Maryland, his stay in England, where he was lionized, and his return to Bondu, after being ransomed by his family, as a friend of the English and of their plans for a greater share of the trade from Bondu and its vicinity.

Bluett knew Job in both America and England. In *The Life of Job*, Bluett functions, he would have his readers believe (and he certainly believed himself), merely in the role of an amanuensis rather than as a biographer. So, he could be interpreted as performing an office in the presentation of a slave narrative not greatly, if any, different from that of some of the white mediators and expediters to whom, approximately a hundred years later, fugitive slaves would "dictate" their narratives. But Job was not, as those fugitives would be, illiterate. We are told that he could reproduce the whole Koran from memory. Certainly he could have written his own memoir and given to Europeans a picture of his own mind. Instead, Bluett's *Life of Job* gives a picture of Bluett's mind, most arrestingly, it well may be, in Bluett's presentation of Job as if Job were a noble savage considerably advanced, it is true, beyond primitivism by, if nothing else, his Mohammedism, but still essentially as much a child of Rousseauistic nature as the protagonist of Aphra Behn's *Oroonoko*. Nor is Bluett a Mohammedan. He writes like the thorough Occidental he is, leaving little doubt that *The Life of Job* is a narrative, not by a slave, but by someone acquainted with that slave. There were some "slave narratives" in the eighteenth century which were mendacious to the extreme, complete forgeries, as, for instance, *The Life and Adventures of Zamba, an African King; and his Experiences of Slavery in South Carolina, written by Himself*, in Philip Curtin's well-informed opinion, one of the "more blatant" forgeries.[6] *The Life of Job* is no such forgery. It is not pure invention. There was a Job. The account of his life written by Bluett should be associated with genuine slave narratives. It should hardly be identified as one of them.

One more possible precursor, individually and as a type, to the genuine slave narrative remains to be mentioned. In Massachusetts in 1745 appeared *The Declaration and Confession of Jeffery, a Negro, who was executed at Worchester, October 17, 1745, for the murder of Mrs. Tabitha Sanford, at Mendon, the 12th of September Preceding*. This *Declaration and Confession* was a broadside, as would be *The Life and Dying Speech of Arthur, a Negro Man, Who was executed at Worchester, October 20th, 1768 for a rape committed On the Body of one Deborah Metcalfe*. In the eighteenth century, of course, before the day of the rotary press and of newspapers and newsmagazines capable of huge, rapid multiplications and circulations of themselves (to say nothing of a similar competence exponentially greater in its effect possessed by the awesome forces of wireless media), the confessions, the dying speeches, and other like effusions from criminals, printed as broadsides or chapbooks and hawked abroad, offered about as facile an approach as any to the pockets and the attention of a mass audience. How much of any particular broadside or chapbook purported to be a criminal's outpouring of himself was the authentic, unaided expression of the criminal who was supposed to have uttered it, rather than the work of a literary ghost, will almost surely never be known. Some caution, therefore, must be exercised in asserting that Jeffery wrote all, or even most, of his *Declaration and Confession*. He quite possibly did not. Arthur, also, may not actually have written much of his *Life and Dying Speech*. However, whatever feats of authorship Jeffery and Arthur did, or did not, perform, the works attributed to them are criminal narratives, and criminal narratives, like Indian captivities, in the eighteenth century constituted a recognizable element in the presumed wisdom about his environment of the then average man. Jeffery's *Declaration and Confession* and Arthur's *Life and Dying Speech* were not the only criminal narratives credited to black criminal authors in early America. There seem to have been, by 1800, between thirty and thirty-five such narratives, all short, and none the preparation of which without some complicity from an anonymous

---

6. Philip Curtin (ed.), *Africa Remembered: Narratives by West Africans from the Era of the Slave Trade* (Madison, Wis., 1968), 6.

collaborator (singly or collectively) in its authorship is a matter of sworn and credible certitude.

Slave narratives in the manner most representative of the slave narrative as a phenomenon of consequence in Afro-American literature did not develop from criminal narratives, not even from those criminal narratives concerning which their publishers stipulated that they had been written by black criminals. The great period of the slave narrative falls between 1830 and 1860. In these particular thirty years just before the Civil War, the slave narrative was at its best in the sense that it exhibited then the characteristics generally considered now most typical of it. Prominent among such characteristics, understandably, was the fierce attack launched and maintained by that slave narrative against slavery. Slavery was not an issue in black criminal narratives. Yet evil was. Moreover, both in the slave narrative as it would be in its most representative form and in the black criminal narrative as it was in the era of Jeffery and Arthur, or at any time, sensationalism played a role. Resemblances in content, then, do link the black criminal narratives and the most representative slave narratives. Inevitably, also, the two genres exhibit resemblances in form, since both genres are quintessentially narrative. Hence, however much by parallels that merely happen to be parallels, there are elements within the black criminal narrative which do reappear in the most representative slave narratives. To that extent, at least, as well as in its eighteenth-century setting (earlier than the 1830–1860 period) and the race of its declared authors, the black criminal narrative qualifies as a precursor of the slave narrative in the very guise that genre would eventually assume after it had shaped itself consciously to be, above all, a voice for the freeing of America's slaves. It should be added here that the blacks who wrote, or were said to have written, the black criminal narratives did tend to be slaves. Consequently, in terms of one criterion only, the criterion of whether its announced authors were free or slave, the black criminal narrative was, thus circumscribed, very definitely a slave narrative.

About one slave narrative published in the eighteenth century there is nothing that can be cited against the legitimacy of its right to be regarded as a "true" slave narrative but much that can, and probably should, be adduced in support of its recognition as a work of prime importance in early Afro-American literature. That slave narrative is *The Interesting Narrative of the Life of Olaudah Equiano, or Gustavus Vassa the African, written by himself*, which was first published in London in 1789, and which, for a generation, until nearly 1840, was enough of an attraction in the judgment of the book-buying public throughout the English-speaking world to go through many editions in both England and America. In addition, Equiano's *Narrative* may be the best of the slave narratives written before the period of 1830 to 1860. The narratives of Briton Hammon and Marrant both are short, not as long, indeed, as a large percentage of the chapters in most books or of articles in most magazines. Equiano's *Narrative*, at approximately sixty thousand words, is genuinely book-length, even though not sufficiently extensive to make a large book. It alludes to most of Equiano's life, excluding only the final third thereof, and it does so in a mode of English speech which, while it is by no means the fine instrument English prose did become when used by such eighteenth-century virtuosos at the glorification of style in their own language as Addison, Steele, Swift, and Samuel Johnson, is still a medium which serves to unfold a protracted tale clearly, often interestingly, and never with a hint that its employer is affecting a vernacular decidedly not that which he, as it were, imbibed with his mother's milk. There is, however, more than a hint of propaganda in Equiano's *Narrative*. Equiano did reach a point in his life, before he wrote his *Narrative*, when he could speak his mind much as he genuinely desired. For him that meant, among other things, an active advocacy of the antislavery cause. His *Narrative* is not a tract. Above all else it recounts a series of memorable events in the history of a very real and individual human being. Yet, unlike the narratives of Briton Hammon and Marrant, it does combine its autobiography with polemics, in strategically selected moments excoriating both slavery and the slave trade, the contribution of which to the prolongation of slavery Equiano patently and perceptively does not underestimate.

Equiano's *Narrative* begins in Africa. Therein it is further unlike the narratives of Briton Hammon and Marrant—or, for that matter, the poetry of Terry and Wheatley, even though Terry and Wheatley, like Equiano, were "salt-water Negroes." Indeed, Equiano, in his *Narrative*, is the first black writer associated with America who speaks in any particularity of an Africa remembered. Equiano was born, by his own account, in 1745 in southeastern Nigeria, a member of the Ibo people and a resident of "a charming fruitful vale, named Essaka." Equiano's recollections of life in "Essaka" are fairly circumstantial. He summoned them for use in his *Narrative* perhaps more than thirty years after he had quitted Africa.

They apparently returned to him little, if any, harmfully distorted by lapses or errors of memory. Comparisons of them with the increasing knowledge about eighteenth-century Africa of present-day Africanists who have documented their research suggest that the picture they give of Equiano's homeland as it must truly have been when Equiano lived there is reasonably reliable. African kidnappers, moving by stealth through Equiano's village while its adults were tending their fields out of eyeshot of the village, bore away to African slavery both Equiano and his sister when Equiano was about ten years old. The African slavery Equiano found neither as harsh nor as degrading as the white man's slavery into which, separated from his sister, he was introduced near the Gulf of Guinea months only after his capture in "Essaka."

Possibly, Equiano's references in his *Narrative* to life in Africa, including especially his allusions to African slavery, are as kindly as they are in order to enhance his denigrations of slavery in Europeanized America. Equiano, on a slaver, was taken from the Gulf of Guinea to Barbados, where he was not considered a good slave to buy. Earlier we conjectured that Wheatley may have arrived in Boston as "refuse," a term the special meaning of which in the slave trade could apply to slaves scorned by potential purchasers in the Caribbean slave marts. As "refuse" Equiano arrived in Virginia. There Michael Henry Pascal, an officer in the English navy, bought him. He remained Pascal's slave throughout the Seven Years' War, securing thus a heavy dose of exposure to battle scenes. He was, for instance, with his master, on an English fighting ship at both Louisburg and Belle Isle. In 1763 he was sold to Robert King, a Philadelphia Quaker and an owner of ships which traded in West Indian and American ports. Three years later he bought his freedom from King, who, although a Quaker, was loath to accept his money and release him from his state of bondage. As a free man Equiano traveled in the West Indies, to the Levant, and to the western Mediterranean, with John Constantine Phipps, afterward Lord Mulgrave; on an Arctic expedition searching for a northeast passage and the North Pole; and in the land of the Mosquito Indians on the Nicaraguan coast of Central America. Eventually Equiano did settle down in England, where, from his first visit to it, he had longed to live. In 1792 he married an Englishwoman, a Miss Susan, or Susanna, Cullen. He had been deeply involved in the movement to establish, for the black poor, the colony of Sierra Leone and, as a matter of fact, had expected to accompany the founding expedition to the colony as its commissary for stores. Intimations from him of looseness in the handling of the funds for the movement, added to other differences between him and some of the people with whom he would have had to work in Sierra Leone, led to his dismissal as commissary for stores. Even so, and despite his marriage, he retained an interest in Africa. He may never have abandoned, it seems, a hope of returning there as a missionary or an explorer. The date of his death is uncertain. It has been said that he died in London in 1797.[7]

It can be argued, in respect to Equiano, that he never actually lived in America and that it is, therefore, an unwarrantably liberal use of language to speak of him as an American author. His direct acquaintance with America admittedly was limited. He spent some weeks in Virginia, apparently near a river, before his first master, an Englishman from Old England, as Equiano called England within the British Isles, bought him. He was bought by his second master, not in America, although that master was American as we conceive Americans, but in Montserrat, one of the Leeward Islands of the West Indies. As long as he belonged to his second master tiny Montserrat was his home. He only visited, during that time, the much larger American mainland, albeit once as far north there as Philadelphia. Both before and after he was free, he came in trading expeditions to South Carolina and Georgia, so that he did spend some time, in days, not in weeks or months, actually within the boundaries of cities like Charleston and Savannah. Settled in England, he yet continued, for ten years, to travel, but never to the English colonies on the American continent. His America was much, much more the Caribbean than it ever was the colonies which have become the United States. Yet in the eighteenth century the English possessions in the Western Hemisphere constituted a unit as those same lands, all of them now liberated from a mother country, do not today. In his *Narrative* it is clear that Equiano feels himself, in terms of his sense of where he belongs, as much at home (and at odds with slavery by whites) in continental, as in Antillean, America. As an account of an Anglo-American world, his *Narrative*, following the unmistakably habitual practice to be expected in its day, tends to view that world—the mother country and the colonies, whether islands in the Caribbean or land along the American coast—as substantially an undivided whole. The American part of that whole was both,

7. Paul Edwards (ed.), *Equiano's Travels* (New York, 1967), xv.

and rather indifferently to Englishmen before our Revolution, the islands off the American shore and the American shore itself. Even so, the West Indian America, with its dominant sugar plantations and mills and its over nine blacks to every white, was never quite the same as the America of the English colonies along the American shore. The degree and kind of Equiano's Americanism must, therefore, always be subject to qualification. With that proviso, strong as it is, he probably still does remain continentally American enough to be permitted in a pantheon of continental America's black authors.

There is one more eighteenth-century true slave narrative by a black who had, like Equiano, no trouble recalling, for his narrative, a childhood some of which was spent in Africa. This black, however, quite unlike Equiano, did live his life outside Africa, both as a slave and a free man, within the confines of present-day America. His name was Venture Smith, and he acquired his odd first name for the reason (a nice illustration of the variety of opportunities for avid enterprising in the slave trade) that the steward of the vessel which brought him from Africa, before the ship set sail across the Atlantic, purchased him for a private experiment in slave trading.

Venture's *A Narrative of the Life and Adventure of Venture, a Native of Africa But Resident Above Sixty Years in the United States of America* was first published in 1798. In this *Narrative* Venture reports himself as being born in 1729. By his own testimony, then, he was in his seventieth year of life when his *Narrative* appeared. He seems to have come from a region of West Africa east, by not a tremendous distance, of present-day Ghana. His father, we learn from him, was a king of monumental stature and great bravery who was killed when an African army which seems to have been collecting slaves and other plunder overran his father's kingdom. His father died in battle. Venture apparently inherited his father's size and strength. In Connecticut and nearby Long Island, where he spent all of his long American years, he was renowned for both. He might well have been renowned also for his persistence and success in reordering the conditions of his American existence. By the time he was forty-six years old, he had purchased his own freedom and that of his wife, his oldest child, a daughter, and three Negro men. At the time he wrote his *Narrative*, he tells us, he was possessed of more than one hundred acres of land and three "habitable dwelling houses," and he had, at one time or another, "of boats, canoes and sail vessels . . . [owned] not less then twenty."[8] But, although Venture speaks of his father with pride and of his childhood in Africa in terms reminiscent of Equiano's fond recollections of his own African background, Venture's *Narrative* is as much an unabashed defense of the British and American petty bourgeoisie as it would have been had it been written by the steward who had named him Venture. The memorable complaints in Venture's *Narrative* are not against slavery but against people, white and black, who have, through chicanery or what Venture represents as violations of commercial contracts, cost him money or property. Venture could not escape his African birth. The more querulous passages in his *Narrative* unwittingly emphasize his failure to escape the mentality of a Western small entrepreneur. The color of his skin was something of an oddity in Connecticut. His embrace of a Protestant work ethic and of the values of Western capitalism in the eighteenth and nineteenth centuries was not.

And yet Venture, of course, may have been more of a "race" man, a champion of his people, than can be easily discerned in the pages of his *Narrative*. His deepest motive, indeed, for writing his *Narrative* could have been a desire of his to speak out for black people, to show what he had done, under certainly a set of trying and extremely adverse circumstances, with his own life as an example of his race's capabilities and a protest against the proposition that Negroes were created only to be slaves. His *Narrative* is a very pedestrian piece of writing. He was clearly not a writer by trade or an artist driven, by some daemon which would not let him rest, to practice his art in a furious pursuit of beauty and of truth. In no sense was literature his life. Rather, writing, for him, at most was an avocation, something he did to seek a satisfaction which had little, if anything, to do with an aesthetic conscience. So, also, writing may well have been for some others of his color in his day of whom, less private in their lives than he, it could be said that race leadership, whether they were altogether aware of it or not, had become, more or less, their actual vocation and one so demanding on them that everything else they did—including, sometimes, writing—was an avocation forced upon them, in their judgment, to improve their practice of their vocation.

There are, probably, no more clear-cut instances of such others, of race leaders in Venture's day who wrote, truly, in extenuation of their race leadership, than Prince Hall and Richard Allen. Hall, born in Bar-

8. Venture Smith, *A Narrative of the Life and Adventure of Venture, a Native of Africa But Resident Above Sixty Years in the United States of America*, in Venture Smith et al., *Five Black Lives* (Middletown, Conn., 1971), 23.

bados in 1748, migrated to Boston in 1765, and died there in 1807, but not until he had, while becoming a relatively affluent soap maker and property owner in his personal affairs, founded Negro Masonry. His was the initiative behind the establishment of a lodge of Negro Masons in Boston by the Masons of a British army regiment in 1775 and the eventual granting of a charter to that lodge, by the Grand Lodge of England in the 1780s, which provided the legal base for all of black Masonry in America. A charge of Hall's delivered to the African Lodge at Menotomy, Massachusetts, outside Boston, on June 24, 1797, constitutes his most considerable contribution to Afro-American literature.

Richard Allen may have been the most outstanding leader of his race before Frederick Douglass. Born a slave in Philadelphia in 1760, sold to a proprietor of land in Delaware when he was four years old, he bought his freedom from that proprietor in 1783 and was back in Philadelphia, where he lived the rest of his life, by 1786. He was involved in an incident, in the white St. George's Methodist Episcopal Church in Philadelphia in 1787, a sequel to which was the founding of the Free African Society of Philadelphia and of two churches, one of which was Bethel, the so-called mother congregation of the African Methodist Episcopal church, the familiarly known AMEs, largest connectional denomination of black America (Baptist churches are, in strict legality, separate congregations), of which Allen was, except for an almost never remembered day-only incumbency by Daniel Coker, the first bishop. Allen died in 1831. His funeral, described as the largest, until that time, accorded an American Negro, attested to the place he held in the black America of his day. He could, therefore, hardly have avoided writing something. As a matter of fact, he did write an undated autobiography, *The Life, Experience, and Gospel Labors of the Rt. Rev. Richard Allen, to Which Is Annexed the Rise and Progress of the African Methodist Episcopal Church in the United States*, which was not published until 1880. His "Letter on Colonization," an emphatic statement of his anticolonization views, appeared in the first Negro newspaper, *Freedom's Journal*, on November 2, 1827. He collaborated with his close friend of many years, Absalom Jones, in *A Narrative of the Proceedings of the Black People during the Late Awful Calamity in Philadelphia; and a Refutation of Some Censures Thrown Upon Them in Some Late Publication*, published in 1794. An epidemic of yellow fever in Philadelphia in 1792 and 1793 was the "late, awful calamity." The white Matthew Carey, in his *Short Account of the Malignant Fever*, published in Philadelphia in 1793, had severely taken to task Philadelphia's blacks for what he charged was intolerably gross and even criminal misconduct on their part while Philadelphia was ravaged by disease. Carey predicated his *Short Account* on the arbitrary hypothesis that blacks, naturally, one must suppose, possess an immunity to yellow fever which whites do not have. It had been an obligation, therefore, of their condition for them to have taken care of the whites during the calamity. Instead, they had tried to capitalize on misery. They had done less as nurses than they should have done. They had demanded exorbitant payments for what services they had provided in attending to the sick and burying the dead. And they had pilfered and plundered outrageously. Allen and Jones not only, in their *Narrative of the Proceedings*, question Carey's charges. They also remind him that he was not in Philadelphia during the epidemic. Fear for his own safety had impelled him elsewhere. The longest work, however, of any kind bearing Allen's name is his collaboration with Jacob Tapisco on *The Doctrine and Discipline of the African Methodist Episcopal Church*, published in 1817.

Absalom Jones not only collaborated with Allen in the writing of *A Narrative of the Proceedings*. He had also been with Allen in St. George's Church when the incident occurred that led to the Free African Society. One of the two churches, Allen's Bethel AME Church, which developed from the Free African Society, has already been mentioned. The other was St. Thomas' Episcopal Church, having Absalom Jones as its rector and, in 1795, the first black rector of an Episcopalian congregation in America. Jones had been born a slave in Sussex, Delaware, in 1746. He was, thus, older than Allen and, indeed, in the warm harmony between the two, although there could be no doubt of Allen's preeminence, Jones was, apparently, something of a father figure. Jones was not brought to Philadelphia, by a master new to him, until 1762. He bought the freedom of the woman he married before he eventually purchased his own freedom in 1784. He stayed in Philadelphia and there became the solid, trusted, venerated leader it took an Allen to outshine. He pastored St. Thomas' for twenty-two years until his death in 1818. In addition to his collaboration with Allen in *A Narrative of the Proceedings*, he is remembered in Afro-American literature for *A Thanksgiving Sermon, Preached January 1, 1808, in St. Thomas's, or the African Episcopal Church, Philadelphia; on Account of the Abolition of the African Slave Trade*, which was published in Philadelphia in 1808, the year that America, insofar as the law declared, ended its importation of slaves from abroad.

Benjamin Banneker was an early race leader who, in at least one respect, differed greatly from Allen and Jones, or for that matter from Hall. Allen, Jones, and Hall were race leaders in a very overt and highly visible way. They lived and worked with groups of Negroes in whose midst they were while they performed quite public actions which identified them as tribunes in the people's interest for all the members of their race. Banneker, from childhood through old age, was something of a recluse. Moreover, there were circumstances about his family and the location of his normal residence which limited his association with blacks. He had, to begin with, a curious genealogy. His grandmother, Molly Welsh, or Walsh, convicted in England of stealing a pail of milk which rumor averred she did not tamper with at all dishonestly, but which a cow kicked over, arrived in Maryland under a forced indenture, worked out her indenture, acquired land hardly ten miles from a Baltimore then nonexistent, increased her holdings in land, bought two slaves off a vessel "in the bay" straight from Africa to help her work those increased holdings, freed both her bondmen in a few years, and married one of them, whose African name of Bannka or Bannicky (or some such collocation of sounds) became, in English, Banneker, and by whom she had four children, all girls. Bannka was said to have been an African prince. He did not live nearly so long as his wife. His oldest daughter, Mary, born in 1700, tall, handsome, well proportioned, and stalwart, in 1730 married another "salt-water Negro," Robert, who took Banneker for a surname. Benjamin Banneker, born in 1731, was the only son of Mary and Robert Banneker; their later three children were all girls.

Everything we know about the Bannekers, although not remarkable for its total volume, suggests that they were a very closely knit family the members of which tended to keep much to themselves. When Molly Welsh married Bannka, she violated Maryland law. But, whereas in the late twentieth century five million people live in the combined Baltimore and Washington metropolitan areas, in the late seventeenth century, when Molly was clearing land, raising tobacco, and becoming, in effect, a sturdy yeoman farmer and small planter, as well as later, in the eighteenth century, when her children and grandchildren were growing up under her eyes and often her tutelage, Maryland along the Patapsco River, near which Molly lived, was sparsely settled. Unless she exerted herself to advertise it, few people then would ever know of her illegal marriage, and those few would tend to be, like herself, quietly secluded in what was still, to some extent, a wilderness.

Benjamin Banneker learned his letters from his grandmother Molly, one of whose most prized possessions was a large Bible which she had had sent out to her from England. He knew his grandmother well. Robert Banneker, his father, in spite of giving a willing and generous hand to Molly in the cultivation of her land, had rather quickly, after his marriage, become a landowner, too. Indeed, he owned, not only a small tract of land of twenty-five acres called Timber Poynt, but also a larger farm of one hundred acres which he had purchased in both his son's name and his own. Robert Banneker died in 1759. Benjamin Banneker never married. In addition to the loving instruction he received from his grandmother, he attended, for a few months in each of several years, a one-room schoolhouse near his home. But the bulk of his life was spent, largely in solitude, on his farm, of which he seems, in his prime, to have been an efficient husbandman. Between other members of his family and himself there seems always to have been genial and steady intercourse. He was retiring, but not one to make a point of shunning his fellowman. He played the violin and the flute. Moreover, when he was twenty-two years old, after having seen only two timepieces, a sundial and a pocket watch, and using only a minimum of iron and brass, he carved, from hard-grained wood, a clock which both ran accurately and struck the hours correctly. In the valley of the Patapsco his clock made of him a celebrity. Two members of a family named Ellicott would contribute to his life in ways that would make him, even outside the valley of the Patapsco, relatively well known.

The Ellicotts were Quakers who began their American careers in Pennsylvania. As builders of mills for grinding corn and grains, they invaded, and greatly transformed, the Patapsco Valley. They were affable, able, imaginative, and industrious. To support their mills they built roads, stores, and warehouses. Around their mills, stores, and warehouses, in the 1770s and 1780s, communities developed. Banneker, no longer young, was drawn somewhat out of his shell by the Ellicotts. There was an Ellicott store near his farm. His mother was still living, and she had an arrangement to supply some of the provisions which the Ellicotts thought they needed. Meanwhile, Banneker fell into the habit of loitering, taciturn but observant, at the aforementioned store. He and young George Ellicott, twenty-nine years his junior, formed an attachment based on their mutual interest in astronomy. George let him have books and instruments he could use in studying the heavens. By the 1790s Banneker, undoubtedly a born mathematician, began to think of calculating an ephemeris from which an almanac could be constructed.

For his first ephemeris, which would have provided the basic component of an almanac for the year 1791, he almost, but not quite, found a printer. His work on a second ephemeris was interrupted by the great adventure of his life. One of the Ellicotts was a leading surveyor of the time. This Ellicott was commissioned to lay out the ten-mile-square Federal Territory, or District of Columbia, as it has now long been called. He chose Banneker as his assistant. From February until late April, 1791, Banneker left his farm and worked with this Ellicott on the District survey. It was the only time in his life he absented himself from his farm for a period longer than a matter of hours. His employment with the survey, however, merely delayed his completion of his second ephemeris, which did appear in an almanac for the year 1792. This almanac, printed in Baltimore and made available for distribution in Baltimore, Philadelphia, and Alexandria, was to bring Banneker no small measure of fame, largely because of its promotion by antislavery Quakers. An almanac bearing Banneker's name and featuring an ephemeris by him appeared in every year from 1792 through 1797. Banneker died at his home in 1806.

The ephemeris of an almanac is, of course, not belles-lettres. Still, it is writing of a sort, as is any scientific treatise. And there was much writing, other than simple predictions about the seasons and the weather, in an eighteenth-century almanac. There were, in such almanacs, proverbs, parables, poetry, incidental intelligence—space occupiers of all kinds. Banneker's almanacs were no exception to this general rule. Most of the material, however, which padded the almanacs and presumably increased their sale tended to be selected by printers. Here, again, Banneker's almanacs were no exception to a general rule. It has been conjectured that "A Plan for a Peace Office," which appears in a Banneker almanac for 1793 and proposes the establishment of a department in the president's cabinet to advance the cause of peace, was written by Banneker. A recent discovery of this "Plan," however, in a collection of essays published in 1798 by Benjamin Rush establishes beyond question that Rush was its author.[9]

Banneker did versify a little, and it is almost a certainty that some of the "fillers" in his almanacs, prose or poetry, if not both, were products of his pen. It has been said that, among papers which he left by will to George Ellicott, but which were later destroyed by fire, were dissertations, written by him, on the habits of bees and locusts and some rimed

9. Silvio A. Bedini, *The Life of Benjamin Banneker* (New York, 1972), 186–87.

problems in mathematics which it was Banneker's rather habitual pastime to compose for the delectation of his friends.[10] Nevertheless, in addition to his ephemerides only one piece of writing associated with Banneker or his almanacs can safely be attributed to him. Prior to the publication of his first almanac, Banneker sent a copy of his ephemeris for it, with an accompanying letter, to Thomas Jefferson, then George Washington's secretary of state. The letter related the ephemeris to animadversions upon the Negro's capacity to think. Jefferson responded graciously to the letter, in his reply noting that he had sent the ephemeris on to his friend and member of the Société des Amis des Noirs, the noted French scientist and revolutionary Condorcet. Both Banneker's letter to Jefferson and Jefferson's reply to it were published in connection with the appearance of Banneker's first almanac.

10. Loggins, The Negro Author, 40.

3. More Early Writers of Prose

Banneker's identification as a leader of his race depended very obviously, and probably somewhat curiously, on what he symbolized—although that, in his day, was considerable—rather than on any maneuvering on his part of Negroes into actions directed at the progress of their race. A similar observation may be made, with even greater truth, of Lemuel B. Haynes, who may have seen and talked with, during his entire life, even fewer Negroes than Lucy Terry. In the summer of 1753 in West Hartford, Connecticut, a white woman, possibly of the servant class, bore, by a black man, a male child whom she almost immediately abandoned. Deacon David Rose, who was emigrating to Middle Granville, Massachusetts, accepted the child, Lemuel Haynes, under an arrangement which indentured Haynes to Rose until Haynes was twenty-one. But Deacon Rose and his wife were not unkind to Haynes. Neither Haynes's color nor his low estate prevented the Roses from treating him as if he were their own son. In the humble school of their town, Haynes received as much formal education as such a school allowed. In the intensely religious atmosphere of the Rose home, he received a thorough immersion into a stark, zealous Puritanism. He was never to forget the apple tree under which, while (as he said) he was mourning his wretched state, he felt that he had achieved conversion. A sense of God and of this world and the next like that of Jonathan Edwards would accompany him all of his life.

Haynes was a minuteman and, later, a private in the Continental army. He first saw Vermont with a military force en route to Ticonderoga. After the war he began to prepare for the ministry. Licensed to preach in 1780, he was ordained a Congregational clergyman at Torrington, Connecticut, in 1785. He had married, in 1783, a white woman, Elizabeth Babbit, ten years younger than himself and a member of the church in Middle Granville which, at the time of his marriage, he was serving as a supply pastor. He was never to become more than a supply pastor at Torrington, either, some thought because of his color. In the twenty years between 1785 and 1805, he and his wife were to have ten children. He at last became the pastor in the fullest sense of the term of a church when he was called, in 1788, to the West Parish of Rutland, Vermont, where he remained for thirty years. His color may have entered into his eventual separation from this church. He had been a noted divine there and a highly respected preacher. He was moderator of the Vermont General Convention in 1813. During more than one season he preached as a Congregational missionary in parts of Vermont not as settled as Rutland. But in 1818, even in Vermont, color could arouse to open expression more latent racism than it did when Haynes first came to Rutland. After 1818 Haynes served for five years as the pastor of a Congregational church in Manchester, Vermont. For the last eleven years of his life, he pastored a Congregational charge in Granville, New York, just across the border from Vermont. He was in his eightieth year when he died from a gangrenous infection in one of his feet.

Among early American Negro writers Haynes was relatively prolific. Among them, moreover, he was also more than ordinarily literate. The two clergymen who tutored him for his profession taught him Latin and Greek. Possessed of a prodigious memory, which he strengthened through constant exercise, he could quote verbatim an astonishing portion of the Scriptures as well as virtually all of Milton's *Paradise Lost,* Edward Young's *Night Thoughts,* Isaac Watts's psalms and hymns, and much of some other authors. Indeed, Middlebury College in 1804 conferred upon him a master's degree, *causa honoris,* probably the first of its kind in black America. *Sketches of the Life and Character of the Rev. Lemuel Haynes, A.M.,* by Dr. Timothy Mather Cooley, in the words of Loggins a "full-length biography" and the product of "one of the eminent Congregational ministers of the time," was published in 1839, six years after Haynes's death. It probably demonstrated, again in the words of Loggins, "the high esteem in which . . . [Haynes] was held by his denomination."[1] The *Sketches* con-

---

1. Vernon Loggins, *The Negro Author: His Development in America to 1900* (New York, 1931), 118.

tains a goodly number of letters written by Haynes between 1795 and 1818. But he was a divine, like many divines of the present and the past, who wrote out sermons. Moreover, he lived at a time when it was not unusual for sermons to be published and read. Among his sermons the first, apparently, to be published in his lifetime, printed at Litchfield, Connecticut, was *The Character and Work of a Spiritual Watchman Described: A Sermon Delivered at Hinesburgh, February 23, 1791.* In keeping with its title, this is an ordination sermon. His *The Important concerns of Ministers, and the People of Their Charge, at the Day of Judgment,* published at Rutland in 1798, a funeral oration for a deceased minister, constitutes, in effect, an ordination sermon in reverse.

Haynes, perhaps rather anomalously in view of his color, clung with notable tenacity to conservative positions in both politics and theology. He was, incidentally, more liberal in theology than in politics. He could stomach, that is, "New Light" doctrines, with their relaxations from the "Old Light" strictness of the original New England Puritans, so long as those "New Light" doctrines were not extreme. But in politics Washington and John Adams were his heroes. The Federalists were his party. He could not stomach Jefferson, or the French Revolution, or the anti-Federalist War of 1812. In his sermons, *The Influence of Civil Government on Religion,* printed at Rutland in 1798, and *The Nature and Importance of True Republicanism,* printed at Rutland in 1801, his Federalist sentiments are easily discernible. Nevertheless, an altercation over an issue in theology occasioned his most famous sermon, the one widely and popularly known as *Universal Salvation,* of which at least twenty editions were printed and circulated in America and Europe. This sermon replied to a sermon by Hosea Ballou, a leading exponent of Universalist doctrine, which questioned predestinarianism and argued that all men, through the agency of the gospel, might well be saved. In *Universal Salvation* Haynes presents the spectacle, surely rather astounding to twentieth-century eyes, of a Negro defending the exclusivist doctrine of the elect. And yet it must be said of Haynes that he is no mean controversialist. He had learned something which reflected well his ability to discipline himself, and his sense of humor, about the uses of wit. Against Ballou he summons to his aid a text from the fourth verse of the third chapter of Genesis, "And the serpent said unto the woman, 'Ye shall not surely die,'" and performs so adroitly with the implications of his text that he does make of both Ballou and Universalist doctrine serpents in Eden, devils in disguise, speaking words superficially fair, but false, and, if not perceived as the sophistries they are, a certain avenue to the very death they seek to disclaim.

Haynes, often enough in his sermons, walks with the ponderous tread all too frequently encountered among sermonizers of many generations. But he is not always devoid of art. Moreover, the chance did once come his way for him to show the qualities of a good raconteur, particularly of a raconteur with a talent for telling a tale spiced with mystery and crime. While Haynes was pastoring in Manchester, Russell Colvin, a resident of the town not always as fully in command of his faculties as his own safety might require, disappeared and, after a passage of time, was declared dead. He had disappeared more than once before, but now his wife's pregnancy seemed to demand, in the interest of her child, a ruling as to her husband's whereabouts. Somehow, in a classic mishandling of the investigation and prosecution of a possible crime, the woman's two brothers, Stephen and Jesse Boorn, both Haynes's parishioners, were accused and convicted of her husband's murder, although no body of her husband had been found. One brother was sentenced to be hanged; the other, to prison for life. Fortunately, before any execution occurred, Colvin returned from New Jersey, where he had been all the while working on a farm, and his brothers-in-law were set free. Haynes had never believed in the guilt of the brothers-in-law. He had visited them daily in their prison. The sermon he preached, on the Sunday after they gained their freedom, *The Prisoner Released. A Sermon delivered at Manchester, Vermont, Lord's Day, Jan. 9th 1820, on the remarkable interposition of Divine Providence in the deliverance of Stephen and Jesse Boorn who had been under sentence of death for the supposed murder of Jesse Colvin,* was published, in Hartford, Connecticut, in 1820, with a pamphlet, *Mystery Developed; or Russell Colvin, (Supposed to be Murdered), in Full Life, and Stephen and Jesse Boorn, His Convicted Murderers Rescued from Ignominious Death by Wonderful Discoveries.* Both the sermon and the pamphlet show, as do all of Haynes's sermons and letters, when they touch upon the political economy of our universe, that Haynes believed as steadfastly and devoutly in the doctrine of Providence as Briton Hammon or Marrant or any other early black American author. But the pamphlet shows, also, that Haynes may have missed somewhat his calling. He had undoubtedly not failed in the Christian ministry. Yet years of activity in solemn homiletics still had left unextinguished in him some of the instincts of a writer of detective fiction. *Mystery Developed* permitted him to indulge a little those instincts.

James Forten ranks at much the same level, and belongs in much the same category as a race leader, with Richard Allen. Also like Allen, he is associated with Philadelphia, where Forten was born in 1766, the grandson of a slave brought from Africa, but son of that slave's American-born son who had bought his own freedom and married a free black woman. Forten, then, was never a slave. He attended the Quaker Anthony Benezet's school for free blacks in Philadelphia and, after volunteering, served as a powder boy in the American navy on a Philadelphia privateer during part of the Revolutionary War. For a while, however, before the war ended, the British held him captive near New York in one of their prison ships. For a year after the war he dwelled in England, drawn there by his ardent desire to experience existence in a country free from slavery. When he returned to America, he apprenticed himself to a sailmaker. By the age of twenty he was foreman of the shop where he had been an apprentice. Twelve years later he owned the business. It is recorded that he invented a device for handling sails, profits from which greatly expedited his becoming genuinely rich. Certainly the manufactory which he had purchased prospered. It employed forty workers, black and white. In a large, fine house on Lombard Street in Philadelphia, Forten, ever a man who enjoyed his family, lived with his wife, who died long before him, his five sons, and his three daughters. It was not unusual for a score of his children and their children to break bread with him at his board. But Forten was more than a patriarch to his own kin. He was a man of high ideals and a strong sense of civic duty. Over the years he became increasingly a patriarch of good causes, especially of those involved with the advancement of the Negro. Moreover, when he espoused a cause, he invested in it, not only time, but money. His offspring were like him. From the whole Forten family streamed a constant assault upon the evils in the social order which the Fortens thought should be corrected.

Of these evils, obviously, the most objectionable was slavery. Forten had eagerly consorted with English abolitionists like Granville Sharpe throughout his year in England when he was young. He played a prominent role in the organization and operation of antislavery societies in America. He strongly supported William Lloyd Garrison's paper, the *Liberator*, helping it with cash and the collection of subscriptions. Garrison, too, became his close personal friend. For the Forten hospitality was justly famous. Leading abolitionists stayed and held meetings in the Forten home. John Greenleaf Whittier wrote a poem, not discovered until 1906 by one of Forten's granddaughters, "To the Daughters of James Forten," which is a testament, not only to Whittier's appreciation of the Fortens as people, but also to the whole concept of civil rights which the Fortens espoused.

To the same degree that Forten championed abolition and black civil rights he assailed colonization. The colonizationists had wooed Forten in the hope that they could publicly project him as one of their leaders. Forten seems temporarily to have not denied the colonizationists a hearing.[2] As soon, however, as the colonizationists, in December, 1816, and January, 1817, formally organized, under the revealing name of the American Society for Colonizing the Free People of Color of the United States, which was shortened, in ordinary parlance, to the American Colonization Society, Forten allied himself with the opponents of the new organization. In January, 1817, he chaired a protest meeting at the Bethel AME Church in Philadelphia which adopted resolutions against the colonizationists. Later in August of the same year, again in Philadelphia, at a schoolhouse he chaired another protest meeting against colonization attended by three thousand people, who unanimously adopted and issued the anticolonizationist *Address to the Humane and Benevolent Inhabitants of the City and County of Philadelphia.* The colonizationists had privately painted for Forten a picture of himself as a high potentate in Liberia, a ruler living with virtually the powers and the perquisites of a king. But Forten thought not merely that colonization was wrong. He also thought that it was absurd. To the insinuation that he belonged back in Africa he responded, on one occasion in 1833, first with a reference to his third-generation status as an American and his nearly sixty years of domiciliation in his own person on American soil, and second, with the not easily misunderstood observation: "Yet some ingenious gentlemen have recently discovered that I am still an African; that a continent, three thousand miles, and more, from the place where I was born, is my native country. And I am advised to go home. Well, it may be so. Perhaps if I should only be set on the shore of that distant land, I should recognize all I might see there, and run at once to the old hut where my forefathers lived a hundred years ago."[3]

Until he died in 1842, Forten looked with scorn and loathing upon the

2. On this point, decidedly at variance with traditional accounts of Forten, see Sheldon H. Harris, *Paul Cuffe* (New York, 1972), 68, particularly footnote 129.

3. Samuel J. May, *Some Recollections of the Antislavery Conflict* (Boston, 1869), 287, as quoted in Ray Allen Billington (ed.), *The Journal of Charlotte Forten* (New York, 1953), 17.

colonizationists. Like many of his contemporaries, he worked actively for more than one good cause. He was, for instance, a teetotaler who allied himself with temperance societies, as with organizations which promoted universal peace and women's rights. He was a founder and president of the American Moral Reform Society, a group of Negro men in Philadelphia banded together in the interest of "Education, Temperance, Economy and Universal Liberty" according to the statement they proudly flaunted in the magazine they published, the *National Reformer*, the first magazine, be it noted, to be published by any blacks in the United States. Forten was also a prominent participant in the conventions of Negroes, in addition to the two he chaired in 1831, held in the 1830s to continue opposition to colonization and thus, of course, to slavery.

Undoubtedly, Forten had a hand in the writing of such documents as the resolutions presented and generally adopted at the conventions in which he participated, always prominently. The *Address to the Humane and Benevolent Inhabitants of the City and County of Philadelphia*, for instance, is attributed to his joint authorship with a young Negro student of theology named Russell Parrot. Forten has also been credited with *Letters from a Man of Colour*, anonymously published in Philadelphia in 1813, a work sufficiently important in the nature of its topicality, the historic significance of the subject it addresses, and its obvious indebtedness to a well-established literary fashion of essays in epistolary form on issues of public concern and debate, to make of itself something of a landmark in early Afro-American literature.[4] The introduction of a bill in the Pennsylvania legislature passage of which would have closed the state to further in-migration by free blacks occasioned the letters, five in number, all emphatically opposed to the anti-Negro bill. Loggins says of the *Letters* that the diction in it is "homely" and the phrasing "unimaginative."[5] But it is possible that no reader of the *Letters* in 1813 failed to feel and be affected by the vigor and power of its argument, crude though were the rhetorical skills of the arguer. The *Letters* speaks of the same kind of a birthright to America for free Negroes that Forten assigned himself in his arraignments of the colonizationists. And the philosophy which informs it accords with the philosophy which could justify for young Forten his

---

4. Carter Woodson, without hesitation, in reprinting one of the letters in *Negro Orators and Their Orations* (Washington, D.C., 1925) regards Forten as their author. Ray Allen Billington follows Woodson's lead in Billington (ed.), *Journal of Charlotte Forten*, 14. Loggins, *The Negro Author*, 64, only surmises that *Letters from a Man of Colour* were written by Forten.

5. Loggins, *The Negro Author*, 66.

involvement on the American side in the Revolutionary War. It was a philosophy which equated in natural rights blacks with whites. The bill which the *Letters* opposed did not reach the floor in the Pennsylvania legislature before the legislature's adjournment in 1813. It was not revived in subsequent sessions of the legislature, whether or not because of influence exerted on the legislators by the *Letters* no one has yet been able to say.

Almost without exception the race leaders in black America of Forten's time were, like Forten, strongly anticolonizationist. One who supported colonization, however, was Paul Cuffe. Moreover, probably because of Cuffe's great reputation for probity, his advocacy of colonization seems not to have cost him the respect of other Negroes, leaders and followers alike, in early nineteenth-century America. In 1728 a boy ten or eleven years old, from the evidence of his name—that (Kof, Koffa, or Cuffe) given by Fantees to boys born on Friday—probably a native of Ghana, had come, of his own volition, across the ocean and been landed in the Buzzards Bay area of Massachusetts. As Cuffe Slocum this boy was enslaved. He bought himself free in 1744, married Ruth Moses, a Gayhead Indian descended from the Wampanoags of King Philip, in 1746, lived for a while on tiny Cuttyhunk, the largest of the Elizabeth Islands, where he farmed, fished, and had ten children by his wife, but died in 1772 on the farm of 120 acres on the Massachusetts mainland in Westport which he had bought in 1766.

Paul Cuffe was the youngest son among Cuffe Slocum's ten children. Even so, it was to Paul, as well as to his older brother John, that Cuffe Slocum's farm was bequeathed. Paul, however, took to the sea when he was only sixteen. Beginning as an ordinary seaman, he first established himself independently with vessels he owned in the coastal trade. His horizons, however, constantly broadened. He acquired a fleet. Ships he owned, altogether or in part, sailed as far from Massachusetts as the Gulf of Mexico, Sweden, Portugal, and around the southern tips of both Africa and South America. His property in Westport faced the Westport River. He added to it a wharf and warehouse. The signs of his wealth were real. With his land, his ships, and the cargoes he bought and sold, he did rule a small empire. Yet, although he never demeaned himself unduly, there was nothing offensively imperious about him. Rather, he was notable for his tact in dealing with others. Powerful white contemporaries of his, like the Rotches of his state and the Browns of Rhode Island, were his staunch admirers and friends. He married in 1783, like his

father, a Wampanoag. Negro men in his day and his part of Massachusetts rather tended to marry Indians. By 1808 he formally joined the
Quakers, who esteemed him so that once he spoke at their Arch Street
Meeting House in Philadelphia. He and his wife had seven children, two
sons and five daughters, but Westport had no school. On his farm, in
1797, he built a school the use of which was free for all the children of his
community. The Westport Quakers badly needed a new meetinghouse.
In 1813 they were able to erect one, approximately half of the cost of
which was borne by Cuffe.

Cuffe was undoubtedly public-spirited. He was also, as he grew older,
increasingly concerned about problems which his color, in effect, forced
into his consciousness. He was, of course, both a Negro and an Indian,
a particular half-and-half hybridization known where and when he lived
as mustee. His first involvement in an issue which would hardly have
touched him as it did had he not been what he was occurred in 1780,
when Cuffe and his brother John sought relief, along with others penal-
ized for their color, from the payment of property and poll taxes, specifically on the grounds, surely familiar to their countrymen, that, since
they could not vote, they were suffering taxation without representation.
Cuffe and his fellow petitioners did not get the relief for which they pled,
even though Cuffe and his brother for a while refused to pay the taxes in
question and actually did, once, spend a few defiant hours in jail. At
times, in fighting what he regarded as the injustice of having to pay taxes
when suffrage was denied him, Cuffe represented himself as an Indian.
At other times thereto he spoke of himself as black. As he grew older,
however, he became decidedly more bemused by his African, than by his
Indian, ancestry. It seems, moreover, that he was at least as interested in
the good which he could do for the Africans left in Africa as for the
Americans of African extraction in America. He accepted Christianity
wholeheartedly. He wanted, therefore, to Christianize Africa *in toto*. But
he wanted, also, to introduce the blessing of Western prosperity to Africa. Through Western ways of economic enterprise and trade between
Africa, Europe, and America, he dreamed of an Africa which would be-
have in its economy substantially as did he and his neighbors in Massachusetts or anywhere else in the West. The slave trade, as he saw it, was
both ruining Africa and sustaining slavery in the Americas. Furthermore,
in his eyes, for far too many Africans, cooperating with the slave trade
had become a way of life. To a horrendous degree, then, it seemed to him
these Africans and the whites for whom they gathered slaves had turned

Africa's would-be economy into a shambles. And, of course, it was not only Africa's economy that suffered from the slave trade. In acquiescing in the brutalization and theft of its own sons and daughters Africa was losing both its soul and its hope of ever improving its own civilization. The vision which animated Cuffe was no small essay in wishful thought. He sought a redemptive force which would affect at least two continents, if not three.

Cuffe, largely through his Quaker contacts, had friends both in America and in England. He was much aware of the British experiment in Sierra Leone. In 1811, on his own ship, *Traveller*, he sailed to Sierra Leone to initiate conditions there suitable for the kind of trade he envisaged between Africa and the West and for the transportation to Sierra Leone of American Negroes who would foster in the colony Christianity and Western developments in commerce and technology. Much was tentative, he found, and not everyone received him well in the still young colony, and so Cuffe went on from Sierra Leone to England, where he and his intentions for the colony were warmly acclaimed and the approvals he required to do business as he desired in Sierra Leone were readily granted by appropriate authorities.

Sailing back to the colony from England, Cuffe assisted in establishing in Sierra Leone a cooperative trading organization called the Friendly Society of Sierra Leone, which was sponsored, despite its name, not by Quakers, but by a Methodist church in the colony. Early in 1812, he returned to America with a cargo of exotic woods. In America he ran afoul of the embargo, although it was not Madison's, but that of Madison's predecessor, Jefferson. His cargo was impounded after *Traveller* was intercepted by a Newport customs cutter. Through talks in Washington, D.C., with Secretary of the Treasury Gallatin and President Madison, both of whom were apparently quite well taken with him, he obtained the release of his cargo. He had hoped, in the ambitious perspective of his long-term planning, to visit Sierra Leone at least once each year. Now the War of 1812 disrupted his design. Nevertheless, as soon as he could when hostilities ceased, he sailed again, later in 1815, for Sierra Leone, on this voyage, again on *Traveller*, bearing to the colony, at his own expense, thirty-eight American Negroes, eighteen adults and twenty children. He found the Friendly Society doing well. In 1816, after his return to America, the colonizationists, especially the Reverend Samuel J. Mills and the Reverend Robert Finley, both white and both founding fathers, as it were, of the American Colonization Society, began to importune him for information and support. He did not discourage their approaches. But neither did he ever return to Sierra Leone. He died in America in 1817.

Cuffe's unpublished papers in the New Bedford Free Public Library contain scrapbooks, notebooks, account books, letters, and the journal he kept throughout 1811 and 1812, the years during which he made his first trip to Sierra Leone. He did send back from Sierra Leone to friends of his in New York a communication, twelve pages when printed, which was published in New York in 1812 as *A Brief Account of the Settlement and Present Situation of the Colony of Sierra Leone in Africa.*

Another colonizationist was Daniel Coker, already mentioned here in connection with Richard Allen and the fledgling AME church. Coker was born in Baltimore County in 1880. His mother was white, and Coker was not visibly black. As a child he accompanied to school a white boy who, apparently, would not have gone to school at all if Coker had not gone there with him and who, also, may well have been Coker's half-brother. Coker, incidentally, during this period had yet to become Coker. He had been christened Isaac Wright. It was not until, still less than full grown, Coker ran away to New York City that, for the obvious reason of greater protection for himself, he assumed the name of Coker. In New York City, Coker exercised vigorously his not inconsiderable abilities as a leader. Active among the Negro Methodists there, he was ordained into the Methodist ministry by the great Bishop Asbury himself. In 1807 a group of Negroes were so anxious for him to return to Baltimore and teach the school for black children they were determined to establish there that four of them supplied the money with which his freedom was secured. By 1819, however, he had become interested in colonization. He sailed for Africa in 1820 on the *Elizabeth.* The pioneering colonists on the *Elizabeth* were actually, in due time, to become the nucleus for the American-inspired country of Liberia. But, in Africa, the *Elizabeth* first halted at length in Sierra Leone, and it was, after performing some services helpful to the American Colonization Society, in Sierra Leone that Coker settled down. He accepted an appointment as superintendent of Hastings, a village then newly founded by the British to receive former Negro captives whom they had liberated on the high seas. In acting as chief executive for Hastings and in developing the congregations of a church, called the West African Methodists, of which, after playing a leading role in its organization, he became the first head, also with the title of superintendent, Coker spent, as a figure of consequence in a small

corner of the world, rather admirably the rest of his life. He died, a victim of malaria, in 1835 and was buried in Hastings.

Coker was better educated than most of the early Negro leaders. He
may also have been possessed of more of what might well be called a native aptitude for literature than such diamonds in the rough in letters as
Richard Allen and James Forten, to whom fate seemed surely to have
entrusted a greater capacity for performing with exceptional competence
in the world of practical affairs than for writing good poetry or prose.
Coker, it is known, wrote some poetry. He published in 1810, in prose,
A *Dialogue between a Virginian and an African Minister,* excellently described by Loggins as "an ingeniously arranged and well written anti-
slavery tract."[6] His record of his voyage to Africa appeared in 1820 in
Baltimore as the *Journal of Daniel Coker, A Descendant of Africa, from the
Time of Leaving New York in the Ship Elizabeth . . . on a Voyage for Sherbo
in Africa, in Company with Three Agents and About Ninety Persons of Colour . . . with an appendix.*

Among the earliest Negro American leaders, Prince Saunders was
unique because of his ties with Haiti. Saunders was born in Vermont,
where he grew to manhood. Around 1806, he taught a school for blacks
in Colchester, Vermont. But he went to Haiti and rose to become a per-
son of some eminence there, a minister of education under the emperor
Henri Christophe. He seems to have been representing Christophe in
England in 1816 when he published in London his rather considerable
Haytian Papers, which combined Haitian laws as they appeared in the
Code Henri with an extensive gloss apparently of Saunders' authorship.
Dismissed by Christophe from the Haitian government, by 1818 Saun-
ders had returned to America. He lived in Boston and Philadelphia. In
Boston he oversaw the publication of an American edition of his *Hay-
tian Papers.* In Philadelphia he published *An Address Delivered at Bethel
Church . . . Before the Pennsylvania Augustine Society, for the Education of
People of Color* and *A Memoir Presented to the American Convention for
Promoting the Abolition of Slavery, and Improving the Condition of the African Race,* both short pieces of no distinction and both published in
1818. Before the end of 1820, however, Saunders was back in Haiti,
where Christophe's suicide had cleared the way for a new government.
Under the new conditions Saunders prospered. He died in Haiti in 1839
as the country's attorney general.

6. *Ibid.*, 63.

Perhaps the last of the early Negro leaders in the sense of when and how he was active in the epoch for which racial stalwarts such as Hall, Banneker, and Allen may be considered representative was Peter Williams, Jr. He had been born about 1780 in New Brunswick, New Jersey. But his father, Peter Williams, Sr., had been bought as a slave, and immediately liberated, by the John Street Methodist Church of New York City, which Peter Williams, Sr., a man of no formal education, but far from devoid of ability and character, then chose to serve as its sexton for the rest of his life. In New York City, Peter Williams, Jr., whose exceptional intellectual gifts distinguished him as a child, was trained for the Episcopalian ministry, despite the conspicuous role played by his father in promoting Methodism among the Negroes in New York. In 1820, indeed, Peter Williams, Jr., was ordained an Episcopal clergyman and appointed the rector of St. Philip's, which he pastored until his death in 1840. His prestige and influence in the black Manhattan of his day were unquestionable. But, also, in several important ways, he epitomized the leadership of his race before the Age of the Abolitionists.

Many of the abolitionists, of whom Frederick Douglass was the prime example, would come from the South. The first Negro leaders tended to be northerners unacquainted in person with any part of the South. The abolitionist leaders were, by and large, fugitive slaves. When they went north, as they invariably did, they went with a price on their heads. Early Negro leaders were free, either from birth or through purchase. And it was their civil rights they tended to want. Of their freedom they had already taken care. Of course, they fought slavery, and, increasingly as the years advanced, they gave unstinting encouragement and aid to the efforts which would generate and sustain the clamorous and indefatigable abolitionist crusade of the thirty years before the Civil War. We have seen, for instance, the close relations between James Forten and William Lloyd Garrison. Even so, the early Negro leaders tended to incline toward an eighteenth-century pattern of the philosophe steeped in the doctrines of John Locke and Montesquieu, the man of reason appealing to the Shaftesburian constitution and benevolence of all his fellow human creatures. But the Douglasses and William Wells Browns were much more propagandists and incendiaries than philosophes. They were fighting, not only slavery, but a system of which they were vividly aware, the plantation South. To the end of his days Peter Williams, Jr., never had quite their nineteenth-century minds. He had never quite their vision either of Armageddon or of America. Three things he wrote seem to belong to the permanent literature of his race. His *Oration on the Abolition of the Slave Trade; Delivered in the City of New York, Jan. 1, 1808* was published in New York as a pamphlet in 1808. His *Discourse, Delivered on the death of Capt. Paul Cuffe, before the New York African Institution, in the African Methodist Episcopal Zion Church, October 21, 1817* was published in New York in 1817. Finally, his *Discourse Delivered in St. Philip's Church, for the Benefit of the Coloured Community of Wilberforce in Upper Canada; on the Fourth of July, 1830* was published, also in New York City, in 1830.

4. George Moses Horton and David Walker

The strangest of all the early Negro writers was George Moses Horton. Where he really belongs in Afro-American literature, if he must belong exclusively in some one place, it is usually difficult to say. The years generally accepted as those of his birth and death, although they certainly do not fail to give at least a sense of when he lived, are nevertheless of little help in providing guidance for attaching him wholly to a specific epoch of Afro-American literature. It may well be a sound assumption that he was born in 1797. Unquestioned, incidentally, is the place of his birth, a township called Rich Square in the northeastern quadrant of North Carolina. But birth in 1797 permitted him formative years, and some adulthood as well, within the world of Lucy Terry, Jupiter Hammon, Benjamin Banneker, and Richard Allen. If, then, he lived, as is most often supposed, until 1883, he survived into a world so different from the world of these representative and undeniably early Afro-American writers and so long after them that it certainly can appear to be quite possibly something of a *tour de force* to associate him only with them. Even so, it may also appear equally as much of a *tour de force* to associate him only, if at all, with the classifying generalizations usually considered applicable to black writers of the next age in Afro-American literature, the age of William Wells Brown and Frederick Douglass. To some extent the difficulties of placing Horton may be attributable to Horton's relative isolation—and it was hardly less than that—from the South, the classic plantation-dominated antebellum south, that is, while living, paradoxically, on southern soil through years when the South was increasingly assertive of its southernness.

To another, and possibly greater, extent these same difficulties may be as readily attributable to Horton himself. He was, as a person, uncommon. What would have happened to him had he been born a field hand on one of the huge, comparatively impersonal plantations operative upon the rice lands of South Carolina or distributed here and there throughout the cotton kingdom of the Deep South defies, of course, ordinary conjecture. The power, almost incredibly strong in him, that would not let him rest until he created poetry may have withstood the pressures which the dehumanizing environment and the crippling rigors of an existence so cruel and physically exhausting would have imposed upon it. But such an even greater miracle than the miracle he actually was did not, and thus now will not, occur. No poet more enslaved, *de jure* and de facto, than Horton ever has written, or ever will write, poetry in America. And yet Horton did write poetry, in the often paranoid slaveholder's South. He wrote there, moreover, the poetry, whatever its merit or demerit, of a true poet, of one for whom, indeed, the writing of poetry, whatever its nature or subject, was an inescapable accompaniment to the very act of breathing. There has been argument as to how racial a poet Horton was. There can be no argument as to how compulsive were his years of cultivating his muse. He was, in his own small way, a Villon, a Poe, a Rimbaud, an Ezra Pound, a fated and doomed follower of an art for that art's sake. He did not need, then, to write against racism. The kind of person, and artist, he was did that for him. For all of his life he was black. Yet, also, for most of his life he was an object lesson in the irrelevance of color to aesthetic sensibility. He was, in other words, a living refutation of racism's major premise, that Negroes are born unlike other people because they are born less human.

The Horton plantation on which Horton first saw the light of day was more farm than plantation. All the Horton slaves, except Horton's mother, were his older sisters. Horton seems to have been not over six years old when William Horton, his master, concluded that the tobacco he had been growing had worn out the soil he owned, and abandoned his plantation near Rich Square for land in Chatham County within ten miles of the infant University of North Carolina. In Chatham County, also, William Horton abandoned tobacco, becoming, on eventually between four and five hundred acres, more a subsistence farmer than a producer of a marketable staple crop. He grew now crops that he could both sell and use, such as corn and wheat, and he fed and watered cows to benefit his crops as well as to enlarge and vary the private larder of his household. George Moses Horton, until he was a well-grown adolescent, tended the cows. But he had acquired a desire, truly a passion, to learn to read. Combining, apparently, intuitions from his observations of white schoolchildren with a rigorous analysis of, in his own words, "dim and promiscuous syllables in my old black and tattered spelling book," which he had acquired he does not say where, he taught himself to read, additionally using, in the process, it seems, the Bible and a Wesley hymnal owned by his mother. His slightly younger brother, incidentally, motivated by sibling rivalry, not only learned to read, at first more proficiently than he, but also learned to write, an accomplishment not encompassed by Horton for at least another twenty years.

In 1814 William Horton, beginning to divest himself of some of his holdings, transferred the ownership of George Moses Horton to his son, James, who had remained in Rich Square. For a brief period, then, George Moses Horton may have returned to his birthplace. But James moved soon to Chatham County, bringing Horton, if Horton had not stayed in Chatham County, back there with him. At some time after 1813, but before 1820, Horton, joining in a well-established practice, began walking up to Chapel Hill on Sundays from the Horton farm to peddle primarily, if not solely, fruit from the farm to the undergraduates of the university. He thus began an involvement with Chapel Hill and the university which was to last for almost fifty years.

The Chapel Hill undergraduates relished extorting entertainment from their Sunday visitors before they released their cash in payment for anything their visitors brought that they might agree to buy. They quickly decided that Horton must orate, or "spout," as they called it, for their special pleasure, almost surely with a picture, uproariously amusing (no doubt) to them, vividly in their minds of the contrast between Horton, with his walnut-brown, though not black, skin, and the light-complected forensic models from classical antiquity whom they revered as the paragons of oratory. Horton did, for a brief term, oblige them by "spouting." But no matter how he may have appeared to others, Horton seems always to have perceived clearly, in his own conceptualization of himself, what it was he wanted to be, and to have displayed, especially when it is remembered that he was a slave, a remarkable proclivity for being Horton's Horton rather than someone else's. While Horton was learning to read, he had also discovered his congenital and insatiable interest in poetry—

which, incidentally, and not too illogically, he connected with a similar interest of his in music. It was not his ability to extemporize a public speech of which he wanted Chapel Hill undergraduates to be aware but rather his talent for creating poems. And it was not long before he acquainted them with Horton, the poet, and presented this aspect of himself so ingratiatingly to them that his Sundays quickly became occasions when he was selling poems in addition to his fruit.

Many of Horton's poems were acrostics on the names of, as he said in his short autobiographical preface to his *Poetical Works,* "the tip-top belles of Virginia, South Carolina, and Georgia" (his omission here of North Carolina can intimate an inclination of his to emphasize how widely his poetry traveled). Since he could not write, he dictated his acrostics, and other poems, to student agents of his who took orders for verse by him from their fellow students, in Horton's presence or absence, and delivered the orders every Sunday to him. During each succeeding week he composed and stored in his mind until the following Sunday, again in his own words, "at the handle of a plough"—for he had graduated from cowboy to farmhand—the poems to fill his weekly order. The standard price for one of his acrostics or love poems was twenty-five cents. Sometimes for a poem, or a poem and a letter, he was able to command as much as fifty or seventy-five cents. He could expect at least a dozen orders a week. An undergraduate of the time might well receive from fairly indulgent parents not more than a dollar a month for his allowance to spend on himself.

Thus it transpired that, as the years passed into decades and the decades moved on toward another century, the University of North Carolina assumed and maintained in Horton's life the function of a home, much more the place where he lived than the Horton farm. When he first started walking up the road from his master's land to the university, Chapel Hill itself was only a hotel, a blacksmith shop, two boardinghouses, two stores, and about a dozen residences, and there were only about 100 students in the University of North Carolina. In 1860, on the brink of the Civil War, over 700 people lived in Chapel Hill, and the University of North Carolina, with 460 students, was second in size among American colleges only to Yale.[1] As the town and university both grew, Horton became a robust, continuing legend associated with them

---

1. Richard Walser, *The Black Poet* (New York, 1966), 19.

both. At some point in the 1830s, he consummated an agreement with James Horton through which, for twenty-five cents a day, he bought his time to dispose of it as he chose. He had, then, to interrupt no longer his residence in Chapel Hill with reluctant retreats to the Horton farm. When James Horton died, he became, at the auction of James's assets, the property of Hall Horton, James's bachelor son, a tanner as well as a farmer. This Horton continued to let him buy his time, but raised the price for the privilege to fifty cents a day, and so the price remained until Horton became free.

Two presidents of the university knew Horton well, Joseph Caldwell, the Princetonian president who died in 1835, and David Swain, a former governor of North Carolina who was still the university's president in the 1860s. Apparently Horton was on better, and closer, terms with Caldwell than with Swain, although, apparently also, he could, and sometimes did, ask virtually anything of either. Generation after generation of Chapel Hill undergraduates adopted him as a cherished extension of their college life, with inevitable and appropriate regard, of course, for the circumstance that he was a Negro to be kept in a Negro's place. Even so, the undergraduates gave him books, in deference to his literary tastes, clothes (there were times when he was, by the most exemplary standards, accoutered like a beau brummel), and, especially in his middle years, sometimes too much to drink. So he acquired a library which included, among its titles, Murray's English grammar, Dr. Johnson's dictionary, *Paradise Lost*, James Thomson's *Seasons*, parts of the *Iliad* and the *Aeneid*, Plutarch, the *Columbian Orator*, Young's *Night Thoughts*, and selections from Shakespeare and Byron. His reading in his library undoubtedly affected his poetry. One of his favorite poets seems to have been Thomas Campbell, as one of his favorite poems may well have been Campbell's "The Pleasures of Love." Yet his own activity as a poet was stimulated not merely by reading. In 1826 Caroline Lee Hentz came to Chapel Hill as the wife of Nicholas Marcellus Hentz, a native of Metz, France, who was joining the faculty of the university to teach modern foreign languages, but who was also a devoted entomologist. Mrs. Hentz, poet, dramatist, and novelist, would become one of the best-known and most successful of the group of novelists, all distinctly female and popular, whom Nathaniel Hawthorne would one day acidulously categorize for the nature of their appeal (they vastly outsold him) as a "damned mob of scribbling women."

Mrs. Hentz's perhaps best-remembered novel, published in 1854, was the widely circulated *The Planter's Northern Bride*. In her *Lovell's Folly*, published in 1833, she included a character who was very clearly only a thinly disguised Horton. Moreover, during the five years which the Hentzes spent in Chapel Hill, Mrs. Hentz sedulously promoted Horton as a poet. One of Horton's poems, "Slavery," was published in the *Lancaster Gazette*, a newspaper in her home town in Massachusetts, because she sent it there. It would be republished in 1834 in William Lloyd Garrison's *Liberator*. And she may have called Horton to the attention of the never-identified "philanthropic gentleman" who took the lead in an effort to raise money to free Horton in 1828—an effort which, although not successful, spread as far north as New York City, where *Freedom's Journal* expressed its wish that every Negro in New York would contribute a penny to the Horton freedom fund. Mrs. Hentz certainly aided a second effort to free Horton, the publication in 1829 in Raleigh, North Carolina, of his book of twenty-one poems, *The Hope of Liberty*, proceeds from the sale of which were intended to pay Horton's fare to Liberia, but did not.

The Hope of Liberty was reprinted in Philadelphia, without Horton's knowledge or consent and with no change in what it contained, but with a change of name, as *Poems by a Slave*, in 1837. The publisher was the white abolitionist Lewis Gunn. In Boston in 1838, another white friend of abolition, Isaac Knapp, with no more resort to Horton than Gunn, included *The Hope of Liberty*, still as *Poems by a Slave*, in a volume the first part of which was the *Memoir and Poems of Phillis Wheatley, a North African and a Slave*. Meanwhile, in Chapel Hill, Horton had learned to write, not very late, apparently, in the 1830s. It seems that it was also in the 1830s that he married, as much as a slave could, a slave woman, still unidentified, who was apparently the property of a landowner near the Hortons named Franklin Snipes. By this woman Horton seems to have had a son, Free Snipes, who died in Durham in 1896, and a daughter, Rhody Snipes, who had married a Van Buren Byrum and was still living in Raleigh in 1897.

Other evidence about Horton's marriage is nonexistent. It appears to have had very little effect upon him or his way of life. He continued to live in Chapel Hill, supporting himself through his poetry and supplements to his income from services to the university or to students or from mendicancy performed with a flourish which may have often presented, as its *pièce de résistance*, an uninvited recitation by him of one, or more, of his poems. By the early 1840s, Horton seems to have assembled a second volume of poems, which he was calling *The Museum* and which he never published, although two poems of his, printed in the *Southern Literary Messenger* in 1843, sent there by Chapel Hill professor William Mercer Green, apparently were taken from it. In the 1840s, also, perhaps because of a distaste for Hall Horton, Horton was evincing new interest in securing his own freedom. He composed a letter to Garrison of the *Liberator* asking Garrison's aid in publishing a volume of his poems. He did not, however, send the letter directly to Garrison. He gave it, instead, to the university's president, Swain, with the request that Swain send it to Garrison. Swain kept the letter, apparently without revealing to Horton that he had done so.

With ninety-nine subscribers, eighty-one of them Chapel Hill students, and with his own autobiography until he was thirty years old as a preface, Horton did have published at Hillsborough, North Carolina, in 1845, a second volume of poetry, *The Poetical Works of George M. Horton, the Colored Bard of North Carolina*. But the book did not sell well. It provided Horton with no money that could be used to buy his freedom. Nevertheless, Horton had finally managed to elicit from Hall Horton a price for himself. It was $250. Horton addressed a letter to Swain asking the university president to advance him the money with the implied understanding that Horton, through the sale of poetry, would pay Swain back. Swain's response was to counsel a redirection of Horton's request to the attention of another possible Maecenas, Horace Greeley, whose wife, although a native of Connecticut, had once taught in North Carolina, whence she had acquainted Greeley with Horton and his work. Horton, therefore, did pen a letter to Greeley, an appeal for money containing the same implication of a conceivable return of aid as Horton's letter to Swain, but also bearing, on the verso side of the paper in the letter, a poem, "The Poet's Feeble Petition," of which the fourth, and last, stanza implored

> Then listen all who never felt
>   For fettered genius heretofore—
> Let hearts of petrifaction melt
>   And bid the gifted Negro soar.

Swain, however, treated Horton's letter to Greeley as he had Horton's letter to Garrison. Without revealing to Horton what he was doing, he kept this letter also.

It was now 1852. Three years earlier, at the request of Chapel Hill students, Horton had delivered, in Gerrard Hall on the campus, a Fourth of July speech. Stylistic peculiarities indicate the strong probability that some of the poetry published in the *North Carolina University Magazine* after its reestablishment in 1852 was ghostwritten by him. In 1859, in the midst of a commencement season at the university when 2,500 visitors and President James Buchanan had descended upon Chapel Hill, Horton delivered, again in Gerrard Hall, and again in response to a request made by Chapel Hill students, but, for this occasion, from a manuscript, an oration, "The Stream of Liberty and Science: An Address to the Collegiates of the University of North Carolina, by George M. Horton, the Black Bard."[2] But the inexorable march of national events would quickly convert this address retroactively into something of an unwitting valedictory. The university did not officially close for the Civil War. Its students, nevertheless, did virtually all disappear, to fight, of course, for their beloved South.

Precisely how Horton spent the war years is not known. It seems most reasonable to surmise that he divided them, somehow, between the Horton farm and Chapel Hill. On the day after Easter Sunday, 1865, Union troops from Sherman's army entered Chapel Hill. Horton may have joined these troops in Raleigh. He may have waited for them in Chapel Hill. Certainly he attached himself to them and found a patron for himself and his poetry in Captain Will H. S. Banks of the 9th Michigan Cavalry Volunteers. When Captain Banks's company, as part of its larger unit, left Chapel Hill, Horton went with it, under Captain Banks's protection. The company moved, never leaving Piedmont North Carolina, to Greensboro, Lexington, Concord, and back to Lexington, where it was mustered out. With the Union soldiers Horton was again a working poet. He once had written acrostics for students at the university on the names of girls these students had left behind them in southern places away from Chapel Hill. Now he wrote acrostics for the Union soldiers on the names of girls to whom these soldiers had breathed adieus and spoken, probably, of enduring ties in far-off northern villages and farms. He and Captain Banks, however, were collaborating on a project to which both were enthusiastically committed, a third published volume of Horton's poetry. When, therefore, Banks left the army, he and Horton went to

2. *Ibid.*, 83. Buchanan seems to have been the commencement speaker.

Raleigh. There they saw through the press *Naked Genius*, Horton's largest, and last, volume of verse, 134 poems, including all but 3 of the 45 in *The Poetical Works*, although with only 2 selections from *The Hope of Liberty*, but composed, in the main, of poetry written by Horton during his weeks of living with the Union troops.

Captain Banks and Horton had planned another volume of Horton's poetry which they intended to call *The Black Poet*. They advertised it in *Naked Genius* and issued from the introductory material of that book an invitation for "energetic young men, especially those who had become disabled by the casualties of war," to sell *The Black Poet* and thus repair any damage to their fortunes. By 1866, however, Banks had resumed his civilian life in Michigan. He was never to be in contact with Horton again. In 1866, moreover, Horton—nearing, if not beyond, his seventieth birthday—appeared in Philadelphia, then a city of about 600,000 inhabitants with a colony of some 20,000 Negroes which was in a state of rapid and feverish postwar expansion easily understandable as an effect of the location of the city near the southern boundary of the North. Into this colony Horton made an entry which could have redounded much to his personal advantage. The Banneker Institute, an organization of thirty of the leaders of black Philadelphia, held a special meeting in his honor. Banneker members were, apparently, expecting to receive Horton as an addition to their own exalted fellowship. There had even been mention among them of financial, as well as moral, support from the Banneker Institute for at least the publishing of *The Black Poet*. But the members of the institute, when they experienced Horton, seem to have recoiled from him. It has been reported that they found his vanity intolerable and considered what they interpreted as his gaucherie far from amusing. So, according to one biographical tradition, he disappeared from view in Philadelphia and may have died there, or he may have returned to North Carolina and died in that state.

A professor of geology from North Carolina, Collier Cobb, in another version of Horton's final years, testifying as a witness with, as we shall see, special knowledge, declared that, in Philadelphia, Horton had some success in selling to papers and magazines stories from the Bible, told in prose and translated, with appropriate changes in character and settings, out of the several antiquities of the Scriptures into modern times. Horton even sold upon occasion, according to Cobb, the same story to more than one paper or magazine, thus qualifying for recognition as one of the pioneers, if not the pioneer, in the syndication of journalistic features. Cobb had relatives in Philadelphia who employed Horton now and then. In 1883 Cobb, in Philadelphia to visit these relatives, also paid a call on Horton. In a letter dated 1929, Cobb specifies 1883 as the year of Horton's death, although no documents in Philadelphia have been found which confirm this date.

It is possible, if not probable, that Horton wrote, for his student clientele in Chapel Hill, to say nothing of his later customers from the North, several hundred acrostics. Dispersed, however, as they were into many hands, understandably no collection of these products of his ingenuity exists. Moreover, only five of his acrostics have been found in individual copies. Composed, from quite convincing external evidence, in or about 1835, one of those five celebrates, as follows, a Julia Shepard:

> Joy, like the morning, breaks from one divine—
> Unveiling streams which cannot fail to shine.
> Long have I strove to magnify her name
> Imperial, floating on the breeze of fame.
> Attracting beauty must delight afford,
> Sought of the world and of the Bards adored;
> Her grace of form and heart-alluring powers
> Express her more than fair, the queen of flowers.
> Pleasure, fond nature's stream, from beauty sprung,
> And was the softest strain the Muses sung,
> Reverting sorrows into speechless Joys,
> Dispelling gloom which human peace destroys.

This is obviously occasional verse in which the commercialization of a talent plays a commanding role, even to the toleration of constant incoherence throughout its text. As such, an unmistakable instance of an artist quite blandly prostituting himself for gain, it illustrates one of the several paradoxes which complicated Horton's character as a person and his performance as a poet, for we have already dwelled upon the sincerity and compulsiveness of Horton's practice of his art. Whatever claims, positive or otherwise, may be advanced about the level of Horton's poetic accomplishment, a just appreciation of him must contain an admission of the fact that he was not a simple, or simple-minded, fellow whether as an individual in a social order or as a writer seeking the voice that suited him. No one who has written of him has been so imperceptive about him as to characterize him as a mere clod, aware only of himself animalistically. Yet Richard Walser, sympathetic biographer of Horton as he intends to be, perhaps inclines too much toward the view of Horton articulated in Collier Cobb's account of the poet, "An American Man of Letters," which, after presentation in the *North Carolina University Magazine* in October, 1909, was published as a pamphlet. Cobb's Horton is essentially incapable of creditable thought at any impressive level of intellectuality or of a genuinely sophisticated range of perspectives in his assessment of men and the world men have made. "George never really cared for more liberty than he had, but he was fond of playing to the grandstand," Cobb, perhaps too confidently, informs his readers of the inner versus the outer Horton.[3] So, to Cobb, Horton appeared, beneath his layers of pretense, as very much the contented slave who avoided work when he could, wore his feelings rather lightly on his sleeve, took little, if any, thought of tomorrow, and found the *summum bonum* of his existence in fishing or reclining half-comatose in fields or woods. Walser's Horton is not nearly so hopelessly arrested in his development as Cobb's. But a chapter in Walser's life, *The Black Poet*, although far from divesting Horton of an inner self significantly at odds with the one attributed to Horton by Cobb, does bear a title, "Troubadour in Motley," which suggests that Horton had a penchant for self-dramatization.

Still, in the literature on Horton, it is Loggins' Horton who closely parallels Cobb's, for Loggins' Horton, like Jupiter Hammon preeminently the possessor of a primitive Negro mind, is inescapably, thereby, as much of a child as Cobb's, with a difference between the two in only form, not substance. Hence, Loggins can aver of Horton, as he does, that in "Horton's grotesque music and bizarre imagination something which is foreign to the Caucasian mind is delightfully revealed." Loggins, moreover, aware of Horton's exposure to poets considered major in the literature of the world, such as Shakespeare, Homer, Virgil, and Milton, can also insist, as he does, that Horton lacked the endowment in necessary cerebral power to profit truly from such an exposure. Of Horton and his comprehension of the music of these masters, Loggins, thus, simply declares that Horton "got it all mixed up." Furthermore, pursuing a line of review and evaluation parallel to his about Horton and the masters' music, Loggins adds that Horton's "imagery is a . . . hodgepodge, made up of free borrowings from the masters and homely conceits of his own coinage."[4] To a

---

3. Collier Cobb, "An American Man of Letters," *University of North Carolina Magazine* (October, 1909), 6.
4. Vernon Loggins, *The Negro Author: His Development in America to 1900* (New York, 1931), 117, 116.

decisive degree, then, Cobb and Loggins dismiss Horton as substantially something other—and, presumably, less—than he might have been had he not been subject to limitations in himself resulting from his race. Horton may be someone they can see as a disparate person, but he emerges from all of their references to him—whether to his life or to his poetry—consistently in accord with the stereotypes about the Negro which prevailed in American popular folklore until within recent years and to which all too clearly Cobb and Loggins uncritically cling.

The black critic of Afro-American literature J. Saunders Redding spoke early in his career about Horton. He did draw one conclusion about Horton which allies him, as far as it goes, with Cobb and Walser. He observed, that is, that "Horton was an incorrigible actor and laughter-baiter, never missing an opportunity (at the cost of no matter what falsehood) to dramatize himself." But Redding, also, observed as "remarkable" Horton's imagery, which seemed to Redding, while "generally as confused and wasteful and rich as a tropic sunset . . . [nevertheless] sometimes astonishingly fine and telling." Similarly "remarkable," in Redding's view, are Horton's "turns of humor," the presence of which, Redding maintains, in a statement of opinion distancing him from Cobb, "deny the simplicity of . . . [Horton's] mind and character." The white Joan Sherman does not simply echo Redding when she speaks of Horton. But she does see Horton through eyes much more like Redding's than Cobb's. She utters strictures, it is true, on Horton's love poetry. His early verse dealing with this perennial object of poetic scrutiny she ruefully deplores as weak. Subsequent verse of Horton's anent this same object tends overly, in her judgment, to suffer from "hackneyed and bombastic diction, obscure allusions and careless thought." Yet when she passes a general verdict on Horton and his poetry, she states that "he displays unusual skill with meter and rhyme, firm control over content, and sensitivity to language. Moreover, a joyous sense of life, originating in Horton's naive enthusiasm for nature and for his Muse, enlivens many of his poems."[5]

The Horton of Redding and Sherman, then, is neither merely a curio nor an American racial stereotype. There are no manifestos in his favor from either Redding or Sherman which would, if accepted, elevate Hor-

5. J. Saunders Redding, *To Make a Poet Black* (Chapel Hill, 1939), 13, 117; Joan Sherman, *Invisible Poets: Afro-Americans of the Nineteenth Century* (Urbana, Ill., 1974), 13, 12.

ton to the status of a major figure in America's literature or even of a leading writer of his time. Still, clearly, Redding and Sherman believe that there is more to Horton than his sheer oddity and more to his poetry than the simple wonder that it was written at all. Caroline Lee Hentz once said of Horton, "Instead of the broad smile of the African, he has the mild gravity of a Grecian philosopher."[6] It was her most sympathetically intended, although racially patronizing, way of asserting a quality in Horton, a quality which belied what her world expected of his color and his condition. Walser's "troubadour in motley" also asserts a quality in Horton. It implies the possession of at least a minimal measure of a genuine artistic consciousness. And that, of course, is the actual arresting oddity in connection with Horton and his poetry. Not gibberish or balderdash, his poetry is far less crude than poetry can be. It is, for instance, decidedly less crude than the poetry of Jupiter Hammon. It is more versatile, both in form and sense, than the poetry of Phillis Wheatley. Whether it would have been even more versatile had Horton never been a slave obviously no one can say. What is true of it, as it is, is that it displays an amazing range of interests and proficiencies which would have done credit to many people in Horton's day who were not in chattel bondage.

Horton liked to rhyme, and he was facile at it. He seems, indeed, to have written only one poem in free verse, "Division of an Estate," the subject matter of which can be shown to have a factual basis for itself in the family history of the Hortons. But Horton applied an attentive and indefatigably acute ear to more than rhyme and rhythm in the sound of his verse. He had an affinity for refrains, simple or incremental. Of the three poems on slavery in *The Hope of Liberty*, one is called "The Slave's Complaint." It opens as follows:

> Am I sadly cast aside
> On misfortune's rugged tide?
> Will the world my pains deride
>   Forever?
> Must I dwell in Slavery's night
> And all pleasure take its flight
> Far beyond my feeble sight
>   Forever?

6. Hentz, quoted in Walser, *The Black Poet*, 103–104.

And so it proceeds. Each of its seven stanzas ends on the word *forever*.
One of the poems of Horton's which appeared in the *Southern Literary
Messenger* begins:

> I would be thine when morning breaks
>   On my enraptured view,
> When every star her tower forsakes,
> And every tuneful bird awakes
>   And bids the night adieu.

The same four monosyllables, "I would be thine," introduce all the stanzas in this poem of five stanzas except the last. That final stanza employs
an increment. "I would be thine" becomes "let me be thine." But rare,
indeed, if not completely lacking, is any poem by Horton without some
sequence of sounds involving repetition. He does not ignore sense in his
poetry, self-taught though he was. It would be an egregious error to describe him as a rapt musician only, beside himself with glee merely if his
pattern of accents, his vowel coloration, his sibilants, his assonances and
alliterations, and similar effects, contrive a satisfyingly pretty tune. As a
matter of fact, the reader of Horton may be constantly surprised at the
variety of topics in which Horton shows an interest. Even so, the resources of sound are tremendously important to Horton. His poetry may
not start with them. It never tires of experimenting with and exploiting
them.

Sherman notes approvingly Horton's vocabulary. She calls it "extraordinary," and so it was, and would have been even had Horton not been a
slave. Rather extraordinary, also, she notes, as we have noted earlier
here, is Horton's versatility. He affected numerous verse forms. He
changed attitudes. He explored a variety of themes. His poems on slavery, although only a meager lot, as has also been already noted here, are
still almost surely, for any reader now, surprisingly frank in their denunciation of the institution. Yet Redding introduces a possible nuance about
Horton's "anti-slavery" poems which, if true, can cast their frankness in a
new light. Redding came to feel that "although . . . Horton fully realized
the bitterness of bondage, he tasted its gall only for himself . . . [and
seemed] to have thought that slavery was created for himself alone." It is
possible, therefore, to read most, if not all, of Horton's antislavery poems
as cries of distress, not for the plight of all the slaves in America, but
against the special injustice done by slavery to one man. This is not,

however, a distinction made by the critic who stipulates that, of the twenty-one poems, excluding the invocation, in *The Hope of Liberty*, three are on slavery, five on death, "four on nature and pastoral life, four on love, three on God and his might, and one each on poetry and loss of innocence."[7]

Another critic, while arguing that "Division of an Estate," which appears in Horton's *Poetical Works*, is an antislavery poem, again without Redding's distinction, lists as themes other than slavery treated in *The Poetical Works* "religion, patriotism, money, drinking, fame, scholarship, poetry itself," and love. The same critic places the poems in *Naked Genius* in the following twelve thematic categories: "love lyrics, religious verse, anti-slavery verse, philosophical musing, poems in praise of famous and not so famous men, patriotic paeans, humorous verse, campfire and battle pieces, antithalamia [this critic's admitted self-coinage to represent Horton's poems against women, love, and marriage], and miscellaneous."[8] Even without the addition, then, of a unique category of protest for at least some of Horton's antislavery verse, it is very apparent that, as a poet, Horton addressed a veritable host of issues and that he was, therefore, neither much afraid to talk on whatever caught his fancy or, having chosen a subject, to speak on it just about as he chose. Accordingly, one may well contend that not often, if ever, does it seem to have been Horton's custom to act in a manner compatible with orthodox notions of the psychology of a slave. The ultimate paradox in his conduct may have been that he was both a "troubadour in motley" and yet, at his heart's core, more an irrepressible cynic than a fellow of infinite jest—that his mock, even when he was outwardly most a mountebank, was inwardly dry.

In December, 1849, when the Hungarian patriot Louis Kossuth was toasted in Raleigh with verse from an English poet, Horton directed to a Raleigh newspaper a letter which said, in part:

I always have been and am still opposed to every exaltation of foreign over native talent. I am for developing *our own* resources and cherishing native genius. I may never be before the People for any office, and therefore cannot be personally affected by any seeming assent to what I do most cordially disapprove. But as a

7. Sherman, *Invisible Poets*, 5; Redding, *To Make a Poet Black*, 16; John L. Cobb, "George Moses Horton's *Hope and Liberty*: Thematic Unity in Early American Black Poetry," *College Language Association Journal*, XXIV (1981), 446.

8. William Carroll, "Naked Genius: The Poetry of George Moses Horton, Slave Bard of North Carolina, 1797–1883?" (Ph.D. dissertation, University of North Carolina at Chapel Hill, 1977), xlviii, lxiii.

North Carolina patriot, I ask, Why leave our own to stand on foreign soil? Why go *abroad* for poetry when we have an infinitely superior article of domestic manufacture. I am too modest to speak of my own, but surely there *is* poetry of native growth, even of your fair City of Oaks, good enough for a toast to Louis Kossuth, without straying off into foreign parts.[9]

No matter how capable of self-mockery Horton may have been, this is a remarkable letter. Assuming its sincerity, it demonstrates that, in very much the unprovisional fashion in which James Forten thought of himself as American, so, apparently, did Horton. It is, of course, anachronistic to try to impart to either Forten or Horton twentieth-century notions of blackness without serious qualifications. But, in twentieth-century terms, both were integrationists. Neither was a black nationalist. If Horton was less forthright, and less the social crusader, than Forten, it may have been because Horton possessed the plain common sense to recognize that he should not attempt in the South some things which he might much more safely have done in the North. But it may also have been because of Horton's temperament. He seems not only not to have been a community leader. He seems also, by disposition, to have been inclined toward a contemplative life. It was probably, therefore, not a hardship for him to preserve a sufficient detachment within himself from the events around him—in an outer world of which he did not approve—to inhibit him from the violent attacks upon society of a Nat Turner or even from the nonrevolutionary activism of a Paul Cuffe. He idealized neither women nor marriage. Indeed, he seems to have harbored a low opinion of both. The propensity of whites, like his master, to get drunk, as well as their aversion to literature, if they could read, or to any pastimes except the idlest sports, whether they could read or not, did not escape his sardonic gaze. He certainly might well not have felt that these whites were better than he. Some of the Chapel Hill undergraduates he knew were to become personages of great eminence nationally as well as locally. James Knox Polk became president. How heroic these personages ever were to him probably should be open to serious question. In great likelihood his slavery was always, to paraphrase Redding, nominal.[10] It affected very little, if at all, his original gifts. Those did not incline him toward a literature epic in theme or structure. In spite of Mrs. Hentz's observation, he did not have the gravity of a Greek philosopher, at least not in most of

9. Quoted in Walser, *The Black Poet*, 73.
10. Redding, *To Make a Poet Black*, 14.

his moments of creativity. One of his best poems is his "Creditor to His Proud Debtor," some lines from which read

> My duck bill boots would look as bright,
> Had you in justice served me right;
> Like you, I then could step as light,
>   Before a flaunting maid.
> As nicely could I clear my throat,
> And to my tights my eyes devote;
> But I'd leave you bare, without the coat
>   For which you have not paid.

> Then boast and bear the crack,
> With the sheriff at your back,
> Huzzah for dandy Jack,
> My jolly fop, my Jo!

In verse of this sort Horton was at ease in his true métier, the adroit pillorying of man in his relatively petty misdemeanors, not the arraignment of humanity before some high tribunal where everyone speaks as portentously as in the Book of Job. Yet it will not do not to notice the occasional presence in Horton of a certain possibly delayed resonance, a conceivable second (and, sometimes, third) meaning, that may be there because Horton was aware of it and wanted to speak through it, even if he could not, as may happen with any artist, be quite sure he knew how it had gotten where it was. So, for example, "Creditor to His Proud Debtor" could be, quite circuitously, a poem with an antislavery dimension. Could not any of the three Hortons who had "owned" George Moses, or most, if not all, of the masters profiting anywhere from their human chattel, be, in their way, "proud debtors"? We cannot say now how devious Horton may sometimes have been. We can only say that, of the poets whom we have become accustomed to regard as the first four in Afro-American literature, he was certainly the one who experimented most with the possibilities of verse. That is decidedly true. Moreover, his experimentation existed in both what he said and how he said it. One close observer of him has discovered in *The Hope of Liberty* a thematic unity inherent in Horton's attraction to the phenomenon of soaring.[11] This observer connects what he detects as Horton's obsessive incorporation into his verse of images of flight with a powerful both conscious and subliminal impulse in Horton toward any artistic expression which could

---

11. Cobb, "Horton's *Hope of Liberty*," 441–50.

be, in its sense and form, a method of conveying, and relieving, his visceral reactions against slavery. Of Horton's resentment of his own bondage there should be little, if any doubt, in spite of Collier Cobb. Horton must have been, when all is said and done, unhappy about any slavery. Yet, granting that his "soaring" in *The Hope of Liberty* is a metaphor, it may not be the end of wisdom to correlate that metaphor only with abolitionism. To some extent, at least, surely it can be correlated additionally with his need to express himself, and to be thereby emancipated, through the creation of verse. It is reasonable to believe that Horton abhorred slavery. It is imperative to know that he loved poetry. His "soaring" could have been, and probably was, an objective correlative for states desirable to him either as a man or as an artist, but, in great likelihood, as both.

Horton, we have seen, was an old man when he left North Carolina and went north. David Walker was, like Horton, a North Carolinian, born in Wilmington, the thriving seaport south and east both of Rich Square and Chapel Hill. Walker's father was a slave who died, it is understood, before his son's birth in 1785. But Walker's mother was free. So, therefore, was he. He is our authority for the information that he traveled widely in the South, where, apparently, everything that he saw of slavery—and he says that he saw of it a great deal—made him hate the institution with a truly monumental hate. He was, however, unlike Horton, still very much in the prime of his life when he settled permanently in the North. By at least the 1820s he had become a resident of Boston, where, by 1827, on Brattle Street, near the docks in the heart of the harbor district, he was operating a shop through which he bought and sold secondhand clothes. Almost as soon as *Freedom's Journal* was founded, Walker allied himself with it as its Boston agent. He also contributed copy to it. Meanwhile, he was speaking, as well as writing, against the great hatred of his life, starting with small groups, but so accommodating himself that, by 1828, he was lecturing against slavery to fairly large crowds. In September, 1829, he wrote, apparently in white heat and at great speed, the long pamphlet *David Walker's Appeal in Four Articles; Together with A Preamble, To The Coloured Citizens of the World, But in Particular, And Very Expressly, To Those Of The United States of America*. He paid for the printing of his *Appeal* from his own pocket. It has been persuasively conjectured that, since he seems to have received, from bartenders in the neighborhood of his shop, garments bartered by sailors for drinks, he abetted the distribution of his *Appeal* by surreptitiously inserting copies of it into the pockets of these garments, so that sailors who renewed their wardrobes in his store could end up helping him by ridding themselves of his *Appeal* in distant, and often, perhaps, southern ports.[12] By June, 1830, he had written, and had published, a third edition of the *Appeal.* But on June 28, 1830, his corpse was discovered in the street near his shop. It is suspected that he was murdered, probably by poison.

Walker's *Appeal* obviously and deliberately modeled its form upon the form of the Constitution of the United States, possibly, if not probably, because Walker thus intended even that aspect of his work to express his sense of the irony represented by racism within the American democracy. In the very first paragraph of the Preamble of the *Appeal,* he asserts that the "coloured people of these United States . . . are the most degraded, wretched, and abject set of beings that ever lived since the world began." He enforced this assertion with references elsewhere to slavery and enslaved peoples in countries other than America, always with the unmistakable purpose of demonstrating that in none of these other countries did slavery equal, in its dehumanization of the slave, slavery in the United States. His four articles are entitled, in order, "Our Wretchedness in Consequence of Slavery," "Our Wretchedness in Consequence of Ignorance," "Our Wretchedness in Consequence of the Preachers of the Religion of Jesus Christ," and "Our Wretchedness in Consequence of the Colonizing Plan." He repeats himself. He raves. Yet detectable in his "wretchedness because of ignorance" is an attack on Negroes for not helping themselves as much as they could and should. He damns the church for its hypocrisy on slavery, particularly with an anecdote of his about a sermon he had heard in South Carolina the white deliverer of which quoted from the Bible admonitions to his slave audience to obey their masters. He is utterly disdainful of the colonizationists, fortifying his attack upon them with the inclusion in his fourth article of an anticolonizationist letter by Richard Allen which had been printed in *Freedom's Journal.*

Despite its faults as literature, then, the *Appeal* did function well enough as propaganda to frighten many Americans of its day. Copies of it quickly reached the South, where reactions against it, including a price on Walker's head, were immediate, bitter, violent, and widespread. Wanted posters, of course, promised more for him dead than alive, in his native North Carolina ten times as much. For, as Charles Wiltse aptly says, the *Appeal* takes "dead aim at the argument used then [in Walker's

12. Charles M. Wiltse (ed.), *David Walker's Appeal* (New York, 1965), ix.

time] to sanction slavery . . . the argument that the Negro is a different species, not quite human and therefore not to be confused with all those men who, according to the Declaration of Independence, were created equal."[13] But it also constitutes an exercise in incendiary, and elementary, logic. In effect, it presents as incontrovertible facts two major premises, that life in America for Negroes, slave or free, is intolerable and, yet, that life elsewhere for those same Negroes, the colonizationists notwithstanding, is inconceivable. It can only be concluded, then, that American Negroes, if they do not kill themselves, must change the conditions under which they live—in other words, rebel. The clamor of the South against the *Appeal* was based, of course, on its fear of a slave insurrection.

The future spoke through David Walker. He looked forward toward the extinction of slavery. With him, and Afro-American writers who would follow him, the age of the earliest Afro-American writers was dead. In 1843, thirteen years after Walker's death, at the National Negro Convention in Buffalo, New York, a Negro of a later generation, Henry Highland Garnet, would cry out, loud and clear, and unequivocally: "Brethren, arise, arise! Strike for your lives and liberties. Now is the day and hour. Let every slave throughout the land do this, and the days of slavery are numbered. You cannot be more oppressed than you have been—you cannot suffer greater cruelties than you have already. Rather die freemen than live to be slaves. Remember that you are four millions!" Appropriately, in 1848 Garnet's *Address* was coupled with Walker's *Appeal,* and the two were published together in a single volume the financial support of which came from John Brown.

13. *Ibid.,* vii.

Part Two ❧

The Age of the Abolitionists, I

5. Frederick Douglass, Plus the Early Black Press

In mid-May, 1870, Baltimoreans of color staged the largest, and possibly the most elaborate, of the many celebrations by black Americans of the ratification two months earlier of the Fifteenth Amendment, the addition to the Constitution of the United States which ostensibly eliminated color as a factor in the enfranchisement of American males. The celebrants were acting, of course, before the era of motorcars and other forms of autonomously powered transportation. Thus, the huge parade which gathered to start a long and memorable day was headed by twenty carriages propelled by horses, not by any of the more miraculous agents which tend to drive our carriages today. In these carriages sat the dignitaries whom the occasion sought to distinguish from a common horde. But the parade, indeed, was huge principally because of the twenty thousand black Baltimoreans from precisely that common horde who, with something of a hallelujah in their every stride, tramped on foot through Baltimore streets to a point locally familiar as Monument Square. Brass bands playing lively airs tramped along with the twenty thousand. At Monument Square all the music and marching ceased, and florid oratory, which would last well into the night, became the order of the day. The protracted round of festivities terminated with the thunderous adoption of eight resolutions, the last of them a tribute to Frederick Douglass, cited in the resolution, amid "loud acclaim," as "the foremost man of color" of his time.

The resolution did not lie. Douglass was the foremost man of color of his time. Students of our national past increasingly are conceding that he was also one of the foremost Americans of that, or any, American era.[1] And so he is a shining example of the phenomenon of eminence sprung from the deepest and direst obscurity. Born a slave in Talbot County near the town of Easton on Maryland's Eastern Shore, apparently in 1818, not 1817, as has hitherto been quite generally supposed, he spent the first eight years of his life always within a radius of fifteen rather easily traversable miles, or less, from his rural birthplace. The next seven years, except for a brief return to Talbot County during the settlement of his first master's estate, he spent in urban Baltimore, where he somewhat surreptitiously taught himself to read and write. Ownership of him had passed from his original master to that master's daughter and then on to the daughter's husband, a man named Thomas Auld, after the daughter, like her father, died. It was with Thomas Auld's brother, Hugh, that Douglass was lodged in Baltimore. A disagreement between the brothers precipitated Douglass' return to Talbot County in 1833. He was now a man in size, but too city-bred for immediate efficiency on his part in work associated with a farmhand's pursuits. Nature, however, had endowed him with a truly magnificent physique (he was over six feet tall) as well as a superior mind. He could, and did, acquire expertise at doing what, in that day on the Eastern Shore, a farmhand should. But there came a time, in 1836, when he was suspected of being the leader and master plotter in an attempt by five slaves (including himself) to escape. He was jailed in Easton. His master vowed vociferously to sell him south, then quietly sent him back to brother Hugh in Baltimore. Douglass now learned the calker's trade. His affairs so prospered that he was permitted to become semi-independent, selling his own time, although by far the bulk of what he earned went into Hugh Auld's pocket, and living outside his work hours much as he pleased.

In the late summer of 1838, one delay by Douglass in his delivery of the weekly levy from his pay to Hugh Auld resulted in an abrupt revocation of the privileges Auld had granted him. In early September, 1838, Douglass, posing as a sailor, left Baltimore by train. The next day he was a homeless but happy fugitive in New York City. Within a fortnight Anna Murray, the free black woman eight years his senior to whom he had become affianced in Baltimore and who had, with virtually all her meager savings, helped finance his escape, joined him in Manhattan,

---

1. Note the treatment of Douglass as a very minor figure in the monumental works on America by such historians as James Ford Rhodes, Edward Channing, and John B. McMaster. McMaster could not even correctly spell Douglass' name.

where the two were wed by James W. C. Pennington, an earlier black
fugitive from the Eastern Shore. Hours after their wedding the bride and
groom moved on to New Bedford, Massachusetts. There Douglass, who
had come north as Frederick Johnson, heeding the cautionary advice of a
leader in New Bedford's black community that he not retain a surname
which might identify him to slave catchers, became Frederick Douglass
(this community leader had been reading *The Lady of the Lake*). Racism
forestalled Douglass' employment as a calker. He worked however he
could, shoveling coal, sawing wood, and at other varieties of strenuous
manual labor. Anna worked, too, as a washerwoman or domestic. The
pair had their first child, Rosetta, in 1839. Their first two sons, Lewis and
Frederick, Jr., were also born in New Bedford, in 1840 and 1842 respectively. Late in 1842 the Douglasses moved to Lynn, Massachusetts, where,
in 1844, Charles, their last son and next-to-last child, a namesake of the
noted black orator Charles Lenox Remond, was born. But in August,
1841, Douglass had appeared as an unscheduled speaker before five hundred abolitionists convened for a meeting on Nantucket Island. He was,
to put it mildly, in this first display of his exceptional platform skills, a
great success. The Massachusetts Anti-Slavery Society immediately hired
him as one of its lecturers.

Through the early 1840s Douglass toured an abolitionist circuit in
Massachusetts, Rhode Island, New York, Pennsylvania, Ohio, and Indiana. He quickly mastered his role on the lecture platform. He was the
opponent of slavery who spoke from his experience of slavery. However,
for such a role he employed an English too pure and presented an appearance too elegant and assured to satisfy a number of his hearers who could
not quite believe that someone looking as he looked and talking as he
talked could ever have been a slave. Partially to confound these skeptics,
Douglass curtailed his lecturing during the winter of 1844–1845 and
composed his *Narrative of the Life of Frederick Douglass, An American
Slave, Written by Himself*. This *Narrative* appeared in May, 1845. In August of the same year Douglass sailed for the British Isles. He stayed
abroad for twenty months and was no less a success overseas than he had
been with his 1841 American audience on the hitherto mentioned island
of Nantucket. He returned, moreover, to America no longer a fugitive.
The British, led by two sisters who lived in Newcastle-on-the-Tyne, had
raised seven hundred dollars with which they purchased his freedom. Additionally, they gave him more than two thousand dollars, accompanying
this money with their urgent admonition that it be used to start a news-

paper. Douglass was a protégé of William Lloyd Garrison, who most pontifically warned Douglass that any essay by him into the field of independent journalism would be a gross mistake and offered Douglass, instead, a regular columnist's space in the white-owned *National Anti-Slavery Standard.* Douglass, however, moved himself and his family to Rochester, New York, in the fall of 1847. There, before the new year, he had launched his own abolitionist weekly, the *North Star,* on a press which he had purchased with much of the money he had brought back from Great Britain.

More than a newspaper was to contribute to a widening rupture between Douglass and Garrison. Staunch abolitionist though he was, Garrison yet affected a philosophy which might well trouble a born pragmatist like Douglass. Garrison and the Garrisonians, a considerable faction of the abolitionists, absolutely abjured politics. It seemed to them without question that the American Constitution was a proslavery document. Hence, to electioneer, to vote, or to hold office in America was to enter into a compact of evil with the slavocracy, advocates of the devil. Garrison and Garrisonians would resort only to what they, and others, called moral suasion to end slavery. But abolitionists did exist who did not abjure politics. Some of these abolitionists who were not so unrelentingly perfectionist as the Garrisonians formed the Liberty party, which nominated candidates on a national ticket in 1840. In 1848 the Free-Soil party, primarily committed to the restriction of slavery to the South, was able to persuade Martin Van Buren to be its candidate for president. Both the Liberty party and the Free-Soil party would substantially end as elements of the Republican party. And Douglass would not only fight slavery through his paper. He would also be involved with the Liberty party, the Free-Soilers, the Radical abolitionists, and the Republicans. His paper, indeed, when it changed its name to *Frederick Douglass' Paper* in 1851, absorbed the paper of the Liberty party. For Douglass not only came to terms with politics as Garrison would not. Once he entered the world of politics he never quit it. To him it was important, not only that Negroes be free, but also that they fight, on the same terms as any other Americans, for their civil rights.

Douglass knew and respected John Brown. He visited Brown in Brown's home in Springfield, Massachusetts, in 1848. Douglass' home in Rochester, incidentally, was a station on the Underground Railroad. Brown stayed there, for three weeks, as Douglass' guest in 1858. Brown and Douglass conferred clandestinely in an old stone quarry at Chambersburg, Pennsylvania, only eight weeks before Brown's attack on nearby Harpers Ferry. It was at this Chambersburg meeting that Brown futilely sought to enlist Douglass into his intended guerrilla army of liberation. "Come with me, Douglass," Brown pleaded. "When I strike, the bees will begin to swarm and I shall want you to help me hive them." But Douglass was too prudent to accept Brown's invitation. Even so, to avoid a very possible prosecution, after Brown's apprehension Douglass waited hardly overnight to flee to Canada and then to England. His youngest child, Anna, a favorite of his, died while he was in England. Douglass returned by May, 1860, to an America which, with a crucial election in the very immediate offing, had quickly lost much of its interest in tracking down accomplices of Brown, whoever they might have been.

Douglass, of course, did all that he could to support the Union cause in the Civil War. He recruited black soldiers. Two of his sons served with the 54th Massachusetts. From June, 1858, until July, 1860, Douglass had published both *Frederick Douglass' Paper* and a new periodical, *Douglass' Monthly*, intended primarily for a British audience. The weekly that had begun as the *North Star* and continued as *Frederick Douglass' Paper*, like all the other abolitionist papers, as well as all the other antebellum newspapers published by blacks, experienced chronic financial difficulties. Yet it never missed an issue until Douglass, feeling he could no longer tolerate its deficits, abandoned its publication in July, 1860. But he abandoned the publication of *Douglass' Monthly* in the summer of 1863 for the quite different reason that he actually expected to go to Mississippi as a commissioned officer to, in his own words, "assist . . . in the organization of colored troops." He never received a commission and never went to Mississippi. Yet he did get to know Lincoln well enough for Mrs. Lincoln to send him, after Lincoln's assassination, the martyred president's cane.

Douglass' home in Rochester burned in 1872. He moved to Washington, D.C. There in 1874 he permitted himself to be elected president of the Freedman's Savings Bank, only to discover such a parlous state in the bank's affairs that he did what his senses of honesty and responsibility demanded and helped to initiate the bank's closing. Three years earlier, as an accommodation to President Grant, who wanted the United States to annex Santo Domingo, he had accompanied a commission of inquiry to the eastern end of the island which Columbus had named Hispaniola. He was marshall of the District of Columbia under President Hayes. President Garfield appointed him recorder of deeds, a post he retained under President Arthur and even, for a year, under the Democratic president Cleveland. He would be sent in 1889, by President Benjamin Harrison, as the minister resident and consul general from the United States to Haiti. In 1878 he had bought the fifteen-acre estate on a hill rising from the Anacostia branch of the Potomac which he called Cedar Hill. The estate surrounded the twenty-room house within which he would reside for the last seventeen years of his life. Anna, almost paralyzed in her last years from rheumatism, died in the summer of 1882. Seventeen months later, in January, 1884, Douglass married the white Helen Pitts, a native of Rochester twenty years his junior. With her, Douglass made his last trip overseas, a leisurely promenade of sorts that began in September, 1886, meandered through England, France, and Italy to Egypt and Greece, and then returned to Paris, where Helen parted from Douglass to hasten to the bedside of her ailing mother while Douglass lingered on the other side of the Atlantic for further visits with old friends of his in England. The Haitians had grown very fond of Douglass while he was America's emissary to their country. They persuaded him to act as their commissioner for their exhibit in the world's fair, the Columbian Exposition, at Chicago in 1893. His death came suddenly at Cedar Hill in 1895.

The *Narrative*, published by Douglass in 1845, ranks as a classic of our national, as well as of Afro-American, literature. In comparison with most books it is short, except for its appendix easily less than forty thousand words in length. William Lloyd Garrison wrote a preface for it which lauds Douglass as both a speaker and a writer. A commendatory letter from Wendell Phillips to Douglass follows Garrison's preface. For there had developed by the 1840s, in the typical slave narrative, a drastic change of its dominant function from what that function earlier had been, and these clearly polemical panegyrics affixed as introductions to Douglass' *Narrative* from two of slavery's most ardent foes suggest the nature of that change. Briton Hammon's slave narrative, written in the eighteenth century, did not advocate abolition. Douglass' *Narrative* decidedly does. And thus, emphatically in a very important regard, it resembles all but one of the extant slave narratives published between 1830 and 1860, the unquestionably most celebrated period of the genre, when slave narratives assumed the character erroneously, if also almost universally, taken for granted as prototypical of every slave narrative whenever and wherever it might have been composed. Moreover—and perhaps equally as emphatically for the student of slave narratives—Douglass' *Narrative* resembles virtually all other slave narratives published in its day by its repetitions within its pages of distinctive categories of form and content so thoroughly common to all these narratives as to constitute proof positive that such narratives—the abolitionist slave narratives they might well be called as a class—are, in truth, a subgenre of a genre.

So, Douglass' *Narrative* is shaped as a linear account of a personal history set mainly within a southern scene and culminating in a slave's escape to freedom in the North. All other abolitionist slave narratives are similarly shaped, even to an occasional long and complicated ending which is truly less an ending than an opening into a very new beginning. Douglass' *Narrative* is quite the picaresque tale. It strings together in loose array episodes from Douglass' life which, in aggregate, constitute a conducted tour, for a person of no greater perspicacity than most persons in this world, of the special world every American slave would be expected to know, and share, in the real world of Douglass' day. All other abolitionist slave narratives are similarly picaresque. Finally, Douglass' *Narrative* is candidly and pronouncedly melodramatic. It dichotomizes the people it portrays, and most of the action it presents, quite symmetrically according to a formula which surrounds with a bright and presumably celestial light all that is antislavery, including the slaves, and shrouds within a Stygian gloom the exact opposite of a heavenly radiance everything and anything of supposed aid to slavery. All other abolitionist slave narratives are similarly melodramatic.

In terms of content, Douglass' *Narrative* abounds with episodes which are nothing more or less than case studies illustrative of the inhumanity of slavery to the slave and of this very slave's humanity in spite of his inhuman treatment by southern, and many northern, whites and in obvious contradiction to such pseudoscientists as Dr. Josiah Nott of Mobile, who would, by 1850, deny that blacks and whites even belonged to the same genus of the animal kingdom. Atrocities are committed, in the *Narrative,* as far as, allegedly, in at least five cases, the extreme of coldblooded murder, by whites upon blacks. No atrocities are committed there in any way by Negroes. Black women are preyed upon sexually, in the *Narrative,* by white men. Of course, no white women in the *Narrative* are subjected to the venery of black men. And while the slaves in the *Narrative* live meanly—poorly housed, poorly clothed, and poorly fed—instance after instance of their unquenchable propensity to care for one another in the role of a responsible parent or a grateful child or a loyal friend and to observe, in general, an especially magnanimous version of the golden rule toward all their fellow men, demonstrates their ability to rise above their circumstances and to practice those domestic and civic virtues which are the basic underpinnings of a human society in an advanced stage of man's elevation of himself from savagery. One thing more of special note appears in the Narrative, a series of pictures revealing the hypocrisy of white southern Christianity. Douglass' voice in the Narrative is never more charged with condemnation, contempt, and ire than when he shows some of his white neighbors at worship and then moves on to add, as tellingly as possible, vignettes of these same white neighbors, with their psalms and scriptures still ringing in their supposedly pious ears, abusing their slaves unmercifully. His voice in this regard is a voice found in all other abolitionist slave narratives, just as the case studies of slaves and their masters which supply the content of his Narrative are but duplicates of similar case studies distributed copiously throughout all other abolitionist slave narratives.

Once, however, Douglass' acquiescence in the habitual practices of writers associated with the abolitionist slave narrative is recognized, acknowledgment should then be made of what he does which, in his Narrative, redeems his resort to those practices from a mere hackneyed reproduction of a prevailing fashion. And what he does thereby constitutes a genuine tribute to his own original powers and his individual cultural growth. He pours, as it were, into old bottles representative of the customs to which he is deferring a fresh and often delightful vintage compounded from effects directly attributable to aesthetic sensibilities which were his and his alone. As an orator he had held live audiences spellbound, not simply because of his appearance, much to the advantage of any public figure as that appearance was, or of his voice, a rich bass-baritone which he could inflect at will and project, without artificial aid, into the ears of hearers on the farthest edge of the not infrequently large crowds that he addressed. But he was, sometimes while he spoke, among other things, a superb mime. He liked, for example, occasionally to turn his platform into a pulpit from which a southern white preacher, a lackey of the slaveholding South, could be seen and heard preaching to slaves, warning them to obey their masters and brandishing over their heads, like a would-be fiery sword, gospel verses in defense of slavery. When he became this preacher, an organic mixture of the real thing and of broad caricature, Douglass was availing himself of talents in his possession which a literary artist might well exactly so have used. It was of these same talents, involving, as they did, a genuinely artistic apprehension, re-creation, and enhancement of reality, that Douglass availed himself in his Narrative.

Contemporary reviewers on both sides of the Atlantic received the *Narrative* with encomia which would certainly gratify the heart of any author. The New York *Tribune*, for example, on June 10, 1845, said of it, "Considered merely as narrative, we have never read one more simple, true, coherent and warm with genuine feeling." *Chambers' Edinburgh Journal* on January 24, 1846, in a somewhat different vein which stressed approvingly the impression of veracity it considered easily derivable from the *Narrative*, was, even so, hardly less effusively eulogistic. Reviewers, however, tend not to be too analytic of the subtler processes possibly connected with a writer's art. More than a century after the reviewers, Benjamin Quarles, although a historian and not a literary scholar, brooded (perhaps as perceptively as anyone has, or probably ever will) over the precise identity of the attributes within the *Narrative* which account for its appeal. Quarles found the answer to the problem he had posed in a quartet of virtues specifically describable as Douglass' ability to write a simple and direct prose; the "sensitive" descriptions within the *Narrative*, whether of inanimate things, like places, or animate things, like people; the skill with which Douglass, in his book, when he wishes to evoke pathos, achieves his wish without cheapening his appeal to sentiment; and, finally (surely the consummate accomplishment for a propagandist), the success with which, at various points throughout the *Narrative*, while maintaining sufficiently his storyteller's stance, Douglass invests his incident with argument.[2] Quarles seems, with his quartet of virtues, to have made the right discoveries. The *Narrative* lacks magnificence. It ranges over no vast areas of thought or speculation. Nothing about it is elegant or grand. But it is everything which Quarles says it is and possibly more. Research, allowing for some misspelled names, has substantiated virtually all its claims of fact, except for a possible injustice to the brothers Auld, who may have treated Douglass, and his grandmother in her dotage, much more compassionately than Douglass admits. If the brothers are distorted, however, there the *Narrative*, apparently, does succumb to what could have been too great an urge on Douglass' part to accommodate reality to the picture he wished to paint of slavery. Still, elsewhere, in the main, and to an impressive degree, the *Narrative* remains, on one level, a transcript, remarkable for both its eloquence and its accuracy, of a significant single life. On another level, modest as its habiliments are,

2. Quarles's analysis occurs in his excellent Introduction to Benjamin Quarles (ed.), *Narrative of the Life of Frederick Douglass, an American Slave, Written by Himself* (Cambridge, Mass., 1960), xvi–xvii.

it yet penetrates the regions of myth and epic, for it speaks, at that level, repeatedly, in terms direct and indirect, of the persisting saga of a people.

Douglass was to spend, after the *Narrative*, a long life as, in effect, the tribune of all black Americans. It may be tempting, therefore, to suppose him a partisan of blackness and an outstanding exemplar of distinctively intraracial cultural traditions. Very little, apparently, could be farther from the truth. Existing records indicate that Douglass' ancestors, with a strong sense of their locality, had lived on the Eastern Shore from at least the turn of the eighteenth century, and that, indeed, they may have, with surely as much of probability from Barbados as from Africa, arrived in the county of Douglass' birth virtually when Englishmen first settled that county around 1660.[3] As slaves they could possess no family name. Yet enough of them were somehow associated with the name, under various spellings, of Bailey for Bailey to serve as more or less a cognomen for their entire clan. They seem rather quickly to have acquired an admixture of Indian blood. Douglass, moreover, may not have been the only one of them of whom one parent was white. In any case, by Douglass' time their roots in America were solid, conscious, and deep. They could not but transmit to Douglass an awareness of an American background which was its equal in intensity to that of any of their neighbors, black or white.

Douglass' first close companion was his maternal grandmother, who lived, however humbly, more in the spirit of a Jeffersonian yeoman than of a slave. His second close companion was Daniel Lloyd, the twelve-year-old son of the Colonel Lloyd who was, at the time, master of the great Lloyd home plantation on which Douglass' master lived. Douglass, some five years younger than Daniel, was elected to be Daniel's special slave. In the freemasonry of childhood, he and Daniel spent most of their waking hours together at a period when Douglass was especially susceptible to such habits of Daniel as Daniel's mode of speech. In Baltimore, after Douglass learned to read, he bought, and studied diligently and passionately, the Columbian *Orator*, whence he absorbed, from their speeches therein, the thinking (as well as the language, pure or in translation) of Socrates, Cato, both Pitts, Charles James Fox, Washington, Richard Brinsley Sheridan, Napoleon, Daniel O'Connell, and other exemplary exponents of the Atlantic civilization which clearly governed

3. Cf. the first chapter of Dickson J. Preston, *Young Frederick Douglass: The Maryland Years* (Baltimore, 1980).

the attitude toward life of Caleb Bingham, the New Englander, very much a product of his geographical section, who had, in assembling the *Orator*, added to it poems, playlets, and dialogues written by himself. In Baltimore also, during the two years just before he escaped, Douglass became a member, albeit illegally, of a secret club known as the East Baltimore Mental Improvement Society. The other five members of the society, which existed primarily to foster intragroup debates, were young free blacks. Topics for their debates ranged from "the status of blacks in Maryland to classical theology" and, once, in a debate, Douglass alluded—seriously, it may well have been—to his intention some day to occupy a seat in the Senate of the United States.[4] By no means was Douglass what he would have called a traitor to his race. But he interpreted his advocacy of the best interests for Americans of his color in integrationist terms. His opposition to the colonizationists was inveterate, pronounced, and anything but passive. In the weeks immediately succeeding Lincoln's election, when Lincoln was clearly exerting himself to hold the South within the Union at conceivable costs that seemed to Douglass much too dear, Douglass did falter and plan a trip to Haiti to investigate the prospect of emigration there. Yet that was only once, and then in an exceptional moment, for Douglass, of almost utter despair. Otherwise Douglass never doubted where he belonged and what he wanted.

The nine-room, two-story brick house which Douglass inhabited in Rochester and his small estate at Cedar Hill are excellent symbols of his "acculturation." The lecture he delivered oftenest for pay was called "Self-Made Men," and he was a self-made man. But, also, some nineteenth-century Americans were dedicated to reform. They believed enough in the doctrine of the perfectibility of man to additionally believe, as a necessary corollary, that it was their duty to work for changes in human institutions which, in their judgment, would set men on the road to an earthly paradise. These Americans crusaded for many causes. Such crusading was a mark of their epoch. And Douglass crusaded with them. He was not only an abolitionist but also a temperance man. And he was one of the male participants in the convention at Seneca Falls, New York, in July, 1848, which initiated a systematic fight for women's rights. Indeed, he persevered throughout all of his life in the fight for women's rights. The last meeting he attended, on the day of his death,

4. *Ibid.*, 148–49.

was a women's meeting for a women's cause. He persevered, likewise, in the broadest of American conceptions of idealism and success. He was even able to permit himself to stomach governmental maneuvers aimed at American imperialism. One of his reactions to his experience of Santo Domingo was his comment, "If this is all my poor colored fellowmen have been able to do in seventy years, God help the race." It was not that he dissociated himself from blacks in Santo Domingo, Africa, or elsewhere. But just as he could see nothing wrong with judging black West Indians by the standards which allied him with the Columbian *Orator* and Cedar Hill, he could also see no wrong in other black Americans thinking as he thought. American was what he was, even when he evaluated blacks in other places. He copied his political ideas from Rousseau and Jefferson.[5] His dress, his speech, the style of life which he unselfconsciously affected were equally American. And so was his *Narrative*. It was protest. But protest couched in American terms to change American habits in American ways.

Douglass wrote the story of his life, not once, but thrice. It should not be forgotten, incidentally, that each of these autobiographies was—not only technically, but actually—a slave narrative. Nor should it be forgotten, either, that all of these autobiographies are, in at least one truly interesting way, somewhat singular forms of protest. They are all about winning, not losing. But, indeed, the abolitionist slave narratives are, as a class, the most positive of all works in black American literature. And none of them outshine, in this particular, Douglass' account of his own enslavement and his transcendence of it. His *Narrative* does not end until he is free and has proven his abilities at Nantucket. His second autobiography, which he called *My Bondage and My Freedom* and which appeared in 1855, rehearses, as does the *Narrative*, his birth and growth to manhood under the yoke of slavery. It extends its account of his life, however, into the years after the establishment of his paper in Rochester, with some attention, therefore, to his first trip abroad and its ensuing sequel of his long sojourn in the British Isles. *My Bondage and My Freedom*, moreover, reflects his break with Garrison. More than three times longer than his *Narrative*, it is considerably richer in its provision of detail, not only, it seems, because of its greater length, but also because the Douglass who wrote it was free and no longer a fugitive slave, obligated,

5. Laura E. Richards (ed.), *Letters and Journals of Samuel Gridley Howe* (2 vols.; Boston, 1909), II, 575, quoted in Benjamin Quarles (comp.), *Frederick Douglass* (Englewood Cliffs, N.J., 1968), 256; Quarles (ed.), *Narrative*, xii.

as a man of honor, not to reveal all of his past. Yet it has increasingly been overshadowed by the *Narrative*. It did, incidentally, sell well when it was published, even though not as phenomenally as the *Narrative* (which exhausted, in America, five editions totaling almost twenty thousand copies and an equal number of editions totaling almost thirteen thousand copies in England by 1850). And it remains to this day a superior slave narrative. But the relative brevity of the *Narrative* to it may well add to the superiority of the *Narrative* over *My Bondage and My Freedom* as a work of art.

Some passages in the *Narrative* rival the best of etchings in the manner in which, while avoiding a superfluity of inscriptions, they yet catch the essence of whatever it is the artist wishes to portray. Surely Douglass' disquisition on the singing of the slaves, culminating in his assertion of a genuine sadness at the heart of that singing underneath its surface gaiety, and his account of his fight with Covey, from his recital of the incidents out of which the open altercation grew to his notation of Covey's forbearance toward him once the physical struggle had terminated in Covey's defeat, are two of the finest, as well as best-known, moments in the *Narrative*. In neither moment does Douglass say so much that his point is lost, nor in either is there an inclusion of anything, overtly or by implication, which does not contribute to his main intent. *My Bondage and My Freedom* should not be dismissed as a great decline artistically from the *Narrative*. It never, however, is quite as powerful, or as gemlike in its brilliance, as the *Narrative* at its best.

Douglass called his last autobiography *The Life and Times of Frederick Douglass*. Whereas his *Narrative*, as we have seen—and, indeed, *My Bondage and My Freedom*, also—sold well, both in America and the British Isles, *The Life and Times* never approached the level of commercial success of either of the earlier books, whether at home or abroad. *The Life and Times* first appeared, in an American edition, in 1881. A second American edition was issued in 1892 and a third, somewhat revised, in 1893. *The Life and Times* was published, with an introduction by John Bright, in England in 1882. A Swedish edition, published in Stockholm, appeared in 1895. Even longer than *My Bondage and My Freedom*, like that work, *The Life and Times* by its length alone, if by nothing else, also seems to be prevented from rivaling the *Narrative* as an artifact constructed with truly superlative craft. Again, like *My Bondage and My Freedom*, *The Life and Times* is, however, far from an execrable example of the autobiographical art. If it has no other value, it must be accepted

as history told by a participant of some consequence in actual great occurrences concerning which he was privileged to provide an insider's
view. Douglass, incidentally, as American minister to Haiti was perforce
involved in an American attempt to secure from that country a concession which would have rendered possible the installation of an American
naval base on Haitian soil. In spite of protocol, Douglass' role in the attempt (which failed) was subordinate to that of an American admiral.
Nevertheless, Douglass was criticized, as well by proponents of the attempt (who attributed to Douglass ineptitudes which may well have been
the admiral's) as by opponents of the move whose censorious attitudes
originated either, or both, in general qualms about the possible birth and
growth of a new American imperialism or in a specific perception of
Douglass, in an act of high treason against his own color, willfully unit-
ing with whites in the duping, and degradation, of blacks, or both. The
final editions of *The Life and Times* contain Douglass' version of the nego-
tiation for the Haitian territory, a promontory called the Mole St. Nicholas, on which the American naval base that did not materialize would
have been built. There seems little doubt, either from Douglass' defense
of himself or from a full survey of all of the available evidence, that
Douglass, even under the disadvantage of a slight from his own country,
behaved remarkably well, whether as a man of character, a loyal American, or a responsible Negro, during the whole approach by America to
the Haitians and that he certainly operated on higher planes of integrity
and professional efficiency than the admiral who had temporarily superseded him as a diplomat. Nothing, however, rescued *The Life and Times*
from its failure to sell. It may well be that, in the lengthening perspective
of literary history, relatively free from the possible parallax errors of a special, particular moment, the book can well be seen for what it truly is,
considerably far from a masterpiece, but, still, a respectable example of
autobiography almost surely rendered more valuable than most autobiographies because of, among other good things in it, the importance
and singularity of the life it portrays.

But Douglass wrote much more than his three autobiographies. In at
least one instance he tried his hand at fiction, or fictionalized biography,
with his composition of the short story "The Heroic Slave," which appeared in 1853, first in four installments in his own paper and then in
Autographs for Freedom, a miscellany, containing poetry and prose, which
was the brainchild and the editorial feat of Julia Griffiths, the Englishwoman, for eight years Douglass' invaluable aide in his newspaper office,

who had conceived the *Autographs* as a means of raising money to reduce the deficits accrued by Douglass in the maintenance of this paper. Behind "The Heroic Slave," which may be the American Negro's first venture into the novella, was a stirring sequence of actual events in the life of an actual man. That man, Madison Washington, had escaped from slavery in Virginia to Canada, furtively returned from Canada to liberate his wife, been captured and reenslaved in Virginia, put on the brig *Creole* at Richmond, with a cargo of tobacco and 129 other slaves, and thus dispatched for sale in New Orleans. But Madison, thirteen days after his departure from Richmond, on the high seas, led an uprising which succeeded. He, with accomplices, seized the *Creole* and sailed it to Nassau in the British island of New Providence. There the British refused to return the Negroes from the *Creole* to slavery. All the British did, after more than a decade of discussion with the American government, was to pay, in 1853, an indemnity of $110,000 for these Negroes to American slaveholders.

So, Douglass' "The Heroic Slave," when it appeared, was highly topical. Indeed, it could easily remind its first readers, not only of the *Creole* affair, but also of the affair of the *Amistad*, which had begun when blacks, newly brought from Africa and sold as slaves in Havana to Cuban Spaniards, at sea like the blacks on the *Creole*, had mutinied and seized a ship. Eight weeks after the mutiny the *Amistad* was taken into custody off eastern Long Island by an American Coast Guard cutter. The bitter ensuing argument over the disposition of the Africans from the *Amistad* did not end until 1841, when the venerable John Quincy Adams, once the first citizen of his homeland, in a moving plea before the Supreme Court of the United States, struck the final blow which won for the Africans their freedom and the right to be repatriated in their homelands. Sentiment ran high during the 1840s and early 1850s among many Americans over both the *Amistad* and the *Creole*. That very sentiment, although much too diluted and adulterated by the arch sentimentality so oppressively omnipresent in all the popular fiction of the 1850s, pervades "The Heroic Slave." Disdain of bondage takes the most uncompromising of uncompromising positions in this tale of valor and derring-do. Its protagonist makes it clear that he either will be free or die. He permits himself no other choice. Douglass divides his story into four parts, the first three of which are presented through the consciousness of a white Ohioan named, as insinuatingly as the characters in Restoration drama (or *Pilgrim's Progress*), Mr. Listwell. Part IV develops from conversational ex-

changes between sailors in a Richmond coffeehouse. In Part I, Mr. Listwell, quite unseen, overhears a slave, tall, manly, and black enough,
presumably, not to be a mulatto, alone in a Virginia forest, declaring
aloud his resolution not to continue to accept his own enslavement. This
slave, it turns out, is Madison Washington. His soliloquy, incidentally,
closely parallels a true colloquy which, in his *Narrative*, Douglass reports
he once had with himself as he stood, without companions, on an outpost of Covey's farm looking north up Chesapeake Bay. In Part II, chance
delivers Washington into Mr. Listwell's residence in Ohio, whence Mr.
Listwell conveys him to Canada. In Part III, Mr. Listwell, again in Virginia, discovers Washington in a gang of slaves that is to be shipped to
New Orleans. Washington's sortie back into the South to get his wife has
precipitated the double disaster of his wife's death and his own recapture.
Part IV provides an account by the mate of the *Creole* of the loss of the
vessel to Washington and the slaves Washington commands. The mate's
account, very clearly a thematic summary of Douglass' tale, emphasizes
the concept of Washington as a genuine hero.

Douglass' three autobiographies and his one short story, however, far
from demonstrate how prolific a writer he truly was. From 1847 on, if not
before, he busied himself constantly with assignments that required of
him arduous activity with the pen. It was in 1847, as we already know,
that he began the *North Star*. With it, its successor, *Frederick Douglass'
Paper*, and its successor's extension, *Douglass' Monthly*, which was actually more a newspaper by that day's standards than a magazine, Douglass
was attached, for a decade and a half, to a medium which, in effect, guaranteed that he would do a certain amount of writing virtually every day.
And in his own periodicals Douglass did write virtually every day, not
only editorials, but also a variety of other items such as reviews of books
(and of at least two plays), propaganda pieces, polemics, news accounts,
and comments on many issues of the day. In the early 1870s, to the
Washington-based *New Era* and *New National Era*, Douglass contributed,
in addition to money and his name, editorials and, sometimes, the kind
of ruminations about the news which, in the twentieth century, have
come to be associated with syndicated columnists. In the year he started
the *North Star*, he maintained a working connection with the *Ram's
Horn*, a newspaper published in New York City by the free Negroes
Willis A. Hodges and Thomas Van Rensselaer. He wrote for white newspapers as well, for example, upon occasion, for the New York *Independent*

and New York *Tribune*. For magazines, moreover, such as *Scribner's*, the *North American Review*, the *Atlantic Monthly*, *Harper's Weekly*, *Cosmopolitan*, and the *Century*, Douglass authored articles which, certainly by the 1870s, were eagerly sought. Negro magazines were, of course, no less hospitable to his work than were these magazines published under white auspices.

In the many causes with which he identified himself, Douglass tended not to shirk journeyman labors with the pen. He wrote his share of open letters, as, for instance, the one he addressed, in 1847, to Henry Clay about colonization, or another, directed by him in 1853 to Harriet Beecher Stowe, expanding upon ideas he had expressed to her, at her home in Andover, Massachusetts, favoring the establishment of a manual-training school for Negroes. He participated in the conventions held by northern blacks in the 1840s and 1850s. The convention of 1848 issued an "Address to the Colored People of the United States" of which he was the principal, if not the sole, author. It was a committee chaired by him which wrote "Claims of our Common Cause," the report of its work and hopes issued by the convention of 1853. The volume of the statements of one kind or another representing cooperative endeavors to which Douglass contributed of his time and skill as a writer is, indeed, impressive. And Douglass eventually acquired the habit of consigning to manuscript most, if not all, of his speeches. When he began his career on the podium, he did eschew prepared expressions. A two-hour address called "The Claims of the Negro Race Ethnologically Considered," which he delivered as the guest of the Philozetian Society in July, 1854, during a commencement season at Western Reserve College, now part of Case Western Reserve University, seems to have been his first departure of consequence (if not altogether) from dependence on a mere extempore platform appearance. By 1860, apparently, he had wedded himself, however, to the custom of preparing and writing down his speeches before he delivered them, and so for much of his life his oratory was no longer that of the improviser creating, and losing, his material in the very process of his performance but rather that of the essayist from whom a formal written literature can emanate. Yet, as an orator, as in other aspects of himself, he was preeminently a creature of the America of his day. He spoke in the manner of Webster, Clay, Edward Everett, and James G. Blaine. Understandably, his subjects tended to be racial. But, if he never sat in the American Senate, no one who did could have been rhetorically more in tune with his own historic moment and its contemporary tastes than he through the kinds of diction, the rhythms (with their *cursus* and their cadences), and the poetry in prose often affected by him in his speeches.

Douglass lived at a time when the great orator was expected to fulminate, to pile Ossa upon Pelion with a succession of long, rolling periods of language studded with "big" words. Nor was the great orator then expected to be short-winded. His audiences were not averse to hearing him talk literally for hours. Douglass, the orator, fulminated. Sometimes, when he spoke, he fulminated at great length. Even so, upon occasion he spoke as gracefully and as concisely as his friend Lincoln at Gettysburg. And always, running through his oratory, as through his autobiographies, his essays, and his journalism, in a way much like the way the very same phenomenon would later run through all the recorded expression of his great successor, W. E. B. Du Bois, is a note of protest memorable for its powerful components of both intelligence and passion. Douglass was of the breed of David Walker, not of Jupiter Hammon. Pragmatist and visionary, he reconciled within himself an intense Americanism with an equally, if not more, intense antiracism. A major figure in Afro-American literature who never spent a day in school, he was his own self-made man as he was his own heroic slave.

Douglass' eminence and importance in Afro-American literature stems mainly from his *Narrative* and his other two autobiographies. His *North Star*, however, connects him prominently with the black press, in which he was an early, but not the first, pioneer. For, in the latter part of 1826, the colony of Negroes in New York City quite understandably reacted with concern against a campaign in the press, supplemented by ugly rumors on the street, which most aggressively and viciously supported the notion that Negroes, criminal and dissolute as they tended all to be, both male and female, constituted a grave menace to the peace and safety of white New Yorkers. The white Mordecai M. Noah, an entrepreneur in more than one way and a newspaper owner, apparently was a principal instigator and expediter of the campaign. A group of leading New York Negroes, meeting in the home of Boston Crummell, decided to employ, as one means of countering Noah and his fellow detractors of blacks, a newspaper. These New York Negroes were to name their newspaper *Freedom's Journal* and to accomplish their newspaper's debut on Friday, March 16, 1827. Thus the Afro-American press was born.

Two young men, Samuel E. Cornish and John Browne Russwurm, edited *Freedom's Journal.* Posterity has not been kind to Cornish, the newspaper's designated senior editor, although it has to Russwurm. Born about 1795 in Delaware, raised largely in Philadelphia and New York, and educated in the African Free School of New York City, Cornish early became one of the outstanding Negroes of his time. He founded the first Presbyterian church for Negroes in New York City. For years his was a respected voice among the free Negroes of the American Northeast. But references to him in Negro history are almost nonexistent and tend to be vague when they do occur. On the other hand, Russwurm's name has long been a virtual byword to students of Negro history, if only because it was once customary to distinguish Russwurm as the first black to finish an American college. Historians now know that an Alexander Twilight finished Middlebury in 1823 and, in addition, that an Edward Jones received his baccalaureate at Amherst on August 23, 1826, two weeks before Russwurm was graduated from Bowdoin in September. Moreover, Russwurm was not only not the first black to finish an American college. He was also, although he was schooled in both Quebec and Maine, not a native of mainland America. He had been born in Port Antonio, Jamaica, of a white man, who was a merchant, and of a free mulatto woman. He might never have gone to Bowdoin had not his father married a woman (as white as he) who resided in Maine (near Bowdoin, therefore) and who insisted, even after Russwurm's father had died and she had married again, that Russwurm be treated as one of her own children, even to the provision of as much schooling as could be supported for him. Nor did Russwurm end by living permanently in America. He and Cornish, at *Freedom's Journal,* soon reached a parting of their ways, for Cornish was committed to fighting his battles as a black man in America while Russwurm grew increasingly enamored of colonization. Cornish severed his connection with *Freedom's Journal* (and, really, with Russwurm) in September, 1827. When, however, in February, 1829, Russwurm finally announced unequivocally his complete conversion to the cause of the colonizationists and, in effect, his own belief that Negroes should return forthwith to Africa, the black leaders responsible for *Freedom's Journal* in the first place, none of whom shared Russwurm's emigrationist sentiments, branding him a traitor to his race, ousted him from their paper and recalled Cornish to its editorial chair. Russwurm, acquiring a master's degree from Bowdoin before his departure, did go to Africa, specifically to Liberia, where he served immediately as superintendent of public schools for the entire country and founded a paper, the *Liberia Herald,* which he also edited. In 1836, however, he was appointed governor of the Cape Palmas District, site of the Maryland Colony within Liberia. In this position he achieved his greatest eminence and genuine fame. As governor of Cape Palmas he died in 1851.

Lerone Bennett, Jr., has drawn an excellent picture of *Freedom's Journal.* Of it he says:

The paper, in truth, was a modest thing. In structure and conception, it was more a magazine than a newspaper. Not more than two of the sixteen columns were devoted to foreign and domestic news. The remaining columns were filled with material not unlike the stories and features in *Ebony* and other black-oriented magazines. The first issue, for example, contained the first installment of the "memoirs" of Paul Cuffee . . . a report on the illegal imprisonment of a poet, articles on the "Common Schools of New York," and "The Church and the Auction Block," "A True Story," an essay on "The Effect of Sight Upon a Person Born Blind," antislavery material, entertainment and variety departments. There was even an article with disguised sex appeal, "On Choosing a Wife By Proxy." Also included in the paper were notices of marriages, deaths, and court trials. Commercial advertisements were printed on the last page.[6]

This is, however, a picture, not only of *Freedom's Journal,* but of every Negro newspaper in antebellum America. They were all, except for their publication schedules, more magazines than newspapers. And so they were quantitatively, if not otherwise, a relatively extensive (and, perhaps, the most relatively extensive) source of antebellum black literature. For belles-lettres, not news, was truly their forte. And, before the end of the Civil War, there had been some thirty-five or forty of them: two in Canada; two actually on the West Coast in San Francisco; three (all in New Orleans) in the South; seven, apparently, scattered from the Alleghenies westward in Pittsburgh, Cleveland, Cincinnati, and Lawrence, Kansas (during the significant years 1855–1857); four in Philadelphia (one of which is often listed as a magazine and another of which may actually have been a Philadelphia edition of a paper primarily published in New York City); one in Boston; and all of the rest either in New York City or New York State. Thus, it may be seen, the antebellum Negro press was almost exclusively a phenomenon of nonslave America in spite of the circumstance that, by 1860, there were nearly ten times as many slaves (approximately four million) as free Negroes in America, more free Negroes—83,900 and 58,000, respectively—in the slave states of Maryland and Virginia than in any other American states, slave or free, and

6. Lerone Bennett, Jr., *Pioneers in Protest* (Chicago, 1968), 63.

more blacks, 27,900, in slaveholding Baltimore than in any other American city, again regardless of whether that city was slave or free.

The three black antebellum newspapers in New Orleans hardly constituted an exception to the free-state character of the black antebellum press. New Orleans, with its Gallic traditions and its relative liberality in its treatment of its fairly numerous *gens de couleur,* could not be classified as a typical antebellum southern city. One of the papers in New Orleans, incidentally, the New Orleans *Creole,* which survived from June, 1856, to January, 1857, was a daily, the first black daily in America, as it was, also, the first black newspaper in the South. The two other black New Orleans papers, both published in the 1860s, were also both bilingual, the *Union,* or *L'Union,* and the New Orleans *Tribune,* or *La Tribune de la Nouvelle-Orléans.* Yet all three of the New Orleans papers fitted the generalization of newspapers which were more magazines than newspapers. And they were typical of black antebellum newspapers in another way. They were highly sensitive to the issue of the black person's civil rights. The black press in the antebellum North, as we have seen, did attack slavery. It was abolitionist as, for instance, the New Orleans *Creole* dared not be. But it fretted at least as much over the plight of Negroes after they were free as when they were slaves. So, one continuity of emphasis was established early in the Negro press which has never left it. That press has been constantly sensitive to the issue of equality for the individual Negro. And, accordingly, it has campaigned from its beginnings against American color caste. To see it, then, as ever concerned primarily with slavery may be not to analyze it as perspicaciously as one should. From its very beginnings, its fundamental note of protest may have been, in the most accurate terms, exactly the one which has dominated Afro-American literature since at least the days of David Walker's *Appeal.* That note has been the cry of outrage by black writers in successive generations against the conception of the Negro as someone not good enough to be permitted to mingle indiscriminately with other Americans. The status sought for Negroes in Afro-American literature has always been more than mere emancipation of the body. It has always been the elimination of color caste.

Antebellum black newspapers tended to be short-lived. Most were fortunate if they survived as long as two or three years. Some ceased publication in a matter of weeks, or months. When, for instance, Cornish returned to the editorship of *Freedom's Journal,* that paper at first interrupted its schedule of publication only temporarily but, subsequently, soon made its last appearance before the public forever. Cornish then, still before the year 1829 was over, began from scratch a new paper in *Freedom's Journal*'s place, *Rights of All*, which managed to maintain itself merely into the succeeding year, 1830. The free Negro Philip A. Bell started the *Weekly Advocate* in New York City in January, 1837. In March of the same year this paper became the *Colored American*. Cornish, free from *Rights of All* for seven years, now took the place of Bell as the editor of the *Colored American*, which was also, later, to be edited by the prominent free Negroes Dr. James McCune Smith and the Reverend Charles Bennett Ray (a daughter of whom, Henrietta Cordelia, wrote poetry) before its own gentle subsidence into the limbo of lost causes in 1842. And thus it was that transitoriness, rather than a penchant for longevity which might have given to some twentieth-century black newspapers existences decades in duration, tended to be a distinctive attribute of unit after unit of the black antebellum press. Partly this was so, quite understandably, because that press was always in dire financial straits. After all, both its mission and, therefore, its market were limited. But partly, also, its various newspapers may have owed their lack of staying power to the unfortunate fact that all too typically the Negroes wont to begin and try to maintain them refused to confine the use of their time and talents to the exclusive prosecution of any single endeavor. They would not heed the maxim that he who would succeed with a small business must virtually consecrate to that business his entire life. It was almost as if each of these Negroes felt that only he was available to do all that needed to be done to succor the whole Negro race.

There was, for example, the black newspaper the *National Watchman* in Troy, New York, in the 1840s. The handsome mulatto William G. Allen, in effect, took it in hand. But not for long. Elsewhere in the state, at Central College in McGrawville, he became one of the three Negroes added to what seems to have been America's first interracial college faculty. It was, of course, a time when one concept of the Negro insisted that Negroes could not learn Greek. Central College appointed Allen "professor of Greek and German languages and of Rhetoric and Belles Lettres," a position he surrendered, after only a brief tenure, to flee prudently to England with Mary King, a white student of his who had married him. Hence, apparently, assertions of his disagreement with stereotyped limits upon Negro behavior drew at least as much upon his black activism as upon his newspaper publishing. He was, moreover, a public foe of drink. Yet even in him the *National Watchman* had possessed a chief executive who did not begin to match, in the number of pursuits in which he engaged, such multiple careerists connected with the antebellum black press as Henry Highland Garnet and Martin R. Delany, of both of whom more will be said here later. Garnet and Delany spoke and acted against slavery and the humiliation of Negroes on three continents. There was hardly any reform dear to their century they did not espouse, not with moral support alone, but in ways requiring of them often time-consuming labor. And there were more Garnets and Delanys in the black antebellum press than Allens. There were certainly, with the possible exception partially of Frederick Douglass, no Pulitzers.

The black press, however, did experience something of an increase in stability and a decided growth in size after the Civil War, although not immediately so. A time did come, then, after not too long, when it could count as among its own a paper like the New York *Age*, which, started in 1887, was still being published when its most famous editor and columnist, T. Thomas Fortune, died in 1928. In the nineteenth century the great era of expansion for the black press was the decade of the 1880s. There were, apparently, 31 black newspapers in America in 1880. In 1890 these had proliferated to 154, 114 of which were published in the South.

6. Slave Narratives, 1830–1860

All that the decade of the 1880s was to the black press the three decades from 1830 to 1860 were, and more, to the slave narrative. That these same three decades constitute also the very period when American abolitionism was at its zenith, both in the intensity of its onslaught against slavery and in the number of its supporters willing to be known as such, represents, of course, no mere coincidence. The abolitionists and the authors of slave narratives written during the Age of the Abolitionists were consciously united, consciously marching, shoulder to shoulder and step by step, as it were, in a common holy crusade. Hence, there was much for them to share, kindred intentions and visions of a sweeping social revolution, passionate conviction of a monstrous evil to be crushed and a sense of their own righteousness in a world where the powers upholding that evil were bent, not only on preserving it, but even on expanding it until it covered at least the whole of the Western Hemisphere. All abolitionist slave narratives, therefore, if nothing else, tend to be morality plays. And, as all morality plays obviously should do, they tend also to be aware of purgatories and paradises, of bogs of evil and many forms of iniquity and of pilgrims' progresses that should pass from darkness into light. Their greatest fault, perhaps, is that their greatest sinners are never saved.

The frequently highly intrusive presence of authorial collaboration in these narratives may occasion some questions, here and there, about their authenticity. Testimonials from whites are a familiar accompaniment of a significant percentage of all early publications by black authors, slave narratives or not. As much of an intellectual prodigy, for example, as Phillis Wheatley was reputed even in her own time to be, the governor and lieutenant governor of Massachusetts, along with sixteen other estimable white citizens (including seven divines) of the then colony of His Britannic Majesty George III, felt constrained to "assure the world" that Phillis Wheatley's *Poems on Various Subjects, Religious and Moral* was actually a collection of verses written by a black female of that name. Who could be sure, after all, that any Negro, despite instruction from whites like the indulgent Wheatleys, could quite be equal, genetically, to the sophisticated disciplines required of any nonwhite hopeful of writing as creditably as respectable white writers? The abolitionist slave narratives, moreover, were not written by slaves from households as lenient toward black advancement as the household of the Wheatleys. Slaves in the Calhoun South, quite to the contrary (as is well-known), were anything but encouraged to learn to read and write. In fact, instructing blacks, slave or free, in the three Rs, was increasingly illegal there. A number of abolitionist slave narratives, consequently, were "dictated" by illiterate black fugitives from slavery to white northern abolitionists, who tended to be, oftener than not, so antislavery as to regard without revulsion the use of their own talents to "improve" what was confided to them by these fugitives in ways more injurious, they assumed, than they might otherwise have been to any sympathetic concepts of the South. Overwhelming evidence exists that Frederick Douglass, William Wells Brown, and other fugitive slaves of their caliber, however little they may have experienced of formal schooling, did write the narratives attributed to them with certainly no more help—if as much, by probably a considerable degree—than they might get from the editorial staff of a contemporary publisher. At the other end of what might be termed a spectrum of veracity, there were so-called slave narratives which not only were not written by the fugitive slaves announced as their authors but were actually altogether fabricated as fictions by the whites who truly composed them. The two of these about which students of slave narratives have said most are the historian Richard Hildreth's *The Slave: or, Memoirs of Archy Moore*, published in 1836, and *Autobiography of a Female Slave*, published in 1857, by Mattie Griffiths, a white Kentuckian and schoolteacher turned, rather ardently, abolitionist. Neither of these works is essentially any less an original creation or, in genre, any less a novel, than *Uncle Tom's Cabin*. Both attracted, in their time, eager readers.

Possibly as much a figment of fantasy as either of the above may have been the *Narrative of James Williams, an American Slave, Who Was for Several Years a Driver on a Cotton Plantation in Alabama*, published in New

York City in 1838. By chance John Greenleaf Whittier, dedicated abolitionist as he always was, happened to be in New York at an opportune moment for Williams to be introduced to him. Whittier, delighted at the bonanza which fate had virtually thrust upon him, from interviews with Williams produced Williams' "dictated" narrative. Williams, then, clothed in new celebrity, proceeded on to England. A storm soon arose, however, in America, over the credibility of the account of slavery he had left behind him. Proslavery southerners who loudly asserted absolute knowledge of very precisely everything they needed to know to take the position they took denounced, as an arrogant collage of flat and filthy falsehoods, Williams' version of Alabama. He could not have spent the merest second in the real Alabama, they insisted, since he spoke constantly of places and people which had never been part of an Alabama scene. A chagrined abolitionist press suspended further editions of Williams' *Narrative*. Whittier himself remarked that abolitionism needed "no support of a doubtful character." It was rumored, furthermore, that Williams was a free Negro who had spun his narrative out of his own too agile and active (as well as unscrupulous) imagination from anecdotes about slavery he had heard which may or may not have either been true or had Alabama settings. In the American North, as abolitionist sentiment there increased and sentiment for aiding fugitive slaves sometimes expressed itself in ways which could easily be converted into cash by an unprincipled wayfarer, occasional impostors of Negro blood did appear out of a nonslave past they felt they could dissemble and did masquerade as escapees from a South where masters and overseers—not to mention other whites—had tormented them unmercifully. Perhaps Williams was one of these. Yet James Birney, who had once actually been a slaveholder in Alabama, as soon as he subjected Williams' *Narrative* to a critical review, maintained that the Alabama he remembered in many specific particular details accorded very well with that he found in the pages of Williams' book. In such a case, then, Williams' *Narrative* probably was, and is, not as bad—not as spurious—as Hildreth's *Archy Moore* or Griffiths' *Female Slave*. It was, and is, only (at worst) a possibly extreme example of a "dictated" narrative—a "dictated" narrative, that is, in which all of the elements of literary presentation, as distinct from whatever those elements present, are the contribution, and the property, not of the "dictator," but of the party to whom the "dictator" has "dictated." And, if the *Narrative* is (as well may be) any—or, even, most—of the above, it is very much the counterpart of probably the most famous of all "dictated" slave narratives in the history of America, *The Confessions of Nat Turner,* the one slave narrative of any consequence written during the Age of the Abolitionists which is not (or at least was not meant to be) abolitionist.

Consensus among historians distinguishes as the three most memorable of American slave revolts Gabriel's insurrection in Richmond, in 1800, Denmark Vesey's intended uprising in Charleston in 1822, and Nat Turner's rebellion (the only one of these three attempts at slave resistance to reach an effective level of overt action) in Southampton County, Virginia, in August, 1831. Nat Turner was captured late in October of that same year. His rebellion had lasted about forty hours, involved as participants between sixty and eighty slaves, occasioned the deaths of perhaps as many as sixty-five whites, and expended its momentum before it reached either Jerusalem, as the county seat of Southampton County then was called, or the Dismal Swamp. In Jerusalem were arms which Turner's men could have used to great advantage. The Dismal Swamp, of course, was a hiding place where they might have evaded capture for years. Turner himself was the last of his band to be apprehended by the authorities, although he never left Southampton County and eventually surrendered meekly to a stripling whom he faced alone in a secluded woodland glade. Of such a would-be captor Turner could hardly have been afraid. It is not difficult to believe that Turner, a self-proclaimed mystic, sought the final act which his trial and execution added to the drama of his revolt. Nor is it difficult to believe, also, that his statement made from prison to the white southern lawyer Thomas R. Gray and first published, under the title *The Confessions of Nat Turner,* in Baltimore in 1831, was granted, as Gray avers, voluntarily. Without *The Confessions* Turner's moment of most uncivil disobedience could not be nearly so resonant of a larger meaning as history has found it. With *The Confessions* Turner rounded off his life with more than his own death.

Gray places his transcript of Turner's utterance in *The Confessions* between an introduction and a conclusion, both of which Gray wrote. Nothing in either says anything other than what probably should be foreseen, given similar circumstances, from any of the many Grays in the South of 1831. Gray was a lawyer, and his profession, perhaps, does show in his manner of handling items of description which might serve purposes of identification. In such circumstances he tends to incline his style toward the precision of a legal brief. He speaks, nevertheless, with a stereotypical tongue as he refers, in his introduction, to Turner, as a "gloomy fanatic" leading a "fiendish band" of "savages" impelled by "hellish purposes" to the "conception and perpetration of the most atrocious and heart-rending deeds." Yet he, apparently, tampers little with the information he receives from Turner, and it is very possible to feel a sense in *The Confessions* of a presence not always so altered by Gray's intervention as to be thoroughly, or even too significantly, lost within Gray's own prescription of what Negroes are born to be. This presence is of one who decidedly believes himself to be a prophet, appointed by the Lord to perform a mission of momentous import and acquainted by a spirit from above with his singular status in his very early childhood. Turner's parents, apparently, taught him to read and write before Turner's father ran away, never to be recaptured or seen again in his neighborhood. Turner himself had visions. Voices spoke to him, as to Joan of Arc. He did some preaching, and once baptized a white man. A solar eclipse seems to have been the sign which he interpreted as the signal for his insurrection. He was, according to Gray, explicit in not repenting of his challenge to man-made authority, comparing himself, as he faced the gallows, with Jesus, as Jesus approached Golgotha.

The Confessions was followed in the 1830s by slave narratives which were unequivocally abolitionist. In fact, after *The Confessions* there was never anything again of its peculiar nature in Afro-American literature. Only a few years after *The Confessions*, in 1836, appeared *Slavery in the United States: a Narrative of the Life and Adventures of Charles Ball, a Black Man*. This was a hardy narrative. An edition of it called *Fifty Years in Chains* was issued in 1858. It was also a relatively unhurried account (well over ten times longer than Nat Turner's brief *Confessions*) of experiences, beginning before the end of the eighteenth century, which forced upon its alleged author, finally (we are told) safely domiciled near Philadelphia, an inside view of southeastern slavery extended over the better part of forty years. Vernon Loggins thinks Charles Ball and Archy Moore are equally fictitious, although he ventures to suppose *Slavery in the United States* "in many respects a more exciting romance" than *Archy Moore*. Conversely, Nichols, in his *Many Thousand Gone*, refers repeatedly to Charles Ball in a manner unmistakably indicative of Nichols' absolute faith that there was once a Ball as real as anyone could be. Nor does Nichols ever seem to doubt that Ball, "a tall, wellbuilt Negro," in Nichols' terms, reports reliably and truthfully upon the life he led as someone else's chattel and upon his two escapes, once by land and once by sea, from Georgia.[1]

With Moses Roper's *Narrative*, first published in London in 1838, no problems appear to be associated insofar as it purports itself to be a true relation of its subject's actual life. Its degree of "dictation" remains conjectural. English friends of Roper's clearly were involved in its composition. Whether Roper could have written even any of it depends, apparently, if on nothing else, surely to some extent upon how rapidly he, precocious though his life demonstrated him to be, acquired a proficiency in reading and writing not available to him until he arrived in England only months before his *Narrative* was consigned to print. Roper, unless his story errs, was no more than six when he was put to work as a physician's assistant and little older when he began to do, under orders, other kinds of work, some of it heavily manual, expected of adults. A native of Caswell County in north-central North Carolina, he was the son of a slave girl whose young mistress was married to his white father shortly after his conception. Moreover, he was thought to be, physically, the very image of his father in everything including color. To the astonishment of no one in Caswell County he was sold south. Ball had been taken, by comparison, as far in that direction as Georgia. Roper, who may not have been quite twenty-one when he escaped from slavery—so that his narrative is, after all, but an account, strange though it may be, of a childhood and its succeeding adolescence—served two masters, one good and one bad (as Roper judged them), in Florida, before he made his way to the vessel which brought him from Savannah to freedom on Staten Island in New York. Most fugitive slaves escaped from points of departure much nearer the North.

Roper had not grown out of boyhood when he began trying to steal away from the South to freedom. Once he started his attempts at escaping slavery, he repeated them no matter how often he was caught. His color, which, with his facial features, had so infuriated his father's wife, undoubtedly benefited him as a bondsman on the loose in the very heartland of slavery. He could be—as he certainly sometimes was—easily mistaken for white. But perhaps one of the anomalies of slavery which has probably not been awarded the prominence it deserves in pictures of the antebellum South is the relatively great amount of movement in that

1. Vernon Loggins, *The Negro Author: His Development in America to 1900* (New York, 1931), 98; Charles H. Nichols, *Many Thousand Gone: The Ex-Slaves' Account of Their Bondage and Freedom* (Bloomington, Ind., 1967), 17.

South by slaves who were following their own wishes, not their masters'. Some slaves, individually or collectively, lived for years, if not for most of their entire lives, in southern hideaways. Indeed, the slaves who established themselves as a permanent semioccult presence in the Dismal Swamp overlapping the border between Virginia and North Carolina became, in their own time, a living legend. But even more on the humbling subject of the defiance by actual human behavior of experts' (and laymen's) generalities concerning their fellows may be learned from knowledge of the slaves who simply took vacations from their slavery somewhere near their place of enslavement and then returned, often unpenalized, to resume their slavery as it was before their brief, entirely self-initiated respites from it. They attest to the incidence of laxities inseparable from attempts at rigid, repressive control through codified restraints in any situation where a large number of human beings, who cannot escape diversity of character, are supposed to apply this control uniformly to another large number of human beings who are, themselves, diverse in character also. The abolitionist slave narratives are often better history than, probably, their writers intended them to be. It was their intent to emphasize the darker side of slavery. More or less elliptically, they also illustrate the ameliorative effects upon that very darker side inherent in the very scale of southern slavery as a phenomenon of southern life.

Octoroons like Roper are figures of note among the authors, purported or real, of abolitionist slave narratives. They may well be regarded, incidentally, among other things, as proofs, like slave vagabondage, that slavery in action was not always consistent with its own official professions. William Wells Brown, of whom much more will be reported here later, was one octoroon who authored a slave narrative. Ellen Craft, who coauthored a slave narrative with her husband (again, as will be noted here later), was essentially as octoroon as Brown or Roper. And Lewis Clarke was no less "white" than any of these. His mother was the daughter of a slave owner in Kentucky, the state in which, near Lexington, Clarke was born. His father, a journeyman weaver who had fought, and been wounded, in the Revolutionary War, was an ethnic and legal white born in Scotland. But the death of his mother's father, who had promised to free his mother and all of her children, and the somewhat suspicious failure to find the will which this father may well have executed, seemed to doom Clarke perpetually to slavery. Clarke had already had forced upon him direct knowledge of how bitter slavery could be, not by his mother's father, but principally by a white half-sister of his mother, a resident of Lexington, to whom he had been granted in his seventh year as part of the dowry given to this daughter of his grandfather when she married. For ten years this actual aunt of his, whose malevolence toward Clarke had been rabid to an extreme, abused him before she sold him to a planter of tobacco who was equally abusive. Clarke was serving another, and much more lenient, owner when a turn of affairs occurred as ominous to him as the disappearance of his grandfather's will. His lenient owner died, and hints too strong to be ignored appeared of his own imminent sale to Louisiana. So, with another slave and with the scheme, since he looked so white, for him to pose as his companion's master, the two slaves started north. Quickly they realized, however, that their absolute illiteracy imperiled overmuch their enterprise, and they furtively crept back to their homes in slavery, where Clarke stayed, nevertheless, only two weeks before he returned north alone.

Clarke moved in stages now, by way of Cincinnati, and Cleveland, to Canada. He was to live a long life. He was born in 1815. He died almost at the end of the century in 1897. He became a most successful abolitionist lecturer, for he possessed, like Douglass, a retentive memory and the ability to dramatize his recollections. Living in both Canada and the United States, he led a life so distinguished that, upon his death, his body, by order of the governor of Kentucky, lay in state in Lexington, where he had died, in the city auditorium while whites and Negroes alike paid tribute to him. He was buried in Oberlin, Ohio.

Clarke's sense of family was strong, as was his determination to do more than talk in assisting slaves, kin to him or not, in making their way to freedom. He participated repeatedly, therefore, in rescue missions into slave territory even at the cost of sometimes journeying in his own person with such a mission. One of his sisters escaped from slavery without his help. So compelling was her beauty to a Frenchman who saw her that he fell in love with her, bought her, took her to Mexico, where he married her, and, at his death, left her all he owned. Other siblings of Clarke's— like, for example, his brother Cyrus—did benefit directly from Clarke's ventures back to the south of the Ohio River. Indeed, a classic vignette of abolitionist literature, recounted by Clarke, tells of Cyrus, once he had crossed the Mason-Dixon line into the southernmost part of Ohio, insisting on delaying the party which was conveying him north until he had drunk some water flowing from free soil, sat on a log in the free air, and rolled in the grass on the slope of a free hill.

Clarke published his own abolitionist slave narrative, *Narrative of the Sufferings of Lewis Clarke, during a captivity of More than Twenty-Five Years among the Algerines of Kentucky*, in 1845. With his brother Milton, another beneficiary of Clarke's attachment to his close blood kin as well as of his general hatred of slavery, he published, in Boston in 1846, the abolitionist slave narrative *Narrative of the Sufferings of Lewis and Milton Clarke, Sons of a Soldier of the Revolution, during a Captivity of More than Twenty Years Among the Slave-Holders of Kentucky, One of the So Called Christian States of North America*. Both narratives bear statements explicitly indicating that they were dictated. Both narratives, also, replete as they are with vivid incident, are scathing indictments of slavery. Clarke's denunciatory portrait of his mother's white half-sister fittingly illustrates his antislavery animus throughout both these narratives. He dwells upon this representative of the slavocracy whom he perceives, female though she be, as a foul fiend, with a husband no less revolting than herself. The spouses match each other in the constancy and excess of their resort to alcoholic drink and profanity. The wife derives particular pleasure (and, apparently, some satisfaction of a thirst for vengeance against Clarke because he is her kin) in tormenting Clarke, into whose eyes she delights to fling vinegar, and whom she kicks and curses, sorely tasks at pulling herbs in the hot sun in the hope of darkening his complexion, and offers as a special target for ill-treatment to her children after she has goaded them into a spiteful fury against him.

The 1846 narrative representing the brothers as collaborators outsold Clarke's 1845 narrative. Very popular among abolitionists and a highly marketable item at abolitionist meetings, the later work commanded, indeed, one of the widest audiences of any, or all, slave narratives. But Clarke obtained a place in American literature of special interest because of the effect of his 1845 narrative upon one reader, Harriet Beecher Stowe. Mrs. Stowe not only read Clarke's narrative. She conversed with him about himself and his family more than once in her own home. Eventually, after *Uncle Tom's Cabin* had swept into its great prominence on two continents, she was to state unequivocally, in *The Key to Uncle Tom's Cabin*, that her George Harris in *Uncle Tom's Cabin* was derived from Clarke.

It may be important to note that Clarke's narrative not only links him, as a partial source, to *Uncle Tom's Cabin*. It also links him to other slave narratives in which, as in his, may be readily discerned a notable concern for the integrity and preservation of a family. Slave families, of course, constituted absolute nonentities in antebellum American law, which recognized slave mothers (perhaps to avoid an absurdity not even tolerable in the madhouse of slavery) but proceeded, in theory and in fact, as if slave children were immaculately conceived insofar as slave fathers may have contributed to their existence. A whole literature has accumulated, moreover, in the social sciences, almost obsequiously sympathetic to the premise of a doleful weakness in the black American family—a weakness, incidentally, one supposedly unwholesome consequence, and symptom, of which, according to this premise, has been the inclination of the black American family toward a matriarchate. Clarke was a patriarch, not a matriarch, who went, as we have seen, to extraordinary lengths to maintain as intact as he could a family—his. Evidence in the abolitionist slave narratives abounds—rather than is hard to find—which suggests that Clarke was far from atypical and, in all likelihood, a member of a majority among male slaves in his esteem for the ties which connected him to his own parents (though one of his was white) and to his siblings in his own immediate family circle. Frederick Douglass after the Civil War built on his property in Rochester a "snug little cottage" for his half-brother, Perry, who had never been able to escape from slavery (Perry landed, in fact, while still young, in Texas) and whom Douglass had not seen for almost fifty years. The cottage was, significantly, before Douglass finished with it, a new home for Perry's entire considerable family of six. And Charles Ball's first priority, after he returned to the Maryland neighborhood of his earlier life from his long, illegal captivity in the Deep South, was a reunion, which he was unable to effect, with his family. Moreover, at least three of the better-known abolitionist slave narratives are largely, distinctively, and almost passionately chronicles of a black father's patriarchal interest in his family.

The earliest of these three was, apparently, truly written by Lunsford Lane, the former slave to whom its authorship is attributed. Lane's mother was a bonded house servant of Sherwood Haygood (owner of 250 slaves) near Raleigh, North Carolina. She was relatively well treated. So, in his infancy and early youth, was her son. For Lane remembered his own childhood as little short of a taste of paradise. He played with his master's children, on equal, affectionate terms with them, until the inevitable coming of the time when the differences began to creep into his relations with them which let him know he was abjectly their inferior. The master's children, for example, were taught to read and he was not, while in countless other ways, big and small, the master's children devised strata-

gems and single acts designed to impress upon him that part of his growing up was to learn of the impassable gulf between him and any white.
Yet he suffered no immersion into the brutish status of a plantation hand.
On the contrary, he served, for a while, as a "waiter and messenger" for
two governors of North Carolina. But it was as an entrepreneur for himself, both before and after he bought his own freedom, that he truly prospered. He earned pourboires from whites. He sold them peaches and cut
them firewood. Most of all, he throve from the sale of pipes which he
made and tobacco which he blended, even sometimes inventively, and
did so well that, eventually, he merchandised his products in Fayette-
ville, Salisbury, and Chapel Hill, as well as in Raleigh.

As slave and freeman, Lane had adjusted to the antebellum South.
It is he who tells of the deliberate circumspection, to avoid the giving of offense, of his behavior in the presence of whites. Nevertheless,
there were whites who viewed him with disfavor, almost surely because
they envied his accomplishments, obviously beyond those which they
felt should be permitted to a person of his color. Because of statutory
obstacles in North Carolina, he had been manumitted in New York
State, though by a friendly white North Carolinian. His return to Raleigh precipitated the invocation against him of a law which limited the
residence in North Carolina of a free Negro from another state to twenty
days. Helped by white friends, he delayed for four months his compliance
with this law through a court appeal, which he lost. He went north, accompanied by the only one of his six children who was then also free,
and took up residence in Boston. His sole return to North Carolina
proved almost fatal for him. He was tarred and feathered, although he
did survive his brush with death to return to Boston. Obsessed with his
need to have his family with him, he spoke at abolitionist meetings in
the North and begged from door to door to raise money which he could
transmit to an agent in the South who might complete the purchase of
the freedom of his wife and five remaining children and send them north.

Through such determined exertions, Lane accomplished the recon-
stitution of his family as a cohesive unit under his supervision outside the
South. To help pay for his recovery, and retention with himself, of his
family, he published in Boston in 1842 *The Narrative of Lunsford Lane*. It
may be added here that Lane was, apparently, one of those people who,
wherever they go, tend to be regarded respectfully and pleasurably by
other people. His troubles in the South had little, if anything, to do with
the way most whites (as well as blacks) whom he met there, or anywhere,

reacted to his public personality. In the North a writer in Garrison's *Liberator* spoke of him as a "modest, intelligent man, very prepossessing in appearance." But Lane seemed all of this also to northerners who were not necessarily of the abolitionist persuasion. Moreover, his amiably tempered impression on the Boston community stood the test of time. In 1863, twenty-one years after *The Narrative of Lunsford Lane* was first published, the Reverend William G. Hawkins felt sufficiently moved by his awareness of Lane's sterling character as a person and a practitioner of good will to others to write and publish *Lunsford Lane; or Another Helper from North Carolina*. Hawkins' very well-intended biography is considerably more than five times as long as Lane's narrative. Moreover, Hawkins had been subjected to nothing like the exclusion from access to the world of literacy through which Lane had had to fight for his command of a writer's skills. Even so, it may well seem, measured against *Another Helper*, that *The Narrative of Lunsford Lane* is the better, as well as much briefer, book.

A second abolitionist slave narrative a salient feature of which is the light cast by it upon a male slave's concern for family is Moses Grandy's *Narrative of the Life of Moses Grandy, Late a Slave in the United States*. Published in Boston in 1844 on the heels of an English edition, this narrative represents, unlike *The Narrative of Lunsford Lane*, an additional example of the dictated slave narrative. The leading English abolitionist George Thompson committed it to the form in which it reached its readers. Nevertheless, an attentive perusal of it suggests very strongly that Thompson was not being either merely modest or crassly duplicitous when he declared, in a prefatory statement, for himself the role much more of simply an obedient amanuensis than of an author in his penning of what he heard from Grandy. Certainly it seems that it was Grandy, not Thompson, who invested Grandy's *Narrative* with a concern for family similar to that found in the narratives of Clarke and Lane. Grandy recalls of his mother that, when he was but a child, she would spirit him and her other children into the woods adjacent to the plantation of her master whenever she feared (as she did on numerous occasions) their sale away from her by her master. On such occasions she fed herself and her children largely on anything that came to hand, such as the berries she could find growing wild, and quenched their thirst, when need arose, from puddled water cradled in her palms. Her family was, however, as well might have been expected, eventually separated, beginning with the sale of one of her sons, younger than Grandy, to a bargainer willing to

pay a price satisfactory to her master. Then, indeed, it became quite evident to her that her master had theretofore been deterred from such a
sale not so much by her disappearance with slaves of his into a forest as by
his determination to get for any of his slaves the margin of profit he
wanted whenever he marketed one of them. Surely he reacted with telling vigor when Grandy's mother physically intervened to retain her son.
He had her whipped. Moreover, later in Grandy's life, a pregnant sister
of his obviously near the end of her term with her child, was so severely
flogged, in the fields, that she lost her child. And Grandy's first "wife"
was sold away from him in a transaction of which he was totally unaware
until he accidentally noted this "wife's" presence in a coffle of slaves
headed south. Bitter experiences induced in Grandy a perhaps unusually
active sense of family. Nor did his own freedom come lightly. He was
forced to buy that freedom three times over and, finally, to sue for it, for
one of his masters was thoroughly unprincipled and another was a compulsive gambler who became bankrupt. After his own manumission and
removal to the North, Grandy earned enough, principally as a seaman,
to buy, through an agent, his second (and truly legal) wife, who joined
him in the North. But when he went in person to Norfolk, Virginia, to
buy a son of his, he failed completely in his mission and was so threatened himself that he was relieved to quit the Tidewater unharmed.

The third of the abolitionist slave narratives to be cited here particularly for its evidence of a slave father's interest in his family, *A Narrative
of the Life of Noah Davis*, was published by Noah Davis in Baltimore in,
apparently, 1859. Davis claimed, in an explicit statement, that his narrative was written by himself. He also claimed, at the time his narrative
appeared, to be fifty-nine years old. Like Lunsford Lane, he had experienced a childhood as a slave which he could recall more with pleasure
than with pain. His father, black though he was, had occupied the rather
enviable position in an agricultural community of head miller of a mill
large enough to be a vital cog in the economy of a somewhat extended
neighborhood. This father was able to keep his family with him, to nour-
ish in his children a consciousness of their kinship with one another, and
even to determine, almost virtually unhindered, how they would be trained.
Thus Davis was taught shoemaking and so, with what he was able to put
by for himself from working on his own time, paid for his own manumission. The Baptist religion played no small role in Davis' early life. He
cites in his *Narrative* the custom, upon which his father placed great emphasis, of reading the Bible in his house to a reverent family circle every

Sunday of his childhood. Davis himself, once free, became a Baptist preacher, the pastor of the Saratoga Street Baptist Church in Baltimore. His *Narrative*, he says, he wrote principally to raise the money to buy his two children still enslaved in 1859.

Ten years before Davis, Henry Bibb, a native of Kentucky, undoubtedly as the principal (if not sole) author, wrote his abolitionist slave narrative. Perhaps only Douglass' *Narrative* exceeds Bibb's as a work of art, although Bibb lacks much of Douglass' apparently inborn abundance of what Keats called negative capability—the ability, that is, of not saying what might be well left unsaid while saying very appropriately what is said. Yet Bibb had the writer's knack for recalling telling incidents and equally, if not more, telling, although seemingly random, details within those incidents. Bibb begins his account of his own life with his birth, in 1815, not too far from the Ohio River in Kentucky. His mother was a slave; his father, a white Kentuckian and state senator. Bibb was as white as his father, a circumstance that helped him in each of his escapes from slavery. An aura from the world of romantic love (that would be ultimately only an unwitting prelude to the bitterest experience of Bibb's life) clings to Bibb's *Narrative* as to no other slave narrative. Before he was twenty years of age, Bibb fell deeply in love with the beautiful slave girl called Malinda who, in addition to her other charms, sang like the angel she appeared to be. Malinda reciprocated Bibb's love. He and Malinda "married" and had a daughter before he ran away, with the help of people whom he knew and did not know (particularly, of a Quaker, one he did not know, who glowed for the rest of Bibb's life in Bibb's memory as the good Samaritan of all good Samaritans), and made his way along the Underground Railroad to Michigan. He did, however, return soon to Kentucky with the intention of shepherding to freedom his "wife" and child. Thus, however, he plunged himself into a sea of troubles. Captured, he was, with Malinda and this child, sold to a trader who disposed of all three in New Orleans to a planter, from the Red River country of Louisiana, an ostentatiously sanctimonious Christian who, decidedly to his own delectation, treated his new purchases (as he did his other slaves) with calculated cruelty of a most sadistic sort. Gamblers bought Bibb, but not his wife and child, from this hypocrite, close replicas of whom occur frequently in other slave narratives. The gamblers treated Bibb much better than had the Christian, eventually passing him on, for a good price, to an aged, affluent Indian.

Upon this Indian's death, Bibb fled again to the region of the Great

Lakes. He saw, after his sale in New Orleans and under conditions which he describes with credit to his powers of observation, considerable areas of Louisiana, Texas, Arkansas, and Missouri. His survival, however, of a harrowing ordeal was not for him an unmixed blessing. He did make one more trip to the South, for Malinda, only to discover that she had yielded sufficiently to the pressures put upon her by her master to become a prostitute. In the North, Bibb established himself as a noted lecturer on the abolitionist circuit, and understandably so. Like Douglass, often he resorted to more than oratory to regale the audiences he faced. He could make those audiences laugh and he could make them cry, as he both told and acted out his accounts of his experiences as a slave. One of the features of his antislavery appearances was his mournful singing of "The Slave Mother's Lament." He also turned to politics in his war against slavery. He was one of the earliest activists, and speakers, in the Liberty party. He married, in 1848, the talented Mary Miles from a well-known Negro family of Boston. The Fugitive Slave Act of the Compromise of 1850 sent him and his wife scurrying to Canada, where they continued with unstinted energy and zeal their abolitionist labors. Bibb started the first newspaper edited and published in Canada by a Negro, the *Voice of the Fugitive,* in 1851. He died, still young, in 1854.

Bibb was quite obviously a person of superior abilities, even though he happened to be regarded in America as a Negro. Like Bibb was James W. C. Pennington, much darker in complexion than Bibb, but no less blessed than Bibb with talents beyond those of the so-called average man. Pennington was born a slave on the Eastern Shore of Maryland. He was trained as a blacksmith. When he was around twenty-one years of age, he fled slavery. A Quaker was of special help to him in his transition from bondage to freedom, as another Quaker had been to Bibb in a similar circumstance. Pennington achieved a high level of literacy. He is even supposed to have received a doctorate of divinity from the University of Heidelberg. He entered the Presbyterian ministry, notably in Hartford, Connecticut, and New York City, where, for a while, he pastored the famous Shiloh Presbyterian Church. He first went abroad in 1843. He went abroad again in 1850, fearful of what might happen to him in consequence of the new Fugitive Slave Act, but his manumission the next year occasioned his swift return to America. His last years were clouded by his addiction to alcohol. He died in 1870 in Jacksonville, Florida, where he had gone mainly to recover from the fondness for the bottle which had darkened his career.

Pennington published, in 1841, A *Text Book of the Origin and History . . . of Colored People*. Some of his addresses and sermons were also published, as *Covenants Involving Moral Wrong Are Not Obligatory Upon Man: A Sermon*, in 1842, and his *The Reasonableness of the Abolition of Slavery*, in 1856. His slave narrative, *The Fugitive Blacksmith*, first appeared in London, where it was published in 1849. It attracted readers and went through at least three editions. No doubt exists of its composition by Pennington himself. But Pennington lacked Bibb's genius for narrative. He cannot tell his story without pausing to sermonize. He clutters what he is trying to say with too many gratuitous (and banal) advices to his anticipated readers expressive of his lofty humanitarian, religious, and abolitionist sentiments. And this admonitory Pennington is tedious. Nowhere in *The Fugitive Blacksmith* can anecdotes be found that vivify his story as do many of the anecdotes—such as Bibb's placement of himself among the white deck passengers on an Ohio river vessel during his first escape or his descriptions of his Red River days—in Bibb's *Narrative*, where, moreover, the moralizing is much less intrusive than it is in *The Fugitive Blacksmith*. Neither Pennington's intellect nor his earnestness improve as a slice of life *The Fugitive Blacksmith*. But not even Bibb's polemics prevent his *Narrative* from being a well-told story.

Among abolitionist slave narratives, two, if no others, reflect in high relief the familiar figure from Afro-American folklore of the trickster, the Brer Rabbit of the Uncle Remus tales, in his mastery of dissimulation, the Uncle Tom of Negro accommodationism, and, more than superficially, a special form of the *eiron* of Old Greek Comedy from whom irony derives its name. One of these narratives is attributed to William Hayden; the other, and much the better-known, to Josiah Henson, by many, including discreetly himself, proclaimed as the prototype for Harriet Beecher Stowe's Uncle Tom.

Hayden's *Narrative of William Hayden Containing a Faithful Account of his Travels for a Number of Years Whilst a Slave in the South* was published in Cincinnati in 1846, and may well have been more or less substantially written, as it claimed, by himself. Hayden was born in 1785 in Stafford County, Virginia. His years as a slave were numerous, forty in all. But they were not rebellious years, although Hayden, in his *Narrative*, unequivocally asserts that becoming free was always a deep desire of his. Hayden was only five when he was sold to a master in Georgetown near Lexington, in the heart of the bluegrass region of Kentucky. This new master gave Hayden to his daughter with the promise that Hayden would be manumitted when this daughter attained marriageable age. Moreover, Hayden, a house slave, as a youth was treated kindly, even being taught, by his white "family," to spell and read. As he approached maturity he acquired a trade. His master was a rope maker, and Hayden was inducted into rope spinning. Additionally, he was permitted to make money from the sale of fish which he caught and from service on the staff of a neighboring inn in his spare time. The problem which developed for Hayden, however, was a change of masters more than once because of all of his masters' penchants for getting themselves into financial difficulties. Nevertheless, wherever he went, Hayden, whatever his inner yearnings, insinuated himself within the good graces of his masters and of white folks in general. Indeed, his fellow blacks regarded him with suspicion and distaste, an indication, as a matter of fact, of their good judgment, up to a point, of him, for he once went so far as to betray an intended slave revolt to the whites. Still, he was really a trickster, with the true trickster's loyalty, at bottom, solely to his own skin.

Hayden's last master, a man named Phillips, was something of a trickster himself, but a sufferer also, not only from his chronic lack of character but from, as well, an equally chronic inability to avoid insolvency. Hayden had paid Phillips a sum of three hundred dollars, which Phillips had agreed would purchase Hayden's freedom. Phillips, however, in thoughts he kept to himself, planned to sell Hayden as soon as he conveniently could. He reckoned without regard to thoughts, and knowledge, Hayden had kept to himself. At the appropriate moment Hayden produced papers, signed by Phillips, which he had assured Phillips he had destroyed, that established his freedom. So the wily Phillips was bested by the wilier Hayden, who proceeded north, if not with Phillips' genuine approval, at least with Phillips' legal sanction.

Of major stature in the abolitionist slave narrative, Josiah Henson reflects even more powerfully the trickster image of the black accommodationist than Hayden. But much of this reflection, subjected to analysis, reveals room for doubts and contradictions. A widespread legend said of Henson that he was Harriet Beecher Stowe's Uncle Tom. And Henson, as already intimated here, lent some credence on his own to that legend. Yet there is cause for wonder in how he did so. For years he never really said anything which could be truly characterized as an unequivocal statement by him that he was Mrs. Stowe's Uncle Tom. Neither, for that matter, actually did Mrs. Stowe. At last, when he was old and his powers were failing, Henson, on at least one occasion, addressing himself to a large audience from which he had finally to be led away (so increasingly incoherent were becoming the words he tried to utter), did refer repeatedly to himself as Uncle Tom. But before *Uncle Tom's Cabin* was published it does not seem that Henson and Mrs. Stowe met and talked directly with each other, in spite of any intimations to the contrary. Nor does Mrs. Stowe, in her *A Key to Uncle Tom's Cabin*, published a year after the appearance of her famous novel, identify Henson in any way which would establish him as the genuine and undisputed prototype for her Uncle Tom. Nevertheless, with so little actual help from either Henson or Mrs. Stowe, over the years a popular notion flourished that Henson was the original of Uncle Tom, and Henson, by merely not refuting that notion, basked in the glory and the advantages which it conferred upon him. The truth is, moreover, that Henson was not, in his character, at all like the saintly figure created by Mrs. Stowe. He was, if nothing else, too vain to be so. He was also too ebullient and too crafty. And it is almost the cream of a monstrous jest to call him an Uncle Tom in the sense of a term which, by the twentieth century, if not before, had come to mean, especially among Negroes, a "white folks' nigger."

Henson was born in 1789, the year that Washington was inaugurated as America's first president. He died in 1883, almost twenty years after the end of the Civil War. Both as a slave and a freeman, he lived an eventful life. His place of birth was in the little corner of Maryland between the city of Washington, D.C., and the western bank of the Chesapeake Bay. There Henson grew up, becoming, according to a famous passage in his narrative, by the age of fifteen a "lively . . . young buck . . . [who] could run faster, wrestle better, and jump higher than anybody" in his neighborhood. His father had been lashed, mutilated, and sold to Alabama for thrashing an overseer who abused Henson's mother, his father's "wife." By his late adolescence, even so, Henson had become the trusted body servant of his third master, Isaac Riley. Riley's dependence on him, indeed, was so great that Henson was, in effect, an overseer himself. Still, he also suffered from his special favor in Riley's eyes. Another famous passage in his narrative tells of his rescue of a drunken Riley from a party of white men under circumstances which required the use by Henson of physical force and occasioned the subsequent major injury to both of Henson's shoulders by one of these white men—a major injury which lasted, for Henson, a lifetime. In any case, Riley was not only a roisterer. He was also a poor manager of his own affairs. A time came, therefore, when, in order to retain possession of some of his slaves he had

Henson, alone, to convoy them to his brother in Kentucky. This brother eventually sent his son to New Orleans with Henson, having given his son a secret order to sell Henson in the New Orleans market. Henson divined the order. One night, as he tells us in what may be the most famous passage in his narrative, he planned, while the boat carrying him was still southward bound, to murder with an axe the boy who was to sell him, as well as the three other persons on the boat. He was poised to strike when his own Christianity (Henson is fervent on this point) stayed his arm. In New Orleans his would-be deceiver took so ill that he was saved only by the ministrations of Henson, by whom he was glad to be taken home.

Before this trip to New Orleans, Henson had already lost faith in his master in Maryland, who, with Henson's money in hand—money which satisfied an agreement for Henson's release from bondage—had raised the price of Henson's freedom. Riley's brother in Kentucky lived within a few miles of the Ohio River. Carrying his two smallest children in a sack on his back and accompanied by his wife and their two older children on foot, Henson now escaped under cover of darkness to Indiana. It was 1830. He was forty-one years of age. He would never be a slave again. In Canada he achieved an eminence which made his name something of a byword on two continents. He interested himself, especially in connection with the community called Dawn, in a manual-labor school and a sawmill. He traveled to England twice. He had audiences with the archbishop of Canterbury, Prime Minister John Russell, and Queen Victoria. President Rutherford B. Hayes received him and his wife. Once he settled in Canada, however, he never resided in the United States again, although he did return there as a conductor on the Underground Railroad. He died in Dresden, Canada.

Henson's first narrative, with the title *Life of Josiah Henson, formerly a Slave, Now an Inhabitant of Canada, Narrated by Himself*, appeared in Boston in 1849. Its true author was Samuel Eliot, a former mayor of Boston. As competent intellectually as Henson undoubtedly was, he never seems to have achieved the kind of literacy the writing of a narrative undoubtedly would have required. A professing Christian at eighteen, before he escaped Kentucky he was already a preacher in the Methodist church. But he was a preacher who could not read or write. In Canada a twelve-year-old son of his who had quietly noticed that Henson was repeating from memory, with some telltale lapses, a passage of Scripture which he was pretending to read began to teach him his letters and initiated for him an acquaintance with the rudiments of a formal education. But Henson, in Canada, was a man long past the flush of youth. His late start at mastering reading and writing, if nothing else, meant that he would never be a Douglass or a Bibb. So he did not write, also, the second version of his narrative, considerably revised from the first, presenting a preface by Mrs. Stowe and with a title reminiscent of Lord Byron (whose widow Mrs. Stowe had chosen to champion), *Truth Stranger than Fiction: Father Henson's Story of His Own Life*. This second version, like the first, was published in Boston. Like the third version to come, the first edition of which would not appear until 1877, when it would be published in London, not Boston, this second version would differ from the original, 1849 version partly in that it was a cumulative account of Henson's life and his very active public career.

The third version of Henson's narrative, just cited, bore the quite significant title *"Uncle Tom's Story of His Life": An Autobiography of the Rev. Josiah Henson (Mrs. Harriet Beecher Stowe's "Uncle Tom"), From 1789 to 1876*. It was written by its "editor," the Englishman John Lobb, who followed it within the year with his *The Young People's Illustrated Edition of "Uncle Tom's Story of His Life" (From 1789 to 1877)*. Although, of course, none of Henson's narratives approached by far the phenomenal commercial success of *Uncle Tom's Cabin*, they were all, even among slave narratives, unusually popular. The number of editions of the various narratives, particularly of the version "edited" by Lobb, is still not authenticated completely, although surely, in some form (or forms), this 1877 narrative was published elsewhere than in England. Strange, then, was not only Henson's life but also the uses made of descriptions of it both during Henson's own lifetime and after he had breathed his last. Whatever Henson was in his many various guises from his birth to his death—local hero, accomplice of dishonest masters, sometimes himself a trickster, evangelist for Christ, first citizen of a free black Canadian community, and celebrity on two continents—he was never an epitome of meekness and self-effacement, and he was certainly not an instrument of accommodationism as Booker T. Washington or any other Negro too fearful of pitting himself against the white establishment, in the years between Henson's death and the Harlem renaissance, was to be.

Nothing strange, apparently, is to be noted about either the life or the aftermath thereof of Henry "Box" Brown. But Brown assumed his nickname because of the strangeness of the means by which he made his way to freedom. His narrative, published in Boston in 1849, followed by an

English edition in 1851, bore the title *Narrative of Henry Box Brown, Who Escaped from Slavery, Enclosed in a Box Three Free Long and Two Feet Wide; Written from a Statement of Facts Made by Himself*. Brown may have, in his "statement of facts," reported a somewhat slimmer box than he actually used. The two feet of the title, that is, may have been two and a half feet. Even so, in his flight from bondage, he subjected himself to a truly excruciating test. He entered his box in Richmond with a "beef's bladder" of water. The box, of course, was securely shut. He endured transportation in this close, blind, and very still confinement, sometimes on his head, as a secret item concealed within the bulky freight consigned to a company known as Adams Express, for twenty-seven hours until abolitionists in Philadelphia, alerted to expect his box, uncrated it, and he leaped forth from his stifling chamber no longer in slave territory. Brown had brought with him, incidentally, a five-stanza hymn of thanksgiving which he sang as soon as he emerged into the open air.

Another narrative notable for the strangeness of the method of escape it recounts in its relatively brief text was first published in London in 1860. Its title, *Running a Thousand Miles for Freedom*, is somewhat misleading, for it really focuses on a journey made from the Deep South—and the title does pay tribute to that rather abnormal aspect of a flight from slavery—not on foot but by means of the then available ordinary modes of public conveyance in constant association with other passengers who were, by law, genuinely white and, hence—every one of them—a potential menace to the Crafts, who "ran" the thousand miles. William Craft, in a preface to *Running a Thousand Miles* of less than two pages in length, asserts that he himself wrote this narrative, as very probably he did. A slave in Georgia, he married, as much as slaves could, the attractive slave girl Ellen. William and Ellen were about the same age at the time of their extra-legal nuptials, in their very early twenties. William was brown of skin. Ellen was a pronounced octoroon. Her mistress, indeed, was her half-sister, and Ellen had become the property of a Dr. Robert Collins, a leading citizen of Macon, and owner of a railroad, a bank, a home on a four-acre estate, ten thousand acres of plantation land, and sixty-two slaves, when Dr. Collins and Ellen's mistress embarked upon their own quite legal marriage with each other. William, a cabinet maker, belonged to the cashier of Dr. Collins' bank.

Because the Crafts were as different as they were in color, the thought occurred to them that they might actually be able to travel north as a white attended by a slave. But, for such a ruse to work, Ellen was almost surely of the wrong sex. Young white women in the antebellum South, as in America of all generations, were not in the habit of traipsing around the countryside, whatever their condition, accompanied only by equally young male blacks, free or slave. So, during the Christmas week of 1848, the Crafts left Macon, with Ellen in masculine attire and apparently so invalided that she could neither write (Ellen was thoroughly illiterate) nor comfortably mingle with other people. William assumed the role of an ailing master's solicitous slave. The two went by rail from Macon to Savannah, by boat from Savannah to Charleston, where they lodged in a hotel for several hours, by boat, also, to Wilmington, North Carolina, by train from Wilmington to a point just beyond Fredericksburg, Virginia, by boat from there to Washington, D.C., in a horse-drawn omnibus from Washington to the train station in Baltimore, and, finally, with their nerves very much on edge, from Baltimore to Philadelphia by train.

Running a Thousand Miles fortunately is, throughout most of its entire length, in a plain, simple, declarative style, a reconstruction of the five days in the life of the Crafts occupied by their activities above. It does contain a few digressions from its function of travelogue. Like any good and proper abolitionist slave narrative, for example, it devotes some pages to a description and denunciation of the heartless separation of William from the other members of his family who were sold away from him. But such descriptions and denunciations, as rather emphatically hitherto noted here, were virtually obligatory in all abolitionist slave narratives. About the last fourth of *Running a Thousand Miles* conducts the Crafts on from Philadelphia into England. In Philadelphia they had met the influential and wealthy free Negro Robert Purvis, had been given their first lessons in writing by friends and members of the family of Barkley Ivens, the philanthropic Quaker with whom they were quartered with due regard for secrecy, and had made their initial acquaintance with William Wells Brown, who was sent by some of his fellow abolitionists to make as certain as he could their unmolested passage from their sanctuary in Pennsylvania to Massachusetts. They lived in Boston for two years, during which time they were married—in a ceremony they treasured as the one they would have liked to have had in Georgia—by the celebrated white divine and abolitionist Theodore Parker, and reveled, as it were, in a situation in which William could practice freely his trade of cabinet making while Ellen, just as freely, learned to be a seamstress. At the end of their two years, however, they fled from Boston. As with many fugitive slaves, the Fugitive Slave Act affected their lives. Indeed, after this law's adoption, while not, physically, for one moment removing his watchful eye from the direct observation of all his property in Georgia, including his slaves, Dr. Collins dispatched two slave catchers to Boston to bring the Crafts both home to Macon. Boston resisted the slave catchers. Yet it was deemed best for the Crafts to leave America. Through Maine and Nova Scotia they hastened to a ship which bore them to Liverpool.

William (who, as well as Ellen, went to school in England), or William with help, in *Running a Thousand Miles,* produced one of the more effective and convincing slave narratives—one which, in great likelihood, presents itself as attractively and persuasively to its readers as it does precisely because with so commendable an absence of heat it casts real light upon its stated purpose, its account of the "running," with the subterfuges it required, by the Crafts from an old condition to a new. Memorable, incidentally, as was that prolonged feat of valor, of poise, and of staunch adherence to a dangerous plan, it did not render all of the remainder of their lives merely an anticlimax to this one experience of theirs which had been so unusual in its nature and so sweeping in its alteration of who they were. Quite to the contrary, it only provided them a point of departure from which they moved, in effect, onward and upward to demonstrate how sterling were the qualities in themselves which slavery had repressed.

The Crafts resided for almost twenty years in England, where, admirably, they educated themselves, lectured against slavery, engaged in productive labor, and acquired, as their own offspring, four sons and one daughter. But when the Civil War was over, they returned to their native land and even to Georgia, their native state. There, with money given them by abolitionist friends of theirs in both England and America, they bought land near Savannah and settled down, as they grew older, virtually where they had grown up as slaves, to devote the years that were left to them, after their own good fortune, to the education and economic betterment of the not so fortunate former slaves (and their children) they had left behind them. Their only daughter married the eminent Dr. William Crum, sometime collector of customs for the port of Charleston, who was appointed, in 1910 by President Taft, minister resident and consul general from the United States to Liberia.

Strange, but strange in a different way, a double reversal of direction in both cases, from either the narrative of "Box" Brown or the narrative of the Crafts, was *Twelve Years a Slave,* subtitled the *Narrative of Solomon Northup, a Citizen of New York, Kidnapped in Washington City in 1841, and Rescued in 1853, from a Cotton Plantation Near the Red River in Louisiana. Twelve Years,* which appeared in 1853 and represented a collaboration between Northup and the white David Wilson, who lived in the vicinity of Northup's home in upstate New York but who was not, necessarily, an abolitionist or, as pragmatic as he was generally inclined to be, an ideologue of any kind. *Twelve Years* sold well, over thirty thousand copies in three years. Its success may be attributable, at least partly, to its publication when the impact of *Uncle Tom's Cabin* on the emotions of Americans was at its height. *Twelve Years* and *Uncle Tom's Cabin* are obviously reminiscent of each other. But the success of *Twelve Years* may also be attributable, again at least partly, to David Wilson's desire, in his rendition of the tale he heard from Northup (for the style of *Twelve Years* is clearly Wilson's own), quite sensibly to guarantee, above all, that an account of an adventure inherently entertaining if only allowed to be merely itself would not be transformed unduly into a tedious and clumsy vehicle for propaganda.

What happened to Northup, as revealed in *Twelve Years,* was by no means unique. Northup was a free Negro—so born and so raised, in the free state of New York—who was shanghaied into slavery. Such a violation of personal status occurred with sufficient repetitiveness in America before the Civil War for it to constitute an ever-present potential danger of which all free Negroes tended to be constantly aware. That Northup, therefore, of whose high intelligence notice would be taken by whites and blacks alike in Louisiana when he got there, should have permitted this particular violation to have been imposed on him still appears the consequence of an act of will on his part astonishingly inconsistent with his usual apparent capacity for keeping his wits about him at all times. Cupidity, for some reason, must have greatly outweighed caution this once, if nevermore, in his life. In any case, on a day in 1841, purely by chance, it seemed, in Saratoga Springs, New York, Northup fell into a conversation with two white men who were complete strangers to him. As one of his marketable skills, Northup performed upon the violin. So charmed became Northup by promises of employment as a violinist made by his new acquaintances that he accompanied them to Washington, D.C., where he awoke, from a sleep he had not sought, drugged, beaten, and chained—he could not remember when or how—and, even worse, discovered himself in the custody of a slave dealer who almost immediately added him to the other poor wretches in a boatload of slaves destined for New Orleans. It was from an auction block of Theophilus Freeman's widely notorious slave-trading establishment in New Orleans that Northup was sold as a slave to a master who lived in the so-called Red River country near Alexandria in the heart of Louisiana.

Thus Northup came to the part of the world with which his narrative is most concerned. He had his troubles there. But an arresting feature of *Twelve Years* is its refreshing objectivity. In this narrative every white Louisianian whom Northup meets is not a devil. Both blacks and whites, in his view, are good and bad. Moreover, Northup, in Louisiana, was an assiduous observer. One may learn from *Twelve Years* not only important facts about the treatment of slaves in the Red River country in the 1840s but also revelatory details about the country itself—about its topography and vegetation; about its crops, including what was done with them after they were harvested; and about its inhabitants, white, black, and red, in regard both to their histories as individuals and to the impact upon them of the parochial culture of which they were a part. Northup, of course, had come to the Red River country an outsider rudely thrust into a new world as a person unpleasantly born again. His narrative indicates that he was, even so, an outsider with an active and able eye for seeing, in an atmosphere obviously not stimulating to his most buoyant energies, a signal amount of all that was there to be seen, as well as a felicitous faculty for sorting out what he had seen with a sure sense of the appropriate for his purposes, when the opportunity arrived for him to recall for publication his experiences in a distinctive portion of the Deep South. Northup, as might have been expected, was deprived of his true name when he became the fraudulent property of his kidnappers. In Louisiana he was known as Platt. His skills as a carpenter and a musician served him well when he was Platt as they had served him well when he was Northup. It was partly his carpentry which expedited his return to his home in New York State. Confidences he found he could safely share with an itinerant, Canadian-born white carpenter named Bass led to Bass's notification of white friends of Northup's in New York about Northup's plight in Louisiana. One of the white friends came in person to the Red River country and, assisted by more cooperation from Louisiana officialdom than might have been anticipated, returned to New York State with a Northup blissfully extricated from his twelve years of nightmare far from his family and home.

There was, within three years of the publication of *Twelve Years*, a second account of the illegal enslavement of a black. It was a slave narrative, however, which made no pretense of being autobiographical. The white woman, Kate Pickard, who wrote it and took full credit for its authorship, had taught school in Alabama. The narrative, *The Kidnapped and the Ransomed Being Personal Recollections of Peter Still and His Wife "Vina," after 40 Years of Slavery,* was published in Syracuse, New York, in 1856. Peter Still, a brother of the William Still conspicuous in Afro-American history for his long service in Philadelphia to the Underground Railroad (about which *he* wrote), was seized by his captors in New Jersey and carried, as a slave, to Kentucky and Alabama. One white man, Seth Conklin, actually lost his life trying to bring back Peter Still, with his wife and children, to the free states. Still bought his own freedom but returned to the South, where he stayed until he was able to accomplish the rescue of the other members of his family. That Pickard "improved" her "true" relation of the enslavement of the Stills with novelistic touches of her own invention is a possibility not to be lightly dismissed.

Several of the fugitive slaves most well known as fugitives, and as laborers in the cause of abolition, not surprisingly were runaways from Maryland's Eastern Shore. One of these was Samuel Ringgold Ward, born a year before his fellow Eastern Shoreman Frederick Douglass, in 1817. Ward died in 1866. He was only three years old when his parents, fearing his mother's sale to the Deep South, fled to New Jersey with him and his two brothers, one younger than himself. The Wards, however, lived in New York City for most of Ward's youth, and it was in New York City that Ward attended the Mulberry Street School with such other matriculants there as Henry Highland Garnet and Alexander Crummell, who would become, like him, among the best-known Negroes of their time. Ward was physically large enough to seem almost a giant. His skin was dark, so dark that a notable number of his contemporaries remarked about the intensity of his sable hue. Yet he pastored two white churches. He was especially esteemed as an orator.

Abolitionist that he was, Ward played a leading role in the founding of the American Missionary Association (which has lasted to contribute significantly to Negro higher education) in 1846. But a more outspoken and direct manifestation of his abolitionist zeal was his participation, in Syracuse, his home at the time, in the rescue from prison and the immediately subsequent transportation to Canada, *vis et armis,* of a fugitive slave. This flouting of authority occurred in 1851. With a heightened consciousness, because of it, of the Fugitive Slave Act of 1850, Ward moved to Canada, returning from his haven there once only to the United States when, after becoming active, and quite prominent, in the affairs of Canadian Negroes, in 1853 he took ship from New York City (and the last visit he would ever make to his mother) for England. Ward continued his abolitionist labors in England. A wealthy Englishman gave him fifty acres of land in Jamaica. So, in 1855, Ward changed his residence for the last time. He spent the final eleven years of his life in Jamaica. Of Ward's ability and eminence there can be no question. In 1866 he published *Reflections of the Jordan Rebellion,* of which no copies seem to exist and about which, from its title, it is probably accurate to assume a focus on things Jamaican. He also wrote articles for Bibb's *Voice of the Fugitive* and Garrison's *Liberator.* His slave narrative, *Autobiography of a Fugitive Negro: His Anti-Slavery Labours in the United States, Canada & England,* published in 1855, in view, especially, of the richness of his experience of life and the exceptional abilities in communication he otherwise displayed, compares unfavorably with such a narrative as Northup's *Twelve Years.*

As a matter of fact, *Autobiography of a Fugitive Negro* hardly justifies its title. It says very little, relatively, about Samuel Ringgold Ward, and that very little almost exclusively at the beginning of a text rather formidably long. After four short chapters collectively designated as an autobiography, it presents the bulk of its content under the rubric "Anti-slavery Labours." But Ward was both educated and a public man. In this narrative he feels constrained, therefore, to draw upon his knowledge of Negro history, his store of animadversions upon the false philosophy and the questionable behavior of proslavery Americans, his contacts with, and high opinions of, leaders, white and black, of the antislavery cause whom he has met in America, Canada, and all parts of the British Isles, and, not least of all, his own general reflections about virtually every aspect of human conduct. So his slave narrative disappears into a miscellany of somewhat random thoughts and anecdotes. He is earnest. He is, all too patently, a grammarian of parts. Victorian decorum and the punctilios of a public man aware of his position inform his prose. But little, if any, of a Samuel Ringgold Ward speaking from uninhibited intimate recesses of himself about slavery and freedom, and his reaction to them, appears in this text. Such adjectives as *run-of-the-mill* apply to it. It may well be, of all slave narratives, considering the conceivably pertinent qualifications of its author, the most disappointing.

Somewhat like Ward a racial leader a phase of whose career connected him to Canada was Theophilus Steward, author of the slave narrative *Twenty-Two Years a Slave, and Forty Years a Freeman,* published in Rochester in 1857. Steward was born a slave in Virginia in the 1790s. He was taken, while still a child, to New York State by a master who was seeking, in a new environment, to reverse a record of failure. When Steward was twenty-two years old, he took advantage of a provision of New York law which made him free. For a while thereafter he remained in that state, reaching the high-water mark of his New York career as a grocer in Rochester. To help his fellow blacks, he betook himself and his family to Canada in 1831. There he became the president of the Wilberforce Colony. But this colony, after a somewhat auspicious beginning, came to no good end. By 1837 Steward had returned to the United States. After his Canadian venture, incidentally, he never regained the prosperity he had previously enjoyed in the United States. He speaks conscientiously in his narrative, but with little spark. He does not fail to deplore slavery. But black venality significantly accountable for the disruption of the Wilberforce Colony also is a target of his disapproval.

It was probably inevitable that at least one abolitionist slave narrative, if not more, would focus on sex and, specifically, on the history of a black woman in bondage to whom the protection of herself from the lust of white men legally empowered to use her body as they might choose had been a matter of prime concern. Such a narrative is *Incidents in the Life of a Slave Girl,* published in Boston in 1861 as the autobiography of Harriet Jacobs, a pseudonym for Linda Brent. The veteran writer and abolitionist Lydia Maria Child edited *Incidents,* a circumstance highly suggestive of Child's translation of recollections dictated to her into a text of her own composition. *Incidents,* however, does seem what it proclaims itself to be, insofar as it does apparently recount, whether or not as originally as claimed, events actually experienced by a female slave in the antebellum South. Jacobs, to adopt the nomenclature of *Incidents,* was apparently the kind of woman ideally, in an imagined scenario, suited to suffer as she claims she did. She was a mulatto of an attractive physique and a house servant often present in her master's eye. According to Jacobs, her seduction became virtually the one driving obsession of that master's whole existence, so much so that, in desperation, she gave herself to another white man, by whom she had a succession of children, in order thus to avoid the even worse degradation of herself she firmly believed submission to her master would have entailed. Incredibly, Jacobs hid for seven years, separated from her children, in an attic and finally accomplished her escape to the North a desperate stowaway at sea. In justice to *Incidents*, it must be said that Jacobs manages, with all of her attention to her problems with white men, also to testify on other aspects of slavery. Like Northup, she was a good observer, and so, although her role as a black Pamela invests her narrative with its major distinction, her story may be read with profit solely as a thoughtful slave's picture of what slavery had meant to her.

7. Perpetuations and Close Relatives of the Slave Narrative

Between approximately 1830 and the end of the Civil War, some fifty slave narratives, in round numbers, appeared which share the characteristics of what we have called the abolitionist slave narratives. Of those fifty the ones cited in the previous chapter are representative. Obviously the abolitionist slave narrative was dated, as was abolitionism itself. With the end of slavery, both lost the special ill which they attacked so uniformly and so resolutely and which conferred upon them a reason for being as they were. But the end of slavery did not mean the end of people who had been slaves. Many of the former slaves, quite as was to be expected, continued to live after slavery perished, some well into the twentieth century. In two ways which can be rather sharply distinguished from each other, these survivors of slavery perpetuated, more or less, the slave narrative. A select few—Frederick Douglass, as we have seen, among them—wrote, and published, after 1865, accounts of their own lives, not excluding their years as slaves, which can still be called slave narratives. Slave narratives, we know, tend to deal with slaves who became free. Nor do they tend to speak only of the slavery and not of the freedom. This, then—the narrative by the single former slave written and published after slavery's end—is one of the two ways through which the slave narrative extended itself after slavery, and we shall return to it in a moment.

The other way has produced, as it were, instead of portraits of (and largely by) individuals, composites of groups, since these composites tend to be collections of interviews granted to auditors by former slaves. Moreover, these composites tend really to be secondhand accounts—edited transcripts of whatever was originally articulated, even though they are repeated almost always in the first person. Actually, an example of these composites perhaps too important to ignore appeared before the end of slavery. Its title may be given as *The Refugee: A Northside View of Slavery or The Narratives of Fugitive Slaves in Canada Related By Themselves.* It was published in Boston in 1856, the work of Benjamin Drew, a Boston educator and journalist descended from ancestors who arrived in Massachusetts in 1660. A Boston clergyman named Nehemiah Adams, after a trip into the South, had published, in 1854, *A Southside View of Slavery*, an abject capitulation, it clearly seemed to people like Drew, to the South in that region's most abominable defenses of its peculiar institution. Adams, indeed, even asserted that Negroes were happy to be slaves. He also pilloried *Uncle Tom's Cabin* as a mountain of untruths. So, whereas Adams had traveled south, Drew went to Canada, seeking evidence about slavery from some of the more than 30,000 black fugitives from the United States residing there in 1855. His interviews with 113 of these fugitives scattered through 14 Canadian communities became the collection of slave narratives—authentic recollections although edited into his own English by him without, he obviously hoped, alterations of intended meanings—which forms the composite picture of slavery, quite different from that of Adams, provided by *The Refugee*. Drew clearly was not a lazy man. His responses from many of those he interviewed were sufficiently substantial to be translated by him into several pages in *The Refugee*. His narratives, therefore, are often not like the many "narratives" only a paragraph or so long frequently presented as the recollections of former slaves. In no sense, additionally, do the narratives in *The Refugee* support slavery. Whatever Adams found in the South, he speaks, in *A Southside View of Slavery*, of a country different from the land remembered by Drew's blacks in Canada. They were happy no longer to be slaves.

In the early 1930s, however, long after slavery, a team of social scientists under the direction of Charles S. Johnson (whom we shall later connect with the Harlem Renaissance and who died as president of Fisk University) invaded Macon County, Alabama, to undertake a study, a classic of its kind, called *Shadow of the Plantation* and credited to the authorship of Johnson, which was published in 1934. Tuskegee Institute, it may be interesting to observe, is located in Macon County. But Johnson and his team concentrated their attention, not on Booker T. Washington's school, Washington's shadow, surely, but on the Negroes resident in Macon County, whom they regarded collectively as a model exhibit of the black peasantry of the South contemporary with their study. Among the 612 families they selected as the objects of this systematic scrutiny, they found a few former slaves and so were able to elicit from some five of their informants reminiscences which appear in *Shadow of the Plantation* as edited slave narratives in capsulated form. One of their informants, incidentally, remembered slavery as better than freedom and, thus, would have gratified Nehemiah Adams' proslavery sentiments, although more typical of the former slaves of Macon County than this one black defender of the Calhoun South probably was an aged black matriarch— herself also born in bondage—who cautioned Johnson's team not to believe "no nigger when he says he rather be . . . [a] slave."[1]

In any case, the slave narratives in *Shadow of the Plantation* constitute a prelude, along with somewhat similar brief narratives in Frederic Bancroft's *Slave Trading in the Old South* (1931), John B. Cade's "Out of the Mouths of Ex-Slaves," published in the *Journal of Negro History* in 1935, and Orlan Kay Armstrong's *Old Massa's People: The Old Slaves Tell Their Story* (1931), to the monumental collection of reminiscences of former slaves made from 1936 through 1938 under the aegis of the Works Progress Administration, by both black and white interviewers attached to the Federal Writers Project. These interviewers searched out ex-slaves in eighteen states: Alabama, Arkansas, Florida, Georgia, Illinois, Indiana, Kentucky, Louisiana, Maryland, Mississippi, Missouri, North Carolina, Ohio, Oklahoma, South Carolina, Tennessee, Texas, and Virginia. By 1939 the process of depositing typescripts of the slave narratives thus collected, along with some other materials, in the Library of Congress had begun. In this manner were accumulated within the rare-books division of the library, among other related materials, the seventeen volumes in thirty-three parts of the Federal Writers Project entitled *Slave Narratives: A Folk History of Slavery in the United States from Interviews with Former Slaves.*

More than two thousand former slaves, about one in fifty of all the former slaves alive in the United States in the second Roosevelt's early administrations, provided the interviews which appear as narratives in *Slave Narratives: A Folk History of Slavery.* Obviously, not one of these more than two thousand seniors of their tribe was older than a child or a young adult in 1865. So in at least one sense they could not be representative of America's total slave population as it ever, at any time before

1. Charles S. Johnson, *Shadow of the Plantation* (Chicago, 1934), 20.

emancipation, actually was. Some slaves then were middle-aged, and some were even well past their prime. On the other hand, the former slaves who had survived to be interviewed for *Slave Narratives: A Folk History of Slavery* were far more representative generally of all the slaves—the real and true rank and file of black folk—who experienced American slavery than the relatively very few ex-slaves from whose tiny special corps emanated the authors of the abolitionist slave narratives. The ex-slaves interviewed for *Slave Narratives: A Folk History of Slavery* had not, for instance, as slaves, largely lived in border states. Rather, they had resided under bondage, like most slaves, in the Deep South. Moreover, as they were of every skin complexion, of both sexes and of every size, while they also had participated, as slaves, in all the occupations in which slaves tended to participate and had been located on small farms with almost no fellow slaves or on big plantations where slave gangs could be huge in proportions of their sum commensurate with the historical distribution of slaves on the southern land before the Civil War, they did (and do) constitute a sample, however random, that essentially repeats with marked fidelity most of the characteristics of the whole of which they were once a part. Thus, the great virtue of *Slave Narratives: A Folk History of Slavery* as a voice from the past is clearly apparent. It does possess almost absolute authenticity and authority as a direct, vital expression of a history of slavery delivered from a black perspective. It is as much, if not more, a testimonial by the Negro folk as a Negro spiritual or the juba dance or the animals of Afro-American folklore. So it could be a notable resource in the study of the American Negro, and so, in spite of its original limited accessibility in the Library of Congress, it has become.

For America, as it entered the 1940s, under the impact of the Great Depression, a global conflict and the expanding therapy of an ebbing of passion from the high tide of anti-Negro hysteria too long a feverish accompaniment of the so-called redemption of the South, was beginning to undergo a sea change in its attitudes toward race. A black voice like that of *Slave Narratives: A Folk History of Slavery* might well have been left to languish not only unpublished, but also unregarded, in the days when scholars such as Ulrich B. Phillips, a masterful historian but also a dedicated defender of color caste, set the lines of demarcation for documentation of the Old South. It was then for blacks to speak only through white interpreters who intuited the mind and soul of blacks. It would not be so in the 1940s. It would be even less so as America, after World War II, turned upon itself to examine, for its own salvation, its own possible deviations from its own democratic creed. Meanwhile, *Slave Narratives: A Folk History of Slavery* would start to live as it could never have flourished merely at the level of its typescripts and its immobilized contents immured therein.

Its first experience of some release into a wider sphere of availability resulted from the publication, in 1940, by the Virginia Writers Project, of *The Negro in Virginia*. The Virginia Writers Project was, unlike the Federal Writers Project, an all-black unit. Most of the interviews obtained by it and used in *The Negro in Virginia* were not deposited in the collection assembled as *Slave Narratives: A Folk History of Slavery*. Even so, a significant minority of the slave narratives reflected, if not more literally represented, in *The Negro in Virginia* are items within *Slave Narratives: A Folk History of Slavery* and thus belong to the narratives gathered, and retained in a separate state collection, by the Virginia Writers Project. In 1976, incidentally, Charles L. Purdue, Jr., Thomas E. Barden, and Robert K. Phillips, after a thorough examination of the pertinent materials in both the Library of Congress and the archives of the state of Virginia, exhumed, as it were, most of the interviews represented in *The Negro in Virginia* (whether they were in Washington, D.C., or Virginia) and published them in *Weevils in the Wheat: Interviews with Virginia Ex-Slaves*. The first genuinely extensive audience, however, for the narratives (or materials therefrom) in *Slave Narratives: A Folk History of Slavery* resulted from the publication, in 1945, of *Lay My Burden Down*, by the eminent folklorist B. A. Botkin. This book, aside from Botkin's attractively soft-toned introduction to it, is composed of selections from the narratives—far from always without omissions—so arranged as to emphasize themes suggestive of the folk mind and folk conditions of the slaves (*Lay My Burden Down*, like the collection from which it came, is subtitled *A Folk History of Slavery*).

In 1970, in Norman R. Yetman's *Life Under the "Peculiar" Institution: Selections from the Slave Narrative Collection*, one hundred of the narratives in *Slave Narratives: A Folk History of Slavery* were published in their entirety. Two years later, at last appeared, in nineteen volumes edited by George P. Rawick, *The American Slave: A Composite Autobiography*, containing all the narratives amassed for *Slave Narratives: A Folk History of Slavery*. The first of these nineteen volumes, individually entitled *From Sundown to Sunup: The Making of the Black Community*, is not a collection of narratives but a setting for all of them within a general picture, as conceptualized by Rawick, of slavery. The last two of these nineteen volumes also do not contain narratives from *Slave Narratives: A Folk History of Slavery.* They are composed of narratives based on interviews with ex-slaves in the 1940s by interviewers sent out from Fisk University. Finally, *The American Slave: A Composite Autobiography* was expanded to forty-one volumes with the addition of the twelve volumes, edited by Rawick, Jan Hillegas, and Ken Lawrence, entitled *The American Slave,* Supplement Series 1, and the ten volumes, edited by Rawick, entitled *The American Slave,* Supplement Series 2. In these additional twenty-two volumes may be found narrative-interviews from many states, in libraries and other depositories throughout the country, gleaned by workers for state units of the Works Progress Administration or for various writers projects or for projects independent of governmental auspices.

It has been estimated that all of the American slave narratives of every kind, wherever and whenever they were published, total now at least six thousand. As a force upon the American imagination, they have, if nothing else, increasingly influenced American scholarship. Students of American history and culture, especially since 1970, have welcomed the perspective these slave narratives provide upon a most important component of the American past. In a carefully conceived article, "Ex-Slave Interviews and the Historiography of Slavery," Yetman cites, as scholarly works of consequence about slavery which have used—to repeat from Yetman an exact single term—"extensively" the slave narratives available now in print, Eugene Genovese's *Roll, Jordan, Roll,* published in 1974; Olli Alho's *The Religion of the Slaves* and Herbert Gutman's *The Black Family in Slavery and Freedom, 1750–1925,* both published in 1976; Lawrence Levine's *Black Culture and Black Consciousness,* published in 1977; Albert Raboteau's *Slave Religion* and Thomas Webber's *Deep like the River: Education in the Slave Quarter Community, 1831–1865,* both published in 1978; and Paul Escott's *Slavery Remembered* and Leon Litwack's *Been in the Storm So Long,* both published in 1979.[2] Yetman also refers to the probable effect of the large collections of slave narratives upon John Blassingame in *The Slave Community: Plantation Life in the Antebellum South,* published in 1972, and *Slave Testimony,* published in 1977. In these two works of his, Blassingame, while laying great (and justifiable) stress upon his urgent concern that all personal documents from the slaves themselves should be used by scholars only with the utmost of

2. Norman R. Yetman, "Ex-Slave Interviews and the Historiography of Slavery," *American Quarterly,* XXXIV (1984), 181–210.

critical care, has fashioned accounts of slavery in which such documents—ranging from the older slave narratives published before emancipation through the letters and speeches of slaves and former slaves and communications in interviews by them to several kinds of interviewers, as well as autobiographies not necessarily slave narratives—provide the sense he seeks of slavery as it may well have seemed to the slaves.

Of the ex-slaves who wrote individual accounts of their lives which were published after 1865, the first both to be born, at Dinwiddie Court House in Virginia in 1825, and to issue an autobiography in print after the Civil War was Elizabeth Keckley, like Harriet Jacobs in the bloom of her youth an attractive female mulatto slave. Like Harriet Jacobs, also, Keckley would pay a price for her physical attractiveness as an apparently consenting partner in a sexual intimacy she would eventually testify she did not relish with a white man for whom she certainly never harbored a really deep affection. From this intimacy, in Hillsborough, North Carolina, she acquired a son of whom, however, she was most fond. In St. Louis, Missouri, she married a Negro who lied to her when he assured her that he was free. He proved, moreover, as dissolute as he was dishonest—so dissolute that she was most sincerely grateful for the end of the eight years it took her to get rid of him.

Keckley's skill as a modiste and her good character won her white friends in St. Louis who expedited her purchase of freedom for herself and her son. She established herself as a fashionable dressmaker, quite respected among society's leading matrons, in Washington, D.C., during the very months when the South was separating from the North. One of her clients, Jefferson Davis' wife, so prized her as to propose that she move south as the Davises did. But Keckley by this time had met Mrs. Abraham Lincoln. She remained in Washington, to sew for Mrs. Lincoln and become a familiar within the White House as well as, she proudly believed, Mrs. Lincoln's bosom friend. For many years after the Civil War, she taught at Wilberforce University as "Director of Domestic Art." Her long life ended in Washington, D.C., in 1905. The son on whom she had so doted died in battle with Union forces in Missouri in 1861.

Keckley called her narrative *Behind the Scenes: Thirty Years a Slave and Four Years in the White House.* It appeared in 1868. Less than a fifth of it deals with her years as a slave, but that fifth, at the beginning, of course, of her book, mirrors in many important aspects of theme and content the conventional abolitionist slave narrative. Keckley is flogged, for example, on more than one occasion, and a southern Christian minister is largely responsible for these unchivalric and most un-Christian assaults on her weak woman's body and her sometimes supposed ethereal woman's soul. Most of *Behind the Scenes*, nevertheless, is a gossip about the Lincolns during Lincoln's presidency and, furthermore, about Keckley's continuing relation with Mrs. Lincoln for the first years after the president's death. A notable passage in the book sets forth in possibly too ample detail, but very sympathetically for Mrs. Lincoln, Keckley's attempt to help the widowed first lady, now badly in need of money, to dispose of remaining items from her White House wardrobe at a profit large enough to relieve her financial distress. Mrs. Lincoln's cash returns from this effort, incidentally, fell far short of what she had hoped. *Behind the Scenes*, therefore, greatly resembles the domestic fiction by those feminine authors so popular in America in the 1850s who formed a school of which, however greatly critics of so-called serious literature may ignore it, those who treasure a true and total sense of America entire must acknowledge for the light it casts upon America as it was throughout much of the middle period of its existence until now. And so *Behind the Scenes* reflects its moment and milieu. It is genteel. It is sentimental. It sees its world through the eyes of a woman who could have stepped, except for her color, directly from the pages of *Godey's Lady's Book* or, in England, Coventry Patmore's *Angel in the House.* Yet this very woman could, and did, support, in St. Louis, a large household, black and white, completely from her needle. Keckley appended to *Behind the Scenes* letters she had received from Mrs. Lincoln (who usually addressed her as "Lizzie"). The publication of these letters, if nothing else about *Behind the Scenes*, so mightily offended Robert Lincoln, the Lincolns' son, that he effected a rapid suppression of the book.

Of all the autobiographical works written by ex-slaves and published after the Civil War, easily the best-known, of course, is Booker T. Washington's *Up from Slavery*, which we shall discuss later when we speak more fully of Washington. *Up from Slavery* was published in 1901. A year later appeared, in Boston, a small volume, *Reminiscences of My Life in Camp*, by Suzie King Taylor, who had been born a slave near Savannah in 1848. As a child in Savannah, Taylor learned to read and write. Her marriage to a Negro who became a soldier and noncommissioned officer in the first regiment of black soldiers organized by the Union accounted for her presence in the area of coastal South Carolina and the Sea Islands where the famous Port Royal experiment took place. She can be said to have been at least a witness, if not a part, of that experiment. Her primary interest at the time, understandably, was her husband and the soldiers associated with him. She lived within the orbit of their daily lives, taught some of them their letters, and, in other ways, such as nursing and laundering, did what she could to contribute to their comfort. She even accompanied them on a mission involving actual fighting to Florida. But she also taught the children of the black Sea Islanders whom the Yankees had liberated around Port Royal. Hence, her reminiscences, slight as they are, and highly anecdotal, as well as prolonged into her life long after the war, possess something of a special value because she and her husband were located, for historians, at so much of an appropriate place at equally so much of an appropriate time. Her husband died soon after the South surrendered. Taylor married again and eventually moved north to Boston. In her *Reminiscences,* in spite of her title, she follows her recollections of her youth, by means of which she obviously retrieves in memory a season—too remotely and utterly defunct—of hope, with vignettes of her life, not from her days at Port Royal, but from her long sequence of years afterward during which that season of hope dwindled into the disillusioning reality, for her and other Negroes, of post–Reconstruction America.

A final gleam of the slave narrative as written by individuals who once were slaves—although admittedly no more than a gleam—may be discerned in John Roy Lynch's *Reminiscences of an Active Life* and Ida Wells Barnett's *Crusade for Justice: The Autobiography of Ida B. Wells.* The publication of both these works was considerably expedited by John Hope Franklin, who included them in the Negro American Biographies and Autobiographies, for which, at the University of Chicago and through the University of Chicago Press, he was the series editor. Both books appeared in 1970.

Lynch was born in 1847 on a plantation in Louisiana, but only a few miles from Natchez, Mississippi. His mother was a decided mulatto; his father, a native of Dublin; and Lynch was as octoroon as Henry Bibb or Ellen Craft. Possessed of ability, character, and a personable nature, Lynch prospered both in business and as a Republican politician in Natchez during Reconstruction. He was only twenty-two years of age when he was appointed a justice of the peace. Not only was he elected to the Mississippi legislature. He became there the speaker of the house. At the age of twenty-five he went to Washington, D.C., as a member of Congress. Possibly his greatest public honor was his selection as temporary chairman and keynote speaker for the Republican national convention which nominated for the presidency James G. Blaine in 1884. He owned, and sold, plantations in Mississippi. He studied law and passed the bar. As a paymaster and officer in the United States Army, he traveled widely and saw the world. A year after his retirement from the army and his second marriage he moved, in 1912, to Chicago, where he resumed the practice of law, more than dabbled in real estate, and existed very comfortably until his death, as a nonagenarian, in 1939.

Lynch had, of course, participated in Reconstruction. The version of it perpetrated by the whites who wrote about it at the turn of the twentieth century, and closely thereafter, some of whom claimed to be serious historians, outraged Lynch with what he considered its monstrous and savage libels of the American Negro. He tried to provide an effective corrective in articles he wrote and the book *Facts of Reconstruction,* which he also wrote, and published in 1913. He thus battled a force he could not stem at the time he exerted himself to combat it. He was a slave long enough for his life during slavery to provide an element of interest in his *Reminiscences of an Active Life.* But it is Reconstruction, rather than slavery, which occupies the center of attention in his narrative of his years as slave and freedman.

Ida Wells Barnett was born Ida Wells, a slave, in Holly Springs, Mississippi, in 1862. The Civil War and slavery obviously were over before she was barely past her infancy. As a young woman she taught school in Mississippi, in Memphis, and in rural neighborhoods near Memphis. There was never a time when she was not an intrepid defender of the Negro's civil rights. She became involved in journalism while she was still in southwestern Tennessee. Her crusade against lynching attracted national attention and expanded to international dimensions with the trip she took to England to speak overseas against what she defined as the barbaric evil of this form of vigilante vengeance. She took up residence in Chicago in 1894. In 1895 she married the lawyer Ferdinand Barnett, member of a prominent Negro family, and published *A Red Record: Tabulated Statistics and Alleged Causes of Lynchings in the United States, 1892–1893–1894.* She raised a family but never lost her vigor as a public figure, whether in local affairs or, especially in her work with Negro women's clubs, as a Negro leader nationally. It was in 1928 that she decided to write the story of her own life, and she finished the manuscript of *Crusade for Justice* only shortly before her death in 1931. Her daughter, Alfreda M. Duster, edited the manuscript before entrusting it to John Hope Franklin.

Crusade for Justice, as could hardly be otherwise, touches only very lightly and in only a very few pages upon slavery. The portion of the abolitionist slave narrative in its heyday which it most repeats is the portion telling of a fugitive's new life after his escape to freedom. In a sense, then, it well may be a fitting coda to all the slave narratives of antebellum times. They made a great thing of a promised land. Barnett, even more than Suzie Taylor, lived long enough to know how sadly the writers of all such narratives, had they lived longer than they did, would have been forced to realize that their hopes were only dreams, and dreams no nearer, it seemed, of coming true in 1920 than in 1875.

Three works which can hardly qualify as slave narratives and yet which surely belong in a category that closely identifies them with genuine slave narratives are the journals of William Johnson and Charlotte Forten and the autobiography of John Mercer Langston. William Johnson was born a slave in Natchez in 1809. A white William Johnson freed the slave-born William Johnson's mother, Amy, in 1814. Amy Johnson had had a daughter, Adelia, whom this same white William Johnson freed in 1818, even though he found it necessary to send her to distant Philadelphia to do so. In 1821 the white William Johnson, certainly continuing to act like the father of Amy's children, freed the slave-born William Johnson. The freeman lived his whole life in Natchez. His sister, Adelia, had married a free Negro named Miller, who, at the time of their marriage, was Natchez' leading barber, irrespective of color. Miller took Adelia's brother under his wing as an apprentice barber as soon as young Johnson was freed. When the Millers moved to New Orleans in 1830 for Miller to practice barbering there, young Johnson took over Miller's shop in Natchez and barbered in his native town until, in 1851, he was killed from ambush by his adversary in a dispute about a boundary between the adjacent lands of the disputants. He had lived a life in many respects—although, of course, not quite entirely—indistinguishable from the lives lived by Natchez' most thriving white men. His barbershop, situated on the street which was, and was named, the main street of Natchez, grew to have six chairs. He owned a bathhouse and two one-chair barbershops. He made money as a moneylender. He owned the building on Main Street containing his barbershop and other buildings in the immediate vicinity. He also owned, eventually, fifteen slaves. He speculated, at times, in land, but he, in addition, became a landowner, the proprietor, indeed, of the very plantation possession of which provided the proximate cause of his death. He married, in 1835, the free Negro woman Ann Battles, by whom he was to have ten children and with whom nine of these children were to survive his death. In the same year in which he married he started a diary, which he continued until he died.

Johnson's diary, however, remained virtually unknown for almost a hundred years. Scholars became aware of its existence in 1938. Edited by William Ransom Hogan and Edwin Adams Davis as the first volume in the series Source Studies in Southern History, a project of Louisiana State University Press, it appeared, in 1951, under the title *William Johnson's Natchez: The Ante-Bellum Diary of a Free Negro,* and were it nothing more than the nonpareil it is, it would be memorable. But it also accumulates, within the broad, comprehensive composite it provides of an American town in the period within that town's greatest fame, telling miniatures, little pictures inside the big picture, with each little picture a gem of statement about, in scattered segments, the customary actions, the familiar scenes, and the occasional, sometimes exciting departures from the usual events of the day which constitute the fabric of normal human lives at any place and time. Thus, it is history of a very good and special kind, a past recovered precisely as it was before it died. Moreover, the sort of person Johnson apparently was may well enhance the sense of authenticity in his miniatures. For, superior though he always showed himself to be in the management of his estate, otherwise he seems sufficiently unexceptional to be the perfect reflector of the ordinary world around him. Not for him were the critical perceptions, the assertions of individualized consciousness (or conscience), of a Douglass, or an Alexander Crummell, or, even, a Henry Bibb. Certainly, too, not for him, as for such Negroes, was the use of the intellect to explore the too abstruse or the too loftily ideal. And, if he had any semblances of the talent of such Negroes for brooding over the mysteries of the cosmos or of social justice, those semblances he most assuredly did not complicate with sentiments which impassioned him to crusade against a *status quo.* He wrote as he lived. And so, as a diarist, he was the perfect ingenue. His were the eyes of an average man in a Natchez where, to accord with the dominant collective point of view, although more blacks inhabited Johnson's Natchez than whites, the average man was white. Essentially, then, Johnson was white. Nor did he keep his diary to object to his ethnic orientation. He looked in virtually every way a white man. He reasoned in virtually every way as he looked. His pen, therefore, could not subscribe to a black identity which was not his. Here is an excerpt from the entry in his diary for December 20, 1836:

Yesterday in the afternoon I Let Mr Ingraham have my Little Sorrill mare on tryal to wride out home, and he Promised me to send Her in Early in the morning and it is now night and she has not been sent in yet, I am beginning to think that He has made off with Her—I sold Mr R. Evans a pair of handsome Razors to day on a Credit for $6 and I also Sold a pair to Mr John Coleman of Jefferson County, very handsome Ones for five Dollars Cash—I wrode out this Evening by the Oil Mill and there I saw a large Fox Squirrill on a tree quite close to the House—Col Bingaman Closed a Race to be ran ten Days before the Jocky Clubb Racess—He runs a Sorrill mare that He calls the Lavender Girl against Naked Truth, 4 miles heats—He made the Race with Mr Lee Claibourne, This mare that the Col Runs is the one that Jumped over Board off the Steam Boat

Except, perhaps, for some of its titles of personal address, the passage above could have been written, complete with its misspellings and other marks of lack of schooling, by almost any of the new white frontier aristocrats of the Old Southwest, one of whom, Andrew Jackson, it is easy to remember, no less illiterate than Johnson, ascended to the presidency of the United States. Jackson's rough edges, however, did not prevent him from building the Hermitage. Those who succeeded among young America's adventurous commoners were rarely, if ever, slow to reveal that they, too, respected civilization's graces. Had Johnson been white he could not have followed more faithfully the pattern of a prevailing regional culture. As soon as he was able, he furnished his own dwelling in Natchez with tokens of the "aristocratic" refinement he sought to make a part of his life and, even more, almost surely, of the lives of his children. He purchased, of musical instruments alone, long before his children grew up, a piano, a guitar, a flute, and violins. Still, he unwearyingly kept his eye on the wellsprings of his prosperity. Numerous entries in his diary begin with references to his business, which is described, for example, variously as "tolerable," "dull," "good," "Tolerable fair," "very Good," "getting very Dull, indeed," or comparably so through a whole scale of gradations, expressive of the acuteness of his regard for the health of his many sorties into the pursuit of profit, although no related acuteness ever taught him to spell *business* other than "buisness."

In a world where business counted, Johnson refrained from ever underestimating its value. Like the whites in this world, whose minds and feelings he had internalized, he worshipped business. After business, when and where business permitted, he lived the rest of his life, also always like the whites of the class to which he might well have belonged had he been altogether white. We have cited his obeisance to the arts. In somewhat different forms of pastime not unseemly for white males in Natchez with his financial and social assets, he hunted, he fished, he gambled a little, particularly on horse races, and he owned, free Negro as he was, some of the horses that ran in these very races, which he was allowed to watch unsegregated, whether or not he was betting on them. He traveled north-east once, to Philadelphia and New York, as well as south, more frequently, to New Orleans. He treated his own slaves with relative benevolence (as would have, presumably, the white he might have been), although he did not hesitate to punish them upon occasion, even with the lash. From a distance safe for himself, he observed politics and politicians. From an equal distance, albeit somewhat more warily (as well as with actual testiness when, in his view of the passing scene, he thought he detected injudicious behavior on the part of a free Negro or an unemancipated black), he steadily maintained his own private surveillance, and analysis, of the nonwhites of Natchez. Understandably, he appreciated, and approved, the advantages which free Negroes enjoyed over slaves in his community, if not ubiquitously in the South.

A wisp—and only a wisp—of the fever of abolitionism did reach Natchez in the 1840s. It was a wisp which received no welcome and no fanning of its potential flame from Johnson. With what might well be considered, for antebellum Natchez at any date of its existence, a minimum of violence, the wisp of abolitionism was deflected elsewhere. It came, and went, without the slightest visible impact upon Johnson and his relations with Natchez. Nor did it affect discernibly the Johnson of the diary. Almost like a test, it confirms his taste for moderation (if that is what it was). Of some things in his diary he simply will not speak. With something of the restrictions of a Vermeer, he crowds upon his canvas the outer trappings of human individuals accommodating themselves to the circumstances of their society. He goes, substantially, no farther. There may have been, somewhere, a Johnson who yearned, like Socrates or Plato or St. Augustine, to know what is ultimately real, or to conceive of, as many men have wished, social justice and the best of states, or even, as many American blacks have aspired, to apprehend what is needed in America to end the problems between America's whites and America's blacks. No such Johnson, either in whole or in part, appears in Johnson's diary. That diary is matter-of-fact, so matter-of-fact, indeed, as to be, if not substantially a flawless reproduction of a Negro who, in a southern antebellum setting, fulfilled to the last distinctive detail the twentieth-century Black Militant's definition of an *oreo* (a Negro, usually bourgeois, cravenly determined to be white), then a masterpiece of duplicity, and the masquerade of a superb dissembler, wherein a divided soul displays to others only his blandest demeanor while hiding completely from everyone but himself the part of himself in torment. Whichever Johnson's diary is, Johnson's family reverently preserved it. The bulk of it was retrieved from the attic of the widow of Johnson's grandson, a medical doctor who had accepted the change of the family name to Johnston but had not, thus, repudiated his ties to the diarist of an earlier day.

This diarist and Charlotte Forten, except that they were both free Negroes during slavery, whiter in physiognomy than most blacks, and exempt from financial cares, were otherwise arrestingly unlike, as distant from each other in temperament and training as the Philadelphia where Forten was born in 1837 from Natchez in Johnson's day above or below its hill. Forten was an idealist from whose intensest cerebrations issues of social justice, very much including slavery and personal ethics, were never absent. She worried about her color, not because she rejected it, but because she wanted the world to know, certainly from all of her own words and deeds, how meritorious Negroes could be and how utterly despicable it was that any whites should mistreat blacks solely because those blacks were not white. James Forten was her grandfather. Her favorite aunt, one of James Forten's three daughters already mentioned as the subjects of an adulatory poem by John Greenleaf Whittier, was married to Robert Purvis. Whether in her grandfather's palatial mansion on Philadelphia's Lombard Street, where she lived (and her grandfather died when she was only five), or at Byberry, Purvis' gentleman farmer's farm fifteen miles away in the Pennsylvania countryside, she existed in luxury. So, however, she was only more conscious of her obligation to her race. Her grandfather, her father, and Purvis, like all their friends, some of whom were influential whites, and the whole Forten-Purvis family axis, were fervent abolitionists. Until the end of slavery Charlotte Forten would be a dedicated and active opponent of slavery.

Forten was sixteen when she was sent to school in Salem, Massachusetts, in part to both escape and protest against racial discrimination in education in Philadelphia. She wrote the class poem for the class with which she graduated in Salem. She would write more poetry in her life, but she was never seriously a poet. She taught in Salem and then went home to Philadelphia at an early manifestation in herself of what, in her day, was sometimes called "lung fever." When the Port Royal experiment

was instituted, she was free to go south, as she did, and join it as one of
the northern teachers who undertook, through it, to help prove that liberation of Negroes from slavery was not an anathema to nature. After the
war she moved to Washington, D.C., where she met Francis Grimké,
one of the Grimké brothers sired by a Charleston aristocrat from his slave
mistress, Nancy Weston. Forten was thirteen years older than Grimké,
but she married him, in 1878, and bore him a daughter who died in
infancy. Grimké, incidentally, never ceased to worship her. She was, he
said, "one of the dearest, sweetest, loveliest spirits that ever graced this
planet." He was pastor of the Fifteenth Street Presbyterian Church when
he married her. For three years in the 1880s, he served a Presbyterian
church in Jacksonville, Florida. He went there because he also had problems with "lung fever." He and his wife, however, returned from Florida,
his health improved, to his Washington pastorate, which he did not re-
linquish, except as an *emeritus*, until his death at the advanced age of
eighty-seven in 1937. His wife, fragile as she always appeared to be, had
then been dead for a quarter of a century, but still had lived well past the
scriptural threescore and ten.

Forten, who published poetry in various periodicals, articles, notably
two poems about Port Royal in the *Atlantic Monthly*, and a translation, in
1869, of M. M. Erckmann-Chatrian's *Madame Thérèse; or, The Volunteers
of '92*, began her journal in Salem in May, 1854. She continued it, more
regularly than not, until May, 1864. Then she apparently put it aside,
not to write in it again until she made scattered additions to it intermit-
tently, and not too frequently, throughout the years from November,
1885, until July, 1892. Preserved in manuscript, her journal eventually
was edited by Ray Allen Billington, with considerable deletions in its entries from 1854 to 1862 and complete omission of all entries after 1864,
and published, as *The Journal of Charlotte Forten: A Free Negro in the Slave
Era*, in 1953. This version of it appeared as a paperback in 1961.

No crudities of composition comparable to those so often to be found
in William Johnson's diary occur in Forten's *Journal*. She was, of course,
trained to be a schoolmistress. A photograph reproduced on the cover of
the paperback edition of the *Journal* shows her, her every feature unmistakably Caucasian, a book held lightly by hidden hands on her lap, ear-
nestly and steadfastly looking out upon the world around her. Earnestness and steadfastness, indeed, set the tone for her *Journal* as for her entire
life. Refined she intended to be, as well as stalwart in her championship
of her race. She enters in her *Journal* for Tuesday, January 23, 1855:

Read a report of one of Lowell's lectures on English Poetry. They are interesting and contain many beautiful thoughts which only a true poet could have. In the evening took a pleasant walk with my dear teacher [Mary L. Shepard?], as far as the entrance of Harmony Grove. The moon was shedding a soft light over the beautiful spot, and the perfect quiet was only broken by the music of a tiny waterfall which the dark evergreens concealed from our sight. It was a lovely night. We stopped at Mrs. Putnam's [a colored resident of Salem] and spent some time there in very animated conversation about slavery and prejudice.

Forten seems most true to herself in such an entry. She reads Lowell's lectures, and she engages in a discussion of slavery and prejudice. So her world turned. Nor are other deeply rooted sensibilities of hers absent from this entry. A creature of her age, she regarded nature with Wordsworthian (as well as somewhat Gothic) inclinations, keenly aware of the moon, the waterfall, and the beauty of the night. She was a romantic as well as something of a genteel revolutionary, an apostle of beauty as well as a consecrated acolyte of the intellect. A goodly number of the "best people" in the reform movements which flourished in her day were familiar to her. She knew them in person as they knew her. And so she measured herself against exalted standards, and although her *Journal* is not, for example, *Praeterita* or the autobiography of John Stuart Mill, it is a respectable self-portrait of a person who sincerely sought a lofty level of cultivation for her mind and soul.

Forten may be at her best in her southern entries. Port Royal and its environs were like an exotic foreign country to her. She went to the former slaves there with the same missionary spirit as the white Yankees who labored as did she in the Port Royal experiment. Her *Journal* indicates her conscientious discharge of her duties toward the blacks she had come south to aid. But passages of it record impressions from her of the South either anthropological or aesthetic, or both, in their primary interest. She was only disembarked for a few hours off the steamer which had brought her to the South Carolina coast from New York when she found herself, during a sunset the glory of which she ecstatically remarked, in a boat propelled by a crew of Negro oarsmen whose singing, as they rowed, profoundly affected her with its "sweetness, strangeness and solemnity!" Among the numbers they rendered was a "Roll, Jordan, Roll" which she thought was grand, and she, apparently, made a note of their

Jesus make de blind to see
Jesus make de deaf to hear

> Jesus make de cripple walk
> Walk in, dear Jesus

with its refrain, "No man can hender me." Avidly, throughout her stay at, and near, Port Royal, as if she were a folklorist on assignment, she listened to, and remembered, the Negro singing she was privileged to hear, none of which, it seems, from what her *Journal* says, was secular— never a work song or a forerunner of the blues or the lyrics of jazz—but all of which fell within the related provinces of the spirituals and shouts. And she was no less a folklorist as she reacted to such aspects of the life of the southern Negroes she encountered as their family relations, the role of their elders in their community, their comparisons of their new, free status with their lot under slavery, and their perceptions of the cultural ties which bound them to the other members of the special black community their relative isolation within their particular locality had fostered. She went once, for example, to a collection of Negro houses known in the Port Royal neighborhood as "The Corner," where lived, among others, a black great-grandmother named Venus and a woman who gave Forten some tanias, edible roots which, boiled, Forten failed to find appetizing but may well have recognized as an expression of group mores, a gesture of appreciation which the inhabitants of "The Corner" probably felt the circumstances of Forten's visit to them required.

Race consciousness, as should be expected, can be repeatedly detected in the southern entries of Forten's *Journal*. One of her talks to the children she was teaching lauded Toussaint L'Ouverture. In Beaufort she was able to spend some time in the company of Harriet Tubman. The experience excited her and was good for her sense of racial pride. Of the black soldiers under Colonel Thomas W. Higginson in the regiment of 1st South Carolina Volunteers she was sympathetically aware. And of the black 54th Massachusetts, terribly repulsed at Fort Wagner, she says in her *Journal*, "Thank Heaven! they fought bravely!" But another kind of repercussion from her race consciousness also is probably intimated by her *Journal*. She undoubtedly resented color caste, but, apparently, her rebellion against it did not encompass intermarriage on her part. Almost surely she considered such a concession to white masculinity a betrayal of her race and a desertion of her fight to demonstrate that whites were not genetically superior to blacks. In an entry dated May 18, 1863, she speaks in her *Journal* of a certain Mr. Thorpe, a young white companion of hers in the Port Royal experiment. She explicitly stipulates that rumor imparts to Mr. Thorpe amorous sentiments toward her of a nature normally associated with proposals of marriage. Whatever, however, is in Mr. Thorpe's mind, she clearly does not envision as a development to which she would accede a future with him as his wife.

Of another young white man, also a companion of hers in the Port Royal experiment, a Dr. Seth Rogers from Worcester, Massachusetts, she does speak rather often in her *Journal,* always in terms of admiration tempered with a tenderness not discernible in references by her to anyone else she met in the South. And yet a palpable reserve accompanies this tenderness, as if she very consciously wants her *Journal* to show that marriage with Dr. Rogers is a possibility she never contemplates. Candor, sometimes read between the lines, yet more frequently fiercely, proudly overt, is one of the great merits of Forten's *Journal.* So, too, is its measure of provision of evidence which helps to fill in a woeful gap in historic Americana. For far too long, conventional recollections of the American past have tended to exclude women of the Forten stamp. Her *Journal* makes both herself, and her kind, less invisible.

Johnson and Forten kept their records of their lives—at least ostensibly—not necessarily for public scrutiny. They wrote of themselves, apparently, above all else to talk to themselves about themselves. John Mercer Langston's *From the Virginia Plantation to the National Capital,* published in 1894, is neither a journal nor a diary, but an autobiography clearly intended to reach as large an audience as it might attract.[3] It is written in the third person, somewhat felicitously, for it is, from beginning to end, an arrantly shameless laudation of the man who wrote it. Langston, however, may be forgiven, in some degree, his high opinion of himself. He was a person more endowed with abilities he could turn to good use for himself and the general welfare than all except a decidedly minuscule minority of humankind. And he did lead a life worthy of much commendation. That life, moreover, began as an element of a story contradictory to almost everything traditional in a love story about American lovers.

Langston, born in 1829, was the last of four children, a daughter and three sons, borne by Lucy Langston to Captain Ralph Quarles, who had fought valorously on the American side in the Revolution, owned a relatively large, benevolently administered, and fairly prosperous plantation

---

3. John Mercer Langston, *From the Virginia Plantation to the National Capital* (Hartford, Conn. 1894).

in Louisa County, Virginia, and was a collateral descendant of Francis Quarles, the Cavalier poet. Through a second son of his, Charles, by Lucy Langston, he would be a great-grandfather of Langston Hughes. There can hardly be any other way to describe his attachment to Lucy Langston than as a true and deathless love of remarkable constancy and intensity. He never married. Obviously, in antebellum Virginia he could not have married Lucy. She was part Indian and part black. But he treated her, until his death, as his fervently adored wife and the respected mistress of his plantation (on which, incidentally, no white, except himself, resided). Even so, it does not appear that his love for Lucy, and fidelity toward her, were any greater than her love for him, and its attendant controls of her conduct. Perhaps significantly, in 1834 he and she (he first) died within a few weeks of each other, following which, to their unusual love story, was added an equally unusual aftermath. Captain Quarles had left a will which, among other provisions, stipulated that Charles and his younger brother, our Langston, should be sent north and educated. So Charles and the last of the offspring of the captain and the woman he treasured above conformity to the mores of his moment and milieu were conveyed to Ohio, where both of them did go to school. So, too, the circumstances surrounding Langston's birth and youth diverge dramatically from what may have been expected of them in his day.

In Ohio, Langston lived, well cared for by friends and relatives, in Chillicothe, in Cincinnati, and then in Chillicothe again. Neither in Chillicothe nor in Cincinnati was he to experience any problem with his formal education. Indeed, in Chillicothe, during his second stay there, he was a pupil of George Vashon, the Negro poet of whom more will be said here later. Langston acquired degrees at both the bachelor's and the master's level from Oberlin College, studied law in the offices of Judge Phileman Bliss, was admitted to the Ohio bar, was elected town clerk (not concurrently) in both Brounhelm and Oberlin, communities near each other in northern Ohio, married in her senior year at Oberlin College a Caroline Wall, who had fled North Carolina for greener pastures with other members of her free-Negro family, and made a name for himself in northern Ohio with his string of triumphs in defenses in court, where, as counsel for an accused, he seemed sometimes to surmount formidable opposing odds. In the one exercise of his legal skills which, probably, he never matched for brilliance, he saved from conviction of murder Edmonia Lewis, whom the state had charged with killing a white fellow woman student of hers at Oberlin College. Lewis became, in her later life (and in Europe), the first black woman sculptor of note.

The Civil War and some of the changes it precipitated separated Langston, and his family, from northern Ohio. As an inspector general for the Freedmen's Bureau, he traveled widely through the South before 1870. At Howard University he was the founder and dean of the school of law and a vice-president and acting president of the university. Rutherford B. Hayes appointed him resident minister and consul general to Haiti, as well as, concurrently, chargé d'affaires to the Dominican Republic. His diplomatic career ended with the ouster of the Republicans from the White House by Grover Cleveland. Returning to the academic world and to the state of his birth, he served as president of the Virginia Normal and Collegiate Institute, now Virginia State University, from December, 1885, until December, 1887. After a struggle to be seated, he served a portion of a term in the United States House of Representatives, the only Negro yet to reach Congress from Virginia. He died in 1897. Douglass, for whom he lost no love, and who lost no love for him, outshone him as the premier American Negro of their joint day. Almost surely, only for Douglass could such a claim be made.

Langston's autobiography covers virtually all of his life. He, like Samuel Ringgold Ward and Douglass, achieved an enviable reputation as an orator in his own time. Like Ward, and unlike Douglass, he possessed few of the qualities which could have lifted what he wrote into a sphere of excellence comparable with that of what he said to the live audiences he never seemed to fail to captivate. The prose he penned is pedestrian, and nowhere in his autobiography does he demonstrate an artist's ability to endow with life a reproduction of reality. Indeed, in his autobiography he writes as if he were a petty bureaucrat preparing an official report padded, moreover, with letters and documents few people would care to read. Undoubtedly, he enjoys himself most when he is presenting (as he far too often does) views of himself in action which obviously he thinks illustrate his superiority invariably to mortals who must contend with him. He says, for instance, of his closing speech in the hitherto mentioned trial of Edmonia Lewis:

Finally, when the State had made its last argument, the prosecuting attorney closing his lengthy, admirable address amid the plaudits of his associates and a large proportion of the people, after an adjournment of thirty minutes Mr. Langston was permitted to make his closing argument in support of his motion. His argument, whose delivery occupied all of six full hours, as his friends and the journals claimed at the time, was replete with learning upon the subjects involved, addressed with the greatest care and skill to the court, clear, forcible and effective, from first to last commanding the closest attention, and at times moving all who heard it to tears, with manifestations, even to outbursts, of the deepest feeling.[4]

This unabashed panegyric upon himself fairly represents Langston as an autobiographer. Such is his stature as a monument of the Afro-American past that his autobiography can hardly be ignored. Otherwise, little that is good can be said of this contribution to Afro-American letters.

Langston, in truth, wrote much in the vein of Horatio Alger. Not only was he never a slave, champion of justice for his race though he undeniably was, and near contemporary of most of the writers of abolitionist slave narratives. All, if any, resemblances between his autobiography and abolitionist slave narratives are faint and, quite possibly, coincidental. The temptation to attribute to the abolitionist slave narrative more impact upon Afro-American life and letters than it actually had may easily exist. Since the upsurge of interest in the Afro-American past allied to the great increase of activism for black civil rights and the corresponding increase in emphasis on black pride beginning in the 1960s— although not, be it carefully noted, in quite the same ways as during the Harlem Renaissance—everyone, as it were, seems to know of slave narratives and to honor them. It was not always so—far from it. The abolitionist slave narratives essentially disappeared from the public consciousness with the actual achievement of abolition's big goal, the end of slavery. Not only in white schools but in black as well, whether before college or afterward, the generations of Americans who reached maturity as the twentieth century approached and, later, as the century moved on to pass its midpoint, heard of many things, but rarely, if ever, of slave narratives. In the white schools, of course, the failure to talk about slave narratives was only part of the general failure there to talk about Negroes at all, unless disparagingly. In the segregated schools, where, for their elementary and secondary education, black children congregated, an occasional black teacher might include in the curriculum black poetry such as, for instance, Paul Laurence Dunbar's "Ode to Ethiopia." But departures, even so limited, from the texts, all of them "white," universally prescribed then for the American school required, on the part of any

4. *Ibid.*, 179.

teacher, white or black, daring as well as independence. Not even in black normal schools and colleges then was a student too likely to encounter any literature other than that purveyed at the white institutions of higher learning where the supposedly best-trained teachers of Negro youth in that day took their advanced degrees.

On their own black campuses, where law and custom herded them, Negro students, for almost a century after the Negro's emancipation, heard, with only few exceptions, of Chaucer, Shakespeare, Tennyson, and other writers equally white. It is, happily, too much to say to charge that no black teachers brought to the attention of their black students any black writers. Even so, the black writers of slave narratives were not the black writers whose memories, for years, black teachers tended to preserve. Benjamin Brawley's *A Social History of the American Negro*, published in 1921, is virtually altogether silent about slave narratives.[5] J. Saunders Redding's quite estimable account of Negro literature, *To Make a Poet Black*, published in 1939, hardly is less silent than *A Social History*. Finally, in the epochal anthology *The Negro Caravan*, edited by Sterling Brown, Arthur Davis, and Ulysses Lee, and published two years after *To Make a Poet Black*, the section entitled "Autobiography" includes excerpts from the slave narratives of Milton Clarke, Josiah Henson, Solomon Northup, Frederick Douglass, and Elizabeth Keckley. So *The Negro Caravan* heralded a resurrection. For more than two generations the slave narratives were too ignored to constitute the vade mecum of the black writer's consciousness they are sometimes said to be.

5. Benjamin Brawley, *A Social History of the American Negro* (New York, 1921).

8. Antebellum Black Leaders

During the very years when the abolitionist slave narratives flourished, there were, as earlier in Afro-American history, some blacks not particularly interested in writing as a vocation but prominent for their qualities of leadership, especially in representing the aspirations of their fellow blacks, who did sometimes turn to writing in conjunction with their activities as racial leaders. The earliest of these blacks in our Age of the Abolitionists seems to have been Theodore S. Wright.

Wright, like Peter Williams, Jr., and James Forten the child of free black parents, no less than Williams and Forten asserted constantly his pedigreed Americanism, if only as an intended exhibit hopefully of great weight in his never-ceasing argument that he should not be treated by Americans except as merely another American. He was born, it has been said, in Providence, Rhode Island, but more probably in New Jersey, in 1797. His father was to be a person of consequence in the national Negro conventions of the quarter of a century beginning in the early 1830s. Wright himself was first educated at the African Free School in New York City. Supported by De Witt Clinton, Arthur Tappan, and others, at the rather advanced age of twenty-eight in 1825, he enrolled in the Princeton Theological Seminary, from which he became, three years later, of that institution, its first black graduate. Almost immediately thereafter, he succeeded Samuel Cornish as the pastor of the very influential (among blacks) First Colored Presbyterian Church in New York City. He then had only nineteen years of life left to him. He died in 1847. It is remarkable how actively he spent the less than a double decade of mortality left to him. He did, incidentally, marry, an Adaline T.

Turpin of New Rochelle, New York, in 1837, one month before his for-tieth birthday.

Leadership of a high order Wright gave to his own congregation. But he also involved himself with Presbyterians who were not his parish-ioners and not necessarily black. Indeed, he was elected, in 1845, moder-ator of the Third Presbytery of New York. In his day, as we have previ-ously noted, reformers tended to embrace more than one reform and to crusade on more than one front. Wright was typical of the reformers of his day. He served a term as an officer of the New York City Temperance Society. He did not shy away from politics. Staunchly he affiliated him-self with the Liberty party at its birth, never deserting it as long as it existed in spite of his broad conviction against Negroes tying themselves too tightly to any political party. He followed closely the fortunes of the *Amistad* mutineers, as he had followed closely the emancipation of slaves in the British West Indies, for his ardor to improve the lot of man was little, if any, affected by geography. His heart bled for people he knew. It also bled for people he would never see. So he was, in 1841, one of the founding fathers, and the first treasurer, of the Union Missionary So-ciety, which dedicated itself to spreading Christianity both in America and abroad—abroad to the society meaning, especially, Africa. And he was very interested in Africa, partly because of his vehement opposition to colonizationism. Five years after its founding, the Union Missionary Society would be, with three other groups, absorbed into the American Missionary Association, of which, for a year until his death, he would be one of the five vice-presidents. But he would still have time to work with the New York Committee of Vigilance (and thus with, among other things, the Underground Railroad) in the schism between the Garrison-ians and anti-Garrisonians, to play a rather prominent role in the forma-tion of the new American and Foreign Antislavery Society, and, as an advocate far forward in the front ranks of advocates among his fellow Negroes of the doctrine of Negro self-help, to become a vice-president of the Phoenix Society of New York and, then, shortly before his death, president of Phoenix High School, a project of the society.

Wright spent much more of his life performing as a live speaker than as a writer. Some of his speeches were printed, however authoritatively or not, in his own day in, for instance, the *Colored American* and the *Libera-tor*. Two of his speeches, considered among his best and delivered to an antislavery convention at Utica, New York, in 1837, appear in the well-known *Negro Orators and Their Orations*, which Carter G. Woodson edited in 1925. One of these speeches is entitled "The Progress of the Anti-Slavery Cause," the other, "Prejudice Against the Colored Man." A pastoral letter from his pen, dated June 30, 1832, may be found in *Early Negro Writing, 1760–1837, Selected and Introduced by Dorothy B. Porter*, published in 1971. One of his more ambitious attempts to exploit the written word for purposes dear to him occurs in the pamphlet *Prayer of a Colonizationist*, which he coauthored with Samuel Cornish. The *Prayer*, a satire not notable for its subtlety, purports to emanate from a colonizationist, an excellent example of all his fellow colonizationists, whose distaste for Negroes and hypocritical parades of virtue color virtu‐ally every syllable he utters. To this colonizationist blackness is its own hereditary curse, and every black person should be subject to social con‐trols which recognize the inescapable inferiority of blacks to other human beings.

Yet Wright, bitter and never-failing as was his own revulsion from whites too much, in the actual flesh, replicas of his caricature of them in his fictive colonizationist, harbored no sentiments which made him at all a replica in reverse of the whites he hated. He held nothing against any whites simply because of their whiteness. Rather, he prized highly some attitudes and codes of conduct which, while he might well have encoun‐tered them among both blacks and whites, he certainly regarded as com‐ponents of the most virtuous elements in white American culture. So he speaks, it may be said, both as a defender of his black identity and, yet, as the practitioner of an ethic of Christian charity shared by him with many whites when he tells, in probably his most widely noticed publication (dated 1836), his "Letter to Rev. Archibald Alexander, D.D.," of some‐thing which happened to him at Princeton, where the Reverend Mr. Al‐exander had been one of his highly respected teachers. The something which happened was outrageous. Wright, quite innocent, it seems, of any motive that could have been termed "ulterior," but merely as a fond old graduate returning to a scene he had learned to love, had attended an annual meeting of a literary society at Princeton in the chapel of the seminary. Just when the meeting was virtually over, a young, thickset Princetonian, a perfect stranger to Wright, shouting "Out with the Nig‐ger," grasped Wright rudely and ejected him from the chapel. It is clear that Wright corresponds with his former teacher to provide for himself a forum by means of which he can castigate a blatant racist. But he ends his remarks to the Reverend Mr. Alexander with an expression of his own desire always to abide by principles that will not let him retaliate in kind against people like the Princetonian who had laid unfriendly hands on him.

Of Wright, apparently, it must be said that he was genuinely (or genuinely tried to be) as impartial and far seeing of perspective as he could in his views on American racism. A similar tribute seems due to William Whipper, a worthy forerunner of Martin Luther King in his advocacy of a philosophy of nonviolence. Whipper's affluence placed him in the same advantageous position for championing the interests of his fellow Negroes as Paul Cuffe and James Forten. Rather curiously, however, as prominent as he was in his own day, two versions of his life, especially in its earlier phases, are current still among scholars of the Afro-American past.

According to one of these versions, Whipper (the grandfather of the actor Leigh Whipper) was born in Little Britain Township in Pennsylvania, probably (although not certainly) in 1804, and lived a youth about which no facts are truly known. He first appeared distinctly in Philadelphia in 1828, where he was then engaged in trade as a cleaner of clothes who sanitized his customers' garments by resort to a process called steam scouring; later, in Philadelphia still, by 1834 he appeared even more distinctly as the proprietor of a "free labor and temperance" grocery store which he had opened in a building immediately adjacent to Big Bethel, the mother church of African Methodism. He moved away from Philadelphia in 1835 to Columbia, Pennsylvania, at which place he married, in 1836, a Harriet Smith and soon became a business partner of the wealthy Negro lumber merchant Stephen Smith, who has not been identified as a relative of Whipper's wife. This version of Whipper's life stipulates 1876 as the year of his death.

In the existing alternate version of his life, Whipper was born in 1801 but did not die until 1885. His youth, far from being shrouded in obscurity, was spent in Columbia, Pennsylvania, where he was born to a well-to-do white father and a black household slave of this man. Moreover, with important results for the man Whipper was to become—a man at home, and happy, with the world of letters—he was raised in his father's house, sharing a tutor with his younger, white half-brother until his half-brother went off to college at Swarthmore, after which, even so, his half-brother brought home to him the lessons the half-brother had received at college for Whipper to absorb the learning in them also. Both versions of Whipper's life agree as to Whipper's proprietorship of the grocery store in

Philadelphia and his partnership with Stephen Smith. Indeed, they agree on virtually everything about Whipper's life after 1835 other than the year of his death.

The Smith and Whipper firm prospered mightily. With a portion of the profits from the lumber it sold, it bought railroad boxcars and operated a highly lucrative freightage service to Philadelphia. Whipper came to own the land, with a fine, large residence on it, surrounding the free-soil end of the bridge across the Susquehanna River at Columbia. Thus he was able to establish a very active station of the Underground Railroad. Fugitive slaves from Maryland and Virginia arrived by stealth at Whipper's house and grounds, where there were, of course, secret nooks and crannies for their concealment. Some of these fugitives were sent west to Pittsburgh by boat. Others went on northeast to Philadelphia, often, if not always, in the false end of a Smith and Whipper boxcar. Still others were convoyed as far as Canada, while a not inconsiderable number remained in Columbia, within the island of relative security there largely made possible by the aid, comfort, and protection Whipper was never too immersed in his own affairs or too weary of playing the good Samaritan to extend to them. Whipper additionally gave a thousand dollars every year from 1847 to 1860 to the abolitionists, although he purchased, in 1853, land at Dawn, the colony for free Negroes in Canada, near Dresden, probably both alarmed and depressed, as were many other Negroes, by the Fugitive Slave Act of 1850 and the dangers it posed for all Negroes in the North, fugitive slaves or not. During the Civil War, in one cash contribution, he gave five thousand dollars to the Union's fight against the South. After the Civil War, he lived, at separate times, both in Philadelphia and New Brunswick, New Jersey. He was an officer of the branch of the Freedman's Savings Bank in Philadelphia. He died, after an illness that persisted for almost three years, in Philadelphia.

Whipper apparently wrot: no books, nor is there extant, it would seem, any collection containing a sampling from the many pieces of largely expository prose he published during his lifetime. For, impressively industrious and successful though he was, both at adding substance to his own store of worldly goods and at devoting time, energy, and skill to the campaign against the mistreatment of the Negro, he was still able to live the life of someone who could not turn his back upon the invisible, insubstantial realm of speculation dear to those determined to use as fully as they might their own capacities for exploring the nature and nuances of noumena. Like Thomas Browne, he loved what Thomas

Browne was wont to call an "O Altitudo." He lacked only, when he wrote, the disciplines upon his style and natural aptitudes he might well have acquired had he not been forced to educate himself so excessively through his own interpretations of materials he studied alone. He is, indeed, a prime example of why men and women who seek to develop cultivated intellects suffer, almost always, a fatal deprivation when they must forgo, as they mature, the exposure of their experiments in learning to the critical examination of trained observers other than themselves. The Whippers of this world, the self-made practitioners of the traditions of intellectualism, too often turn out like Whipper. There are communally developed ways to say what they want to say and think what they want to think, elements of taste and discretion with which they are not familiar because they have not been properly socialized in their attempts at literacy in its most polite and gracious forms. There are infelicities in Whipper's prose at times, bombast and prolixities especially, which should not be there and which it is easy to suspect are probably attributable to the solitariness of his training. But there is, also, persistently in Whipper's prose a sense of the presence of a strong, healthy, vigorous cerebration insisting on the exercise and externalizing of its own vitality, and so there is never, in Whipper's prose, a complete absence of ideas worthy of careful and sympathetic examination.

With no significant exceptions Whipper's written compositions tend to be essays, speeches, or letters. He flourished as a writer almost exclusively from the 1830s until the 1850s and then fell almost totally mute. He published in quite a number of periodicals, including Garrison's *Liberator*, the *Emancipator* (organ of the anti-Garrisonian abolitionists), the *National Anti-Slavery Standard* (of which James Russell Lowell was, for a while, one of the editors), the *Demosthenian Shield*, both Douglass' *North Star* and *Douglass' Monthly*, the *Pennsylvania Freeman*, the *National Enquirer*, and the *Anglo-African*, the last perhaps as ambitious a project as any among all the various kinds of periodicals of the early Afro-American press. Moreover, Whipper tried his hand at editing. He had zealously supported the convention movement. Indeed, he seems to have been the only supporter of that movement who attended every convention sponsored by it between 1830 and 1835. Out of somewhat the same impulses as those responsible for the convention movement there had come into being, by the middle of the 1830s, an organization called the American Moral Reform Society, most of the members of which were black Philadelphians. The Moral Reformers, however, placed a premium upon transcending the problems of blackness and, thus, upon the desirability of integration. They sought a royal road to an earthly paradise shared without color bars by everyone. Whipper was one of their most dedicated spirits and the editor of their magazine, the *National Reformer,* the first magazine edited by an American Negro, which published its first issue in September, 1838, and its last in December, 1839.

Very possibly no single work by Whipper was better known during his own lifetime than his "Address on Non-Resistance to Offensive Aggression," which appeared in four consecutive installments in the *Colored American* in September, 1837. As its title suggests, this work is a plea for nonviolence. It recommends, as a fitting and necessary corrective to man's physical assaults upon his human neighbors, nonviolent resolutions of human conflict based upon admonitions from divine law and principles of conduct compatible with the dictates of human reason. The Whipper who wrote this work strongly advocates integration. He is still an almost starry-eyed Moral Reformer. But the Whipper who anticipated Martin Luther King, Jr., in his attitude toward nonviolence also anticipated W. E. B. Du Bois in a shift of his position, as he grew older, vis-à-vis integration and black nationalism. In the 1830s and 1840s Whipper objected even to the use of words like *colored* and *African* by Negroes in their references to themselves, and he vigorously decried any disposition on the part of Negroes to exclude whites from events or movements supervised by Negroes. By the 1850s, a Whipper saddened by the virulence and intransigence of American color caste was speaking favorably of Negro emigration to Canada. By the first year of the Civil War, he was one of the vice-presidents of the African Civilization Society, the members of which preached, not universal benevolence (and integration), but black nationalism. After the Civil War he did stay in the United States. His interests in championing causes which could benefit the civil rights and welfare of American Negroes remained sincere and profound. His fellow Negro leaders had always thought of him as consistently high-minded in both his precepts and his practice even when some of them counseled courses of action of which he did not approve. Their sterling regard for the nobility of his character never wavered. Nor should it have. Whatever changes reshaped the world around him, however his final convalescence reduced his youthful verve, the probity of Whipper's inner self remained, until his death, the same.

Like Whipper's father, the father of Robert Purvis was both white and rich. But it was much more in the image of John Mercer Langston's father than of the elder Whipper that Purvis' father treated Purvis' mother and his sons by her. The tale of the Purvises is another of those stories which depart from the expected in the relations of a white to a black in America.

Purvis' father, William Purvis, born in England, came to America about 1790, became an American citizen, and, in America, made a fortune as a cotton broker. Meanwhile, a girl named Harriet was growing up. Her mother had been born in Morocco, at the age of twelve kidnapped into slavery, freed at nineteen, and eventually married to a German Jew, Baron Judah. Harriet was the daughter of Baron Judah and his Moroccan wife. She was a free woman of color. William Purvis married her. They lived in Charleston, where they had three sons, of whom Purvis, born in 1810, was one. At the age of nine Purvis was put, with his brothers, into a private school in Philadelphia. The school owed its existence to his father. Purvis also attended Amherst, then in its infancy as an institution. Purvis' father died when Purvis was only sixteen. He left Purvis an inheritance of $120,000. Ever afterwards Purvis lived like a prince, but a prince with a social conscience and an unswerving commitment to the abolitionism inculcated into him by—according to Purvis himself—his father, abetted by books his father gave him before his father died.

Purvis, therefore, was only a youth when he purchased Byberry, the fine estate near Philadelphia, with its large, tree-lined lawn and prizewinning livestock, on which he dwelled as a gentleman farmer until his own death, ripe in years, in 1898. He married Harriet Forten, daughter of James Forten. Of his eight children, one especially—his son Charles, the first doctor to attend President Garfield when Garfield was shot in the railroad station in Washington, D.C.—was to make him very proud. Charles, who would live a life only one year shorter than his father's, was to count, among his many honors, incumbencies as surgeon-in-chief of Freedmen's Hospital in Washington, D.C., and dean of the medical school at Howard University.

Even before he married into the family of a dedicated abolitionist, Purvis became active of his own initiative as a fighter for the freedom of slaves. He made the acquaintance of both Benjamin Lundy and William Lloyd Garrison. Each man impressed him mightily, although it was to Garrison that he gravitated more. Indeed, he adhered to Garrison even when other black abolitionists like Douglass had deserted Garrison for an abolitionism not contemptuous of politics. As a matter of fact, Purvis persevered as a staunch Garrisonian in spite of his own rather constant involvement in activities that could hardly be described as anything other than political. In 1832, for instance, when a bill was proposed to the Pennsylvania legislature the effect of which would have been, had it passed (as it did not), to prohibit further settlement in Pennsylvania by Negroes, he was very prominently connected with the organized expressions of opposition to any such discrimination against the Negroes already resident in Pennsylvania.

The incident of authorship for which Purvis is best remembered possessed its own strong political overtones. In 1838 Pennsylvania engaged itself in the adoption of a new state constitution, one for which an article had been formulated which would bar Negroes from voting. Purvis chaired a committee of seven, all blacks, which sought to articulate the reaction of black Pennsylvanians—hostile, of course—to this proposed article. The eighteen-page pamphlet, *Appeal of Forty Thousand Citizens Threatened with Disfranchisement to the People of Pennsylvania,* issued by this committee and unsuccessful in its object, since the article was adopted, was largely, if not entirely, written by Purvis. Incidentally, its main theme repeated the very argument of the men who fostered the American Revolution, that of taxation without representation amounting truly to tyranny. Incidentally, further, a time came in the 1850s, by one of those unforeseen and opportune strokes of circumstance which all too rarely occur, when Purvis was able to illustrate, with notable clarity, the theme of his *Appeal* by a deed, quite political, rather than by mere words. Byberry Township fatuously closed its public schools to Purvis' children, who were octoroons, as were both Purvis and his wife, because the children were not white. Purvis, the largest taxpayer by far in Byberry, then simply refused to pay his school taxes, whereupon the exclusion of his children from the schools of Byberry was immediately rescinded. Purvis, however, could not do to the Philadelphia Chicken Fanciers what he did to the bigots of Byberry Township. Poultry of his, for three successive years in the early 1850s, took the first prize at the chicken fanciers' annual exhibition. The fanciers thereupon closed their competition to Purvis, claiming that they did so because he was not white. Against the fanciers Purvis could only fume. No power he could bring against them, either moral or political, could overcome their obduracy, whatever their real reason for it.

The Purvis, of course, who fought the disfranchisement of Negroes because they were Negroes and withheld his school taxes in Byberry was a civil libertarian. The Purvis who was an abolitionist started young and stayed the abolitionist course until slavery was ended after the Civil War. The earliest formal organization of abolitionists in America, the Pennsylvania Society for Promoting the Abolition of Slavery, the Relief of Free Negroes Unlawfully Held in Bondage, and for Improving the Condition of the African Race, was founded in Philadelphia in 1775. Benjamin Franklin once belonged to it. Purvis, barely in his majority, became its first—and, until 1859, its only—Negro member. When, in December, 1833, sixty-three delegates from eleven states gathered in Philadelphia to form the American Antislavery Society, with which Garrison was associated, Purvis was one of the three Negroes who participated in the meeting. In 1837 he helped to organize the Pennsylvania Anti-Slavery Society, which he served for five years as president, from 1845 until 1850, when he refused a sixth presidential term. In 1836 Purvis played the role of generalissimo in the planning and execution of what has been justifiably termed one of the most celebrated early cases of the transportation by the Underground Railroad of a slave to freedom, that of Basil Dorsey. Purvis was a model of elegance in his own handsome person, in his manners in his daily intercourse with others, and, indeed, in his whole mode of living as the patrician gentleman he undoubtedly was. But he was a guerrilla for the masses when help was needed to speed a fugitive slave away from bondage. He had some hand in the aid given to hundreds of the hunted creatures whom the Underground Railroad accepted as its passengers. He was elected president of the Philadelphia Vigilance Committee, an arm of the Underground Railroad, when it was established in 1838. He was chairman of its successor, the General Vigilance Committee, when it was organized in 1844. And his home, a cherished citadel of family life though it was, served for years as a station on the Underground Railroad, complete with a room reached only by a hidden trapdoor reserved for human shipments en route via the Railroad from the South to destinations well above the Mason-Dixon line.

During early Reconstruction, like Douglass and John Mercer Langston, Purvis refused an invitation from President Andrew Johnson to lead the Freedmen's Bureau. Like Douglass and Langston, he did so not because he disdained working in the South but because, again like Douglass and Langston, he disdained President Johnson. He had been irate over the Dred Scott decision and had eulogized John Brown. So he evinced the radical extremism of his convictions about injustices to the American Negro. It was a radical extremism which accompanied him to his grave.

After the 1860s he curtailed his participation in public affairs, but only, it would seem, because of his increasing age, not because he had moderated his antipathy to racism. Of the sixty-three zealots who formed the American Anti-Slavery Society in 1833 he was the ultimate survivor. He was nearly ninety when an attack of apoplexy terminated his long life.

An undated pamphlet, now rare, entitled *Letters and Speeches*, contains a collection of brief works in prose by Purvis. Two eulogies known to be by him are *A Tribute to the Memory of Thomas Shipley*, published in 1836, and "Eulogy on the Life and Character of James Forten," which was orally delivered in 1842, the year of Forten's death, and included in an abridged form in William C. Nell's *The Colored Patriots of the American Revolution*, published in 1855. Shipley, who was white, through the role he had played in hundreds of judicial proceedings decided favorably for Negroes whose freedom was at issue, had died a hero of the antislavery cause. Purvis coedited R. C. Smedley's posthumous *History of the Underground Railroad in Chester and the Neighboring Counties of Pennsylvania*, published in 1883, to which Purvis also added an autobiographical statement, as a letter, of some of his involvement with the Underground Railroad, notably in reference to the rescue of Basil Dorsey.

As there are occasional poets, Purvis was certainly a writer of occasional prose. He eschewed abstract reflection on general topics to react invariably to some immediate need. His purpose was always clear, whether he was seeking to bend the public will toward an end he deemed desirable or praising a public figure in whom he perceived fitting elements of virtue. He pretended to be only what he was, a journeyman writer for the causes he espoused. And he was nothing more than he pretended to be, a propagandist and a polemicist who used his pen, not because he sought to embellish art, but because the written word was one expedient available to him in the performance of his obligations, as he perceived them, toward his race and nation. There was nothing exceptional about him as a rhetorician. Among the many who have assumed the literary stance for reasons much like those which led him to write, he ranks as neither very good or very bad. No notion of his is memorable for its originality. He is only a type, but a type which must be appreciated fully to appreciate Afro-American literature.

Of Henry Highland Garnet we have already made some comment in connection with David Walker. Each has achieved a lasting presence in Afro-American literature on the basis of one utterance. In the case of

Walker, of course, that utterance is his famous *Appeal*. In the case of Garnet it is his "Address to the Slaves of the United States of America."

Garnet was born a slave on a plantation near New Market on the Eastern Shore of Maryland. His slave father, a shoemaker, was reputedly the son, or grandson, of a Mandingo king, and certainly pride in an African ancestry given unusual luster by its reputedly long complement of warriors and rulers who were both free and strong was one of the sentiments deeply instilled into Garnet by his parents. Garnet's father escaped from slavery when Garnet was only nine. But Garnet's father proved to be a worthy representative on his own account of his forebears' historic valor. He took with him, in his flight, his whole family—his wife, Garnet, and Garnet's sister. So, in New York City, the Garnets began life anew. Garnet worked when his family's fortunes required that he should, mostly on sailing vessels in the New York area, and went to school when he could, at the African Free School, where he first met fellow scholars, like Alexander Crummell, with whom he would share warm friendships terminated only by death. Slave catchers, however, scattered the Garnet family in 1829 and actually carried Garnet's sister back to slavery. Apparently, too, they roused in Garnet a passion to which some of his vehemence as an abolitionist may be attributed.

In 1835 Garnet enrolled at Noyes Academy in Canaan, New Hampshire, where, during the previous year, twenty-eight whites and fourteen Negroes had been educated interracially. The townspeople of Canaan, even so, were not abolitionists. What would have been Garnet's first year of Yankee schooling had hardly begun when these Canaanites, using a hundred oxen, pulled the building housing the Noyes Academy into a swamp and left it there. The Negro students at the academy were run out of town, and, in the judgment of Alexander Crummell—who had gone to Canaan in the same stage which had borne Garnet, unable to ride inside because of a bad leg, strapped to its top—had not a warning shot from Garnet induced in the Canaanites some second thoughts, the Negro students might well have been killed. Garnet finished, in 1840, the Oneida Institute at Whitesboro near Utica, New York. There he had received, among other immediate boons, training for the ministry. It was not a wasted tuition benefit. Garnet became one of the most eminent Presbyterian clergymen of mid-nineteenth-century America. He pastored first in Troy, New York, to a congregation largely white. During the Civil War he shepherded the flock of the very fashionable (for Negroes)

Fifteenth Street Presbyterian Church in Washington, D.C. It was during this pastorate that, with a sermon which he delivered before the House of Representatives on Sunday, February 12, 1865, as a "Memorial Discourse" in celebration of the Emancipation Proclamation, he achieved the distinction of being the first Negro to speak in a chamber of the Congress of the United States. Both before the Civil War and afterwards, he pastored at the important Shiloh Presbyterian Church in New York City.

Preaching, nevertheless, did not suffice to exhaust Garnet's abilities and energy. For a while in Troy he taught school. There he also edited, in rapid succession, abolitionist newspapers, notably, among them, the *Clarion.* As an abolitionist lecturer, he almost rivaled Douglass in the frequency of his appearances on a public platform in opposition to the South's peculiar institution. He almost rivaled Douglass also in the effectiveness with which he thus championed the abolitionist cause. Indeed, he could be theatrical in one way that Douglass could not. The bad leg he had carried with him to New Hampshire, and which he had originally injured working as a youthful farmhand on Long Island, he finally lost by amputation. Tall like Douglass and blessed, like Douglass, with a magnificent speaking voice, in lecture hall or church he faced his hearers with one of his hands gripping well the crossbar of a crutch. Accordingly, where Douglass possessed only hands to aid his arms, when Garnet gestured with his right arm he could, and often did, manipulate this crutch essentially as if it were actually a flesh-and-blood extension of his arm and fist. He capitalized on resort to this maneuver. Without his crutch he usually mesmerized an audience. With it, he astounded as he entranced.

Garnet was never mild in his opposition to slavery. He went abroad in 1850 as one more Negro impelled to put additional distance between himself and the South by the Fugitive Slave Act of 1850. Audiences in the British Isles and on the Continent responded enthusiastically to his abolitionist tirades. The Scotch Presbyterian church sent him as a missionary to Jamaica. But by 1855 he had returned to America. Always aware of his African background, he accepted, in late 1881, an appointment as America's envoy to Liberia and arrived at his new post in December of the same year. His African residence was brief. He died in February, 1882. He was buried in Liberia near the ocean. An outpouring of Liberians, including virtually all of that country's high officialdom, attended his corpse to its grave.

In 1840, while he was still studying at Oneida Institute, Garnet had delivered an incendiary philippic against slavery at an annual convention of the American Antislavery Society. Three years later, to repeat again a previous allusion, he made the speech at the Negro convention in Buffalo on which his fame, contemporary and continuing, mainly rests. He begins this "Address to the Slaves" with a reminder to his hearers in Buffalo and their kind, free Negroes in the North, East, and West, that they tend actually to think almost exclusively of themselves when they talk about, or act on, the problems of their color. They, with hardly any exception, he asserts, ignore their sisters and brothers in the slaveholding South. Garnet appears to anticipate, it clearly seems, in his censure of the northern Negroes presumably activists of his day, a charge made against the black bourgeoisie of the twentieth century (if not from the 1890s on). He indicts, that is, his northern Negroes for the same type of a breach of racial solidarity which, for instance, some blacks, his juniors by a generation or more, insist they detect in the behavior of all Negroes so fearful of not coursing along with America's so-called mainstream as to recoil from—or not admit to any awareness of—Negroes less "white" than themselves. But he tears himself away quickly from what is, after all, with him for the moment, only a passing reference, although a significant one, and applies himself with no further delay to his main business of the hour, which is to speak to the slaves of America as if they all, rather than the free Negroes actually before him, are truly within his sight and the sound of his voice.

Slavery, he reminds the slaves, has lasted in America almost three hundred years. It antedates the American Revolution. Despite its age— and its therefore obviously indigenous nature—the colonists, who were not hesitant to criticize England for permitting slavery (and the slave trade) in its colonies, did not abolish slavery when they freed themselves from their mother country. They merely strengthened slavery as an institution in their own independent polity. The Negro Jupiter Hammon was once able to reconcile slavery with Christianity. Garnet, although, like Hammon, both a Negro and a preacher of supposedly Christian doctrine, was able to do no such thing. In his "Address to the Slaves," he describes, and defines, slavery, explicitly and unequivocally as a sin against Christianity and the Christians' Almighty God. He eulogizes emancipation in the British West Indies as he praises, for their services to freedom, "Denmark Veazie [sic]," Nathaniel Turner (he uses "Nathaniel" instead of "Nat"), Joseph Cinque of *Amistad* fame, and Madison Washington, hero of the seizure of the *Creole*. Thus he moves into his climactic statement, in which he calls on all the slaves in the South, his brethren, as he says, to rise up and strike, themselves, a mighty blow for their freedom.

Undoubtedly Garnet at Buffalo, a young man only twenty-eight years old, was calling for the slaves in the American South to mount a rebellion, with resort to force, against their masters. His "strike for your lives and liberties" had but one meaning. It could not fail but connote an armed servile insurrection. In spite, incidentally, of the fact that it did, so fully had he charmed the normally quite careful and temperate Negroes listening to him in Buffalo that a resolution from the floor to adopt his "Address to the Slaves," including all of its inflammatory injunctions, as an expression of the sense of the convention, was defeated only by the margin of a single vote. Five years passed before Garnet published his "Address to the Slaves" with a copy of Walker's *Appeal* which he had edited. In the interim Garnet had, apparently, become more careful and temperate himself:

> We do not advise you to attempt a revolution with the sword, because it would be INEXPEDIENT. Your numbers are too small, and moreover the rising spirit of the age, and the spirit of the gospel, are opposed to war and bloodshed. But from this moment cease to labor for tyrants who will not remunerate you. Let every slave throughout the land do this, and the days of slavery are numbered. You cannot be more oppressed than you have been—you cannot suffer greater cruelties than you have already. RATHER DIE FREEMEN, THAN LIVE TO BE SLAVES. Remember that you are THREE MILLIONS.[1]

Thus Garnet moderated his original "Address to the Slaves," delivered orally in an atmosphere he himself had heated to a fever pitch, from a terrorist document counseling open, pitched war into a summons merely for a general strike. The slaves, it is true, neither fought nor struck. Garnet, meanwhile, published other pieces of prose, although he is not notable for the volume of his printed work. His lecture "The Past and the Present Condition, and the Destiny of the Colored Race," more philosophical and decidedly less livid than his "Address to the Slaves," like his "Address to the Slaves" was published in 1848. Contributions from his pen also appeared in various periodicals, among them those he edited, as well as in the *Liberator* and *Douglass' Monthly.*

Garnet's friend Alexander Crummell was born free in New York City in 1819. Crummell's free father had been born in Africa. Yet such was his

---

1. Both this paragraph and the paragraph it replaced appear in Ruth Miller (ed.), *Blackamerican Literature: 1760–Present* (Beverly Hills, Calif., 1971), 136.

strength of character that, for many years, Crummell's father exercised the influence of a patriarch among Manhattan's blacks. A similar influence would be Crummell's nationally among Negroes. The essay "Of Alexander Crummell," in W. E. B. Du Bois' *The Souls of Black Folk,* an unabashed paean to Crummell, is an evidence of the almost idolatrous affection and respect which Crummell inspired among other blacks who felt themselves touched by what they perceived to be the nobility of his mind and heart and the lofty regard for Negro advancement of his career.

Growing up in New York City, Crummell attended the African Free School on Mulberry Street and the Canal Street High School. He worshipped in the Episcopalian congregation presided over by Peter Williams, Jr. To a great extent Williams became for him a model and a mentor. We already know that he was one of the youths chased away about as forcibly as possible from Noyes Academy because of his color. He finished Oneida Institute and sought acceptance into a seminary in New York City which would have none of him on the same grounds, although with milder methods of dissuasion than those of the hysterical New Englanders who visited their racial bigotry upon Noyes Academy. He was able to acquire some of the academically prescribed preparation for the priesthood in Boston and even to be ordained as an Episcopal priest in Philadelphia. But his difficulties plainly attributable to the accident of his race which promised to hinder him in the practice of the priesthood anywhere in America sufficed for him to welcome an opportunity to go to England in 1848. In England such families as those of Froude, Thackeray, and Coventry Patmore received him graciously. Queen's College of Cambridge University, where he studied, conferred a bachelor's degree upon him in 1852.

Crummell chose not to return to America. His next twenty years were spent in Liberia. He went to this African land both for his health, which he had been told sorely needed a warm climate, and as a Christian missionary. Liberia, it may well have been, did improve his health, and unquestionably he performed magnificently his role there as an apostle for his church in an alien and somewhat inhospitable land. But he also became, in Liberia, a leading citizen of the entire republic, especially as an educator and a speaker. He formed a close friendship with the great Liberian statesman (who was actually a native West Indian) Edward Wilmot Blyden. In England, if not before, he had learned to love English thought and English ways. Indeed, he was, sentimentally and intellectually, as well as in his speech, dress, and manner, most profoundly and sincerely an Anglophile. Yet in Liberia he sympathized, not with the often mulatto Americo–Liberians, but with the blacks who defended the interests of the Liberians of African nativity. A conflict between the Americo-Liberians and the African Liberians, which the African Liberians lost and one consequence of which was the jailing of his son, seems to have precipitated Crummell's departure from Liberia. He had never severed his ties with America. During the Civil War, he had returned to the country which had originally nourished him on three occasions for visits. His daughters he had sent to Oberlin to be educated as Americans. And so, in 1873, after twenty years in Africa, he came back to America. He would never revisit Africa. Settling in Washington, D.C., he founded St. Luke's, the Episcopal church of which he was to be the rector until his retirement from the active ministry in 1894. He lectured considerably, in the main on Negro college campuses. After his retirement he did some teaching at Howard University, and in 1897 he brought together forty Negroes prominently associated with the arts and education—among them Du Bois, Kelly Miller, and Paul Laurence Dunbar—to form the American Negro Academy. One year later, at Red Bank, New Jersey, he died of a heart attack. His well-attended funeral was held at St. Philip's in Manhattan, the church where, as a boy, he had learned to admire so greatly Peter Williams, Jr.

In formal education Crummell stood almost alone among the Negroes of his time. He not only went to school. He went to good schools and prospered in their lore. His learning favorably affected his performance as a writer. Decidedly, it improved his control of the mechanics of his expression and the instruments of rhetoric with which he sought to grace whatever he wrote. Loggins says of him, in a judgment which probably should not be taken lightly, that with a "style . . . immeasurably purer than that of any of his Negro contemporaries . . . Crummell was the most literary of all the Negroes who wrote before 1900."[2] Significantly, in all likelihood, the prose Crummell wrote after his exposure to the opportunities available to him at Cambridge differs markedly, and in particulars decidedly to his credit, from the prose of his first publication, *The Man: the Hero: the Christian! A Eulogy on the Life and Character of Thomas Clarkson: Delivered in the City of New York, December 1846*, which appeared in print only very shortly after he left America for England. The bombast, the too-frequent infelicities of phrasing, and the awkward

2. Vernon Loggins, *The Negro Author: His Development in America to 1900* (New York, 1931), 200.

straining after grand effects which mar this eulogy tend not to reappear in his later work.

Crummell never did exert himself to test his creative imagination, if he had one, in composing fiction, whether in prose or in verse. Yet sometimes, during his happiest moments in the prose he did write, elements of a beauty poetic in its nature creep into the phrasings, and the rhythms, from his pen. Even so, not often, if ever, is he prone to induce, in either himself or his readers, that singular state of blissful expansion and intensification of the senses to which Longinus long ago gave the name of transport. It was very much a concern of Crummell's to lift men up out of themselves with a vision of a fairer, finer social order than any the world had known, and in his passion to achieve such a transcendental levitation, he spoke sometimes as movingly as a prophet of the Old Testament—as an Elijah or the Ezekiel who saw the wheel within the wheel. But he was also constitutionally and inveterately something of a social scientist, a collector and dispenser of unpoetic, quantitative data, and he tended to write at least as much in the peculiar fashion of social scientists as of poets. So his open letter to the American free Negro Charles Dunbar, *The Relations and Duties of Free Colored Men in America to Africa,* published as a pamphlet at Hartford in 1861, polemical as is plainly its intention, almost bristles with tables and statistics, as if the Liberia of which Crummell speaks had been assigned to him for a study which might well appear in a journal of political economy or sociology. It was not that Crummell lacked a reformer's zeal. But, even as he crusaded for the utopia of his dreams, the academician he always was never slept. The tradition of scholarship in Afro-American letters begins with him. The Du Bois, the Alain Lockes, the Robert Haydens, in this regard, do but follow in his train.

A selection of Crummell's essays and letters called *The Future of Africa* was published in New York City in 1862. In 1882 twenty of his sermons were gathered, and published, in a volume called *The Greatness of Christ.* His last book, containing sixteen of his speeches and essays, *Africa and America,* was published in 1891. As long as he was connected with Liberia, as well as afterwards, Crummell preached a strong brand of Liberian nationalism. In so doing, he demonstrated a certain consistency of his thinking on matters racial in their nature. *Pan-Africanism* as a term became a popular usage only after his death. But Pan-Africanism as a form of international comity worth dreaming of and working for was something in which he very much believed while he was alive. He experienced no difficulty in espousing it during the very same moments that he honored Anglo-American culture and pronounced as the religion which all human creatures should adopt the Eurasian religion of Christianity. Anyone of African stock, he felt, was not only indissolubly bound to everyone else in whose veins the blood of Africa (however diluted) flowed but was also morally responsible for the welfare of all of Africa's children wherever they might reside.

At Oneida Institute, Crummell had attended a school which, like Tuskegee at a later date, could be said to offer its students both academic and industrial training. Somewhat curiously, considering his intellectuality and fervent racial patriotism (or yet, perhaps, because he hoped to be what he could define as a realist), Crummell applied, with a class-conscious coefficient, Oneida's divided curriculum to his prescription for progress based on self-help by the American Negro. He was, incidentally, very much an apostle of self-help. The black Manhattan in which he grew up drilled its sons and daughters in their need, not only for the sake of their individual salvation, but also for the salvation of "the race," to spare no effort in their pursuit of mental and moral improvement. But in his prime Crummell's sense of this doctrine of self-help, precisely in its intraracial context, became assimilated with a bifurcation of Negroes into those who had minds to be cultivated and others who would be best served by a more "practical" education. Crummell's American Negro Academy, of course, accorded with this concept of a proper program from within the race to expedite the Negro's own advancement of himself, as also it provided a very evident, if unwitting, prelude to Du Bois' later doctrine of the "talented tenth." Crummell was not the man to champion an aristocracy based either upon the patently intended to be self-serving social pretensions of a plutocracy of *arrivistes* or upon the equally ridiculous posturings of self-anointed bluebloods crassly claiming genealogical superiorities over human beings not so blessed as they (according to themselves) with exalted ancestors. He, on the other hand, did believe in an aristocracy of merit. People in this world, he clearly maintained as a truth of great significance, if they did right, raised themselves up by their own exertions into a condition of inward grace and outward prosperity. He preached, especially to Negroes, this anything but recondite, morally oriented gospel from his version of the strenuous life. He certainly tried to practice what he preached. It was his overweening obsession in word and deed. Thus the great bulk of what he wrote tends to be monolithic in theme and didactic in tone. It cannot be said of him that he lacked completely the sheer joy in the exercise of the power to toy with language which true writers share. But he was also a slave to a purpose. His writing was a function of his fulfillment of his obligations, to himself and his race, as a member of the American Negro's "talented tenth."

9. Early Black Historians

It was in Crummell's day, in the Age of the Abolitionists, that Afro-American historiography was born. There were elements of such historiography before the Age of the Abolitionists in the work of, for example, Paul Cuffe and the early black authors of slave narratives. And there were, for blacks in America, always reasons for their own writing of black history—not the least of such reasons very obviously being an easily understandable reflex action on their part against the contemptible position in the American social order of blacks, of all of whom, collectively, it was customary for other Americans to say they were so inferior among the races of mankind as to have no history.

Robert Benjamin Lewis, a native of Boston about whom little seems to be known other than that he was both part Indian and part Negro and that he, very apparently, vastly resented white characterizations of the Negro as a man without an honorific past, in 1836 published *Light and Truth*, which he republished in 1844, enlarged, it may well have been, further to justify its subtitle, "Containing the Universal History of the Colored and the Indian Race, from the Creation of the World to the Present Time." The Creation with which Lewis begins his account of two American minorities is the Creation as given in Genesis in the Holy Bible, where neither blacks nor American Indians, except for a conjectural reading of an exasperated outburst by Noah, manifest any vestige of the slightest appearance. As a matter of fact, Lewis relies upon the Bible, plus hearsay, as the main authority for his history throughout a far and near antiquity in which he identifies as Negroes Solon, Plato, Hannibal, Pompey, Epictetus, and even Homer and Euclid. Documentation of any of his many flat assertions constitutes no problem for Lewis. He simply makes his statements and lets them stand. He says, moreover, in truth, not all that much about the history of either blacks or Indians in America, although he utters a notable amount of gossip (it can hardly be otherwise described) about American Indians and the lost tribes of Israel. Indeed, in spite of his admitted Negro blood, it is certainly possible to argue that the major excuse, to him, for the existence of *Light and Truth* is its interest in establishing the lost tribes of Israel as the progenitors of the Indians.

James W. C. Pennington's *Textbook of Negro History* was published in 1841. It is no more scholarly than *Light and Truth*. It was written for a chosen audience, the Negro children of America, and is organized to catechize these fledglings in learning and life as it informs them and fortifies their racial pride with a succession of questions about black heroes and black achievements for which answers, not to be supplied too prematurely, are also given. Within a year of its original publication it had proceeded into a third edition. But it is not respectable history. It has the flavor of a nursery rhyme and certainly does not show Pennington in a circumstance happy for him, since he possessed more formal education than almost all of his contemporary blacks.

William Cooper Nell, born free in Boston in 1816, was the son of a man friendly with David Walker. Before Nell died in 1874, he had run unsuccessfully for the Massachusetts legislature (on the Free-Soil ticket) but contributed perhaps more than anyone else to the long fight, which did end successfully, for the desegregation of Massachusetts' public schools. Out of his anger at the Dred Scott decision he fashioned the first Crispus Attucks celebration in America. He was, also, after the Civil War, as a postal clerk, one of America's first black federal bureaucrats. Even so, he seems always to have had some appetite for the world of journalism and its neighboring, more exalted universe, that of history. Devoutly an abolitionist and an admirer of Garrison, by the early 1840s he was writing articles and performing other chores for the *Liberator*. From 1847 until 1851, when Douglass broke with Garrison, he lived in Rochester and served as publisher of Douglass' *North Star*. In Boston in 1851, before he left Douglass and Rochester for a permanent return to his hometown, he published the twenty-three-page pamphlet *The Services of Colored Americans in the Wars of 1776 and 1812*, subsequently enlarged in a second edition to forty pages with an introduction by Wendell Phillips.

In 1855, as a book and not a pamphlet, and with an introduction by

Harriet Beecher Stowe, Nell's Colored Patriots of the American Revolution appeared. In a form of excess not unlike the return of Light and Truth to the Biblical Creation, Colored Patriots in actuality roams outside the Revolution. It is subtitled, "With Sketches of Several Distinguished Colored Persons; to which is Added a Brief Survey of the Condition and Prospects of Colored Americans." And so in Colored Patriots Nell actually writes as full a history as he can of the Negro in America. Biography bulks large in his history, which contains brief lives of more than several "distinguished" colored persons. But documents also bulk large in Colored Patriots. Nell was sufficiently the research scholar avidly to seek the relatively unimpeachable verification for his work of written records. He uses these records far too indiscriminately, sometimes incorporating whole a vexing number of the pages of a direct quotation, with no deletions or condensations at all, into his text. Thus, in effect, his history remains regrettably amorphous. It lacks, in the first place, the coherence and firm inner structure present in the work of historians who, as historians should, see in their minds patterns for the pasts they are presenting and are guided by those patterns as they compose their histories. The formlessness of the documentation in Colored Patriots but duplicates, therefore, and so increases, the formlessness of the book's total conception and execution. Yet its respect for sources, and exhibition of them, is an advance in black-American historiography beyond Light and Truth. Only embryonically is Nell a historian. But Colored Patriots at least contains materials historians reliably, if sometimes also only judiciously, can use.

William Still's The Underground Railroad, published in Philadelphia in 1872, resembles Colored Patriots in its preponderant value, not so much as history, but as a treasure trove of source materials for historians interested in the Afro-American past. Still was born in 1821 in the New Jersey town of Medford, the eighteenth child of a man who had purchased his release from slavery, but of a woman who had accomplished the same end by flight from Maryland into free territory. Still lived a long life. He died in 1902 in Philadelphia, his home after his migration to that city in 1844. He became a man of substance, both in his accumulation of houses and other real estate and in his financially very rewarding operation of a coal business. He was also active in more than one respect in efforts to advance the cause of the Negro in America, both in the United States and Canada. His lasting fame, however, rests upon The Underground Railroad.

Still was hired to work in the office of the Pennsylvania Anti-Slavery

Society in 1847, the year in which he married Letitia George (by whom he had four children). He was expected to perform the duties of a janitor and clerk. It took him little time, nevertheless, to become associated with additional tasks at the society. Particularly did he become an important source of dedicated labor in the aid given by the society to escaping slaves. By 1850 he was chairman of the vigilance committee organized by abolitionists in Philadelphia whose interest in helping fugitive slaves on their way to Canada—or, at least, away from the South—had been greatly heightened, heated, and amplified that year (the year, as we know, of a new fugitive-slave act much abhorred by people like the members of the vigilance committee). Still played a major role in the activities of this vigilance committee and tended to have, in ways not always safe, a wealth of direct contacts with virtually every fugitive an object of the committee's compassion. He lacked almost altogether any formal schooling. But, self-taught, he did not shrink from performing a writer's chores. Indeed, before he published *The Underground Railroad* he had already written, and issued (strangely enough, it may well seem), mostly for the contemplation of some Philadelphia Negroes who were disturbed by his campaign against racial segregation in public transportation, *A Brief Narrative of the Struggle for the Rights of the Colored People of Philadelphia in the City Railway Cars.* He, incidentally, won his campaign after the passage of some eight years. On his mind for much more than eight years, however, as he worked with abolitionists, had been, not only the drama inseparable from the very phenomenon of escape from slavery, but also his own perception of how very much the fugitives by their own initiatives and exploits were constantly contributing to the presence of heroism and a measure of happy endings within that drama.

By no means did Still begrudge whites credit for the pains some of them were taking and the dangers to which some of them were exposing themselves in order to help spirit Negroes away from bondage. He admitted, for example, the important role played by the white conductors and the white operators of way stations along the various routes of the perilous secret service the Underground Railroad perforce had to be. Even so, he believed he had noted an insufficient recognition, given the pertinent facts, of what black fugitives, of their own daring, courage, and exertion, and northern blacks like himself together had done to make of this spectacular experiment an institution as effective as it had become. Moreover, Still was steeped in the same doctrine of racial self-help as Crummell. It was a matter of the gravest consequence to him that

Negroes should demonstrate Emersonian qualities of self-reliance and that out of their own might and their own temper they should forge a higher status for themselves in their American home. A theme which unites *The Underground Railroad* is the valor of the blacks within it who risk their lives to free other blacks, as well as, sometimes, their very selves.

Part of the inspiration which underlay *The Underground Railroad* derived from an incident, one of those occurrences which are never supposed (and, certainly, never expected) to happen, that actually did befall Still in August, 1850, when a stranger, in Philadelphia, who gave his name as Peter Freeman, solicited a favor from Still. This stranger, a black fugitive, sought information which might direct him to parents from whom he had been separated for longer than Still's residence in Philadelphia. It developed that this stranger's parents were also Still's and that, therefore, this apparition, as it were, from a void was to Still an older brother of whom he had had no glimpse before that August day. Still's purposive acknowledgment to himself of the fact that he was engaged in the collection of materials which could expedite his preparation of such a work as *The Underground Railroad*, according to Still, truly began on that fantastic, for him, August day which marked the marvelous eruption into his life of this Peter Freeman who was really Peter Still. Hence, Still found himself in a most receptive mood when the society for which he had worked, in a gesture connected with its culmination of its own existence, in 1871 authorized him to put into writing an account of its history and accomplishments.

In no sense, of course, was Still as qualified to perform such a job as might have been Crummell or Charlotte Forten. *The Underground Railroad* reflects all too fully his limitations as a man of letters. Its petty errors which betray his lack of formal schooling are legion. His style is crude almost to an extreme. He was woefully without any conception of how a history should be organized, and so *The Underground Railroad* is nearly eight hundred pages largely of memorabilia of various kinds, a miscellany containing, although in no manner generating from them a coherent work of art or of history, letters (too often quoted at exorbitant length) from slaves, fugitives or abolitionists, excerpts from newspapers, legal documents, tales, biographical sketches, and reminiscences from Still himself. In the discharge of his duties with the society, Still had kept a journal on a daily basis. Thus he was even more prepared than he might otherwise have been to resurrect in detail his privileged view from the inside of the most concerted effort in American history to circumvent an inhumane law. Accordingly, *The Underground Railroad* constitutes a unique and impressive repository of evidence for seekers of a sense of the way some Americans once placed themselves above legalisms which they considered unjust. Nor was it unappreciated in its own time. It quickly went through three editions. Still employed agents to hawk it and, himself, proudly exhibited it at the centennial of American independence in Philadelphia in 1876.

No more than a miscellany also, yet, nevertheless, also with its own claims, limited though they are, to some of the distinguishing characteristics of history, is *Men of Mark: Eminent, Progressive and Rising*, written (really edited) by William J. Simmons and published in 1887. Simmons was a native of Charleston, born a slave in 1849, who died in 1890, only three years after his *Men of Mark* appeared. He was still a child of quite tender years when his mother managed to traverse, as a runaway, the hundreds of miles between Charleston and the free North even as she bore with her Simmons and two of his siblings, daughters of hers (and Simmons' father) not much older than Simmons. He resided, often under trying conditions, in Pennsylvania, Massachusetts, and New Jersey, receiving training in New Jersey as a dental assistant before, a boy fifteen years old, he enlisted in the Union army. During his months as a soldier, the months of the last year of the Civil War, he fought in Virginia and was among the men from the North in uniform at Appomattox when Lee surrendered. He furthered his own education after the war. Indeed, he attended Madison (later, Colgate) University and Rochester University and took both a bachelor's and a master's degree from Howard University. He married and had children, and lived and taught in Arkansas and Florida until eventually, as a Baptist cleric in Kentucky, he became, himself, a Negro man of mark. Before his early death, he served as president of State University, a Baptist institution located in Louisville, where he, additionally, edited the religious newspaper the *American Baptist*. He was the first president of the American National Baptist Convention. To commemorate him, State University, some years after his death, was renamed Simmons University. He made good use of a relatively short life. The evidence is strong that he died probably before his public career had reached its zenith.

Men of Mark represents itself as a collection of biographies. It would be more accurately described as a collection of autobiographies. Most of the biographies it contains were written by the people who are the subjects of the biographies. Scholars now, therefore, exercise caution in using it. One's account of one's own life too often, obviously, may not be trusted for objectivity, even in its rehearsal of the supposedly most neutral and most unimpeachable matters of fact. Simmons had chosen the *Men* in the title of *Men of Mark* with highly conscious regard for a disposition into separate categories of black men and women. In the introduction to *Men of Mark,* a portion of the book which Simmons did unquestionably write, he expresses the hope that Negro youth, both male and female, will read *Men of Mark* and, from their knowledge thus acquired of the lives of some older people as Negroid as themselves, increase their stock of racial pride. Even so, *Men of Mark* includes, in its biographies of 177 persons of color, not a single woman. It was Simmons' intention to produce a companion volume in which would appear biographies solely of black women. Conceivably, his death prevented the completion of this companion volume and thus deprived him of a chance to show, in spite of his separation of the sexes, that he was, even in his own benighted time, not altogether a male chauvinist.

Men of Mark does not restrict only to America and Americans the array of black males who, in its pages, are displayed, as we have noted, largely for their possible good effects on the morale of other blacks. Thus, among its biographies are lives of Toussaint L'Ouverture, Alexandre Dumas père, and Edward Wilmot Blyden. *Men of Mark* retreats into the American past as far as Crispus Attucks. The book, incidentally, is not alphabetized. It may not be proper, therefore, to call it a dictionary of any kind. And while it does offer biographies of such American Negroes as Richard Allen, Frederick Douglass, and Booker T. Washington (albeit a young Washington before his apotheosis at Atlanta), of whom it can never be said that they would not be eminent in whatever company they found themselves, however stringently they were judged, for a notable percentage of its biographies a statement similarly ecumenical would constitute, unfortunately, an excursion into fantasy as well as a large distortion of the truth. These subjects of biography—whether all or merely most of them—may well have been sufficiently exceptional in both character and ability to share power and glory with the actual paramount dignitaries of their world. But all, or most, of them, nevertheless, tended to occupy, in veritable fact, positions among all Americans only modest at best by the most generous of standards. Millions of white Americans held jobs better in every way than either such jobs as these subjects of biography, in their real flesh and blood, ever did secure or even any to which they reasonably could have aspired. For, if *Men of Mark* does nothing else, it reflects with absolute fidelity the antiblack intolerance of its time, those unhappy last two decades of the nineteenth century, when rabid racism in white America was, in both intensity and savagery, rising to a peak higher than any comparable peak before or since.

Yet *Men of Mark* does do, also, something else for which it deserves remembrance. In Afro-American literature, biography is a strong constituent element. At one chronological end of this possibly most formidable genre among all the genres of Afro-American literature, the slave narratives hold sway. At the other end of black biography's extension through time, well into the twentieth century, are the outstanding autobiographies, in their fullest concentration of bulk and quality, of all Afro-American literature: James Weldon Johnson's *Along This Way*, Du Bois' *Dusk of Dawn*, Richard Wright's *Black Boy*, Claude Brown's *Manchild in the Promised Land*, and the collaboration of Alex Haley and Malcolm X, *The Autobiography of Malcolm X*. Between these two extremes, although anything but a commanding phenomenon because of any virtues peculiar to it, lies *Men of Mark*. Editions of Douglass' final autobiographical work immediately precede, and closely follow, it in publication dates. Thus it divides with only a lone other work of biography the honor of sustaining, through what might well have been an absolute break in a line of progression, the active tradition of black biography. So it is part of a grand continuum, a humble part admittedly, but strategically a part of singular value to a very important whole.

In 1888, a year after *Men of Mark* appeared, Joseph T. Wilson published his *The Black Phalanx: A History of the Negro Soldiers of the United States in the Wars of 1775–1812, 1861–'65*. Wilson, who was born in Virginia in 1836, traveled widely in his youth. He was living in Massachusetts when his wanderlust carried him outside the United States, and it was from Santiago, Chile, that he returned, posthaste, after the outbreak of the Civil War, to enlist in Louisiana, the first state he reached in which he could, as a black bearing arms against the Confederacy. Throughout much of the war, however, he served in a Massachusetts regiment. He essayed history first in 1882 with a small work called *Emancipation: Its Course and Progress from 1481 B.C. to A.D. 1875*. This work and his activism as a veteran attracted sufficient favorable attention from other veterans to occasion, by a post in Virginia of the Grand Army of the Republic, his selection to write an account of the experience during the Civil War of the Massachusetts regiment to which he had been attached. Thus he wrote *The Black Phalanx*. He died in 1891.

The black historians who preceded Wilson all tended to function significantly in the capacity of the historian as bard. They eschewed, of course, the medium of verse. Still, they tended to recount, as an exercise in the retention of versions of the past dear to themselves and their fellows in a tribe, the exploits of heroes of the tribe. So even though they wrote in privacy rather than recited in public, they tended closely to repeat one another very much in the manner of harpers of old, orally transmitting tales prescriptively uniform in content and adulatory tone which they were extracting from an already existing, time-hallowed oral tradition. If these black historians were slavishly committed to the familiar and the highly sanctioned by custom, that, too, was part of the tradition. They were but observing their duty to keep intact an account of the tribal experience in whole and in all of its parts precious to the tribe.

To a degree which should be recognized, Wilson, in *The Black Phalanx*, continues the role of the black historian as racial bard. But Wilson also is a figure of transition in black historiography. As he stands with one foot in the past, he stands also with his other foot in an atmospherically different future. Enough of *The Black Phalanx* constitutes historiography in accord with conventions and principles of scientific research regarded as obligatory guides for historians and critics of historians in recent times for it not to be dismissed too summarily as quaint and musty primitivism in historiography. Wilson accepts the importance of documentation. He does not always handle his documentation well. Far too often he quotes directly from his sources at excessive length. But he does vastly prefer identifiable sources to hearsay. He is more critical than the bardic tradition.

In the bardic tradition, perhaps, *The Black Phalanx* begins with the Revolution and the War of 1812. But it lingers long with neither of these earlier historic events. And there is a pattern which makes good sense in the treatment by *The Black Phalanx* of the Civil War. It gathers its initial impetus with chapters on the introduction of Negro recruits into the United States Army after a protracted delay of such recruiting in deference to the volume of sentiment in the North against the training of blacks to kill any whites. Next, it rehearses, in rather ample detail, the performance of these Negro recruits in the various regional theaters of the war, in none of which, Wilson obviously believes, were Negro soldiers ever free of the necessity to prove their worth in battle and in other military functions. So, it moves from Louisiana and the valley of the Mississippi to the Southeast, the Department of the Cumberland and Virginia, where Negro troops participated in the final assaults on Richmond. It concludes with two chapters on the Negro after the war, a somewhat perfunctory bibliography, and appendices which refer to particular units of black troops.

The Black Phalanx is illustrated. Its frontispiece displays Wilson himself, in uniform, bemedaled and cradling a sword in the curve of his left arm. Wilson, however, succumbs very little, if at all, to the vices of exhibitionism and personal vanity in his history. He sticks with commendable zeal to the task he has appointed for himself. Just as his ability to conceive a logical order of progression appears in the sequence of his chapters, so his basic good sense as a writer of history appears in his prose style. Fundamentally, a historian is a teller of tales. Narrative is his métier. And Wilson is no pitiable and gross incompetent in the practice of the storyteller's art. Quite to the contrary, he seems to have been born with an affinity for declarative sentences and verbs in the indicative mood which prepares him for narrative and provides the main discipline for his sense of the appropriate throughout *The Black Phalanx*. Few flights of fancy, few digressions, and almost no extended bombast impede, therefore, the flow of narrative in *The Black Phalanx*. Wilson, it must be admitted, is no great writer (as he is no great historian). He is not to be read as can be read the finest of essayists. What he himself read as a youth, if he read anything at all (and, with or without formal schooling, he surely did read something), we do not know. It may be suspected that his access to finer letters, in comparison to what it might have been had he had a different birth from that he did have, was limited in more ways than one. Possibly—almost surely, probably—he was, like Frederick Douglass, a self-made writer and historian. And, like Douglass, he was—in this regard, at least—anything but his own worst enemy.

About the Civil War, of course, a voluminous literature exists. Voices have spoken of it, or of some aspect of it, from many quarters. In this chorus, it pays to hear a Negro voice occasionally. Statements occur, therefore, in *The Black Phalanx* which are arresting if only because they are not part of the common lore concerning the war to be found either in the work of scholars or, most certainly, in the awareness of the national past of the average American. Perhaps such statements acquire an added value from this very circumstance which helps to make them so arresting.

In effect, such statements, moreover, also operate as instruments in the service of justice, like witnesses too long denied a hearing in a court where all the rulings from the bench have favored the stronger side. Thus *The Black Phalanx* stoutly asserts as a fact, not merely probable, but beyond dispute, a significantly larger number of Negro soldiers in the Union army than official records imply (more than approximately 180,000) since "a practice prevailed [in Negro fighting units] of putting a live negro [sic] in a dead one's place" and of having the live Negro assume, then and thereafter, the identity by name on the army rolls of the vanished fighter he replaced. Indeed, *The Black Phalanx* further maintains, some mulattoes passed for white and fought in the Union army as white soldiers, but even more to the point, as white officers commanding white enlisted men. Some mulattoes, likewise, according to *The Black Phalanx*, officered in the Confederate army.[1]

Perhaps nowhere in all its length is *The Black Phalanx* more memorably and eloquently a witness too long unheeded but finally heard than in a rather extended vignette about a Union expedition into Florida. The expedition occurred in February, 1864. It was launched on a high tide of optimism, under the command of a General Seymour, from the vicinity of Charleston. Six thousand men, black and white, went with the general by water to Jacksonville. Wilson, in his black Massachusetts regiment, was one of these men. Union intelligence, it was thought by the appropriate Union high command, had taken good note of a dearth of Confederate forces in Florida. Union strategists of high rank foresaw an opportunity too excellent to be ignored to divert from the Confederacy cotton and lumber the South could ill afford to lose and the North could gratefully receive, very probably to find more Negroes who could be inducted into the Union army, and even, possibly, to detach the whole state of Florida from the Confederacy and restore that state to the Union.

General Seymour encountered only negligible enemy opposition in, and around, Jacksonville. He proceeded westward along the line of the Florida Central Railroad with more enthusiasm than caution. About forty miles from Jacksonville a Confederate force larger than his own trapped him between two swamps, dealt his command heavy casualties, and sent his routed troops reeling back to Jacksonville. Wilson tells the full story of Seymour's folly, but within it, all the more vividly, he paints a picture of the valor and the unquenchable morale of the Negro regi-

---

1. Joseph T. Wilson, *The Black Phalanx: A History of the Negro Soldiers of the United States in the Wars of 1775–1812, 1861–'65* (Hartford, Conn., 1888), 123, 179, 180.

ments which accompanied the general. As he does so, at least twice he adds to his canvas touches of notable artistry. He tells of the band of the 54th Massachusetts, at the edge of the battle during one of its bitterest moments for the North, undauntedly playing "The Star-Spangled Banner." Later he describes the black troops, once the fury of the fight at its worst has abated, in their withdrawal from their ambush, taking pains to recover their living casualties, loading them on flatcars standing on rails without engines there available at all, attaching ropes and vines to the flatcars, and then, exhausted and unfed, themselves becoming engines, through the long night and early daylight thus trundling back to Jacksonville their helpless wounded comrades.[2] So, without unseemly grandiloquence in his prose, in a dying fall of the black historian as bard, Wilson contributes to the bardic tradition one of its finest moments. But he, at the very same time, tells here a story from the Civil War as worthy to be held in the national remembrance as many better-known stories of the war—as, for example, the stories of Pickett's charge at Gettysburg or of the bloodiness at Shiloh or Antietam. In such a story he is both racial bard and national and international historian. He is here at his best in both respects. In addition, he is here his own primary source. Amateur at the historian's trade he well may be, but he is not such an amateur without some saving graces.

George Washington Williams is a pivotal figure in black American historiography. Generally he is considered the first black American to write history at a level of competence entitling him to serious designation as a genuine forerunner of such black historians as John Hope Franklin and Benjamin Quarles. Without academic training in the writing of history, he wrote history which historians so trained far from view askance. Moreover, within the province of black culture, if not more extensively, he is sufficiently the littérateur—sufficiently, it may be reasonably declared, a Gibbon or a Parkman in his feeling for writing as an art—to be treated, in a history of literature, as a literary figure. He was born in 1849, over ten years later than Wilson. Yet he died in 1891, the same year as that in which Wilson died. And the two works of history by which he is remembered were both published in the 1880s. Wilson, it will be recalled, also published his histories in the 1880s. Facts, therefore, justify a view of Wilson and Williams as contemporaries. The good things which may be said of Wilson's historiography are even more applicable to the his-

2. *Ibid.*, 269, 273.

toriography of Williams. Moreover, Williams seems, in fewer years, to have lived the fuller, richer life of the two. It does appear, indeed, as if some daemonic spirit, not evil, but virtually impossible to please, drove Williams from his youth to his early death. He could not find, it would seem, ever enough things to do. The wonder is that, restless as he was, he was able to perform so ably as he generally did in so many different pursuits of difficult ends.

Williams was born in Bedford Springs, Pennsylvania, on free soil, of humble, but free, black parents. Negroes were excluded from combat with Union forces in the Civil War until 1863, when Williams was only fourteen years old. Immediately then, from Massachusetts, where he may have added some formal schooling to the barber's trade taught him in Pennsylvania, having assumed the name of one of his uncles and lied about his age, Williams contrived to enlist in the northern army. His double deception discovered, he was mustered out. Nevertheless, he managed to reenlist. The story that, after the war, he joined the Mexican army, serving with the forces of Benito Juarez against the French intruder Maximilian, and rising to the rank of a Mexican lieutenant colonel, seems to be a myth. He did, however, become a trooper in the 10th Cavalry of the American Regular Army, stationed in Indian country, remaining so from 1867 until 1868. He had been wounded near Fort Harrison in Virginia during the Civil War. He was wounded in his left lung during his tour of duty with the cavalry. He studied at both Howard University and Wayland Seminary in Washington, D.C., before being admitted to the Newton Theological Seminary in Massachusetts, from which he graduated as one of the commencement orators in 1874. He pastored the Twelfth Street Baptist Church in Boston, one of New England's finest black congregations, for fourteen months. He pastored, also, the Union Baptist Church in Cincinnati in 1876. Between the two pastorates he edited a magazine, the *Commoner*, in Washington, D.C., and when the magazine, in spite of its support by prominent Negroes such as Frederick Douglass and Douglass' arch rival, John Mercer Langston, showed no signs of vitality sufficient to justify its continuation, worked in the Washington post office.

Williams was most enterprising during his years in Ohio. He retained his ministry in Cincinnati barely a year. But he studied law with Alphonso Taft, father of the then future president Taft, and entered politics while proceeding through the tenures, first, of a position as a storekeeper in the internal-revenue division of the United States Department of the

Treasury and, next, of a secretaryship in the office of the auditor of the Cincinnati Southern Railway. He was elected, in 1879, to the house of representatives of the state of Ohio. He did not run for reelection. He had written in 1876 an 80-page history of the church he was, at the time, pastoring in Boston. An address he had delivered on the Fourth of July in 1876 had concerned itself with the history of American blacks. Increasingly the writing of history—and, particularly, the writing of a history about American blacks—attracted him as the one thing, above all, he yearned to do. As he served in the Ohio legislature, he spent hours in the public library in Columbus. He examined documents from the Boston Public Library, the Library of Congress in Washington, D.C., and the Lenox Library of New York City. Over a period of six years he delved, if his personal testimony is to be believed, into 12,000 books, as well as thousands of pamphlets and newspapers. He availed himself of information from the War Department, the *Congressional Record* and *Congressional Globe*, the AME church, the *Journal of the Confederate Congress*, orderly books of general officers, newspapers, other histories, and talks with many people whose special intelligence he thought he could use. Thus he engaged in a truly Herculean labor of research. In 1883 his *History of the Negro Race in America from 1619 to 1880* appeared. It was published by G. P. Putnam's Sons, exceeded 1,100 pages in length, and was available either in two volumes or in a popular edition of the two volumes in one.

History of the Negro Race had a decided immediate impact. A gratifying number of reviewers from respected journals applauded it. A smaller number of reviewers from journals equally respected were not so kind. But an audience perhaps surprisingly large read it. Because of it Williams was called upon to lecture widely. He traveled in Europe and the Near East. Early in 1885 Republican president Arthur appointed him American minister to Haiti, but Democratic president Cleveland, on his accession to office in the same year, annulled the politically sensitive appointment. Meanwhile, Williams had already embarked on another venture in the writing of history. In 1888 appeared his *History of the Negro Troops in the War of the Rebellion, 1861–1865*, published by Harper and Brothers, wherein he acquitted himself as a historian with no less superiority over his black predecessors and contemporaries in the field of history than he had already in his *History of the Negro Race*.

Williams had not lost, however, his appetite for activity on more than one front. In Europe he had met King Leopold II of Belgium. The Congo interested him. Indeed, he fancied that American Negroes might well find a fertile field in that, to Westerners, undeveloped land for careers mutually beneficial to themselves and to the natives of the Congo, who were, of course, every American Negro's racial kith and kin. By 1890 he was in the Congo. He saw the country and the people and followed the Congo River itself to its headwaters at Stanley Falls. Even more to the unwelcome point, considering his own anticipatory optimism, he saw the cruelty with which Leopold II—obviously an exploiter, of the most sadistic kind, of a defenseless people—treated the unfortunate natives of the Congo in his inordinate lust to wring from them and their homeland every bit of plunder, however soaked in human blood, that he could. Not the least of what Williams saw was the actual maimings of Africans by Europeans acting in Leopold's name. In *An Open Letter to His Serene Majesty, Leopold II, King of the Belgians*, Williams trumpeted to the world Leopold's greed and heartlessness. He also wrote articles for the young but expanding McClure syndicate about the Congo and published *A Report Upon the Congo-State and Country to the President of the Republic of the United States* and *A Report on the Proposed Congo Railroad*. The articles and reports belong to the year 1890. He had returned to England by 1891, his interest in the Congo unabated and his attention now devoted to an additional work, much longer than any he had done in 1890, in which he intended to picture, with more room for telling the full, revolting truth, the situation in the Congo. But his health failed him. Taken, by friends, to Blackpool for the sea air there, he succumbed to tuberculosis and pleurisy. His corpse was interred in a cemetery in Liverpool. In 1975 the most distinguished of his successors as a writer of American Negro history, John Hope Franklin, made a pilgrimage to his grave. Moreover, Franklin bore the cost of the headstone he had deliberately tarried to see placed on Williams' grave.

When Williams left the United States cavalry in 1868, he went to St. Louis from the currently still more open farther West. In St. Louis he was baptized. Although still less than twenty years of age, he was mature by then, not a child acceding to an elder's bidding, but a veteran of military strife who had looked his own death in the face more than once. A historian he would eventually become. Yet he was also, as long as he lived, to remain a faithful Christian who could never ignore the Bible, although it should not be forgotten how reputable were his publishers in both 1883 and 1888. So he begins his *History of the Negro Race* with "Preliminary Considerations," in part an account of man's prehistoric past which is, as

Loggins says, "a compromise between the Biblical and the scientific."[3] But it is decidedly a historian wedded to scientific methods of research and documentation that he strives to make of himself, and consciously prefers to remain, elsewhere in his *History of the Negro Race*. He declares, in his preface to this work, that he has written it, not as "the blind panegyrist of my race, nor as the partisan apologist, but . . . to record the truth, the whole truth, and nothing but the truth," and these words are more than idle boasting. The portion of his "Preliminary Considerations" in which he attempts to provide some sense of the American Negro's African background, as well as a related sense of modern West Africa, is much freer, therefore, of the taint of his religiosity and much more expressive of his intent to represent himself as an objective historian committed to reliance upon records and verifiable evidence than his account of man's creation and beginning. He deals with the Negro in colonial America colony by colony. Collectively, thus, he assembles the second part of the first volume of *History of the Negro Race*. The third part of this first volume carries the American Negro through the Revolutionary War.

The second volume of Williams' *History of the Negro Race* is also divided into parts, five of them. It turns to the first thirty years of the nineteenth century with an emphasis upon Negro opposition to slavery then and, at notable length, with a picture of the Negro in the War of 1812. Its next part concerns itself with the antislavery agitation of the 1830s and the 1840s. The following part, the sixth part of the two volumes of the history, is called "The Period of Preparation." It presents the years of which it speaks in terms highly sensitive to the character of those years as a season of direct prelude to the Civil War. Part seven of the history is about the Civil War. The eighth and concluding part, treating of the Negro in America's first decade, or so, of his freedom after slavery, ends with a section called "The Decline of the Negro Governments," an obvious reference to Reconstruction as judged by a censorious Williams, which (surely not as Williams must have intended) consequently closes his whole history of black America on a note hardly calculated to lift up any hearts. Impartiality as a historian did not, accordingly, imply to Williams the impassivity—and, hence, the possible readiness for any point of view—of a tabula rasa. He did seek the organizing power of interpretation, exempt (he hoped) from the biases of ideological or racial

3. Vernon Loggins, *The Negro Author: His Development in America to 1900* (New York, 1931), 276.

prejudice, which would confer upon his history an infrastructure indicative of his conclusions about the significant interdependence of historic facts. So he includes in his work some biographical sketches and some chapters of social and cultural history, to extend and fortify the sense of background introduced by him with his allusions to man's beginnings and to the Negro in Africa both before and after the Negro's importation to America.

Williams was not, however, as accomplished a historian as he might have been. After all, he came to the writing of history not only as a preacher with a preacher's experience of promulgating the Christian faith. He came also as an orator steeped in the tradition of the gross spellbinding oratory of his day. How meager, indeed, when he embarked on the writing of his *History of the Negro Race*, were his contacts with the world of the trained historians in comparison with the extent and intensity of his conditioning by the worlds of the fundamentalist ministers with whom he consorted and the popular speakers he had learned to emulate must be appreciated truly to comprehend the quality of his achievement by the time his history was done. Even so simple an acquisition of the properly trained scholarly historian as a conventionally approved *apparatus criticus* was a bagatelle he did not possess. Often he fails to speak, in a footnote, as clearly or as fully (or both) as he should, or, even more reprehensibly, fails to attribute credit specifically to a source which he should mention. Like Still and other black forebears of his, he sometimes overquotes. And his penchant for spellbinding oratory possesses its distressing counterpart in too many lapses of style in his written composition. His language, that is, sometimes suffers from the unction of its phrasing, its excess of grandiloquence, and its shoddily ornate conceits. At such moments, of course, he loses his way both as a literary artist and as a historian. Nor is he always a grammarian beyond reproach. Yet his good instincts, relatively untrained though he was, sufficiently prevail to rescue him from ever speaking too long in a bad way and to invest his history with admirable measures of lucidity, fluency, coherence, vividness, and charm. As a matter of fact, typically he speaks directly and is easily read. Moreover, he covers his subject well. He has set out to write a comprehensive history of the Negro in America, and so he does. Not for more than half a century, in such a regard, would any black historian supersede him.

In his introduction to *A History of the Negro Troops in the War of the Rebellion*, remembering especially America's stereotyping of its Negroes,

Williams avers: "The part enacted by the Negro soldier in the war of the Rebellion is the romance of North American history. It was midnight and noonday without a space between; from the Egyptian darkness of bondage to the lurid glare of civil war; from clanging chains to clashing arms; from passive submission to the cruel curse of slavery to the brilliant aggressiveness of a free soldier; from a chattel to a person; from the shame of degradation to the glory of military exaltation; and from deep obscurity to martial immortality." Williams did not like the British. They had participated in the slave trade. He harbored no overly sympathetic notions about Africa or Africans. To him the Africans were idolators. Slavery, of course, he thoroughly abominated. He wrote, therefore, of the Negro in the Civil War with perhaps more passion than he had written earlier of the Negro merely in America. In his *History of the Negro Race* he had unequivocally aligned himself with Western culture and Christianity. It was Western racism and abuses by capitalism of what he conceived to be its own principles which, in his *History of the Negro Race,* he decried, not Westernism itself or Christianity. His vaunted program for Africans and for American Negroes, simply stated, was for them to become more Western and more Christian.

In the light of such a program, his *History of the Negro Troops in the War of the Rebellion* acquires an added meaning, and the quotation from his introduction given above is more than an orator's flourish. It presents the Civil War, that is, as the first seizure to a degree that mattered by the American Negro of an opportunity to cross a great divide, to show himself possessed of capabilities which would enable him to facilitate his entry into a new estate, equal in esteem with that of any other group of immigrant Americans and certifiable as his badge of membership, with no reservations, in the civilization with which white America was most identified and black Americans most acquainted. In general form, his account of the Negro's Civil War differs little from Wilson's account of the same war in *The Black Phalanx.* It does not differ really, for that matter, from *The Black Phalanx* in its interpretation of the significance of the Civil War for Negroes and for America. It demonstrates, in other words, the completeness of agreement between Wilson and Williams as to what should be the Negro's prime objective in America. For both of them the American Negro's most pressing obligation to himself, as to America, was to make himself as American as he could be. For both of them, in their attempts at history and literature, as in the pattern of their personal lives, an integrated America was the America of which they dreamed, an

America which would be the consummation of their version of right and truth.

Williams' objectivity as a historian is impressive. Whether he is reconstructing the Negro plot in New York City in 1744, as he does in his *History of the Negro Race,* or telling of the bravery, and slaughter, of Negro troops in action against Fort Wagner, as he does in his *History of the Negro Troops in the War of the Rebellion,* he scrupulously adheres to his policy of being guided by the facts. Even so, however, he is never divorced from something more than that policy, his own predilection for what he would consider an ideal world. He does, therefore, write propaganda as well as history. But never does his propaganda separate him from the land, or the culture, into which he was born. And never, in his propaganda, whether as an abolitionist or as an integrationist, is he anything of a gradualist.

Part Three ❧

The Age of the Abolitionists, II

10. *Early Abolitionist Poets*

The finest poetry created by black Americans during the Age of the Abolitionists, the Negro spirituals, cannot be credited to any individual authors. In that sense it must, apparently, forever remain anonymous. More will be said about it later. However, during the years between Walker's *Appeal* and Douglass' death, Negroes who can be identified by name did write and publish verse—indeed, at least one hundred of them, including four Methodist bishops. Among their number about one in five have attracted the attention of literary historians.

Noah Calwell W. Cannon was born free in 1796 in Sussex County, Delaware, the son of parents both born free in the same county. When he was sixteen years of age, according to a story he delighted to tell, an angel visited him while he, recumbent on his bed, lay peacefully drowsing or asleep and certainly not expecting a celestial guest. His extraordinary intruder clutched in one of his fists a candle two feet long, the source of the more tangible form of illumination which abetted Cannon's faculties of perception as the angel conducted him on a tour through hell and heaven until, at last, having witnessed an astounding (to Cannon) succession of wonders, he and the angel culminated their sweeping inspection in the very presence of the Savior himself. Cannon returned to the bed from which the angel had transported him very conscious of the injunction carefully, he could not fail but note, and somewhat prayerfully (he felt) delivered to him by the angel, as the angel bade him farewell, for him to preach the gospel of the risen Christ. He could do no less, then, than ally himself with the Christian church, as he, in haste, did do immediately. Moving to Philadelphia, probably in 1818, he became a member of the AME denomination and was soon an AME clergyman.

From the relatively little we know of him, Cannon must have proceeded throughout his entire life with absolutely no formal schooling. Even so, he was a famed exhorter, as well as one decidedly peripatetic. The circuit he traveled extended from Pennsylvania into Ohio, Maryland, Delaware, and Washington, D.C. He lived at a time when camp meetings flourished in America, and he seems to have been greatly suited, in his practice of homiletics, to these camp meetings and the special emphases on evangelical fervor they bred. Undoubtedly, the seekers after God's grace who heard him at camp meetings tended to exalt him as a sympathetic counselor to them unusually competent at communicating with them in the special manner of a spokesman for the Lord to which they had become accustomed. It seems to have fallen to his lot, in 1844, to bring home to Philadelphia from eastern Canada the ailing AME bishop Morris Brown, the second (in chronological order of incumbency) prelate of his denomination, after whom an AME college in Atlanta is named. Cannon seems also, subsequently, to have made Canada his home. He died there in 1850.

Cannon published, in 1833, a book called *The Rock of Wisdom*, which was principally in prose, yet did contain, in its final pages, 16 hymns in verse and a poem of 32 lines entitled "The Ark." There appears to be, incidentally, no good reason why "The Ark" should not likewise be termed a hymn. In decidedly the fashion of a hymn, it celebrates the apotheosis possible for Christians who emulate the dedication of themselves to their God of Joshua, Joseph, Elias, Moses, and other heroes of the Scriptures, both in the Old Testament and in the New. The prose of *The Rock of Wisdom*, throughout its 120 pages, tends to demonstrate repeatedly, as a fundamental tactic for increasing its own vigor and appeal, a penchant for the kinds of figurative expressions and categories of rhythms in speech generally associated with poetry, not prose. Rhyme frequently occurs within it, although it is not divided into verses. It inclines toward an affection for tone color in its vowels and for theatrical sound effects, such as sibilance, in the selection and arrangement of its consonants. Cannon writes prose, that is to say, which might well suggest that, for him, it is poetry which is his true first love and, so, that it is wrong of him, and a denial of his own best interests as a literary artist, not to make of the writing of poetry the prime concern in his attempts at writing anything at all.

This suggestion from *The Rock of Wisdom* may well appear to coincide with Cannon's performance as a camp-meeting preacher. A camp-meeting preacher, whatever else he was or was not, and whether he was black or white (but especially, perhaps, if he was black), it has long been a scholarly consensus to describe as, in part, an exponent of a distinctive form of extremely histrionic oratory heavily dependent for much of its singularity upon its willingness to infuse within its prose practices borrowed from the peculiar aesthetic of poets. To study historically, therefore, the black folk preacher is, inevitably, to conceive of him as, among other things, a poet in a pulpit. But no suggestion of an affinity for poetry in Cannon which might emanate either from acquaintance with his "poetic" prose in *The Rock of Wisdom* or from reflections upon his behavior during his many years as the kind of preacher preaching to the folk in a manner which report assures us made his spoken prose also poetic finds convincing confirmation in any of his hymns or "The Ark." Nowhere in his writing that he calls poetry is he other than banal, mediocre, and dull. The following stanza, with its limp in its last line, from one of his hymns typifies all of his poetry:

> This is the glorious day
> That our redeemer made,
> Let us rejoice and sing and pray,
> Let all the church be glad.

The Cannon who, it would seem, dared to be as vivid as he could when he was on display and shaping his thoughts for oral export to an attentive camp-meeting congregation seeing and hearing him as an audience with which he could react, once he retired to wherever he wrote poetry rather than transmitted aloud and directly his message to those he wished to reach, became only a tame copy of a thousand ignominious other poetasters whose unhappy misadventures with language and imagination disbarred them eternally from creating ever the miracle which true poetry is. With a pen in hand, Cannon was simply not a poet. He was neither literate enough, nor sufficiently endowed with inborn talent, to write verse worthy of the name. An angel with a massive candle may, indeed, on one rare occasion have led him mystically to a favored place in heaven. That angel, mystically, or otherwise, led him on no excursion which took him even near where he could drink deeply, rather than not at all, of Pope's Pierian spring.

Ann Plato was an aspiring lyricist no more able as a poet, apparently, than Cannon to discover (although she was better educated than he) how good poetry really can be written. At Hartford, Connecticut, in 1841, she issued her *Essays; Including Biographies and Miscellaneous Pieces in Prose and Poetry.* Among Afro-American women authors, only Phillis Wheatley antedates her as the publisher of what may, however guardedly, be termed a volume of poetry. In her *Essays; Including Biographies and Miscellaneous Pieces,* a book 122 pages in length, are 16 essays, 4 biographies, and 20 poems. All of the essays are relatively short. They conscientiously address such subjects as education, religion, and benevolence with all the wit, verve, and originality of a hopelessly spinsterish schoolmarm giving advice on life and love to her captive charges in a seminary for well-bred females. The four biographies—like the essays, uniformly brief—all refer to friends of Plato's, presumably all of them black, certainly all of them obscure, and, conceivably, none of them long-lived. These biographies are as much an unrelieved diet of tasteless pabulum as the essays. The twenty poems which complete Plato's volume fail to lift Plato as a poet on to a level of art superior to that mounted by her as an essayist-biographer. Her greatest, if not sole, significance in Afro-American literature is historical.

The famed James W. C. Pennington, who identified Plato as one of his parishioners, wrote the introduction to *Essays; Including Biographies and Miscellaneous Pieces,* the only source thus far for personal information about Plato. But in it Pennington says nothing to help picture Plato as an individualized human being once he has cited her connection with his church. From passages in Plato's poetry, it has been conjectured that she, when she wrote these poems, was either already a teacher (though still an adolescent) or in the process of preparing herself to teach and that she may have been, then, as young as fifteen years old. It might well be difficult, from a review of her poetry and with no other evidence in hand, to ascertain that she was black. One of her lyrics, "In the First of August," eulogizes the emancipation by the British of their slaves. Elsewhere she makes no statement in verse which might betray her race. The subjects which move her most to poetize are religion and death—death, in spite of the fact that she seems, in 1841, to have been hardly more than beginning what may well be regarded as the years in her life when she might very possibly be most alive. She did try her hand at one love poem, of eight stanzas and a refrain, which says, in part:

> When the last rays of twilight fall,
> And thou are pacing yonder hall;

When mists are gathering on the hill,
Nor sound is heard save mountain rill,
When all around bids peace bestill,
  Forget me not.

But Hartford is not a place for mountain rills. Plato speaks of a lover almost surely more a literary phantom than a real person. She was a romantic, not, of course, as were Blake and Keats, but as were many other
young ladies in her day who could, like Cannon (although trying themes
Cannon never seems to have essayed), only be poetasters rather than
poets and whose romanticism came, diluted, insipid, and cloyed with
saccharinity, from second-class Gothic novels and feeble imitations of
sentimental verse such as Thomas Moore's. Pennington, we have seen,
was a leading black abolitionist. From the little we know of Plato, she
was as "white" as Lucy Terry, albeit, of the two, Terry, for all her primitivism, undoubtedly must be reckoned the better poet.

Plato was a free Negro in New England. Far from her in the 1840s,
some other free Negroes, members of the strangest of all the widely distributed enclaves of free Negroes in antebellum America, also were writing poetry. Their claims for recognition in the field of Afro-American
literature, both for the quality of the poetry they wrote and for their historical significance in the total canon of creative literature by black
Americans, greatly surpass those of Plato. They were all Louisiana black
Creoles, and under the editorship of one of their number, Armand Lanusse, in 1845 in New Orleans they published, in French, the first anthology of verse by blacks in America, *Les Cenelles*. The title of their
anthology may be anglicized as *The Holly Berries*.

The black Creoles of Louisiana are, of course, one of America's most
striking and extreme deviations from conventional Americana. They
originated early in the most primal days of Louisiana when Louisiana was
as French as, for instance, early Virginia was English, but when, also, a
great disparity existed in white Louisiana between the relative proportions there of the sexes. Not surprisingly for a frontier outpost of Western
culture, it was the white women who were in short supply. No more surprisingly, since black women in Louisiana were more available then to
their white masters, or other white men, than females of any other color,
a notable incidence of white-black miscegenation, in this Louisiana, occurred and with little, if any, less of its initial momentum continued to
occur. Frequently enough, however, to occasion a trend, the contacts of
an intimate physical nature in Louisiana between white men and black

women, as the years wore on, ceased to be unfailingly merely casual couplings to gratify quickly a white man's lust. Sometimes, that is, a white man who had the means and the social position to do much as he chose would take a black woman as his mistress and treat her, except for marriage and an abandonment of his white wife and family, as if she were, to him, at least a second wife. Indeed an institution developed called *plaçage* which supplied a formula for such a not-so-clandestine polygamy. The black women who entered into these permanent liaisons with white men were called *placées*. Typically, a *placée*, black though the law denoted her, was visibly as white, or almost so, as any legally white woman in Louisiana. Typically, also, she was, in all of her animal attributes, a thing of beauty. But *placées* tended to be more than courtesans adept at the arts of the bordello. The chances were, by the time *plaçage* in Louisiana was in full flower, that a prospective *placée* would be reared by a mother who was herself a *placée*. Such women were keenly aware of their obligations toward their daughters. Their all-encompassing concern was to inculcate in those daughters a capacity for, not simply snaring the favor of a rich, aristocratic, white male, but also for charming him throughout a lifetime with the amenities of an attractive domesticity.

These women placed a premium upon the induction of their daughters into *plaçage* as unsullied virgins. They supervised the exhibition (the marketing, as it were) of their daughters at so-called quadroon balls, to which they welcomed only white men of the proper kind. And they did not forget that even men of supposedly the highest credentials of gentility may not always be completely trusted. It was they who, normally, as a sort of final fulfillment of their maternal care, took the pains to be sure, if it was at all possible, that their daughters performed no function of *plaçage* without advance security. So each such mother expected to restrain her daughter from the ultimate surrender of her person in *plaçage* until that daughter held in irretrievable possession from her white suitor, however importunate he be, a house, as well as, ideally, in addition, a goodly sum of cash.

The children of *placées* tended not to be neglected by their parents of either race. They were domiciled, understandably, in the residences of their mothers. But their white fathers tended to be familiar with them as any affectionate and indulgent fathers might well be familiar with any of their most cherished offspring. Moreover, from their white fathers they could, and not seldom did, receive bounties which permitted their education and their acquisition of perquisites in life which sheltered them from want and from the grosser indignities to their bodies and their spirits most blacks in antebellum America were forced to endure. Some of the children of *placées* inherited plantations from their fathers. Some owned slaves, either as appanages of the plantations bestowed upon them by white fathers or from transactions involving the slaves alone. Questions of racial identity were tortuous when a *placée's* child considered them, and the attitudes of the children of *placées* affected tremendously, as they also paralleled, the thinking of all of Louisiana's other antebellum black Creoles.

Hence, *Les Cenelles*, written in the very period when the sentiments of abolitionists dominated black American literature and published in the same year as Douglass' *Narrative*, is not an exercise in abolitionist rhetoric. It is not even an exercise in black racial protest. The contributors to it were not, and none of them had ever been, slaves. They may well have been, had they felt free to speak their minds openly—as, very conceivably, in New Orleans, they did not—opposed to slavery (but then, again, they may not have been). It is true that, apparently, they esteemed greatly their whiteness above their blackness. They were, for instance, almost desperately anxious not to be regarded, by either whites or blacks, as the degraded equals of blacks other than themselves. They even wanted to be distinguished from free blacks in Louisiana who were not, as they were, Creole. For they were highly conscious of their ties to France (and, thus, they did at least ally themselves with a nation free of slavery).

They spoke French. The more fortunate of them in their own eyes went to France. They took a special interest in French Haiti, where there were, moreover, black French Creoles virtually mirror images of themselves—born comrades of theirs in essentially every respect—with whom they maintained correspondence and exchanged visits. They never expected to wield a hoe or to drudge in fields of sugarcane. Whether their mothers were *placées* or not, the chances were that, as children, they had been drilled in the etiquette and badinage of fashionable drawing rooms and had been educated by French Catholic priests and nuns. The contemporary literature they read tended to be the literature of French romanticism—literature written by young men very much like whom they conceived themselves to be. So they were romantic, too, as were their brothers and models in distant France.

Les Cenelles contains eighty-five poems by seventeen authors. Editor Lanusse, who also wrote the introduction and a dedication for the volume, contributed to its content the most poems, eighteen. He used fourteen poems by Camille Thierry; twelve by Pierre Dalcour; eleven by Val-cour B., who so signed himself in *Les Cenelles* although his name seems actually to have been B. Valcour; and eight by Mirtil-Ferdinand Liotau. No other contributor to *Les Cenelles* is credited with the authorship of more than three poems. Some contributors are credited with the author-ship of one poem only. Victor Séjour, for example, perhaps the best-known literary figure connected with *Les Cenelles,* is represented only by the last poem in the volume, "Le retour de Napoléon." Bowers, who signs himself somewhat pseudonymously as "Boiors" in *Les Cenelles,* is represented only by "The Orphan of the Tombs," Desormes Dauphin only by "Adieu," Nicol Riquet, although he wrote hundreds of songs and poems (ascribing, incidentally, their authorship to other writers whose reputations he hoped thereby to help), only by "Double Rondeau," and even Lanusse's younger brother, Numa Lanusse, the victim of an early death, only by "Couplets" (or "Verses Sung at the Marriage of a Friend") and "Justification à Mademoiselle. . . ." The other contributors to *Les Cenelles* are the brothers Jean and Louis Boise, Nelson Desbrosses, the good friends August Populus and Michel Saint-Pierre, Joanni Questy, considered one of the best poets in the volume, and Manual Sylva, whose name suggests what is true, that he, alone, of the contributors to *Les Cenelles,* was not black and French but black and Spanish.

Editor Lanusse was born in New Orleans, in 1812, where he died fifty-five years later and after the end of the Civil War. There are conflicting reports about his education, not as to its quality, unfailingly described as excellent, but as to whether or not some of it was received in Paris. Dur-ing Lanusse's early maturity, a certain Madame Convent, upon her death, willed land which she stipulated should be applied to the creation of a school for indigent black orphans in a designated part of New Orleans. She further stipulated that a certain Father Manchault should direct the school. Father Manchault worked strenuously to insure that the school projected by Madame Convent was brought into actual existence. So, for that matter, did Lanusse. A Félicie Cailloux, from 1848 to 1852, was the first principal of the school, which was called the Catholic School for Indigent Orphans of Color. Lanusse, however, in 1852 became the school's second principal and remained its principal until his death. So his influence in the New Orleans of his time was considerable. During the Civil War he served in the Confederate army and, after the North captured New Orleans, at first refused to have a northern flag on the grounds of "his" school. His sentiments had changed, however, by the time of his death. It was then the South and southerners he was advising Negroes to reject. His interest in poetry was deep-seated. With some of the other contributors to *Les Cenelles*, he established in 1843 a journal, *L'Album Littéraire: Journal des Jeunes Gens, Amateurs de Littérature!*, as an instrument for the publication of poetry by Louisiana's black Creoles. *L'Album Littéraire* was to appear monthly. It ceased to exist within a year but obviously paved the way for *Les Cenelles*. Lanusse, incidentally, is the only contributor to *Les Cenelles* to refer in any way to *plaçage*, and he speaks of it only once, or perhaps twice. In a terse satire, "Epigramme," he allows, wittily and obliquely, that it may be a sin. In "To Elora," if there he does refer to *plaçage*, he attacks it as a venality as sordid as prostitution.

Three of the contributors to *Les Cenelles* were conspicuously the children of *placées*. Pierre Dalcour was the son of wealthy parents. Although born in New Orleans, he was educated in Paris. He lived and died, moreover, in Paris, after his one attempt to reconcile his Parisian experiences with a Louisiana setting sent him scurrying back to Paris and his familiar association with historic figures as eminent as Alexandre Dumas père and Victor Hugo. Like Dalcour, Victor Séjour, whose full name was actually Juan Victor Séjour Marcou, was born in New Orleans, but Séjour's wealthy white father, a dealer in paints, was a native of Santo Domingo. From 1836 until his death in 1874 at the age of fifty-seven, and his burial in Paris in the famed cemetery Père Lachaise, Paris was Séjour's home. He returned to Louisiana only on occasional visits to his mother, for whom his strong affection never waned. He shone in Paris as a playwright and, no less than Dalcour, moved in circles where he met on familiar terms the Dumases and the Hugos. He lived long enough, however, for fashions in Parisian drama to change, and his last years were those of a former favorite in eclipse as well as of a man of means sunk into relative poverty. Camille Thierry, although born in New Orleans, was the son of a white Frenchman, well disposed in worldly goods, who had planned to provide for Thierry the best education available in both New Orleans and France, did live to see Thierry receive excellent schooling in New Orleans, but died just as Thierry was to continue his schooling in France. Thierry himself divided his life thereafter between New Orleans, Paris, and Bordeaux. His inheritance from his father, with the active administration of which he was much involved, served him well for most of his life and permitted him an indulgence, virtually unchecked, in literature, the focus of his most precious concerns. He died in Bordeaux, ruined by bankruptcy and in broken health, in 1875 at the age of sixty.

Of the other contributors to Les Cenelles, apparently only Valcour B. made the pilgrimage so coveted by them all to Paris for an education in France. Louis Boise was a tailor who was born in New Orleans and never left the town during his entire life. Neither did his brother Jean, who suffered from mental problems and died young. Desbrosses may be of special interest because of his residence for some years in Haiti, where he acquired sufficient command of Haitian mysticism, probably of forms of vodun, to become an established medium in New Orleans upon his return there. Questy was a teacher. In fact, he taught, as a subordinate of Lanusse's, at the Catholic School for Indigent Orphans of Color. Riquet was a cigar maker. Like the Boises, he was born in New Orleans and lived and died there without ever setting foot outside the town of his nativity. Populus was a stonemason who eventually became fairly affluent. Saint-Pierre was a fencing master of such skill that he was known in New Orleans as the "Creole Bayard." At least once he seriously considered suicide but was cajoled into continuing to live by Populus. Of Liotau little is known except that he died in New Orleans, the city of his birth, in 1847.

The poet who seems to have wielded the greatest influence upon the contributors to Les Cenelles is Alphonse de Lamartine, whose Méditations Poétiques, published in 1820, may well have served all, or most, of them as if it were a textbook from which they learned the secrets of their art. They were not unaware of, and sometimes were deferential toward, traditions and practices in French poetry which antedated Lamartine. For example, they could, and did, write alexandrines, a feature of their art subject to loss in English translation. Moreover, there are echoes, however faint, of neoclassic Gallic satire in their verse. But it was not so much the world of the satirist as of the dreamer to which they turned, and turned as would an impressionable youth seeking a voyage to some Cythera in a visionary sea bemoaning a fate to him most lamentable and undeserved. The themes which captured their imaginations have been well listed as "escape, fantasy, melancholy, liberty . . . individualism . . . suicide and death, desired and untimely; love, chaste, unrequited, or tragically ended; nature; and faith."[1] These are, of course, the themes of the French romantics, and their popularity with the contributors to Les Cenelles is only

1. Armand Lanusse (ed.), Les Cenelles, trans. Regine Latorture and Gleason R. W. Adams (1845; rpr. Boston, 1979), xii.

additional evidence of the hold which these French romantics had upon the imaginations of the contributors. To read a slave narrative of the 1840s or 1850s and, then, to transfer one's attention to any poem in *Les Cenelles* is truly to move from one world to another of a far different nature. And it is certainly not to trace the influence of one black tradition upon another.

Lanusse's introduction to *Les Cenelles* is both a defense of learning and an apology for poetry. As a defense of learning, it speaks briefly, but with no hint of doubt as to the unassailable infallibility of its position, about the benefit of formal schooling. As an apology for poetry, it refers both to poets and to those who make a point of treating poetry, and poets, with a sweeping disdain based upon their belief that nothing marks a man as in full possession of his right mind other than the proper pursuit of so-called practical affairs (in other words, than the scramble to make money). These scoffers at verse Lanusse presents only, of course, so that he may oppose them and, in opposing them, chide society in general for its failure to value poetry as highly as Lanusse feels it should be valued.

Lanusse's New Orleans of *Les Cenelles*, although a town, belonged to an agrarian world, a world presided over by a landed aristocracy. Lanusse, therefore, does not complain for poets and against nonpoets quite in the same vein as, for instance Matthew Arnold bemoaning the increasing discomfiture of art and artists in a world dominated by the culture of those whom he branded as Philistines and whose close counterparts Sinclair Lewis later would pillory as Babbitts. Arnold and Lewis, and many others like them within the last century or so, would connect the plight of their artist with a complex of effects deriving from the world as remade by the Industrial Revolution, a world belonging not to a landed aristocracy but to an urbanized bourgeoisie. So Arnold, Lewis, and their kind would perceive a force in their social environment, as in the conditioning of men and women, inhospitable to art precisely because, to a significant extent, it represented, and represents, the spirit of its age, the age of a new ruling class not lordly or manorial but moneyed, scientific, and based atop cosmopolis. Lanusse has no problem with such a force or such an age. He had not come so far, undoubtedly, because his New Orleans was still essentially as free of the changing culture to its north as he thought it was. Lanusse's complaint was old. It stretched back through centuries. In an extreme form a Horace might have said it of a Petronius. Always any poet may have felt it about the most of his less poetic neighbors. And, certainly, in his New Orleans, Lanusse felt it about whites as well as blacks, if not, indeed, more with reference to whites, since blacks were hardly those to whom he devoted his dearest time and affection.

Revolution, then, of any kind does not rear its ugly head anywhere in *Les Cenelles*. Nor, for that matter, does the crude primitivism of a black poet like Noah Calwell W. Cannon, who could not have had the experience with literature of Lanusse and the other poets in *Les Cenelles*. As a matter of fact, possibly one of the more interesting aspects of *Les Cenelles* is the evidence it supplies of a state of mind common to its band of authors which indicates a measure of entrancement among them with, as it were, the games they could play as poets—games not requiring of them any intensities of social purpose akin to those they could hardly have avoided had they, for instance, been committed to the writing of racial protest. So there are acrostics in *Les Cenelles*. There are poems which can be set to music. There are stanzas and rhyme schemes of various kinds, some of them quite fanciful. In one of his poems Dalcour accepts the challenge—extended to him, he says, by his friend Armand Lanusse—to write a poem each stanza of which will conclude with the word *character*. He meets his challenge, quite happily, it may be inferred, in his eyes, in a lyric wherein *character* appears in its designated place four times. Sylva performs a similar feat, in a poem also four stanzas long, with the term *soudain*. Liotau, in his poem "Verses, Sung at a Wedding," quite consciously and deliberately writes an epithalamium (thus, incidentally, playing a game not readily to be associated with the games played by slaves, who could not marry). And Valcour B.'s "My Dream" is a whole poem based, as he is careful to point out, on a single line quoted from a poem of Lamartine's.

Love and death figure prominently in *Les Cenelles*. The love may be, perhaps, more literary than real. It certainly accords with love as that emotion appears in much of the more sentimental poetry and all of the correspondingly sentimental novels of the nineteenth century. It is a love articulated through a battery of phrases and images all too commonly employed by the least inventive poets contemporary with *Les Cenelles*. Surely, however, a sight to watch in *Les Cenelles* is the coloring of the maidens who are loved. Their complexions typically are white. Their eyes typically are blue. Death in *Les Cenelles* tends to be melodramatic: it takes to a tragically early grave a young girl at the height of her loveliness; a son loses most pitifully the mother he adores; in what could be a tribute to the vogue of Werther, a young man commits suicide;

and from Armand Lanusse, in his "A Brother at His Brother's Grave," emanate echoes of Catullus' classic "Ave atque Vale."

In summary, then, *Les Cenelles* simply does not fit as a volume of black literature if, in black literature, blackness is all. It contains absolutely no links with the flaming philippics against white racism of David Walker or the intransigent black nationalism of post–1960 Black Militants. Its decorous Roman Catholicism distances it by far from the Methodist reliance on an individual conversion (in which one's dungeon shakes) of Jupiter Hammon or the fervid evangelical proselyting of Noah Calwell W. Cannon. And, certainly, nowhere in *Les Cenelles* is there any hint of the kind of experience with religion out of which the Negro spiritual derived its unique attributes of beauty both as an artifact and as an expression of faith in a divine will. The antebellum tradition of blackness, as already hitherto noted, embraced a glaring illiteracy. Valcour B.'s "Letter to Constant Lepouze," an epistle to a Frenchman who had immigrated to New Orleans and there had taught the young Creole, thanks Lepouze for his introduction of Valcour B. to the poetry of Horace and Virgil. In the Red River country of Louisiana, Solomon Northup found blacks being introduced to something altogether different. It is true, incidentally, that *Les Cenelles* does present a poem by Valcour B., "The Louisiana Laborer," in which the poet praises the dignity of honest toil (presumably with the hands), expresses himself as, in sympathy, at least, a man of the people, and even expresses his firm attachment to his "only goddess," Rose, a "woman of the people," a "beauty plain" who, in addition, dresses simply without the fine, elaborate, expensive gowns and accessories to their wardrobes of the more privileged maidens of higher social rank than Rose to whom the "people" are surely a nonentity. But in "The Louisiana Laborer," Valcour B. seems almost certainly to be writing, as it were, his own version of a pastoral. He is as much a man of the people in the later sense of a Eugene Debs or of the workers in the turpentine camps visited by Zora Neale Hurston in her collecton of folklore as Theocritus was a shepherd. So, undoubtedly, he well represents *Les Cenelles.*

The very name *Les Cenelles*, it seems, was chosen for the volume it adorns because holly berries are indigenous to Louisiana and because, also, these berries are only a modest form of vegetation as vegetation goes. They constitute no example, in taste, appearance, or any combination of the two, of the eye-feasting, richly appetizing fruits nature can produce at her botanical most lavish. To artists identifying themselves with such a special closed and narrow world as that inhabited by the contributors to Les Cenelles, the mere quality of being indigenous might well be reckoned, if only as a readily calculated sop to their own self-esteem, a virtue of the highest order. But virtue or not, it is certainly a decided, as well as (probably) highly exotic, curio in the conceivable range of gradations in the defensive thinking of the black American ghetto. No less certainly the poetry in Les Cenelles is modest in its level of achievement. It may, indeed, be more modest than indigenous.

Like New Orleans, Charleston is a port town. During the period of slavery Charleston, again like New Orleans, developed a community of mulattoes, strikingly octoroon, that lived, as did the very similar community to which belonged the poets of Les Cenelles, in a strange universe between two other worlds. An anecdote, however apocryphal, which has flourished in Negro intraracial lore for several generations tells of a Negro church in Charleston with a front door the lintel of which was tinted ivory. According to the anecdote, no one darker in complexion than the lintel was ever, in the good old days, permitted to join the church. But Charleston also was the home of Denmark Vesey. There were free Negroes in Charleston, then, as well as slaves, who thought as did James Forten and Black Gabriel. Daniel Payne was born in Charleston in 1811. Both his parents were free. His father, incidentally, like the mother of John Marrant, had been born free in the North and had voluntarily come south. So Payne, no mulatto, was born free. He would grow up with easy access to Negroes hardly distinguishable, if at all, from the contributors to Les Cenelles in their attitudes towards whites and other Negroes. But it was the Negroes who consorted with Denmark Vesey that were far more of his breed. And, when he died, only the sainted Richard Allen, in whose footsteps he could be said to have trod and whose mantle he could be said to have assumed, was considered a greater black churchman than he.

Physically, Payne was relatively frail, and certainly anything but prepossessing in size, in spite of the fact that he lived into his eighties. Both of his parents died before he was ten. A great-aunt raised him. To book learning he was introduced while he was still very young through his enrollment in a school maintained by some free black Charlestonians. With the instruction thus received he was soon able to mingle knowledge acquired from a very good private tutor. But it was largely by means of his own independent study that he made himself, especially for his epoch, a genuine savant. He became proficient, for example, not only in basic literacy, but also in mathematics and science, as well as in, for his time, such elitist languages as French, Latin, and Greek. Yet he was also trained to work. Before he was eighteen he had, in effect, served successive apprenticeships to a shoe merchant, a carpenter, and a tailor. Religion was always important to him. His most vivid memory of his parents may well have been of them at their daily prayers or performing other acts of pious devotion in the home he shared with them. It was a memory dimmed by nothing which occurred in the household of the great-aunt who raised him. At eighteen he experienced conversion, in the white Methodist Episcopal church. Events so transpired, nevertheless, that, at about the same time, he started a school. It was, at first, just a little school for three slave children. However, it grew. Soon enough, it required a building of its own. For Payne was a teacher with a golden touch. His school, therefore, was an institution of considerable size and standing among black Charlestonians when, in 1835, because of a recently adopted South Carolina law denying the benefits of schooling to blacks, he was forced to terminate it. His best-known poem, "The Mournful Lute, or the Preceptor's Farewell," is an obvious accompaniment of the closing of his school.

Without his school to hold him, Payne chose no longer to stay in the South. He went north. In New York City he had a thought-provoking conversation with the white abolitionist Lewis Tappan. He studied at the Lutheran Seminary in Gettysburg, Pennsylvania, and pastored a Presbyterian church in East Troy, New York, before opening another school in Philadelphia. By 1841 he had become an AME, and by 1843, an AME minister. He pastored AME churches in Washington, D.C., and Baltimore, but he quickly became a figure of consequence throughout the whole AME connection. His love of learning did not desert him in the pulpit. To the discomfiture (and anger) of many, he actually crusaded against an illiterate clergy. He compounded his departure from amiable complacency by inveighing against a kind of song very popular with the rank and file of AME communicants which was full of gibberish from untaught minds and, thus, of that very illiteracy, often even in denser forms, already objectionable to him in the language of the presumptive spiritual leaders of these communicants. He called examples of the rude tunes with their ruder words which he so deplored "cornfield ditties," and it eased his spirit none that such "cornfield ditties" were usually chanted, supposedly in holy worship, as those who uttered them were caught up in the animal hysteria of violent and antic, if not obscene, contortions of

their physiques. In any case, in 1852, although in disregard of his strenuous protest, he was elevated to the AME episcopacy. In 1863 it was he
who engineered (with financial aid from one of Du Bois' ancestors) the
purchase by the AME connection, from the Methodist Episcopal church,
of Wilberforce University. He served as president of Wilberforce, without surrendering his bishopric, from 1863 until 1876. Yet there may have
been no sweeter single moment in his entire life for him than that ecstatic instant, in 1865, of his return to Charleston exactly thirty years to
the day after his departure therefrom, where he, before he turned north
again, as one talisman of the changing times, established a South Carolina conference of his beloved AME denomination.

Payne was married twice. His first wife died within a year of her union
with him. His second wife survived him. He made two trips abroad, once
to England and once to England and France. On both occasions he went
to meetings of associations related to his vocation as a priest. He was
commissioned in 1850 to write a history of the AME church. On his own
initiative, he had shown a disposition to visit and examine AME congregations. To gather material for his history, he traveled America from
Canada to New Orleans, undaunted (it is surely worthy of note) by the
menace of such travel to a free Negro below the Mason-Dixon line before
the Civil War. He did, incidentally, complete his history. It was published in 1866 as the *Semi-Centenary and the Retrospection of the African
Methodist Episcopal Church*. But his first book had been poetry, the small
volume *Pleasures and Other Miscellaneous Poems*, published in 1850. He
winnowed his own thought and drew upon his own experiences in positions of public trust and responsibility to write the *Treatise on Domestic
Education*, which he published in 1885. Undoubtedly, however, his autobiography, *Recollections of Seventy Years*, to which the estimable and eminent Francis J. Grimké (Charlotte Forten's husband, it will be remembered) added an introduction and which was published in 1888, easily
takes precedence in interest and importance over anything else he wrote.
He presided at a session of the Chicago World's Fair in late September,
1893, and had planned, as was usual with him in his later years, to winter
in Jacksonville, Florida. But he died at Wilberforce in November, 1893.
He was buried in Baltimore.

What we know about Payne's life, with the tremendous demands he
permitted it—eagerly, it seems—to place upon the long hours he chose
to devote to exhausting work, using therein all the talents and developed
skills he could command, as well as the picture we have of him as a per-

son, so grave, so meticulous, so stern, so committed to the rigorous discharge of sorely taxing duties, and so apparently uninvolved with an "artistic temperament," may incline us toward a highly fallacious underassessment of his passion to be a poet. It is true that the older he grew the less rein he gave to that passion. His labors for his church, the AME, and his people, all of America's Negroes, did increasingly preoccupy him once he had begun to become, certainly no later than the early 1850s, the Payne by whom a multitude of communal concerns were supervised. He made thousands of speeches, far from all of them sermons, but none of them in a voice so captivating and easy to project as that of Frederick Douglass. In the 1850s, and until the Civil War, he never missed a chance to give his aid to the abolitionists. He was the Negro who joined Carl Schurz in pleading with President Lincoln for the freeing of the Negroes in the District of Columbia. His years as president of Wilberforce University were both crowded and productive. And after those years, he retired into no retreat. Most of the poetry he wrote, therefore, was written in his youth. It is lyric poetry. It suggests limits on his imagination—that he could plod, but hardly soar. But he must, when he did seek to poetize, have worked hard at his chosen task—must have given it a portion of himself he deeply prized—and dreamed for it some flights into lyricism too ambitious as attempts to reach the difficult-to-gain haunts of beauty for his powers of creativity to summon them into actual existence.

It is, as has been stated here before, "The Mournful Lute" by which Payne's poetry circulated to its widest audience. And "The Mournful Lute," for good or ill, does tend, in virtually its every principal aspect, reliably to represent all of his verse. It is a poem which, although written in 1835, employs exclusively the neoclassical heroic couplet. Nor is it neoclassical in prosody alone. A half a century after Phillis Wheatley's death, Payne shared with her the same set of assumptions about how poetry should be conceived and written which had animated her. He shared with her, also, proficiency in the mechanics of making verse. His ability to rhyme is far from crude. He does not forget occasionally to invest his flow of auditory effects with alliteration. And with sufficient frequency, it may well be, for conscientious poetry, he resorts to figures of speech, among them notably the similes, often Homeric, at least to some degree, which neoclassic poets loved, but in which they typically lacked the capacity to achieve that special alchemy of synthesizing parts into a whole so that the disparity of the parts helped, and did not hinder, the desired sense of a single revelatory insight indispensable from true meta-phors. He was, in short, a proper poet, one who blotted no line or syl-lable from an absence of sincere intent, but also one whose strength of determination to compose for his muse was not matched by anything within him that actually did transmute rhythmic prose into the magic which is real verse such as, to illustrate, the something which worked through Keats in Keats's great odes. There was, moreover, always some-thing terribly inhibited about even his approach to poetry. If he sorrows, for example, it is always only with sighs and sobs, never with an outburst of grief so lost in abandoned emotion as tears.

"The Mournful Lute" begins with a tribute from Payne to his parents and, especially for its effect on him, their steadfastness in their faith. From his contemplation of their adoration of the Lord, it is but a step for Payne to the proclamation of his own apprehension of, and submission to, God's will and God's intelligence. So, indeed, he traces his mission as a teacher back to the very heart of the Eternal throne. For it is through what he has learned of God that he has also learned the actual nature of ignorance, a condition induced in man only by the devil's evil curse and industry and, therefore, a condition not merely reprehensible but a sin. Payne, then, serves God directly and attacks nothing less than a would-be citadel of Satan when he affords instruction to the pupils he has brought within his care. For him to rejoice—as he does (and should)—over the success of his school is for him, truly, to take delight both in his pupils' individual accomplishments and in his own perception that their en-lightenment extends the kingdom of God. Thus, for more than one rea-son, he declares:

> Oh, here's my bliss, that I the way have shown
> To lovely youths which was before unknown;
> From scientific shrines plucked golden fire,
> And thrilled with notes divine the sacred lyre.

Nevertheless, Payne exhibits no tendency to rail at God for the situa-tion, the closing of his school, which occasions, as it were, his lute to mourn. He does remember how once the Lord attended Abram when Abram was driven to roam abroad from his home. And he does indulge himself, if only rhetorically, in one hope which he absolutely knows is vain. He speaks, that is, of arresting time, of holding back any further passage of the sun until the "lads" and "modest virgins" of his school have completed a curriculum he has prescribed for their education. He cries aloud, therefore: "Oh! that my arms could reach yon burning sun / And stop his motion till my work be done!"

But Payne cries aloud, of course, not as one who truly expects a miracle to happen on the scale of that which ushered Joshua into Jericho. He merely resorts to what is, after all, a hyperbolic image as a means of articulating with some degree of adequacy his sense of loss from his contemplation of that which now will never be consummated (as much as he had so devoutly wished it) at his school. And so he advances themes in reference to which sound criticism could hardly argue a fault in their selection. The finest of poets have expatiated on similar themes. The parents he describes, his meditations about them and God, the unhappy turn of events for his school and his reaction to that disaster all are worthy of a poet's attention. Of conception he is not bereft. It is in execution that he fares too often somewhat amiss, without emancipation from the sterility of imagination which, apparently, dooms his poetry always to be never quite free—or free enough—of nonpoetic elements. He writes, in "The Mournful Lute," 186 lines of verse in 22 stanzas of 8 lines (or 4 couplets) each and a concluding stanza 10 lines (or an extra couplet) long. His progression through the 186 lines is steady and sensible. In the longest (and most Homeric) simile of the poem, some lines after the couplet just quoted here, he portrays himself:

> As when a deer does in the pasture graze,
> The lion roars—she's filled with wild amaze,
> Knows strength unequal for the dreadful fight,
> And seeks sweet safety in her rapid flight—
> So Payne prepares to leave his native home,
> With pigmy purse on distant shore to roam.

Thus, he announces, as it were, a calm succeeding a storm. In the dramatic structure of his poem, he has arrived at its falling action. Now he can end his poem on a note of reconciliation with himself, and hope, as Milton ends his *Lycidas*. Payne's final couplet says: "A useful life by sacred wisdom crowned / Is all I ask, let weal or woe abound."

Payne is something of a nonpareil among black poets. Charles Reason and George Boyer Vashon, however, are two of his contemporaries who, as black poets, seem to invite consideration as a pair. As free-born northern Negroes of the same generation, much which they did, and said, was of a pattern common to both of them. Yet as poets they differed, even though they tended to address the same theme, freedom. And the manner in which they differed is well worth some attention. Reason could versify. But he was really at least as bound to the prosaic and commonplace in poetry as Payne. Vashon, on the other hand, possessed the true native talents of a poet. Indeed, of all the black poets of the nineteenth century, perhaps only Albery Whitman was more the poet in the fullest, finest sense of the term than he.

Reason was born in New York City in 1818, the oldest of three sons of a Martinican father and a Haitian mother. He went to the African Free School, where Henry Highland Garnet, Alexander Crummell, James McCune Smith, and Ira Aldridge were among his fellow students. Although he displayed a decided talent for mathematics, he sought entry into the same Episcopal seminary as that which rebuffed Crummell, with the same result. He was rebuffed, too. Educated thereafter at McGrawville College, in 1849 he joined the faculty of the newly founded, abolitionist New York Central College, located in McGrawville, as the first of the three Negroes who would serve on its faculty. In 1852 he became the principal of the Institute for Colored Youth in Philadelphia, from which, incidentally, Cheney State College descends. He was very successful with the institute. Nevertheless, in 1855 he returned to New York City, the city of his birth, to teach there. He spent the rest of his life, either as a teacher or a principal, in the schools of New York City. Not even the partial paralysis which he eventually suffered prevented his maintenance of his career as a teacher-administrator. He died, still active in his profession, in 1893.

Reason was a Negro of light complexion. His contemporaries tended to consider him handsome. They also tended to remark his cultivated behavior and good manners. No one could fault his loyalty to his fellow Negroes. Much of his support of racial causes occurred, as it were, however, behind the scenes. He wrote, for example, more than his share of resolutions and reports and attended many committee meetings without losing the relatively low profile he—rather deliberately, it seemed—maintained as a public man. Still, those who knew him well were prone always to speak of him in uniformly commendatory terms. He may well have been a model exhibit of what is supposed to be meant by the phrase "gentleman of the old school."

Reason issued no volume of his own poetry, and only four poems attributed to him are, apparently, still extant. How much poetry he did write is subject to conjecture. The assertion has been made that poems by him, during his own time, did appear, upon occasion, in newspapers. Of his poems still extant, the two by far best known are "The Spirit Voice, Or, Liberty Call to the Disfranchised," an ode summoning the Negroes of New York to oppose their exclusion from the ballot box, and "Freedom," a eulogy to the great English abolitionist Thomas Clarkson. "The Spirit Voice" first appeared in 1841. "Freedom" first appeared in 1846. It can hardly be said that the subject of admission to the ballot box inherently appears to promise the excitement presumably inherent in a tale of murder or an account of young love or, even, in a relation of some exploit like a hunt for treasure or the shooting of big game. Nor does it seem that Reason was the kind of poet who might well have written in a lively style about such things. He, apparently, just did not possess the kind of sense of drama out of which he might have rendered his verse both more graphic and less tame. He does achieve some eloquence at times within "The Spirit Voice." And he never falters in emulating the behavior of a polite littérateur in the formal aspects of his verse. But he also never does anything more, at least not in terms of setting imaginations on fire. His way with poetry (and the dead weight of his subject) throughout "The Spirit Voice" appears reliably in the following lines near the conclusion of his poem:

> Come! rouse ye brothers, rouse! nor let the voice
> That shouting, calls you onward to rejoice,
> Be heard in vain! but with ennobled souls,
> Let all whom now an unjust law controls
> Press on in strength of mind, in purpose bent,
> To live by right; to swell the free tones sent
> On Southern airs, from this, your native State.

In "Freedom," Reason resorts to personification. Accordingly, he describes, in order, a creature, more or less a goddess, it would seem—or certainly at least a somewhat disembodied spirit with godlike powers—who (or which) animates the Jews of the Old Testament leaving Egypt; then, in their finest moments, the Classical Greeks and Romans; next, the Western Europeans, like the Swiss opposing Austrian tyranny (but never any Asians east of Asia Minor or black Africans); and, finally, the abolitionist Clarkson in his crusade against the slave trade and slavery.

Vashon was the son of a free-born Virginian who had fought in the War of 1812. Vashon's father was to spend the bulk of his life in Pittsburgh as the solidly affluent owner of a bathhouse, a leading figure, conspicuous for his unselfish labors for the common good, among the free Negroes of Pittsburgh, one of the best-known Negroes nationally in the

America of his time, a wily and indefatigable abolitionist not averse to contributions from his purse, as well as from his time and energy, to the fight against slavery, a very active functionary of the Underground Railroad, and something of a doting parent able to give Vashon a finer start in life than most youngsters in any era might expect from their immediate sires. Vashon, who was born in Carlyle, Pennsylvania, in 1824, five years before his family's move to Pittsburgh, indeed, in 1844, was the first Negro to finish Oberlin. His hopes of practicing law in Pittsburgh were dashed when, because of his color, he was not even permitted to take an examination for the bar. Understandably resentful, he left Pittsburgh for Haiti. Yet, on his trip to the West Indies, he chose an itinerary sufficiently devious to allow his pausing long enough in the state of New York to take and pass there a state bar examination to which he was admitted.

For thirty months in Haiti, Vashon taught at the College Faustin in Port au Prince. The thirty months were momentous for Afro-American literature. A clear connection exists between them and Vashon's memorable poem "Vincent Ogé." In the summer of 1850, however, Vashon returned to the United States and practiced law in Syracuse until 1854, when he entered upon three years of service on the faculty of New York Central College. In 1857 he resumed residence in Pittsburgh, where, of course, he had grown up. He continued to teach school. Uniformly his contemporaries described him as a great teacher. John Mercer Langston, as has been noted earlier here, was once one of his pupils. In 1857, also, he married Susan Paul Smith of Boston, from a family virtually as noted in the national community of free Negroes as his own. Whether he ever taught at Howard University and was dean of the law school there, as has been repeatedly stated, is open to question. There is, as a matter of fact, a need for the clarification of his biography during the last years of his life. He may, or may not, have perished as a victim of a yellow-fever epidemic in 1878 in Rodney, Mississippi, as is commonly assumed. In any case, his wife, who had borne him seven children, survived him by thirty-four years, until 1912, dying in St. Louis, where a high school was eventually to bear the name Vashon.

As with Reason, so with Vashon. Little poetry by Vashon is extant. It is not supposed of Vashon, however, that he may have written much more verse than that to which we have access now. A restless, as well as a brilliant, man, he seems constantly to have had too many irons, often at too high a temperature, in the fire to turn his mind, other than most infrequently, to the writing of poetry. In "A Life-Day," published in

1864, he tells, without descending excessively into the maudlin, about a white southern planter deserted by all, as his health appears to fail, except his beauteous and devoted female slave, who nurses him back to at least a semblance of the man in both body and spirit he once was and whom he marries, only for this angel of mercy and her two children by him to be sold as slaves after his death. His "Ode on the Proclamation of the Fifteenth Amendment," published in 1870, is precisely what its title says it is, a declamation in verse (of no particular breadth of the imagination) welcoming the addition to the Constitution by which the Negro, according to the letter of the law, was enfranchised. Solely in "Vincent Ogé" does Vashon demonstrate how ably he could speak when at his best in essaying poetry to express himself.

There was a real Vincent Ogé who was a genuine martyr to a genuine cause. But Ogé was far from black. He was a pronounced mulatto, a quadroon if not an octoroon, who occupied in colonial Haiti (where quarterings according to color were carried to absurd and fantastic lengths) a position in society closely analogous to that of the poets of *Les Cenelles* in the society of antebellum Louisiana. Ogé's mother, like him a free Negro, owned a large plantation, and slaves, in Haiti. It had been no problem for her to educate Ogé in France. Moreover, Ogé was in Paris in 1789. There he could not but be well aware of much of the turmoil and challenge to an ancien régime which history rightfully associates with the imminence of the French Revolution.

White Haitians of the planter class were most decidedly conscious of the same turmoil and challenge. Some of these white planters lived in Haiti. But some of this identical brand of the Haitian upper class were absentee owners, most of them living in Paris and belonging to a club which they had formed for themselves and called the Club Massiac. When, in May, 1789, the States General was summoned to meet at Versailles, it seemed to members of this club that the time had come to seek from the homeland, France, dominion status, or as near its equivalent as possible, for the colony of Haiti. The Club Massiac, therefore, in Haiti's interest, as they conceived it, although they limited that interest to prerogatives for Haitians of exactly their exalted rank and kind, arranged to send commissioners to the States General. But the white Haitian planters who were not in Paris (or France) and not in the Club Massiac—it may well have been because they were so distant from the scene of the central action—were bolder in their moves than their fellow planters in Paris. Understandably, officials sent out from Paris to represent the French government were stationed in Haiti. These officials, as was to be expected, frowned upon dominion status for Haiti and opposed all activity designed to reduce the colony's obligations and subservience to France. The white Haitian planters in Haiti, in a clear confrontation with French officialdom on their island, chose to elect from only their own highly exclusive, and very white, inner circle persons whom they sent to Paris, not as commissioners to negotiate with the States General, but as delegates fully to share in whatever the States General did. The States General, which had become the National Assembly, accepted the delegates from the white planters of Haiti and granted to that colony a colonial assembly, essentially what the white Haitian planters had asked for, especially since this colonial assembly was to be one the members of which were to be elected according to terms proposed by the white Haitian planters— terms calculated to place into the hands of these planters complete control of the colonial assembly and, so, of Haiti.

But the free Negroes of Haiti had their man in Paris, also, the young, rich, well-educated Julien Raimond, who had lived in Paris for years; who had made friends with such notable Frenchmen as Lafayete, Brissot, Gregoire, and Robespierre; whom the free Negroes of Haiti designated as their commissioner to the National Assembly; and who actually did receive, and well employ, the opportunity of speaking before the National Assembly, where his remarks fell on some ears quite sympathetic to his pleas on behalf of the Haitian free mulattoes. Hence, as well as because of the spirit of innovation already present in the unstable political climate of France in 1789 and for some years afterward, the decree granting a colonial assembly to Haiti did permit an interpretation not quite that insisted upon by the white proprietors of Haiti. Under the decree, extension of the franchise to the free Negroes of the colony (but no slaves) could have been arranged. As a matter of fact, the ambiguities in the decree were not only not lost upon the white Haitian planters. These very ambiguities, an invitation to change as they might be construed, rendered the planters, individually and severally, even more adamant, and choleric, in their determination that the free Negroes of Haiti would not be relieved of a single one of their disabilities, including, obviously, the disability of their exclusion from the franchise. The election of a colonial assembly for Haiti was to proceed, the white Haitian planters undertook to guarantee, with no free Haitian mulattoes involved. The planters' intransigence did not stir Raimond from France, sincere as was his concern for an improvement in the status of his fellow mulattoes. Ogé, however, who was also in France, of his own free will decided to return to Haiti and institute measures, of which a resort to arms might be a part, to secure the vote—and, possibly, other rights—to Haiti's free Negroes.

It should perhaps be emphasized here that, sub specie aeternitatis, Ogé did believe in the abolition of slavery, albeit not in its immediate end. Like his friend Raimond, he favored a gradual emancipation of the slaves. Yet, also like Raimond, he consorted as a true believer with members and supporters of the Société des Amis des Noirs, an organization which was abolitionist, and not in terms which would delay emancipation. Ogé, nevertheless, was returning to Haiti specifically and exclusively to organize and fight for Haiti's free Negroes. He had made no plans in France to lead a slave insurrection. He made no such plans after he returned to Haiti. The 300 men he armed there and gathered round himself as a band of committed warriors could argue their own championship of legality, inasmuch as it was their mission, by the reasoning they announced, to expedite the proper observance of a decree from the National Assembly. Ogé and his men actually fought two battles. In the first, against a force almost three times larger than their own, they were not vanquished. In the second, facing 1,500 antagonists equipped with artillery, they were demolished. Ogé escaped to the Spanish part of the island, whence the Spaniards returned him to French Haiti. Some of his captured followers were sent to the galleys. Some were hanged. Ogé, in 1791, was broken on the wheel and drawn and quartered, after which his dismembered body was placed conspicuously on public display in four cities of Haiti. In 1792 the slaves in Haiti did revolt under a leader who came to be known to history as Toussaint L'Ouverture.

Although Ogé was a genuine martyr for a cause he thought sufficiently noble to give to it his last full measure of devotion, he was hardly a genuine martyr for black people. It is not difficult to believe that he could easily have been persuaded to espouse the rights of blacks. Even so, it requires some imprecision of historical fact to associate his martyrdom with the black struggle for freedom and equality. Be that as it may, however, in "Vincent Ogé," Vashon uses Ogé as a symbol representing the fight of everyone, including blacks, to achieve freedom, especially from tyrannies imposed on others by a privileged class. With its 391 lines, "Vincent Ogé" clearly is not truly a long poem. On the other hand, neither is it short. Still, Joan Sherman, in a very able reading of it, refers to it as an epic.[2] For Sherman is impressed by qualities she finds in it which she associates with poetry of the epic kind—not least among those qualities its theme and the manner in which Vashon relates his treatment of that theme as magnificently as he does to what may be called the immortal longings and yet, also, the conditioning by their unhappy past of an entire people.

Of Vashon in "Vincent Ogé," Benjamin Brawley, not one to distribute praise lavishly, says, "He does not give a straightforward narrative, but uses the rhythmic, discursive, and frequently subjective manner of Byron and Scott, sometimes with surprising effect." Sherman inspects more meticulously than Brawley Vashon's discursiveness. She finds in it some highly creditable art. "Vincent Ogé" is divided into eight uneven parts within which events and human beings, according to Sherman, exist (most significantly) in a state of "Heraclitan" flux. Vashon, Sherman asserts, "sustains an ambience of unstable activity throughout the poem with an image pattern of flickering light, storms, blood, and warfare; by shifts from classical to prosaic to metaphorical diction; by abrupt changes in metrical and stanzaic form; by intermittent use of descriptive, narrative, and subjective voices; by movement in temporal and spatial scene; and by direct statement of theme such as, 'Life is a changeful thing.'"[3]

It is a measure of the complexity, the sophistication, and the level of mastery of an art in "Vincent Ogé" that Sherman may speak of it in detail as she does without fear that she greatly misrepresents her subject. In "Vincent Ogé" there is, indeed, a persisting ambience of unstable activity—an ambience, far from incidentally, the result not of haphazard chance but of its creator's intent—and this ambience, this more than a mere fleeting impression, is fabricated, even though, as always in high art, somewhat inexplicably, to no small degree by resort to precisely those methods of articulating thought and feeling which Sherman itemizes above. Moreover, the notion of life as a changeful thing is a theme which one does encounter in "Vincent Ogé." In truth, it more than seems part of the excellence of "Vincent Ogé" that, throughout the poem, Vashon not only describes and tells. He also broods. Thus themes, really subthemes, such as his subtheme of life as a changeful thing, are

2. Joan Sherman, *Invisible Poets: Afro-Americans of the Nineteenth Century* (Urbana, Ill., 1974), 58.

3. Benjamin Brawley, *Early Negro American Writers* (Chapel Hill, 1935), 262; Sherman, *Invisible Poets*, 57.

available to provoke the reader's appetite for probing into profundities, here and there, from the beginning of the poem to its end. But the central theme, the big theme, of the poem is still political, still the theme of freedom and its achievement. One of the ends, therefore, which Vashon accomplishes in "Vincent Ogé" that Payne, for example, could not accomplish in "The Mournful Lute" nor Reason in "Freedom" is the rescue of an abstraction from its abstractness. It is, indeed, not only Vincent Ogé, his insurrection, and his death, which become instilled with life in "Vincent Ogé." It is, likewise, ideas themselves—conceptions about the nature of this world and of the significance within our cosmos, in both a limited and a rounded, full perspective, of the incidents connected with Ogé—which "Vincent Ogé" endows with meaningful vitality.

Brawley links Vashon with Byron and Scott. Certainly Vashon is a poet of their exalted order. The opening lines, alone, of "Vincent Ogé" show convincingly how little was he a mere poetaster. In them he says:

> There is, at times, an evening sky—
> The twilight's gift—of sombre hue,
> All checkered wild and gorgeously
> With streaks of crimson, gold and blue;—
> A sky that strikes the soul with awe,
> And, though not brilliant as the sheen,
> Which in the east at morn we saw,
> Is far more glorious, I ween;—
> So glorious that, when night hath come
> And shrouded it in deepest gloom,
> We turn aside with inward pain
> And pray to see that sky again.

So, in these lines, Vashon prepares his reader well for the whole of his major poem which these lines, in effect, allegorically summarize with one swift coup of perception while, at the same time, they set a tone and invite a mood both of which foster in a human consciousness the kind of cognition which seems reserved for seers.

There is, then, in "Vincent Ogé" at its most elementary level a simple narrative which may be traced through all the apparent disjunctions in the internal structure of the poem. It is a narrative foreshadowed by the poem's opening lines. It pictures Haiti, when Columbus found it, as a semiparadise, an Eden. It does not picture Haiti with slaves as such. But there does come a new day in France. Clearly, therefore, a new day should not be unthinkable in Haiti. Yet, like the sky we may be forced to accept as a phenomenon of our existence even after a bright new prospect we thought we saw there has failed to be redeemed, so Ogé has tried to introduce to Haiti a dispensation fairer than the old and has failed in his attempt. His defeat and death have woefully terminated a valiant undertaking by a hero worthy of permanent renown in the annals of man's fight for freedom. But in "Vicent Ogé" there is always, also, more than a simple narrative. There is always, in "Vincent Ogé" additionally, at a level above that of the unadulterated narrative, the brooding cited here earlier, the play of a contemplative mind upon stark incident and unvarnished fact, searching for connections and hidden meanings which might illuminate that which we tend to find unduly inscrutable in our world. "Vincent Ogé" contains no certain answers to its own brooding. But, through that brooding, it invests itself with a powerful dimension of suggestion. Through its search for light, however dim, within the obfuscations which tend to hide the contours of truth so often when most we wish our vision could be clear, it reflects upon the whole of human life as well as upon the lamentable fate of Vincent Ogé.

11. *Later Abolitionist Poets*

Vashon was a close contemporary of Joshua McCarter Simpson, who was born about 1820 in Morgan County, Ohio, and died in 1876 in Zanesville in the same state. For some reason Simpson was sometimes, even to other writers, known as Joshua C. McSimpson, John McCarty Simpson, or J. S. McCarter. At the age of three Simpson was apprenticed to an Isaac Kay, a stonemason and farmer, who mistreated him so badly that representatives of the law removed him from Kay and reapprenticed him, until he would be twenty-one, to another farmer. With very little schooling, Simpson entered the preparatory department at Oberlin College in 1844, the year in which Oberlin, it will be remembered, granted a bachelor's degree to Vashon. Simpson remained at Oberlin until 1848. In 1847 he was married in Zanesville. At the time of his death, he was pastoring a Baptist church in Zanesville, but also, allegedly, serving those who wished his ministrations as a herb doctor.

Herb doctoring hardly seems an avocation in keeping with the faith of a good Baptist. If it intimates, however, a quirk of the mind which deterred Simpson from being a respectable poet, it is misleading. The genre of poetry affected by Simpson differed greatly from that to which Vashon turned his hand in "Vincent Ogé." But just as Vashon was talented for epic, so Simpson was talented for the kind of thing he wrote. Abolitionism was a cause he espoused, just as colonizationism was a cause he abhorred and despised. Principally, he wrote songs for abolitionism and wrote those songs with telling effect. People, singly or in groups, liked to sing his songs. Harriet Beecher Stowe heard Sojourner Truth lustily roaring his "Away to Canada," which appeared in 1852 in Garrison's *Libera-*

tor, and Stowe noted how the woman who had grown famous for her dramatic diatribes against slavery seemed to take as much delight in voicing the words and music of a Simpson song as she did in uttering her own oratory.

Simpson, respectable evidence suggests, began publishing his verse as early as 1848. Some of his poetry apparently he circulated in pamphlets. In 1874 he published *Emancipation Car,* in which he collected fifty-three of his songs along with an autobiography and two of his own essays. In one of these essays he attacks colonization and emphasizes his belief that he and all other blacks are Americans who should keep themselves firmly stationed in America. In the other essay, "A Consistent Slaveholder's Sermon," under the pretense of reporting word for word a white bishop's homily to his slaves, he satirizes rather effectively white Christianity's defense of slavery. For he was gifted, not only as a creator of singable songs, but also as an artist in the use of the dry mock. Just as he had a knack for convenient diction—for restraining himself to words not so long that they would tie into knots and hobble the tongue of an ordinary person—in his songs, so, in his satire, he tended not to overdo his ridicule or his righteous wrath. He even often showed a certain genius in the selection of the tunes to which he attached his songs, as when, for instance, he matched his "Warning to the White People of America" with the melody of "Massa's in de Cold, Cold Groun'."

The art of satire found a home in which it could take some pride not only, however, in Simpson's verse but also in the verse of another black poet of Simpson's time, Elymas Payson Rogers, who was born in Madison, Connecticut, in 1815. An ancestor of Rogers had been one of the slave survivors of the shipwreck of a slaver off the Connecticut coast in the very earliest years of the eighteenth century. From the memory of that ancestor, as well as from his zeal to propagate universally the Christian faith, Rogers seems to have derived a resolution to return to Africa which was of signal importance to him throughout his life. Rogers' childhood was not easy. His parents were poor. He did eventually manage, in Hartford, after he was fifteen years of age, to attend school. In Rochester, New York, he taught as a member of the faculty of a public school for black children. From Rochester he went to the Oneida Institute at Whitesboro to study for the ministry. His first love was the pulpit, not the schoolmaster's desk. By alternating his teaching and his enrollment at Oneida, he graduated from the institute in 1841, the same year in which he married. Then he moved to New Jersey, where he became the principal of a public school for black children in Trenton. But he was also extending his studies in theology. In 1844 the New Brunswick Presbytery licensed him, and he immediately assumed the pastorate of a Presbyterian church in Princeton, New Jersey. He ceased to teach. In 1846 he moved from his pastorate in Princeton to one in Newark. In his fourteen years in Newark, he greatly expanded the membership and the influence of his church. Nevertheless, in November, 1860, he sailed from New York City for Africa. He had never abandoned his youthful dream to spread the gospel there. Victim of a fever, he died on the western coast of Africa in January, 1861.

Rogers wrote two satires which entitle him to some recognition in Afro-American literature. Both were published in Newark, "A Poem on the Fugitive Slave Law" in 1855, and "The Repeal of the Missouri Compromise Considered" in 1856. As their titles suggest, they are both highly political and highly topical. "The Fugitive Slave Law" refers to the legislation adopted as part of the Compromise of 1850 which went to what many northerners regarded as excessive and possibly crime-inciting lengths in its provisions for the return of fugitive slaves to their southern owners. "The Repeal of the Missouri Compromise Considered" refers, not to an actual repeal of the famous compromise (which, of course, never happened), but to the passage of the Kansas-Nebraska Act, the effect of which was, however, an end to the protections against the territorial extension of slavery embodied in the compromise and, hence, an accomplishment of the very triumph for the South which a literal repeal of the compromise would have allowed.

It is highly probable that Rogers wrote both his satires for declamation to an audience. Even so, either poem might well companion a reader in a library. As William H. Robinson has accurately observed, Rogers possessed "a wry, sardonic humor."[1] He tends, therefore, in his verse to avoid long, dreary stretches of statement and commentary in which nothing original or interesting is said. "The Fugitive Slave Law," although a little shorter than "Vincent Ogé," is not truly a short poem. "The Repeal of the Missouri Compromise Considered" is two-and-a-half times "Vincent Ogé" in length. But in both "The Fugitive Slave Law" and "The Repeal of the Missouri Compromise Considered," Rogers' satire benefits, in great likelihood, from his sense of humor enough to prevent the poem from becoming a tremendous bore. Still, in both poems

---

1. William H. Robinson (ed.), *Early Black American Prose* (Dubuque, Ia., 1971), 60.

Rogers is angry, just as in both poems he presents himself as an apostle of righteousness. In "The Fugitive Slave Law," as if he were a Thoreau, a Gandhi, or a Martin Luther King, he invokes the proverbial law higher than human law to condemn the Fugitive Slave Act of 1850. In "The Repeal of the Missouri Compromise Considered," he continues to speak for a tribunal above courts of law subject to human fallibility and human vice. He utters some remarks which are hardly complimentary about Stephen A. Douglas. And he obviously discerns behind the Kansas-Nebraska Act that very dream, so cherished by some ambitious southerners and their accomplices, of a slave empire encompassing all of the United States and much, if not all, of Latin America which was the true motivation of the remarkable Ostend Manifesto of 1854.

Humorist or not, Rogers was sometimes savage in his arraignments of American racism. Perhaps, at times, even more savage in the same sort of attack, and undoubtedly almost always bitterer, was James Monroe Whitfield, an ardent supporter in the 1850s of Martin R. Delany's colonizationism. Yet Whitfield, genealogically at least, was very much an American. Born in New Hampshire in 1822, he was certainly no less than a third-generation New Englander. Barbering was the trade by which he lived, anything but opulently, for virtually all of his adult life, although it seemed to some prominent Negroes of his time (Frederick Douglass among them) a pity that, with the talent they attributed to him for leadership, he should be so immersed (hopelessly, according to their observation) in a poor, yet demanding, way of making a living which circumscribed as straitly as it did what could have been his freedom to devote himself, not to the mere eking out of his animal subsistence, but to the playing of a substantial role in the fight to improve the Negro's lot in America. By 1850, and probably earlier, he was living and barbering in Buffalo, in a basement shop. It was in the 1850s that he evinced his most activist zeal for colonization. He followed closely and approvingly the emigration schemes mainly advocated by Delany and seems, in the years between 1859 and 1861, to have traveled in Central America as a commissioner for the Delanyites, seeking good places there in which black Americans might profitably resettle themselves. But by 1861 he had gravitated to California, where, except for brief sojourns in Oregon and Nevada, he was to spend the remainder of his days. As he had in the East, in the West he continued to rely on barbering as the source of his livelihood. He did, in the West, reduce his advocacy of colonization. He did not there, however, completely withdraw from the world of public affairs. He was, for example, Grand Master for the Prince Hall Masons of California, and he dabbled in politics in Nevada as well as in California. He died of heart disease in San Francisco in 1871, before his fiftieth birthday.

Whitfield collected poems he had written in *America and Other Poems,* published in 1853. Racial protest was, very possibly, the one big concern never absent from his mind. Even so, not every poem in *America and Other Poems* involves itself with America's transgressions against the Negro. The slender book contains also lyrics about love and some occasional verse. These poems by Whitfield not intended primarily as instruments of social engineering afford a fairly clear picture of his basic virtues as a poet. They reveal him, whatever kind of poetry he chooses to write, as the possessor of a good ear for appropriate diction in his verse and of equally as excellent an ear for the selection and orchestration of the sounds of the spoken word in ways calculated to enhance the value of that diction as an attribute of his poetry. They reveal him also as something of an adept in the handling of poetic rhythms and as a craftsman in the mechanics of versification of whom it cannot be said that he is ill suited to his vocation. These basic virtues to be found in his poetry without protest occur, undiminished in their strength, in his poetry of protest. They help to lift his verse, even in the realm of his protest, above the level of simple pamphleteering.

Most of the poems in *America and Other Poems* distinctly belong to Afro-America's large literature of antiracist propaganda. But also, they plainly identify Whitfield as an exponent of black separatism. The title poem of the volume, "America," and a second long poem therein, "How Long," may well be examined to follow the process of ratiocination upon which his black separatism depended. Fundamentally Whitfield believed, as these two poems indicate, that life in America for Negroes is barren of virtually everything required to make a human life worthwhile. White Americans, Whitfield notes, speak glowingly of American democracy and the equality of man. But they not only tend shamelessly to subvert their own words in their mistreatment of the Negro. They give every evidence, additionally, in Whitfield's eyes, of being determined never to change. To Whitfield, then, every hour spent by a Negro in America is a precious waste of time fatuously and cravenly allowed by that Negro to extend his own experience of his own degradation and dehumanization. Moreover, as Whitfield sees it, to make the whole dispensation worse, America is a Christian nation, and Christianity, as practiced by white

Americans, aids and abets the white American in his persecution of the Negro. Whitfield's separatism is gentle only in its failure to advocate physical violence. It is not gentle in the picture it paints of American racism. Nor is it gentle in the program it proposes to end that racism, although Whitfield never asks, necessarily, that every Negro in America seek another home. Many American Negroes, Whitfield readily admits, probably should not move at all from where they are in America. But many other black Americans should, with as little delay as possible. And the many to whom, in Whitfield's mind, departure from America would almost surely prove of greatest benefit are certainly not, in his same mind, the black Americans least favored, by either nature or nurture, in their qualities of body and soul.

Barbering, we have seen, was Whitfield's trade. Plastering was the trade of James Madison Bell, who bore, like Whitfield, given names reminiscent of an American president. Bell was born in Gallipolis, Ohio, in 1826. At the age of sixteen he moved to Cincinnati, where his brother-in-law, George Knight, a plasterer himself, apparently of no mean skill, taught Bell to plaster. It was Bell, however, of his own volition and on his own momentum, who betook himself to a Cincinnati high school for black citizens and who divided his year so that he could give all of his time to study in the winter but curtail his pursuit of a formal education to nights only in the spring, summer, and fall, when, primarily, he plastered. Bell married Louisiana Sanderlin in Cincinnati in 1847. He and his wife had children. In 1854 Bell moved himself and all his family to the province of Ontario. When John Brown went to Canada in 1858 to hold his provisional convention, he lived with Bell and made Bell's home his headquarters. Still, Bell did not go with Brown to Harpers Ferry. Yet Bell made no secret of his activity in enlisting men and soliciting money for Brown's sortie into the South. Without his family, therefore, which he left in Ontario, in 1860 Bell prudently withdrew from an area associated with Brown and went, far away, to California. He rejoined his family and relocated with them in Toledo in 1866.

For all of his adult life, Bell was an active and prominent layman in the AME church. In politics, after the Civil War, he was a Republican. Ohio sent him as a delegate to the Republican national convention, in Philadelphia in 1872, which nominated Grant for his second term as president. But neither politics, religion, nor plastering at any time in Bell's life interfered seriously with his composition of poetry. As he aged, he became increasingly a well-esteemed friend of the AME prelate Bishop

Benjamin Arnett. It was at least partly because of pressure from the bishop that Bell's poetry—much, if not all, of it—was published in 1901, from Lansing, Michigan, as *Poetical Works of J. M. Bell.*

To a notable extent, Bell, the "Bard of the Maumee" eventually to many who knew, or knew of, him, represented the troubadour tradition in poetry. He made a career of reading his poetry to living audiences. In fact, as William Robinson has pointed out, he did more than read, thus, his poems. He acted them out, so much so that Robinson speaks, seemingly, with great felicity when he suggests that Bell's poems almost always should be regarded, rather than as poems, as, actually, scripts.[2] For Bell, who, according to the lengthy biography of him contributed by Bishop Arnett to *Poetical Works,* tended to exist with "a trowel in one hand and his pen in the other," once slavery had been abolished, toured north and south in America, especially to cities of appreciable size, delivering in person from a stage, as a one-man show, his poetry. He was, incidentally, rather handsome in appearance. He died in 1902.

It may well be that Bell could have used much to his own advantage some of Rogers' wit and humor. Bell was eminently a facile versifier. He was informed about the issues of his time which affected American Negroes. He spoke, in his poetry, in terms of which an enlightened champion of the Negro's civil rights could hardly not have approved. Without quite writing doggerel, however, Bell wrote verse too easily forgotten. "The Day and the War" and "Modern Moses, or 'My Policy' Man" are probably the two of his poems most familiar both to his contemporaries and to literary historians. "The Day and the War," it is reported, was first declaimed, by him, in 1864 in Platt's Hall, San Francisco, as part of a celebration of the first anniversary of the Emancipation Proclamation. Dedicated to John Brown, it undertakes, in some 750 lines, an account of black America from slavery to freedom. In a sense "Modern Moses," a satire on Andrew Johnson, complements "The Day and the War." The later poem, not unexpectedly, paints Johnson as virtually Lincoln's satanic alter ego, a force as hostile to the Negro's emancipation as Lincoln's proclamation was friendly to it. Bell attacks, however, not only policies of Johnson such as the president's attempts to sabotage the Freedmen's Bureau, but also Johnson's personal failings, including his drunkenness. "The Day and the War" is not as lively as "Modern Moses." Yet not even "Modern Moses" is anything but a lampoon made of perishable

2. *Ibid.,* 82.

material. There is about it no less an evanescence than that which haunts day-by-day journalism and the professional work of newspaper columnists. It need not be claimed, to evaluate Bell, that he wrote poetry only to entertain. He certainly thought of more than entertainment in his support of John Brown. To accuse Bell of dilettantism, then, in his own conception of his function as a poet may well be, hence, to ignore the totality, depth, and sincerity of his commitment to the advancement of his race. Bell's poetry lacked weight, not because of anything he did (or did not) want to do, but because of his character—as light as a passing breeze—as a poet. He wrote what he could. Nevertheless, if he is nothing else, he is a reliable historian, as only those with an artist's interests can be, of his abolitionist era.

Of this abolitionist era a black poet who sought to place it too ambitiously within a perspective of more or less all of the human past was Francis A. Boyd, a minor figure even in the context of Afro-American literature, about whom virtually nothing is known except that he was born free in Kentucky in 1844 and that he is not be confused with the West Indian John Boyd, author of The Vision and Other Poems, in Blank Verse, published in London in 1834. Francis A. Boyd is credited only with the publication, in Chicago in 1870, of the long poem (occupying a volume of sixty-nine pages) Columbiana or the North Star, which Boyd clearly intended as an epic.

Freedom, personified as a dedicated maiden who drives a winged chariot, is the protagonist of Columbiana. Boyd's verse joins her in ancient Eypgt and follows her progress toward the goal of the North Star through Israel and Greece into America, where, of the personified evils she encounters, Secessia, obviously a would-be allegorical figure for the South and southerners who formed the Confederacy, is her main opponent. Columbiana is divided into cantos, five of them. It permits Boyd to range over a variety of rhyme schemes, poetic rhythms, modes of organizing his narrative, and ways of structuring his poem. The use of this variety Boyd enjoys rather lavishly. But Columbiana is grandiose, not grand, a poem to poetry as oversized and unwieldy as the dinosaur appears to have been in comparison with other beasts.

Quite different from Columbiana are the sixty-three poems in Lays in Summer Lands, a volume of verse written by the Negro leader J. Willis Menard, and published by him in 1879. Menard's "lays" tend to be lyric in tone and nature. None of them are epic in structure or length.

Some of the white Menards in Menard's family tree were anything but nonentities. Apparently the white Menards who came to America first settled in Canada. One of them, after drifting down into the United States, became the first lieutenant governor of the state of Illinois. Another founded Galveston, Texas, and there are Menard counties in both Illinois and Texas. J. Willis Menard was born in Kaskaskia, Illinois, in 1838. He grew up on an Illinois farm, attended college in Ohio, and, shortly after the Civil War, turned up in Washington, D.C., where he became, among other things, the first black American appointed to a federal clerkship. Menard rivaled Whitfield in the intensity of his commitment to black separatism. No less than Whitfield, it seems, did he attribute to white racism an existence, from all that he could predict, as durable, in prospect, as the hills. One of the missions he performed for the federal government was a trip to British Honduras in 1864 to bring back a report on how well he thought that country might serve as a place to which American blacks could emigrate. Even so, he was living in New Orleans by 1865. He ran for the United States Congress in 1868. Governor Henry Warmoth of Louisiana certified his election. His white opponent, Caleb Hunt, challenged Menard, and Menard became the first Negro to address the House as one of its candidates for membership. The House, however, seated neither Hunt nor Menard. Racism may well have influenced its decision. But, then, political campaigns in Louisiana in the late 1860s were not tea parties. Fraud and violence tended heavily to beset them, and the contest between Menard and Hunt had been fought with no holds barred. Eventually the House declared that neither man had won, and awarded each claimant fifteen hundred dollars in compensation for what he may have lost. Menard then moved, in 1871, to Florida, where he lived for seventeen years and some months. In both Louisiana and Florida he published, and edited, newspapers. He returned to Washington, D.C., in 1889. There he died in 1893.

Perhaps nothing—especially in view of Menard's life and his views about white racism—so marks *Lays in Summer Lands* as the relative absence within it of racial protest. This is not to say that one may go from the beginning to the end of this book without encountering a single blast against slavery and color caste. Indeed, Menard the poet does not retreat so far from the actual world in which ambitious men seek every advantage they can give themselves as not, in verse, to take a potshot here and there at white supremacists and their iniquities. Just as, moreover, he sometimes castigates racists and racism, he also eulogizes, for instance, Garrison, Douglass, Sumner, and Lincoln, as well as Phillis Wheatley and Madame Selika. But *Lays in Summer Lands* is dedicated to an anonymous lady friend of his "of past years," and a goodly number of its poems are simply brief exercises in amorous expression addressed to maidens who are obviously fictitious. Just why Menard, a man of serious stature in the public affairs of the age of Reconstruction, should have devoted the time he did to such escapist verse, especially when the sophomoric character of every line of his intended lyrics to love demonstrates his lack of talent for following in the footsteps of a Villon or Herrick, must, apparently, forever remain a mystery. He speaks of the nameless lady in his poem "Just Over the Sea" at the level of art representative of his performance always as a servant of Venus when he says of his subject:

> She's a sweet, fairy one,
> Whose soft, mellow voice,
> Has made me rejoice
> In hours that are gone.

This, of course, is most undistinguished lyricism, the kind which invites a doubt that the author of it has experienced any genuine feeling before resorting to his pen. In Menard's case, moreover, another circumstance connected with his love poetry notably obtains. The women he celebrates with his tokens of affection are no blacker than those immortalized in the verse of *Les Cenelles*. They have Caucasian features. If they do not betray a subconscious yearning of Menard's to be white, they at least deprive his verse of terms which, by their very nature, would confirm in him no true uneasiness with being black.

For relative absence of racial protest in the poetry he wrote, the saintly Alfred Islay Walden may well be paired with Menard. No better a poet than Menard, Walden is yet a most appealing person. He suffered from a terrible affliction, a near blindness which haunted him all of his life. Even so, he fashioned for himself a highly respectable record of individual achievement. Beyond that, as if he were a nineteenth-century St. Francis of Assisi, he showered the blessings of his own benevolent acts upon his fellow humans, particularly those of his acquaintance in distress. His personal lot was certainly hard enough. That he was, nevertheless, so unceasingly the good Samaritan sets him aside for special honor as a lover of his kind.

Walden was born in 1842 in Randolph County, North Carolina. During his slave childhood, at least two of his successive masters profited financially from their public exhibition of him as a child prodigy gifted with the ability to perform at astounding speeds intricate arithmetical calculations in his head. Still a slave, he had, for some years, been a driver of mules in the North Carolina gold mines when the Civil War ended. Despite his tricks with figures, he had remained illiterate. But he yearned for an education. Equally, he yearned for ordination as a minister of the gospel. All the way from a western area of his native state, he began a grueling pedestrian journey which deposited him, months later, in Washington, D.C. There, and in New Brunswick, New Jersey, he acquired the formal schooling which made him literate. Yet, in both places, he instituted and maintained projects which alleviated the wants and improved the spirits of indigent, abused black children. He studied at the normal school of Howard University and at the New Brunswick Theological Seminary. It was in New Jersey that he achieved the license to preach which had been long and profoundly a wish of his. In 1879, under the auspices of the American Missionary Association, he returned, as a Christian evangelist, to Lassiter's Mills in the county of his birth. There both whites and blacks welcomed him home with genuine cordiality. Pastoring a congregation which, at first, met in a forest clearing, he soon built, almost exclusively from the voluntary manual labor of his parishioners (whose numbers quickly grew from twenty to sixty), a school and a church. The church was given a name, the "Promised Land Church." Gratifying, however, as were these results of his ministry, he died in 1884.

During his sojourn along America's eastern coast, Walden was sorely pressed to find means by which he could provide himself with the necessities of life. One such expedient of his, for instance, was the delivery of a lecture on anatomy and hygiene which he had memorized from a textbook on anatomy. Another such expedient, for him, was the writing of poetry which he could sell. Thus, in 1872, in Washington, D.C., he published *Miscellaneous Poems*, a second edition of which, enlarged, he published a year later. Further to help support himself, in 1877 in New Brunswick he published *Sacred Poems*, a collection of thirteen hymns. Walden harbored no illusions about his own poetic talents. He wrote pleasantly about trivial subjects. Race seemed, as it were, no problem to him. He dealt with slavery by virtually avoiding any reference to it. For Reconstruction and its prospective aftermath apparently he counseled a policy of reconciliation exempt as far as possible from pain, although such a policy obviously conceived of pain in terms too generous to a *status quo*. If the diction of his verse, like its rhythms, tended to be almost naïvely childlike in its simplicity, so, too, did the level there of his

dim and limited commentary on the social scene around him. His es-
pousal of his God was, of course, uncompromising. It may not be, therefore, too harsh to him to think of him as one less worldly than a true
prophet for his era might well have been.

Walden spent part of his life in New Jersey. Alfred Gibbs Campbell
seems to have spent all of his days there. But Campbell, a much too neglected figure in black literature, remains a virtual cipher insofar as knowledge about him as a person is concerned. He seems to have been born
somewhere in New Jersey, perhaps in 1826. He certainly married in
1852. In Paterson, William Carlos Williams' city, Campbell published,
for a while in the early 1850s, a lively newspaper, the *Alarm Bell,* which
provided him with a forum to express his decided opposition to slavery
and drink, as well as his equally decided support for women's rights. In
1883 he published his one book of poetry, *Poems.*

As a poet Campbell easily surpassed Menard. Menard wrote poems
about religion. So did Campbell. But Campbell's poems on a subject
which might well have touched Menard in the very center of his being
possess, in both thought and form, qualities nonexistent in any of Menard's verse on any subject. Some of the selections in *Poems,* even though
the volume appeared almost twenty years after the end of the Civil War,
are abolitionist. It may be, however, that Campbell is at his best when he
inveighs against rum. Certainly he is then at his cleverest and wittiest,
and clever and witty, as well as fervently sincere, he often is.

Easily a competitor for the title of the most refined, or most effete,
Afro-American poet of the nineteenth century (not excluding Charlotte
Forten), Henrietta Cordelia Ray, who liked to call herself H. Cordelia
Ray, was born in New York City, possibly in 1852 and certainly no later
than the early 1850s. Her father was Charles Bennett Ray, of an old
Cape Cod family. As an eloquent clergyman and a persistent journalist
who ardently supported the cause of abolitionism, he was a leading American Negro especially in the decades before, during, and immediately after
the Civil War. He fathered seven children, five of them girls. Three of
his daughters survived to their maturity. Charlotte, a graduate of the law
school of Howard University, became the first black woman to practice
law in Washington, D.C. Neither Cordelia Ray nor her immediately
younger sibling, Florence, ever married. The two, both the recipients of
excellent training in the humanities, were devoted to each other in an
age when spinster sisters as compatible and genteelly bred as they were,
and not direly in want, were a species of social animal which spoke vol-

umes about the life of woman prior to the changes for her which have accompanied her most recent history. Ray taught for approximately thirty years in the schools of New York City. Florence, incidentally, also taught, although she eventually became an invalid. For a long while Charles Reason was Ray's principal. Languages seem to have long been Ray's field of highest expertise. Yet after her retirement from the public schools, she tutored individual pupils, not only in languages, but also in music and mathematics. Moreover, to classes of teachers she gave instruction in English literature. She died in 1916.

No child—and certainly no child as intelligent as Ray—could have grown up in her father's household without direct knowledge of the true nature of this world. Ray's father used his home as a station on the Underground Railroad. That there were far too many moments when life was nasty, ugly, and cruel surely was a fact of which Ray was anything but unaware. Even so, preeminently Ray projected in her poetry a universe of dainty fancy as free from grime and pain, and as full of a delicate (if somewhat meretricious) beauty, as a landscape of Watteau. It cannot, perhaps, be accurately said of her that, in her poetry, she never shows her race. She wrote a goodly number of poems which appeared in periodicals. She also collected poetry of her own making in two volumes, *Sonnets*, published in New York City in 1883, and *Poems*, published in New York City in 1897. Her predilection in her poetry for subjects and themes, as well as modes of utterance, which identify her with the white culture of Western civilization is most apparent. Yet she wrote poems to William Lloyd Garrison, Wendell Phillips, Charles Sumner, Abraham Lincoln, Robert Gould Shaw, and Harriet Beecher Stowe, obviously because of their interest in the Negro. She eulogized Frederick Douglass and Paul Laurence Dunbar in verse. It is at least arguable, moreover, that she wrote no better sonnet than the following to her father:

> A leaf from Freedom's golden chaplet fair,
> We bring to thee, dear father. Near her shrine
> None came with holier purpose, nor was thine
> Alone the soul's mute sanction; every prayer
> Thy captive brother uttered found a share
> In thy wide sympathy; to every sigh
> That told the bondman's need thou didst incline.
> No thought of guerdon hadst thou but to bear
> A long part in Freedom's strife. To see
> Sad lives illumined, fetters rent in twain,
> Tears dried in eyes that wept for length of days—

> Ah! was not that a recompense for thee?
> And now where all life's mystery is plain,
> Divine approval is thy sweetest praise.

It can hardly be said, therefore, of Ray that she never remembers her color. Nor can an absolute abjuration of true experience, even of events in real life with which she had some actual connection, be charged against her. Her father, after all, did, in his actual person, listen to his captive brother's prayer, did, in that same person, bear a long part in Freedom's strife, and similarly did exert himself to see that some fetters were truly rent in twain. But even into Ray's sonnet to her father the word *guerdon* creeps. The sonnet itself is impeccably Petrarchan (and there is no reason that it should not be). Freedom, in the sonnet, is personified. It is a sonnet which, even while it identifies Ray's race, also identifies her tastes. She was a lady of the same school as many wives and sisters of northerners who affected literature.

Ray was clearly more a Tennyson than a Browning, with, apparently, no little of the spirit of Pre-Raphaelitism lurking in her bones. To some extent, sheer prettiness could captivate her for purely its own sake. In her poem "A Thought on Lake Ontario," for instance, the ease with which the spell of a cheaply won hedonism could dominate all of her critical faculties is there most unforgivably apparent. There, indeed, swooning to teasing sounds and vapid images, she speaks:

> The lucent lake was lit with sheen,
> Shining the crested waves between,
> And through the purpling air
> The young birds trilled their lightsome lays,
> To join the hymn of Nature's praise,
> And earth was passing fair.

Whatever fugitive slaves she had seen, and however much her heart, sincerely, had bled for them, the little inner shrine she worshipped treasured beauty in the terms of what she ultimately most was, a true believer in an escapist's dreamlike beauty that never was on land or sea. Not accidentally, she alliterated *l*'s, rhymed *sheen* with *between*, conceived of birds trilling lays, and thought, in her own mind, of Nature as might a Greek who imagined nymphs in field and stream and goddesses not too far off from mortal men. The technical side of her vocation as a poet Ray had mastered admirably. She could write a sonnet or a ballad with due attention to every requirement of the accepted form for each kind of poem. She moved, quite capably, from one conventional stanza to another. She even seems to have invented a new stanza form here and there. She possessed a Spenserian love for allegory and for scenes in which appear ladies with names like Luna as well as knights whose names seem equally appropriate for the world of *The Faerie Queene*. Generally, she took her subjects from the great abstractions, such as nature, love, and literature. In pursuing such subjects she followed tried and true paths already existing in the literature which had been taught to her in the schools belonging to the *status quo* of her time. As she was no great adventurer in race, she was no great adventurer in verse. She wrote safely. She did not write poorly. And, as she seems to have found solace in her sister Florence, she seems also to have found solace in her art.

George Clinton Rowe may well be thought of as the last in time of the black poets from New England who probably should be associated with the Age of the Abolitionists. Rowe was born in Litchfield, Connecticut, in 1853. He grew up in his native town, received his education in New England, and married a girl from Litchfield in 1874. But, as with Alfred Islay Walden, a missionary spirit animated him. He went south in 1876 and never returned to the North. As part of his education, he had served an apprenticeship on the Litchfield *Enquirer*. He had also privately prepared himself for the ministry. At Hampton Institute he worked in the school printing office and started, away from the school, a religious mission. Thus the pattern of his life as a journalist and a clergyman—incidentally, in the Congregational faith—was set. Moving farther south, he edited, preached, and pastored, and indefatigably exerted himself in movements which he considered for the public good in Georgia and South Carolina. He died, survived by his wife and seven of their nine children, in Charleston in 1903.

Rowe was a prolific writer, as he was a familiar figure in the pulpits and on the secular platforms of Georgia and South Carolina. He was not a revolutionary but a Christian gentleman whose brand of Christianity tended to be orthodox. He was, however, also nonviolently, decidedly a "race" man, and he agitated with equal fervor for the kingdom of God and the improvement of the lot of the American Negro. His collection *Thoughts in Verse* appeared in 1887, and a second collection, *Our Heroes: Patriotic Poems*, in 1890. In 1891, his poem *Decoration* was individually published. Almost without exception, in *Thoughts in Verse* Rowe touches on no racial themes. His poetry there reflects, in themes and subjects, as well as excessively in style and tone, the homilies he must have tended to deliver from the many pulpits he occupied during his career as a missionary. The heroes of *Our Heroes*, nevertheless, are black, and in his tributes to them Rowe obviously seeks to work for black advancement. But no sparks of genius ignite Rowe's verse. He was, as a poet, a plodder, albeit often at a singsong gait. All was commonplace with his poetry. His sincerity, in verse, was his long suit.

12. *Frances Ellen Watkins Harper and Albery Allson Whitman*

Until the advent of Paul Laurence Dunbar, Frances Ellen Watkins Harper was undoubtedly the most widely known and widely read of black American poets. A mammoth and important distinction, not too incidentally, between Dunbar and Harper was the composition of their audiences. Of these two highly visible representatives of black America's literary urge, Dunbar attracted far more attention from white editors, critics, and readers than the less conciliatory Harper ever did, although there was, even so, a time when a volume of Dunbar's poems, often looking extremely like the family Bible, seemed to be in the parlor of every Negro home anywhere within the length and breadth of the entire United States. But the occupants of these Negro homes, especially if there were parents or grandparents among them at the turn of the twentieth century, frequently were at least as familiar with Harper as with Dunbar. Moreover, some of these occupants might well have seen Harper in the flesh and heard her, in her living voice, speak as a lecturer or read her poetry, or do both. For, whatever else may be said of Harper, she was an indefatigible strolling minstrel to her own poetic talent. In her long life, on thousands of occasions in public settings of every kind, and in America north and south (except Texas and Arkansas), she held a band of listeners, small or great in number, spellbound as she recited verse which she had produced out of her own powers of creativity.

Harper was born, as Frances Ellen Watkins, in Baltimore, with its relatively large colony of free Negroes, in 1824. Both of her parents were free. Her mother died in 1828, and an aunt of hers immediately assumed the duties of a parent relinquished by the new orphan's deceased mother.

Another relative of hers, her uncle William Watkins, conducted the school where she was educated. This uncle, a pillar of Baltimore's black community, believed in the rigorous inculcation into his charges of the three Rs. No less did he believe that it was his rightful and sacred duty to instruct his pupils in religion—by which, of course, he meant Christianity—and, equally, in abolitionism. He left an indelible impression on his niece. She went to work, to support herself (apparently, out of need), while she was still an adolescent. Her first job placed her as a housekeeper and seamstress in the home of a white Baltimorean who owned a bookstore. She availed herself, therefore, of her access to her employer's library to amplify her education. Meanwhile, she began to write, and both poems and essays from her pen appeared in Baltimore papers during the 1840s. But in 1850 she secured employment in Union Seminary, a trade school near Columbus, Ohio, which the AME church had established and which that same denomination would, only a few years after 1850, consolidate with Wilberforce University.

In 1852 Harper, still Miss Watkins, transferred her employment to a school in York, Pennsylvania, where she was to spend a year. But in York, also, two dramatic instances of the abuse of fugitive slaves so affected her as to change the course of her life. She now dedicated herself wholeheartedly to the cause of abolitionism, which her uncle William had preached so relentlessly to her and her fellow students in Baltimore. Moving to Philadelphia in 1854, she lived at the Underground Railroad station in that metropolis with its excellent location for anyone eager to aid fugitive slaves. She became a friend of William Still's, and her letters to him are a precious part of the correspondence on which Still drew in his preparation of his book on the Underground Railroad. In 1854, additionally, she published, in Boston, her *Poems on Miscellaneous Subjects,* to which William Lloyd Garrison contributed an introduction. She seems to have published earlier the no-longer-extant *Future Leaves.* But she, also, in 1854, spoke in public for the first time for the cause of abolitionism at a meeting in New Bedford, Massachusetts. As with Frederick Douglass, so with her. One speech of hers on abolitionism was sufficient for the abolitionists to insist on further use of her obvious oratorical abilities in their crusade against slavery. The Maine Anti-Slavery Society seized forthwith upon her as a lecturer and sent her out in the North to spread its message. Soon, the Pennsylvania Anti-Slavery Society followed suit. During the last years of the 1850s, Miss Watkins spoke as an abolitionist in more than eight states. Moreover, her speaking was not only virtually a daily exercise. Sometimes she spoke to two, or three, audiences a day. She gave of herself without stint to the fight against slavery. She contributed money, as well as time and effort, to this cause which seemed now to her of such prime importance. For the two weeks before John Brown's execution she lived, in Still's Philadelphia home, with Brown's wife. Never at all daunted by the might of those opposed to Brown and abolitionism, she dispatched works of cheer and packages containing items meant for their comfort to the imprisoned survivors of Brown's raid.

In 1860, however, Watkins became Harper by marrying the widower Fenton Harper in Cincinnati. For four years, until Fenton Harper's death, she lived, in mid-Ohio, the life of something of a recluse on the farm which she and her husband had purchased near Columbus. She bore her husband a daughter, Mary Harper. This daughter, her only child, never married, living with her mother until she died two years before her mother breathed her last. With her husband gone, Harper emerged from her bucolic retreat, where she had, apparently, contented herself with the quiet role of wife and mother. Slavery had become a thing of the past, but the world without slavery showed no lack of good causes which she could support as she had supported abolitionism. To several of these causes, such as moral reform, women's and children's rights, and education, Harper attached herself, but principally to the cause of temperance. And she returned to lecturing, whether for temperance or some other cause or interest of her own. Now she went everywhere, both above and below the Mason-Dixon line, addressing audiences which varied in size and dignity—even, on one occasion, directing her guest remarks to the legislature of South Carolina, in which, during Reconstruction, Negroes sat. Her reputation as a speaker tended to draw for her overflow crowds. Once, at least, it is reported, she stood in the doorway of the edifice intended to harbor the audience to which she was supposed to speak so that she could simultaneously be apprehended through both eye and ear by a divided throng of people, one part within and the other part without the portal where she had stationed herself, for every member of that throng, however remote from her, was determined, if it were at all possible, not to miss the import of the slightest syllable which issued from her lips.

Harper's appeal as a lecturer was quite understandable. Her appearance aided her greatly. She was anything but an unsightly female, no titaness in size, with a fair figure, long, lustrous hair, and facial features pleasant to behold. Moreover, she did not overdo her performance as an employer of elocutionary skills. She was sparing, if graceful, of gesture. She avoided ranting. And while she was deeply committed to enlightening America as she believed with all her might she should, she was not given to speaking above the level of capacity for understanding ideas of those who had altered the normal pattern of their lives in order to take the time and trouble required to attend a meeting at which she would speak. So her success as a lecturer was far from a matter of good luck alone. With little reflection upon her sincerity, one may say that it was essentially a result of calculation, of her knowledge of the experience of life of her auditors, who were mainly the almost totally anonymous, ordinary black people of her time, and of her ability to use her profound empathy with these auditors in crafting her message to them. They did not read *On the Origin of Species, Das Kapital,* or, later, Nietzsche or William James. Intellectualism so advanced was far beyond them. They sang the spirituals of an old-time religion, looked back (many of them), as travelers who had been there, upon slavery and emancipation, hungered for simple forms of personal advancement, and were still, in probably the majority of their number, just beginning to try to reconcile what they thought they had learned from a hoary order of feudal agrarianism with the all-too-different, and more complicated, kind of world it appeared they would need to cope with in an America moving into an urbanized, industrial, imperialistic twentieth century. It was to such auditors, consciously, that Harper lectured and for such auditors, consciously, that she wrote her poetry. The nature, and the limitations, deliberately imposed or inescapably inborn, of her expression of herself when she lectured were part and parcel of her expression of that same self when she wrote her poetry.

Once Harper had established her residence in Philadelphia, she kept it there. She bought and lived in a three-story, brick house, eking out the cost of the purchase of this property from her lecturing and the sale of her poetry. It was her practice to publish her poetry in pamphlets, which she could take with her and sell on her lecture tours. Her pamphlets, that is to say, were at least assembled at her Philadelphia home, and, so, much remains to be done in the authentication of a bibliography of her published work. She had been bred in youth a Unitarian. For certainly no less than half a century, and more, she worked closely, and fraternized much, with the AMEs, who were proud of her and liked to claim her as one of their own, if only by adoption. But when she died, in 1911, only three years short of her ninetieth birthday, she still considered herself a Unitarian, and it was as a Unitarian that she was lowered into her grave.

In addition to her *Poems on Miscellaneous Subjects*, at least twenty editions of which had appeared within twenty years of its original publication, Harper's most notable volumes of verse (none, it will be remembered, other than booklets or pamphlets) are *Moses, a Story of the Nile*, in its second edition by 1869, and *Sketches of Southern Life*, issued first in 1872 and enlarged in 1896. Harper is credited with the authorship, in 1859, of the first short story, "The Two Offers," by a black woman. Indeed, were it not for Frederick Douglass' "The Heroic Slave," already discussed, Harper would possess the distinction of being the first black American of either sex to publish a short story. Harper's one novel, *Iola Leroy or Shadows Uplifted*, was published in 1892. Of it more will be spoken later. She wrote much in prose, in letters, essays, and a tale or two, as well as in verse. And her pamphlets tended to contain repetitions of items included by her in pamphlets she had published previously. A task yet undone, as has already been intimated here, is a scholarly canon of her work.

One poem, virtually any poem she wrote, may well suffice to convey a correct impression of Harper's character as a poet. For Harper, as a poet, had few strings to her bow. Her last was narrow, and to it she clung with notable tenacity. The following, therefore, "The Slave Mother," is approximately illustrative of all the poetry she ever wrote:

> Heard you that shriek? It rose
> So wildly in the air,
> It seemed as if a burdened heart
> Was breaking in despair.
>
> Saw you those hands so sadly clasped
> The bowed and feeble head
> The shuddering of that fragile form
> That look of grief and dread?
>
> She is a mother, pale with fear,
> Her boy clings to her side,
> And in her kirtle vainly tries
> His trembling form to hide.
>
> He is not hers, although she bore
> For him a mother's pains;
> He is not hers, although her blood
> Is coursing through his veins!
>
> He is not hers, for cruel hands
> May rudely tear apart
> The only wreath of household love
> That binds her breaking heart.

This is, as may be readily discerned, a specimen of verse in which the vocabulary is modest, a collection of terms not taxing to the humble mind, the rhythms and the rhymes, like the stanzaic forms, as simple and elementary as the modesty of the vocabulary, and the ideas and values on which the poet's message rests as modest, as simple, and as elementary as everything else in the poem. It cannot be said of this poem that it does not dramatize an incident. But it must be said of it that it performs its dramatization at the level of a lesson in a primer. It eschews profundity of thought, plays to herd emotions, and asks of its social consciousness no perceptions and assumptions which the freedmen Charlotte Forten once observed in South Carolina might not share.

Harper, then, was a poet to whom the common man and common woman could give ear. She spoke out on broad issues only. She was not a cultist. She peddled no strange doctrines as would later a Father Divine or an Elder Micheaux. She kept, instead, safely within the confines of a largely accepted *status quo.* Like the women novelists who sold well in her time, she made much of chaste females at the mercy of lascivious males. She echoed loudly and clearly other speakers for American democracy who emphasized the application of America's professed principles of equality and fair play to all Americans. And she was as steadfast in her advocacy of Christianity as had been Jupiter Hammon or as were her friends on the bench of bishops of the AME church. She was integrationist. Not for nothing had she bought her little foothold of land on American soil in Philadelphia. America was hers to cling to, as were the virtues of family, religion, and citizenship she had learned in the Baltimore in which she grew up. Superlatives are out of place in relation to Harper's art. She operated within set boundaries. Within those boundaries, however, she knew her way around and made the most of what therein was palpably hers to command.

In *Moses,* Harper is, as well it seems she should be, a writer of narrative, rather than lyric, poetry. *Moses* is unrhymed. But it is not blank verse. Neither is it a departure in any significant way, in its picture of Moses, from the picture of Moses provided by orthodox Christianity, the God-appointed leader of the Hebrews nearly into their promised land, who lives in the Negro spirituals as he did in the homilies of the black preachers to whom America's black folk turned for solace, guidance, and spiritual uplift during slavery and Reconstruction. Harper's *Moses* begins with the parting of Moses from the Egyptian princess who has raised him as her son since the strange discovery of him, an infant in the bulrushes of the Nile, by her handmaidens. A break with Moses is a rupture which the princess does not desire, but upon which Moses insists. His real mother, he has long come to think he knows, is his old Hebrew nurse. From this nurse Moses has learned a history of the Hebrews in the perspective of a Hebrew concept of the world and God. Relying only upon himself, therefore, Moses leaves the Pharaoh's palace, and Harper then conveys him down a path, familiar to readers of the Scriptures, into Goshen and his slaying of the brutal Egyptian taskmaster, from Goshen to his long exile in Midian, and back to Egypt to conduct the Hebrews, after the plagues upon the Egyptians, miraculously through the Red Sea and, despite occasional tribulations, almost into Canaan. On Mount Nebo, Harper's *Moses* draws to its conclusion as angels bear Moses' body to its secret place of interment. So, in *Moses*, Harper merely tells an old story in an old way. The parable that story has always seemed to provide to American blacks in relation to their experience of American life hardly could have been less apparent to Harper, or less of a partial reason for her retelling of the story, than it was, or would be, to other black American artists, notably Zora Neale Hurston.

Sketches of Southern Life is, in form, a dramatic monologue, uttered by one Aunt Chloe, whose full name, incidentally, is Chloe Fleet. Statements to the effect that *Sketches* entitles Harper to recognition as a pioneer in the use in poetry of Negro dialect and, hence, in that regard, as a direct forerunner of Paul Laurence Dunbar, should not be accepted as warranted by the relevant facts. Very scanty (as well as questionable), in truth, are any locutions used by Aunt Chloe which could justify calling Harper a dialect poet. Moreover, Aunt Chloe tends to talk at a rather high level of literacy, conceivably by design. For she works in the big house. She neither plants nor tills nor picks a crop on her master's land. But she clearly consorts, day after day, with her master, her mistress, and their son in the residence her owner's family occupies.

Aunt Chloe has children of her own, two sons. *Sketches* begins when she learns that these sons, because of her master's financial distress, are to be sold away from her. These sons do vanish, victims of America's domestic slave trade. But Aunt Chloe's master, in an even more ultimate sense, vanishes also. He dies, it turns out, to the good of his plantation, which his son restores to the prosperity of an earlier day. After Fort Sumter, however, this scion of the planter aristocracy departs to fight. He dies—whether in battle or not is obscure. So fate does eventually serve Aunt Chloe better than it serves her mistress, since both of Aunt

Chloe's sons are reunited with her during Reconstruction. During Reconstruction, moreover, Aunt Chloe, old as she is, learns to read, as do some other freedmen and freedwomen of her age. She joins with the blacks in her community in the construction of a church which they can call their own. And she manages to accomplish the erection of a small home, though large enough for her reunited family, which she can call her own.

A vital period of transition in the history of a nation provides the backdrop for Aunt Chloe's monologue. But that it does is not a circumstance beneficial to Harper. The extent to which Harper does not make of the world within her poetry a rich and full simulation of the real world upon which her poetic world is based becomes even more glaringly apparent than it might otherwise be when Aunt Chloe's monologue is placed beside any adequate depiction of America as it was during the period of *Sketches*. *Sketches* is not only superficial. It is thin. Like thistle in the wind, it drifts away. Clearly all of Harper's verse tends to be topical. So, if only so, it courts evanescence. However, it is not only so. Artists who live beyond their own era tend to do more than please ordinary tastes. If they write, as Harper did, a poem about a slave auction, they are able, somehow, to say something about the auction meaningful for human values when slave auctions are no more. But Harper was trapped on a petard of her own design, her popularity in her own time, which feasted, as does journalism, more on the perishable and the easily depicted in human conduct than on perceptions which belong to the timeless present of enduring art. The vulgar enslaved Harper. The petty secured her within its grasp. Her eyes never raised themselves, truly, to any hills. Nor did her poetry. In no way is it touched with the sublime.

But, whatever may be said, or not said, of Harper, a growing consensus of critical opinion distinguishes as possibly the finest black poet of the abolitionist era Albery Allson Whitman. From Whitman's pen a fairly large body of verse remains extant. If it can be said of him, as quite apparently it should be, that he was possessed by an irrepressible urge to write poetry, just as apparently it must be said of him that this compulsion which he could not avoid was anything but one which led him far afield from his true self. He was no stepchild of the muses. His talent, like his taste, for poetry was innate, a happy accident of the natural endowments which the gods conferred upon him when they presided at his birth.

That birth occurred in May, 1851, near Munfordville and the Green

River in Hart County, somewhat north of the famous part of Kentucky where Mammoth Cave is located. Both of Whitman's parents were slaves. He remembered being put to work in the fields while he was still a child. It was, he also remembered, not easy labor. Yet he tended, after he matured, not to recall his childhood with bitterness. His reminiscences about his youth include little or nothing about Negroes and certainly no references to experiences of slavery which he thought brutalized him. Moreover, he seems to have acquired a genuine fondness for the vicinity of his birth. He appreciated there, if nothing else, a beauty in nature on which he looked back with delight for all of his days. His mother died in 1862; his father, in 1863. With (or, perhaps, before) emancipation, Whitman became more or less itinerant. He lived in Louisville for a while and then in Cincinnati. In Troy, Ohio, he worked first in a shop which made plows and next as a construction hand on the railroad. In Troy he was able to go to school, apparently for seven months in all. He taught school in Carysville, Ohio, and in Kentucky near his birthplace. In 1870, or thereabouts, he became a student at Wilberforce University, even if for only six months. That six months ended Whitman's brief exposure to formal education. But it also brought him within the orbit of Bishop Daniel Alexander Payne, with whom Whitman established an enduring relationship not too dissimilar from that of a son to a father whom the son much admires.

Whitman published his first book of verse, *Essays on the Ten Plagues and Miscellaneous Poems*, probably in 1871. It sold approximately 1,000 copies. No copies of it survive. His *Leelah Misled* appeared in 1873, and his *Not a Man, and Yet a Man* in 1877. *Not a Man* is over 5,000 lines long. It was, thus, the longest poem by a black poet until the publication, with a preface assigning the publication to Baltimore, 1903, of the Reverend Robert E. Ford's *Brown Chapel, a Story in Verse,* the 21 cantos of which are over 3,500 lines longer than *Not a Man.* With, or without, proper ordination, Whitman had become an AME minister, as well as, for a limited time, general financial agent for Wilberforce University. By 1877 Whitman was pastoring an AME church in Springfield, Ohio. His poetry, of course, occasions his renown in generations later than his own. But in his own time, and certainly among AMEs, Whitman was also a figure of consequence because of his preaching. Many of his contemporaries considered him an extraordinarily effective pulpiteer. The AMEs used him, not only to hold together old churches in their denomination, but also to start new ones for them. And so, to a somewhat unusual degree, they kept him on the move, pastoring or evangelizing in Ohio, Kansas, and Texas.

Whitman did have a grievous fault, an addiction to the bottle which he seemed unable to cease or even to diminish and which sometimes affected his deportment as he sermonized. Moreover, his alcoholism undoubtedly shortened his life, although it did not prevent his marriage to a beautiful woman who steadfastly refused to desert him, whatever his faults, and who also bore him two beautiful daughters. These daughters, incidentally, collaborated with their two half-sisters, born to their mother after Whitman's death, to form a vaudeville team, the Whitman Sisters, singers and dancers, successful and celebrated for twenty years or more both in America and abroad. Whitman's wife, Caddie Whitman, while never a vaudevillian professionally, gave something of a vaudevillian's help to her husband. He, like Harper, for instance, promoted his own poetry by reading it in public. Unlike Harper, however, he frequently had Caddie read on the same program with him. Whitman was almost white. Caddie was even more nearly white. Indeed, it has been conjectured that she was actually a woman legally white concealing her status in law presumably to ease her accommodation to her marriage. Especially in Caucasian terms, both Whitman and Caddie were strikingly handsome, and neither was inexpert in addressing the audiences they often faced as partners in the oral interpretation of Whitman's verse.

The store of Whitman's poetry from which he and Caddie could read grew rather steadily during his lifetime. Whitman followed *Not a Man* with *The Rape of Florida*, published first in 1884, somewhat revised and issued as *Twasinta's Seminoles* in 1885, and, in 1890, combined for further publication under the same cover with *Not a Man* and a group of lyric poems called *Drifted Leaves*. In 1893, the year of the Chicago World's Fair, Whitman published a pamphlet, *The World's Fair Poem*, containing "The Veteran" and the longer "The Freedman's Triumphant Song." In 1901 Whitman published *An Idyll of the South*, also containing two poems, "The Southland's Charms and Freedom's Magnitude" and "The Octoroon." But 1901 was the final year of Whitman's life. As the 1890s drew to a close, he was given a charge where he might have stayed long enough to feel that he was settling down, St. Philip's in Savannah. A storm and fire, however, destroyed St. Philip's. He esteemed this charge sufficiently to plan to rebuild it. In a development which, nevertheless, could hardly have displeased him, he was transferred to Allen Temple in

Atlanta. It was as the pastor of Allen Temple that, on a visit to Anniston, Alabama, in the summer month of June, 1901, he contracted pneumonia. Brought home to Atlanta, before July was over he was dead. He was buried in Atlanta.

Du Bois was wont to say, to the public at large as well as to his friends, that one of the reasons he objected to racism was the capriciousness of the incidence of genius. Whitman, like Du Bois himself, is a convincing illustration of the sagacity of Du Bois' perspicacious witticism. For Whitman had absolutely no business being a poet, except that, to speak repetitively, nature had made him one. And of Whitman it certainly seems that the composition of verse was the one thing he wanted most to do. The very strength of this determination of his to poetize may at least partially explain the relative lack of racial protest in what he wrote. Notable about him was the eagerness and yet indefatigability with which he incorporated into his own verse a variety of verse forms. Poorly schooled in formal terms as he was, on a typical black person's limited income, living in the cramped world void of virtually all of the amenities of scholarship and culture of the Negroes of his time, it was purely and simply a feat of personal exploration and acquisition that he should discover and familiarize himself with such phenomena as the Spenserian stanza, ottava rima, free verse, couplets of several kinds, sonnets, and meters as diverse as trochees, dactyls, anapests, and iambs, in addition to the rhyme schemes he must have found only from reading on his own the poems of many poets. Quite obviously, not even his unslakable thirst for drink deterred him from the ardent pursuit of his first love, examining and writing poetry. No less for him than for a poet like Poe, art was an absolute and a poem its own excuse for being. Always there have been writers who avail themselves of their skills in writing primarily to save the world through their advocacy of some good cause or causes. No such writer was Whitman.

Yet, to do Whitman justice, it is not fair to dispose of him as one who never as an advocate thought, for a better world, of Negroes and their problems in America which separated them from other Americans. Nor can it truly be said of him that he never uttered remarks that could—perhaps, should—be considered racial protest. But everything which Whitman said about blacks and whites—or, for that matter, about blacks and not necessarily also about whites—marked him as a man to whom, apparently, nothing should rank higher in any individual's hierarchy of values than that individual's pride in himself and determination to use to the utmost for his own good and the good of others whatever abilities, great or small, providence had seen fit to grant him. Whitman did not argue that America, for the Negro, had been a bed of roses. He dedicated Not a Man to those whom he called the "Abolition Fathers." The praise of freedom is a recurring theme in his work. That all men should live unhampered by subjugation to others of their kind he, both in and out of his poetry, maintained as fervently and constantly as he, both in and out of his poetry, worshipped beauty, nature, and God. And he certainly did not close his eyes to the circumstance that, in America, the Negro had not always been free. He admitted slavery, just as he admitted the woes, and sometimes shortcomings, of the black freedmen and freemen around him, many of whom were his contemporaries. His prologue, in verse, to Not a Man, indeed, is a tribute, among other things, to the valor and the aspirations of blacks who had borne arms with other Americans in both the Revolution and the Civil War. But the preface, in prose, to Not a Man, which comes before the prologue, is a tribute to Wilberforce University, principally because Wilberforce, in Whitman's eyes, represented an attempt by Negroes to help themselves. In preliminaries to The Rape of Florida, Whitman would speak scathingly, in almost direct terms, about Negroes who wasted their time, and demeaned themselves otherwise, by "whining" over how badly slavery, or white oppression of any kind, had crippled them. In virtually the same breath Whitman would add that, to him, "petition" and "complaint" constituted the "language of imbecility and cowardice." So, in connection with his two longest poems, he clarified for himself and whoever cared to read him his own position on race.

Whitman spoke, of course, before the day of the often so-called welfare state. He seems not to have been a liberal intellectual. There were such creatures in Whitman's time, and even then they had wisely begun to consider the impact of a powerfully skewed and perverted social environment, one in which investors' syndicates and huge industrial combinations flourished, upon the true independence of the individual. Whitman, however, as we shall see, was not only a romantic in his art. He was also a romantic in his view of man. Almost as if he were a genuine Galahad in the days when knighthood was supposed to be in flower, he clung to the beau ideal of every man a champion who should not repine when he had to act alone. Men should merely do their best at all times, whatever their own limitations or the external odds against them. Thus Whitman felt he had tried to do when he went to Wilberforce. Thus every American Negro should attempt, whatever injustices America forced upon him. Thus, Whitman reasoned, the Negro would prevail in America, by clenching his teeth and biting his tongue and exerting himself against every obstacle he faced, however great. Whitman over-simplified both the increasingly complex real world around him and the problems of the Negro in America in the 1890s. Yet, he did not over-simplify, or misrepresent, his own belief in self-reliance and unwearied struggle.

One cannot say of Whitman that dark-skinned Negroes appalled him. He, for instance, as we know, unreservedly revered the very black Bishop Payne. Even so, Negroes of sable hue and features strongly African in ancestry play a very minor, if not nonexistent, role in Whitman's poetry. The first poem of Whitman's which may be called, as it were, vintage Whitman, although the vintage would improve, was his *Leelah Misled*. For Whitman was not only a good lyric poet. He also had a flair for nar-rative. He could tell a story well. Yet Whitman never could altogether overcome his passion for asides, and in *Leelah Misled* all three aspects of his characteristics as an artist which are, perhaps, most notable in him—his often mellifluous and, not less often, enchanting lyricism, his profi-ciency with narrative, and his fondness for digressions—are apparent to a degree worthy of remark. Actually, the story in *Leelah Misled* is simple and familiar, the tale, as old as sexual play between the sexes, of seduc-tion, and particularly of the seduction, by a male, of an innocent female. In *Leelah Misled* it is not tortuous, nor does it involve a long campaign of intrigue and maneuver extending through many years. It is a brief series of incidents that can be quickly recounted as, indeed, they are, except that Whitman interrupts and delays his recital of them with sortie after sortie into the interminable thickets of discourse, so pleasant to him, bred by his personal observations on any subject which enters his mind.

Leelah, the titular heroine of the poem, is a well-meaning young girl. She is very white. No suspicion of Negro blood attends her. Moreover, she is decidedly blonde and "of form and feature neat" (Whitman had an eye for ladies' figures), with eyes of ethereal blue and cheeks in which the red glow of health and happily exuberant vitality add to the many other attractions, such as her soft, long hair, of her delightful femininity. She falls easy prey to the blandishments of McLambert, a practiced philan-derer, and surrenders to him her chastity, only for him, in keeping with his custom, to abandon her. If her tale has a moral, that moral must lie in the charity of Leelah's spirit. And certainly no moral for it can be found in Whitman's multitude of digressions.

Rodney, the heroic protagonist of *Not a Man*, does possess some Negro blood. Yet, he is "eighty-five percent Anglo-Saxon." At the beginning of *Not a Man*, he lives in the frontier village of Saville, Illinois, the sole slave there, a bondsman of Sir Maxey, Saville's local magnate and the father of the lovely and sweet-tempered Dora. Rodney is twenty years old and six feet, three inches, tall. Unmatched in Saville as a hunter and a woodsman, a Sampson in athletic strength, he is also noble of character. Mean thoughts never cross his mind, although he shrinks not from engagements with romantic love. Existence in Saville tends to be idyllic in the pattern of Rousseauistic primitivism. Nevertheless, an element of evil is there, represented by the racism, not only of Rodney's enslavement, but also of the xenophobia shared by too many of the villagers in their attitude toward Indians. For, not far from Saville, a band of Sacs, following their ancestral ways, are gathered in their own village, presided over by their revered chief, Pashepaho. Like Sir Maxey, Pashepaho has fathered a daughter, Nanawawa, and, moreover, like Dora, Nanawawa epitomizes maidenly beauty at its height.

To the Sacs, Whitman imparts a primitivism even more Rousseauistic than that of the inhabitants of Saville. The Sacs, for instance, harbor no inhumane intentions towards their white neighbors. And Nanawawa, merely expressing, it would seem, the dictates of her own young heart in the choice of a mate without regard to any vicious doctrines of class or caste, falls in love with White Loon, taken in war by the Sacs and retained by them in bondage (although not, as Rodney is, in chattel bondage). To this White Loon, not at all an unrequiting or ungrateful recipient, she gives herself, on a little lake of pristine beauty, during a night of rapture for her, certainly for White Loon, and, judging from the tone of his verse, for Whitman also. But trouble comes to paradise. Villagers from Saville, in a hunting party led by Sir Maxey—but unaccompanied by Rodney, who, as a slave, is not permitted to ride a horse—plunder the Indian village, opportunely visiting it at a moment when its braves are absent while they seek out game by which they can help to feed their tribe. Pashepaho, incidentally, full of years and honors, already earlier has been gathered to his fathers. The Indian braves, however, return to their home before the white hunters are able effectively to disappear from the scene of their orgy of destruction. Moreover, the braves discover that some white fiend has wantonly murdered Nanawawa. The braves pursue the whites and kill them all except Sir Maxey, whose fleet horse saves him.

In a related sequence of events, Rodney returns to a Saville awaiting a retaliation, which the villagers see no hope of repulsing, from the Indians. He hastens to Fort Dearborn hoping to obtain there help which, it develops, is not forthcoming. Retracing his tracks, he finds Saville demolished and Dora in the possession of the Indians. Singlehandedly, he rescues Dora and takes her to Fort Dearborn. Throughout Rodney's exertions Sir Maxey has been at Fort Dearborn, pleading for someone to undertake the recovery of his daughter and pledging to anyone who restores her to him money and Dora's hand. When Rodney does appear, however, with Dora, the two of them obviously drawn to each other, Rodney's reward is his sale into further slavery in the Deep South.

From Fort Dearborn Rodney is sent to Memphis, about which as a symbol for slavery and racism Whitman wrathfully remarks. But it is in Florida—where Whitman surely never pastored and may never even have evangelized—that Rodney has his second long experience as a slave. Thither he has been transported, and there he has become the property of one Mosher Aylor, the unwed, yet anything but celibate, last survivor of a family, originally New Englanders, the men of which fought for the colonies in the Revolution and one of whom, after marrying a fine New England girl, emigrated to Florida. In Florida the Aylors prosper. They acquire land and slaves, build the proverbial elegant mansion in the best tradition of *Gone with the Wind*, and, for a while, do embody in their conduct much of the noblesse oblige ideally attributed to a planter aristocracy. But degeneracy overtakes them. Mosher Aylor is a horrible caricature of what once they were. He is lewd with women, despotic, sometimes sadistically, with his underlings, and bereft entirely of sympathetic feelings for anyone but himself. Even so, Rodney, performing diligently and quietly his assigned tasks and, then, retiring to be alone with himself after his hours of labor when he can at least recall the happier moments of his past, lives as Aylor's slave without running afoul of Aylor's venomous spite.

But a dawn arrives when Rodney, after a night of solitude in the woods, is proceeding, silently and unseen, toward the spot of his next daily toil only to see, from a hidden point of vantage, the comeliest of maidens admiring herself nude in a forest pool. Rodney at once is smitten. He does not know that Aylor, as unseen as himself, has also beheld the maiden in her unclothed state. The maiden robes herself and leaves her temporary boudoir, quite obviously, it seems, to wend her way home. Rodney follows, as does Aylor, but Rodney, becoming aware of Aylor's presence before the latter realizes that he is not the only voyeur in the woods, prudently abandons the maiden's trail before she has come to, or near enough, her destination for him to collect some clue which may help him to see her again. Aylor, however, perseveres in his pursuit. Thus he discovers that the maiden is a quadroon slave from New Orleans named Leeona, the property of a neighbor of his, and for an exorbitant price, he purchases this paragon of nubile charm, his senses seething with lustful fantasies of future dalliance with her. Of course, Rodney and Leeona meet, once they are both Aylor's slaves. With equal inevitability they fall deeply in love with each other. It is impossible that they should do so without Aylor's eventual awareness of their new condition. He is, after all, as busy as he can be trying to bed Leeona. Moreover, he has, in great likelihood, never been angrier, and more frustrated, than he is now from his absolute lack of success in having his way with, to him, a prospective courtesan whom, by law, he owns and should be able to do with whatever he wills. Finally, Aylor imprisons Rodney. But Rodney, with Leeona's help, escapes to a cave where she can visit him. Aylor, however, rapes Leeona and impregnates her. Dogs are sent after her when she, with her infant in arms, ultimately flees the Aylor household. Rodney, who has maintained, as much as he can, vigil over her, joins her in her flight and kills Aylor's dogs.

Rodney and Leeona, with Aylor's child, at last turn northward. The hunted trio do not make their way to freedom uneventfully. They are sometimes separated. Along their way Leeona, but not Rodney, encounters White Loon—a White Loon sadly a wreck of the splendid youth Nanawawa had loved. Rodney and Leeona end their long odyssey (which passes through Kentucky) in Canada. Leeona's child has died just after Leeona, for the first time, has touched free soil. There, they settle comfortably and serenely in a little green cottage in the hamlet of Sussex Vale. They remain there without further tribulation for the remainder of their lives, quite blissfully free of bondage and gracefully growing old. Two incidents befall them, nevertheless, with which Whitman chooses not to leave his readers unacquainted. Dora is living in nearby Montreal, contentedly married to a man of considerable wealth and great compassion. Father Eppinck, the parish priest of Sussex Vale, brings her, during a Christmas season, to the dwelling of Rodney and Leeona. So Dora and Rodney get to know of each other that each has come, in the end, relatively unscathed through life's vicissitudes. And Rodney, at the age of sixty, fights in the Civil War, conceivably the oldest rifleman ever in

Union arms. His two sons by Leeona accompany him as Union soldiers also. Somewhere in the South, in Tennessee, perhaps, or possibly with Sherman's troops marching to the sea, Rodney and his sons come upon a dying Confederate soldier who turns out to be Mosher Aylor. As Aylor expires, in his last, barely audible utterance as a mortal man, beset agonizingly with remorse, he begs forgiveness of Rodney and Leeona.

Whitman does not end *Not a Man* without a coda which serves the poem in the manner of a dying fall. Freedom has been the sole major theme of *Not a Man*. The love of freedom, indeed, strongly aided and abetted by an unquenchable resolve not to suffer forever the ignominy of slavery, fundamentally determines, in *Not a Man*, all of its protagonist's actions, even his twin affections for Dora and Leeona. So, in his coda, Whitman addresses explicitly this theme of freedom. He says nothing novel as he speaks on his great subject. Yet he does approach his eulogy of it through a plea for reconciliation of the North and South, which may seem, from a black in the 1870s, somewhat strange. Assuming a stance, then, of a sectional impartiality which represents a decided departure from what might well be expected of him, he says:

> And may no partial hand attempt a lay
> Of praise, as due alone to blue or grey.
> The warrior's wreath may well by both be worn,
> The braver man than either ne'er was born.
> They both have marched to death and victory,
> They both have shown heroic misery,
> And won the soldier's immortality.
> But scars of honor that they both yet wear,
> The proudest testimonials of their valor are.[1]

With such sentiments, arrestingly magnanimous on his part, spoken as they were during the very years when the South had already begun its campaign of "redemption," a euphemism for "putting the Negro in his place," Whitman proceeds thereupon, after a swift presentation of an abbreviated history of freedom, to a paean about peace in America enhanced by his picture of a new national solidarity, most desirable and altogether possible, in which freedom and equality reign and a country and a people prosper, secure in their democratic faith and practices and heedful of a wise, benevolent deity who keeps alive in them the flame of liberty as he has for all who have believed in him and followed his com-

---

1. Albery A. Whitman, *Not a Man, and Yet a Man* (1877; rpr., Miami, 1969), 205–206.

mandments since, long ago, he shepherded Moses and the Israelites through the parted waters of the Red Sea, away from Pharaoh and his army, who were to drown. There can be no doubt that, in this coda, Whitman is sincere. He may be naïve. And he is certainly neither doctrinaire nor a self-appointed counselor who speaks in carefully detailed terms of a program of political and social action which he is specifically recommending. He is only a poet writing poetry who wishes and dreams. And should his wishes and dreams come true, he makes it clear, America, as he views America's future, at last unencumbered with slavery, from Canada to Mexico and coast to coast, will mature and change into a land benevolent to its laborers and kind to all of its adults and children, with everywhere within it universal education, "free schools, free press, free speech and equal laws," and nowhere within it oppression, so that it will at last be truly living, in its actual existence, its spoken creed. There is in Whitman's coda, consequently, a note of prayer. He could hardly have found a better note on which to end a poem extolling liberty by a Negro in his day.

Its length and the fact of its being a narrative undoubtedly have occasioned references to *Not a Man* as a novel in verse. Such references may well be far from inappropriate. *Not a Man* appeared in a century when a significant number of poems—Browning's *The Ring and the Book* is an excellent example—could be seen to be novels in verse, not a phenomenon concerning genres difficult to understand in an age when the novel had unmistakably become the dominant vehicle for literary art. But, in Whitman's case, if *Not a Man* is thought of as a novel, even though only as a novel in verse, Whitman probably should then be thought of as the best of the very early Negro novelists. For certainly no Negro novelist who published a novel before 1870 contrived to create, in his novel, the qualities of *Not a Man.* To tell a story and not let it get out of hand requires disciplines. In *Not a Man* Whitman conceives a simple grand design and adheres to it. He uses one of the oldest and most familiar of plot formulas, the chase. Throughout all of *Not a Man*, Rodney pursues freedom. Moreover, he attains it. His chase ends happily, even if not at first where he would most have wished it to, for he is free in Canada before he is emancipated in the United States. Nevertheless, there are no loose ends, no obscurities, no incoherences, and no esoterica in Rodney's chase. It hews to a cardinal principle, if not the cardinal principle, of all tales properly told, no matter how long they are, or how short. It chooses to be about one thing only and makes very clear what that one thing is.

Not a Man does not, incidentally, choose so much to dramatize its single and exclusive subject as to picture it. *Not a Man*, indeed, is a panorama composed of two pictures, each adequately distinctive within itself, but both, nevertheless, to Whitman's credit, so complementary to each other as not to destroy the function of either in contributing to the unified portrait of a life which *Not a Man* essentially is. Picture number one presents Rodney in Saville. Its final vignette, as it were, is a rendering of his conversation with Dora in which he learns of the fate immediately ahead of him, an auction block somewhere in the slaveholding South. Picture number two records Rodney's life in Florida and afterwards. Together, the two pictures strongly explicate the title of the poem, which, with their varied detail, they substantiate. Rodney, these pictures say, while he is a slave and even, because of his black blood (slight though it may be), while he is not, suffers the indignity of a denial of his manhood, and so, even of his humanity, by the very society of which he is a part. But both pictures also show that, whatever that society may try to mandate, Rodney's manhood, however tested, as an inescapable, unequivocal force pervading his whole character, is never in doubt. As a matter of fact, not only is Rodney a man. He is, always and everywhere, the best man in *Not a Man*. He chases, therefore, not a change in himself, but a change in his external world. That change, at least in some significant measure, does occur. The literature of racial protest by black American writers almost uniformly dooms its black protagonists to defeat, if not, additionally, to despair. But *Not a Man* not only shows Whitman as a better storyteller than some other blacks. It also shows him as, apparently, a greater optimist. His protagonist of *Not a Man* does not close his tale a loser.

Characters in *Not a Man*, including Rodney, tend toward the stereotypical. Even so, like the narrative they inhabit, they are clearly delineated. Dora, Nanawawa, and Leeona, for instance, all are young women of surpassing charm, but each of them is different from the other two. Indeed, each of them evokes her own stereotype, and not one of them invades the territory, as type or individualized portrait, of any character in the poem but herself. Yet there is an aspect of the characterization in *Not a Man* which may well be more interesting than its measure of stereotypicality. All the characters in *Not a Man*, major or minor, are larger than life. They come, therefore, out of the world of the saga and the epic, where a literary artist may strive for realism firmly based on human beings as they are and on events which may plausibly occur, yet impart to both his dramatis personae and the incidents in his story an excess of certain of their inherent qualities intentionally transcendental in its effect. Thus Rodney is, without being supernatural, a better athlete than any athlete who ever was. Dora is fairer than ever any Evangeline, and Leeona more dazzling to the eye than ever any belle of a quadroon ball. This aspect of Whitman's characterization does not harm his narrative. If it does anything at all, it relates his whole story more universally to his theme as well as to those values, some bad, some good, all men must either make part of themselves or reject.

Nor does Whitman harm his narrative with his variations in verse form throughout his poem. Life in Saville he describes in couplets which, although not neoclassic—they are not closed—nevertheless are reminiscent, especially in their sense of nature and their interpretations of the recurring rituals of human behavior, of James Thomson in *The Seasons* or of Thomas Gray even, perhaps, in his odes. When Whitman enters the Sac village, he turns from his original couplet to trochees so similar to those in Longfellow's *Hiawatha* as to seem, as well they might be, a deliberate imitation. Saville and the Sacs represent two different modes of living the simple life. It is incumbent upon Whitman, from the easily divined general strategy of his poem, to make it clear through the thoughts his words convey that Sir Maxey and his friends and neighbors are culturally strangers to Pashepaho and his tribe. That task Whitman undertakes without failing in it. But his change in the form of his verse signals and dramatizes his passage in his poem from the realm of the Sir Maxeys to the outlying province of the Pashepahos.

The greatest fault in the verse itself of *Not a Man* occurs in the portion of the poem associated with Rodney's residence in Canada. Compared to the verse in the preceding portions of *Not a Man*, the verse of this portion seems almost devoid of inner vitality, much as if to indicate a decline of Whitman's intense involvement in his own exercise in creativity. But peace and quiet have always been, it seems, less of a tonic to artistic talent than turmoil. Evil, for that matter, has always seemed to provoke from artists finer art than good. Yet Whitman does make of Rodney, the good man in *Not a Man*, a sympathetic character. Beyond that, he makes, in *Not a Man*, of freedom a sympathetic theme. Not with declamation (although he does declaim too much as *Not a Man* nears its end), but with a story in no wise ineptly told and verse often so felicitous as to invest simply through itself with a franchise for its existence whatever he is saying, he utters his protest against American racism. So, his narrative comes first; his protest, second. It is the proper order, surely, both for his art and his protest.

Whitman's interest in Florida did not cease with *Not a Man*. He returned to the once-Spanish colony for *The Rape of Florida*, or *Twasinta's Seminoles*, under either name essentially the same poem. The Indian chief, a Seminole, in *The Rape of Florida* who matches Pashepaho of *Not a Man* as a figure of reverence among his people is named Palmecho. Incidentally, the fabled Osceola does appear in *The Rape of Florida*, but only momentarily and certainly not to his own best advantage. Like Pashepaho and Sir Maxey, Palmecho has a beautiful daughter, the tawny Ewald, through whose veins flows a mixture of Indian, Spanish, and Negro blood. Ewald loves, and is loved by, the young Seminole chief Atlassa, in all respects except his lack of Negro blood a counterpart of Rodney from *Not a Man*. The black presence, indeed, in *The Rape of Florida* is even less than in *Not a Man*. Ewald alone of the major characters in the later poem has a touch of Negro ancestry. Yet, in an important way, *The Rape of Florida* is but an extension of *Not a Man*. A quest for freedom dominates the lives of Palmecho, Ewald, and Atlassa and serves as the theme for their poem as, in *Not a Man*, it had dominated the life of Rodney and served as the theme of his poem.

Whitman chose to write *The Rape of Florida* in the Spenserian stanza, the first black poet to be so bold. The poem is less than half as long as *Not a Man*, by no means an indication that it is short (which it is not). Its 257 stanzas are divided into 4 cantos. From first almost to last, it tells a tale of white aggression and perfidy. Its main action begins when an American military force, capitalizing on surprise, attacks Palmecho's village, in the process wounding Palmecho. It may be interesting to note, in view of the record of the Seminoles in actual history, that Whitman attributes to the Seminoles, unless provoked, a taste for peaceful coexistence not unlike that which he had earlier attributed to Pashepaho's people. Palmecho and his people are saved by fellow Seminoles, led by Atlassa, who rush to Palmecho's aid and put to flight the American soldiers. Nevertheless, Palmecho does fall all too soon again into American hands. Under a flag of truce, which he foolishly trusts, he attends a peace conference with the Americans in St. Augustine, where they once more imprison him. Ewald, quite to the contrary, eludes the Americans, who had planned to capture her also, and turns to Atlassa for protection. He places her, he thinks, out of harm's way, in his own village and, with the help of two of his braves, for a second time rescues her father, only to discover, when he returns home, that the Americans now have Ewald. Further conflict between the Seminoles and the Americans is, in a manner, resolved when the Americans, who obtain Palmecho now for a third time, herd the Seminoles and black maroons whom they have not killed onto a ship which is to go to Mexico. The Seminoles and maroons leave Florida in chains. The captain of their transport, however, unchains them. He is more humane than their American captors. Landed in Mexico, they attempt there to start a new life.

The Rape of Florida does not end so happily as *Not a Man*. Yet Atlassa, Ewald, and their comrades in Mexico are free and do have, although they have little else, in their freedom a chance to begin a new life. Carl Marshall, the leading exponent of the thesis that Whitman has been too summarily underestimated by critics as a writer of racial protest, has studied carefully *The Rape of Florida*. Marshall finds ample protest in the poem. He concedes that Whitman is a romantic—a "latter-day romantic." But, to him, Whitman is far from an unthinking romantic. According to Marshall, Whitman conceived of nature as a symbol and, indeed, as such (while Marshall does not say this explicitly), of a kind which permits it to be, in ways discernible to man, if only he troubles himself enough to see what it is possible to perceive, an expression of God's attributes and will. We may wish to remember here Whitman's love of the country—of his external surroundings sheerly as substances of themselves—in the part of Kentucky where he was born and to parallel that love with the feeling for similar aspects of his environment so ardently enunciated by Wordsworth in such poems of his as *The Prelude* and "Tintern Abbey." Neither Whitman nor Wordsworth believed that nature could be as it was without significance for man. Both saw in nature a book, as it were, written by a divine hand, containing knowledge of the utmost importance for men who wanted to live their lives under the most favorable of circumstances. Both, too, saw in nature incontrovertible proofs that God and his universe are ultimately benevolent as well as beautiful. So, Marshall asserts that, for Whitman, nature possessed the power of promoting man's highest qualities, none of which, Marshall further asserts, in Whitman's view, appeared to nature of greater consequence than freedom of the mind.[2]

It was, then, Marshall concludes his argument, no light decision of

---

2. Carl Marshall, "Two Protest Poems by Albery A. Whitman," *College Language Association Journal*, XIX (September, 1975), 50–56.

Whitman's which occasioned his manner of speaking about race. Whitman, Marshall strongly infers, had tried, as it were, to probe the secrets of the cosmos around him, inanimate and animate. Romantic though he was, he had, in effect, said to himself that it was not enough to be sensitive to beauty and truth and to seek to create, through art, simulacra of reality sufficiently faithful to fact in their mimicry as to constitute, for man, a most valid form of vicarious experience. For Whitman, the artist, owed his audience more. He needed to dare to ruminate, to reflect, to cogitate. Without being a metaphysician by trade, a Kant or a Hegel, Whitman yet pondered issues which metaphysicians do tend to consider. His thoughts on eschatology were limited by his religion. He did not seem to be affected at all by the kind of doubts which troubled a poet like Tennyson. Darwinism, that is, cast no shadows on his literal acceptance of Christianity with its versions of the Creation, the Resurrection, and the literal existence of heaven and hell. He could fit in with such a religion his own concept of nature and the lessons it provided, if only they were appreciated, for the control of human behavior. Hence his doctrine of self-reliance and his optimism. To him, the man who took it upon himself to make his own way and who never faltered in his conviction that, in the end, virtue and merit would triumph was only accepting truths which the world of nature demonstrated were part of an eternal scheme. Rodney, therefore, of *Not a Man* was very much a natural man, and the party surrounding Atlassa that was forced to start life anew in Mexico, as Adam and Eve were forced to do both in and out of Eden, was not a party without hope. Neither should be the Negroes recently emancipated, and still under heavy burdens, in America.

The third, and last, of Whitman's major poems, "The Octoroon," the second poem in *An Idyll of the South,* is written all in ottava rima, and so it is the second of Whitman's major poems which experiments with a form of verse not usually to be found in poetry by black Americans. It totals 161 stanzas, and it is, though not as long as *The Rape of Florida,* yet more than 1,000 lines in length. It is a narrative, well-constructed and relatively free of extraneous matter. Moreover, it is a narrative of love. It tells of nothing else except the warm and wonderful amorous emotion of the extremely beautiful octoroon Lena for Sheldon Maury—the handsome and highly principled young white man whose love for her is as great and sincere as hers for him—and of what happens when Sheldon actually plans to marry her. It has been possible for three centuries and more in America to degrade Negroes ultimately because of the robust vitality of one institution, color caste. But color caste itself would vanish were it not for its ban on the marriage of whites with blacks. That ban is the most sacred article in its creed, the taboo which must not be violated, else all of color caste is lost. So, Sheldon's father rises to, for him, a desperate occasion and performs his obvious duty as a defender of color caste. He is not only Sheldon's father. He is also Lena's master. How much of a treasure in her he owns is well indicated by Whitman in the following lines:

> Just in the dawn of blushing womanhood
> Her swan-neck glimpsed through shocks of wavy hair,
> A hint of olives in her gentle blood,
> Suggesting passion in a rosy lair;
> This shapely Venus of the cabins stood
> In all but birth a princess, tall and fair

Nevertheless, obviously it now behooves the elder Maury to rid himself of this treasure, taking care to place her where his son will have small, if any, chance of access to her. The elder Maury does discharge his obligation, excellently, by his light. He sells Lena to a man, closer to his age than to Lena's, who surely, he expects, will debauch her in every way. He has underestimated Lena. She withstands her new owner's attacks upon her, to speak politely of the scheming and pawing of a brute. She even manages to escape her tormentor. But the toll she pays is an effect upon herself which leads to her own death. An anguished Sheldon eventually tracks her down, weakened as she is, in a woodsman's cottage, before she breathes her last. He, of course, still loves her and still wants to marry her. But that desire of his, his parent has thwarted. Lena's life ceases with the cessation of "The Octoroon."

Joan Sherman, probably Whitman's ablest and fullest critic thus far, has said of "The Octoroon" that for "its tight construction, consistent tone, and lyrical beauty . . . [it] is . . . [Whitman's] most artistic endeavor," in other words, his best poem. That special phenomenon it well may be and, consequently, as a matter of some importance, strong evidence, possibly, that Whitman is one of those artists, not as numerous as they well might be, who do grow as they continue to practice their craft. In any case, Sherman's commentary on "The Octoroon," and especially on the poem in its later stages, deserves respectful attention. Sherman calls attention to the manner in which, in the poem, after Lena has been sold away from Sheldon and as her lover is frantically searching for her, "the poetry's spasmodic lines and harsh alliteration convey cosmic dis-

cord as the frenzied lover rides to Lena's rescue through an infernal darkness." To help to prove her point, Sherman quotes the lines:

> And night came on. Earth-jarring thunders roared
>   And rolled afar. Behind the inky banks
> The sun had sunk in terror. Up, up soared
>   The scurrying clouds and spread like serried ranks
> With murky banners flying,—swirled and poured
>   Through lurid arches,—while demoniac pranks
> The vivid lightings cut and onward came,
>   Stabbing the darkness with their spears of flame.[3]

Next Sherman extends her praise to include all of the conclusion of
"The Octoroon." She cites Sheldon's discovery of Lena. Then she adds:

The pathos of reunion and of Lena's peaceful death and simple funeral escapes
effusive sentimentality, for broad nature imagery and abstract theologizing distance the emotion. The poet's thoughts on faith and immortality in the final
eleven stanzas are not overly didactic, and their solemn tone of glad acceptance
blends with the tragic love story, as in this fine stanza [of Whitman's, of course]:

> The wild moose shivers in the north land's breath,
> Where Huron's wave upbraids the fretful shore;
> The marsh fowl far to southward wandereth
> And calls her tribes to milder climes explore;
> All nature seems to sigh: "Remember death,
> For all the living soon shall be no more."
> But mark how Faith sweeps on with Tireless wing,
> To find for e'en the fowl an endless spring.[4]

No power exists which can recover the content of Whitman's mind
during his composition of "The Octoroon." Nor was he a writer who extensively recorded his own meditations. Little of his correspondence, if
he corresponded much, has been preserved, although we do have letters
from him, about his poetry, to (among others) Henry Wadsworth Longfellow and President Hayes (whose last name Whitman misspelled).
Whitman kept, apparently, no semblance of a journal. His nearest approach to an autobiography seems to be very brief statements about himself in the preliminaries to *Not a Man* and *Twasinta's Seminoles*. He did
range, as we have seen, over a wide array of issues, sometimes digres-
sively, in his poetry, in such a manner as to reveal the nature of a number

---

3. Joan Sherman, *Invisible Poets: Afro-Americans of the Nineteenth Century* (Urbana, Ill.,
1974), 124.
4. *Ibid.*

of his most profound convictions. But no matter how he is explored, there is no documentary evidence which even suggests that "The Octoroon" is intended as anything but the love story which Sherman and others have found it, in a gratifyingly disciplined manner, to be. Yet, whatever else is true about it, Whitman's love story is decidedly about intermarriage. Perhaps it would be even more about intermarriage if Lena was less white. A dark-skinned heroine might dramatize more arrestingly the issue of so-called racial hybridization than an octoroon like Lena. But, even so, Whitman's love story, which is only a love story and very good of its kind, does happen to have embedded deeply in the infrastructure of its plot a complication which clearly would not be there if Lena and Sheldon both were white. They cannot marry because of color caste. Should they be free to spend their lives together in holy matrimony? Undoubtedly, Whitman, who has made each of them an exceptionally fine young person, believes they should. He need not say so didactically. His poem speaks for itself. Like *Not a Man* and *The Rape of Florida*, freedom is its theme, but the freedom it most directly espouses is one which would wreck the most inner of the inner sanctums of color caste. However unwittingly, or wittingly, "The Octoroon" does protest, all the better because so unblatantly.

Of Whitman's shorter poems, none of which show him to such advantage as his three long poems, eighteen are appended as "Miscellaneous Poems" to the 1877 edition of *Not a Man*. All eighteen are lyrics. They include eulogies of the black poet Joshua McCarter Simpson and, in "Ye Bards of England," of Chaucer, Thomson, Shakespeare, and Byron. One of the eighteen is a sonnet. Another, "The Great Strike," reveals Whitman as hardly a friend to organized labor. *Drifted Leaves,* which appeared in 1890 with versions of *Not a Man* and *Twasinta's Seminoles*, contains twenty-three lyrics, among them Whitman's only two poems in Negro dialect, at even which, incidentally, he shows the marks of a true poet. His poems "The Veteran" and "The Freedman's Triumphant Song," published together in *The World's Fair Poem,* are run-of-the-mill. "The Veteran," in clichés, eulogizes men who fought in the Civil War. "The Freedman's Triumphant Song" defends the Americanism of America's blacks in peace and war. Like "The Octoroon," with which it was published in *An Idyll of the South,* "The Southland's Charms and Freedom's Magnitude," seventy-four stanzas long, is in ottava rima. Topically diffuse, it manages only to discuss its subject with no surprises and an absence of distinction.

In his own time there were some, Whitman himself among them, who called Whitman the poet laureate of the Negro race. Longfellow spoke a good word for Whitman's poetry, as did William Cullen Bryant and John Greenleaf Whittier. Black writers James D. Corrothers and George Marion McClellan praised him, although McClellan went to some length to make it clear that his commendatory sentiments applied solely to Whitman's verse and not to Whitman the person, whom McClellan reprehended as too unlearned and much too egotistic. The black biographer William Simmons acclaimed Whitman. Bishop Payne, who constantly lamented Whitman's drinking, took pride in Whitman's excellence as a poet. Thus, Whitman far from lacked recognition while he was still alive. Even so, his reputation now is almost surely higher than it has ever been. Estimable critics, prominent among them Louis Rubin, have visited and revisited him with increasing respect for his merits as a poet. Indeed, a growing consensus of respectable opinion seems to have installed him as, in effect, the leading black poet of his century, no less distinctive for his era than Phillis Wheatley had been for hers.

At least one charge, however, sometimes brought against Whitman should always be given serious attention. That charge identifies him as too much the sedulous ape of other poets. Whitman's propensity for mimicry troubled Brawley, who found in Whitman's verse "imitation on every hand." Sterling Brown has also noticed Whitman's reliance on other poets, specifying, for instance, as poets from whom Whitman apparently copies, Lord Byron, Tennyson, Bryant, and Whittier. But the charge of mimicry against Whitman may nowhere, perhaps, have been made more emphatically than by Vernon Loggins in his treatment of Whitman in *The Negro Author: His Development in America to 1900*. Loggins stigmatizes Whitman as a "mocking bird" of some other poets. Exception to Loggins' characterization of Whitman, as to any similar indictment anywhere, has been ably expressed by critic Charles E. Wynes. It is not, says Wynes, so much a question of whether Whitman was notably a mockingbird as of whether he was not also a lark. In his apologia for Whitman, Wynes quotes a stanza from *The Rape of Florida*, one which has caught the attention of other readers of Whitman and which is sometimes called "The Boatman's Song":

> "Come now, my love, the moon is on the lake;
> Upon the water is my light canoe;
> Come with me, love, and gladsome oars shall make
> A music on the parting waves for you,

> Come o'er the waters deep and dark and blue;
> Come where the lilies in the marge have sprung,
> Come with me, love, for Oh, my love is true!"
> This is the song that on the lake was sung,
> The boatman sang it over when his heart was young.

No mere mockingbird, of course, could have written such a stanza. Wynes says as much. For, throughout Wynes's comments on Whitman, he adheres to the simple argument that, fundamentally, Whitman's poetry derived from forces of genius original with Whitman. Critics may delight in asserting that "The Boatman's Song" is a Byronic use of the Spenserian stanza—which, as a matter of fact, it well may be—but there remains a beauty in the stanza which does not come from Byron. It comes from Whitman, from the poet who, as a boy, to quote from a quotation by Wynes of Whitman, before he "could write a letter, . . . was trying to scribble down what the birds and bees and cows were saying and what even the dumb rocks were thinking."[5]

It was always, for Whitman, as for any artist, a compound of his past experiences which went into his poetry. Some of those experiences represented his borrowings from other poets; some, his independent attacks on problems of poetic composition. Yet he was anything but preeminently a plagiarist of other poets' virtuosities. "The Boatman's Song" makes that fact clear. It shows in Whitman the quality of independent creativity which was his birthright and which, above all else that can be said of him, accounts for his deserved eminence in Afro-American literature.

5. Benjamin Brawley, "Three Negro Poets: Horton, Mrs. Harper, and Whitman," *Journal of Negro History*, II–III (October, 1977), 388; *Dictionary of American Biography*, X, 139; Vernon Loggins, *The Negro Author: His Development in America to 1900* (New York, 1931), 341; Charles E. Wynes, "Albery Allson Whitman—The Black Mocking Bird[?] Poet," *Illinois Quarterly*, XI (Fall, 1978), 39–47.

13. Early Folk Literature, Largely Prose

There is left, of the poetry by black Americans in the nineteenth century, the anonymous verse the crowning glory of which would appear to be, beyond any doubt, the texts of those marvelous songs most familiarly known as the Negro spirituals. These spirituals belong, of course, to the rich and fascinating province of American folklore. Where—chronologically, at least, if not otherwise—that province begins it may be difficult to say. There were Indians in America long before the coming of the white man. Their folklore, including a not inconsiderable amount of genuine literature, certainly now, while it will never cease to be (as it always should be) identified with them, like the folklore of all the other, and later, immigrants to the continental United States, has become a component of our common national treasury of folklore. People have trekked to America from diverse Old World backgrounds, bringing with them, among other things, the folklores of the countries from which they came. There exists, consequently, in all American folklore, some residue of archaic Old World importations.

Such residues alone would impart to American folklore a goodly measure of variety. But, moreover, America itself, a land so vast as to seem several countries in one, has also acted to create in American folklore localized elements which are not everywhere the same. For America is a country not easily compressed into a unit as might be a Wales or a Luxembourg. America covers, after all, millions of square miles. It cannot but change as it extends. Its Country of the Big Sky in Wyoming and neighboring states differs markedly from its Down East in upper New England or its Maryland and Virginia Tidewater or its hard-scrabble ridges of the Appalachians or its bayous of central Louisiana or the topography, the climate, the vegetation, and the total physical environment in even other distinctive, separable areas within the whole United States. So America is a medley of landscapes with accompanying natural phenomena which are not uniform and which, to a truly significant degree, have operated to effect, in America, a certain tyranny of place. We do have, in America, subcultures based on where people live. The result—abetted in no trivial measure by such historical incidents as the forced conveyance of Canadian Acadia to Louisiana, the purchase of a Gallic culture in and around New Orleans, and even the annexation of a colonial Spain in the Far Southwest and California—has been the development, in America, of an American regionalism.

This regionalism has been well observed in American literature. Writers like Bret Harte, for example, and Sarah Orne Jewett are cited regularly as regional writers. This regionalism is no less well observed in American folklore, the lines of which sometimes intersect with those of literature. The net effect, moreover, of this regionalism upon American folklore has been to enrich the folklore, to multiply it, to variegate it, and rarely, if ever, to influence unduly its qualitative merit. Whether its manifestation is a snatch of a ditty sung long ago by a trapper of French extraction or the eighteenth-century architecture in a town along the Connecticut River or a tall tale from the Old Southwest, more often than not American folklore gratifies both the historian and the artist we all well may be. It recalls to us our American past in terms that link us not so much to heroic legends as to the familiar lives of ordinary Americans usually so obscure as ourselves that we may feel comfortable with them and yet so representative of our democracy that we cannot fail but take pride in it and them.

Afro-American folklore can be called, in a manner of speaking, a regional American folklore, for black Americans, to an extent hardly only figurative, under the pressure of color caste, have always lived in a region of America all too exclusively their own. Black Americans began early to amass a folklore. Black Americans, too, like other Americans who were not black, had ties with an Old World. For black Americans, obviously, the Old World was Africa. Much attention, therefore, in black American folklore, has focused on dance and song. Africans dance and sing, it has been emphasized. And so black Americans should dance and sing. Moreover, these black Americans should dance and sing in an African way, with a command of rhythms often intricate and exotic, a penchant for the use of percussion instruments (including clapping hands and stomping feet), an affection for contrapuntal chants, and a sense of harmony which can apply both to sounds and to choric moves all reminiscent of Africa. And, as a matter of fact, in their folklore which does dance or sing, or both, black Americans do seem African atavists of a rather avid order. Africa then relives itself in them, although it is never wise in black-American folk dance and folk song to ignore the purely American presence there. But dance and song are only peripherally connected with literature. For Afro-American literature, the black folk have expressed themselves, in prose, mainly through folktales and folk sermons and, in poetry, through secular songs such as the verses which they have sung at work and, preeminently, as we have already claimed, in the spirituals.

Of black-American folktales it well may be that none are better known—or certainly better known about—than the animal stories which America's slaves and freedmen circulated among themselves, with particular, and joyous, attention in them to crafty, irrepressible Brer Rabbit. Animal tales, scholars agree, are universal, found in virtually every culture. Moreover, there are elements indispensable to animal stories, such as motifs and characters, which seem to possess traits and elements as universal in their similarities as the tales. Nevertheless, ancestral relations between old Africa and the animal tales of Afro-American folklore are too obvious to be ignored. If no other affiliation seems true, clearly the animals in both the African and Afro-American tales are the same, as if the ships which bore the slaves across the ocean had brought along also the animals of their tales. Brer Rabbit himself is but the African hare. The African jackal is the American fox. The African tortoise is, in the black-American folktale, a turtle or terrapin. And the African spider is something of an exception to the other animals of the African folktale. He crossed the ocean, indeed, but never reached the continent of North America, stopping in the West Indies to inhabit the Anansi tales which have long been passed by word of mouth among the blacks of the Caribbean.

Brer Rabbit owes a large amount of his popularity to a white man, Joel Chandler Harris, author of the Uncle Remus tales, almost an American institution from the 1890s to the 1920s. Uncle Remus was black, a fictional slave who told his black folktales, featuring Brer Rabbit, to a little white boy, the son of Uncle Remus' owner and master. In dispensing his tales to an auditor who was not black, Uncle Remus broke a cardinal rule for folktales, which must be for, as well as by, the folk. Moreover, white intervention (both that of Joel Chandler Harris and that of the imaginary little white boy) links Uncle Remus with another famous phenomenon of American life in which the black folk were, as it were, preempted and modified by white interpreters. This phenomenon was blackface min-strelsy, and a word about it can hardly be amiss here before we return to Uncle Remus.

The point about blackface minstrelsy to be remembered in connection with Afro-American literature is that, no matter how far it got from where it started, and it did get very far, blackface minstrelsy never lost its origin, however faint, in the behavior of the Negro folk. It was at least based on what somebody white, who had watched Negroes, thought Negroes were like. Constance Rourke has described as the comic trio of early America the Yankee, the backwoodsman, and the Negro.[1] In so doing, she speaks convincingly. A land, especially along its pioneering edge, starved for the relief of humor from its hard, bleak existence, turned eager eyes on all three members of Rourke's comic trio, but probably found no member of the trio more in evidence than the Negro. He could be found not only on the plantations and small farms, as well as around the houses and taverns, of the thirteen original colonies. As America ex-panded, he went west. In what may have been his most sorrowful guise for the casual public eye, he drudged southward in slave coffles, bound for auction blocks in such places as New Orleans. But he was very visible otherwise. He worked for whites who stayed at home. He worked also for whites who traveled. Nor was what many whites considered his peculiar gift for entertainment overlooked. There were masters who had formed bands and minstrel troupes out of their own slaves, at least thus leaving the possible folklore of dancing, singing, and making jokes in Negro hands. But, late in the 1820s, young Thomas Dartmouth Rice of New York City, stagestruck from his boyhood, in either Cincinnati or Louis-ville (but most probably in Louisville), saw a Negro hostler with a hunched-up right shoulder and a left leg stiff at the knee perform a dance infectiously agile and startlingly adroit in view of the unmistakable infir-mity of the hostler. It was Rice who improvised the verse which, with many additions, would sweep the world of the Anglo-American theater and music hall:

1. Constance Rourke, *American Humor: A Study of the National Character* (New York, 1931). See especially the first three chapters of this excellent book.

First on de heel tap, den on de toe,
Ebery time I wheel about I jump dim Crow.
Wheel about and turn about and do jis so,
And every time I wheel about I jump Jim Crow.

So Thomas Dartmouth Rice became Jim Crow, or "Daddy" Rice, for al-most twenty years, until he died a paralytic and impoverished. He en-joyed great success in both America and the British Isles, and blazed the trail for those who would follow him into the true world of blackface minstrelsy.

For "Daddy" Rice was only a single blackfaced impersonator. Black-face minstrelsy evolved into a theatrical institution the sine qua non of which was not one man or woman but a show as full of acts and perform-ers as a three-ring circus. This institution, moreover, developed a vitality which permitted it to last for almost a hundred years. In the days before the movies, the radio, and television, it had no rival anywhere in the world as the favored form of mass entertainment. It thrived, not only in America, but also in Europe and as far afield as Hawaii and Australia (not to speak of a band of Hindi minstrels who played and sang in nineteenth-century India). Probably the first true blackface minstrels were the Vir-ginia Minstrels (one of whom was Dan Emmett, composer of "Dixie") in New York City, either in late 1842 or in 1843. Not until 1928 did the Al G. Field Company ring down the final curtain professionally on black-face minstrelsy. In between the two termini, the blackface minstrels, who tended overwhelmingly to be white, their Negro faces applied with burnt cork, had created and circulated a version of the black folk which reduced all Negroes to "darkies," with shuffling feet, rolling eyes, huge, pendulous lips, petty larceny in their hearts (they stole chickens and wa-termelons), a superstitious dread of graveyards and the dark, and the ar-rested mental development of idiotic, delinquent children. Yet no full sense of black folklore is quite possible without an awareness of blackface minstrelsy. Occasionally, even in the vicious stereotype of the folk Negro this minstrelsy perpetrated, in song or jest, dance or pantomime, an au-thentic bit of Negro behavior genuinely representative of the Negro folk did manage to survive. Even more importantly, the stereotype blackface minstrelsy loved so much and shared so extensively with other white-controlled media of expression, the "darky," a Stepin Fetchit, an Amos and Andy, at best a Mr. Benny's Rochester, dramatized in its unreality, its perversion of the truth, the real folk Negro of actual Negro folklore, who had his faults and could, at times, be ludicrous, but who was never the sorry figure of the Virginia Minstrels and their successors.

So, to resume with Uncle Remus, the prominence of Brer Rabbit, a small, weak animal, in these tales, and his success in outwitting bigger, stronger animals like Brer Bear and Brer Wolf, whom he can obviously not outbrawl, suggest that, wittingly or not, Joel Chandler Harris did retain, in his version of black animal tales, a feature of them which was sympathetically black, not doctrinally white. The Negro in America was in enemy country where the enemy obviously, in terms of sheer physical power, was greatly his superior. The Negro, therefore, who could not play Brer Rabbit's game—who could not, that is, circumvent the white man's wishes with guile—was a Negro doomed never to have his way. It does seem, consequently, that the popularity of Brer Rabbit in the animal tales of black-American folklore was no accident. He articulated through his conduct a lesson the value of which many Negroes considered significant, if only for their survival in any manner not utterly to their shame, while simultaneously he occasioned in some Negroes the pleasure they could feel from believing that there were times in their own lives when they had been, in their own way with the white folks, as clever as might have been the ostensibly unlikely hero of their animal folktales. Moreover, along with Brer Rabbit as a master of guile and chicanery in the animal tales, the human trickster was precisely the same kind of devious opponent in tales not about animals in black folklore, so that these trickster tales, as numerous and highly appreciated by their black-folk originators as they clearly were, constitute, at least conjecturally, a measure of confirmation of the existence of the sentiment already cited here, which accounted for Brer Rabbit's position of esteem in the affections virtually everywhere of the Negro folk. Brer Rabbit was a trickster. Long live all tricksters! And so the trickster story with men as the tricksters—and the tricked—did not do at all badly in the world of the Negro folk. In some of these trickster stories Negroes outwitted other Negroes. In others they did outwit whites.

One of the trickster stories still current orally among the Negro folk as late as the 1920s (if not later), whether or not any version of it has yet been confided to print, achieves its point rather subtly through what might well be called a reversal of the probably expected lesson, with an emphasis upon the consequences to a Negro of any lack of the true trickster's ability to foresee, with commendably unusual acumen, all the possible dangers to himself in a course of action he adopts. In this tale a

Negro with a normally indulgent master, in the middle of a sunny, summer, southern day, is drowsing at his ease along the bank of a stream which flows through his master's plantation. Quite suddenly, yet not abruptly, an alligator rears his head above the stream in the water near the Negro and says, in an even tone, to the Negro, "Nigger, you talk too much." The alligator then submerges, leaving a Negro almost stunned with disbelief in the reliability of his own eyes and ears. But twice more the alligator, without changing his manner, reappears and issues his admonition to the Negro, who, finally, rushes up the bank to his master's mansion, awakens his master from his daily siesta, and insists that his master come with him to witness this marvel of an alligator who talks. After some delay, and with great reluctance, the master does accompany his slave to the waterside, where the alligator, whom the Negro without hesitation identifies as the beast capable of human speech, almost immediately partially surfaces. But the alligator no longer utters any human sound. Eventually the irritated master returns to his siesta after ordering the Negro to be severely whipped. Then the alligator does speak—and says again, "Nigger, you talk too much."

Some of the black folktales were about black preachers. That they were is easily understandable. Black preachers occupied a position of prominence and power among the Negro folk long before the end of slavery and continued as, in effect, father figures to a tribe in the world of the black folk after emancipation. Portraits of these black folk preachers appear in such twentieth-century black novels as Zora Neale Hurston's *Jonah's Gourd Vine* and Margaret Walker's *Jubilee*. A most valuable attribute literarily of black folklore is the black folk sermons, of which, nevertheless, it must be said that scholarly collection, although not analysis, of them seems to have lagged behind their reputation. Perhaps, since they were the product of a largely illiterate people, the day has passed when any considerable number of them will ever be written down. How they could attract the attention and stimulate the activity of scholars and artists, or of persons who were some of both, may be well illustrated by a look at James Weldon Johnson, who taught school in rural Georgia during the summers of his student days at the old Atlanta University. Johnson had grown up in a comfortably bourgeois environment in Jacksonville, Florida. The black folk world he encountered in rural Georgia was relatively new to him. He found it strange, as would have a Frank Norris or a Henry James. It had for him, of course, its appalling side. It spoke to him of a system he hated and despised and of the worst failure, as he assessed it, of a so-called democracy to fulfill its announced creed. Above all, the terror which stalked that world, and too often struck it in its vitals, left its lasting impression upon him.

Yet not everything in black rural Georgia was negative for Johnson. It was there that he found the black folk preacher in what was probably the black folk preacher's most congenial habitat. This preacher Johnson warmly appreciated and intensely studied. His art Johnson tried to reproduce, without his dialect, through the seven poems of God's Trombones. And, in giving short shrift to the dialect, Johnson, as usual with him, acted with great intelligence. What truly mattered in the black folk sermon was its art. Out of that art this sermon was expected to play upon the emotions, to rock the church where it was uttered, and to send its hearers into deliriums of religious fervor as they shouted their amens and hallelujahs. Basically these sermons were theatrical presentations, played out by one performer, sometimes with musical cooperation from a soloist, a choir, or an entire congregation (or of soloist, choir, congregation, and the preacher combined). But the essence of their construction, and of their appeal to those for whom they were intended, was their reliance upon old, long-established, simple principles of drama and, indeed, of melodrama. They wasted no time on involved induction or deduction. They merely dealt, in terms a child could understand, with sin and the devil, the Christian story and the Resurrection, often adding, for good measure, glimpses of eternal delight as it would be in Heaven. These sermons were full of repetitions and digressions to permit the performer to exhibit one, or more, of his special feats in rhetoric and theatricality of which he was most vainly proud. Nevertheless, they were never meant to be dull, at least not for those who were supposed to hear them and to react to them. They were a form of evangelical Christianity, for Methodists or Baptists at best and certainly not for Episcopalians or Unitarians under any circumstances. And they were not from manuscript. The preacher of a black folk sermon simply placed himself, empty-handed and alone, before his people and, then, addressed them. In a sense he was an impromptu speaker. But, actually, and especially if he was an old practitioner of the game, he never was. It was not merely that, as we have intimated earlier, he tended to use material he had used before, much as did William Jennings Bryan in his famous "Cross of Gold" speech. It was also, to be particularly noted here, that he relied heavily on words, sentences, biblical allusions, and even images which were formulaic.

The preacher of the black folk sermon did exactly as poets did long ago when bards freely plagiarized each other, and were expected to. The audiences he faced, moreover, were in no wise offended by their familiarity with a considerable amount of what he was saying. They were like the audiences at the plays popular in Greek antiquity. Those audiences had come to the theater to see dramatized stories with which they were already well acquainted. The black folk in James Weldon Johnson's day, and before, attended church to hear again and again stories from the Bible, not every such story, but the relatively few select stories from the Bible which had become the favorites of their fancy. Yet that was only part of their desire. They wanted what well might be called their stories told in a certain way, *their* way, a formulaic way. They listened for language and imagery which duplicated as exactly as possible language and imagery they had heard before. And so the single black folk preacher could have individual merits. But, unless he was most obtuse, he knew that the black folk sermon was, in effect, a patented artifact with mostly standardized parts. Whoever preached it submitted to following, to some extent, carefully in the footsteps of many predecessors.

Few, if any, of the black folk sermons were more celebrated than John Jasper's "De Sun Do Move," transcriptions of which do exist. Jasper was a Virginian, born in 1812, who lived until 1892, most of the years of his long life in the city of Richmond, where he preached "De Sun Do Move." He learned to read, while he was still a young slave, from a spelling book, with the help of another slave. He says of himself, in "De Sun Do Move," that his conversion to Christianity came after his introduction to literacy, and he may well thus be telling the truth. But he may also be acting here as quite a canny man. For the whole point of his sermon is the worth of the Scriptures. He is, that is to say, an excellent Protestant for whom salvation depends upon, first, direct knowledge of the Word of God and, then, obedience to that Word. Reading the Bible, therefore, and accepting it as literal truth is, hence, for every Christian the categorical imperative of all categorical imperatives. Thus, in "De Sun Do Move," Jasper focuses his attention on the account in the Bible of the people in the city of Gideon, beset upon by armies from their neighboring cities because they have been hospitable to the Jews. In this moment of dire distress, the Gideonites send a message to Joshua for help, and he answers their call. He brings other men and himself to their aid and joins them in battle against their enemies. Nor is he ineffective.

With him on their side, the Gideonites are winning. But the day is wan-
ing, and evening has drawn nigh. Joshua and the Gideonites need more
time, in full daylight, sufficiently to accomplish the victory they desire.
So Joshua, relying upon his God, asks that the sun stand still and day be
prolonged until the foes of the Gideonites are thoroughly subdued. The
sun does stand still. Joshua slaughters every enemy he wants to slaughter.
He gets the victory he craves and in the process demonstrates, according
to Jasper, God's absolute sovereignty over everything, great or small, in
all creation.

Jasper acknowledges, in "De Sun Do Move," that there is an astronomy of modern science which differs from the astronomy of the Bible.
But Jasper puts his faith completely in a cosmos which he derives from his
interpretation of the Holy Scriptures. So, to him, the earth is flat with
four corners (an angel at each corner), and the movement of the sun to
which he alludes is not that of an object rotating on its axis while whirl-
ing through a vast orbit in even much vaster space. Jasper's sun rises from
somewhere in the morning and progresses steadily across an arched sky
until it somehow disappears at eventide. This is the sun that Joshua
stopped, and therefore, it is to the ordinary senses of man, to which the
sun seems stationary, that Jasper addresses his assurance of a sun in
motion.

No traces of his African cultural heritage appear in Jasper's "De Sun
Do Move." Jasper, in it, speaks only as a Christian and an American. As
Joshua fought the followers of alien gods in his day, so Jasper battles the
advocates of modern science. It is, to Jasper, utterly a question of belief.
And Jasper refuses to budge one inch from his belief in the Bible as a sacred text, the source of all knowledge and the arbiter of all disputes. The
light from Jesus, Jasper avers, surpasses any light from the sun, powerfully
as the sun, Jasper remembers, has beaten down on his back in the heat of
a season when he was hoeing in the fields. Moreover, it is only through
the light of Jesus, Jasper never doubts, that he and others like himself will
be led to heaven and the glory of their everlasting life. So Jasper affirms
the supremacy of God and, thus, of the existence of a will, and a law,
above any will or law made by man. Thus, also, he can intimate to his
hearers that rebellion against a *status quo* need not be criminal. At one
point in "De Sun Do Move," he fervently reminds his hearers that God is
a God of war as well as a God of peace. It can be, then, that Jasper
covers, for at least some occasions, with the mantle of God's authority,
even rebels who resort to the use of arms. If so, he allies himself with an

element worthy of note in black folk preaching. Churches historically have tended to be conservative. Nor can it be denied that the voice of black religion in America often has sounded like the opiate of a people. Yet neither should it be forgotten that Nat Turner was a preacher or that black folk preachers were, during slavery, agents who helped in enterprises like the Underground Railroad as they would sometimes be, after slavery, leaders in the Negro's fight against discrimination and segregation. One of the two black senators and Congressman Richard Cain of the thirty-three black members of Congress in the nineteenth century were black clergymen, all nurtured on the tradition of the black folk sermon.

At least two forms of the black folk sermon which were rather special perhaps should not be overlooked here. One of these two forms was frequently called the Heavenly March. The other could answer to the appellation of the Train Sermon. In the Heavenly March, the black folk preacher preached a sermon during which he led his congregation, on a march, of course, from earth through the pearly gates to the Master's throne. Properly done, the sermon involved not merely the tramping on to glory—and some of the tramping could be real marching, within the church—but stops along the way. A good folk preacher found it no problem to make a tremendous occasion of every stop. He could, for instance, have virtually every member of his congregation in a paroxysm of delight at the Evening Star. And at the pearly gates he could pause for a long moment of résumé, and anticipation of reminding his hearers of their earthly trials, in which he could wax eloquent and emotional both about the weaknesses of the flesh and the joys of heaven. The Train Sermon could take two routes. If it operated as what was sometimes known as the Black Diamond Express, it headed downward, making thirteen stops, and arriving at its final stop, in hell, ahead of time. If it took its scheduled run the other way, it became a special version of the Heavenly March. It is obviously the basis, incidentally, for the sermon preached by the blind reverend Homer Barbee in Ralph Ellison's *Invisible Man.*

Relatives, as it were, of black folk sermons were black folk religious testimonials and black folk prayers given by black lay sisters and brothers at prayer meetings, class meetings, revivals, Sunday services, and other functions of the church. These testimonials and prayers live today, even more than black folk sermons of the last century, largely by reputation. To a great extent, also, what they once were, and fairly much seem uniformly to always have been, apparently may be discovered in similar testimonials and prayers still being made in the churches of the Negro folk

north and south today. Another relative of the black folk sermon and the
black folk prayer takes us back to the realm of the black folktale. This
relative is the folktale about the black preacher, and some such tales
there undoubtedly were. Conceivably, such a tale could be invented,
with thus, indeed, no limits to its possible embellishments except the deficiencies, or timidities, of its inventor's imagination. But there were actual black preachers around whom folktales were spun as legends supported by verifiable facts. One of the national leaders, for instance, of
America's Negro Baptists between the two world wars was long the pastor
of a large congregation in Chicago and the president of the National
Baptist Convention, Lacey Kirke Williams. But the Reverend L. K.
Williams, as he was generally known, had started life along the Brazos
River in Texas, where, although his father was a respectable and devout
Christian, as well as a deacon in the church, young Williams acquired,
deservedly, a lurid and rather widespread reputation as a heavy drinker, a
gambler, and a haunter of places of ill fame. The folktale about him begins with an account of his wild behavior, but its drama most inheres in
its accompanying account of his conversion in Texas at a revival into
which he bursts, a sensational repentant, fresh from his last carouse with
Satan. Other folktales connected with religion tell about magic and spirits, such as, in some cases, the voodoo tales of Louisiana. There are also
tales which deal with the why of this or that and so are, in their modest
way, religion as epistemology. In its modest way, the tale about Williams
is a tall tale. A whole small class of tales, sometimes called "lies," are the
tall tales of black American folklore.

14. Early Folk Literature in Verse

An effort almost always must be made to separate black folk poetry, whether secular or religious, from the music with which it is, much more often than not, an integrated unit. Music in America owes a great debt to the Negro. In secular music alone, as is well known, ragtime, the blues, and jazz are offspring of the Negro folk. But the Negro folk have sung at work as well as at play. Among the secular songs, therefore, are work songs and prison songs. It is at least possible that a trace, however faint, of their African provenience occurs in these work songs. A Fisk professor is rumored to have argued similarities between the chants he heard lifted by native laborers near ancient Memphis on the Nile and work songs of which he made note that had been sung by black stevedores moving cotton along the docks at Memphis, Tennessee. In any case, Negroes have sung at work all over, especially in the South. Far back in slavery times, and after, black rowers sang at their oars, some in crews selected for their singing. We remember here, for instance, the singing rowers whom Charlotte Forten heard. Negroes sometimes sang in the fields to ameliorate their exertions as they planted, tilled, or gleaned. Behind the white folks' backs, also, Negroes composed and sang folk songs derisively—and, sometimes, bitterly—critical of the whites.

The verse of all these songs, divorced from the music, was (and is) poetry, and so part of the folk poetry of the Negro. Some of it survived the earlier centuries of Negro life in America. But all of it betrays the circumstances of its origin. One prison song, "Water Boy," would come into the twentieth century (unless it was born after 1900) and find a wide audience outside the land to which it was indigenous. This song would also illustrate a phase of development which could be added to a Negro folk song. For a Negro folk song could be heard by trained musicians who would like it well enough to arrange it and write it down as they did for their other music, thus converting the folk song into what has been sometimes called an art song. As an art song "Water Boy" achieved entry into, most fortunately, the repertoire of the eminent black tenor Roland Hayes. Thousands who heard Hayes heard it, as well as other thousands who heard singers other than Hayes. On the concert stage, and as, titularly, an art song, "Water Boy" retained sufficiently its character as a black work and prison song to convey, wherever it was sung, an authentic taste of secular black folk song. Its opening lines, actually its refrain, supposedly sung by convicts, are as follows: "Waterboy, where are you hiding / If you don't come, gwinetuh tell 'uh yo' mammy." Next come the lines of the first stanza. They usually have been rendered as follows:

> You jack of diamonds, you jack of diamonds,
> I know you of old, boys, yes, I know of old.
> You robba my pocket, done robba my pocket,
> Yes, you robba my pocket, of silver and gold.

"Water Boy" has several stanzas. The refrain precedes every stanza, but it was also sung after the last stanza as the concluding lines of the poem. Singers like Hayes were inclined to picture to their audiences, if not with a preliminary verbal explanation, then through nuances of their delivery as they sang, the scene "Water Boy" was intended to evoke, of a gang of black prisoners, attended by white armed guards, crushing rock with sledgehammers under a southern sky. The sledgehammers were heavy. A hot sun poured its beams down upon the prisoners. Their one amenity may well have been a waterboy whom, although not too often, they could call. Whatever their situation, however, the song blessed them by aiding the rhythm of their work. Possibly they grunted in unison as, in unison, their hammers struck the rock, and so (the *huhs* show when the hammers strike): "Waterboy (huh), where are you hiding (huh)? / If you don't come (huh), gwinetuh tell 'uh yo' mammy (huh)."

To shift from the secular to the religious in black folk song is, at last, to concentrate upon the Negro spiritual. Of an uncertain history, if only for its obscurity through what must have been easily a half dozen, or more, American decades, the spiritual finally began to achieve recognition, not alone in America, but also abroad, shortly after the Civil War. Quickly, when known, it captivated its new-found public. Primarily, its attractiveness depended upon its appeal as music. But the words which provide explicit oral communication to accompany what its music may seem to say are, obviously, possessions of the world of literature. Under inspection, moreover, these words, a folk poetry of their own, turn out to be profoundly interesting solely within themselves. But to approach them properly at all they must first be included, without special reference to them, in a picture of the spirituals as a whole. Their story, as poetry, depends somewhat upon a knowledge, in full, of the songs of which they were, and are, so integrally a part. And those songs as a whole have not only been sung and heard. They have also, and understandably, occasioned curiosity about their origins and close inspection of their character. Inquiring minds seem to agree in wanting to know how old they are, how profuse they ever were, and how they were born. In particular, did one person make them, or a host of anonymities? What, indeed, was the process of their composition? Since they are black folk songs, do they look back to Africa, either some or much, or are they substantially, or, for all that matters, exclusively, American? Finally what about them renders them memorable? What is their character that history should so enshrine them?

It seems virtually certain now that no one will ever be able to say with authority not subject to question how old the spirituals are. In 1867 some of them were published in the book *Slave Songs of the United States*, edited by William Francis Allen, Charles Pickard Ware, and Lucy McKim Garrison. The book was a first of its kind, the first appearance anywhere of the spirituals in print. Allen, Ware, and Garrison all were northerners of the type of sympathizers with blacks who were drawn south during the Civil War by such projects as the famous Port Royal experiment or whose sense of mission and high purpose allied them after the war in efforts to educate or otherwise lend a helping hand to the freedmen whom the war had liberated. Also in 1867, an article by Thomas Wentworth Higginson, "Negro Spirituals," appeared in the June issue of the *Atlantic Monthly*. Higginson was a native of Massachusetts, a graduate of Harvard, of Brahmin stock, and an irrepressible abolitionist in every blue vein of his vigorous and impressive physique. His was the distinction of commanding, as a colonel, the first regiment of Negro troops to serve the Union, the 1st South Carolina Volunteers. He came to know Port Royal well, and there are allusions to the spirituals in his book, published in 1870 in Boston, *Army Life in a Black Regiment*. But John Lovell, Jr., in his exhaustive study of the Negro spiritual, *Black Song*, asserts that the spirituals "were spread all over the slave land of hundreds of years."[1] That can only mean, if Lovell is to be believed, that the earliest Negro spirituals were created in the seventeenth century, the first century of American colonization and of black residence in America.

The spirituals celebrate but one religion, that of Jesus Christ, the sole religion tolerated among the slaves by their white masters. Nor can it be said of America's Negroes that Christianity was not warmly and sincerely accepted by them or that they waited for many years before adopting it. The seventeenth century is not too early to think of the slaves as Christians. It is altogether possible that, before 1700, the Negro folk were composing, and passing on to their children, Negro spirituals. But it is not known, from documents, that they did so. Moreover, it is not probable. On the other hand, the songs collected by Allen, Ware, and Garrison, and referred to by Higginson, from their very nature had not sprung up overnight. Obviously, the black folk who sang them had received the spirituals from their ancestors. Whether those ancestors had received the spirituals from their ancestors, even through more than one generation, remains the issue relative to which conclusive evidence is lacking. It seems safe to assume that the spirituals date back to at least the earliest years of the nineteenth century. Because we know that Negroes were Christianized before that and had their own preachers, some, if not many, of whom were inspirationally evangelical, as well as because we know that blacks were introduced into America in the eighteenth century far more numerously than in any other century and so were merged at least by then into a folk community highly conscious of itself, with inner traits and properties it shared freely only within its own confines, as (not too strangely) all minority communities often do, we may possibly, and, perhaps, even probably, assume that the spiritual was born no later than at some date in the eighteenth century. But the spiritual may not have been two hundred years old at the time of the Civil War, just as it may have been older. It may well not be, then, too bold to say that spirituals were being sung in America by Negroes at least as early as the late 1700s or the early 1800s. Beyond that, little more than almost all sheer conjecture apparently begins.

Lovell, in his *Black Song*, considers the question of the number of Negro spirituals. He is at some pains, incidentally, to mention the findings, anent this point of number, of George Pullen Jackson, leading ad-

1. John Lovell, Jr., *Black Song: The Forge and the Flame* (New York, 1972), xiii.

vocate of the hypothesis that Negro spirituals derived from what Jackson was wont to call the white spirituals of the southern uplands. Lovell stoutly opposes the notion that the Negro spirituals owe anything to white singers of religious songs from the southern uplands or anywhere else. In any case, he cites Chapter 14 of Jackson's *White and Negro Spirituals: Their Life Span and Kinship* (published in New York City in 1943), which contains Jackson's assessment of the actual number of Negro spirituals when absolutely every extant one of them, according to Jackson, has been counted. Jackson, Lovell reports, credits himself with examining 13 collections of Negro spirituals, all published before 1940 and containing, in sum, the titles of 1,413 songs, of which only 500 or 600 are not duplications. In effect, Jackson numbers the spirituals in the middle hundreds while he "clearly suggests," according to Lovell, that his 500 or 600 individual songs constitute all of the Negro spirituals. Jackson's figures, thus, differ considerably from those of Lovell, who claims to have assembled more than 500 *collections* of Negro spirituals published before 1940 and to have cataloged, from these collections, about 6,000 "independent" spirituals.[2]

Lovell, as any test of his veracity and competence will show, and as the accumulation of printed versions of the spirituals confirms, is much nearer to the truth than Jackson. In some form or other, there were several thousand Negro spirituals or, perhaps, even more when the possibilities of spirituals uncollected and of those simply expired of attrition from lack of sustained repetition are taken into account. Indeed, it does appear that only a fraction of the Negro spirituals which did, at some time or other, exist has ever been collected. Moreover, reflection upon the Negro spiritual in terms both of its not inconsiderable age at the lowest reasonable attempted estimate of its length of existence in the Afro-American past and of the fewest thousands of songs it once may have generated strongly suggests that the spiritual was a hardy, thriving, long-lived, and, throughout the antebellum South, almost ubiquitous form of Negro creativity. A Negro who sang spirituals with other Negroes in the upper South during slavery and whom the domestic slave trade may then have transported to Mississippi or Alabama or Texas would have found, apparently, himself able to resume his singing of spirituals with a fresh assortment of black comrades in his new home in the Deep South, wherever that new home chanced to be. It is possible, if not likely, also, that

2. *Ibid.*, 19.

the Negro spiritual was a more private—and, hence, perhaps a more prized—possession of the Negro folk than their dance and song which underlay blackface minstrelsy or than the kind of Negro melodic idiosyncrasies detectable in such lyrics as those—say, "Old Black Joe" and "My Old Kentucky Home"—composed, however, mimetically, by Stephen Collins Foster. Conceivably, the relative lack of reference to the spirituals in the travel literature about the South written by foreigners and by white American natives from the North and the South can be attributed to a tendency among the Negro folk to be less open with their spirituals than with their secular music. And, should this tendency have existed, the less inhibited revelations, as it were, of the spirituals by southern blacks to whites only as slavery was passing, with its emphasis upon the apparently preferential selection of northern whites by blacks to hear their spirituals, could be, for students of the spirituals, an indication of the value which the slaves had placed upon these songs.

That value certainly depended to a great extent upon the fact that the spirituals so truly were a folk product. No Schubert or Samuel Coleridge-Taylor devised them as expressions of an individual genius. Yet to make such an admission may be only to utter a partial truth. It may well be that some of the spirituals at least, if not more than some, did begin their often wide-ranging existence on the lips, and from the creative powers, of a single slave. James Weldon Johnson, in his poem "O Black and Unknown Bards," muses over what he calls "the wide, wide wonder in it all," alluding thus to the aesthetic quality of the spirituals and, additionally, to their great contrast with our knowledge, incontrovertible in its authenticity, of the burdens slavery imposed upon the slave, who worked sometimes from before the break of dawn until after sundown at often stupefying tasks from which he retired to a hovel too frequently unfit for human habitation. But another wonder about the spirituals is the mystery of their method of composition. Surely no collective efforts could be altogether responsible for any of them. A line or two, or more, of each of them must have occurred to some one person who introduced his original creation, a fragment or the whole—at least in embryo, if not in finished form—of a song, to a group. Then, it almost surely was, the group did actually enter in the process of creation.

In perhaps rare instances the group's contribution was minimal. The group may have only altered, or added, words, or words and melodies, or melodies, to fit its tastes and capacities. In other instances, the group may have conceived, through its members working in an assembly, refrains, responses in a call-and-response chant, or stanzas. Every conceiv-able form of interaction of an individual with a group in a situation where a folk song was achieving an identity, of course, could be possible. But the mystery remains. John Livingston Lowes, rifling through records of Samuel Taylor Coleridge's reading, could demonstrate the process of composition of Coleridge's "Rime of the Ancient Mariner." No parallel feat can be achieved for the composition of the spirituals. How they were made can be assumed, and if only because the assumptions appear to cover all the possibilities, the assumptions are probably congruent with the truth. Not only are the spirituals anonymous. Exactly the nature of their anonymity remains unknown. And if we speculate about that ano-nymity, we may, perhaps, most safely suppose that individual artists who originated spirituals were probably young. One-half of the slaves in Amer-ica always were no more than twenty years old. Three-fourths of the slaves in America never lived past their thirtieth birthdays.

Old or young, any slave who initiated a spiritual, in part or in whole, was a mass psychologist. He knew what his fellow black people wanted. His genius was not only aesthetic, but social. His very existence, how-ever, has been called into question by a hypothesis about the Negro spiri-tual which would eliminate him from it completely. This is the proposi-tion, stoutly trumpeted to the world by Jackson, with whose relatively low enumeration of the Negro spiritual it has been already noted here Lovell disagrees, that the Negro spirituals were actually white spirituals appropriated without apology or proper acknowledgment by the black folk. Jackson traces a joint stream of song and group behavior from New England to the South. Jackson begins his progress thus as a sleuth with the fasola people—so called from the notes fa, so, and la, repeated twice in all their scales—who appeared in Massachusetts as early as the 1720s, who fostered many a singing school, and who tended to use notes differ-entially shaped as circles, squares, diamonds, and quarters of diamonds, the so-called shape notation, in writing down their songs.

According to Jackson, the fasola folk, with their shape notes and their fondness for the singing of religious songs, filtered south, moving, after they or their ancestors came to America, actually not so much from New England as from the Delmarva Peninsula, into pioneering regions of their new homeland as remote from their points of departure as Texas. They were ardent participants in the great age of revivals in the last decade of the eighteenth century and the first half of the century following. In-deed, a camp meeting, of the kind Mark Twain apparently loved to describe, was hardly representative of its true character without their songs and their singing. Certain songbooks circulated among them, *The Kentucky Harmony*, *The Columbian Harmony*, *The Sacred Harp*, *The Southern Harmony*, *The Western Harp*, and *The Hesperian Harp*, for instance, and were (some of them, at least) still being used in the twentieth century.

There was, according to Jackson, a German element among the fasola folk, but 50 to 80 percent of them were Celtic, Scotch-Irish, to be specific. These folk congregated, not only on the coastal plains of the South, but in the hills and valleys west of the southern lowlands stretching from Virginia into Georgia. In *White Spirituals of the Southern Uplands*, published in 1933, *Spiritual Folk Songs of Early America*, published in 1937, and *White and Negro Spirituals*, published in 1943, Jackson asserts and insists that the slaves based their spirituals upon the spirituals of these folk.[3] Jackson would have black slaves present, although segregated, at white camp meetings. He finds parallels to white spirituals in black spirituals. And he seems to assume such an inferiority in the black slaves to all whites as would preclude borrowings from the one by the other from going in any direction save white to black. Like Jackson, the white scholars Guy B. Johnson and Newman Ivey White suspect a debt of the Negro spiritual to white predecessors.[4]

It was not, however, in the southern uplands that America's slaves were ever mainly to be congregated. Furthermore, the white spirituals of the southern uplands differ from the black spirituals of the slaves, wherever those slaves were, in a very important and decisive manner—in the manner, that is, that the spirituals sound. If the Negro spiritual is a derivative of any white antecedent, then, whatever it has acquired from Wesleyan or other white sources of song, in its process of becoming part of a black culture, it has undergone such a change from all white music, religious or secular or both, as to destroy altogether a debt of inheritance that could truly matter. Even if some of the mechanics of the Negro spiritual can be associated with white progenitors, nothing of that peculiar beauty and poignancy which so distinguishes the Negro spiritual from all other song can be detected in the body of song described, and championed, by Jackson.

There is some question, nevertheless, as to how African the Negro

3. George Pullen Jackson, *White Spirituals of the Southern Uplands* (Chapel Hill, 1933), *Spiritual Folk Songs of Early America* (New York, 1937), *White and Negro Spirituals: Their Life Span and Kinship* (New York, 1943).

4. See Guy B. Johnson, *Folk Culture on St. Helena Island, South Carolina* (Chapel Hill, 1930), and Newman Ivey White, *American Negro Folksongs* (Cambridge, Mass., 1928).

spiritual is. Does it retain an African sense of rhythm and an African propensity for antiphony? Are there African songs too like particular spirituals for the correspondence to be merely coincidental? As an issue of fact, it has been alleged, for instance, that "Steal Away" is a West African melody. But whether it is or is not is primarily a question to be addressed by musicologists and anthropologists. In the context of the worth of the words of the spirituals as poetry, it does help, however, to know something of the audience the spirituals have achieved. The number of the spirituals, it may not be amiss to interpolate here, possesses considerable significance, also, in the history of Afro-American literature. Since there are thousands of these sorrow songs (to quote Du Bois' appellation for them), they constitute the largest homogeneous body of black lyric poetry in the nineteenth, or any, century. The audience for the spirituals has been huge. And that it has been so extensive has additionally been a fact of great significance in the history of Afro-American literature. The very size alone, in other words, of this audience has given to the spiritual the special kind of audience which Walt Whitman once ordained as a categorical imperative for great poets and, therefore, for great poetry. This audience began to burgeon on the very earliest tours, in the 1870s, of the Fisk Jubilee Singers, traveling in the interest of Fisk University, and singing, initially when they left their campus, both spirituals and songs which were not spirituals. But once the Fisk Jubilee Singers recognized (as it was easy for them to do) the catholicity of the appeal of the spirituals and identified the spirituals as their own major source of appeal to any public, their fortune, as it were, was made. The singers triumphed both in America and overseas. Enthusiastic and grateful crowds received them, and so also, with equal enthusiasm and gratitude, did dignitaries as exalted as Queen Victoria and Kaiser Wilhelm I.

In the Fisk Jubilee Singers' wake, and over a span of years exceeding half a century, followed bands of singers from many institutions, notably the choirs from Hampton Institute and Tuskegee Institute, at their best coached, respectively, by the fine musicians Nathaniel Dett and William Dawson. As Negro artists rose in status on the concert stage, these artists sang spirituals to throngs of eager listeners all around the world. Beginning in the 1920s, Roland Hayes larded his programs with spirituals as well as with German lieder. Paul Robeson sang spirituals. On Easter Sunday of 1939, seventy-five thousand people heard Marian Anderson sing "Gospel Train," "Trampin'," and "My Soul is Anchored in the Lord" at the Lincoln Memorial in Washington, D.C. The Hall Johnson Choir, among other such professional aggregations, took the spirituals to Broadway, most famously in Marc Connelly's play *The Green Pastures*. With the advent of the radio, groups like the Southernaires and the Wings Over Jordan Choir broadcast spirituals. And, all the while, in many places of greater privacy, such as black churches and black schools, spirituals were continuing to be sung until, finally, a president of the United States, Lyndon B. Johnson, placed an accolade upon the civil-rights legislation he had shepherded through both houses of Congress with the words from a spiritual, "We shall overcome."

It was highly fitting for this president to turn as he did to the poetry of spirituals. For the spirituals are the epic verse of black America. An African ethnicity speaks through them in their incremental leading lines, their choral iterations, and their call-and-response chants. But the American experience of the black folk who wrote them governs their thought and tempers their emotion. Their language is simple, the idiom of a humble, unlettered people without the pretensions of an upper, or a leisure, class. No words in them assert, in length or etymology, any acquaintance with learned or sophisticated tongues. Sentences in them are like the words those sentences contain, elementary in every regard. But the simplicity of the language of the spirituals does not eventuate into speech devoid of force or grace or food for thought for the active mind. With their almost never a term beyond a monosyllable and their dearth of dependent clauses, the spirituals, even so, compound a discourse often rich in its pictorial power and intensely vivid in the sense of a people's mentality and range of feeling it conveys. The spirituals project, among many other striking vignettes, Peter going to ring "dem" bells, the Lord handing down to an ecstatic follower of His Son a silver trumpet, all the "little chillun" who want to go to heaven being told to "git on board," the old ark, however, lumberingly, setting itself "a-movering," and a big wheel running inexorably by faith while a little wheel, just as inexorably, is run by the grace of God.

These same spirituals, moreover, fill their private universe with good sound as well as arresting sights, as when Joshua's lamb-ram-sheep horns and trumpets blow before, to their sonorous tumult, is added the bedlam of the walls of Jericho crashing down, or when Little David plays on his harp and then shouts with joy after he kills Goliath, or when the Lord calls in the thunder while the horn blown by Gabriel at Judgment reverberates in an alert and grateful Christian's soul, or even as when, in a pregnant silence stronger in its impact upon the organs of hearing than any clamors of pain or protest, a bruised and mutilated Jesus, crucified and entombed, utters never a mumbling word. To a significant degree, then, the diction of the spirituals replicates a condition of the black folk. The slaves, too, might well have seemed, in their mean habiliments and inferior status to others in their social order, a poor lot. Yet, on more intimate acquaintance with them, qualities of theirs tended to appear which belied their image as creatures only to be reviled and scorned.

The spirituals, of course, assume a Christian universe and a Christian eschatology. Some doubt, however, has been cast upon the Christianity of the slaves. The reputable black scholar John B. Cade, in his article "Out of the Mouths of Ex-Slaves," published in the *Journal of Negro History* in 1935, reported that, of 150 former slaves, all in Louisiana, whom he interviewed, only 10 said they were Christians. But Cade's findings seem exceptional. The slave narratives present Negroes who firmly believe in the Christian God. Even David Walker's radical *Appeal* does not reject Christianity. It only, like the slave narratives, expresses disgust at whites who betray their own self-announced faith. And the black folk's reverence for their black slave preachers of the Christian persuasion is too well confirmed by an abundance of evidence to be denied. In any case, as James Weldon Johnson reflected upon the spirituals, he concluded that Christianity, more than any other single factor, explained their unique quality. He wrote the preface to *The Books of American Negro Spirituals: Two Volumes in One*, a joint venture, originally published in 1925, in the editing and musical arrangement of a group of spirituals resulting from a collaboration of his with his brother, J. Rosamond Johnson, and Lawrence Brown. All serious students of the spirituals visit this preface. There Johnson says, trying to account for what he terms the "advance," particularly in melody and harmony, of the American Negro's music beyond the music which the Negro had brought with him from Africa, "It was because at the precise and psychic moment there was blown through or fused into the vestiges of his [the Negro's] African music the spirit of Christianity as he [the Negro] knew Christianity." Later Johnson adds, "The Negro took complete refuge in Christianity and the spirituals were literally forged of sorrow in the heat of religious fervor."[5]

5. John B. Cade, "Out of the Mouths of Ex-Slaves," *Journal of Negro History*, XX (1935), 294–337; James Weldon Johnson *et al.*, *The Books of American Negro Spirituals: Two Volumes in One* (1925; New York, 1969), 20.

So, to Johnson, without their Christianity, the spirituals would not be as they are. That could be true and, indeed, may be so irrefutable as to be altogether unarguable.

Even so, it also well may be that to speak in terms superior here in their refinement and closer in their identification with the truth would be to recognize the Christianity associated with the spirituals as both an element in the content of the spirituals and a catalytic agent affecting in the spirituals the representation there by the slave of his full experience, religious or otherwise, of life in slave-time America. This slave, a victim of an inhuman economic and social system, felt that experience, the source for him of a gamut of excruciating emotions, not excluding a desire for better things, deep within his being. His sense of the injustice perpetrated upon him was keen, but so, apparently, was his sympathetic appreciation of America, beginning with his love of the American land as a physical entity and extending to his perception of the beauty of the pure, unsullied American dream. It is true, moreover, that what he thought and felt applied both to his perceptions of his lot as an individual and to his empathies with the collective consciousness of the whole slave community in America. Somehow, he needed a medium through which he could express his inner self, this core of his own psyche and psychology, so complex and yet so importunate for relief, through a relatively safe ventilation into an outer world. The spirituals became the expedient he thus needed, and the Christianity within them a way of dissembling much of the possible harshness of their message through allegory. Nothing necessarily was magnified or distorted in the spirituals of the slave's actual religious convictions. He did worship Jehovah and he did accept the Crucifixion. Heaven to him was real and a place he did want to go. But the artistic talent within him, wittingly or not, in effect seized upon a happy chance. Under the aegis of religious meditation, it articulated not too openly his critical appraisal of the secular world around him which occasioned him so much grief and pain.

So, there is a level within the spirituals at which the slave displays his knowledge of the Bible and Christian tradition. At this level he appropriates tales from both the Old Testament and the New and accommodates them to his verse. Here he does not dwell on the Garden of Eden. But he does show some fondness for Father Abraham and Noah and the ark, for Moses' Jehovah and for the plight of those in the fiery furnace, for Joshua the fighter and David, the stripling virtuoso on a stringed instrument and yet the slayer of Goliath, for Jesus and for the Crucifixion

and the Resurrection, for Peter, and for the Book of Revelation. He refers here, also, to the angels and to God, omniscient and omnipotent,
ever keeping watch above His own. At intervals, here, the geography of
the Scriptures concerns him, especially in its other-worldly aspects.

It cannot be said of the allusions to Scripture in the spirituals that they
range comprehensively and proportionately throughout the Bible or that
they suggest in the black folk of the antebellum South biblical scholarship of a very high order. In fact, the opposite is true. The scriptural allusions in the spirituals are those surely to be expected of a largely illiterate
community most of whose knowledge of the Bible is based on hearsay.
These allusions are restricted to a rather paltry few of the many characters and events which the Scriptures, in their entirety, supply in abundance. Moreover, these allusions resemble the black folk sermons in
their tendency to return repeatedly to the aforementioned few characters
and events, saying virtually, also, always repetitious things about them.
Indeed, therefore, in this regard, if in no other, the spirituals, like the
black folk sermons, may be said to be formulaic. It is at this level, probably, that the spirituals can be considered at their most extended in
naïveté, the expressions of a simple, docile, untroubled people as charm-
ingly (and eternally) childlike as the Negroes of *The Green Pastures*. An
observation often made about the spirituals, accordingly, is that they reflect the slaves' (really sensible, some might say) resignation to their lot
on earth, for which their religion of Christianity had come to serve as a
form, quite effective, of consolation. There is, as a matter of fact, a spiritual, "Give Me Jesus," in which occur the actual words "You may have
all dis worl' give me Jesus." Yet, even in this realm merely of scriptural
allusion, another note may be detected or, at least, sometimes suspected
in many, if not all, of the spirituals.

Thus in the spirituals looking toward an afterlife, with all their references to trumpets and bells and chariots, as well as to robes and crowns
and wings, not to mention those spirituals in which the subject explicitly
is death, there remain a marked number of scriptural allusions which are
hardly consonant with the counsel of a contented slave or of slaves apa-
thetically inured to slavery. The spirituals give a notable amount of attention to Pharaoh, as they do to Moses. And the spirituals do not side
with Pharaoh. Moses, the overthrower of Pharaoh, is their man. Nor do
the spirituals ignore Daniel, whom the Lord delivered from a den of
lions, or Goliath, who was done to death by a much punier adversary.
With Pharaoh and Moses, as with Daniel and Goliath, the spirituals are

not apprehensive about the Lord's will in another world. They are quite attentive to problems of power and injustice, and opposition to such problems, in this world. The Red Sea in the spirituals which engulfs Pharaoh and his army is not located beyond the Jordan, nor is Moses operating above the empyrean when he dares to oppose the Egyptian state and lead the cause of abolitionism for the bonded Hebrews. Too often for it to be inconsequential, the spirituals celebrate an activism in human life, and typically an activism on the part of the lowly and op-pressed, which God approves and the success of which enlarges the free-dom and the prosperity of an underdog.

If, then, *Dies Irae*, the sinner's hell, and the persevering Christian's reward in heaven appear in the spirituals, so does an advocacy of con-structive human action in a very present world antecedent to any world conceivable after death. There are trains as well as chariots in the spiri-tuals. In "Git on Board, Little Chillun," the exhortation is to mount a train with a locomotive and a collection of passenger cars like the trains running in the antebellum South which slaves normally could watch but rarely ever ride. Moreover, and very significantly, it well may be, the train of "Git on Board" is classless and capacious. Its fare, the same for everyone, is cheap, and with room "for many a mo'," rich and poor on it, "all can go." Strong in the spirituals is a sense of family. In one after another of the better-known spirituals—for instance, "Stan' Still Jor-dan," "Peter, Go Ring Dem Bells," "Nobody Knows de Trouble I See," "Same Train," and "Walk Together Children"—as well as in numerous others not so well known, the allegiance of a slave to his close blood kin is manifest.

It has been suggested that such spirituals as "Somebody's Knockin' at Yo' Door," "Every Time I Feel de Spirit," "Lord, I Want to Be a Chris-tian in My Heart," and "I Know de Lord Has Laid His Hands on Me," in their verbal texts, as in, possibly (as has been earlier cited here), some musicological phenomena variously present throughout the spirituals, hark back to the slave's African past. In the case of the spirituals just cited, incidentally, and any others to be classified with them, the as-serted African survival is the phenomenon of possession, the entrance of an outside spirit, often supernatural, like the Greek god Dionysus, into the flesh and spirit of the person thus "possessed." And Zora Neale Hurston, in her introduction to her novel *Moses, Man of the Mountain*, insists that she found in Haiti an African Moses typically fused with the highest god in the Haitian pantheon (whose symbol is a snake), Damballa Ouedo Onedo Tocan Freda Dahomey. But this Damballa, Hurston, in her introduction, further insists, originated, not in Haiti, but in Dahomey in Africa. Nor has he tarried out of Africa only in Haiti. As a Moses with godlike powers, more commonly, it seems, than as a Damballa, he is known among the black folk of America. Asseverations of the persistence of Africa in the text of the spirituals—in the spirituals as poetry, that is—as well as in the spirituals as music, should not, then, apparently be summarily dismissed. But neither, apparently, should asseverations of the presence of Moses, under whatever form or name, in America. Neither set of asseverations, obviously, obviates the other. Indeed, moreover, a person may cling to his past, especially if he feels more powerful and more respectful of himself in that past than he does in his present, for the reason that he wants to be successful and strong in the present. The same motivation which may, at least partially, account for an American Negro's retention of Africanisms might well also have occasioned in the text of the spirituals a this-worldism, to coin a phrase, and even too much of this this-worldism for it to be fair to the spirituals to speak of them as always other-worldly.

In any case, no great powers of discernment are required to note in the spirituals evidences of the slave's sensitivity to his mortal state. Clearly in the spirituals he talked about people like his mother, people close and dear to him whose well-being he cherished, because he was not indifferent to their human fate or to his own. The text of the spirituals does constitute a source for evidence related to the continuing controversy associated with the perception of the Negro's sense of family, with its accompanying effects upon Negro behavior in America. Apparently, this evidence suggests, slaves did treasure institutions from which they could derive confirmations of their own identity as well as of their own worth in largely social terms. And this evidence is not inconsistent with a denial of the belief that slaves did not harbor inwardly, even when they may not have rebelled outwardly, a sense of protest against their status, and treatment, as slaves. Of slave rebellions, slave flights, slave sabotage, slave malingering, and other forms of overt resistance by slaves to slavery historians are well aware. In slave flights, spirituals surely were overtly used, as when Harriet Tubman signaled a prospective cargo of hers where and how to gather for a trip toward the North Star on the Underground Railroad by singing such a spiritual as "Wade in de Water, Children, and Be Baptized." But comparably duplicitous with Tubman's resort to spirituals in her activist assault upon slavery are the numerous passages in the texts of the spirituals which applaud heroics aimed at some kind of earthly emancipation, as in, for instance, the spirituals "Go Down Moses," "Joshua Fit de Battle of Jericho," "We Are Climbin' Jacob's Ladder," and "Singin' wid a Sword in Ma Han'."

Within our present context, it certainly should be added that some spirituals, among them not a few of the spirituals of great popularity, lend themselves to substitutions in the language of their texts which convert them into masterpieces of ironic dissimulation as well as possible oblique revelations of the slaves' hatred of slavery. So, "Swing Low, Sweet Chariot" may well be interpreted, read literally and with no suspicions about what might have been, when it was composed, its authors' intentions, quite simply and unexcitingly as no less a sincere expression of a good, truly believing Christian's desire to get to heaven than, for example, "Abide with Me." In both songs, if death is not actually nigh, the thought of it, for the singer, apparently is. Moreover, in both songs it is, apparently, what lies ahead in heaven which accounts principally, if not solely, for the singer's attitudes and emotions. The text of "Swing Low, Sweet Chariot" reads, very ostensibly, in its first verse:

> Swing low, sweet chariot,
> Comin' for to carry me home.
> Swing low, sweet chariot,
> Comin' for to carry me home.
> I looked over Jordan, and what did I see?
> Comin' for to carry me home.
> A band of angels coming after me,
> Coming for to carry me home.

In its second verse, "Swing Low, Sweet Chariot" replaces the lines about the band of angels with the following:

> If you get dere befo' I do,
> Comin' for to carry me home,
> Tell all my friends I'm comin' too,
> Comin' for to carry me home.

Thus, in both of its verses, "Swing Low, Sweet Chariot" seems merely to affirm a statement here already made. It seems merely, that is, to echo the doctrine of the Resurrection so precious to Christians of all the ages and so central to the Christian faith. But both of its verses can be altered dramatically, to make them speak of something other than transportation to heaven, through a translation of the words they contain into terms applicable to a far different and much less reposeful general situation. Merely change Jordan to the Ohio River (or any stream near the border of the North and the South) and the band of angels to companies or agents of the abolitionists, and home becomes freedom outside the South. Using the same kind of simple sleight of hand, getting there before the singer does becomes reaching the North or Canada before the singer escapes slavery, and the message to the singer's friends, should they, indeed, have already reached the North (thus putting themselves, conceivably, in a better position than heretofore to help him follow them), is that he is still planning to "vote with his feet" against the South. Some slaves may well have sung "Swing Low, Sweet Chariot" with no malice in their hearts and only real angels on their minds. Some other slaves, it should be respectfully observed, were probably not so altogether other-worldly.

Nevertheless, no matter what the subjects and themes contained in the spirituals and however the spirituals did, or did not, permit the slave to bare his soul and private thoughts to the outside world, a constant attribute of the spirituals is beauty. To say this is again to commend, in the spirituals, their quality as poetry and to recognize the frequency with which, within them, the conclusive evidence that defines their worth defies the best efforts of clinical analysis. Simply to recite the titles of many of the spirituals is to enter into the magic kingdom of Keats's realms of gold, where the atmosphere is most salubrious, and most inexplicable: "Steal Away to Jesus," for instance, and "Deep River," or "Peter, Go Ring Dem Bells," "My Lord, What a Mornin'," "Who'll Be a Witness for My Lord," "Sometimes I Feel Like a Motherless Child," and, certainly, "Swing Low, Sweet Chariot," itself. The list of such titles for the spirituals—titles so possessed of whatever it is which supplies the substance of beauty as to suffice as poems themselves—is long. These titles alone reveal that America's black slaves, when they truly capitalized on their talents in the field of literary art, could have a genuine way with words.

These titles, moreover, represent with total fidelity an idiom—a folk idiom, clearly a property of the Negro slaves en masse—found everywhere throughout the spirituals. It is an idiom pared to the bone for the task it has chosen for itself to perform, reduced to vocables which would never occasion a slave difficulty with their enunciation or pronunciation, as well as to words and phrases quite familiar to the slave, if not in his daily speech, at least in the universe of special, added discourse he shared with his own folk purveyors of the Holy Word. The beauty of the text of the spirituals, then, is not only real, but also somewhat arresting in its form. There is about it an adherence to the low road linguistically similar to that of the verse in Scottish dialect of Robert Burns, but nothing in it readily apparent to any reader which would link it closely to the genteelly clothed lyricism of Shelley or Thomas Gray. The great secret of its success in creating beauty seems organically related to its power for existing in, or near, the world of metaphor. Perhaps its affinity for metaphor is all the more arresting because of its relative crudities linguistically.

There are, of course, bad spiritual texts, many of them, among the several thousands of such texts. Yet, at their best, and their best are those which have most survived, these texts are rich in the imagery, both sensuous and largely ratiocinative, which they evoke. One of the spiritual texts clearly so endowed is "Lis'en to the Lam's," wherein the effective line is "Lis'en to the lam's; all a'cryin'." "Lis'en" and "lam's" obviously gain in their impact upon a reader because they are united by alliteration. "Lam's," moreover, particularly to good Christians, is inseparable from a whole train of imagery in which Christ, as the central figure, performs acts of love—of tender care and rescue—which show him heeding the supplications of any, and all, of His Father's human creatures who feel the need of a helping hand. The plea for succor in the spiritual, incidentally, may not require application solely (or at all) to religious salvation. The big picture the lambs crying here might well suggest could very readily be that of America's distressed mass of slaves importuning their masters and other Americans for relief. But, however finally interpreted, the conceptualizations possible from the text of "Lis'en to the Lam's" attest to the principal means by which, in the spirituals, humble expression is transmuted into the stuff of poetry. These conceptualizations profit immeasurably from the personification which initiates them.

In a spiritual, on the other hand, such as "In Dat Great Gittin' Up Mornin'," there is never any metaphor in the truest sense, unless to change human beings into angels is to add to personification a new (and sort of fourth) dimension by virtue of which human beings, freed from their animality, assume an etherealized personhood impossible to them on earth. But the imagery which can be summoned into existence by this spiritual, even from the sound and sense of its highly appropriate and resonating refrain of "Fare You Well," constantly hovers delightfully on the edge of metaphor. Much occurs in "In Dat Great Gittin' Up Mornin'." It is one of the busiest of all spirituals with, among other things, preachers folding their Bibles in it and prayer makers praying no more while Gabriel asks the Lord how loud to blow his trumpet ("calm and easy," replies the

Lord). Hell, a'burning, comes uncapped, coffins burst, dry bones creep, the elements melt, lightning forks, the world takes fire, the moon bleeds as stars fall, and, in the end, of course, benignly watched by all the angels, Christ, the Savior, and God the Father Himself, to the rumbling of the thunder, the righteous come a'marching home. There are, really, no metaphors here, but a vivid depiction of stirring events. Yet the sense of metaphor hovers around all the movement and the fabricated vistas in "In Dat Great Gittin' Up Mornin'," which after all, is about a posthistorical event much dependent, for an apprehension of its supposed nature, on a sense of metaphor.

Without such an ambiguity, the metaphors are very real in "Deep River," whose title is clearly itself a magnificent figure of speech for death, if only because a solemnity and majesty inhere in the image of water it invokes that preclude any association of the experience represented by the metaphor with something not inspiring the greatest awe. Even so, the figure of speech of the almost bottomless stream may not be the happiest metaphor in "Deep River." The pilgrim who traverses the Jordan in "Deep River" expresses the desire to "cross over into campground . . . that promised land where all is peace." The "promised land," here, "where all is peace," represents no allusion to heaven unusual or remarkable in its character. But the hereafter as a campground is another matter. So is introduced into "Deep River" a metaphor which, highly expressive of the language of the black folk, reflects an experience they tended to find most agreeable. In the fellowship of their campgrounds, they could restore their appreciation for themselves. Why should not they compare what they hoped to find on the other side of the most portentous barrier they would ever cross to a communal celebration they had learned not to dread?

In any final assessment of the spirituals, it might very well be highly appropriate to focus attention upon aspects of the spirituals associated with the communal existence of the American Negro. One of those aspects, the communal participation of the slaves in the composition of the spirituals, has already been cited here. The slaves, of course, with only the exception of those very few most recently deceased, have all long been gathered to their fathers. But the slaves' descendants in the twentieth century have profited communally from the spirituals. First of all, the spirituals have been, for the Negro of the twentieth century, a particularly convenient, accessible, and vivid form of his usable past. It has often been emphasized (and rightly so) that the slaves, in terms of written documentation about their lives, were almost completely inarticulate. Unschooled for the pen, they left for their posterity no wealth of diaries, journals, letters, or records of their own devising which would mirror who, and what, they were. The spirituals constitute the worthiest substitute for the conventional written documentation of themselves which the slaves did not produce. In this sense alone, the spirituals are a very usable, as well as a very valuable, available past. So, the spirituals have been, for the twentieth-century Negro, a resource for education about himself. Additionally, they have acted upon the twentieth-century Negro to improve his sense of racial solidarity, and they have had beneficent effects upon the twentieth-century Negro's group morale.

On an April evening during Franklin Roosevelt's second administration, W. E. B. Du Bois faced an all-black audience in Louisville, Kentucky. The occasion was the principal session of an annual meeting of the Kentucky Negro Educational Association, the official statewide organization of black teachers in Kentucky, where schools then were segregated. The black church at the altar of which Du Bois stood was crowded. Every seat within it was occupied. Latecomers were positioned in its aisles or crammed together in the space between its rear pews and a wall. Du Bois would deliver that night an impassioned plea for the adoption by the whole national community of American Negroes of a policy of voluntary segregation which—Du Bois had begun (using Hegelian dialectic) to argue, wherever he went—represented an enlightened strategy for the ending, on terms advantageous to Negroes, of all segregation and racial discrimination in America. Just before Du Bois spoke, a boys' chorus from the larger of Louisville's two black junior high schools sang two songs, the second of which was a Negro spiritual. The chorus, it is true, in some quite visible ways did not hark back to the world of the slaves out of which the spirituals had come. Its members, like its director, were clad in storebought clothes. The version of the spiritual they performed had been arranged by a trained musician. Their director, too, was trained, with an advanced degree from a university in music, while they were obviously well rehearsed. Dramatically, at a propitious moment, a boy soprano soloed with flutelike sweetness for them. Much of what they had been taught to do did separate them from their forebears. Yet their choice of a spiritual spoke volumes, as did the reverent reception of their song by the black bourgeoisie who heard it, about the virtual unanimity of black feeling for the spirituals.

Admittedly, not every Negro of the twentieth century who sought upward social mobility for his race never derogated the spirituals. Such a Negro might sometimes murmur against the spirituals on the grounds that too many whites who were committed to "keeping the Negroes in their place" enjoyed immensely listening to Negroes singing spirituals because those whites interpreted the spirituals, and Negroes singing them, as a gesture, by Negroes, of surrender and submission to the institution of color caste. Even so, the prevailing sentiment among twentieth-century Negroes of all classes overwhelmingly honors the spirituals. Nor does it do so out of ignorance. No Negro writer, not even Paul Laurence Dunbar, ever came close to the range and depth of presence within the Negro consciousness of the spirituals. Indeed, there have been Negroes aware of the spirituals who would remain for all of their lives unwitting of the Chicago *Defender*. No form of literature, therefore, written by Negroes has been so completely identified with all Negroes, and known and accepted by all of them, as the spirituals. That is one of the significant observations to be made concerning the spirituals and Du Bois and his audience in Louisville. They were as hospitable to the spirituals as, surely, in his life, was Du Bois' great antagonist, Booker T. Washington, who could serve with Du Bois to define the opposing nether limits—and, hence, the entire breadth—of thought and feeling racially among American Negroes during the first half of the twentieth century. To every gradation of American Negro ideologically the spirituals belonged, tying him to his past, inspiring him with pride in his forebears, and further vitalizing his assurance to himself of his own worth, especially in comparison to the worth of people not as subject to his past as he.

15. The First Negro Novelist

The Negro novel may be said to begin with a novel named *Clotel*. It can be argued—as, indeed, we have seen it has been—that not everything in the slave narratives (quite a number of which antedate *Clotel*) is true, that some of the "improvements" and embellishments in such narratives, no matter how loftily intended or how heavily coated with an intended aura of authenticity, are as categorically—even though too frequently far less delightfully—products of the imagination as *Othello* or *Native Son*. These "improvements" and embellishments are, in other words, according to this argument, often enough, thinly disguised novelistic fiction. But *Clotel* is explicitly and unabashedly, without any pretense of disguise, novelistic fiction. It cannot pretend to be great fiction, novelistic or otherwise. Everyone agrees on that. But it must be conceded to be a historic fiction. Nothing of its genre precedes it. It is the first Negro novel, the first long piece of sheer invented narrative written by an American Negro. It initiates a tradition. Yet, to make an observation which is only half-facetious, it does not do so with all of its credentials quite as obligingly unimpeachable as they might be. Its author was a black man who did not look black. He looked, for all of his life, like a white man. Moreover, *Clotel* is an American novel that was not written in America. It was written in the British Isles and first published in London by the very English firm of Partridge and Oakey of Paternoster Row, in 1853.

The man who wrote *Clotel* was named William Wells Brown, or so he had come to call himself by the time, as well as for some years before, he wrote *Clotel*. But he was born a slave, and christened with only one name, William. That "William," as if to emphasize young Brown's lack of opportunity really ever to choose for himself, was taken from him when it was found to conflict with the first name of a white boy in his household (Brown was renamed Sandford). Slaves, moreover, could claim no surnames, no patronymics of any kind, since they could claim no legal fathers. Nor could they, often, pronounce firmly as to the years in which they had been born. Brown's birth year, for example, is still not determined as indisputably as it might be, although the most convincing calculations do suggest that it was almost surely 1814. His place of birth, however, has been quite narrowly, on creditable evidence, firmly established. He first saw the light of day in the heart of what is often called the bluegrass country of Kentucky, either in, or near, the town of Lexington. His mother was a slave, one Elizabeth, who bore seven children for seven different fathers. She must have been a source of double profit to her owner, a Dr. John Young, for she was not only able to increase his estate with her offspring. She also labored manfully—the expression is no pun—in his fields.

Some special notice, perhaps, should be taken of this Elizabeth. Judging from her son William's appearance, although Brown's father reputedly was white, and in great likelihood a cousin of Dr. Young's, Elizabeth herself still must have been anything but coal black. Indeed, all that we can divine of her cautions us again not to generalize too readily—or, at least, to be prepared for great exceptions to every rule—when we speak of slaves and slavery. She was never, it seems, a house Negro. Neither, for that matter, was the mother of Frederick Douglass. Nevertheless, both of these mothers' famous sons fit perfectly the romancer's recipe for sons of slave women who were rich white men's petted concubines. Black kept women in antebellum times did exist, we already know, speaking again, for example, of the *plaçées*. But the mothers of Douglass and Brown did not belong to the *plaçées*' relatively privileged and soft-handed sisterhood. It was from bitter drudgery at heavy manual chores that Douglass' mother came to him on those few nights which he was saddened to remember that she had been able to spend with him before her death in his early childhood. And one of Brown's most unforgettable recollections during his long manhood was of his hearing helplessly one morning in his own boyhood his mother being lashed for a delay of hers in getting to the fields.

We have no likeness of Brown's mother. It is virtually impossible, nevertheless, to believe that her person was not attractive or that she did not descend from sturdy stock. Her son William once ascribed to her the celebrated Daniel Boone as a father.[1] But William Edward Farrison, the great student of Brown, rules Boone out completely as an ancestor of Brown's and, after a study of Virginia documents, prefers as Elizabeth's father, and Brown's maternal grandfather, a Negro named Simon, or Simmons, Lee, who fought in the Revolutionary War. In one way or the other, then, Brown could not but locate in his genealogical tree a brightly legended forebear. His mother could not but possess a parent through whom she, and William, could advance cogent evidence that they were just as "American" as anyone. And yet, eventually, his mother, for one desperate eruption of her yearning to be free, would be sold downriver. After 1833 Brown never saw, or heard, of her again. He once wrote a poem about her "Roman spirit." It is well to keep the fact and meaning of this poem in mind when one contemplates Clotel, the mother, in *Clotel*.

Dr. Young, Brown's owner, left Kentucky in 1816, taking his chattels, including the infant Brown, with him. Thus Brown was to spend his boyhood in Missouri, not Kentucky. Thus also, Dr. Young, on the northern bank of the Missouri River not far west of St. Louis, farmed, founded the town of Marthasville (named after his wife), practiced medicine, and entered politics. In 1827 Dr. Young moved to the outskirts of St. Louis. St. Louis, as a result, became Brown's home for the final six years of his existence as a slave. For over five of those six years, Brown was still the property of Dr. Young—whom, incidentally, he did physically resemble, to the annoyance, at times, of Dr. Young's wife, whose women friends, especially, saw to it that she remained aware of this particular likeness.[2]

The more one learns of Brown, the more one may well be inclined to conclude that, whatever strictures must be applied to *Clotel*, of Brown himself and his general competence and worth a different story must be told. Dr. Young hired Brown out to various persons, two of them, perhaps, of more than passing interest here: Elijah Lovejoy, who would be martyred by a proslavery mob in Alton, Illinois, and James Walker, a slave trader who was highly impressed with Brown's abilities. Brown, already experienced as a barber, a waiter, and a steward, served Walker as a respected second-in-command in collecting slaves, transporting them to market, and preparing them to look their best before prospective buyers. With Walker, Brown made three trips by water to New Orleans. In 1833, however, Brown was sold, after he made an almost ridiculously futile at-

---

1. William Wells Brown, *The Black Man, His Antecedents, His Genius, and His Achievements* (New York, 1863), 11.
2. William Edward Farrison, *William Wells Brown: Author and Reformer* (Chicago, 1969), 14.

tempt, with Elizabeth under his wing, to reach Canada through Illinois. It was following the recapture of Elizabeth and Brown that Elizabeth was sold off into the dreaded purgatory of the lower South. Brown was conveyed only to another St. Louisan, Samuel Willi, a merchant tailor.

Brown's stay with Willi was brief. Willi sold Brown, for a quick profit, to a commission merchant and steamboat owner named Enoch Price. Price and his wife instantly took a fancy to Brown. They made him their coachman. To try to guarantee his stay with them, they even bought a slave girl whom they hoped he could be induced to "marry." With the Prices and on one of Price's steamboats, in the autumn of 1833, Brown made his fourth visit to New Orleans. Returning north, the Prices and their party detoured from the Mississippi into the Ohio. Their steamboat docked at Cincinnati on the last day of 1833. On the first day of 1834, having sauntered casually ashore, Brown started to walk to Cleveland.

Thinly clad in intense cold, lacking food and provisions, without a map or compass, and traveling by stealth and largely at night, Brown required virtually the entire month of January to traverse Ohio. Along the way, at a moment when his fortunes seemed at their very lowest ebb, he was retrieved from exhaustion and despondency, well rested, and set again upon his northward way, by an aging Quaker, Wells Brown, who also added his own name to the fugitive's simple William in order, as the Quaker said, that Brown might more auspiciously have a proper start in his new life. It was, therefore, as William Wells Brown that Brown arrived in Cleveland and secured employment, working for himself and not a master, at first at anything that came to hand, and then on steamers and in hotels. In Cleveland, also, he too precipitately married, falling in love by the summer of 1834 with Elizabeth Schooner, whom he called Betsy, and contracting a union with her, in 1834, which terminated in separation by 1847.

Brown moved from Cleveland to Buffalo in 1836. In Cleveland, he had studied as he never had, or could have, under slavery. In Buffalo he became a social activist. He joined the temperance movement as a speaker and an organizer. But his concern for temperance, which stayed with him all of his life, was only a prelude to a moral crusade of even greater import to him. Brown had hardly arrived in the North, in Cleveland, before he began helping other black fugitives. In Buffalo, also, his house was a station on the Underground Railroad. He was a conductor, and whatever else he could be, in support of the operation of the Railroad. And by 1843 he had become a familiar face and voice on the antislavery lecture platform. Long before the end of slavery, only men like Frederick Douglass, William Lloyd Garrison, Charles Lenox Remond, Wendell Phillips, and Henry Highland Garnet would be as active and as well known in the antislavery campaign as he. He moved to Massachusetts in 1847, leaving his estranged wife in western New York State but keeping with him the two surviving daughters of their marriage, Clarissa and Josephine. In 1847, also, he published his first book, *The Narrative of William W. Brown, a Fugitive Slave, Written by Himself.* It would become one of the best-known and most widely read of all slave narratives. In 1848 he published *The Anti-Slavery Harp: A Collection of Songs for Anti-Slavery Meetings.* In 1849, not expecting to stay there long, he went overseas.

The immediate occasion for his visit to Europe was attendance at an international conference on peace which met in Paris in August, 1849. He routed himself to Paris, not directly from his American home, but through the British Isles. After the conference, returning to London, he took lodgings in the Strand. They were lodgings which—for many reasons, including the so-called Compromise of 1850 and its stringent Fugitive Slave Act—he was to retain for five years, as busy a five years as he would ever know. It was during these five years that he wrote *Clotel.* But, also, during these same five years he lectured and traveled widely, especially in both England and Scotland (he had made his mark in Ireland before he went to Paris); he brought his daughters over from America and put them to school, first in Calais and then in London; he practiced the trade of journalism, writing for probably three London newspapers as well as for the small monthly periodical the *Anti-Slavery Advocate;* he produced, complete with catalog, a panorama containing twenty-four scenes in the "Life of an American Slave, from his Birth in Slavery to His Death or His Escape to his First Home of Freedom on British Soil." He did more than his stint of sightseeing—he saw, for instance, the Burns country and the country of Sir Walter Scott (where he did not hesitate to spend several hours at Abbotsford), much of the Lake District (piloted through it principally by Harriet Martineau), Stratford-on-Avon, Ludlow Castle, the church of St. Mary Redcliffe, Tintern Abbey (twice), and Westminster—and, even before he wrote *Clotel,* he wrote *Three Years in Europe; or, Places I Have Seen and People I Have Met,* as an English reviewer noted, the first book of travels by an American fugitive slave to be published in England. But English friends of his eventually negotiated the purchase of his freedom from his last owner,

Enoch Price. In 1854, no longer a slave or a fugitive, Brown returned to America.

Brown lived for exactly thirty years more after his return to America. They were years which did not greatly vary from his years in England. Lecturing, writing, reforming, busying himself in many projects, and taking part in public affairs had become a mode of existence with Brown, and age did not so enfeeble him that he was not much the same man during the later years of his life as he had always tended to be in his prime. His first wife Betsy had died while he was in England. In 1860 he married for the second time. This second wife was, prior to her marriage to him, Annie Elizabeth Gray, a young woman, only twenty-five years old on her wedding day, who lived in the Boston area, where both she and Brown were to remain permanently domiciled after they were wed. This second wife also seems to have been much more compatible with him, and his way of life, than his first wife. She joined with him in much of his discharge of what he clearly felt to be the obligations of a good citizen toward society.

Before the end of the Civil War, Brown became a doctor. He did not go to medical school. That he should was not then a requirement for practicing the profession. He continued his practice of medicine until his death. He had never stopped writing. He is credited with the authorship of the first play to be published by an American Negro. It is called *The Escape; or, A Leap for Freedom: A Drama in Five Acts,* and it appeared in print in 1858. But history, particularly as an account of black achievement, became almost an obsession with him in his later publications. Thus he produced, in 1863, *The Black Man, His Antecedents, His Genius, and His Achievements;* in 1867, *The Negro in the American Rebellion: His Heroism and His Fidelity;* in 1873, *The Rising Son; or The Antecedents and Advancement of the Colored Race;* and, in 1880, although not altogether what its title appears to represent it to be, *My Southern Home: Or, The South and Its People.* Actually, his first excursion into historiography had occurred in 1854 in his brief *St. Domingo: Its Revolutions and Its Patriots,* and his interest in Haiti was always keen. He seems to have visited there in 1840, and some twenty-one years later he certainly traveled and lectured in the Northeast and in Canada advocating Haitian immigration for blacks. His *Three Years in Europe,* with some revisions and additions, he had published in America in 1855 as *The American Fugitive in Europe: Sketches of Places and People Abroad.* As we shall see, *Clotel* appeared in three American versions, the last in 1867.

On February 8, 1884, Brown spoke at a memorial meeting for Wendell Phillips, whose funeral had been held two days earlier. Before the end of the year, he was dead. Annie Brown had given him two children, both of whom died young. She survived him until 1902, when she was fatally burned, the victim of a fire in the kitchen of her home.

There is, of course, no prescription for the proper way in which a person, any person, should decide to write a piece of fiction. Nor are we in a position to state all that was in Brown's mind when he conceived *Clotel*. What can be stated on the basis of persuasive clues is that he did embark on it during a lull in a normally crowded and bustling life. His summers in England were the times when the number of his engagements as a lecturer declined. In the summer of 1852, for instance, apparently with some moments of unusual and unwanted leisure on his hands, he composed *Three Years in Europe*. In the summer of 1853, he undertook *Clotel*. He based the novel on a rather persistent rumor that Thomas Jefferson, the author of the Declaration of Independence and a noted apostle of liberty and equality, had had a daughter by one of his own slaves who had once been auctioned off from the block in a New Orleans slave trader's mart.

In Brown's novel—the full English title of which, it is rather important not to overlook, is *Clotel, or The President's Daughter*—Jefferson is represented as having had two daughters, Clotel and Althesa, by a Negro woman, Currer, who was for many years his housekeeper but who, at the opening of *Clotel*, has long resided in Richmond, where she and her daughters are the property of a Mr. John Graves. Mr. Graves has just died. His slaves are sold. A speculator acquires Currer and Althesa. The beautiful, sixteen-year-old Clotel is purchased at a fancy price by Horatio Green, a young white aristocrat of Richmond who received his introduction to Clotel at a quadroon ball.

The speculator disposes of Currer in Natchez to a Methodist parson named Peck. A native of Connecticut, Peck has married a Mississippi heiress. On his wife's death, Peck is left with a town villa in Natchez, a plantation outside Natchez known as Poplar Farm, and a daughter, Georgiana, to whom slavery is an absolute anathema. Currer is attached by Peck to the slaves in his inherited town villa. Althesa has the even better fortune to be bought in New Orleans by a Vermonter, no friend of slavery, but an outsider making his home in a community where the simplest method for him to use in supplying his wife with domestic help is to buy a slave. Althesa's new master has a friend and a boarder, also a Vermonter, the young physician Dr. Henry Morton, who falls in love with Althesa, buys her for himself, marries her (or thinks he does), but inadvertently neglects to manumit her, and has two daughters by her. The Mortons, incidentally, do try, with no success, to obtain Currer from Peck. She dies in Natchez during a plague. She is detained there by Brown apparently to allow him to develop the drama of the differences between Peck and his daughter, both professors of Christianity. When Peck dies, Georgiana marries a northern schoolfellow of her father's who views slavery much as she does. Her own early death comes only after she and her husband have manumitted, and sent north, the slaves whom her father, as her husband had witnessed, treated with little, if any, less rigor than his neighbors.

In Virginia for a while, but only for a while, Clotel and Horatio Green exist in a small, private Elysium. Horatio establishes Clotel in a cottage that provides a charming physical setting for their romance. The two have a daughter, whom they name Mary. But Horatio harbors political ambitions. In pursuit of these ambitions, he marries the sole daughter of a local Croesus who is also powerful in the political arena. This wife eventually discovers Clotel and Mary and their significance to Horatio. She does not rest until Clotel is sold, to the same speculator who had earlier purchased Currer and Althesa. But Mrs. Green brings Mary into her own home, where she can daily hate her and abuse her before Horatio. The speculator takes Clotel to Mississippi and sells her, but in Vicksburg, not in Natchez. From there Clotel escapes, masquerading as a young southern gentleman under a disability traveling with a servant. At Cincinnati her companion and supposed servant, a fellow slave named William, turns toward Canada. Clotel, still in male disguise, resolutely proceeds on to Richmond. Her aim, of course, is to regain her daughter. But she has been sanguine beyond the bounds of reasonable expectation. She arrives in Richmond during a period of hysteria immediately after Nat Turner's insurrection, when all strangers are viewed with suspicion. An examination reveals her true identity. Fleeing from confinement in Washington, D.C., she finds herself trapped on the Long Bridge across the Potomac and leaps to a watery grave.

The fates of Jefferson's three "granddaughters" remain to be described. In Louisiana, where both Althesa and her "husband" perish of yellow fever, their daughters fall into the clutches of, respectively, an old roué and a young profligate. The daughter whom the old roué has bought poisons herself rather than submit to his lecherous advances. The other daughter dies of a broken heart when the young profligate kills her lover as that lover is in the very act of rescuing her from the rural retreat where the profligate has hidden her. In Richmond, Mary, Clotel's daughter, helps her lover, George Greene, who is under sentence of death for participation in Nat Turner's insurrection, to escape. Her lover, incidentally, is a slave as white as she. Transported to New Orleans, Mary is sold, but aided and abetted, as well as chaperoned, by a handsome Frenchman, she escapes to France. She marries her chaperon. Years later her lover, who has, in the meantime, prospered in England, is miraculously reunited with her in France. Her French husband conveniently dead, she and her lover marry.

Seen in the full extent of its much too exuberant plot, *Clotel* is obviously a melodrama, and a rather lurid one at that. Brown apparently was not ashamed of it. He republished it three times. It ran as the serial *Miralda; or, The Beautiful Quadroon. A Romance of American Slavery, Founded on Fact*, in sixteen installments in the *Weekly Anglo-African* from December 1, 1860, through March 16, 1861. Twice in America it was published in book form, in 1864 as *Clotelle: A Tale of the Southern States* and in 1867 as *Clotelle; or, The Colored Heroine, A Tale of the Southern States*. In none of its four versions is *Clotel* ever quite the same. Not only does Clotel become successively Miralda, Clotelle, and Clotelle, the Colored Heroine. As Clotelle she shifts identity and takes the role which Mary plays in *Clotel*. Almost no names are preserved, as a matter of fact, from the earliest version of *Clotel* to the last. Horatio Green, for instance, becomes Henry Linwood; the slave speculator, who starts out as Walker, the name of the slave speculator to whom Brown actually once was hired out, ends up Jennings. All of the women, including Currer, in the original Currer's family change their names. And the lover who finally gets Mary in *Clotel* not only changes his name to Jerome to obtain her as Clotelle in two of the later versions. He also drastically alters his appearance, being metamorphosed, as the versions of the novel change, from a daintily sized near-white into, ultimately, a tall, husky, argumentative, and very sable black.

The later versions do not simply end with the surviving lovers married and in France. First, Mary-Clotelle is reunited, in Switzerland, with her contrite white father. Then, in the second *Clotelle*, she and her black husband add to her reunion with her father, and this father's return to America to free his slaves, their own return to their native land, where Jerome dies a hero's death at Port Hudson and Mary-Clotelle is last seen as the founder of a school for freed Negroes on the old Poplar Farm outside of Natchez. Not least of all, Jefferson disappears completely from the American versions of *Clotel*, undoubtedly in an easily understandable tempering of valor with discretion. An anonymous white senator succeeds him as the paterfamilias of the *Clotel* line.

We have spoken of the melodrama in *Clotel*. Robert Bone, in his *The Negro Novel in America*, anatomizing the early Negro novel (by which he seems to mean any Negro novel before the Harlem Renaissance), articulates what he obviously considers an important truth: that melodrama constitutes a prime ingredient of early Negro fiction.[3] There is no way to avoid agreeing with Bone. Melodrama is a constant element, perhaps the most constant element, in the early Negro novel, however loosely the term *early* in this connection is construed. But Bone, who must be credited, as must also be Hugh Gloster, with the writing of one of the two accounts of Negro fiction of which no committed student of that fiction can afford to be unaware, additionally—in order, surely, that a proper reference to every factor which could possibly be involved may be cited toward a placing of the melodrama of the early Negro novel within an informed and fair perspective—does not fail to remind his audience of the general fondness for melodrama discoverable in American fiction as a whole during the very era when the Negro novel was being born and, in its birth, beginning to form its own tradition.[4] He does not fail, in other words, to find a literary source for the melodrama he discerns in *Clotel* and the other Negro novels he regards as "early."

This possible literary source and its effect upon the Negro novel should not and, truly, cannot be minimized. But it is at least conceivable that the first affinity between melodrama and the Negro novel may correlate that novel, not with literature, but with life. The very solid and substantial outer world, that is, with which the Negro writer, including the writer of early Negro novels, has perennially found himself forced to come to grips may have played its role (a rather decisive one) in turning him, just as perennially, toward melodrama. And it may have played that role—even, perhaps, to the extent of largely determining this writer's dominant interpretation of his external American environment, both in the earliest and latest Negro novels, and all Negro novels in between—

3. Bone's precise words include an allusion to melodrama as the early Negro novelist's "principal literary vehicle." *Cf.* Robert A. Bone, *The Negro Novel in America* (1958; rev. ed. New Haven, 1965), 21.

4. Both Gloster's *Negro Voices in American Fiction* (Chapel Hill, 1948) and Bone's *The Negro Novel* were composed originally as doctoral dissertations, Gloster's at New York University, Bone's at Yale.

with a power and extensiveness which subordinate to its effects upon the Negro writer any influences upon that writer from places of origin as secondary in importance to the real world as the worlds of popular fiction and literary precedent.

Of Brown, indeed, little can be confidently said which truly identifies and gives in detail the absolute nature of literary influences upon him. Assertions, therefore, that he followed the practices of the best-selling novelists of his day (who were, it is true, highly melodramatic) do tend, after all, as very credible as they might well be, to be also almost altogether conjectural. There is surely nowhere a systematic, comprehensive study of Brown's reading. Comments of his, however, which he made when he visited the grave of Burns, the Lake District, Abbotsford, Melrose, and St. Mary Redcliffe, as given by Farrison in his *William Wells Brown*, would seem to indicate that Brown had at least as much familiarity as his average "well-read" contemporary would have had with the authors who had conferred celebrity upon the shrines he visited. These authors, of course, were "good" writers, the kind who became standard for canonical literary history, not the producers of potboilers. Since Brown was self-schooled, there is, moreover, always the strong possibility that he set more store upon what he and most people of any time or place would consider serious reading than he did upon escapist literary fare, melodramatic or not. Farrison says flatly that Brown had read rather widely in historians, including Gibbon, Carlyle, Macaulay, and Bancroft.[5] Brown, incidentally, did actually see Carlyle in the flesh once on a crowded omnibus, and the near tête-à-tête occasioned a passage in *Three Years in Europe* which certainly bears within itself the suggestion that Brown had read Carlyle with some care, if hardly with warm approval. For Brown, apparently—as well as not at variance with what might well be expected of him—thought racially (Carlyle had the reputation of not liking Negroes) in some of his reading. We do know, for instance, that he read William Roscoe's *The Life and Pontificate of Leo the Tenth*, the book which, in *Clotel*, George Green is desultorily perusing in a cemetery in Dunkirk, France, when his path again crosses that of Mary. Leo X was a Medici pope, and a number of Negroes have entertained, and passed on, the rumor that the Medicis at some time acquired a touch of Negro blood.

Whatever Brown read, he, nevertheless, did live in America. We

5. Farrison, *William Wells Brown*, 444.

know of his statement that his own mother at least once was severely scourged and that he overheard, though distantly, her anguished reaction to her ordeal. A white man was whipping her, if for no other reason than that in America whites and blacks were different (and still, to some, are) by fiat and whites could consequently do to blacks things they were not supposed to do to whites. Melodrama thrives upon such arbitrary dichotomies as well as upon often gratuitous violence. Brown was certainly intelligent enough to recognize the dichotomy which subordinated him to Dr. Young and permitted the outrage upon his mother as an arbitrary classification of members of the human species, just as he must also have categorized much of the terrorism generated by American racism as violence gratuitous not only because it tended to be unwarranted but also because it tended to be so too frequently excessive.

It cannot be said of Brown, it may well be, that he was unaffected by the work of Mrs. E. D. E. N. Southworth and her tribe, whose melodrama certainly was to be found in books and could be related to such literary ancestors as the so-called sentimental novel and the gothicism of Walpole's *The Castle of Otranto* or of any of Mrs. Radcliffe's novels, such as *The Mysteries of Udolpho.* But virtually all of Afro-American literature, not excepting its fiction, is saturated with its creators' awareness of their American environment, an awareness almost always similar to that of Brown's when he heard his mother moaning beneath an overseer's whip and, hence, almost always conscious of the melodrama endemic to American racism. Brown, like Dickens' Barkis, was "willing" in his protest and in his attempts to capture faithfully the melodrama he saw as part of the bizarre savagery he undoubtedly felt American racism to be. What he lacked was much of the command of art he could not do without to craft a melodrama felicitously instrumental to his intended criticism of American life. It would remain, therefore, for better black writers of fiction than Brown to do what he could not. Indeed, one of the great continuities in the history of Afro-American literature is the gradually ascending level of achievement by Negro writers of respectable control of their representation of the melodrama of American racism. In that regard, for instance, *Native Son* is a far cry from *Clotel* and an indubitable sign that not for nothing have Negro writers in America labored at the mastery of their trade.

In subject matter, *Clotel* owes a large portion of its content directly to the flow of allegation and anecdote current among the practicing abolitionists of Brown's day and time, although much of the content of *Clotel* may be credited just as directly to Brown's personal experience of slavery and color caste. David Walker had taken some trouble, in his famous *Appeal,* to stipulate that his generalizations about the condition of the Negro in America were based upon the testimony to himself of his own eyes and ears as he had moved about America. In the opening sentence of the "Preamble" of the *Appeal,* Walker refers to having "traveled over a considerable portion of these United States" and thus to having "taken the most accurate observations of things as they exist." Brown had had his chances, too, to observe at first hand, in America, existing things. He could thank, we may remember, another Walker, the trafficker in the domestic slave trade to whose employment of Brown we have already alluded, for providing him, more than once, with what was no less than a grand tour of the main north-and-south artery of the antebellum South, the Mississippi River. And the fact that his original owner thought enough of him to hire him out to others besides this Walker did not hinder Brown's accumulation of personal experience which he could, and did, draw upon in the writing of *Clotel.*

Even so, the extent to which abolitionist song and story figure prominently in *Clotel* is arresting. The very rumor that Jefferson had a mulatto daughter appears in one of the songs, "Jefferson's Daughter," which Brown included in his collection of songs for antislavery meetings, *The Anti-Slavery Harp.* But the song was not original with Brown. It had been printed, before *The Anti-Slavery Harp,* on both sides of the Atlantic by abolitionists, in the British Isles at least in the issue of *Tait's Edinburgh Magazine* for July, 1839, and on the American side of the intervening ocean, at least in the *Liberator* of May 26, 1848. Clotel's escape from Vicksburg, masquerading as a young white planter accompanied by a black servant, obviously repeats the actual subterfuge brought off in their own escape by Ellen and William Craft, whom Brown, acting for abolitionists, had actually conducted to Boston from their first northern haven in Philadelphia and with whom Brown had appeared on many abolitionist platforms in both America and England. And Clotel's final act, her leap from the Long Bridge across the Potomac within sight of the Capitol dome in Washington, D.C., incorporates into her life the "incident" described in a poem by the abolitionist Grace Greenwood included in her *Poems,* published in 1851, under the title "The Leap from the Long Bridge. An Incident at Washington." Analogues, moreover, for the stories, as told in *Clotel,* of Mary and George Green, of Althesa, with her marriage and the fate of her daughters, and of Salome Müller, the white slave, as well as for other bits of narrative to be found in *Clotel*, were also fairly common knowledge among the abolitionists.[6] Brown, indeed, when he composed *Clotel*, had spent almost twenty years in fervent abolitionist activity. He was probably only twenty years old when he escaped from slavery. By such a simple relation of one block of time within his life to another, one may gather some impression of how greatly, in all probability, the universe of myth and legend shared by abolitionists had become, in effect, an intimate part of him. It is understandable that this source—this abolitionist's world of tales and lyrics—should have supplied a considerable amount of the subject matter of *Clotel*.

But Brown's main function as a working abolitionist was to lecture. It has been said that in England alone, during his five years of residence there, he made a thousand speeches. "The great weakness of *Clotel*," according to Vernon Loggins, "is that enough material for a dozen novels is crowded into its two-hundred and forty-five pages."[7] Loggins' observation may well utter its own indictment of *Clotel*. Yet it may be even more perceptive, apropos of *Clotel*, to say of it that what fills its pages is not so much a dozen novels as a dozen, or more, abolitionist lectures. For it is the art of rhetoric, rather than the disciplines of inspired narration, which seems to determine the organization and the style, in addition to the content, of *Clotel*. The novel is an abolitionist *tour de force* not only in its borrowings of subject matter. It is a succession of abolitionist diatribes in the method of its presentation. As it is episodic, it is also a progression, or really a somewhat frenzied scramble, from one *exemplum* in an abolitionist homily to another. And if Brown never creates engaging characters in *Clotel*, and never surrounds his stiffly moving marionettes there with a world that comes alive, it may easily be because he was not able to shed, even in a novel, the habits of thought and modes of literary creativity he had accustomed himself to use on an abolitionist's lecturer's platform.

Clotel's greatest weakness is that it does not come alive as true fiction comes alive. Brown was a contemporary of the greatest of Victorian novelists. Dickens and Thackeray were at the height of their fame and popularity when he undertook *Clotel*. "Where the Victorians succeed so sensationally," Lord David Cecil says of Dickens and Thackeray, and of

---

6. A fuller tracing of these analogues may be found in Farrison, *William Wells Brown*, 174–75, 204–206, 210–12, and 222. Consult also the notes to William Wells Brown, *Clotel: Or the President's Daughter*, ed. William Edward Farrison (New York, 1969).

7. Vernon Loggins, *The Negro Author: His Development in America to 1900* (New York, 1931), 166.

some of their fellow Victorian novelists, "is precisely on their artistic side, in that quality which distinguishes a work of art from a work of thought or a work of practical use."⁸ He is here introducing his belief that the Victorian novelists were gifted to a "supreme degree" with the "quality of creative imagination," the quality that made of all the great Victorian novels little worlds that seem to come alive virtually as if the things and people in them are as real as their actual counterparts would be were they not fictive but historically true. There are great pictorial feasts in the Victorian novel, like, for instance, the fog in *Bleak House* and the night before Waterloo in *Vanity Fair*. The consummate magic, however, of these very feasts is that they can linger in the mind as still pictures without compromising the effect they also give of being hardly less a moment of arrest in an animated scene than a painting by Delacroix or Constable. An inexplicable sense of transport possesses many readers of *Bleak House* or of *Vanity Fair* which permits these readers, where *Bleak House* is concerned, to feel the fog essentially as an actual physical phenomenon and, in the case of *Vanity Fair*, to participate as omniscient, if hidden, spectators in a ball and the hours immediately after it as if a fabricated Brussels of 1815 were not a phantom but truly a tiny portion of our human past somehow miraculously recalled to life.

The genuine creative imagination makes people and things which, first of all, and above all, exist and please because of the vitality which seems to inhere in them. Should a writer wish (as good writers apparently always do) to pursue, through such persons and things, ideas which interest him—to venture, that is, into what Cecil describes as fields of thought of practical use—the necessary trick for such a writer is to not sacrifice, in a work of fiction, the primacy of creating, through pretense, people, settings, and events which seem real. No matter what flights of speculation about the human species in general this writer may care to take, or how oracular he may wish to be in dialectical approaches to truth for its own sake, his fiction stands or falls on its ability to seduce its audience into a willing suspension of its disbelief in the simulated reality of the artifact he has imagined. It is characters like Septimus Harding, convincingly portrayed, and Trollope's triumph in breathing life into a simulacrum of an English town and countryside, not his views on the Anglican church, which impart a significance that matters to Trollope's fictive Barchester.

---

8. Lord David Cecil, *Victorian Novelists* (Chicago, 1958), 10–11.

As a work of thought (and of practical use), *Clotel* may be explored with fair rewards. The student of the Negro novel can and should, for example, conclude that Clotel herself, a stipulated quadroon, embodies the theme of the tragic mulatto, a prominent theme-to-be in the Negro novel until, and even through, the Harlem Renaissance of the 1920s. He may note that Currer, Clotel's mother, who never legally marries, is yet a matriarch, and that *Clotel,* in which men play only secondary roles, is a history of a matriarchate, except for the marriage of one of Currer's daughters to a white man in New Orleans. Thus *Clotel* may be linked, by thought, to the sociology which has expatiated at length upon matriarchy and the Negro. *Clotel* lingers in, and around, Natchez. It is there that Peck, a northerner come South, resides. Brown uses Peck to illustrate the abasement of organized religion when it capitulates to slavery. He also uses Peck the northerner to suggest the economic interest which, in northerners, could, and often did, lead them to sell their souls, in effect, to slavery. Within the penumbra of implication surrounding Peck may be readily discerned, in a reflective analysis, a train of northern shipmasters, northern millowners, northern merchants, northern bankers, and northern moneylenders. But none of the northerners in this train are really shipmasters, millowners, merchants, bankers, or moneylenders. None of them, that is, are properly imagined for a tale of fiction. All of them, if they are seen in any way, appear only because the mind, catching hold of an idea, seizes upon them as pieces that fit in to help to make this idea whole. They are noumena, works of thought, and thus only of practical use. But they should be, as should be Clotel, more than that. Shadowy or not, they should approach us as through a living dream. And Clotel, of course, especially in a novel which is named after her, after a *person,* should cross that magic boundary a transcendence of which would place her beside the convincing characters of the great Victorians. That she does not, simplistic as it may be, is a measure—indeed, the measure above all other measures—of *Clotel's* failure.

The year before the year in which *Clotel* appeared had introduced the sweeping triumph of *Uncle Tom's Cabin.* Brown knew, of course, of *Uncle Tom's Cabin.* There is no reason to doubt but that its success encouraged him. He could, in 1853, not only calculate on finding occupation for his relatively idle moments by producing *Clotel.* He could, if he was in an exhilarated mood, hitch, at least in dreams, his wagon to a best seller's star. He could, that is, daydream of writing another *Uncle Tom's Cabin.* And he could daydream, moreover, of writing it, not merely for his own financial gain, but also for the greater glory of the antislavery cause. Whatever his aspirations and motives, however, whatever his dreams and hopes—they all foundered. *Clotel* did not become another *Uncle Tom's Cabin*. Nor has Clotel ever become another Uncle Tom. She is not, and never was, a household word. Neither is the even more idealized Clotelle. Yet they are what we have, all we have, however they may be limited and bereft, of the first protagonist in a Negro novel. They establish a point of departure. And knowledge of them, whatever their condition and their goods or evils, is indispensable in a full history of the Negro novel.

16. Frank J. Webb and Harriet E. Wilson

Only four years elapsed between the original publication of *Clotel* and the appearance of a second novel by a Negro writer. Interestingly enough, this second novel was published first in England also. It was called *The Garies and Their Friends*. Of its author still almost nothing is known. He was named Frank J. Webb. He was connected with Philadelphia, where most of the action of *The Garies and Their Friends* takes place. He knew, or was known to, Harriet Beecher Stowe, who wrote a preface to the novel. And he dedicated *The Garies and Their Friends* to Lady Noel Byron, of whom he calls himself a "Grateful Friend."

Harriet Beecher Stowe's preface apparently was written in America and sent to England. It came late, so late that the famed Lord Brougham, stalwart campaigner over many a year for Negro rights, wrote another. Both prefaces now precede the novel, the original publisher wisely deciding to dispense with neither. It is in Harriet Beecher Stowe's preface, however, that we learn the little that we do seem to have discovered about Frank J. Webb. Mrs. Stowe refers to him as a "coloured young man" (for us, who would probably, using the same words, say "young colored man," Mrs. Stowe's "coloured young man" is an arresting locution) and gives then the information that he was born and reared in Philadelphia. Where he met Lady Byron, if he ever met her, and whether or not he was in England in 1857, waiting for Mrs. Stowe's preface, remains to be seen. There are certainly reasons to suspect that Webb, although a Philadelphian, may have spent some time in England. The internal evidence of his novel suggests that he may, also, well have been a mulatto. From his presentation of scenes in Georgia and New Orleans, however, it is difficult to believe that he had ever been in the South.

Arthur P. Davis has called attention to one important difference between *The Garies and Their Friends* and *Clotel*. *The Garies,* according to Davis, is better written, "technically . . . far superior," to *Clotel*. It is also, in his view, notable for several "firsts." As Davis calculates these firsts, *The Garies and Their Friends* "is the first work of [Negro] fiction to describe the lives and problems of the free northern Negro; the first to treat in depth the 'mixed marriage'; the first to include a lynch mob in its plot; the first to treat ironically (as Chesnutt was to do later) the problem of the 'color line' . . . and the first to make 'passing for white' a major theme."[1] All of this seems true, as does Davis' observation that *The Garies and Their Friends* is an improvement over *Clotel* in the very elementary sense that Webb writes better than Brown. Yet Webb displays hardly any finer taste than Brown in subject matter.

If we remove the racial factor, the people and incidents of *The Garies and Their Friends* would be at home in vulgar fiction at virtually any time and place for at least the last four hundred years. There is a girl named Caddy (for Caroline) in *The Garies and Their Friends*. She lives to clean house, to abominate dirt and disorder in any form, and to make existence miserable for a harum-scarum lad named Kinch, whom, of course, she marries before the novel ends. Would-be, but overdone, caricature constitutes the wit of *The Garies and Their Friends*. Such caricature is a staple of much poor fiction. But *The Garies and Their Friends* follows also along other pedestrian and hackneyed paths in the narrative tradition. Its knave is as oily a villain as one would ever see. Nor is he a pleasure to the eye. Its chief heroine is a wholesome American girl. An inheritance is lost and recovered in it, all as part of a mildly perplexing family mystery. The weakling son of one family in it comes to grief. His stronger counterpart in another family in the novel learns and prospers. Thus we have the kind of parable which has been told many times. Moreover, *The Garies and Their Friends* in virtually its entirety is of the stuff of melodrama. Indeed, to quote Davis once again, "With its highly contrived plot, its purple patches, its tear-jerking scenes, and its death-bed repentances, *The Garies and Their Friends* [all of it] is typical nineteenth-century melodrama."[2] Even so, Webb is more of a novelist than Brown. Of the two, Webb is easily the one less unable to animate a fiction.

1. Arthur P. Davis, Introduction to Frank J. Webb, *The Garies and Their Friends* (1857; rpr. New York, 1969), i, ii.
2. *Ibid.,* viii.

The action of *The Garies and Their Friends* begins in the South. Mr. Garie, a white man of respected lineage, owns a fine, large plantation near Savannah. Mrs. Garie, a woman, we are told, "of marked beauty," with "glorious" eyes, is a mulatto not his legal wife, whom he bought for two thousand dollars, but to whose Galatea he has played Pygmalion and whom he treats as if the strictest of liturgical vows had joined him to her in holy matrimony. The Garies have two children, a boy named after his father, Clarence, and a girl named after her mother, Emily. Neither of the children shows any sign of their mother's infinitesimal African blood.

Trouble for the Garies comes when they move north, even though not immediately thereafter. They have been at peace in their Georgia retreat. But now Mrs. Garie is expecting a third child. She does not want it born on slave soil, and Mr. Garie, always solicitous of her state of mind, understands her concern. The Garies migrate to Philadelphia. Thus they are brought into the orbit of the Ellises, a couple also originally from Georgia. Both of the Ellises are unmistakably brown of skin. They met and married in Philadelphia. Mr. Ellis, with his own shop, has achieved a modest competence as a carpenter. The Ellises had known, or known of, the Garies in the South. It is the Ellises who prepare the house which the Garies buy and occupy in Philadelphia.

The Ellises have three children, Esther, the oldest daughter; Caroline, the Caddy already mentioned; and Charlie, whose closest friend is the Kinch destined to marry Caddy. The house which the Ellises prepare for the Garies has been obtained from a Mr. Walters, whom Webb unmistakably presents as the most exemplary male character in the novel. Despite a disparity in age, Walters will be wedded, in good time, to Esther, the most exemplary of the novel's female characters. To the free-Negro cousin of Mrs. Garie who is exerting himself to expedite the Garies' removal to Philadelphia, Ellis says of Walters, "He is very wealthy; some say that he is worth half a million dollars. He owns, to my certain knowledge, one hundred brick houses." And Webb's own description of Walters leaves no doubt of Webb's esteem of him:

Mr. Walters was above six feet in height, and exceedingly well-proportioned; of jet-black complexion, and smooth glossy skin. His head was covered with a quantity of wooly hair, which was combed back from a broad but not very high forehead. His eyes were small, black, and piercing, and set deep in his head. His aquiline nose, thin lips, and broad chin, were the reverse of African in their shape and gave his face a very singular appearance. . . . The neatness and care with which he was dressed added to the attractiveness of his appearance. His linen was the perfection of whiteness, and his snowy vest lost nothing by its contact therewith. A long black frock coat, black pants, and highly polished boots, completed his attire.[3]

Walters, a beau ideal for Negro manhood, obviously, as Webb conceives him, with his black skin and hair, but white features and manners, establishes the values which Webb advocates in *The Garies and Their Friends.*

In Philadelphia, fate—or, rather, coincidence—determines that the Garies shall live beside the family of George Stevens. The Stevens children, George and Lizzie, at first play with the young Garies, until Mrs. Stevens makes the hideous discovery that Mrs. Garie is a mulatto. But, privately, unknown to his wife or actually to anyone else, Stevens, a lawyer of such loose principles that he is often called "Slippery George," has made his own discovery. He has learned that he is kin to Mr. Garie through his own dead mother. She was Mr. Garie's only paternal aunt and was disowned by the Garies, who broke off all relations with her when she married, as they thought, beneath their social class. If Stevens can only manage two or three small accidents, although Mr. Garie has legally wedded Mrs. Garie since they have been in Philadelphia, Stevens may well acquire the not inconsiderable Garie fortune.

It happens that Stevens is already one of the prime movers in a conspiracy to foment rioting, arson, and vandalism that may well make it easier for certain whites to buy at greatly reduced prices any property they desire which belongs to Philadelphia's free Negroes. Stevens' chief lieutenant in the generation of the intended disorders is an Irishman named McCloskey. McCloskey has killed a man. Stevens, as McCloskey's lawyer, has saved him from the gallows, but in such a manner as to retain a hold upon him. So it is that Stevens may order McCloskey to do virtually what Stevens wills. He orders McCloskey, soon enough, to lead McCloskey's army of white toughs against Walters' home. Of all of Philadelphia's Negroes, indeed, none affronts Stevens more than Walters. Not only is Walters well-to-do. He also carries himself like a man. But Walters, luckily forewarned, has converted his house into a well-garrisoned fortress. He easily withstands the onslaughts of McCloskey's mob. The Garies, however, later targets on the same night of the mob's fury, do not escape catastrophe. Mr. Garie is murdered, shot to death in his own house by someone in the mob. Mrs. Garie dies of shock and exposure, and her baby, prematurely born during the bedlam, dies with her. Mr.

3. *Ibid.,* 50, 121–22.

Ellis is another casualty of the evening. He is almost killed by whites who stop him on his way to warn the Garies of the mob's approach. When the mob finishes with him, he is never his old self again.

No will is found for the dead Mr. Garie. All the Garies are deceased except the two children and Stevens, who seizes the occasion now, to the consternation of the Garies' friends, to reveal that he is a Garie. Except for a relative pittance, moreover, which he grudgingly allows the Garie children, he inherits the whole Garie estate. He moves to New York City and settles into a luxurious Fifth-Avenue mansion.

The years pass. Walters, who began to acquire a special regard for Esther, the oldest Ellis child, on the night his home was attacked, has made her a fine husband, and she has made him a fine wife. Charles Ellis, with Kinch as his best man and his sister Caddy as his bride's maid of honor, is preparing to marry Emily Garie in the culmination of a childhood romance. Now a skilled engraver, Charlie bids fair to become a second Walters. Likewise, for that matter, does Kinch. But Emily's brother, Clarence, has acquiesced in the living of a lie. He has, in keeping with an older counselor's advice, passed for white. Thus his life will end in tragedy. On the eve of his wedding to the girl of his choice, he will be exposed as a Negro by young George Stevens. There will be no wedding. Clarence will pine away and die. Yet, even before Clarence dies, retribution will have overtaken the Stevens family. In a deathbed statement, McCloskey confesses to his complicity with Lawyer Stevens in the commission of various crimes. He reveals also that Stevens, safely hidden in the mob, was the anonymous assassin who fired the shot which killed Mr. Garie. Indeed, McCloskey has been able to blackmail Stevens for years precisely because both he and Stevens were aware of McCloskey's undisclosed possession of the information that Stevens was an uncaught murderer. Finally, McCloskey surrenders the key to a trunk in which, for years, he has kept concealed Mr. Garie's will, the will which did, after all, transmit the bulk of Mr. Garie's estate to his rightful heirs, his two children by Mrs. Garie.

Stevens has never really enjoyed his ill-gotten gains. An uneasy recluse in his palatial home, increasingly addicted to strong drink, it is as a pitiable relict of what he once was that he commits suicide just before the law arrives to apprehend him for his crimes. Clarence and Emily Garie recover their fortune, much to the distaste of the suicide's son, young George Stevens—yet decidedly to the satisfaction of Stevens' daughter, Lizzie. And at the end of *The Garies and Their Friends*, perhaps more interesting than the weddings is a disposition of much material prosperity. All of the Ellis children are rich. Esther has the wealthy Walters. Charlie has Emily's portion of the Garie wealth. Presumably, with Clarence's death, he has Clarence's portion also. And Caddy has married Kinch, whose father sold old clothes but also purchased land, including lots which appreciated much in value and sold for a pretty profit as Philadelphia expanded geographically. Kinch, an only child, has inherited all of his father's estate. It too, then, in effect, has become part of what the Ellises may call their own.

It is possible that Frank J. Webb may have genuinely believed, even in the 1850s, that money would cure all of the Negro's American ills. It does not seem, incidentally, that in *The Garies and Their Friends* he explicitly sought to receive credit for espousing such a crude and simple faith, at least not in the blatant form represented by the financial acquisitions of the Ellises. Rather, it seems that, with his conscious mind, he intended to write a defense of the quality of life among free Negroes, especially among those residing in Philadelphia. Undoubtedly, indeed, he did intend somehow to include slaves in his brief for Negroes, although it is notable in *The Garies and Their Friends* how few slaves appear, how dimly those who do appear (largely loyal bondmen on Mr. Garie's Georgia acres) are descried, and how well treated and content they appear to be. Even so, *The Garies and Their Friends* is rather curious protest. Whatever Webb deliberately designed, the workings of his plot cannot be gainsaid. His plot declares that Negroes need, above all, in America to get rich.

A certain naïveté attends much of the experiment with aesthetics in *The Garies and Their Friends*. It is to Balch, a reputable white attorney of Philadelphia acting in the interest of the Garie children, that George Stevens the elder first announces that he is the dead Mr. Garie's cousin and heir. The announcement is made in Balch's office in the presence of Walters. Stevens has just said "I am the heir." Balch and Walters react:

"You! —*you* the heir!" cried both gentlemen, almost simultaneously.

"Yes, I am the heir!" coolly repeated Mr. Stevens, with an assured look. "I am the first cousin of Mr. Garie!"

"You his first cousin? —it is impossible!" said Walters.

"You'll discover it is not only possible, but true—I am, as I said, Mr. Garie's first cousin!"

"If you are that, you are more," said Walters, fiercely—"you're his murderer!" At this charge, Mr. Stevens turned deathly pale. "Yes," continued Walters; "you either murdered him, or instigated others to do so! It was you who directed the rioters against both him and me. . . . Now your motive is clear as day—

you wanted his money, and destroyed him to obtain it! His blood is on your hands!" . . .

In the excitement consequent upon such a charge, Mr. Stevens, unnoticed by himself, had overturned a bottle of red ink, and its contents had slightly stained his hands. . . . An expression of intense horror flitted over his face when he observed it.[4]

Only a writer of fiction who was not discriminating and practiced in his trade could have written this passage—or, if he was properly accomplished and did write it, he could have suffered it to leave his pen only with his tongue in his cheek or his fingers to his nose. The melodrama here is bold and unabashed. There are the right confrontations, simple and clear, and so obvious that even a child can thrill to them: the good lawyer against the bad; virtue against vice; the "white" black against the "black" white. There is the language. Only an innocent or a calculating sensation-monger could have used it: "His blood is on your hands!" And almost past belief is the red ink and its suggested symbolism. That ink is too clumsy even to be meant as parody by an author of fiction whose skill would place him beyond the status of a hack.

But this red ink is hardly more naïve, perhaps, than Webb's prescription for the redemption of his race. If money could do everything, one does wonder sometimes at the lack of inward grace of those who have most of it, albeit the poor, in their usually straitened lives, are rarely an argument for the beneficence of poverty. *The Garies and Their Friends*, we have noted, according to Mrs. Stowe is the book of a young man. Reading it, it does seem precisely that. It has the élan of youth about it and none of the crabbedness of age. It does not yield to disillusionment. It is a book that breathes of spring and hope, so that, in its end, not even the elder Stevens is too hateful, and only his despiteful son, who seems to have been born loving to inflict pain, is truly vile and beyond the orbit of the book's good will. But part of this book's naïveté seems to underscore not so much the absence of sophistication in its art as the extreme degree to which it is a document reflective of American culture and of a value system which Webb shared, not with any past of an Africa he knew (or wanted to know) or with any rebels against American society, but with immigrants who had come from places other than Africa to enjoy a virgin continent. The Elizabethan mathematician Thomas Harriot had spoken too enthusiastically of America as an Eden where a man might produce

4. *Ibid.*, 254.

in one day enough food to last himself for a whole year. There were adventurers who came to Jamestown at least half expecting to pick up gold from the ground. Only a few years before *The Garies and Their Friends*, Americans had sent their younger sons posting around the Horn or across the Isthmus of Panama, if not by long overland trails, to California, where yellow dust had been found at Sutter's Mill. Less than a generation after the publication of *The Garies and Their Friends*, Henry James would bemoan, in America, "no sovereign, no court, no personal loyalty, no aristocracy, no church, no clergy, no army, no diplomatic service, no country gentlemen, no palaces, no castles, nor manors, nor old country-houses, nor parsonages, no thatched cottages nor ivied ruins; no cathedrals, nor abbeys, nor Norman churches! no public schools—no Oxford, nor Eton, nor Harrow," and, while James was somewhat unfair to America in the extravagance of his woe, to meditate upon his strictures is to recognize in an impressive manner the extent to which, in America, the plutocratic interest has subsumed all others.[5]

The Ellises of *The Garies and Their Friends* are a very American family. None of them respond to blood kinship and ancestral ties as did once those Africans on slave ships who dreaded the Middle Passage above all because it separated them from their relatives, living and dead. There is no talk among the Ellises of returning to Africa (or even Georgia) lest they should face the horror of spending eternity separated from those with whom they belong. Nor have the Ellises and their friends an African sense of land. Kinch and his father make money from their land. The people of old West Africa regarded land not as a commodity but as a resource to be husbanded since it was ultimately common property. One did not speculate, in old West Africa, with land. Land there was for tillage or for other uses which contributed to survival. The respect for money, the sense of family, and the attitude toward land in *The Garies and Their Friends* all are impeccably American, as are the language, the notions of romantic love, the manners, the clothes, the food, the religion, the landscape and geography, and the very form the narrative takes, for novels are novels, and not the kind of tales which might be associated with an African literary tradition.

It is inconceivable that Webb could have lived among the free Negroes in Philadelphia without knowing, or knowing about, the real Negro James Forten, of whom we have spoken earlier. Like the real James

---

5. Henry James, *Hawthorne* (New York, 1879), 43.

Forten and the imagined Walters, *The Garies and Their Friends* asserts a fact of life. Negroes raised in America tend to be American. So do Negro novels, from their earliest exemplars. Elementary as this pronouncement may appear, it should not be taken for granted or dismissed lightly. Some linguists argue for African survivals in the speech of American Negroes.[6] Other students of the American Negro—preeminently, perhaps, Melville Herskovits in his extensive and often persuasive monograph, *The Myth of the Negro Past*—have detected African survivals among American Negroes elsewhere than in their speech. Whether such authorities are right or wrong is largely immaterial for the appraiser of the Negro novel. To him the Negro novel presents a world that, whatever its shifting shape, contains at least two constants, its penchant for melodrama and its dependence upon the involvement with America of its creators. It is generally agreed that the prime function of all Negro literature, with only negligible exceptions after 1830, is protest—racial protest. And so racial protest does tend to pervade the world of the Negro novel. So, too, does melodrama, recurring repeatedly in effects connected with the protest. So, too, does America. Protest, melodrama, America: each member of this trinity is deep within the fabric of the Negro novel.

The America of *The Garies and Their Friends* locally, as we have seen, is principally the late antebellum world of the Philadelphia of free Ne-groes—such Negroes as those for whom masters no longer existed, if they ever had, but to whom American racism was still a problem. Thus, *The Garies and Their Friends* constitutes, among other things, a novel about Negroes before the Civil War who are not slaves and who do not dwell in the South. A logical companion for it, therefore, may well be the novel *Our Nig*, which is also set in a northern scene before the Civil War and the protagonist of which, a woman, is also a free Negro.

The North of *Our Nig* is small-town New England, either New Hamp-shire or Massachusetts. The novel was published, two years after *The Garies and Their Friends*, in 1859, with a title which, given in full, reads as follows: *Our Nig; or, Sketches from the Life of a Free Black, In a Two-Story White House, North, Showing That Slavery's Shadows Fall Even There.* This is a heading to be respected as a highly conscious statement by the author of her conception of her very deliberate, and polemical, purpose in the writing of *Our Nig*. That purpose was, of course, to argue against

6. See especially J. L. Dillard, *Black English: Its History and Usage in the United States* (New York, 1972).

too much optimism in comparing the lot of the Negro in the North with the corresponding disposition of the Negro in the South. There are no plantations in *Our Nig*, no paterollers, no auction blocks, and, certainly, no sultry subtropical skies. But the protagonist of *Our Nig* does undergo undue suffering which, according (at least) to her author's wishful thinking, must be perceived as an unhappy result of her being black. This protagonist is her author's offering of proof that American racism in the days of the Websters and the Calhouns was not confined to the haunts and precincts of the Calhouns alone. Where Websters were at home and the soil was characterized as free, it is the major thesis of the narrative which flows through *Our Nig*, Negroes were mistreated just as if they were no less legally subject to bondage than their fellow Negroes in the South.

Our Nig languished in virtual oblivion for the better part of a century. It was, in effect, recalled to life by the black scholar Henry Louis Gates, Jr., who not only exhumed its text but also provided, in his introduction to an edition of it in 1983, the information about its author upon which the present account of her is based. Gates, incidentally, in this introduction, properly notes that *Our Nig* is the first novel by an American Negro, male or female, to be published in America, the first novel ever by a black American woman, and one of the first two novels—in conjunction with *Ursula*, by Maria F. Dos Reis, which appeared in Brazil in 1859—to be published by women of the Negro race anywhere in the Western Hemisphere or, for that matter, in the entire world.

The Harriet E. Wilson who wrote, and published, *Our Nig*, was christened Harriet Adams. Both the time and the place of her birth remain to be determined in a fashion which will leave no need or opportunity for speculation. Gates's research has discovered references in the 1850 federal census of New Hampshire to a Harriet Adams born in that state in 1828. But this same research also has revealed, in the 1860 federal census of Massachusetts, references to a Mrs. H. E. Wilson born in Fredericksburg, Virginia, in 1807 or 1808. A Mrs. Wilson of the second instance here, to be the author of *Our Nig*, would have borne a child two or three years after her fortieth birthday, a not impossible, but still unlikely, probability. And she may well have been born, not free, but a slave who eventually managed an escape from Virginia to the North, coming to Massachusetts and remaining there openly even after the dreaded Fugitive Slave Act of the Compromise of 1850, a desired avoidance of the provisions of which drove some Negroes who had evaded the clutches of their masters outside the United States in the early 1850s.

In any case, persuasive conjectures about the life of Harriet E. Wilson may be drawn from statements made in two different kinds of sources for evidence: *Our Nig*, which seems an autobiography of its author to a marked degree; and separate communications, in an appendix to *Our Nig*, from three individuals who announce themselves, like the character witnesses they clearly intend to be, as credible acquaintances of Harriet Wilson. If the autobiographical implications of *Our Nig* are reliable as authority for the early life of the Harriet Adams who became Harriet E. Wilson, her mother was white, her father was black, and both parents died while she was still an infant or a very small child. But Gates has correctly indicated that virtually all the information which appears to be more trustworthy than otherwise about Harriet E. Wilson, the historic individual, applies to her experiences in the ten years between 1850 and 1860 and tends to be supplied by allusions to her life at that time in the aforementioned appendix, albeit with the reinforcement hitherto cited but not specified from the narrative of *Our Nig*. So, it seems that, by 1851, Harriet Adams (who in 1850 had resided in Milford, New Hampshire, with the family of a carpenter named Samuel Boyles) was lodging herself in a town in Massachusetts with a kindly Mrs. Walker, through whose intercessions on her behalf our future author had been helped to secure employment as a so-called straw sewer. Mrs. Walker's home was in a part of the Bay State where working with straw, particularly in the manufacture of straw hats, was a prominent industry. Mrs. Walker, moreover, not only performed admirably as a good Samaritan to Harriet Adams in assisting her in getting a job. When her tenant began to suffer from poor health, Mrs. Walker extended special care to her.

Also in 1851, Harriet Adams, during a presumably recreational stroll, met a fugitive slave from Virginia, described as "young, well-formed and very handsome," as well as possessed of notably polished and engaging manners which he may well have acquired from having been a house servant rather than a hand who labored like a Caliban in the fields under some harsh driver's supervision. With this runaway, one Thomas Wilson (who would hardly seem to be of the right age for a woman born in 1807 or 1808), Harriet Adams, apparently, fell immediately and deeply in love. She and Wilson were married, according to the 1850 census, on October 5, 1851, at Milford. They were soon separated by Wilson's departure, it might well be fairly safe to assume, in an act of sudden abandonment of his wife and, perhaps, for a life at sea.

Wilson had deserted his spouse at a particularly bad time for her. She was with child and without means of support. She seems to have been forced to accept the hospitality of the county house, a governmentally supported and administered refuge for indigents, in Goffstown, New Hampshire, only a few miles from Milford. In this county house her son, and Wilson's, was born in late May, or early June, of 1852 and named George Mason Wilson, conceivably as a tribute to the Virginian George Mason, somewhat widely and deservedly celebrated for his legal mind, his public career in America before, during, and after the Revolution, and his low opinion of slavery. Once, during the 1850s, Wilson did return to his wife and child. For a while, indeed, it seems that he took care of them in, or near, Milford in a manner which gave them comfort and no little delight. But then he disappeared again, never to return. Eventually his wife placed their child with a family, certainly white, which received him as a foster son and is reported to have treated him considerately and lovingly.

Ill health continued to plague Harriet Wilson, at least upon occasion. Her full history of employment in the 1850s is not known. But it seems clear that mere subsistence then was a constant problem for her. In fact, in her brief preface to *Our Nig*, she alleges that an emergency of the most pressing nature has driven her to authorship. She hopes the financial returns from *Our Nig* will enable her to sustain existence for herself and her child. George Mason Wilson died, however, in Milford in February, 1860, not quite six months after *Our Nig* was published. His death certificate attributes his demise to a fever. How long his mother survived him remains a topic for more conclusive investigation.

"Lonely Mag Smith! See her as she walks with downcast eyes and heavy heart." With these mournful words *Our Nig* begins. But Mag Smith had once been a beauteous young woman. She was, however, of humble origins, and she committed the fault of becoming enamored of a philanderer, above her in social station, to whom she surrendered her virtue but from whom she failed to receive the protection of marriage. She left her home and bore, among strangers, a child who lived only a few weeks. Even strangers, however, now disdained her. In her straitened circumstances, she was befriended by a Negro named Jim, a hooper of barrels, who eventually persuaded her to marry him. For a while, moreover, she and Jim were prosperous and happy together. Their union was blessed with two children, the elder of whom, Frado, the Our Nig of the title of the novel, was an exceptionally attractive, and spirited, small edition of her mother.

Years passed. As they did, competitors invaded the fields of work available to Jim and Mag. The two found now a comfortable home of their own only a bitter memory from their past. Also now, most inopportunely, Jim's health declined and he died. A second Negro, one Seth Shipley, became something of a successor to Jim and lived with Mag, although out of wedlock and decidedly without improving Mag's fortunes. At last Mag and Shipley stole away from Singleton, the village near which Mag had lived after she fled her birthplace. They took with them one child, but one child only. Two miles beyond the outskirts of Singleton lived a family, the Bellmonts, in a two-story white house, obviously the edifice of the subtitle of *Our Nig*. To this family Mag committed unsuspecting Frado, using the ruse of asking the Bellmonts to keep Frado merely for a night during which her family could not tend her.

Frado's sojourn with the Bellmonts occupies the bulk of *Our Nig*. The Bellmont household is headed by John Bellmont, who is anything but inhumane and never abuses Frado. His wife, Mrs. Bellmont, is altogether different from him. She is a shrew and a bully whose happiest hours are those she can savor because of what she has done in them to torment someone lacking in the power to retaliate upon her in kind. Mr. Bellmont does not always sit idly by when she is indulging herself with a hapless victim. Upon occasion he is known sharply to restrain his ill-natured spouse. Other members of the Bellmont household are Aunt Abby, or Nab, Mr. Bellmont's sister, as humane as he; the Bellmonts' invalid daughter, Jane; their younger daughter, Mary, whose character is much like her mother's; and Jack, a son who will constantly exert himself to befriend Frado. Mrs. Bellmont dictates largely the conditions under which Frado is inducted into the Bellmont household. This means, for Frado, sleeping in a horribly cramped space in the attic, eating her scanty meals (skim milk and crusts of brown bread for breakfast) standing up, doing countless chores, and receiving beatings from Mrs. Bellmont. But Jack never hesitates to succor her. He even buys her a dog, Fido.

When Frado attains the age of seven, very poorly dressed and tagging, to suit Mary's spiteful pleasure, far in Mary's rear (since Mary abhors any connection with Frado which implies that Frado is her equal), she goes to school. She is to have three years of schooling for three months a year in her whole life. Meanwhile, the tasks imposed upon her by Mrs. Bellmont constantly increase. She toils both within the white two-story house and on the Bellmont farm. Her work on the farm, however, does not oppress her, except in its amount as it is added to the demeaning labor forced upon her by Mrs. Bellmont. The Bellmont farmhands tend to like her. She is pleasingly vivacious as well as sometimes divertingly mischievous. Her pranks enliven the world around her although, beneath them, she is actually a juvenile Pagliacci concealing from all but her dog her face of woe. At the age of nine, she meets the Bellmont son from Baltimore, to whom she will bear an interesting relationship. This son alights from his traveler's coach at the "two-story white house, north," after a flurry of preparation for him in which Mrs. Bellmont has so savaged Frado that Frado has disappeared. With Fido's assistance, Jack, followed by James, the visiting son, tracks Frado to her place of concealment. When she returns to the Bellmont home, protected by Jack and James from Mrs. Bellmont, and puts herself to bed in her cheerless chamber, James stays with her alone for a brief colloquy with her to lighten her distress.

James's visit is not long. After his departure, Frado's vexations grow substantially. The Bellmonts have acquired a flock of sheep. Frado now must tend them as well as the Bellmonts' cows. Nor have any of her chores inside the house diminished or Mrs. Bellmont relaxed the severity of her attacks on Frado's body and spirit as well. Meanwhile, in Baltimore, the personable James, well-favored both in appearance and in his innate gentility, has married a Baltimorean. His wife, Susan, has much to recommend her. Her gentility matches that of James, and her family is affluent. Jane, who has unfailingly been like Jack to Frado, is also to marry. Mrs. Bellmont wants Jane to marry Henry Reed, a neighbor with holdings which Mrs. Bellmont avariciously hopes to merge with the Bellmont farm into a single estate. Under Mrs. Bellmont's pressure, Jane has virtually plighted her troth with Reed. But a young friend of Aunt Abby's, George Means, comes into Jane's life and evokes from her a reciprocal response to his instant, but real, affection for her. Supported by Mr. Bellmont and Aunt Abby and in spite of Mrs. Bellmont's opposition (some of it shamefully secret), Jane marries Means and departs with him for Vermont. Jack goes west, to assume a clerkship in a store. Mrs. Bellmont, pathologically vindictive, sells Fido. Frado feels a darkening of the world around her.

But Mr. Bellmont will not permit Frado to be too dejected. With some effort he retrieves Fido for her. Frado is now fourteen years of age. James has repeatedly urged Mr. and Mrs. Bellmont to visit him in Baltimore. At last they yield to his importunities, leaving their house in Mary's charge, but thus only adding to Frado's burden of work and abuse. Mary in control of a household is essentially as much of a tartar as her mother.

Moreover, Frado is no longer as hale and hearty as she once was. Not only has demanding toil taken its toll of her. She has never been decently clothed at the Bellmonts, her feet even often going completely unclad in the coldest and most inclement weather. So a time has come when Frado is sometimes too ill to stand.

A drooping Frado only exacerbates Mary's sadism: once Mary flings, although with imperfect aim, a carving knife at her. The return of the elder Bellmonts does relieve Frado somewhat of Mary. But James's health is collapsing badly. He comes home from Baltimore, an obvious wreck of his former self. Nevertheless, Frado delights in his presence. He does not delay in demanding, and achieving, a cessation of the barbarous custom of requiring Frado to eat her meals without sitting down. Aunt Abby, ignoring Mrs. Bellmont's proscriptions, has begun to take Frado with her to weekday evening religious gatherings within the Bellmonts' neighborhood. Of this exposure for Frado James highly approves. In talks with Aunt Abby he speaks of his regard for Frado, his concern over the torture she suffers at his mother's hands, and his intention, once he has recovered his health, to remove Frado from his mother by taking her to his Baltimore home.

James has uttered an undertaking he is never to fulfill. Indeed, he is never to return home himself. The ministrations of a surgeon, even, avail him naught. As he weakens, Frado spends much time with him. In his final moments she kisses him, and he promises her that the two of them will consort with each other in heaven. But Frado's days with the Bellmonts are fortunately numbered. She exercises her right to leave them when her period of indenture with them expires on her eighteenth birthday. Mary dies while she is visiting a brother of hers who, like James, has become a resident of Baltimore. Her passing occurs, far more unexpectedly and quickly than the death of James, before Frado withdraws from the Bellmont household. After Frado has severed her connection with the Bellmonts, and in the fullness of time, Mr. and Mrs. Bellmont, Aunt Abby, and Jack and his wife are all to die. Jane, once the invalid, is to survive them all. So is Frado, who works as a straw sewer and sells a product, precisely as Harriet Wilson may well at times have done, and, again precisely as seems true of Harriet Wilson, marries and has a son. Wilson's husband apparently vanished eventually, we believe, without a trace. Frado's husband dies of yellow fever in New Orleans.

Our Nig is a narrative written in the omniscient form of the third-person point of view. It contains twelve chapters. In the last nine of these chapters, the titles do not clash, in their point of view, with the narrative to which they refer. But the titles of the first three chapters of Our Nig are, respectively, "Mag Smith, My Mother," "My Father's Death," and "A New Home for Me." These three titles could tell a story. For they could be further evidence of the autobiographical nature of Our Nig. Perhaps, indeed, they are what might well be called Freudian slips, a possibility which arguably could be increased because they are the first chapter titles of Our Nig, adopted by Wilson before a censor appropriate in function intervened to discipline her in the control of her manuscript. In this connection, moreover, it is interesting to observe the end of Our Nig. Its last chapter is a rapid, almost pell-mell, summary of events, of which those that deal with Frado seem only a thin disguise of what is suspected to have occurred in Wilson's life in the 1850s.

No pictorial images of Harriet Wilson exist. Was she a mulatto, or, for that matter, was she the bastard child of a white mother and a black father, the most proscribed category of human offspring under the code of color caste? The answers to these questions are not yet known. But Wilson, while it hardly seems justifiable to accuse her of a suspiciously strong interest in Frado's physical appearance, does make it clear, in Our Nig, that Frado is a mulatto with straight hair and a complexion between that of blondes and blacks. One of Mrs. Bellmont's prized abuses of her is the shearing of her curls. She has strikingly beautiful and expressive eyes. And of her comeliness Jack has written to James before James ever sees her, although James, once he has beheld her, obviously from what his own eyes tell him, concludes that she is at least as fair to look upon as Jack has said she is, if not more so.

Of Wilson's mind we could have, in Our Nig, more ascertainable auto-biographical reflections than of her face and form. As limited as had been her time in school, Frado, past her childhood, is not without an inclination to rely on the written word. After James enters her life especially, there come moments for her when she absorbs herself in the reading of the Bible. The real Harriet Wilson, according to what has been supposed of her from apparently authentic evidence, was not unversed in the peculiar literacy of the pious Protestantism of her day and time, a literacy which depended in no little measure upon the close and frequent perusal of the Scriptures. One of the communications in Gates's appendix, signed by "Allida," quotes at length from a letter written by Wilson to the Mrs. Walker with whom Wilson had stayed in Massachusetts. In the letter is Wilson's account of her evening before she went to the county house in which her son would be born. On that evening, she packed with care, being sure not to forget to place into her trunk her portable ink-stand, pen, and papers. But her Bible she did not pack, saving it for a place nearer, she said, to her heart. This Bible, she avers additionally, she opened and began to read as soon as she was safely within her room in the county house.

About the mind, however, of the author of *Our Nig* a portable ink-stand, pen, and papers may speak more eloquently than a Bible and Bible reading. All of the chapters of *Our Nig* are preceded by epigraphs, some taken from famous authors, Thomas Moore, Shelley, Byron, Martin Tupper, and Solomon among them, but three attributed to no one. Could these three epigraphs have been composed by Wilson? She did write poetry. A poem of her own, five stanzas long, each stanza of four lines, graces her letter to Mrs. Walker quoted by "Allida." Writing as well as reading, then, figured consequentially, it may be possibly as-sumed, in Wilson's wishes for herself before she wrote *Our Nig*. In the Bellmont household, Mrs. Bellmont and her burden of backbreaking tasks notwithstanding, Frado consults her Bible. Wilson, too, in actuality, suffered privations and deprivations and seems to have read through all of them. It may have been, nevertheless, that she was disposed also to write. And if she was so disposed, that need not signify at all, inciden-tally, that she lied in claiming that she wrote *Our Nig* for money. For her resort to creativity in an extremity for her should focus attention on what seems to have been true of her, that trying to write, by the late 1850s, was no novelty to her and that, in a sense which was probably not true for too many early Negro novelists (William Wells Brown, regrettably to say, among them), writing novels was vocationally apt for her. She may have been, that is, born to write, not simply for a cause, but even more simply because an urge within her would not be appeased until she tried her hand at poetry and imaginative prose.

Surely, in *Our Nig* it is possible to sense an interest in the aesthetics of creating a piece of fiction which does seem a concern with Wilson of greater and prior importance than any, and all, of the kinds of considera-tions which can be associated with writing only to make a controver-sialist's point. There is a way of telling a story which is sometimes called that of the straight-line narrative. *Our Nig* uses this way, and so, in its basic form, *Our Nig* is simple. It merely begins at a selected point in time and proceeds, without complications of any kind—such as, for instance, flashbacks—to a later point in time, where it stops. As simple as the narrative structure of *Our Nig* is its characterization. Some of its characters are sympathetic. Some of them are not. None of its characters are very complex, and none of them, including the protagonist, are remarkable for any singularity. And *Our Nig,* in theme, is as simple as it is in narrative structure and in characterization. It is a novel about the sorrowful plight of blackness. It does not attempt, or pretend, thematically to be anything more.

Elementary, however may be a better term for *Our Nig* than *simple.* From all that we now know, *Our Nig* is a first novel. So were all the novels written by blacks before the Civil War. The 1850s, then, began for blacks in American literature a second age of apprenticeship, the age when Negro writers, having essayed poetry and autobiography, at last ventured to try their wings in a truly sophisticated area of literary expression. The marks of an old hand at a particular game do not exist in *Our Nig.* Wilson is content to produce there a story containing no daring or dangerous experiments in technique but only resorts, in a familiar manner, to often repeated uses of the rudiments of narrative. There are no tricks with time in *Our Nig,* just as there are no streams of consciousness, in embryo or fully developed, no sequences of dreams, no levels of allegory, no impressionism, no symbolism or surrealism or attempts at any achievement except to tell a story with virtually no complications as directly and clearly as possible. Once or twice, like the conformist inhabitant of her century she seems eminently to have been, Wilson slips into the role of an intruding author, perhaps all the more easily because she rarely avails herself of the voice of a mouthpiece character. Even so, *Our Nig* is preponderantly dialogue and action, surrounded by adequate but hardly excessive description. Wilson as a first novelist is tolerable without being, in her craft, either venturesome or innovative. Who her models may have been cannot now be documented. She wrote, however, in the heyday of a host of women novelists whose standard fare portrayed with a genteel brush an all-too-uniform domestic scene. Not without significance, *Our Nig* is effectively set within the Bellmont household. In an age of novels about the family life of Americans, *Our Nig* is an account, whether Frado is an interloper or not, of life within the family of some Americans.

But the feminine presence in the authorship of nineteenth-century American fiction has been closely studied by Nina Baym in her *Woman's Fiction: A Guide to Novels by and About Women in America, 1820–1870.* Baym develops in this work a concept of an overplot—of elements, that is, occurring in the plots of these novels so often and commonly as to constitute a noteworthy phenomenon—and she attributes to this over-plot the significance of being at least one means by which an aspect of feminism from America's past can be identified and analyzed. Gates notes, in his previously mentioned introduction, that elements of Baym's overplot can be found in *Our Nig*. There are, he says, in *Our Nig* 1) the device of pairing two women, as a heroine and a villainess (two heroines may also be paired); 2) the heroine who is an orphan, as well as a poor and friendless child; 3) the heroine who is abused; 4) the plot with a tripartite structure embracing an unhappy childhood for a heroine, an interlude of time during which that heroine must earn her own living, and a conclusion, whether for good or for ill; and 5) enough indictment of social injustice to qualify the book as a "woman's novel" containing "much explicit and implicit social commentary."[7] These elements of *Our Nig* specified by Baym as elements of her overplot constitute evidence suggesting that, however new Wilson was as a novelist with *Our Nig*, she was not immune to some prevailing conditions in the intellectual and sentimental climate of her era. There was a feminist note which could be struck in the nineteenth-century American novel. Although perhaps not loudly, *Our Nig* apparently struck that note.

Characterization is, of course, not plotting. The character of Frado, for obvious reasons, constitutes an object of prime concern in *Our Nig*. Unless Frado arouses a sympathetic response from her audience, her story may as well be left untold. Consequently, she does not ever appear a weakling. If Frado is to be victimized by a system, Wilson, it seems, is at least wise enough to try to make her appear not so much of a cipher, nor so vicious or detestable, as to occasion from anyone the judgment that nothing much, if anything, should be regretted of mishaps to her. At Frado's first appearance in *Our Nig*, when she is six years old, she is pre-sented as a creature with "handsome, roguish eyes, sparkling with an ex-uberance of spirit almost beyond restraint."[8] Her mother thinks of her as a child who means to follow her own desires. And so at least Wilson en-visioned Frado with a logic appropriate for the enhancement of Wilson's indictment of racism. Frado's significance, however, in a history of femi-nism may not be so readily defined. There were hoydens now and then in

7. Nina Baym, *Woman's Fiction: A Guide to Novels by and About Women in America, 1820–1870* (Ithaca, N.Y., 1978); Henry Louis Gates, Jr., Introduction to Harriet E. Wilson, *Our Nig; or, Sketches from the Life of a Free Black* (2nd ed.; New York, 1985), xli–xliii.

8. Wilson, *Our Nig*, 17.

nineteenth-century fiction, and Frado is something of a hoyden. Once, for fun, she mounts the roof of the Bellmonts' barn. On another occasion she fills with cigar smoke the drawer of a male teacher's desk, with the result that, when that teacher opens the drawer, before a class (as Frado has certainly hoped), he panics in the presence of his delighted students. Even so, Frado's manner thus of flaunting convention could be construed as an identification of her author with a type of character not necessarily feminist but rather, perhaps, a sop not too exotic, or rare, for the taste of an audience contemporary with Wilson.

In the treatment of its theme, *Our Nig* disposes contradictorily to what it proposes. Racism undoubtedly was an ugly fact of life for Negroes in the North when *Our Nig* was written. Such racism explained William Wells Brown's ride in a baggage car of a train on which he had anticipated a passenger's reception. It accounted for the antipathy of whites to the spectacle of Frederick Douglass escorting, in no wise as a servant, the white Griffith sisters (who were from England) along a northern street. But Frado's troubles in the Bellmont household hardly seem attributable to her color. Jack Bellmont is her friend. So is his sister Jane and his father's sister, Aunt Abby, while Mr. Bellmont's urbanity toward her never falters. She has problems only with Mrs. Bellmont and Mary, both of whom all who know them regard as cut from the same mold as Cinderella's stepmother. Mr. Bellmont usually walks warily around Mrs. Bellmont, and Mary's schoolmates are overjoyed at any discomfiture to her. Frado has problems with Mrs. Bellmont and Mary not so much because she is black as because they are what they are. Moreover, when Frado first goes to school and the children are prepared to be unkind to her, the teacher, Miss Marsh, with commendable tact, so admonishes them that they suspend judgment on Frado until she eventually becomes a favorite with them. The workers on the Bellmont farm, we have seen, are as enamored of Frado as her schoolmates. And Aunt Abby's minister experiences no difficulty in conducting himself with Frado according to the higher dictates of his calling.

Indeed, in *Our Nig*, Frado's major source of displeasure seems not to be racistic abuse of herself by others but dissatisfaction with her own color. She wants to be white. She asks James Bellmont, almost as soon as she meets him, why God has made her black and not white. She seeks assurance from others that blacks will go to heaven as well as whites. In her prayers she bemoans her color, always with the implication that she would prefer to be white. Wilson would not be the last black author to debilitate an attack on racism with an unwitting expression of a wish to be white. *Our Nig* illustrates, in one regard at least, racial protest gone awry. Autobiographical in form, it does invite comparisons with the slave narrative, which it echoes in form and in such particulars as the helplessness of its protagonist and her ultimate termination of her indenture. And it is a better novel than the first novel written by a black American male. Of Frado and Clotel, Frado is the superior artifact.

17. Black Separatism Enters the Novel

We know of only four Negro novels written before the Civil War. *Clotel, The Garies and Their Friends,* and *Our Nig* are three of these novels, and all three may be called integrationist. But not *Blake, or The Huts of America,* the fourth antebellum Negro novel. *Blake* is a novel for black nationalists. Its protagonist, Blake, the titular hero of his own story, is black of skin, as black as the ace of spades. Moreover, he harbors little love for whiteness. Nor does he preach that, if only Negroes can achieve rapprochement with whites and gain a goodly measure of economic competence, all will be well in the relationship between the races. He thinks in political terms of black enterprise, espouses a revolution of the slaves, and dreams of a distinct black nation. *Blake* is the first manifesto within the Negro novel of black separatism.

Martin Robinson Delany, who wrote *Blake,* was as dark of complexion as the hero of his novel. Delany was born in 1812 in Charles Town, not to be confused with Charleston, in that part of Virginia which has since become West Virginia. Charles Town is near southern Pennsylvania and Harpers Ferry. Appropriately enough, considering Delany's views, John Brown was hanged there.

Delany's father was a slave noted locally for his prodigious strength. But Delany's mother, Pati, was free. When Delany was nine, his mother took him and her other children across the state line into Pennsylvania, to Chambersburg, where her husband, escaping from bondage, soon rejoined them. At the age of nineteen, Delany trudged on foot across the Allegheny ridge to Pittsburgh. There he found, congenially, a colony of free Negroes, some of whom were relatively successful entrepreneurs and virtually all of whom were almost feverishly engrossed in improving the Negro's lot. Indeed, it is one of the minor crimes of Negro history that so much has been said about the free Negroes of Philadelphia and so little about the same people in Pittsburgh.

Delany entered with zeal and great animal vitality into the life of Pittsburgh's Negro colony. His mother, violating Virginia law, had taught him how to read in English. In Pittsburgh, Delany studied the classics and learned something of how to read in Latin and Greek. Within three years after his arrival, also, he began the study of medicine as an apprentice in the office of a white physician. He joined clubs—like, for example, the Philanthropic Society, which justified its existence by aiding and protecting fugitive slaves. With a good friend and fellow student named Molliston Clark, he founded the Theban Literary Society—there was, of course, a Thebes in ancient Egypt as well as ancient Greece—which did interest itself in literature, including the ambitious efforts at original composition of its own members. Alone, he took the lead in organizing a Pittsburgh chapter of the American Moral Reform Society, the national organ of which, the *National Reformer,* had missed by only one month the distinction of being the first of America's Negro magazines.

All the while Delany seems to have had uppermost in his mind the problem of the Negro's manhood. Clearly he agreed, more or less, with David Walker that "we Coloured People of these United States, are the most wretched, degraded and abject set of beings that ever lived since the world began."[1] He was anything but enamored of the American Colonization Society. But he early began to entertain the notion that American Negroes, of their own volition, did need a sovereign state somewhere, populated mainly, if not exclusively, by themselves, where they could work out their own destiny and be their own true masters in every way. In 1838 the supreme court of Pennsylvania, basing its decision upon that clause in the Fourth Article of the Constitution of the United States which stipulates that a citizen of one state in the Union is entitled to all the privileges and immunities of citizens in the several states, ruled that Negroes could not be citizens of Pennsylvania since—strange logic!—there were states, as in the South, where they could not enjoy these same privileges and immunities. In 1839, therefore, Delany took a trip fraught with grave peril for him. He traveled to Texas, at that time an independent republic, in the hope that he might spy out land there on which

1. See the brief statement preceding the text of Charles M. Wiltse (ed.), *David Walker's Appeal* (New York, 1965).

Negroes could settle and establish an autonomous commonwealth. His trip took him through much of Mississippi, Louisiana, and Arkansas, as well as into Texas. It would be reflected in *Blake*. And it only heightened those intentions and passions of his which were based on his growing anguish over the helplessness and insecurity of American Negroes, even when they were nominally "free."

Delany returned from Texas disappointed. In 1843, he married, and then he started a newspaper. There had been a "Daddy Ben" Richards, a butcher, among Pittsburgh's wealthiest Negro citizens, who had sold his meats to such highly lucrative customers as the army and provision markets and prospered so well that he had owned wagons and boats. Surreptitiously, also, "Daddy Ben" had used his boats and wagons to haul fugitive slaves. One of his sons married an immigrant girl from County Cork. It was Catherine, or Katy, Richards, the half-Irish granddaughter of "Daddy Ben" by this son, whom Delany wedded. No other act of Delany's was ever to eventuate so propitiously. Katy bore him eleven children, seven of whom survived the hazards of nineteenth-century infancy and childhood. Delany named them in keeping with his racial chauvinism. His six sons who lived to maturity he called, in order, Toussaint L'Ouverture, Charles Lenox Remond, Alexandre Dumas, Saint Cyprian, Faustin Soulouque (after the Haitian emperor), and Placido Rameses (representing both the Cuban poet and an Egyptian pharaoh). His daughter was named Amelia Halle Ethiope. Katy also— apparently with no rancor and little, if any, fuss—accommodated herself most agreeably and generously to her husband's driving necessity to be a Moses for his people. By all the available testimony, Delany was an able and respected practitioner of the medicine of his day. He was considered, that is, a skillful cupper and bleeder. Supporting his family, therefore, should have presented no problem to him, except that his crusading, with all of its speechmaking, its traveling here and there, and its involvement in many projects, sorely divided his time. With her needle Katy supplemented the family income. She thus provided Delany with almost as much latitude to pursue the ends of altruism as if he had been born a member of a solvent leisure class. The newspaper he began was known as the *Mystery*. He devoted four years of his life to it. Then he met Frederick Douglass. When Douglass launched the *North Star*, Delany abandoned the *Mystery*, accepting an assignment to travel in the interest of the *North Star*.

In 1850, however, Delany spent a term, all that was allowed for him against objections to his color, at the Harvard Medical School. The 1850s were anything but halcyon for American Negroes. The decade was ushered in by the Compromise of 1850 with its harsh Fugitive Slave Act. Voluntary colonization on the part of Negroes now seemed to Delany an obvious imperative. He wrote and published, in 1852, *The Condition, Elevation, Emigration, and Destiny of the Colored People of the United States Politically Considered,* a treatise which expounded his conclusions about the futility, for the American Negro, of not emigrating. He initiated and played a leading role in the National Emigration Convention held in Cleveland in August, 1854. He became president of the national board of commissioners which emerged from that convention. In 1856 he moved his family from Pittsburgh to the town of Chatham in Canada. Looking further, and operating in the interest of the commissioners, in 1859 he went to Africa. A portion of *Blake* was published serially in 1859 in the monthly *Anglo-African Magazine,* before he went to Africa. This portion and the remainder of the novel appeared serially, after his return, in 1861 and 1862 in the *Weekly Anglo-African,* the successor to the *Anglo-African Magazine.*

Delany remained in Africa for the better part of ten months. He saw the old Guinea Coast of the lushest of slave-trading days from Liberia to the fabled Bight of Benin. He was accompanied from Liberia by a young West Indian black, a teacher in Philadelphia, one Robert Campbell. But Campbell was far from the ideal returning African that Delany was. Campbell looked too Portuguese. In Africa, Delany, of whom a white newspaper once observed that he was as "black as the blackest . . . with a bald sleek head, which shines," was lionized. He did seem of the purest African stock. Then, too, Frederick Douglass once declared also that Delany was endowed with a voice "which when exerted to the full capacity might cause a whole troop of African Tigers to stand and tremble."[2] His reception by the Africans could hardly have been improved upon by trembling tigers. The Yoruba country in Nigeria attracted him most. There he negotiated a treaty, at Abbeokuta, with eight African chiefs. Coming circuitously home through the British Isles, where he delivered addresses as far north as Scotland, and bursting with newly intensified hope and optimism, Delany was again in Chatham by the new year of 1861. But 1861 witnessed the beginning of the Civil War. Delany and

2. *Xenia Sentinel,* quoted in Victor Ullman, *Martin R. Delany: The Beginnings of Black Nationalism* (Boston, 1971), 302; *Douglass' Monthly* (August, 1862), quoted in Ullman, *Martin R. Delany,* 259.

Campbell would issue accounts of their African experience, Delany in the *Official Report of the Niger Valley Exploring Party*. Even so, his emigration schemes were never to come to fruition. Greater events had obtruded.

After the signing of the Emancipation Proclamation, Delany helped recruit Negro soldiers for the Union Army. His oldest son joined the 54th Massachusetts. Moving his family back to the United States, he settled them at Wilberforce, less than four miles from Xenia, Ohio. For the rest of their lives, the Delanys were associated with the rather tight little island around Wilberforce University. Early in 1865, however, following an interview with President Lincoln, who cited him to Secretary of War Stanton as "this most extraordinary and intelligent black man," Delany was commissioned as a major of infantry in the army and, with a tumultuous farewell from the school at Wilberforce, proceeded south to South Carolina. Wilberforce for him became, thereafter, the port of origin which he infrequently visited.

South Carolina became now the main arena where the action of Delany's final score of years occurred. He was in South Carolina when Lincoln was shot. He was not mustered out of the army until 1868. Most of his time in uniform he served the Freedmen's Bureau as a subassistant commissioner whose particular wards were the liberated Negroes of the Sea Islands. He lived, after his mustering out, largely in Charleston, where from 1875 until 1879 he was a trial justice. His last newspaper was the Charleston *Independent*, which he kept afloat for four months in 1875. In Charleston also for a while, not too successfully, he tried his hand at business, at selling and handling real estate.

From Charleston Delany watched the whole tragicomedy of Reconstruction. He had some ideas of his own about the South. He preached for a while the gospel of a triple alliance, northern capital, southern land, and Negro labor, to bring about a new day in a "new" South. But his evangelist's exhortations were accorded little, if any, attention or respect. He had been a good subassistant commissioner for the Negroes of the Sea Islands. He had championed their rights and saved them from some of the ranker skulduggery of the times. When some of them, along with other Negroes in South Carolina, evinced an interest in emigration, he resurrected his old dream and as much of his old fire as he could summon and exerted himself in their behalf. They formed a sort of corporation, the Liberian Exodus Joint Steam Ship Company. Delany was a member of the board of directors. They obtained a ship, the *Azor*. One shipload of them got to Africa. But that was all. The *Azor* vanished for obligations which its white captain should never have incurred. Litigation hastened the disappearance of any other tangible assets which might have helped to make this back-to-Africa movement a success.

Meanwhile, as long as Delany was in South Carolina, he was in a vortex of the political strife and intrigue, as well as dishonesty, terrorism, and some heroics, which marked the era of Andrew Johnson, Grant, and Hayes. Moreover, Delany was supremely a political animal. He had been physician, editor, lecturer, author, traveler, quasi-anthropologist and pseudopolitical economist, explorer, diplomat without a porfolio, military officer, civil servant, businessman, and judge. Yet it was undoubtedly politics which should have been his métier. He was born for it, as much as Daniel Webster, Winston Churchill, Tom Mboya, or Mao Tse-tung. Yet surely fate exposed him to a most excruciating titillation in South Carolina. Of the twenty-two Negroes who went to Congress during Reconstruction, eight came from that state. South Carolina did not ever have a Negro governor. But during Reconstruction it did elect Negroes to other of its state offices and to offices on the local level. Delany never won a political contest. He entered the lists. He always lost. He sought a ministerial appointment from the president. That, too, escaped his grasp. Late in 1884, at long last he wended his way back to Wilberforce. He had published his final gesture as an author, *Principia of Ethnology: The Origin of Races with an Archeological Compendium of Ethiopian and Egyptian Civilization*, in 1879. Early in 1885 he was dead.

As it can, and must, be said of the author of *Clotel*, so it can, and must, be said of the author of *Blake*. Both were remarkable men who led remarkable lives. But whether either should have ever attempted to write a novel is at least an issue subject to debate. Storytellers are apparently born. And neither Brown nor Delany seems to have possessed a native aptitude for fiction. Probably, also, Delany had even less of an innate gift for novel writing than Brown. He apparently not only had fewer narrative skills. He also was apparently unable to divest himself of a congenital weakness for florid phrases and cloudy statements which made of his style a thoroughly impossible instrument for fiction. *Blake* is difficult enough to read as a succession of incidents. There are literally moments in it when the most sympathetic reader might well not be confident of what is happening, or why. But as distressing as are these moments, with their obscurities of empirical detail and their flickering inanities of character portrayal, even more distressing, surely, are the moments in *Blake* when the major problem is simply and inescapably the manner in which De-lany tortures the mere basic business of utterance. He can be guilty, for instance, of a passage like the following: "The frequent coming together in general council formed attachments, doubtless, but little thought of previous to the occasion which induced their meeting. The consumma-tion of conjugal union is the best security for political relations, and he who is incapable of negotiating to promote his own personal require-ments might not be trustworthy as the agent of another's interest; and the fitness for individuals for positions of public import, may not be mis-judged by their doings in the private affairs of life."[3]

And such a passage is hardly an exception with Delany. It was his way with prose, at least in *Blake*. The overarching theme of Blake does arouse the imagination. It would be wonderful to find a man who could energize and ennoble slaves and lead them to set themselves free. This would be opposition to tyranny in a most appropriate form, and such a theme has never suffered from lack of appeal. In *Blake* it suffers from an author's wretchedness as a writer. Earnestness, indeed, is *Blake*'s long suit. Its au-thor has as much of a sense of mission as its protagonist. And, after all, *Blake* is of enduring interest in the world of the Negro novel. It does merit remembrance, if only because it is the first expression in fiction of an uncompromising black militancy. It lives then, and should so con-tinue, as a historic moment in Negro fiction. It cannot live as a great work of art.

How *Blake* ends we are not now really in a position to say. We are largely indebted to Floyd J. Miller for a reconstruction of its history of publication. According to Miller's authoritative statement, approxi-mately eighty chapters make up the complete novel. As we have already partially indicated, Chapters 1–23 and 29–31 appeared in the *Anglo-African Magazine* between January and July of 1859. The novel in its en-tirety was apparently published in the *Weekly Anglo-African* from No-vember 26, 1861, until late May, 1862, but the last six chapters of this publication have yet to be recovered. Earlier respected commentators on *Blake*, it is clear, were acquainted solely with the fragment of the novel available in the *Anglo-African Magazine*. Thus, Vernon Loggins, after re-ferring to this fragment, ventures the opinion that "no more of the story ever saw print." Hugh Gloster restricts his "fragmentary 'Blake, or the Huts of America'" to these same installments in the *Anglo-African Maga-*

3. Martin R. Delany, *Blake; or, The Huts of America,* ed. Floyd J. Miller (Boston, 1970), 275.

zine. Robert Bone, however, does attribute eighty chapters to the novel, although he specifies the survival of only the twenty-six chapters found in the *Anglo-African Magazine* and deals with the novel, therefore, on the same basis of its fragmentation as do Loggins and Gloster.[4]

Hence, it can be seen that most of *Blake* was not known to these earlier commentators. It can also be suspected that a true reconstruction of *Blake*'s composition might alter the assumption that Delany interrupted the publication of *Blake* primarily, if not solely, because of his absence from America and the consequent impracticability of his supervision of its printing. For there are passages in the chapters of *Blake* published only in the later *Weekly Anglo-African* which certainly can be explained as reflections of Delany's visit to Africa. Yet the title of *Blake* was always *Blake*. It is so that the novel is entitled both in the *Anglo-African Magazine* and the *Weekly Anglo-African*, although Blake is known only as Henry Holland in the *Anglo-African Magazine* and the circumstances of his christening with the Spanish name which he anglicized to Blake are not revealed until the story has proceeded far into the chapters serialized solely in the *Weekly Anglo-African*. Further contradicting any theory that *Blake*'s composition was materially altered by Delany's personal experience of Africa may well also be *Blake*'s one-page first chapter. Therein are plot suggestions compatible with Blake's travels abroad—travels which enter the story only in the serialization in the *Weekly Anglo-African*.

Blake opens in Baltimore, where a group of gentlemen, American and Cuban, are arranging for the operation of a vessel which they plan to use in the Atlantic slave trade. One of these gentlemen, a Colonel Stephen Franks, upon his return to his home in Natchez, deems it expedient to sell Maggie, a beautiful slave girl who is the highly treasured personal maid of his wife as well as the spouse of his personal man, Henry. Henry is absent when the sale is made—a sale which sends Maggie to Cuba. When Henry does return, incensed that his wife is gone, he openly defies his master and flees from Natchez. But there is more, much more, to Henry's defiance than merely his sense of personal injury. Henry has long been meditating upon the plight of the American slave. He can conceive no remedy for it other than a general insurrection of the slaves them-

---

4. *Ibid.*, ix; Vernon Loggins, *The Negro Author: His Development in America to 1900* (New York, 1931), 185; Hugh M. Gloster, *Negro Voices in American Fiction* (Chapel Hill, 1948), 27–28; Robert A. Bone, *The Negro Novel in America* (1958; rev. ed. New Haven, 1965), 30. Bone repeats himself precisely here in his revised edition.

selves. He forsakes Natchez, therefore, determined not only to recover his wife but also to develop a nationwide organization among slaves which will expedite an insurrection. Before he leaves, he takes into his confidence two fellow slaves to whom he imparts the details of his plan.

Henry's odyssey carries him first to Louisiana and Texas. He visits the Chickasaw and Choctaw Indians in what is now Oklahoma. He arrives in New Orleans during the Mardi Gras season. Turning east, he travels to Mobile and, from Mobile, through Georgia into the Carolinas. In the Dismal Swamp he talks with survivors of Nat Turner's rebellion, meets the High Conjurors of the Swamp, and is inducted by them into their secret brotherhood as a High Conjuror. After months of missionary effort, he returns to Natchez, by way of Virginia, Kentucky, and Tennessee, satisfied that he has laid the necessary foundations for his insurrection. He tarries in the vicinity of Natchez only long enough to gather quietly a group of fugitives that he shepherds north to Canada, and he tarries in Canada, to which his son, a boy, has already been spirited, only long enough to see these fugitives comfortably disposed.

Off again, Henry makes his way to Cuba and there recovers his wife, who has been physically abused almost beyond recognition by a planter committed to wreaking vengeance upon her because of her refusal to become his concubine. Henry gives her money by which, availing herself of Cuban law, she purchases her freedom. It is now disclosed that Henry is of Cuban origin. His father, a free black Cuban, is a man of property and standing. Henry has returned to Cuba as Gilbert Hopewell, but his true name is Carolus Henrico Blacus. The poet Plácido is his cousin. The two were boys together. They were separated when Henry went to sea on a vessel which he supposed was a Spanish ship of war. It was not. Actually a slaver in disguise, it bore Henry, with its crew, to Africa, where it secured the cargo of slaves it was seeking, and conveyed that cargo to America. Henry, who had incurred the ill will of the captain of the vessel, was illegally sold at Key West to Colonel Franks.

Reunited now with his wife, Henry, however, leaves her temporarily. He has reestablished his bonds with Plácido and his father. He intends, as does Plácido, that Cuba's slaves shall be free (the real Plácido was executed in 1844; this story is set in the 1850s). And so he goes again to Africa, as the sailing master of the very ship owned by Colonel Franks and other members of the cabal to which the colonel had attached himself in Baltimore. This ship also secures the cargo of slaves that it seeks, in a lagoon that, except for its location, could be the famous hideaway of

Pedro Blanco. It returns safely to Cuba, with its cargo, despite a blood-curdling chase by warships of the antislavery patrol and a terrifying storm in the Atlantic. But it has been arranged that its cargo will be unobtrusively bought by the blacks in Cuba who are privy to the rebellion which Henry and Plácido, along with others, stealthily are preparing. In the underground organization of these blacks, the Africans will be fresh recruits, dispersed where they may well be able to do the most good. Henry has been made the head, the "General-in-chief of the army of emancipation of the oppressed men and women in Cuba." This army and its supporters are gaining strength and are consulting, but have not struck an open blow, when the narrative of *Blake* arrives at its presently lost final chapters.

Whether these lost chapters return Henry to America or detain him in Cuba, *Blake*, with all of its gaping deficiencies as a work of art, through the travels of its hero and his insistence upon the abrupt termination of slavery, testifies to the fact that Delany was no child at recognizing and defining the great public issue for Americans in the days of his prime. In the 1850s, for Americans Cuba was not irrelevant. The cotton-growing, slaveholding South had become a system that could not stand still. At least so it seemed to itself. It constantly sought more land for its agrarian "Greek democracy" and its "peculiar institution." The Missouri Compromise was a concession to it. Conciliatory gestures toward it, likewise, were the annexation of Texas, the Compromise of 1850, and the Kansas-Nebraska Act. There were even those among its fanatic fringe who dreamed of a slave empire, one single vast hegemony, that would encompass Cuba, Central America, and, perhaps, the whole Western Hemisphere itself. To such dreamers Roger Taney gave some encouragement and a rationalizer's version of anthropological truth in his particular contribution to the nine separate opinions which the Supreme Court issued on Dred Scott. Negroes, pontificated the eighty-year-old jurist, were "beings of an inferior order . . . altogether unfit to associate with the white race, either in social or political relations; and so far inferior that they had no rights which the white man was bound to respect."

Blake contains more than its share of puerile passages, and one would-be historian of Negro literature has categorized early Negro writers as men of small minds.[5] But *Blake* lacks art, not mind. There was, and is, nothing small about Delany's grasp of the realities which meant much to

<hr/>

5. David Littlejohn, *Black on White: A Critical Survey of Writing by American Negroes* (New York, 1966), 3.

his circumstances as a Negro in America in the 1850s. And into *Blake* he carried his perception of those realities, the largeness of his vision of them. What he could not carry into *Blake* was what he did not have, the command of those special skills in divination and inspiration which permit a man or woman who may be otherwise not particularly gifted, and even, perhaps, in some ways naïve, to write a piece of fiction that makes both sense and beauty. As a practical man, Delany, in *Blake*, both could and did try mightily to reproduce with a high degree of fidelity the dialect of ordinary, working southern slaves. He saw the connection between such slaves and his thesis of mass insurrection of the Negro. It was important to him that his readers should know that Henry, at home and abroad, in his plotting against the white power structure, solicited the allegiance of all blacks, whether they were relatively privileged creatures within the master's mansion or driven from dawn to dark as brutes in the master's fields. And it was just as important to Delany that his readers should perceive the enormity of the power structure against which Henry hoped to launch his defiance. It was not a power structure that was small or weak, nor was it given, by the 1850s, or before, to thinking in small terms. It had had its effect, a great one, on the course of an entire nation. And it did dream, as we have already intimated, vast dreams that were, to it, not beyond the bounds of possibility.

Delany was not thinking with a petty mind when he contemplated the proportions and the threat of that power structure. And it can at least be argued that he was not thinking pettily when he conceived his novel. The lesson of *Blake*, as of *Clotel*—for we know more of Delany and Brown than we do of Webb or Wilson—is far from necessarily that the author of either was intellectually incompetent, but rather that art and life are not arbitrarily perfect correlations of each other. The early Negro novels are as they are not so much, it would really seem, because they were written by inferior people. It is hardly amiss, when one thinks of Brown and Delany, to recall Elizabeth Tudor's boast that, were she set down alone in England with nothing but her shift, she would make her way. Brown and Delany had been set down alone in America against great odds, and they had made their ways. For some things their minds were quite big enough. For others their minds were not. Their novels are as they are because the amateurs in a field who wrote them, though large in life, were interlopers in the world of art.

Before *Blake*'s second and final (and presumably complete) serialization began in the *Weekly Anglo-African,* the Civil War had started. There had been the irrevocable shots at Sumter and the trooping of levies and volunteers to the standards of two separate nations, and the North had suffered the disaster of the first battle of Bull Run. Before the serialization ended, Grant and Sherman, although at first only obscure lesser generals, had already appeared in the West. In February, 1862, Grant had captured, in Tennessee, Fort Henry and Fort Donelson. It was, indeed, to the Confederate commander of Fort Donelson that Grant had sent his famous ultimatum: "No terms except an unconditional and immediate surrender can be accepted." In April, Grant had fought at Shiloh, where, in the merciless slaughter, a truly leading light of the Confederacy, Albert Sidney Johnston, had lost his life. But Grant had moved on from Shiloh. Vicksburg, after siege, would fall to him on the day after, in the summer of 1863, in faraway Pennsylvania the lines in blue would be holding at Gettysburg. Then Grant would go east, after Chattanooga, to take charge of all of the Union armies. While Grant hammered at Lee in Virginia, Sherman would be marching to the sea through Georgia. And it would all end, or nearly end, at Appomattox, in a simple ceremony on a spring morning within the McLean House near Lynchburg. But that ceremony could be so simple only because, its two principal characters being who and what they were, it was deliberately austere. It chose to dissemble the magnitude of the social cataclysm which it terminated. A half a million men either did or would owe their deaths to the Civil War. Three million men fought in its four years of bitter strife. Many of these men would never forget its impact on their lives. Nor would millions of other Americans who did not take up arms forget the war. It was by far the most stirring single event of a century full of stirring events. Moreover, it was even more stirring to Negroes than it was to whites. It ended slavery.

Yet the war was not to be remembered very impressively in the Negro novel. Indeed, when one considers what the Civil War meant to Negroes, it is almost (although not quite) in the Negro novel as if the war never happened. And this is, incidentally, not, as it may once have seemed, because for some time after the war Negroes wrote no novels. Benjamin Brawley, Vernon Loggins, J. Saunders Redding, Sterling Brown, Hugh Gloster, and Robert Bone, who have been, until very recently, altogether appropriately, the readiest sources to whom students have tended to turn for information about the Negro novel in its earlier phases, all speak of William Wells Brown, Delany, and Webb. Loggins, furthermore, does discuss at length a prose work, too long to be short fiction, by one Lorenzo D. Blackson (we will speak more of this work later), which he never categorizes by so definite a label as that of novel, and Bone does mention, as a novel, James H. W. Howard's *Bond and Free*. But, except for these two instances, all of the early commentators on the Negro novel leave a barren ground after *Clotel, The Garies and Their Friends,* and *Blake,* of about thirty years.

From *Blake,* and the American editions of *Clotel,* these commentators pass almost without interruption to the 1890s, to novels written by Frances Ellen Watkins Harper and by the two male partners who collaborated under the female-sounding pseudonym Sanda.[6] The accounts of these commentators, of course, were prepared under conditions over which they had little, if any, control. They achieved what they could in a period of scant support for activity connected with Negro literature. Now, with much more support forthcoming for such activity, bibliographers list some dozen novels, and two novelettes, before Charles W. Chesnutt and Dunbar, although subsequent to *Blake,* which are not mentioned in pioneering studies of Negro novels. These are novels written when the Civil War was still a living memory to many, if not most, adult Americans. Over 180,000 Negroes had served in the Union army during the war (well into the twentieth century, a favorite "rhetorical" before black audiences would be Paul Laurence Dunbar's poem "The Colored Soldiers"). Another 30,000, in round numbers, had served in the Union navy. A few, incidentally, had worn, or tried to wear, Confederate gray. And Negroes who did not engage in the battles of the Civil War experienced it deeply and in a way that could be called a Negro way. Indeed, for all the talk, sincere as it often was, of fighting to preserve the Union, and the nobility of the Gettysburg Address (which never mentions slaves), the Civil War could be called a war to free the blacks. Yet actual fighting in the Civil War appears, until the mid-twentieth century, in the Negro novel only, as we shall see, in Frances Ellen Watkins Harper's *Iola Leroy* and, as we have already suggested, in the last *Clotelle,* where women dominate the scene. Moreover, there has never been, unless (very questionably) in Margaret Walker's *Jubilee,* published in 1965,

6. See especially Benjamin Brawley, *The Negro in Literature and Art in the United States* (3rd ed.; New York, 1929), *Early Negro American Writers* (Chapel Hill, 1935), and *The Negro Genius* (New York, 1937); Loggins, *The Negro Author;* J. Saunders Redding, *To Make a Poet Black* (Chapel Hill,

a Negro novel in which the center of action is the Civil War, and no great character in Negro fiction is significant primarily because of his association with the war.

1939); Sterling Brown, *The Negro in American Fiction* (Washington, D.C., 1937); Gloster, *Negro Voices in American Fiction;* and Bone, *The Negro Novel.*

18. A Beginning Ends

In 1862 there did appear a Negro novel, if the appellation is correct, which, while not a novel about the war, is a novel about secession. Written by James Roberts Gilmore under the pseudonym of Edmund Kirke, it bears the title *Among the Pines: or, South in Secession-Time.* A first-person narrative, it represents itself as "not a work of fiction" but "a record of facts," and Edmund Kirke, the "I" of the narrative, as a white man, an antiabolitionist northern Whig, and, indeed, a self-supposed southern sympathizer, who merely happens to be in South Carolina during Christmas week of 1860.[1] He also happens, during this very week, to decide to redeem a pledge which he had earlier made to a South Carolina aristocrat of large means whom he once met in the course of some of his earlier travels. This aristocrat, one Colonel J———, is neither a rice grower nor a cultivator of cotton. A holder of many acres, he resides in the extreme northeast corner of the state, just below the North Carolina line. His extensive domain is thick with pines, from which he, and the nearly three hundred slaves who are his property, extract turpentine and resin. Edmund Kirke and the colonel, thrown together by chance first in Florida, had discovered in each other congenial tastes and temperaments. This colonel had enjoined upon his northern friend the commandment never to come near his residence without visiting it. When Kirke's pursuit of business carries him to Charleston and leaves him there, his mission finished, with some leisure on his hands, he remembers the colonel,

1. James Roberts Gilmore, *Among the Pines: or, South in Secession-Time* (1862; rpr. Miami, 1969), 303.

the colonel's invitation, and his own equally cordial response to it. He sets out for the colonel's part of South Carolina.

Little fault can be found with the manner in which Gilmore feigns his role of Edmund Kirke. We know next to nothing about Gilmore. A statement preceding the text of *Among the Pines* announces "A New Work" of his "Descriptive of Southern Social Life . . . in course of publication" in a periodical given as the *Continental Monthly*. Apparently this "New Work" was being published serially in 1862. Apparently, also, Gilmore lived, or could be reached, in New York City. He may, indeed, have been connected with the *Continental Monthly* and may even have been its publisher. At least he offers as his address the same address as that of the magazine. But confirmation of his true identity and the accumulation of data about his life which would, for instance, settle conclusively whether he was actually from the North or from the South await, it seems, further research. Assuming, however, that the bibliographers who call him black are correct, perhaps the first virtue to be remarked in *Among the Pines* is, as already intimated, that its masquerade does not betray its author's color.[2] A white northern Whig could have written it. Neither its tone nor its style is incompatible with a tone or a style which could have been used, in 1860, by a Yankee who believed in the Union but did not necessarily abominate the South, even if that Yankee was doing precisely what Edmund Kirke purports to be doing in *Among the Pines*.

There are, incidentally, in *Among the Pines* literary echoes. One of them may be traced back to Addison and Steele, to the kind of observation of men and manners for which the *Spectator* is a model. Another links *Among the Pines* to a very American phenomenon, the southwestern humor of Augustus Baldwin Longstreet's *Georgia Scenes*, William Tappan Thompson's Major Jones, J. J. Hooper's Simon Suggs, Joseph A. Baldwin's *Flush Times of Alabama and Mississippi*, and George Washington Harris' Sut Lovingood. Still another recalls John Pendleton Kennedy's *Swallow Barn*. En route to the colonel's pines, for instance, through other growths of pine, all of which give the novel its name, Kirke is forced by an evening storm to spend a night in the filthy cabin of some poor-white clayeaters. And as the colonel's protégé he attends a barbecue and speaking where the white folk of the pinelands disport themselves.

2. Among these bibliographers is Robert A Corrigan, "Afro-American Fiction: A Checklist, 1853–1970," *Midcontinent American Studies Journal*, XI (Fall, 1970), 123.

Neither episode would be out of place as southwestern humor. Yet the general air of *Among the Pines* much resembles that of *Swallow Barn*. Kirke is not blood kin to the colonel as Kennedy was to the pedigreed owners of Swallow Barn, on the James River below Richmond, but he is the kind of friend who can be treated as a relative, and even as a relative in a family the members of which were brought up to be clannish. Gilmore's eye for character and setting, moreover, lead to the same episodic form of a long story as that in *Swallow Barn*. He is not as urbane as Kennedy, not so much the gentle satirist as Horace, whom Kennedy had read and may have consciously been emulating. But he is urbane enough not openly to seem a writer of protest who must be black. In fact, he is urbane enough and good enough at putting his material into the form he imparts to it for *Among the Pines* to constitute a minor landmark in the Negro novel. Not until Chesnutt does he, in the Negro novel—if, to repeat, for added emphasis, he was a Negro—have an equal.

Gilmore's Kirke leaves Charleston by boat. He spends a night at an inn. His description of the inn, where vermin will not let him sleep, smacks of southwestern humor in its wriest mood. The next morning he hires a Newark buggy and a gray and finds a Negro driver to take him on to the colonel's home. What he sees during his holiday, the people and the animals he encounters (including half-wild hogs that can outrun the fleetest of the colonel's horses), his constant gleanings from the natives which tell him of their lives and the tension of the times, and the discoveries he makes about the colonel and the colonel's Negroes are all grist to his mill. He interjects a thread of plot through the colonel's low-bred overseer who shotguns to death in cold blood one of the colonel's Negroes, escapes, is caught and whipped, and then escapes again. He creates some scenes that linger in the memory, not the least of them the night burying of the slain Negro's wife and child, drowned by the wife to rejoin her husband. In the home of one small planter and his wife, both God-fearing and genuinely humane, and neither an aristocrat, he finds a demi-eden. This planter keeps slaves who are in bondage in name only. His slave children read. One of them is something of a prodigy. And no one in this planter's household has any mistaken notions about the blessings slavery confers on anybody.

All in all, Kirke, who obviously considers himself no fanatic for either North or South, spends an edifying week in the pinelands. He gathers local color. *Among the Pines* must be reckoned, in addition to its other virtues, as a contribution to American regionalism. But Kirke also ac-

quires a complex of feeling which is well represented in a passionate outburst made to him by the Negro driver who has conducted him to the
pinelands. Says this driver:

> You kin tell dem folks up thar, whar you lib, massa, dat we' not like brutes, as
> dey tink we is. Dat we's got souls, an' tellingence, an feelin's, an' am men like
> demselfs. You kin tell 'em, too, massa,—'case you's edication, and sic kin talk—
> how de pore wite man 'am kep' down har; how he'm ragged, an' starvin', an' ob
> no account, 'case de brack man am a slave. How der chil'ren can't get no
> schulein', how eben de grow'd up ones doan't know nuffin—not even so much
> as de pore brack slave, 'case de 'stockracy wan't dar votes, and cudn't get 'em ef
> dey 'low'd em larning. Ef your folks know'd all de truf'h—ef dey know'd how
> both de brack an' de pore wite man am on de groun'm and can't git up, ob dem-
> selfs—dey'd do suffin—dey'd break de Constertution—dey'd do suffin' ter
> help us.[3]

Among the Pines, then, is a novel of purpose. Written at a time of trouble
and national indecision, it advocates northern intervention in the South,
in the best interest, it argues, of both black and white. Nor are all of the
whites to be benefited, it also argues, only in the lower class. We have
alluded to discoveries which Kirke makes about the colonel. The colonel
has a wife and a daughter. They are not at home to greet Kirke when he
visits the colonel. Kirke learns that they are usually absent from the colonel's domain. But the colonel has a housekeeper, a handsome woman of
strong character and benevolent impulses, who is at home—always so—
and whom the colonel's slaves adore. The colonel, basically a kind man,
can be impetuous and irascible. He has his share of aristocratic pride, of
the *orgueil* upon which knights placed a high premium in the days when
knighthood was in flower. He is controlled, however, by this housekeeper, who often rescues him from his own excesses and who really runs
his plantation for him.

It does not occur to Kirke at first who this housekeeper actually is. He
assumes that she is white, and truly only a housekeeper. Bit by bit he
learns the real truth. He learns of the housekeeper's Negro blood, of the
love between her and the colonel, and of her two sons by the colonel,
one of whom is studying in Germany and the other of whom, "Master
Tommy," who is clearly unaware of his Negro blood, is still with his
mother, living within the colonel's house. A final touch is given to
Kirke's education when he accepts the knowledge that Jim, the colonel's

---

3. Gilmore, *Among the Pines*, 301–302.

coachman, is the colonel's brother. Kirke takes, undoubtedly for the first time, a really good look at Jim. He sees that

the likeness between the colonel and Jim was not in their features, for Jim's face was of the unmistakable negro type, and his skin of a hue so dark that it seemed impossible he could be the son of a white man [Kirke afterward learned that Jim's mother was a black of the deepest dye], but it was in their form and general bearing. They had the same closely-knit and sinewy frame, the same erect, elastic step, the same rare blending of good-natured ease and dignity—to which I have already alluded as characteristic of the Colonel—and in the wild burst of passion that accompanied the negro's disclosure of their relationship, I saw the same fierce, unbridled temper, whose outbreaks I had witnessed in my host.[4]

It has been noted that Kirke hires an equipage which conveys him into the pinelands. The driver of that equipage not only makes what seems to be the thematic speech of Among the Pines. He also begins the process of what probably should be regarded as the refinement, concerning whites and blacks (and, hence, secession), of Kirke's sensibilities. This driver is named Scipio, and he is, in spite of the fact that he appears only fitfully in Among the Pines once he and Kirke have reached the colonel's house, certainly the most powerfully realized Negro character in all of early Negro fiction. A native African, he was shipped to America from Cape Lopez. Most slaves in the continental United States had come from farther north, above the terrible Bight of Benin. He was landed in Havana, where he was bought by a Charleston resident who brought him to South Carolina. Kirke spends two days largely alone with Scipio as the two travel into the pinelands. He witnesses evidence of Scipio's influence with the slaves, all of whom, whether they have met Scipio or not, seem to know everything about him and to stand in awe of him. Eventually, indeed, Kirke concludes that Scipio is a leader, if not the leader, in an underground organization of the slaves. He comes to respect Scipio very much.

There are many familiar things in Among the Pines. The colonel's housekeeper is only another of the many tragic mulattoes who abound in lore about the South as it once was. The colonel's double family is nothing new. The squalor of the poor whites of Among the Pines can be found repeatedly in comments, fictional and otherwise, on the antebellum South. So, too, can Kirke's tractarian dialogues with southerners about slavery. Moreover, there is a brief afterword to Among the Pines. In

4. Ibid., 194–95.

it Kirke, as is to be expected, returns to the North and resumes his normal existence, but he does receive news from the pinelands. He learns that the colonel is killed in the early fighting in the Civil War. That places the colonel's housekeeper—who, it turns out, as it always does in such accounts, has not been manumitted—at the mercy of his vengeful wife. The colonel, the colonel's housekeeper, the colonel's wife—even Scipio, the heroic slave, and Kirke, like Gulliver, an *ingénu* traveler and narrator—all relate to stereotypes. Gilmore has created no originals in *Among the Pines*. Yet in Scipio he has made what could have seemed merely old seem, instead, rather new, as well as meaningful and true. He has rescued the colonel, too, from the ignominy of being only a stock figure. He has made the colonel breathe and feel. And thus neither stereotypes nor polemics prevent *Among the Pines* from having the character of fiction.

There is probably at least one more good thing, in *Among the Pines*, to be said for Gilmore's skill. The period that the novel describes did not last long. Lincoln was not elected president until November, 1860. It was really only a few months later that the Civil War began. At some time within that few months, it would appear, Gilmore was forced to compose his novel. Otherwise, of course, it could not have been about what it was about. Perhaps he wrote it at white heat. Certainly, highly topical as it was, as topical as a journalist's hurried draft written against a deadline, he had no opportunity for the vision and revisions, the slow crafting, bestowed upon works of fiction which are brought to fruition only after years of composition. He could not linger over his project—could not write and rewrite or wait, as Flaubert once reported of himself, for the cream to set. He had to complete, and issue, his novel immediately. And yet, under the pressures of precipitancy, as well as of propaganda, he did not do badly at all. It does not necessarily follow that he would have done better had he consumed a million years agonizing over what, in truth, he must have written in almost pell-mell haste. But it does help to know that he could do so well in so short a time.

The Civil War had been over only two years when a Negro novel markedly less topical than *Among the Pines* was published by a native of Delaware, Lorenzo D. Blackson. The work was a prose narrative of between 90,000 and 100,000 words in length, supplemented by approximately 700 lines of verse in rhyming quatrains. It bore as its full title *The Rise and Progress of the Kingdoms of Light and Darkness; or, The Reigns of*

Kings Alpha and Abadon. Its hundreds of lines of verse merely reiterate the narrative, which is already tediously recounted in the thousands of words of prose.

In 1867, especially concerning a work written by a black man, the thought may easily have occurred to many people that any references in such a work to kingdoms of light and darkness could easily be so directed as obviously to apply to the new freedom of the Negro and the partisans of that freedom on one side and to those who took a dim view of the Negro's rights and potentialities on the other. *The Rise and Progress*, that is, could have been as topical as *Among the Pines*. But it is not. It is, in fact, about as near as it can be to the opposite and minimal extreme of interest in the here and now. It deals with final things. The world of eschatology is its world. And with that world it is virtually as preoccupied as St. Augustine's classic *The City of God*. It has St. Augustine's heroes and St. Augustine's villains. Its God is St. Augustine's God, less Catholic, of course, and decidedly less magnificent. Its devil is St. Augustine's devil. And its sense of history is St. Augustine's dialectic, the good bishop of Hippo's insistence on the eternal struggle between saints and sinners that will last until the Second Coming of the Son of Man. For *The Rise and Progress* begins at St. Augustine's beginning and ends at St. Augustine's end while, in between, it fights the same good fight as that which St. Augustine attempts to dramatize in *The City of God*.

In a close paraphrase of Genesis, *The Rise and Progress* opens as God creates the world and places Adam and Eve in the Garden of Eden. Then Satan is introduced to play his role of tempter, even as the story pauses briefly to include an account of the prior war in heaven. Thus, of course, Satan's animus against God and man and his presence in the Garden are explained and motivated. Man falls, and is driven out of Eden. In effect, the remainder of the Old Testament next is summarized. Christ, the Messiah, then joins the family of man and is crucified. His disciples and especially the apostles—mainly Paul—assume on earth the burden of the warfare against the kingdom of darkness. As the centuries pass, the Christian community expands. Within its own ranks, however, it has its own fifth column, the pope and the "Beast," the "Beast" being the Catholic church. But, if only to counter the "Beast," there does arise a special class of true believers, true followers of the kingdom of light and of King Alpha. These, inevitably, are the Protestants—of whom, equally inevitably, none are truer than the Methodists. The author of *The Rise and Progress* is a Methodist divine. In time the millennium will come.

That will be after King Alpha has mounted his milk white charger and gone forth to conquer with an army of flaming warriors. King Alpha and his warriors will capture King Abadon and bind the emperor of darkness with a great chain and shut him up in close confinement for a thousand years.

For the true servants of light who have died long ago, this millennium will constitute a first resurrection. Such servants will rise from the dead and reign with the King of Light throughout the thousand years. Yet, at the end of the millennium, Abadon will be released. He will gather forces, among them Gog and Magog, and attempt to capture the very city of Zion. In so doing he will initiate the last great Armageddon. By means of it, after a clash that can never be in doubt, Abadon will be finally subdued. He will be cast forever into a lake of fire and brimstone. His followers will be cast forever into the same enduring torment. For there will be a judgment. King Alpha, from his great white throne, will separate Abadon's followers from his own. The damned will be damned eternally. But the followers of King Alpha, all now risen from the dead, will form themselves into a mighty phalanx, thousands of miles long and in a host of regiments. They will march to the new Jerusalem, the Celestial City, on its twelve foundations, with its jasper walls and its streets of gold. They will be met by another phalanx coming from the city itself, a phalanx led by Gabriel and Michael. The two phalanxes will mingle and merge. Together they will occupy the city. And there they will all, under the benevolent protection of the King of Light, spend the whole of their eternity. As *The Rise and Progress* promises, "There it will be all sweet and no bitter, all joy and no sorrow, and all pleasure and no pain, for the inhabitants having sown to the Spirit shall of the Spirit reap life everlasting, which will fully repay them for their labor and toil in bringing it to perfection . . . so that they who are blessed to be inhabitants of that blessed world will have no employment but giving and ascribing praise and glory and honor to their King."[5]

It has been said of *The Rise and Progress* that it is the work of an illiterate and that it "is the product of what seems to have been a pure African temperament."[6] Both charges are probably untrue. Blackson in *The Rise and Progress* is not always grammatical, although, when one considers his

5. Lorenzo D. Blackson, *The Rise and Progress of the Kingdoms of Light and Darkness; or, The Reigns of Kings Alpha and Abadon* (1867; rpr., Boston, 1968), 236.
6. Vernon Loggins, *The Negro Author: His Development in America to 1900* (New York, 1931), 305.

penchant for marathon clauses and sentences, his ability usually to avoid disaster in the agreement of his subjects and verbs is little short of miraculous. But it is his grammar that occasionally falters, not his literacy. He was relatively well read in books that, for his time, commanded widespread respect. Nor was he without some schooling. He tells us that he was born in 1817 in Christiana, Delaware, and that his father had been a slave who was set free and who then bought his mother's time. His mother had seven children by his father while she was still a slave. Blackson, however, was born after she was freed, as were three other children of these same two parents. His father must have been a man of unusual strength of character. Blackson has nothing but praise for him and for his mother. Moreover, from what Blackson assures us, the elder Blacksons seem both to have had a profound sense of family and of their obligations to their children. It was they who sent Blackson, in his tender years, to Baltimore, that he might live there with a Negro who could tutor him.

Blackson, consequently, learned his letters in Baltimore, but, even so, all was not well with his situation there. Bringing him home, his parents arranged for him to go to school with the white children of the neighborhood. These little sadists would not let him share a seat with any of them or participate with any of them in the convenience of writing with the aid of a desk. They forced him to kneel on the floor and write on the bench which was his seat. In spite of their machinations and abuse, Blackson seems to have received as much from school as they did. And what he received, as well as what he seems to have added to what he received, bears upon the issue of his "pure" African temperament. For Blackson was undoubtedly a pious orthodox Methodist, as pious as he was orthodox, but also as orthodox as he was pious. He had given himself to the church. Indeed, he would have us believe that the biggest moment of his life was the moment of his conversion, when, as with so many other good Protestants, his dungeon shook and his sins were washed away.

Blackson was, in simpler words, not African, but very much the evangelical American. There are African stories of creation. There are African gods and African religions. None of them appear in *The Rise and Progress. The Rise and Progress* depends, instead, entirely upon the Christian Bible, with particular reference to the early books of the Old Testament, the Gospels, the Pauline epistles, and the Book of Revelation. Its fallen angels recall *Paradise Lost*. Its uses of allegory, as well as some of its appeals to ideology, reflect both Bunyan's *Pilgrim's Progress* and the earlier and medieval *Everyman*. A hodgepodge, like Joseph's coat of many colors, it yet contains not one single allusion which cannot be grounded in an Anglo-American source. By a stroke of luck for those interested in piercing the recesses of Blackson's mind, *The Rise and Progress* is illustrated. It has a frontispiece. But that is only a likeness of Blackson himself, who is undeniably a Negro, although he wears a beard much like Uncle Sam's. The other twelve illustrations in the book, however, correlate with the text. And they show King Alpha, whether as the Father or the Son, looking exactly like a Viking prince. King Abadon and his minions tend to look more like Slavs or Latins. But no one in these illustrations looks like Tchaka, the Bantu warrior, or Tenkamenin, the great ruler of ancient Ghana, or even like an emperor of Ethiopia. One must conclude from these illustrations, as from the text they complement, that Blackson, if pure anything, was culturally pure American.

Perhaps only by sufferance can *The Rise and Progress* be called a novel. Blackson may not even have thought of it as fiction. Clearly it is greatly influenced by his commitment to Methodism and his activities as a minister of his religious faith. Its style, prolix as it is, yet on occasion acquires the movement, the roll and surge and even lilt, of the spoken word, and particularly of the enthusiasm of the Methodist sermon delivered before an audience not only listening but ready to join in the worship they are attending with amens and shouts. We seem to have nothing from Blackson which tells us why he wrote it. He does inform us that a number of years intervened between his writing of the first and second parts (*The Rise and Progress* contains five parts), so that the book may well have been begun before the Civil War. As pious and imitative as it is, it is far from being devoid of race consciousness. In more than one passage, Blackson speaks scathingly of persons who profess to be Christians and yet look down on Negroes. He says enough, indeed, on the subject of race prejudice to justify some conjecture as to his authorial intentions. It could be that his book is not altogether as other-worldly as it seems.

Blackson's references to himself in the personal memoir with which he prefaces *The Rise and Progress* suggest that he may have had something of the crusader, as well as of the pharisee and professional do-gooder, in his nature. Always in his day there was a felt need among the Negro masses to know the Bible story. One of the memories which remained with Booker T. Washington all of his life was his recollection from his childhood of old former slaves who expressed the wish, once they were free, to learn to read the Sacred Scriptures before they died. Both the act of reading as a physical accomplishment and fuller acquaintance with the lore of the Christian faith possessed a supreme value to these simple folk. Blackson may have believed that in *The Rise and Progress* he at least improved the chances of many Negroes for their personal acquisition of a connected picture of the content of the Scriptures along with some summary sense of the history of the Christian church. He may have even thought of his book as a text which literate freedmen could share with their illiterate fellows.

And, if Blackson reasoned so, he might also have reasoned further. Congress and Andrew Johnson were at each other's throat by 1867. The Civil War had not settled the American Negro's fate. It had not really guaranteed his citizenship. It had not brought him suffrage. It had left him still much as he was before the war. A note of reassurance to the freedmen and their champions in 1867 could hardly have been amiss. Whatever the moment delivered in Washington, D.C., or the South, God, Blackson may have wished to say, had his plan—the plan which, in the end of all, would triumph. *The Rise and Progress* called attention to that plan. It argued, in effect, that all was well or would eventually be, in God's good time. Today we would call *The Rise and Progress* the effusion of a gradualist. Gradualist, too, it would seem to have been in 1867. But, perhaps, in 1867, the battle for Negro rights may have seemed desperate enough to Blackson for the reminder that God was still in his heaven and that everything would surely all come right in the end to seem also to him well worth saying. Lifted sights may have been, in 1867, what he thought the Negro needed. Certainly lifted sights, in King Alpha and his conquest of Abadon, is what his *Rise and Progress* intends to give.

There is good reason, however, to observe that *The Rise and Progress* was hardly less remote at its date of publication from the real world which surrounded it than at least one other Negro novel written before the turn of the century. James H. W. Howard's *Bond and Free* was this novel, and although published in 1886, it bears the subtitle "A True Tale of Slave Times." Moreover, whether it is true or not, it is certainly about the days of slavery and not about Negroes, or whites, as they were in its own era. It harks back to the Virginia of *Clotel*, to the age of Webster and Hayne, and to life in, and around, the plantation of a blooded and proud slave-owning family named the Maxwells. Of course, one of the Maxwells has had a tragic-mulatto concubine, Elva, by whom, like the good stereotypic slave master that he is, he has had a child, this child a daughter ravishingly beautiful, a quadroon known as Purcey. It is the fate of a darker-skinned bondsman on a plantation near that of the Maxwells to fall deeply in love with Purcey, and Purcey's fate, malgré this bondsman's color, to fall just as deeply in love with him.

When, moreover, Purcey's owner, scenting a possible increase in his possessions, buys Purcey's lover, the only male in all the world for her, the two slaves are permitted a brilliant wedding, with many of the trappings, except for a legal license, that could have been expected in a plighting of the troth between two members of the class they serve. But Elva, Purcey's mother, lives, as she has lived for years, under the spell of an obsessive and nagging monomania. She is a mortal foe of slavery. The cook in the Maxwell household, she moves through it noiselessly, an unsuspected fury, aware of everything that happens there, eavesdropping on every conversation, witnessing, if it serves her purposes, often from places of concealment, all that the Maxwells say and do. Purcey is not her solitary child. She has had, by a black man, two sons and two other daughters. Her two sons, coaxed and coached by her, escape to Canada, taking three other slaves with them. Yet Purcey, the apple of her eye, remains in bondage. Worse yet, Purcey has had, by her new slave husband, fine fellow though he is, a child, a boy. If Elva could have her way, no more slave children would ever be born.

At last, however, Elva's master and half-brother unwittingly sets in motion the chain of events which leads to Purcey's freedom. Mrs. Maxwell, Maxwell's fretful wife, travels north for her health. Purcey is Mrs. Maxwell's maid. Husband and child notwithstanding, there is nothing that Purcey can do but accompany her mistress. Mistress and maid return to the Maxwell plantation in the very hour that Purcey's husband is departing it, presumably forever. He has been lost in a poker game to one of Maxwell's friends, a Virginia cavalier like Maxwell, although somewhat more dissolute. But with her husband gone—a husband whose farewell message, left for his wife in Elva's keeping, is that he will regain her on free soil—Purcey now listens to her mother's importunities. Enlisting the aid of a poor white girl, Sallie Silvers, whom she teaches to read, and taking her child with her, Purcey steals away, under the friendly cover of a summer night, into the North. Beyond the Potomac, Purcey poses as Silvers' slave while, back in Virginia, Elva dissembles, as long as she can, her daughter's disappearance. At approximately the same time, sold by his new owner to a domestic slave trader, Purcey's husband is trudging mournfully towards the Carolinas in a slave coffle. Even so, all ends happily, except for Elva. She dies as the result of a brutal lashing given her for her complicity in Purcey's escape. But Purcey's husband does eventually flee from his captors. In Canada, after many months, he is reunited with his wife and son.

We have spoken of Scipio of *Among the Pines* as a haunting figure from the early Negro novel. Elva, and Elva alone, perhaps of all the characters in this early body of work, is cut from the same cloth as Scipio. She, too, represents a step beyond the hackneyed automata who clutter the fictive world of which she is a part. She, too, is conceived from a deeper well of inspiration than her fellow characters. Her dark brooding over the affront to human dignity of slavery, and the intense fixation of her thought, which she must not betray to the wrong persons, upon the pressing problem of arranging that at least some of her children will not be forced to live out their lives as she has hers, impart to her a semblance of reality which, for instance, a Clotel or a Blake, as well as virtually all of the other characters of early Negro fiction, do not have. *Bond and Free* is slight as a work of art, although its author, like Frank J. Webb in *The Garies and Their Friends*, Harriet E. Wilson in *Our Nig*, and James Roberts Gilmore in *Among the Pines*, does seem less of an interloper at the enterprise of storytelling than William Wells Brown or Martin Delany or Lorenzo Blackson. Nor is Elva sufficient to redeem *Bond and Free*. The novel repeats a familiar—indeed, a too familiar—story line. We have seen all the denouements before. Its characters, even Elva, are all from a well-worked vintage. And its closing felicities occur in Canada. But by 1880 "Pap" Singleton had already led his Negro Exodusters to Kansas, and migration from the South was a topic which Negro leaders were debating with some heat.

A convenient place to read about "Pap" Singleton, incidentally, is the chapter "Leave a Summer Land Behind," in Arna Bontemps and Jack Conroy's work, *Anyplace but Here*.[7] "Pap" (Benjamin Singleton) was born in Nashville in 1809. Although a trained slave artisan, a carpenter and a cabinet maker, he was sold several times to the Deep South, perhaps because he was a troublemaker. By the 1860s he had run off to the North and was probably active, around Detroit and Windsor, Ontario, in diligent work for the Underground Railroad. After the war "Pap" went back to Tennessee. The mistreatment of Negroes in the South, which increased when President Hayes removed the last of the federal troops, spurred "Pap," a self-styled Moses of his people, to lead an exodus to

7. Arna Bontemps and Jack Conroy, *Anyplace but Here* (New York, 1966), 53–71.

Kansas (thus the "Exodusters"). He thought also of Negro migration to Indiana, Illinois, Africa, and the island of Cyprus.

There was, then, in the 1880s, some feeling that the South was not the ideal habitat for Negroes. Southern Negroes, especially, by then seemed to have lost what few gains they might have been conceded to have made during Reconstruction. These southern Negroes were increasingly subjected to terrorism. Many of them were virtually held as slaves by white men who decreed what labor they should perform—usually the tending of cotton—and sank them into impossible debt by underpaying and overcharging them. None of this picture of the 1880s, it is true, appears in *Bond and Free*. But unless such a picture is taken into account, as admittedly, perhaps, Howard tacitly may have done, *Bond and Free* becomes, in addition to its slightness as a story, only escapist reminiscence. Canada symbolizes nothing, no call to present or future action. And the protest in *Bond and Free* is as difficult to construe in flattering terms as its art.

Howard wrote not only *Bond and Free*. He serialized another novel, *The Color Struggles*, in 1889 and 1890, in a magazine, *Howard's Negro American Magazine*, of which he may well have been the editor, if not also the publisher. It does not seem, however, that *The Color Struggles* was ever published as a book. Neither, apparently, were two other Negro novels of the eighties, both by women, which also apparently may be found only in periodicals. These two novels are Clarissa Thompson's *Treading the Winepress*, a feature of the Boston *Advocate* in 1885 and 1886, and a Mrs. Garrison's *A Ray of Light*, which was published in the *A.M.E. Review* in 1888 and 1889.[8] Another black woman, incidentally, Amelia E. Johnson, authored two novels, *Clarence and Corinne, or God's Way* and *The Hazeley Family*, both of which were published in Philadelphia, *Clarence and Corinne* in 1890 and *The Hazeley Family* in 1894. *Clarence and Corinne* is not a novel about Negroes at all, for its cast of characters is white. Indeed, if one grants to Blackson's *The Rise and Progress* a prerogative to be called black because of its animadversions against race prejudice, then *Clarence and Corinne* becomes the first novel by a Negro writer to concentrate on whites, and not on blacks. Even so *Clarence and Corinne* preceded by only two years the novel *Megda* by Emma Dunham Kelley, who sometimes called herself also by the arch

---

8. The *A.M.E. Review* was an organ of the largest Negro Methodist denomination.

pseudonym Forget-Me-Not. *Megda* presents only one Negro character, the footman of a judge and a very minor figure in the book. All of the other characters in the novel, including Meg Randall, the putative heroine, are unmistakably white. The action of *Megda*, a thin pabulum of genteel posturings, is set, moreover, in a small Massachusetts town where Negroes seem not to reside and racial issues apparently cross no one's mind.

In 1871 Thomas Detter had published a novel, *Nellie Brown, or The Jealous Wife* in San Francisco, where few Negroes could have been at the time. Exactly ten years later, T. T. Purvis' *Hagar, The Singing Maiden* appeared in Philadelphia. Of neither novel is it possible to say anything here except that it is a book about which little is known and virtually nothing has been said. A novel that has received considerable notice is Frances Ellen Watkins Harper's *Iola Leroy, or Shadows Uplifted*, published in 1892. Of Harper's life an account has appeared here earlier.

In 1859, a year before she married, Harper had published in the *Anglo-African Magazine* a short story, "The Two Offers," which may have been the first short story put into print by a Negro author. It has been argued that Frederick Douglass' "The Heroic Slave," published in *Autographs for Freedom* in 1853, antedates "The Two Offers." The argument involves, however, not a question of precedence—1853 clearly came before 1859— but the thornier issue of whether "The Heroic Slave" is a short story. In any case, thirty-three years, or virtually half a lifetime, after "The Two Offers," Harper essayed the novel form. Harper, it will be remembered, was a friend of William Still's. He supplied the introduction to *Iola Leroy*. In this introduction he politely praises Harper for *Iola Leroy*, yet not without what may well be considered a disarming, and revealing, candor. For Still admits to having had some rather large misgivings when he first heard that Harper had decided to undertake her novel. He did not, he makes it clear, want her, through an excursion into a literary form hitherto unattempted by her, to tarnish her good name after a lifetime in which, according to Still, she had become, among those who knew, or knew of, her, a byword for fine achievement. He did not want her to "blunder," to use Still's own term.

The well-wishing but apprehensive Still, it develops, did apparently have some opportunity to allay his perturbations about *Iola Leroy* as it passed through its various stages of composition. He first heard a reading, presumably by Harper, of a goodly portion of the manuscript. It would seem, also, that he later either heard or read additional portions of the novel while it remained a work in progress. At any rate his doubts, again to quote him, were "soon swept away." He ended confident in the worth of *Iola Leroy*, aware of its "grand and ennobling sentiments," and opining that "the thousands of colored Sunday-Schools in the South, [we have already noted the possibility that Lorenzo Blackson, a half a century before *Iola Leroy*, may not have been unmindful of these same Sunday schools] in casting about for an interesting, moral story-book, full of practical lessons, will not be content without 'Iola Leroy, or Shadows Uplifted.'"

Iola Leroy may be all that Still affirms it is for Sunday schools. None of its language should offend a Sabbath scholar's ear, unless the curious patois for "Negro dialect" attributed to the novel's darker blacks sounds unseemly. It even has, also, a quite edifying happy ending wherein a son and long-lost mother are restored to each other and a round of hymeneal exercises unites the right people to their proper mates. But as a novel it is hardly better than *Megda*, which it approaches in both saccharinity and milksop gentility, and it is certainly far less entertaining than *The Garies and Their Friends, Our Nig, Among the Pines*, or even *Bond and Free*. Hugh Gloster said of *Iola Leroy* that it was "almost wholly the product of reading Brown's *Clotelle*," and the influence of the earlier work upon it does seem highly probable, especially if one is careful, as Gloster apparently was, not to confuse *Clotel* with *Clotelle* (the after-the-war episodes in *Iola Leroy* could not have been paralleled in *Clotel*).[9]

Yet *Iola Leroy* seems also the product of Harper's poetry and elocution. Her poetry, we have already declared, was sentimental. So was her elocution, although we have been given to understand that she was not one of those declaimers (some were decidedly athletic) who was extravagant with gesture or with movement about the stage. What she did prize, however, was what she undoubtedly regarded (and esteemed) as access to the human heart. She had shown that she did repeatedly and unmistakably in her poetry as well as in her elocutions, and at the age of sixty-seven, she was hardly, it would seem, to be changed in her attitudes by the mere contingency of the writing of a novel. Her way with words—her banality, her play upon easily aroused emotions, her limited store of images and ideas—had been with her too long for that, as had also her self-appointed status as one of the *unco guid*. Strong similarities link *Iola Leroy* to *Clotelle*. Similarities just as strong link it to Harper's poetry, and

9. Hugh M. Gloster, *Negro Voices in American Fiction* (Chapel Hill, 1948), 30.

to her crusades for abolition and against intemperance. Very little in it links it to the 1890s. Very little in it, furthermore, commends it either to us or to its own day.

The titular heroine of *Iola Leroy* is a paragon of all the virtues (not the least of them a figure and face almost beyond compare) and an octoroon. In North Carolina during the Civil War, Iola is rescued from the custody of a slave owner who has the usual lascivious designs upon her. As a nurse very much in the image of Florence Nightingale, she becomes attached to an invading Union force. An uncle whom she has never known, and who is an escapee from his North Carolina owner, is now soldiering as a commissioned officer with this same force. Iola and her uncle both begin, even while they can only speculate about it, to entertain the notion that they may be kin to each other. After the war their blood relationship is confirmed as, through diligent search, they reassemble their broken family—Iola's mother, Marie Leroy, who was the lawful wife of the now-dead white planter aristocrat, but also doting and devoted husband, Eugene Leroy (the young Marie Leroy had been, incidentally, if possible, a greater paragon of all the virtues than Iola); the once almost legendary mother of Marie and Iola's uncle; and Iola's brother Harry, who, like his and Marie's uncle, looks white but has fought in the Civil War with black troops. All the members of the family acquire a postwar experience of life for Negroes in both the North and the South. All of them finally settle in the South. Iola's uncle, prosperous in business, keeps with him his own mother and Marie. Iola's brother marries a girl who is not light enough to "pass." Both he and his wife have dedicated their lives to teaching freedmen and freedmen's children. Iola, after rejecting a twice-repeated proposal of marriage from a very eligible white New Englander and doctor whom she has met during the war, and whom she respects, does marry a brilliant Negro physician, but her husband, unlike Harry's wife, is as octoroon as she.

When William Wells Brown, a fugitive slave abroad in England, wrote *Clotel*, Frances Ellen Watkins Harper, although even then hardly what anyone might have called only a slip of a girl, was, nevertheless, still in the vigor of the prime of youth. The vigor did not noticeably forsake her over the years, but she was nearly a septuagenarian when she wrote *Iola Leroy*, and it was decidedly a different world which she confronted in 1892 from that which she had known forty years earlier and toward which Brown had directed *Clotel* in 1853. Yet one may well have the rather eerie feeling as he reads *Iola Leroy*, and if he simultaneously reflects upon *Clotel*, that, at some point early in her public career, history, for Harper, must have frozen, as it were, in its tracks. Time must have come, for her, almost to a stop. Understandably, Brown's *Clotel* is what may conveniently be called a plantation novel. It is not that its full sequence of events actually does occur within the confines of a place, or places, like the Byrds' famous Westover in Virginia, or Benjamin Fitzpatrick's Oak Grove in Alabama, or Thomas Smith Dabney's four-thousand-acre Burleigh in Hinds County, Mississippi, but that, not only when it speaks of Peck's Poplar Farm, but everywhere it speaks at all, it is committed to a universe in which virtually everything that happens, all that is done or thought, is shaped by the value system and the behavior patterns of the plantation as a dominant factor in a total culture. And so it is not a disconcerting circumstance that Currer, in *Clotel* at her first introduction, should be living, as she has lived for years, in Richmond, a city rather than a plantation, or that some of the important later action of the novel should be set in that candidate for the most cosmopolitan of old American cities, New Orleans. For, after all, before the war—the Civil War—Richmond and New Orleans were as they were only because a regional culture made them so. The bone and marrow of their difference from Boston or New York were sociopsychological as well as geographic. They belonged to, and could not be separated from, the idea, the ethos, and the way of life of the plantation in the Old South.

But by 1866 Henry Grady, in his famous speech before the New England Society in New York City, had proclaimed a new South. He had spoken of the "Georgia Yankee," and if he had been somewhat too sanguine, if it was still true that much of the South was wedded to a feudal agrarianism and a staple crop, as well as to its own past, or legend of its past, it was even truer that his phrase acknowledged changes in America, and the South in particular, which may well have rendered, even for an artist seeing things against a backdrop of extended time, the fundamental cast of an outer world in *Clotel* obsolete. Yet *Iola Leroy* repeats and seems to accept, although forty years later, in every significant detail, the external environment earlier connected with *Clotel*. *Iola Leroy* clings to the plantation, and to the same plantation as that—an antebellum one—contemporary with the publication of *Clotel*.

Interestingly enough, moreover, *Clotel* and *Iola Leroy* are not singular phenomena. The early Negro novel, indeed, is somewhat remarkable for the extent to which it did arrest itself within the shadow of the antebellum plantation. No element, it may well be argued, counts for more in fiction than fiction's people. The characters of a novel are its basic entities. What they are the novel is. The definitive characters of *Bond and Free* and *Iola Leroy*, like the definitive characters of *Clotel, Blake,* and *Among the Pines,* and even the senior Ellises and the Garies of *The Garies and Their Friends,* all tend to have plantation backgrounds. Moreover, they tend to run to types, to be stock figures. Brooding over all is the tragic mulatto, usually in a woman's dress—Clotel, Blake's wife, Mrs. Garie, Colonel J——'s paramour, Elva and Purcey, Iola Leroy and her kin. But, then, there is, often on the scene in the early Negro novel, the always more or less degenerate white aristocrat, like Horatio Green of *Clotel;* Blake's master, Colonel Franks; Jonathan Maxwell and the judge in *Bond and Free;* several North Carolinians in *Iola Leroy;* and, kindly though they may be, even Mr. Garie, Colonel J—— of *Among the Pines,* and Eugene Leroy (nor should it be forgotten that George Stevens in *The Garies and Their Friends* is half Garie). There is also, in this early novel, the heroic slave, like Blake or Scipio, thought-provoking as it may be to realize that neither Blake, the Haitian, nor Scipio, a native African, easily the two most heroic of the early novel's heroic slaves, is of American birth. And there are also, from *Clotel* through *Iola Leroy,* a collection of assorted plantation types. Elva of *Bond and Free* is only one of the plantation cooks. The overseer on Poplar Farm is only one of the overseers. Mammies, "Topsys," and humble "darky" laborers like Tom Anderson of *Iola Leroy* can be found scattered throughout the early Negro novel. This early Negro novel did, in other words, abound in stock figures. Significantly, it took its shape from, and founded its meanings upon, one tradition—the tradition of the plantocratic South.

It was a novel admittedly not conceived with the same intentions as the fiction of white writers, like Thomas Nelson Page, who also existed as writers within the same tradition, but who glorified the southern past and lamented its demise in exudings of sentiment as rapturously elegiac as would be, at a later time, the finer ruminations of Willa Cather looking back upon another vanished era (in another place) of our common American past. The Pages and their ilk loved what this novel hated, for a prime function—if not the prime function—of this novel was to protest. In his first book J. Saunders Redding called the prose of Harper "frankly propagandic," and then proceeded to repeat Harper's own statement that *Iola Leroy* was written "to awaken in the hearts of our countrymen a stronger sense of justice and a more Christlike humanity on behalf of those whom the fortunes of war threw homeless, ignorant, and poor,

upon the threshold of a new era."[10] Thus Harper may, in her own calculations, have sought to rationalize *Iola Leroy*. The question still remains, however, whether any Negro writing protest after the Civil War
could have served well the cause cited by Harper using such an instrument as the plantation orientation endemic to the early Negro novel.
The question still remains, that is, whether, whatever protest should be,
it should ever be, especially in an obviously futile way, a part of the very
thing against which it purports to protest.

The earliest of the early Negro novels originated in a world we may
find it difficult to reconstruct, a world which tolerated human slavery.
The later of the early Negro novels would be created during the years
when America would finish spanning a continent—the golden spike joining railroad lines from east and west would be driven at Promontory Point
in 1869—and when America would also follow in the wake of its own
breed of kings and barons into the twentieth century. Gone would be any
vestiges of a Jeffersonian agrarianism. Gone, too, would be the dream of a
vast slave empire. The great plains would be freed of Indians and buffalo.
Their places would be taken by cattle and by homesteaders while, farther
west, in the ledges of the Rockies, miners would seek, and find, not
merely gold and silver, but also baser metals like lead and copper, alumi-
num and zinc. Oil, too, would be extracted from the earth, although not
until 1901 would Spindletop in Beaumont shower the Texas earth with
the biggest gusher of all time.

From Europe, moreover, would come hordes of immigrants. Of
76,000,000 Americans in 1900, fully one-third would be immigrants or
their children. The older immigrant strains had been English, Irish,
Scotch, and Germans. Scandinavians now would grow wheat in the
upper reaches of the Louisiana Purchase. From southern and eastern Europe, Italians, Slavs, and Polish and Russian Jews, as well as people from
the Balkans, would pour into the cities of the Atlantic coast and the
growing hinterland metropolises along and beyond the Appalachians.
For America would be becoming citified. In 1900 there would be over
three million New Yorkers, over a million Philadelphians, and a million
Chicagoans, and three other American towns would have attained populations of a half a million or more. On the West Coast, Orientals would
be migrating in from China and Japan. Wheat, corn, and hogs would

---

10. J. Saunders Redding, *To Make a Poet Black* (Chapel Hill, 1939), 10. Harper's statement is
extracted from the note which she appended to the end of *Iola Leroy*.

have become the great export staples of America. Railroads would have supplanted old arteries of trade and travel like the Cumberland Road and the Erie Canal. By 1890, with 170,000 miles of track, America would possess by far the greatest railway network of any country in the world.

Inventions, too, would be transforming, in America, both life and a way of life. The telegraph would seem as nothing beside the telephone. Steel, sewing machines, farm machinery, barbed wire, typewriters, the electric light, premonitions of the horseless carriage—there seemed to be no end of American ingenuity in mines, in factories, on the farm, and even in the home. And climaxing it all, in America, was the human drama of the men—crafty, avaricious, bold, and, some of them, imaginative—who plundered everything and everybody, gobbled up huge land grants from the government, owned the railroads, the ore steamers on the lakes, the belching mills around Pittsburgh, and new towns like Gary, conceived and brought into being the first great corporations, developed finance capitalism, and established the dynasties of today's ruling American families.

It must be an interesting aspect of the early Negro novel that so little—virtually nothing—of this then-new America appears in it. Although at the turn of the twentieth century, of 8,833,994 American Negroes, 7,922,969, or almost 9 out of every 10, still lived in the South, and only 880,771 and 30,254, respectively, resided in the North and the West, while, furthermore, the vast bulk of southern Negroes, approximately 4 out of every 5, were rural residents, it is yet true that the American Negro was a part of the large American picture of his time. Neither Europe nor Asia nor South America—nor, even, Africa—was his home. The domestic hearth for him was America, and had been, for 250 years. He belonged where he was. But, even so, the great paradox of his whole existence was the extreme and bitter degree to which his belonging was a nonbelonging. As American as he was, he existed almost solely in the crevices and dungeons, as it were, of his native land. Judged, then, in terms exclusively aesthetic, the early Negro novel leaves much, far too much, to be desired. Quite differently, viewed through a perspective which refracts the conditions of its authors' lives, the early Negro novel becomes a reliable transcript of a social fact. That America so invisible in the early Negro novel was, after all, the America essentially forbidden to Negroes, the America reserved for whites and seen by Negroes, in W. E. B. Du Bois' famous phrase, only through a veil.

The scientific value of the early Negro novel is no greater than that of all of Negro literature from its beginnings to the turn of the present century. Indeed, if Negro literature as a whole is nothing else, it is Negro history of a peculiarly valid kind. It is also a continuum and, thus, a tradition of significant worth because of its impact upon a group, its actual content, and its age. The novel, however, was the last form of literature to enter this tradition. With the advent of the novel, therefore, the configuration of Negro literature into its major divisions was complete. Autobiography, not too incidentally, was almost the first form of literature essayed by Negro Americans (appropriately enough, considering the history of black Americans), through a slave narrative, the one written by Briton Hammon. Understandably, the slave narrative has not endured indefinitely as an active vehicle for Negro authorship. But elements of it, especially of forms and themes it favored, have been recalled to life by black writers, particularly as the great-grandchildren of the slaves and their offspring have become aware of their racial heritage. Meanwhile, the components of the tradition of Afro-American literature, whether in poetry, fiction, drama, or other forms of belles-lettres, have all been constantly growing. The black writers of the Age of the Abolitionists tended to be hardly, if any, less apprentices at their "dreadful" trade than their forebears of the very first age of Afro-American literature. That is not to say that sometimes—like, for instance, in Douglass' slave narrative—they were not, in what they wrote, artists too good and too important to be dismissed as historic nonentities. Nevertheless, almost surely as a group they signify above all else in the literature of their people a bridge. The developing tradition which they inherited they augmented and passed on. It was not for them to have a renaissance or a golden age. In effect, they were journeymen of letters. But collectively, also, they are a testament to the vitality of the people and the continuum they represent.

Bibliographical Essay

Virtually since its first appearance in 1947, and with good reason, the best-known and most highly regarded history of Negro America has been John Hope Franklin's *From Slavery to Freedom: A History of Negro Americans* (New York, 1947), updatings of which have brought it into the 1980s and the later versions of which are available in paperback. Franklin's virtues as a historian are solid, beginning with a scrupulous concern for fact, even in a field where partisanship has often seemed to rule would-be scholarly pens. Franklin, incidentally, writes well and very readably. Nevertheless, *From Slavery to Freedom* is a big book, almost encyclopedic in size, as it is clearly encyclopedic in its coverage of its subject. It may be used with decided profit and a sense of absolute security merely as a work of reference. Yet it constitutes a narrative which can be absorbing and which certainly invites its attentive perusal in full. With great appropriateness, however, a wide consensus of informed opinion esteems as the father of Negro history the West Virginian Carter Woodson (1875–1950), founder of the Association for the Study of Negro Life and History; the *Journal of Negro History*, of which he was the first editor; and, especially for every Negro with at least a modicum of racial pride, Negro History Week. Sentimental reasons, therefore, if none other, advocate awareness of his revered *The Negro in Our History* (Washington, D.C., 1928). But not for nothing did Woodson (like Franklin, later) earn a doctorate in history from Harvard. Indefatigible and far-ranging in his resurrection of the American Negro's past, Woodson published major studies of the education of the Negro before the Civil War, Negro migration, the Negro church, Negroes in the professions, the Negro's African background, Negro orators, free Negro owners of slaves, and the mind of the Negro as reflected in letters written by Negroes between 1800 and 1860. Such a dedication to one subject could not but manifest some of its zeal in ways almost unfailingly positive in *The Negro in Our History*, which, like *From Slavery to Freedom*, begins in Africa and does not ignore the experiences of transplanted Africans in the Americas outside the United States.

By the very titles of their general histories of black America Franklin and Woodson indicate their inclinations toward an integrated America. Of a disposition similar to theirs in this respect are Benjamin Quarles in *The Negro in the Making of America* (New York, 1964) and J. Saunders Redding in *They Came in Chains: Americans from Africa* (Philadelphia, 1950). Quarles, a distinguished veteran in the writing of black history, places a premium on succinctness, with no appreciable sacrifice of scope or depth, in *The Negro in the Making of America*, possibly as an accommodation to the larger interest, and more diverse audiences, in black studies since the Kennedy-Johnson era. But his volume omits nothing about the Negro's past, including Africa and a Pan-American perspective, to be found in Franklin and Woodson. Redding, as is well known, made his far from inconsiderable reputation much more in the worlds of belles-lettres and literary criticism than in professional historiography. Even so, *They Came in Chains* is no tyro's adventure into the field of serious history but a reliable account, done with adroit dispatch, of Afro-America as it has been until now. Perhaps no other general history of the American Negro quite matches it in vividness.

Of the general histories of the American Negro written by the generation of Negro historians younger than that of Franklin and Quarles, the generation now in its prime, conceivably the most accessible to the greatest number of potential readers is *Before the Mayflower: A History of the Negro in America* (New York, 1962), by Lerone Bennett, Jr., of which reprintings, revised editions, and paperbacks all exist. Bennett, a native Mississippian, attended Morehouse College, where, for three of the four years he spent there, in an intimate environment tremendously affected by the inspirational presidency of Benjamin Mays, he was a fellow undergraduate with Martin Luther King, Jr. King went on, of course, to become world famous and a martyr to the cause of the Negro's civil rights. Bennett became a figure of consequence in journalism, a senior editor of *Ebony*. It was his way, it may well appear, of pursuing best with his abilities the same goals as those of King. *Before the Mayflower,* accordingly, is Negro history consonant with Mississippi's Freedom Summer and the 1963 march on Washington. Objections have been raised to some of its conclusions on the grounds that they are too polemical, if not also sometimes inadequately documented. In some quarters judgments upon its respectability have certainly not been helped by the circumstance that its author is no academician. Even so, Bennett is not prone easily to desert principles of objectivity for propaganda. His highest crime (if crime it is) may be the acuteness of his instinct to protect black history from any defilement or distortion by white racism—not least, from such defilements or distortions in the work of black historians. There may be, in addition, too lavish an anecdotal quality attached to his historiography. But his is history to be enjoyed in the reading. And his appendix to *Before the Mayflower*, "Landmarks and Milestones," with its rapid tour of memorable dates and incidents in Negro history, does provide as effortless an approach to at least a cursory acquaintance with Negro history as may be desired. *Before the Mayflower* also contains a bibliography. The bibliographies of all the histories thus far cited here are worth recognition and examination. All of them, that is to say, represent well-stocked repositories of pertinent directions to excellent materials for further study of the Negro, and none of them are without the power to engender an impulse toward just such an exercise in targeted research.

There are some general histories of the American Negro rather more special than those already named. Benjamin Brawley was born in 1882. Like Redding, he evinced admirably a range of interests as a man of letters in scholarly disciplines although he, too, was, above all, a literary critic. Of his age he was, for Negroes, conspicuously a spokesman, and almost surely fittingly so. Thus the past speaks doubly through him, in the subject matter of his *A Social History of the American Negro* (New York, 1921) and in the fullness of his identification with his own generation of American Negroes. He does attempt to write, as his title proclaims, a social history, and not badly for his time and temperament. He could not, very patently, avail himself of the studies of the Negro by social scientists published after his death, nor was he ever unaffected by his interest in the arts. A whole chapter on Liberia is included in his history. Mary Frances Berry and John W. Blassingame have collaborated on *Long Memory: The Black Experience in America* (New York, 1982). Both are black, and both are far from nonentities either in the field of higher education or in American public life. Blassingame's discipline is history. Berry is trained in the law. *Long Memory* is not history as narrative, but is organized totally as a discussion of themes: Africa and slavery, free Negroes, the black family and the black church, sex and racism, black political participation in America, and so on. It promotes the black perspective of the "black is beautiful" school of the 1960s and 1970s. Warm emotions tend to color it and an argumentative tone to incline it toward occasional departure from the ideal of the neutrally transparent eye. Somewhat in its vein, but more eloquent and a narrative, like, for instance, *They Came in Chains*, is Vincent Harding's *There Is a River: The Black Struggle for Freedom in America* (New York, 1981). But *There Is a River* is also projected as part of a larger work—a history of the black experience in America extended into three volumes. Thus, *There Is a River* ends with slavery only yesterday extinguished, Andrew Johnson in the White House, and the possibilities—and problems—of freedom just beginning to be explored by the former bondsmen of the South. It also ends with a dramatization of the final incidents it portrays, which is characteristic of its several raconteurs' virtuosities throughout its entire presentation.

There Is a River, incidentally, is not the sole single-volume history of black America now existing as a portion of a much more ambitious work in progress.

Philip S. Foner's *History of Black Americans: From Africa to the Emergence of the Cotton Kingdom* (Westport, Conn., 1975) is the first volume of a planned four-volume excursion into Negro history, the next two volumes of which have appeared as *From the Emergence of the Cotton Kingdom to the Eve of the Compromise of 1850* and *From the Compromise of 1850 to the End of the Civil War* (both Westport, Conn., 1983). Foner is white, but a seasoned, accomplished, and respected scholar in the field of black history. His first volume, which transports the American Negro from Jamestown in 1619 (and, really, somewhat before) to the era when, for instance, Americans anxious about their country's future were woefully conscious that sectionalism in the nation they cherished could no longer be safely ignored, is no slight publication, but decidedly a formidable tome some seven hundred pages long. Foner has been one who has burrowed in the black American past and sought, with singular success, a close, detailed, but still abundant knowledge of it. One may choose, obviously, as one will in any exploration of the Negro in American history. Should one choose immersion with saturation, there is Foner of whom to take advantage.

Finally, here, for those with an inclination, great or small, to look behind the histories for instruments of authentication or for parcels of information aperitive to further study, there are at least *A Documentary History of the Negro People in the United States* (Secaucus, N.J., 1962, 1964), in two volumes, edited by Herbert Aptheker; Robert L. Clarke (ed.), *Afro-American History: Sources for Research* (2 vols.; Washington, D.C., 1981); and Dwight L. Smith (ed.), *Afro-American History: A Bibliography* (2 vols.; Santa Barbara, Calif., 1974). An interesting encounter with a variety of ways in which to think about Negro history may be derived from a collection of essays preserved by Darlene Clark Hines (ed.), *The State of Afro-American History: Past, Present, and Future* (Baton Rouge, 1986), in which such universally acknowledged experts in the field of Negro history as John Hope Franklin, Eric Foner, and Eugene Genovese, among others, speak evaluatively of black historiography. And, if only as a meritorious example of an account of Negro history applied to the inspection of a single big issue legitimately connected with both American and Afro-American history, there is, by Eli Ginzberg and A. S. Eichner, *The Troublesome Presence: American Democracy and the Negro* (New York, 1964). Ginzberg and Eichner, white professors at Columbia University, although not historians, wrote, in *The Troublesome Presence*, what they hoped would be (as they themselves say) a history of race relations in America—not quite the same thing, they realized, as a conventional history of black America. They were clearly, in their joint exertions on *The Troublesome Presence*, affected by the interracial climate of America in the 1950s and the 1960s, with its unusual impetus toward a review of the attitudes whites and blacks in America have tended, through a rather protracted cycle of historical eras, to assume toward each other. But *The Troublesome Presence*, while undoubtedly more exposed to pressures from a special historic moment of storm and stress than most scholarly analyses of a complex problem, nevertheless quite manages to retain sufficiently the character it should have, that of a study in the name and spirit of disinterested knowledge, rather than that of an evanescent journalism. Moreover, if there is any propaganda in *The Troublesome Presence* (and there seems to be reasonably little), that propaganda can hardly be defined as brash pamphleteering.

No one, perhaps, should pay any serious attention to Afro-American literature (and thus, if only thus, to Afro-America) without at least some delving, however minimal, in the history of Africa. For laymen, as well as for specialists, Roland Oliver and J. D. Fage's *Short History of Africa* (New York, 1962), with succeeding paperback editions and reprintings, is difficult to surpass in either convenience of access or suitability as a sort of primer on a subject, if pursued into its nooks and crannies, of dauntingly immense dimensions. The early chapters of the *Short History* concentrate on Africa during the Stone Ages and are a distinct departure from the scorn for Africa that lay behind the pictures of the "races of man" once conspicuously displayed in the geography books of elementary-school pupils in America. Oliver and Fage (who are, incidentally, both British) do very well also, without prolixity, in their treatment of history after the Stone Ages in those portions of Africa most likely to be associated with the American Negro's African background. There is no dearth now, however, of competent Africanists who explore every conceivable aspect of Africa, past and present. The also British Basil Davidson's *The Growth of African Civilization: West Africa, 1000–1800* (London, 1965), revised in an Anchor Books edition, and published in 1966 as *A History of West Africa to the Nineteenth Century* with the assistance of the two West Africans F. K. Buah and J. F. Ade Ajayi, performs a valuable service in its provision of knowledge about West Africa before and during the period of the Atlantic slave trade. Its text is liberally supplied with maps, and intent as it is upon sound scholarship, it is yet conditioned by its obvious determination to avoid a racist treatment of the West African past. Of special interest, if only because of its author, may well be W. E. B. Du Bois' *Black Folk, Then and Now* (New York, 1939). Of special interest may also well be Paul E. Lovejoy's *Transformations in Slavery: A History of Slavery in Africa* (Cambridge, Eng., 1983).

Blacks, of course, were introduced into America largely by the Atlantic slave trade. A pair of books about that trade which any reader should find interesting as well as informative are Basil Davidson's *Black Mother: The Years of the African Slave Trade* (London, 1961) and Daniel P. Mannix and Malcolm Cowley's *Black Cargoes: A History of the Atlantic Slave Trade, 1518–1865* (New York, 1962). For the very serious student of the trade, there are, never to be forgotten, the often-cited and widely approved Elizabeth Donnan's *Documents Illustrative of the History of the Slave Trade to America* (4 vols.; Washington, D.C., 1930–35), as its name implies, a source of primary evidence for scholars with questions about the trade, and *Minutes of the Evidence* (4 vols.; London, 1789–91), a report on the slave trade to the House of Commons which is difficult to find in the United States, although microprint copies of it, in whole or in part, are obtainable from London, where they are filed under *British Sessional Papers, 1731–1800, House of Commons, Accounts and Papers, XXVII (1789) to XXXI (1791)*. It is certainly not inappropriate here to note that the prominent English abolitionist Thomas Clarkson compiled a six-hundred-page *Abridgement* of these *Minutes* and, furthering his purpose of making the (in his eyes, at least) distressing human story revealed in the *Minutes* even more available to a general public, in 1791 issued an *Abstract of the Evidence* considerably shorter than his own *Abridgement*. Donnan's *Documents* is somewhat famed among specialists in the study of the Atlantic slave trade for, among other things, its conclusions in the introduction to its third volume about the relationship of New England to the trade in slaves, particularly with reference to the economic importance of that trade to New England and the interdependence of that same trade with a commerce in rum.

To W. E. B. Du Bois' *The Suppression of the African Slave Trade to the United States of America, 1638–1870* (New York, 1896) a goodly measure of the stature of a landmark in its field has now long adhered. This was Du Bois' doctoral dissertation at Harvard but was published as the first volume in Harvard's series of studies in history, a testimonial, certainly of no mean value, to its worth. The fact that it is now virtually a hundred years old should not be held against it. It has stood well the test of time. For able recent accounts of the Atlantic slave trade, however, resort may be had to Herbert S. Klein, *The Middle Passage: Comparative Studies in the Atlantic Slave Trade* (Princeton, N.J., 1978); James A. Rawley, *The Transatlantic Slave Trade: A History* (New York, 1981); and Edward Reynolds, *Stand the Storm: A History of the Atlantic Slave Trade* (London, 1985). The role of England alone in the bringing of blacks from Africa to America is explored in Kenneth G. Davies, *The Royal African Company* (London, 1957). The role of the United States alone in performing the same mission is examined in Peter Duignan and Clarence Clenenden, *The United States and the African Slave Trade* (Palo Alto, Calif., 1963). The first American vessel to bring black slaves to America sailed from New England. Two books which concentrate on New England's participation in the Atlantic slave trade are Jay Coughtry's *The Notorious Triangle: Rhode Island and the African Slave Trade, 1700–1807* (Philadelphia, 1981) and James B. Hedges, *The Browns of Providence Plantation* (Cambridge, Mass., 1968).

Some merit may be inherent in particularized glimpses of the Atlantic slave trade. Rather appropriately, the great Elizabethan freebooter John Hawkins, in what may well be as fortuitous as possible a stroke of chance, stumbled, as it were, into the action which eased England into the slave trade. Hawkins' African voyages are recounted in (of all delightful places!) Richard Hakluyt's *Voyages* (London, 1582), and, indeed, in the third volume thereof. John Newton is known to many for his fame in the history of eighteenth-century pietism (as well as for his connections, hence, with the circle of early Methodists which included

William Cowper). But Newton had had his moments in the slave trade and recorded some of them, as may be discovered from his own reminiscences, in *The Journal of a Slave Trader (John Newton), 1750–1754,* edited with an introduction by B. Martin and M. Spurrell (London, 1962). The readily apparent virtues of listening directly to actual participants in the business of ferrying captured blacks from Africa to America may be further exploited by recourse to Captain William Snelgrave, *A New Account of Some Parts of Guinea, and the Slave Trade* (London, 1734); Alexander Falconbridge, *An Account of the Slave Trade on the Coast of Africa* (London, 1788); and Brantz Mayer (ed.), *Captain Canot, or Twenty Years of an African Slaver* (New York, 1854). Mannix and Cowley concluded, incidentally, that Canot (sometimes Conneau) should be considered more credible than was once thought.

One of the most memorable, telling, and horrible single occurrences connected with the slave trade was the deliberate drowning, in deference to a desire to convert a maritime disaster into a huge cash settlement from insurers, of the entire cargo of a slave ship, the *Zong,* an account of which may be examined in Prince Haar (ed.), *Memoirs of Granville Sharp* (London, 1820). Mungo Park's name tends to appear so often in references to the slave traders and their world (see, for instance, the beginning of E. Franklin Frazier's *The Negro Family in the United States*) that surely advisable is acquaintance with Park's *Travels in the Interior Districts of Africa Performed under the Direction and Patronage of the African Association in the Years 1795, 1796, and 1797* (2nd ed.; London, 1799). The *Amistad* mutiny, like Park's travels or Hawkins' slaving, tends to be one of those items connected with the slave trade about which much (not improperly, it would seem) has been made. An excellent account of the mutiny and its several years of historically important aftermath appears in William A. Owens, *Slave Mutiny* (New York, 1953).

No review of the Atlantic slave trade covers all it should unless it gives some notion of the trade's suppression, in which the British navy took the lead. As unsavory as was the trade, suppressing it was vexatious in more ways than one. Details of a mission illustrative of some of this vexation are rehearsed in Christopher Lloyd, *The Navy and the Slave Trade: The Suppression of the African Slave Trade in the Nineteenth Century* (London, 1949). Cooperation between England and America in ending the slave trade involved joint cruising against the slavers by vessels of the British and American navies. This joint cruising is a matter of major concern in Andrew Hull Foote, *Africa and the American Flag* (New York, 1849). Foote was an American officer whose name is not obscure in American naval history. Two other accounts of the participation of the American navy in the sweeping of the slavers from the sea, both with touches of special interest to them, are the Reverend Charles W. Thomas' *Adventures and Observations on the West Coast of Africa* (New York, 1860) and Horatio Bridges' *Journal of an African Cruiser . . . by an Officer of the United States Navy* (New York,

1845). The Reverend Mr. Thomas was the chaplain of the American squadron engaged in the British-American joint cruising from 1855 until 1857. Bridges' *Journal* was edited by Nathaniel Hawthorne, a friend of Bridges from the days when the two had been fellow students at Bowdoin College (where both had met John Browne Russwurm).

Of all the speculations about the American Negro, perhaps none has generated more concern (not to mention ardor) than the question of how American the Negro is. To some considerable extent answers to this question seem to depend upon the degree of African-ness attributed to Afro-Americans. Cliometrics is brought, with no little fanfare, into the numbers game of the slave trade, which clearly bears upon the Afro-American's African-ness, by Robert Fogel and Stanley Engerman in their *Time on the Cross: The Economics of American Negro Slavery* (2 vols.; Boston, 1974). Statistical data, with accompanying tables, charts, and graphs, are of importance in *Time on the Cross*, where there is argued an overwhelmingly American provenience (and, hence, probably culture) for the American Negro. In Philip D. Curtin's earlier *The Atlantic Slave Trade: A Census* (Madison, Wis., 1969), the same argument, not so noticeably dramatized by the theory and practice of cliometrics, obtains. Herbert Gutman's *Slavery and the Numbers Game: A Critique of Time on the Cross* (Urbana, Ill., 1975) is, as its title indicates, a review (somewhat the reverse of laudatory) of the performance of Fogel and Engerman. Whether anyone hearkening to the now perennial debate over the degree of blackness or whiteness in the American Negro should fail to read E. Franklin Frazier's *The Negro Family in the United States* (Chicago, 1939) is at least debatable. Admittedly, there are other (and probably equally, if not more, pressing) reasons for the student of the American Negro to read *The Negro Family*, to which, therefore, we shall return later. But the famous opening passage of *The Negro Family*, incorporating a borrowing from Mungo Park, powerfully introduces a major contention of the whole book. *The Negro Family*, in a way its readers should find hard to forget, leaves the African family in Africa. Frazier's American Negro family, indeed, is an American institution, its variations in form and function during its American history dictated by American conditions and shaped by American modalities. This is one side of an argument. The other side may be met, and pondered over at some length, in Melville J. Herskovits' *The Myth of the Negro Past* (Boston, 1958), a superbly orchestrated statement, with an almost stunning array of presumably supporting evidence, of the view that Afro-American culture retains a significant volume of African survivals. Herskovits' condensed outline of the myth of the Negro past at the beginning of this book is, incidentally, both good and justly famous. For the record, Frazier, a sociologist, was black; Herskovits, an anthropologist, was white. The bulk of Afro-American literature almost surely inclines, with hardly any qualification, toward Frazier's view. Herskovits, however, is no solitary voice crying unheeded in a wilderness.

Much of the battle about the amount of blackness in America's black people has swirled around black speech. A pioneering work asserting African survivals in Afro-American speech is Lorenzo Dow Turner's *Africanisms in the Gullah Dialect* (Chicago, 1949). Turner, a black scholar, turned to the Gullah speech, with the Africanisms he was sure he detected there, significantly because it represented to him a conveniently spectacular phenomenon preserved startlingly intact from disruption by a more powerful culture, presumably because it had managed to do a fair job of keeping away from that very culture. Claims decidedly greater, however, for a black speech in America may be observed in J. L. Dillard's *Black English: Its History and Usage in the United States* (New York, 1972). Blacks tended to bring with them to America, Dillard avers, an English pidgin which they had acquired in the barracoons and slave factories of the West African Coast. Retention of this pidgin as the basis for a Creole the subsequent decreolization of which has not utterly destroyed its distinctive character accounts, according to *Black English*, for a language among American blacks separate from that of American whites. Scholarly enterprise in support of Herskovits' point of view, the championing of Africanisms in the life of the American Negro, has flourished now in America for many a year. For a sample of such enterprise that does not deal with speech, one may turn, for instance, to William Bascom, *Sixteen Cowries: Yoruba Divination from Africa to the New World* (Bloomington, Ind., 1980). More summary of the whole subject of African survivals in an Afro-American setting is available in Robert G. Weisbord, *Ebony Kinship: Africa, Africans and the Afro-American* (Westport, Conn., 1974).

At some point in any study of the American Negro, or of matters connected with him such as literature, the urge to dwell on him and the "problem" he constitutes in fairly general terms may well become irresistible. The staunchest attempt to satisfy as completely as possible this very urge resides in Gunnar Myrdal, *An American Dilemma: The Negro Problem and Modern Democracy* (2 vols.; New York, 1944). As is well known, many scholars, black and white, assisted the Swedish Myrdal in the preparation of *An American Dilemma*. Time has brought to bear new facts upon some of it. Yet a perhaps sobering amount of it (suggesting, certainly, that too much of the "problem" remains) appears not to have lost its currency. It is far from too late, for example, to read with care its chapters on Negro leadership. To what extent Myrdal's Scandinavian sensitivities (and political liberalism) affect interpretations and conclusions in *An American Dilemma* is, of course, a decision each reader of the volume must make for himself.

Two books not at all as comprehensive in scope as *An American Dilemma*, but of the kind which stir reflections on the whole subject of race and racism despite their concentrations on relatively narrow areas of interest in the American past, are Eric Williams' *Capitalism and Slavery* (Chapel Hill, 1944) and W. J. Cash's *The Mind of the South* (New York, 1941). Williams, a black, came to study in

America from the West Indies, to which he returned for an impressive career, including a prime-ministership. *Capitalism and Slavery*, with admirable poise and no little persuasiveness, develops the thesis that disposable income from the slave trade, largely in the hands of new British tycoons of humble origin, provided the money (or much of it) needed to fund England's industrial revolution. Cash, a white southerner who (at forty-one) committed suicide within a few months of the publication of *The Mind of the South*, in that work treats roughly, despite the beauty of his prose, the notion that the antebellum South was glorified by the presence there of a breed of scintillating aristocrats. Aristocracies, according to Cash, whatever else may be said of them, do not spring up overnight. Cash grants the planters who built the cotton kingdom less than two generations of consolidating their class and their culture before the Civil War. A scion of the South, he mercilessly reveals the absurdity of his South's most prized pretensions. Revisionism has been, since the passing of such white historians as James Ford Rhodes, William Archibald Dunning, James Schouler, and Ulrich B. Phillips (of whom more later), the controlling influence in historiography about the South, America, and the Negro. It can hardly be said of books like *An American Dilemma*, *Capitalism and Slavery*, and *The Mind of the South* that they, above all other possible catalysts, occasioned this revisionism. But they did affect its temper. And they were books which got read and talked about. A true grasp of scholarship in the study of black America demands a knowledge of them.

Obviously race itself, whatever it is, if it is, constitutes a matter of prevailing interest for students of Afro-American literature. No dearth exists of books on the subject. It well may be, however, that no treatment of race excels in amplitude or rationality Thomas F. Gossett's *Race: The History of an Idea in America* (Dallas, 1963). Oliver Cromwell Cox, the black sociologist who was never comfortable with the establishment, working for years, produced the monumental *Caste, Class and Race* (New York, 1948), which may be marred somewhat by a touch of pedantry and ostensible limitations in Cox's knowledge about caste. Indispensable in the present context is Winthrop D. Jordan's *White over Black: The Development of American Attitudes Toward the Negro, 1550–1812* (Chapel Hill, 1968). The "Winthrop" in Jordan's name reflects his descent from the Winthrops of New England birth. *White over Black* confirms his possession of qualities consistent with his ancestry. It is conscientious, in a very good sense of the term, placing its first reliance upon an assortment of evidence directly derived from whites who lived, and revealed their attitudes about blacks, during the years with which *White over Black* is concerned. In effect, George Frederickson's *The Black Image in the White Mind: The Debate on Afro-American Character and Destiny, 1817–1914* (New York, 1971) extends *White over Black* for an additional hundred years. Both books are invaluable for the immediacy of contact they provide with the thought and feeling, the pervasive ideas and emotions, within whites which seem to account to a decisive degree for the strange treatment in America of the American Negro.

Before the end of the 1660s, slavery had become the expected lot for American Negroes. There is merit in not viewing slavery in America solely on its own terms but placing it within perspectives which benefit from their preoccupations with slavery elsewhere. Frank Tannenbaum's *Slave and Citizen: The Negro in the Americas* (New York, 1947) offers good opportunities for extending and multiplying the contexts in which American slavery is considered, as do David Brion Davis' *The Problem of Slavery in Western Culture* (Ithaca, N.Y., 1966) and his *Slavery and Human Progress* (New York, 1984). Respectful comment on Tannenbaum and Davis is sufficient to suggest attentive reading of the work of both. They should be supplemented with an at least equally attentive reading of Gilberto Freyre's *The Masters and the Slaves: A Study in the Development of Brazilian Civilization* (rev. ed.; New York, 1956), which assimilates a clarity and breadth of vision and a copious provision of detail to an engaging compassion for the victims of enslavement in the striking picture it paints of slavery in Brazil. That American slavery looked toward the Caribbean, where Englishmen also, and with an earlier start, were practicing slavery, is a staple of historical scholarship, as is the knowledge that Americans did more than observe black slavery in the Caribbean. They borrowed practices and principles from it. Bryan Edwards' *The History, Civil and Commercial, of the British Colonies in the West Indies* (2 vols.; London, 1793–94) long has been, justifiably, an approved source of information about slavery in the West Indies. Edwards was no traveler to the Caribbean. He lived and cast his fortunes there. A further look at black slavery in the Caribbean may be acquired from acquaintance with Richard B. Sheridan's *Sugar and Slavery: An Economic History of the British West Indies, 1623–1775* (Baltimore, 1974). One may well wonder, perhaps, after reading Edwards and Sheridan (both of whom can be capable raconteurs as well as historians), and waiving moral issues, how much of Caribbean black slavery was suited for importation into America.

Time was, as late as, and throughout, World War II, when the work of Ulrich B. Phillips dominated the history of American slavery. It still, surely, remains desirable and important to read Phillips, although he has now been superseded in his attitude toward Negroes and to some extent discredited in his methods. Hardly less than a Thomas Nelson Page, Phillips perpetuated a tradition, the one that supported the golden legend of an antebellum South which it was a tragedy for the Civil War to end. Phillips established himself magnificently with his *American Negro Slavery* (New York, 1918), to which his *Life and Labor in the Old South* (Boston, 1929) adds a potent postscript with no modification of Phillips' original intent or results in *American Negro Slavery.* Phillips does not equivocate about whites and blacks. His position is simply and absolutely that the two races differ because whites are genetically and culturally superior to all, and any, human creatures of African ancestry. To Phillips slavery in America acted as more of a blessing than a curse on blacks, schooling them in ways which mitigated their savagery. For Phillips is a wishful thinker of anything but feeble commitment to his own interpretations of reality. Nor is his work devoid of solid information about the world which slavery made or the kinds of people who inhabited it. He is an unusually able apologist for the regime he champions, as well as a rather seductive stylist in prose. Surely no serious student of American slavery should leave him unread. To see the South of slavery, incidentally, through the eyes of another highly respected white historian of Phillips' generation who was not quite so entranced as Phillips with Phillips' image of the southern past, one may consult William E. Dodds's *The Cotton Kingdom, a Chronicle of the Old South* (New Haven, 1919). But a picture of slavery which very consciously advances an antidote to Phillips is Kenneth M. Stampp's widely applauded *The Peculiar Institution: Slavery in the Ante-Bellum South* (New York, 1956), an example of revisionism with a vengeance by a scholar whose credentials and talents rank him at least as high in eminence as Phillips.

Critical views of slavery from more or less theme-oriented stances are not difficult to find. One may begin here with black Harvard professor Nathan Irvin Huggins' *Black Odyssey: The Afro-American Ordeal in Slavery* (New York, 1977), a most un-Phillipsian depiction of slavery in which it is not an elevation of savages but an inhumane attitude toward the slave which is cited as slavery's capital distinction. C. Duncan Rice, in *The Rise and Fall of Black Slavery* (1975; rpr. Baton Rouge, 1976), parallels Huggins in his attempt to speak comprehensively and with the supporting documentation of the most recent scholarship to contemporary students of American slavery. But a view of slavery which invoked immediately a genuine furor in academic circles when it appeared is Stanley Elkins' *Slavery: A Problem in American Institutional and Intellectual Life* (Chicago, 1959). Slavery, Elkins contends (using, as he builds his case for the perverse conditioning of a group, references to Nazi concentration camps), developed in the American Negro a "Sambo" personality which lingers as a hardly welcome incubus from the past upon America and the Negro. Stringent evaluations of Elkins' *Slavery* may be found in Ann J. Lane (ed.), *The Debate over Slavery: Stanley Elkins and His Critics* (Urbana, Ill., 1971). And a shift from psychiatry to fields of contemplation wedded more to data-bound research and measurements in solid figures characterizes Paul David *et al.* (with Herbert Gutman among the others) in *Reckoning with Slavery: A Critical Study in the Quantitative History of American Negro Slavery* (New York, 1976), as well as another work that theorizes somewhat but still employs disciplines cherished by academicians, Eugene D. Genovese's *The Political Economy of Slavery: Studies in the Economy and Society of the Slave South* (New York, 1965). Interestingly enough, one may, if one is so minded, compare this volume of Genovese's with Ulrich B. Phillips' *The Slave*

Economy of the Old South: Selected Essays in Economic and Social History (Baton Rouge, 1968), edited by Genovese. Leslie H. Owens' *This Species of Property: Slave Life and Culture in the Old South* (New York, 1976) is not, of course, a mere reckoning of slaves as commercial objects but an attempt, also, at a comprehensive account of slavery. Mark V. Tushnet's *The American Law of Slavery, 1810–1860* (Princeton, N.J., 1981) is a specialist's study, devoted to what its title suggests it should be and, hence, to explorations of slavery as slavery was articulated in legislation or litigation. *The American Law* may well serve as a reminder of the existence of another increasingly venerable classic of scholarship in the history of slavery, Helen T. Catterall (ed.), *Judicial Cases Concerning American Slavery and the Negro* (5 vols.; Washington, D.C., 1926), long a most attractive option for the researcher upon slavery to whom time spent with primary sources is time to be fruitfully (and enjoyably) employed.

John Hope Franklin addressed himself to the mind of the antebellum South, in terms somewhat different from those which governed the meditations of W. J. Cash, in *The Militant South, 1800–1861* (Cambridge, Mass., 1956), if nothing else, rather an excellent propaedeutic for Robert E. May's *The Southern Dream of a Caribbean Empire, 1854–1861* (Baton Rouge, 1973). Further insight into the convenient fantasizing of southerners to whom the way of life of the cotton plantocracy had become an earthly paradise to be preserved at all costs may be gained from recourse to Reginald Horsman, *Josiah Nott of Mobile: Southerner, Physician, and Racial Theorist* (Baton Rouge, 1986). Pseudoscience about the Negro and his putative differences from whites reached almost insuperable heights of antic nonsense in the anatomy, biology, and physiology of Dr. Nott. Three relative contemporaries of Dr. Nott who did not live in Mobile, or share with Dr. Nott his strong attachment to the ideology of the plantocratic South, were Frances Anne Kemble (the English actress Fanny Kemble), Theodore Weld, and Frederick Law Olmstead. Kemble, an independent spirit, provides a British eye upon American slavery in her *Journal of a Residence on a Georgia Plantation in 1838–1839* (New York, 1863). Theodore Weld was a white abolitionist. His *American Slavery As It Is: Testimony of a Thousand Witnesses* (New York, 1839) is a record of slavery's wrongs. Olmstead, almost surely most widely remembered for his brilliantly creative role in the genesis of New York City's Central Park, traveled in the South, alert to all he saw there, in the eventful (for slavery and its opponents) 1850s. He put his tourist's observations into three books, *A Journey in the Seaboard Slave States, with Remarks on their Economy* (New York, 1856), *A Journey through Texas; or, a Saddle Trip on the Southwestern Frontier* (New York, 1857), and *A Journey in the Back Country* (New York, 1860). Olmstead, by his own admission, wanted a good, close look at slavery and, as he said himself, at the cotton kingdom. His impressions of the South just before the Civil War deserve careful reading. No one could accuse Olmstead of being a fanatic. For that matter, neither could such an indictment be leveled at Fanny Kemble. In no way, of course, could Theodore Weld not be rightly called an inveterate foe of slavery. Yet neither Kemble nor Olmstead, much like Weld, finds a golden age in America's slave South.

Ventures into systematic inspection at various selected locations throughout the South of slavery, subject to the constraints of scholarly enterprise, exist in a number of books. One such is Elinor Miller and Eugene D. Genovese's *Plantation, Town, and County: Essays on the Local History of American Slave Society* (Urbana, Ill., 1974), a highly competent investigation of typical life at close range in the antebellum South, where the South was most at home. Another such book, which chooses to abide at one site in the heart of the very country from which came some of the fire-eaters of the Civil War, is Theodore Rosengarten's *Tombee: Portrait of a Cotton Planter with the Journal of Thomas B. Chaplin, 1822–1890,* edited by Theodore Rosengarten and Susan W. Walker (New York, 1986). *Tombee* is an account of the way things were at Tombee, a plantation on the sea island St. Helena, off the coast of South Carolina. Not the least of the dividends to be garnered from *Tombee* may well be the access it provides to Chaplin's entries into his journal, on a more or less daily basis, from 1845 to 1858. Chaplin was a master. In James O. Breeden (ed.), *Advice Among Masters: The Ideal in Slave Management in the Old South* (Westport, Conn., 1980), are gathered more than one hundred treatises and opinions, by masters, on slave management, all originally published in southern agricultural journals during the South's antebellum years. A picture of the master's wife, replacing the mythology of antebellum idolatry with sober research, appears in Catherine Clinton, *The Plantation Mistress: Another Side of Southern Slavery* (New York, 1982). An important book, a pathfinder in its time, is John Spencer Bassett's *The Southern Plantation Overseer: As Revealed in His Letters* (Northhampton, Mass., 1925). With this may be combined William Kauffman Scarborough's *The Overseer: Plantation Management in the Old South* (Baton Rouge, 1966). But not all southern slaves lived on plantations or even in agrarian environments. Hence, the great utility of Richard C. Wade's *Slavery in the Cities: The South, 1820–1860* (New York, 1964).

There are, of course, regions within the regionalism of the South—reminders, each subregion in its own way, that (as more than one observer of the South has noted) there are several Souths historically (as well as now), every one of which possesses value both for its uniqueness and its southernness. A rather sizable literature exists about these subregions as they seem to have been at various times during slavery. Far outside the South, incidentally, only one year after the end of the Civil War, George H. Moore's *Notes on the History of Slavery in Massachusetts* (New York, 1866), somewhat misleadingly titled in view of its interest in Massachusetts slavers (not slavery), connected a region outside the South with the traffic in human flesh from Africa in no uncertain terms. But, to return to southern regionalism, several studies of slavery in the area drained by the rivers that flow into the Chesapeake Bay throw light on more than one aspect of the relation of slavery to localized customary behavior in America. A regional way of life and slavery, and how, together, they grew, are definitely under scrutiny in Allan Kulikoff's *Tobacco and Slaves: The Development of Southern Culture in the Chesapeake, 1680–1800* (Chapel Hill, 1986). The peculiar plight in a nation part slave and part free of a border state, exposed to conflicting mores as states not so ambiguously positioned as it never were, is examined in Barbara Jeanne Fields, *Slavery and Freedom on the Middle Ground: Maryland During the Nineteenth Century* (New Haven, 1985). A variation of the theme introduced in Kulikoff's *Tobacco and Slaves* establishes the perimeters for Ronald L. Lewis' *Coal, Iron and Slaves: Industrial Slavery in Maryland and Virginia, 1715–1865* (Westport, Conn., 1979). More in keeping thematically with Fields's *Slavery and Freedom on the Middle Ground* is Robert McColley's *Slavery and Jeffersonian Virginia* (2nd ed.; Urbana, Ill., 1973). So, although with something of a difference, is James Hugo Johnston's *Race Relations in Virginia and Miscegenation in the South, 1776–1860* (Amherst, Mass., 1970). This last has a foreword by Winthrop Jordan.

Of more than passing interest, if only because it does not follow familiar lines of inquiry, is Todd L. Savitt's *Medicine and Slavery: Disease and the Health Care of Blacks in Antebellum Virginia* (Urbana, Ill., 1978). Additional studies relating slavery to the staple crop of a subregion of the South are Daniel C. Littlefield's *Rice and Slaves: Ethnicity and the Slave Trade in Colonial South Carolina* (Baton Rouge, 1981) and Julia Floyd Smith's *Slavery and Rice Culture in Low Country Georgia, 1750–1860* (Knoxville, 1985). Attesting to the westward course of the slave South's expansion are J. Mills Thornton III's *Politics and Power in a Slave Society: Alabama, 1800–1860* (Baton Rouge, 1978), Harriet E. Amos' *Cotton City: Urban Development in Antebellum Mobile* (University, Ala., 1985), and Joe Gray Taylor's *Negro Slavery in Louisiana* (Baton Rouge, 1963), a volume which should not be disdained because it antedates the latest revisionism in southern history. The tertium quid of the South, the often octoroon Negroes who sometimes lived in voluntarily isolated colonies and interbred all too much with themselves, is represented in Gary B. Mills, *The Forgotten People: Cane River's Creoles of Color* (Baton Rouge, 1977), and also, under the guiding hand of a professional writer, in Lyle Saxon's *Children of Strangers* (Boston, 1937). The linkages between Negroes and Indians in the South of slavery—as, for instance, in Albery Whitman's *Twasinta's Seminoles*—may be traced and studied in two works by Daniel F. Littlefield, Jr., *Africans and Seminoles: From Removal to Emancipation* (Westport, Conn., 1977) and *Africans and Creeks: From the Colonial Period to the Civil War* (Westport, Conn., 1979). Of a disposition somewhat (but not quite) similar to that of these works of Littlefield's is R. Halliburton, Jr., *Red over Black: Black Slavery Among the Cherokee Indians* (Westport, Conn., 1977).

A welcome form of revisionism in the history of slavery has been, within the present generation of historical scholarship, a growing regard for the testimony of the slave about slavery as well as for a decidedly less perfunctory and much more clinically rigorous anatomizing of the slave and his world from what might well be defined as deep within the visceral interior of both. A major role in the accomplishment of this change has been played by the black historian John Blassingame. A work of his, therefore, which cannot be avoided in the acquisition of a sense of slavery now tolerable as informed opinion is his carefully wrought *The Slave Community: Plantation Life in the Ante-Bellum South* (New York, 1972), an intelligently ordered (and generally esteemed) experiment in the involvement of the slave in the depiction of his own slavery. A verdict of a jury of Blassingame's peers upon *The Slave Community* exists, incidentally, in Al Tony Gilmore (ed.), *Revisiting Blassingame's "The Slave Community": The Scholars Respond* (Westport, Conn., 1978). Of a piece with Blassingame's work, and worthily so, is George P. Rawick's *From Sundown to Sunup: The Making of the Black Community* (Westport, Conn., 1972). Phillips, Stampp, Blassingame, and Rawick (who is white), taken all together, go a long way toward providing the kind of ecumenically sound view of a particular past which conscientious scholars anxious to be as free as possible of subservience to preordained thought cherish mightily.

John B. Boles, *Black Southerners, 1619–1869* (Lexington, Ky., 1983), represents as ambitious a treatment of slavery as anyone reasonably could want, using, as it does, a variety of scholarly disciplines, including demography and anthropology, incorporating into itself the latest discoveries and developments in theory dealing with slavery, ranging over virtually every conceivable aspect of its subject, and ending, actually, not with the end of slavery but with the new improvisations of a resurgent (even though obsolescent) agrarianism of an ancien régime, such as sharecropping, with which southern Negroes were forced to deal during Reconstruction. A most impressive use of the same ways and means in historiography for blacks as those so excellently employed by Blassingame enriches Charles Joyner's *Down by the Riverside: A South Carolina Slave Community* (Urbana, Ill., 1986), which has been called, by Rawick, the finest work ever written on American slavery. Voices of the slaves may be heard unimpeded in B. A. Botkin (ed.), *Lay My Burden Down: A Folk History of Slavery* (Chicago, 1945), a famous winnowing of quoted recollections of ex-slaves compiled under the auspices of the Great Depression's WPA Writers' Project, as also in Randall M. Miller (ed.), *"Dear Master": Letters of a Slave Family* (Ithaca, N.Y., 1978), and in the solo tones of James P. Thomas, *From Tennessee Slave to St. Louis Entrepreneur*, ed. Loren Schweninger (Columbia, Mo., 1984).

For many strong and valid reasons, attempts to do justice to the slave in interpreting America's slave past lack proper substance and scope if they ignore special attention to the slave family. The classic work on this family is, of course, Frazier's *The Negro Family in the United States*, already cited here. One result of the powerful influence of this volume upon the thinking about Negroes in America has been no little responsibility attributable to it for the relatively wide and great popularity of a belief in an American Negro matriarchy with roots extending back into the too-typical absence of Negro fathers from their families and children during slavery. It was in full awareness of Frazier's black family, and in opposition to some of Franklin's conclusions, that Herbert G. Gutman constructed his picture of the black family in *The Black Family in Slavery and Freedom, 1750–1925* (New York, 1976). A study of black men in America that merits consultation is Robert Staples, *Black Masculinity: The Black Male's Role in American Society* (San Francisco, 1982). There were Negroes not members (unless most rarely) of white families who, nevertheless, did the bidding of white people in a most strategic manner as overseers of black labor. A picture of such Negroes appears, well documented, in William L. Van Deburg's *The Slave Drivers: Black Agricultural Labor Supervisors in the Antebellum South* (Westport, Conn., 1979). But there were, happily, at the other end of a spectrum, as it were, Negroes who had managed, in a slave South, not to be slaves. Negroes of this condition are profiled in Ira Berlin's *Slaves Without Masters: The Free Negro in the Antebellum South* (New York, 1974). A single family of free Negroes is examined in Michael P. Johnson and James L. Roark, *Black Masters: A Free Family of Color in the Old South* (New York, 1984).

Actually, much of the black American past as it truly was constitutes a reminder of the extent to which slavery, however and wherever it flourished, never did utterly encompass the life of American Negroes. Lorenzo J. Greene's very able *The Negro in Colonial New England, 1620–1776* (New York, 1942) has yet no rival, or successor, as a source for reliable information about the Negroes in the place and time it elects to study. A similar credit may be granted to Benjamin Quarles's *The Negro in the American Revolution* (Chapel Hill, 1961). Quarles, incidentally, is also the author of *The Negro in the Civil War* (Boston, 1953). Obviously, to speak of the Negro in early New England or in America's military adventures is to call attention to antebellum black America's refusal ever to be altogether reconciled to the status of enslavement. A general introduction to the incidence of slave uprisings in the Western Hemisphere may be obtained from Eugene D. Genovese, *From Rebellion to Revolution: Afro-American Slave Revolts in the Making of the Modern World* (Baton Rouge, 1979). The probably most utilized study of slave revolts in the United States is Herbert Aptheker's *American Negro Slave Revolts* (New York, 1943), a work which affords Aptheker some opportunity to challenge, as he does with relish, the notion that a natural docility in Negroes fitted them uncommonly well for slavery. The black scholar Joseph Cephas Carroll (who taught me at Wilberforce) partially paved the way for Aptheker with his *Slave Insurrections in the United States, 1800–1865* (Boston, 1938).

A detailed observation of one of the three most famous slave revolts is provided in John Lofton's *Denmark Vesey's Revolt: The Slave Plot That Lit a Fuse to Fort Sumter* (Kent, Ohio, 1983), while in Henry Irving Tragle's *The Southampton Slave Revolt of 1831: A Compilation of Source Material* (Amherst, Mass., 1971) access is offered to material from which a documented account of Nat Turner's insurrection may be formulated. An anecdotal picture of the Underground Railroad, told in a manner of slippered ease (although not always with all the safeguards of impeccable scholarship), exists in Homer Uri Johnson's *From Dixie to Canada: Romance and Realities of the Underground Railroad* (Orwell, Ohio, 1896). Ex-slaves who maintained themselves in independent and understandably stealthy enclaves within a larger world of slavery around them are identified and examined in Richard Price (ed.), *Maroon Societies: Rebel Slave Communities in the Americas* (2nd ed.; Baltimore, 1979), part three of which, by Aptheker, focuses on such societies inside the boundaries of the United States. Finally here may be cited three volumes, in no necessary order, each in its own special way a graphic footnote to the psychopathologies induced by an addiction to slavery. Thus dark and ugly repercussions from American slavery are gathered for inspection in Lathan A. Windley's *Runaway Slave Advertisements: A Documentary History from the 1730's to 1790* (4 vols.; Westport, Conn., 1983), an ingenious provision of some prime examples of the extent to which human callousness may go; Stanley W. Campbell's *The Slave Catchers: Enforcement of the Fugitive Slave Law, 1850–1860* (Chapel Hill, 1970), with its further appalling evidence of incidences of the same callousness; and Walter Ehrlich's *They Have No Rights: Dred Scott's Struggle for Freedom* (Westport, Conn., 1979), a painstaking summation, from the standpoint of political liberalism, of the case, with which everyone is acquainted, that afforded a chief justice of the United States the podium whence he declared all Negroes without rights whites needed bother to respect.

Abolitionism was once, and long, a vigorous effort toward reform in America. Books about it, or touching on it, are not rare. Clearly, here only a selection of such books appears. A good first book to read concerning the opposition to slavery is Dwight L. Dumond's *Antislavery: The Crusade for Freedom in America* (Ann Arbor, 1961), which Dumond, a distinguished white historian at the University of Michigan, did not attempt until his fledgling experiences in his profession belonged by many years to his expired youth. *Antislavery* is not nonpartisan. The passion of the abolitionists lingers in it. Nor does it appear intended for a limited audience. Its vividness, stylistically and pictorially, invites the attention, not only of trained scholars, but also of readers not from the relatively small world in which trained scholars ply their trade. It may be supplemented, at least in its comprehensive treatment of the antislavery movement, by Terence Brady and Evan Jones's *The Fight Against Slavery* (New York, 1977). The dialectic of abolitionism receives an informed, as well as sympathetic, treatment in Jane and William Pease (eds.), *The Antislavery Argument* (Indianapolis, 1965). The Peases are no amateurs in their interest in black subjects. Direct contact with the voices of abolitionism is afforded in Martin Duberman (ed.), *The Antislavery Vanguard: New Essays on the Abolitionists* (Princeton, N.J., 1965), and a use of abolitionists' lives to tell the story of abolitionism is made also a form of direct contact with such voices by the Peases in their *Bound with Them in Chains: A Biographical History of the Antislavery Movement* (Westport, Conn., 1972).

There were black abolitionists. An excellent account of them may be found in Benjamin Quarles's *Black Abolitionists* (New York, 1969), the virtues of which are enhanced, to no small degree, by the contributions to it from Quarles's admirable knowledge of black (and American) history in general. The earliest years of American abolitionism, years which have tended, in comparison with the era of abolitionism after the rise of William Lloyd Garrison, to go relatively unnoticed, are accorded their due attention in Roger Bruns (ed.), *Am I Not a Man and a Brother: The Antislavery Crusade of Revolutionary America* (New York, 1977). An important aid to a clear and connected picture of the extinction of slavery outside the South is Arthur Zilversmit's *The First Emancipation: The Abolition of Slavery in the North* (Chicago, 1967). We are all prone to wonder, sometimes, what might have happened in our world if only this or that had come to pass. The Jeffersonian South, with its sometimes high hopes for black emancipation, experienced, as it were, its final interment in the vote upholding slavery of the Virginia legislature during its deliberations of 1831 and 1832. The story of that fateful moment in American history (which revealed, among other things, Virginia's divided mind about slavery) is told in Alison Goodyear Freehling's *Drift Toward Dissolution: The Virginia Slavery Debate of 1831–1832* (Baton Rouge, 1982). A different story, less plagued with crises of consciences, accompanied the cause of abolitionism farther north. Portions of that story are unfolded by Lawrence Lader in *The Bold Brahmins: New England's War Against Slavery, 1831–1863* (New York, 1961).

Just as Dumond engrosses all of the antislavery agitation in America as the province for his book on abolitionism in America, so, in Leon F. Litwack's *North of Slavery: The Negro in the Free States, 1790–1860* (Chicago, 1961), an attempt is made to cover the entirety of a subject, in this instance, the plight of the Negro in the North before the Civil War. For its extensiveness alone, then, if for no other reason, *North of Slavery* is another of these books obligatory in a full library about American slavery. Of special interest, in terms of how blacks fared in Litwack's North, are Thomas D. Morris, *Free Men All: The Personal Liberty Laws of the North, 1780–1861* (Baltimore, 1974), and, a gratifying example of the work of an unusually able historian, Russell B. Nye, *Fettered Freedom: Civil Liberties and the Slavery Controversy, 1830–1860* (Urbana, Ill., 1972). In Eugene H. Berwanger's *The Frontier Against Slavery: Western Anti-Negro Prejudice and the Slavery Extension Controversy* (Urbana, Ill., 1967), a forceful argument is made for the somewhat arresting proposition that prejudice against Negroes, rather than opposition to slavery, was a major factor in preventing the westward expansion of slavery. Slavery and politics may be examined in various guises in Richard H. Sewell's *Ballots for Freedom: Antislavery Politics in the United States, 1837–1860* (New York, 1976); Frederick J. Blue's *The Free Soilers: Third Party Politics, 1848–1854* (Urbana, Ill., 1973); John Mayfield's *Rehearsal for Republicanism: Free Soil and the Politics of Antislavery* (Port Washington, N.Y., 1980); and Herman Belz's *A New Birth of Freedom: The Republican Party and Freedmen's Rights, 1861 to 1866* (Westport, Conn., 1976). Of the furor between North and South in the 1850s a painstaking picture is drawn in Henry Harrison Simms, *A Decade of Sectional Controversy, 1851–1861* (Chapel Hill, 1942).

Differences between life on the land and life in the city did not wait for Negroes until the twentieth century. A virtually indispensable study for the seeker after wholeness in his concept of the American Negro prior to the Civil War is Leonard P. Curry, *The Free Black in Urban America, 1800–1850* (Chicago, 1981), commendable for its research, its insistence upon the special effects of urban environments upon the free blacks within them, the intelligence of its organization, and its reminder, for those who might still carry in their heads too naïve a picture of the South during slavery, that blacks before the Civil War could be found living in southern, as well as northern, towns of consequence. Exceptions to a general rule should not be ignored, and may have a value of considerable worth, in the composition of a sense of a people's past. In Juliet E. K. Walker, *Free Frank: A Black Pioneer on the Antebellum Frontier* (Lexington, Ky., 1982), such an exception may be encountered with profit for an encyclopedic acquaintance with the black American past. Free Frank was born a slave in South Carolina in 1777. He died free in Illinois seventy-seven years later in a town he himself had founded. No fugitive, he had bought himself, as well as his wife and sixteen members of his family, out of slavery. An expression of the same resistance to servitude as that exemplified in Frank's freeing of himself and his relatives, albeit with nothing even near the splendor of Frank's, may be scrutinized in Philip S. Foner and George E. Walker (eds.), *Proceedings of the Black State Conventions, 1840–1865* (2 vols.; Philadelphia, 1971–1980), an annotated publication of primary sources. Forms of Garveyism before Garvey's time, distinct from the kind of thinking behind the colonization efforts of the white colonization forces, are examined in Floyd J. Miller, *The Search for a Black Nationality: Black Emigration and Colonization, 1787–1863* (Urbana, Ill., 1975). There were black writers in the nineteenth century, it will be remembered, not averse to separating themselves and others like themselves from white America. Complementary, then, to *The Search for a Black Nationality* can be Bill McAdoo, *Pre-Civil War Black Nationalism* (New York, 1983). Anything, however, but similarly complementary would be Michael P. Johnson and James L. Roark (eds.), *No Chariot Let Down: Charleston's Free People of Color on the Eve of the Civil War* (Chapel Hill, 1984), which presents, as part of its restoration of the past, letters, recovered in 1935, that recall William Ellison of the Sumter district of South Carolina, richest freedman in the South, who owned a plantation and at least one business and some slaves, bought the house of a former governor of the state, sent his grandchildren north to school, and was valued, for his possessions, in the 1860 census at a worth exceeding $100,000.

Blacks long suffered badly in accounts by whites of the Civil War and Reconstruction, particularly of Reconstruction. In James Ford Rhodes, *History of the United States, 1850–1916* (8 vols.; New York, 1909–17), and James Schouler, *History of the United States of America Under the Constitution* (7 vols.; New York, 1894–1913), the notion that Reconstruction was a great mistake, a foolish, and often vicious, attempt to put the bottom rail on the top, from which white southerners eventually were able, fortunately, to extricate themselves, goes unchallenged and is, indeed, canonized. Bias at its worst about Reconstruction may well be reached in Claude Bowers, *The Tragic Era: The Revolution After Lincoln* (New York, 1929), and George Fort Milton, *The Age of Hate: Andrew Johnson and the Radicals* (New York, 1930), heatedly vituperative attacks upon whites like Charles Sumner and Thaddeus Stevens abetted by excoriations of black politicians in the South during the days of Reconstruction, and no good words for such attempts to help the former slaves as the Freedmen's Bureau. One may learn much about the effects of spleen and bias upon adjectives in *The Tragic Era*, while in *The Age of Hate* Stevens is represented as a clubfoot Caliban. Neither Bowers nor Milton, incidentally, was a professional historian.

Reference has been made here earlier to an account of the military involvement of blacks in the Civil War by Benjamin Quarles. Other such accounts by historians of Quarles's general temperament on the subject of the genetic endowments of Negroes, and contrary to the beliefs of Bowers and Milton, may be explored in James M. McPherson, *The Negro's Civil War* (New York, 1965), and Dudley Taylor Cornish, *The Sable Arm: Negro Troops in the Union Army, 1861–1865* (New York, 1956). Of some interest in connection with the admission of Negroes to combatant status in the manpower of the Union armies are attitudes in the North toward the Negro at that time, one reflection of which, fittingly vigorous in its nature, is recalled in Adrian Cook, *The Armies of the Streets: New York City Draft Riots of 1863* (Lexington, Ky., 1974). Negroes were victims of violence, and some Negroes were killed, in these riots. But 1863 was also the year of the issuance of the Emancipation Proclamation. A clear picture, uncluttered by flights of rhetoric, of how the proclamation came into being, with an obviously proper interest in Lincoln's monitoring of the public pulse as he prepared it, is presented ably and expeditiously in John Hope Franklin, *The Emancipation Proclamation* (New York, 1963). An account of conditions in a part of the world much on Lincoln's mind when the proclamation was issued exists in V. Jacque Voegeli, *Free but Not Equal: The Midwest and the Negro During the Civil War* (Chicago, 1967). A book highly esteemed ever since its first appearance is Willie Lee Rose (white and female, despite the "Willie Lee"), *Rehearsal for Reconstruction: The Port Royal Experiment* (Indianapolis, 1964). It is a book which benefits from its subject. In a manner of speaking, everyone is interested in Port Royal and its environs during the months and years of the Civil War after Port Royal fell into Union hands. Of equal interest to this same "everyone" has tended to be Port Royal and its environs during Reconstruction. In *Rehearsal for Reconstruction,* Rose does a masterful job of recalling a past, and especially of permitting that past to speak for itself through the witnesses she, like the able barrister she is, subpoenas. Port Royal and Edisto, a sea island off the South Carolina coast, are not far apart and, indeed, share the same regional subculture and history.

In Mary Ames, *From a New England Woman's Diary in Dixie in 1865* (Springfield, Mass., 1906), there is more, really, of *Rehearsal for Reconstruction,* although even with less of what might well be called outside intervention. For Miss Ames was one of the New England teachers who went south to serve with the Freedmen's Bureau in the education of the freedmen. Her diary is exactly what it claims to be, a memoir of her experience with a significant social experiment. A memoir from someone with Miss Ames's pro-Negro sympathies, but of a status much higher in the hierarchy of command than hers, is John Eaton, *Grant, Lincoln and the Freedmen: Reminiscences of the Civil War with Special Reference to the Work for the Contrabands and Freedmen of the Mississippi Valley,* in collaboration with Ethel O. Mason (New York, 1907). Eaton was a top official in the Freedmen's Bureau and, before that, a leading figure in the organized efforts during the actual hostilities of the Civil War to succor blacks in the South. The response of Lincoln's administration to the problems created for it in the handling of former slaves by the successes of Union arms is chronicled in Louis S. Gerteis, *From Contraband to Freedman: Federal Policy Toward Southern Blacks,* 1861–1865 (Westport, Conn., 1973), and a lawyer's eye is turned upon essentially this same response extended into the era of Andrew Johnson in Mary Frances Berry, *Military Necessity and Civil Rights Policy: Black Citizenship and the Constitution, 1861–1868* (Port Washington, N.Y, 1977). Abolitionists did not close shop when the South fired on Fort Sumter. Their maintenance of their fervors in the world depicted in Gerteis and Berry is described in James M. McPherson, *The Struggle for Equality: Abolitionists and the Negro in the Civil War and Reconstruction* (Princeton, N.J., 1964). When Du Bois, who could be called an abolitionist of the twentieth century, set for himself the task of reviewing the Civil War and Reconstruction, he had already embraced Marxism. So, Marxist reasoning can be detected in his *Black Reconstruction in America* (New York, 1966), wherein also a poet lives with a historian. But so, also, does a vestige of the novelist who wrote *The Quest of the Silver Fleece.*

A climate of revisionist historiography conditions Hans L. Trefousse, *Impeachment of a President: Andrew Johnson, the Blacks and Reconstruction* (Knoxville, 1975), as it does the symposium provided by the collection in Richard N. Current (ed.), *Reconstruction in Retrospect: Views from the Turn of the Century* (Baton Rouge, 1969). Various aspects of Reconstruction, each as some salient feature of it may seem to confer upon it elements of distinctiveness, are isolated and examined in David Herbert Donald, *The Politics of Reconstruction, 1863– 1867* (Baton Rouge, 1965); Joseph B. James, *The Ratification of the Fourteenth Amendment* (Macon, Ga., 1984); Joseph G. Dawson III, *Army Generals and Reconstruction* (Austin, 1957); Eugene H. Berwanger, *The West and Reconstruction* (Urbana, Ill., 1981); Howard N. Rabinowitz (ed.), *Southern Black Leaders of the Reconstruction Era* (Urbana, Ill., 1982); and Annjennette Sophie McFarlin, *Black Congressional Reconstruction Orators and Their Orations, 1869–1879* (Metuchen, N.J., 1976). Of carpetbaggers, about whom, throughout the eras of Reconstruction and "redemption," much was heard (and seldom in gentle terms), at least a glimpse may be obtained from Otto H. Olsen, *Carpetbagger's Crusade: The Life of Albion Winegar Tourgée* (Baltimore, 1965). A phenomenon of post-Appomattox America perhaps as interesting in the line of social documentation as the carpetbaggers may be observed in James L. Roark, *Masters Without Slaves: Southern Planters in the Civil War and Reconstruction* (New York, 1977).

Focuses on the former slaves are of prime importance in Donald G. Nieman, *To Set the Law in Motion: The Freedmen's Bureau and the Legal Rights of Blacks* (Millwood, N.J., 1979); Claude F. Oubre, *Forty Acres and a Mule: The Freedmen's Bureau and Black Land Ownership* (Baton Rouge, 1978); and William Preston Vaughn, *Schools for All: The Blacks and Public Education in the South, 1865–1877* (Lexington, Ky., 1974). Concentrating on the campaign by a host of idealists, a large proportion of them women, to bring the blessing of literacy to the former slaves are Robert C. Morris, *Reading, 'Riting, and Reconstruction: The Education of Freedmen in the South, 1861–1870* (Chicago, 1982); Ronald E. Butchart, *Northern Schools, Southern Blacks, and Reconstruction: Freedmen's Education, 1862–1875* (Westport, Conn., 1980); and Jacqueline Jones, *Soldiers of Light and Love: Northern Teachers and Georgia Blacks, 1865–1873* (Chapel Hill, 1980), which draws liberally on the most recent advances in historiography as well as upon relevant manuscripts and primary documents in combining a probe of institutional behavior with personal anecdotage. Also in this vein are Rossa Belle Cooley, *Homes of the Freed* (New York, 1926), which tells about three generations of teachers and students at the Penn School, founded in 1862 on the island of St. Helena, the first of the schools for the freedmen; and Elizabeth Jacoway, *Yankee Missionaries in the South* (Baton Rogue, 1980), a return by a scholar a half century later to the Penn School of *Homes of the Freed.*

Two books which investigate the contribution of religious organizations to the education of the freedmen are Joe M. Richardson, *Christian Reconstruction: The American Missionary Association and Southern Blacks, 1861–1890* (Athens, Ga., 1986), and Clarence E. Walker, *A Rock in a Weary Land: The African Methodist*

Episcopal Church During the Civil War and Reconstruction (Baton Rouge, 1982). The American Missionary Association represented, of course, white church people, and Richardson, who is white, has to his credit a history of Fisk University, one of the black colleges largely indebted to the American Missionary Association for its existence. *A Rock in a Weary Land* is actually not limited to the role in education of the AME church during the 1860s and the 1870s. It is a rather convincing attempt to justify its title, an assertion that all was not wanting in racial self-help in the largest black Methodist denomination during a trying time in the history of the American Negro. Donald Spivey, *Schooling for the New Slavery: Black Industrial Education, 1868–1915* (Westport, Conn., 1978), argues (as is not novel) that the so-called industrial education, à la Hampton and Tuskegee, for example, constituted a major force in teaching Negroes subserviency. One very special, and quite appalling, attempt to teach Negroes subserviency is described in John F. Marzalek, Jr., *Court-Martial: A Black Man in America* (New York, 1972), an account of the expulsion from West Point in 1880, in an outrageous miscarriage of justice, of black cadet Johnson Whittaker (who did live on, incidentally, to lead a successful life as a lawyer and a teacher).

A good introduction to the whole subject of the problems of the freedmen arising from their race is available in Forrest G. Wood, *Black Scare: The Racist Response to Emancipation and Reconstruction* (Berkeley, Calif., 1968). The unseemly stampede of white southerners to devise and enact legislation essentially reenslaving the Negro is presented in helpful detail in Theodore B. Wilson, *The Black Codes of the South* (Tuscaloosa, 1965). One form of the resort to terrorism to cow the freedmen, the form which thrived for a time above all other vigilante harassments of the Negro, receives close scrutiny in Allen W. Trelease, *White Terror: The Ku Klux Klan Conspiracy and Southern Reconstruction* (New York, 1971). A somber tale, not of terrorism, but of a catastrophe for Negroes in which blacks as well as whites were guilty of dishonesty and greed, is related by Carl R. Osthaus, *Freedmen, Philanthropy and Fraud: The History of the Freedman's Savings Bank* (Urbana, Ill., 1976). Lifted sights add welcome dimensions of enlarged perspective to Eric Foner, *Nothing but Freedom: Emancipation and Its Legacy* (Baton Rouge, 1983), wherein, among other good procedures, including a wise appreciation of the role of property in determining the positioning of whites and blacks apropos of each other, a comparative method is used to demonstrate how adjustments to emancipation in the Caribbean and Africa were duplicated in the American South. More on the effects of the distribution of property upon the members of a social order is to be found in Jay R. Mandle, *The Roots of Black Poverty: The Southern Plantation Economy After the Civil War* (Durham, 1978).

For the American Negro, the years immediately subsequent to Reconstruction, after Hayes had struck his venal bargain with the white South which guaranteed him the presidency in 1876, were crucial. Those were the bitter years in which the children of the freedmen were growing up. The story of the coming-of-age of this generation of blacks is the harrowing tale of their attainment of maturity precisely at the moment when America was least disposed to grant them even the smallest mite of the self-respect, and progress, they desired. The term used by the white South (and too many others) to identify the extension, even into a new century, of much of the world of slavery was "redemption." And so, in the South, Reconstruction was followed by an age of "redemption." Events leading into this age are presented and critically reviewed in William Gillette, *Retreat from Reconstruction, 1869–1879* (Baton Rouge, 1979), as well as in Michael Perman, *The Road to Redemption* (Chapel Hill, 1984). Six essays address both Reconstruction and "redemption" in Otto H. Olsen (ed.), *Reconstruction and Redemption in the South* (Baton Rouge, 1980). Developments in the world of politics of importance to the children of the freedmen are the subjects of discussion in Lawrence Grossman, *The Democratic Party and the Negro: Northern and National Politics, 1868–1892* (Urbana, Ill., 1976). Aspects of economics in the South of Reconstruction and "redemption" are given careful scrutiny in Gavin Wright, *Old South, New South: Revolutions in the Southern Economy Since the Civil War* (New York, 1986); Patrick J. Hearden, *Independence and Empire: The New South's Cotton Mill Campaign, 1865–1901* (DeKalb, Ill., 1982), with its surely unwitting reminders of Charles W. Chesnutt's *The Colonel's Dream;* and A. Daniel Novak, *The Wheel of Servitude: Black Forced Labor After Slavery* (Lexington, Ky., 1978), a scathing review of such abuses of the Negro as peonage. Works of genuine worth on a subject far from trivial—both of them well researched and carefully thought out—are Joel Williamson, *The Crucible of Race: Black-White Relations in the American South Since Emancipation* (New York, 1984), and Howard N. Rabinowitz, *Race Relations in the Urban South, 1865–1890* (New York, 1978). Like a goodly number of the scholar-authors represented in this essay, Williamson and Rabinowitz are devoted students of the American Negro.

Indispensable for any serious study of the South since the Civil War is, in the judgment of all expert opinion, C. Vann Woodward, *The Strange Career of Jim Crow* (2nd rev. ed.; New York, 1966), a convincing, timely, and far from inconsiderable reminder to the American people after the Brown decision that southern racial segregation in the 1950s was not part of a divine plan, or even hallowed by age. That such segregation all too faithfully represented the temper of an America exceptionally disposed to be harsh to its Negroes in the last quarter of the nineteenth century is part of the message sought to be conveyed in Rayford Logan, *The Negro in American Life and Thought: The Nadir, 1877–1901* (New York, 1954), a book the thesis of which, with no reservation, stigmatizes the epoch of its concern as the worst in American history for the Negro. In providing what he obviously intends as proof for his contention, Logan relies heavily on direct quotations from America's daily press as it expressed itself in news and opinion during the so-called age of redemption. Neither *The Strange Career of Jim Crow* nor *The Negro in American Life and Thought,* incidentally, failed to acquire a respectable audience when it appeared. Nor did, for that matter, August Meier, *Negro Thought in America, 1880–1915: Racial Ideologies in the Age of Booker T. Washington* (Ann Arbor, Mich., 1963), a thorough, reliable, and insightful digest of the revelatory expression which is the object of its contemplation. A special interest of some value is afforded attention in Henry Lewis Suggs (ed.), *The Black Press in the South, 1865–1979* (Westport, Conn., 1983), while a story more heartwarming than otherwise for supporters of the American Negro is told with scholarly discretion in J. M. McPherson, *The Abolitionist Legacy: From Reconstruction to the NAACP* (Princeton, N.J., 1975). A splendid valediction to study of the American Negro's lot from Reconstruction onwards might well be Willard B. Gatewood, Jr. (ed.), *Slave and Freeman: The Autobiography of George L. Knox* (Lexington, Ky., 1979). Knox was born a slave in Tennessee. When he died in Indiana in 1927, he had become a genuine pillar of a large community. His autobiography was published for the first time in 1894 and 1895 in the Negro newspaper, the Indianapolis *Freeman*.

Quite probably, it may be convincingly argued that more work has been done in the writing of general histories about black America than about black American literature (and one is certainly at liberty to wonder why this is so). More than half a century has elapsed since the appearance of Vernon Loggins, *The Negro Author: His Development in America to 1900* (New York, 1931), essentially a doctoral dissertation at Columbia University. Loggins, not a Negro, certainly wanted to be fair in his treatment of his subject. It may seem to many, however, that his mind was stored with preconceptions about the Negro, widely shared in his time, which unduly affected his history. Even so, no history of black American literature has yet matched in comprehensiveness his attention to Negro literature until the turn of the twentieth century. Moreover, Loggins did consult, among others, Arthur A. Schomburg (after whom a famous Negro collection in New York City now is named), Benjamin Brawley, Charles S. Johnson, James Weldon Johnson, and Monroe Work. In the compilation of his bibliography, he availed himself of advice and counsel from Dorothy Porter (as she was then) and Bella Gross. The last poet treated in *The Negro Author* is Paul Laurence Dunbar; the last novelist, Charles W. Chesnutt. Loggins seems to place a premium upon plainness and clarity of utterance. A deficit unavoidable in *The Negro Author* is the absence from it of information about the writers it discusses which scholarship since 1930 has supplied.

Much separates *The Negro Author* stylistically from J. Saunders Redding's *To Make a Poet Black* (Chapel Hill, 1939). Redding was always the gifted essayist whom Loggins, with no reflection upon Loggins' competence of statement, never was, or could be. No extant history of Negro literature surpasses *To Make a Poet Black* as a delight to read. To begin with, its title constitutes a happy and very ingenious coup de grâce, extracted as it is from Countee Cullen's famous sonnet "Yet Do I Marvel," and, indeed, from the very couplet in that sonnet which announces the poem's race-conscious theme, "Yet do I marvel at this curious thing / To make a poet black and bid him sing." Moreover, in *To Make A Poet Black*, Redding (still then in his scholarly youth) is at his superb best in several ways—in the spinning of a narrative, by virtue (partially, at least) of his command of Negro history, which imparts coherence to what might, under less skillful and knowledgeable hands, have been more a medley than an organic whole; in the able and unflagging exercise of his critical faculties both on single works of literature and in his summary evaluations of individual writers; and, not least of all, in his thoughtful, yet not unimpassioned, defense of the hypothesis, so clearly an article of faith with him, that Negro writers in America have tended so much as they have toward a literature of protest because of the hostility of their social environment toward themselves and all other Negroes. Here, therefore, in *To Make a Poet Black*, may be found Redding's most sustained justification of his well-known contention to the effect that Afro-American literature has substantially been, surely until the collapse of the Harlem Renaissance, with which *To Make a Poet Black* comes to its end, "a literature of necessity."

The bibliography at the end of *To Make a Poet Black* is much shorter than the bibliography of *The Negro Author* and lists almost no works other than those attributable to the authors Redding discusses in his text. But, then, *To Make a Poet Black* is decidedly a smaller work than *The Negro Author*. It is, indeed, what might well be called an extended essay, although, as such, it is certainly not to be derided.

For early Negro writers, those published by 1895 (as well as, indeed, those, also, published between 1895 and 1930), the third literary history probably of most value is Kenny J. Williams, *They Also Spoke* (Nashville, 1970). It bears—properly, it would seem, in view of its content—the subtitle "An Essay on Negro Literature in America, 1787–1930." An essay, as a matter of fact, it is, no less (although about twice as long) than *To Make a Poet Black*. To a general reader, one among that multitudinous throng which claims no great knowledge of, or special virtuosity in, the reading of any literature (Afro-American literature surely not excepted), forays into the pages of *The Negro Author* or *To Make a Poet Black* should present no problems. He who can read an article in a daily newspaper or a magazine such as *Harper's* or the *Nation* should find either account of Negro literature readily intelligible. So, likewise, can it be said of *They Also Spoke*. What additionally seems true, however, of *They Also Spoke* is that it has never possessed even nearly, in size or acclaim, the audience of *The Negro Author* or *To Make a Poet Black*. It ought not be allowed to continue to languish in this undeserved measure of obscurity.

In brief prefatory remarks to *They Also Spoke*, Williams establishes with no hesitation or qualification her lack of sympathy with black separatism. Her position is forthright and clear. She does not question, or necessarily decry, the fact that the Negro's experience of life in America has been sufficiently sui generis to occasion a literature special enough to have its own name and character. Still, as she sees it, there are cultural forces in America which so affect all Americans that, ultimately, all Americans are American. Ultimately, too, she certainly also believes, Afro-American literature is American. It is, thus, an ingredient of a whole throughout which something common to that whole is never missing from any of its parts, however distinctive some part, or parts, of it may seem, particularly at first glance, to be. She begins her history of Negro literature, as did Loggins and Redding, with Jupiter Hammon, almost surely because she was still unaware of Lucy Terry. She concludes her narrative, as did Redding, with the conclusion of the Harlem Renaissance.

Daughter (and only child) of the man who, for a good number of years, was the national head of the organization of Negro Baptists constituting, with its millions of communicants, the largest federated ecclesiastical body of Negroes in America, in her history Williams dwells at length, and with both a convincing fervor and more than adequate learning, upon the Negro spiritual. She also does not scant the slave narrative. Her treatment of individual authors provides her with opportunities, on which she capitalizes, to display her skills as a critic and a rhetorician. And, like Redding, she has a unifying hypothesis for her entire work—a hypothesis again, as in the case of Redding, implicit in the title she has given to her history of her people's literature. It is a hypothesis which may well possess a power to redeem as well as to induce coherence, for it, without any hint or shadow of apology, attributes to the black writers who wrote soon enough to be in her book, after carefully noting their divergences in thinking about blacks and blackness in America from much of the dogma and doctrine of the black writers of the 1960s and 1970s, a pride of race not less than the racial pride of the writers of the later era just specified. In the black literature of the past, her hypothesis avers, black writers did speak out for black people. That these earlier writers were not exclusivist did not, in any way, deprive them of their "black" credentials. In fact, *They Also Spoke* maintains, their very resistance to an exclusivist position would seem to have enhanced their defense of their blackness.

An appendix, "Bibliographical Notes," follows immediately the text of *They Also Spoke*. This appendix combines references to works about the American Negro (like, for example, books and articles on Negro history) with references to works about Negro writers and their work. Relatively succinct, it does, however, not infrequently accompany its recitation of titles with descriptive commentary. But selectivity, rather than any attempt to leave no stone unturned, obviously is the guiding principle in its choices of the works it lists.

The relatively recent Roger Whitlow, *Black American Literature: A Critical History* (Totowa, N.J., 1974), avoids the massive. It is essentially no larger a text than *To Make a Poet Black*. It does include Lucy Terry, and it pursues its subject until the advent of the 1970s. Its opening chapter, however, directs its attention, not toward written literature, but rather toward the oral tradition of the Negro folk, from which have emanated the spirituals, secular songs, and the various species of Negro folktales. Not all the early black writers to whom it could have alluded appear in its pages. This work selects with an obvious concern for its own total effect, clearly intended to be that of an exercise in critical approval and evaluation as well as of an exhumation of fact. It perceives the crux of the triple enlightenment it seeks to provide to be its apprehension, not only of perennials in Negro literature—of which the theme of protest, for example, is one—but also, within the corpus of Negro literature, of such manifestations of change as an improvement in craft, a recently adopted preoccupation (nowhere more than in the work of Richard Wright) with urban realism, and a high incidence, from 1960 on, of a trio of continuities: satire; an interest in the past; and, in Whitlow's phraseology, "themes of Armageddon." This is a good short history of Afro-American literature, beyond anything even suggesting insincerity or naïveté in its attempts at fairness, as well as—for all that it does not pile Ossa on Pelion—a guide which omits from its pages little or nothing essential to a full understanding of its subject in its tour of Negro literature. In an appendix *Black American Literature* presents a bibliography of more than 1,500 titles of works about criticism. There are works from such disciplines as history and the social sciences, clearly to help in the building of a proper sense of background for Negro literature.

It may well be that no one with a strong desire for an acquaintance with the historiography of Afro-American literature which includes every perspective possible to that historiography should fail to read David Littlejohn, *Black on White: A Critical Survey of Writing by American Negroes* (New York, 1966). David Littlejohn is white and was in his late twenties when he wrote this work. A year before its appearance, he had achieved, as a sole editor, the publication of *Dr. Johnson: His Life in Letters.* This Dr. Johnson is, lest there be any question, the Samuel Johnson of the inner sanctum of approved English scholarship. Littlejohn was trained as an undergraduate at Berkeley. His master's degree and doctorate are from Harvard. *Black on White* became available for potential readers when what could surely be termed an unprecedented vogue in black studies was beginning to approach its peak.

But *Black on White* is no encomium for black literature. It disposes, incidentally, of all Afro-American literature before the Harlem Renaissance in less than a page. Of early Negro poetry, including that of Phillis Wheatley, *Black on White* pronounces flatly that none would be in print had that poetry's authors not been Negroes. To Afro-American literature before Richard Wright it assigns the name of the Dark Ages and finds therein, with the "possible" exception of Langston Hughes, no writer of genuine merit. It is, however, quite probably in the introduction and conclusions to *Black on White* that it reveals most tellingly the reactions to Negro literature of its author. The condemnation of whites in Negro literature he rebukes, if on no other grounds, for, as he sees it, the utter failure of Negro literature to simulate, justly and capably, whites. Worse yet, perhaps, a similar failure he detects in the Negro writer's performance in creating Negroes. Indeed, the final paragraph of his aforementioned conclusions begins with the flat, plain, broad statement that we are all still waiting for the Negro writer—any Negro writer—who will convincingly (and credibly) convey to non-Negroes what it is like to be a Negro. The reproofs of Negro literature contained in *Black on White* (which is, of course, not absolutely negative on its subject) have their place in any consideration of Afro-American literature as, ideally, such a consideration should be. *Black on White* completely eschews a bibliography.

What can well, and quickly, be exploited as an intriguing bypath for the student, amateur or otherwise, of Afro-American literature may be comments from historical figures of importance on Afro-American literature in Thomas Jefferson, *Notes on the State of Virginia* (London, 1787), and Henri-Baptiste Gregoire, *De la Littérature des Nègres* (Paris, 1808). Jefferson, despite his deserved fame from the use of his pen, wrote only one full-length book, *Notes*, a response to an articulated desire of certain liberal and influential Frenchmen of his time, keenly interested in America, particularly as sympathizers with the American Revolution (for *Notes* was completed, though not revised, by 1781), to increase their knowledge of America and Americans. A portion of *Notes*, essentially a chapter, entitled "Query XIV," contains remarks by Jefferson about slavery, an institution to which, as is well known, he was opposed. It does not follow, however, that he ever matched this opposition with a high regard for Negroes. Rather, in "Query XIV," he compares the Negro's appearance unfavorably with that of whites and questions also the Negro's mentality and disposition. His famous specific reference to Phillis Wheatley—no poet, he calls her—a relative triviality though it well may be, justifies his identification as a voice which should at least be tendered a hearing in the criticism and history of Afro-American literature. He was, that is to say, Thomas Jefferson, and his slightest utterance about anything which can be deemed a subject of significance must be heeded. Moreover, it is he who is connected prominently with Negro literature as the father of the titular character of *Clotel*, the first Negro novel.

De la Littérature des Nègres does engage itself with some early black writers, not all of them, as its title and the nationality of its author might well imply, Afro-American. Were it not, indeed, for its internationalism, it might, conceivably, qualify as the first history (although, as such, very meager) of Afro-American literature. It certainly qualifies as a deliberate exercise in propaganda. The Jesuit-trained Catholic cleric who authored it and who, relatively unscathed, supported the French Revolution stoutly championed the equality of man. To call attention to Negro literature was, for him, one method of demonstrating the integrity of his belief in liberty, equality, and fraternity.

Other books in which attention to Afro-American literature is combined with extraliterary interests, quite amenable to the study of literature as those extra-literary interests undoubtedly can be, are Benjamin Brawley, *The Negro in Literature and Art in the United States* (3rd ed.; New York, 1929), and Margaret Just Butcher, *The Negro in American Culture* (New York, 1956). Additionally, these two works may easily be seen as further resembling the works of Jefferson and Gregoire in that the people involved in their composition, as well as the contexts of historic incident associated with them, possess a cachet of their own of the kind which not seldom lends a special value and attraction to an exploration into a past. Brawley (who somewhat rewrote *The Negro in Literature and Art*, after it had gone through more than one edition, as *The Negro Genius*, published first, before two reprintings, in 1937) is the Negro scholar in Negro literature of whom no serious student of that literature should be unaware. In the role assigned to him by fate, that of an intellectual born and bred, and doomed to live his entire life, as a citizen of that world within the veil more than once described by Du Bois, he was a giant among his peers and certainly the leading black academician in English of his time.

A native of South Carolina and son of a college president, Brawley earned two bachelor's degrees, the first from Morehouse College and the second from the University of Chicago. From Harvard he acquired a master's. A doctorate, living when, and as, he did, he really did not need. So great a figure of eminence and reverence did he become on the black college campus contemporary with him, largely because of the wide and worshipful circulation of the legend of his classroom teaching at Shaw and Howard universities and Morehouse College, that it may be difficult to believe that, at his death in 1939, he was only fifty-seven. But he was also a scholar who wrote in graceful and elegant prose and never vapidly (even though sometimes priggishly) in thought. Poetry, too, incidentally, he, upon occasion, essayed. His articles on Negro literature and Negro culture were fairly numerous. In addition to *The Negro in Literature and Art* and *The Negro Genius,* he is to be remembered for, in Negro literature, his biography, *Paul Laurence Dunbar: Poet of His People* (Chapel Hill, 1936). Brawley was a mulatto, a gentleman with whom, but for his touch of the tarbrush, J. P. Marquand's the late George Apley might well have spent many a congenial moment, and he was inalterably, in his sensitivities as a critic of literature, of the mold of a Richard Watson Gilder or a Barrett Wendell. For the enfants terribles of the vigorous and outspoken black aesthetic of the 1960s and the 1970s, he clearly was, as surely at least some of these very enfants terribles must have deeply felt, the complete embodiment of every conditioned reflex of the black bourgeoisie which aroused their disapproval, their ridicule, their scorn, and, often, their incandescent rage.

About a third of *The Negro in Literature and Art* is directly applicable to the pursuit of information about Negro literature before 1900. As with Loggins' *The*

Negro Author, The Negro in Literature and Art suffers from its inability to incorporate into its content data from research appropriate for it but, in its day, yet undone. It reflects the state of mind of the generation of Negro intellectuals to which Brawley belonged, and, so, it is doubly an adventure into history. Its first chapter, significantly entitled "The Negro Genius," reveals, willingly or not, Brawley's attitude toward Negroes of the lower class, whom he calls "peasants." Much of the book is devoted to Negroes in the arts—in painting, the theater (actors especially), sculpture, and music, particularly composers and performers wedded to the same modes of self-expression as Brahms, Paganini, or Paderewski. Three appendices of *The Negro in Literature and Art* republish articles by Brawley on Negro literature. A bibliography which lists both books and articles may well be most interesting and serviceable for its expedition of a browsing in the past.

The Negro in American Culture (New York, 1956) was originally projected as his magnum opus by Alain Locke. Locke sickened and died before he had completed any but a small fraction of it. He had collected much material to stand him, he hoped, in good stead in his preparation of it. To Butcher, whom he had known, almost as if she had been his own daughter (he never married), since her infancy and whose father, the biologist E. E. Just, his distinguished colleague at Howard and a Springarn medalist, was his close friend, he explicitly transmitted the, it must be called, sacred task of bringing to a fitting conclusion his unfinished work. Undoubtedly the text of *The Negro in American Culture* is almost wholly the work of Butcher, a professor of English, not (as was Locke) of philosophy. Still, Locke clearly had envisioned an interdisciplinary treatise, a last word, as it were, fortified with appropriate documentation, about the acculturation, including any departures therefrom, of the Negro to his American environment. Butcher adheres, in a manner worthy of the finest principles of trusteeship, as well as of collaborative scholarship, to the grand design for *The Negro in American Culture* which Locke conceptualized as of his own idea and will. This design would seem, in any case, an intellectual construct of which Butcher approved. More than a decade was to elapse after Locke's death before the "gap" appeared which alienated two contiguous generations of black scholars from each other.

Not much in *The Negro in American Culture* applies directly to Afro-American literature, especially to such literature as it was before 1900. All of the arts concerned Locke, nor was he unmindful of the great relevance to his subject of white creativity in America. So, one may acquire from *The Negro in American Culture* no small acquaintance with white art, particularly if that art expresses white assumptions about the Negro. The Harlem Renaissance was decidedly more hospitable to black folklore than Brawley was. So was Locke, a stalwart of the Renaissance. So, for that matter, was Butcher, from her vantage point of a later generation of black scholars than the generation to which Locke and Brawley both belonged. There is, then, in *The Negro in American Culture* a recognition of black folklore, as well as of, also, the slave narrative, not available in Brawley. This recognition, however, offers little hope to anti-integrationists and does not see black folklore as a tremendous repository of Africanisms. It accords with the obvious prevailing temper of *The Negro in American Culture*, precisely that of the scholars who assisted Gunnar Myrdal in the preparation of *An American Dilemma* and of the lawyers and other experts who contributed their time and talent to the NAACP in the winning of the Brown decision from the Supreme Court. It should not, under any circumstances, be alleged of *The Negro in American Culture* that it is a prodigious accumulation of detailed facts about black literature in America. But it is a book which still may be valuable for the insight it can afford into a type of mind significantly associated with the criticism of Afro-American literature.

Decidedly unlike general surveys of southern literature antecedent to it, Louis D. Rubin, Jr., *et al.*, *The History of Southern Literature* (Baton Rouge, 1985), commits itself to an ungrudging inclusion of the work of black southern writers in its text. As with *The Negro in Literature and Art* and *The Negro in American Culture*, its Afro-American literary history is part of a larger subject and dispersed somewhat in bits and pieces, in a manner of speaking, throughout a body of material major elements of which contribute only indirectly to an understanding of black literature. The earliest black writers, Lucy Terry, Phillis Wheatley, and the two Hammons, Briton and Jupiter, were all northerners. Of them, therefore, nothing is said in *The History of Southern Literature*. But a considerable percentage of black writers have been southerners. Such writers receive respectful treatment in *The History of Southern Literature*, and not from scholars, either white (as some of them are) or black, of whom it can be said that they are treading on unfamiliar ground. The slave narrative, for instance, is given careful, although not prolonged, inspection in this book. But, then, dispatch rather than protracted attention governs the flow of narrative and commentary throughout all of *The History of Southern Literature*. To some of the authors in its pages, black as well as white, it grants a whole chapter about one of these authors only. An indication, minor as it may be, of its authority in Afro-American literature is its awareness of *Les Cenelles*. From its organization, and its general tone, neither of which ever appears to be shunting Negroes off into some cramped and menial special place in its treatment of its subject, it seems determined to insist that its writers, whether white or black, all possess legitimate claims to a membership in the pantheon of southern writers. So, if for no other reason, it may well be a useful addition to any bibliography of books about Afro-American literature.

Of John Herbert Nelson, *The Negro Character in American Literature* (Lawrence, Kans., 1926), it may be somewhat similarly observed as it was of the works of Brawley, Butcher, and Rubin and his fellow editors. The sole important intended function of Nelson's work is not an inventory, with or without a complement of criticism, of Afro-American literature. Nelson is interested primarily in reporting on the depiction of Negroes by white American authors. Along the way in his book, he does find occasion to examine for their faults or virtues (and he sees only a dismal dearth of virtues) black authors who would undoubtedly belong in a history of black literature in its presentation of early Afro-American literature. Among such black authors are William Wells Brown and Frances Ellen Watkins Harper, on both of whom he casts a harshly censorious eye. Nelson wrote *The Negro Character,* in the version first to emerge from his hand, as a doctoral dissertation at the University of Kansas. Like Loggins, he was white, as were the professors to whom his image of the (to him) true Negro occasioned no qualms of the mind or conscience in their affirmation of its accuracy. That image was one which, for instance, rejected as harmful and fallacious characterizations of the Negro from Albion Tourgée and George Washington Cable while endorsing, as faithful replicas of reality, the Negroes of Kennedy's *Swallow Barn* (except for the failure of the Negroes there to speak sufficiently in Negro dialect) and the slaves and ex-slaves of Thomas Nelson Page's fiction, whose behavior is terrifyingly disoriented when they are permitted above the powerless state where, naturally, they belong, but who do realize their finest potential in fawning subordination to whites like the young master of "Marse Chan."

In stark, and commendable, contrast to *The Negro Character* are the reactions to race prevalent throughout Seymour L. Gross and John Edward Hardy (eds.), *Images of the Negro in American Literature* (Chicago, 1966), and Jean Fagan Yellin, *The Intricate Knot: Black Figures in American Literature, 1776–1863* (New York, 1972). Gross, Hardy, and Yellin all are white but from a grove of academe salubriously swept with some radical winds of change since Nelson faced his doctoral committee in session in the 1920s. Gross and Hardy's *Images* is a book of essays. Three essays are by eminent black men of letters: Ralph Ellison, Arthur P. Davis, and James Baldwin. But these three essayists address only aspects of the manufacture of images in Afro-American literature not connected with that literature prior to the twentieth century. There are also, however, in *Images,* essays by, respectively, Milton Cantor, Tremaine McDowell, Theodore L. Gross, Leslie Fiedler, Sidney Kaplan, Severn Duvall, and James M. Cox, which not only deal with literacy activity in America before 1900, concentrating on that activity in manners consistent with a no longer Negrophobic analysis of the presence of racism in America's interpretation of itself, but which also invite, if only because they are more learned, less bigoted, and intellectually far more elevated in quality than Nelson's blatant genuflections to a *status quo,* close reading as enlightened discourses upon the shapes and shadows Negroes have historically assumed in the consciousness of Americans as America has developed its sense of its own identity. There are, to shift to Yellin's work, chapters on both William Wells Brown and Martin R. Delany, as well as more than casual references to abolitionist literature (and, thus, to the slave narrative) in *The Intricate Knot.*

Bibliographies, neither of which is (or, to speak in fairness, attempts to be) exhaustive, are appended to both books.

The issue of white attitudes toward Negroes, especially as those attitudes may be examined in the art, written and otherwise, attributable to white Americans, does, surely, bear a significant relationship to the study of Afro-American literature. However much may be the light shed on this issue by works such as *The Negro Character, Images,* and *The Intricate Knot,* it still may well be that the one voice (in literature, at least) which must not be left unheard upon the subject of American whites revealing their true feelings about American blacks is that of Sterling Brown. Actually, perhaps, the sort of miracle of comprehensiveness, yet cogency, on a matter of no little consequence to all Americans which Richard Wright brought to pass with his creation of the character Bigger Thomas in *Native Son* it can be argued Brown achieved (and published), not in a book, but in an article which first appeared in the second volume (January, 1933) of the *Journal of Negro Education.* The journal was then edited by Charles H. Thompson with much of the same inclination to print in it anything, and everything, that might seem to him to advance the welfare of black America as Charles S. Johnson had appeared to harbor for *Opportunity* when he was that periodical's editor.

In any case, Brown's "Negro Character as Seen by White Authors," the article spoken of here, has become, as it should have, a sine qua non of full scholarship on the American Negro. White American writers, this article avers, have historically tended to place all Negroes in seven categories: 1) the Contented Slave, 2) the Wretched Freeman, 3) the Comic Negro, 4) the Brute Negro, 5) the Tragic Mulatto, 6) the Local Color Negro, and 7) the Exotic Primitive. The designations by Brown of some of these categories are now so extensively used as for them to have come to constitute rather familiar bywords (surely, nothing less) in the common parlance of the criticism of Afro-American literature. Brown did, incidentally, publish in 1937 work precisely, in the major object of its scrutiny, a counterpart of Nelson's *The Negro Character,* but in two books, both now available under one cover as Sterling Brown, *Negro Poetry and Drama and The Negro in American Fiction* (New York, 1968). Incisiveness and wit, as well as brilliant perceptiveness, seem never absent from the utterances about literary art attributable to Brown. Moreover, Brown's authority as a commentator on virtually all aspects of life pertaining to the American Negro has long been great. This authority, along with the pleasant and profitable retreat to another generation of scholarship provided by a visit to Brown in his now-distant youth, can impart added dimensions of interest and worth to readings in *Negro Poetry and Drama and The Negro in American Fiction,* whether the Brown so encountered is reflecting upon the treatment of Negroes by white writers or upon the treatment of Negroes and whites by authors of his own color.

There are books even less connected directly and openly with Afro-American literature than any books thus far mentioned here which yet seem to transmit ideas and generate reflections which render them of substantial value to the contemplative review by anyone of the work of black writers. Three such books now are cited here. There may be still nowhere a finer product of its kind than Constance Rourke, *American Humor: A Study of the National Character* (New York, 1931). Merely as an achievement in prose, it is, of course, a thing of beauty. But, then, Rourke had not only thought deeply about her subject, tremendously aided by a philosophic mind and a wealth of information which she had assimilated into syntheses she could articulate in mordant and limpid phrases that, individually, spoke volumes. She also wrote, not for paltry ends, but out of a great love of learning in its most attractive mien. She did "know" America, as few Americans have ever taken their country, with its almost boundless harvest of human thought and feeling, into their minds and hearts. In America's crafts, its song and speech, its music and its dance, she found patterns that revealed to her the very essence of America's past. Obviously she believed that past owed much to humor, the humor Americans had created to help themselves survive whatever may have seemed to them their most harrowing ordeals. And her book is justly famous for its projection of what she calls the comic trio of early America—the Yankee, the Negro, and the backwoodsman. Especially in her chapter "That Long-Tail'd Blue" does she treat the Negro, and there she adduces facts and pursues trains of thought none of which should be omitted from an ideal understanding of the Negro.

In Ralph Ellison, *Shadow and Art* (New York, 1964), a collection of essays supplemented by two interviews and a review of *An American Dilemma,* and Albert Murray, *The Omni-Americans* (New York, 1970), again, as in *American Humor,* generalizations about Afro-Americans and their expression of themselves in forms of art, rather than a detailed systematic treatment of Afro-American literature, in whole or in part, are the treasure to be found. At least two of the essays in *Shadow and Art,* "Change the Joke and Slip the Yoke" and "Richard Wright's Blues," have been closely noted by critics of Afro-American literature. *The Omni-Americans* is subtitled "New Perspectives on Black Experience and American Culture," thus, if in no other way, suggesting its utility for students of Afro-American literature. Both Ellison and Murray were once students at Tuskegee Institute. They are old friends who share a "renaissance" mentality (to speak as Ellison sometimes has) incompatible with the racial chauvinism of the black separatism which appeared strongly in the black aesthetic of America after the Brown decision. It is within the context of their own integrationist beliefs that both Ellison and Murray examine Negro literature. Their refusal to withdraw from the family of man—or, for that matter, of Americans—does not prevent them from an appreciation of the Negro folk and Negro folklore which may seem both more authentic and more intuitive than black-separatist ideology to some because, essentially, it derives from principles of discovery and description not foresworn to divisiveness among ethnic groups.

Additional studies of summary representations of the American Negro by artists of various races include Lemuel Johnson, *The Devil, the Gargoyle, and the Buffoon: The Negro as Metaphor in Western Literature* (Port Washington, N.Y., 1971); William J. Scheick, *The Half-Blood: A Cultural Symbol in 19th-Century American Fiction* (Lexington, Ky., 1979); Wilson Jeremiah Moses, *Black Messiahs and Uncle Toms* (University Park, Pa., 1981); Minrose C. Gwin, *Black and White Women of the Old South* (Knoxville, 1985); and Ronald Takaki, *Violence in the Black Imagination* (New York, 1972). Recent literary theory, with its emphasis upon scientific approaches to knowledge, even in the humanities, is put to sterling use in all of these works. Explicit allusions to early black writers prior to the twentieth century somewhat abound in the first third of *Black Messiahs and Uncle Toms*. For some of the early writers, these allusions, in the manner in which a number of them can pertain to a single writer (such as, for instance, in the case of such allusions to David Walker), may be organized and unified, albeit without lessening the emphasis upon Messiahs and Toms that sets the tone and mood of all of *Black Messiahs and Uncle Toms*, so that, in effect, they become rather comprehensive portraits of individual black writers whom someone may wish to study. Within limits, therefore, *Black Messiahs and Uncle Toms* does qualify as a history of Afro-American literature. It is even, in its own modest way, something of a history of early Afro-American literature.

Black and White Women of the Old South reviews fiction and biography for the treatment in these two genres of literary works of both black and white women from the world of antebellum America in the states which, after Sumter, joined to form the Confederacy. It perceives these women, laws and social customs notwithstanding, as creatures caught and bound, it could not but be, to each other within the same web of violence, a violence grounded in the racism of the South. It is obviously but a step from *Black and White Women of the Old South* to Takaki's *Violence in the Black Imagination*, which does, incidentally, concentrate on black thought in pre–Civil War America, turning particularly to the fiction of Delany, William Wells Brown, and the Frederick Douglass of "The Heroic Slave."

In the long years of the virtual absence of histories of Afro-American literature, some anthologies were (as might surely be safely said) for such histories a form of surrogation. Thus it was especially for Sterling A. Brown, Arthur P. Davis, and Ulysses Lee (eds.), *The Negro Caravan: Writings by American Negroes* (New York, 1941), as influential a single work, most probably, as any ever published about Afro-American literature. Surely, *The Negro Caravan* has been highly visible and highly regarded, too, in circles where a premium is placed on genuine familiarity with Negro literature. During its preparation, Brown and Davis were fellow professors of English at Howard University, where each remained until he retired. The late Ulysses Lee was a professor of English at the now Morgan State University in Baltimore. The success of this trio's collaboration (and their partnership was, patently, very successful) was abetted by their physical proximity to one another. But, above all, this success received by far most of its inner substance from the fitness for their task of this team, to every member of which Afro-American literature was not something to be taken lightly. Each of them was soundly accomplished, and fulsomely practiced, in the study and discussion of the history and criticism of Afro-American literature. Not one of them was merely an "instant" scholar on any significant aspect of black life.

In *The Negro Caravan*, Brown, Davis, and Lee produced a monument to their pride in their own race. They wanted to be comprehensive, even chronologically, in their work. Their anthology includes selections of every mode of literature in which they possessed evidence that the American Negro had been active and is, incidentally, organized into sections by genres, not by historical epochs, although chronological sequence is observed within its sections. Since it was published in 1941, its comprehensiveness in time stops at the beginning of World War II. Unlike many, if not most, anthologies, excerpts from novels do appear in it. One of its sections presents folk literature. The slave narrative, quite properly, is not assigned to this section, but to the section on autobiography. There is a general introduction to the whole volume and introductions to each of the sections devoted to the genres. These introductions are, in themselves alone, if amassed *in toto,* an excellent brief history of Afro-American literature and, as such, moreover, are well supplemented by the headnotes on individual authors and texts. At the end of the book may be found, in parallel columns chronologically coordinated, a listing of memorable events in the history of America and the history, literary and otherwise, of black America. There is no bibliography.

Updatings of *The Negro Caravan* were contemplated but never completed. Its most direct successor is Arthur P. Davis and J. Saunders Redding (eds.), *Cavalcade: Negro American Writing from 1760 to the Present* (Boston, 1971). With Davis and Redding as its editors, the superior quality of the scholarship in *Cavalcade* was assured. Possibly because of its awareness of *The Negro Caravan*, relatively little of it is devoted to Afro-American literature before 1940. There is, indeed, in its preference for attention to Afro-American literature after 1940, the suggestion that it is, to some degree, an extension of *The Negro Caravan*. It is, however, chronologically organized, and it does possess a selective bibliography.

Probably the most attractive value of Ruth Miller (ed.), *Blackamerican Literature: 1760–Present* (Beverly Hills, Calif., 1971), is the direct access it provides to texts of black literature often not easily available to many potential readers of these texts. A sufficient number of such texts were written before 1900 to make of *Blackamerican Literature,* in this regard, a work of possibly unusual interest to students of early Afro-American literature. Excerpts from slave narratives and black folk literature are part of the content of *Blackamerican Literature*. But this is not an anthology which tends to expatiate at length about authors or, for that matter, about conditions generally in the literature it treats. Its bibliography is almost, but not quite, exclusively a recital of primary sources—of, that is, texts written by the black authors of whose lives and thoughts it speaks with clarity and a respect for proven fact.

An interracial team prepared Richard Barksdale and Keneth Kinnamon (eds.), *Black Writers of America: A Comprehensive Anthology* (New York, 1972). Barksdale is black. Kinnamon is white. The pair were colleagues at the University of Illinois when they collaborated on their anthology, weaknesses in which, save as suspected by carping critics, are difficult, if not impossible, to find. Indeed, *Black Writers of America*, anthology only though it be, is no mean history of Afro-American literature, early or late. Anthologies by their very nature tend to omit some writers—always those deemed of less consequence than their fellow writers better situated than they in a rivalry for status—who may well achieve recognition, however small, in histories of literature. Even so, the total array of writers included in *Black Writers of America* is gratifyingly numerous, as well as helpful in conveying a valid concept of the variety and extent of Afro-American literature. Readers of *Black Writers of America* should be thoroughly comfortable with its introductions to the work of individual authors, which are always essays (not hurried headnotes) aptly and adeptly combining thoughtful biography with equally thoughtful literary criticism. The book is divided into parts chronologically. Each part begins with an introduction which places, in the manner and with the means confident scholarship tends to generate, the writers of the period it is intended to depict within their proper setting of an epoch of American life and history. A commendable bibliography, affording references both to primary sources and secondary sources of various appropriate kinds, supplements the book itself.

There is an anthology specifically of early Afro-American literature. It is Benjamin Brawley (ed.), *Early Negro American Writers* (Chapel Hill, 1935). Except for the lack of a bibliography at its end, and any unexplored possibilities of its subject it may have been forced to leave in limbo because of its not being able to use the fruits of research available to *Black Writers of America*, it possesses the virtues of the later anthology. Time spent with Brawley on matters pertaining to Afro-American literature is never, in any case, time altogether wasted, in spite of, as we continue to charge, Brawley's punctilios in taste.

At this moment Eugene B. Redmond, *Drumvoices: The Mission of Afro-American Poetry, a Critical History* (Garden City, N.Y., 1976), stands alone as the only work which seeks to tell the story of Afro-American poetry from its beginning (and beginning here does mean Lucy Terry) until the present. There is nothing dilettante or grossly lacking in intellectual quality about this work.

Moreover, it is replete with circumstantial detail both of the kind delightful and rewarding to literary historians and of that stimulating sort of critical comment which inquisitive minds tend to find tonic for their own creative thought. Redmond is simultaneously a black poet and a university professor. This double identity he exploits to good advantage in *Drumvoices*. He also, in *Drumvoices*, displays an excellent sense of due proportion in his allocation of attention to the different eras of black American poetry. The student of black American poetry will discover essentially all he could want in Redmond's selection of topics to be covered, for Redmond addresses, not only the careers of individual poets, but also group efforts, such as *Les Cenelles* and folk poetry, religious (the spirituals) and secular. He treats with an open mind, and more than an adequate erudition (although he is never pompous and, as a matter of fact, writes prose very well), the issue, too addictive to ideologues, of the relative impact upon black American poets of their African past and their American environment. An extensive, even though selective, bibliography of primary and secondary sources accompanies this work.

The first of the two essays in Blyden Jackson and Louis D. Rubin, Jr., *Black Poetry in America: Two Essays in Historical Interpretation* (Baton Rouge, 1974), reviews black poetry from 1746 until 1923. This essay, by Rubin, emphasizes the urgency apparently felt by the poets of whom it speaks to fashion a language suitable, in their judgment, for their needs. It also recognizes rather notably Albery Whitman's stature as a poet of more than ordinary ability among the black poets of his time. Although sharply focused on one issue and understandably silent about early black poets except those who anonymously contributed to black folk expression, Bernard W. Bell, *The Folk Roots of Contemporary Afro-American Poetry* (Detroit, 1974), a booklet in the Broadside Critics Series, with its judicious deliberations upon more than one theory concerning folk art and its applications of these deliberations to its own examination of selected black poetry, can be valuable in an inspection of Afro-American poetry, whatever that poetry's time of composition. Its title does not prevent Jean Wagner, *Black Poets of the United States from Paul Laurence Dunbar to Langston Hughes* (Urbana, Ill., 1973), from possessing an introductory chapter which is a most competent short history of all of Afro-American poetry, formal and folk, before Dunbar. It may be (and probably should be) added here that Wagner's work has been well received by recognized authorities on Afro-American poetry. Wagner is French. This book, a doctoral dissertation, was originally published in French in Paris.

A work undoubtedly deserving special citation in this place, Joan Sherman, *Invisible Poets: Afro-Americans of the Nineteenth Century* (Urbana, Ill., 1974), remains yet the fullest record of black poetry in its chosen period of time presently available. Twenty-six writers of verse receive close scrutiny within its pages. By design Paul Laurence Dunbar is not one of these twenty-six. Sherman is white, but happily emancipated from the demeaning misrepresentations of Negroes to which Loggins and Nelson were obedient in their day. Both as a biographer and as a critic, she is to be respected. Like *Drumvoices*, *Invisible Poets* probably should be an obligatory item in the library or works consulted of anyone determined to have more than the usual pittance—if that—of knowledge by most Americans of black poetry in America. But Sherman may well have deliberately curtailed her range of ambition in *Invisible Poets*. Protracted excursions into the world of abstruse literary theory do not engage her, nor does she ever depart to any appreciable extent from her provision, throughout her book, of a decidedly forthright (although never too simplistic) marshaling of information very convenient for newcomers to her subject about the individual authors whom she has elected to portray.

Two works must be cited here as usually the first two to be brought to mind when the subject is the history of the Afro-American novel. One of these works is Hugh M. Gloster, *Negro Voices in American Fiction* (Chapel Hill, 1948). The other is Robert A. Bone, *The Negro Novel in America* (New Haven, 1958), of which there have been revisions and paperback editions. Gloster is black and was, quite illustriously, Benjamin Mays's immediate successor as the president of Morehouse College. Bone is white. His scholarly life has been devoted ably and assiduously to the criticism of Afro-American literature. *Negro Voices in American Fiction* examines collections of short stories, as well as novels, by Negro authors. It stops with Richard Wright and some of his black contemporaries. Its bibliography is essentially a checklist of some of the works of fiction it discusses plus recommended titles of anthologies and other works, both books and articles, conceivably useful for the understanding of Negro fiction. The first edition of *The Negro Novel in America* includes Ralph Ellison. Later editions proceed beyond him. Novels solely, and not collections of short stories, as should be expected, are subjected to examination in its pages. Its bibliography somewhat resembles that of *Negro Voices in American Fiction*, although it lists no anthologies. Of both *Negro Voices in American Fiction* and *The Negro Novel in America* it is important to remember, along with an appreciation of their conscientious scholarship, that they constitute still often- and widely used reference works in their field. They both survey the first black novelists.

The temper of a time not like that of the 1940s and the 1950s can hardly fail to capture quickly and powerfully a reader's attention in Addison Gayle, Jr., *The Way of the New World: The Black Novel in America* (Garden City, N.Y., 1975), which occasioned more than a ripple of excitement in circles where black literature is esteemed when it first appeared. Certainly to some older critics of Afro-American literature, this spirited and always purposeful review of its subject may well have seemed at least as much political polemic expressive of a generational gap among black intellectuals as either literary history or literary criticism. Gayle, it must be admitted, in *The Way of the New World* is aggressively the black militant, a champion of a black aesthetic, and a highly vocal excoriator of the black bourgeoisie, who, in his view, have shamefully betrayed the black folk in their bourgeois desire to be white, as the black critics from this same craven (in Gayle's eyes) enclave of black snobbery have played the role of Judas to the masses of black folk in their criticism of black literature. It is a matter of tremendous import with Gayle as to whether Americans of African extraction are called black or Negro. *Negro*, of course, is the term he cannot abide. But, polemicist or not, Gayle is no mean scholar and should be read, if for no other reason, because of his proficiency in the practice of his profession. Moreover, *The Way of the New World* is a significant work because of the audience it has attracted. It does, incidentally, take quite seriously its obligation of depicting without indefensible omissions or grave errors in critical judgment the early black novel. It does not linger in the nineteenth century. But neither does it leave that century so abruptly as to preclude a much more than cursory inspection by it of the first black novelists and their works. That inspection it reconciles, perhaps too anachronistically, with its mandatory mission of evaluating the black novel largely according to Gayle's convictions about the loyalty of that novel to his and his ideological faction's definition of the best interests of black folk. Gayle has softened his animadversions upon the targets of his first attacks, it is only fair to him to report here, with the passage of the years.

No great difference of intended function separates Bernard W. Bell, *The Afro-American Novel and Its Tradition* (Amherst, Mass., 1987), from *The Way of the New World*. Both books seek to explicate elements of sentiment and craft, pervasive (in the judgment of both Gayle and Bell) throughout the corpus of the Afro-American novel, which contribute to a distinctive identity for that novel. Bell is black and, obviously, not co-opted by whites. Blackness as a cult, however, plays no unseemly role in *The Afro-American Novel and Its Tradition*. Actually, *The Way of the New World* and *The Afro-American Novel and Its Tradition* cover much of the same territory without neophytic gaffes and with due regard for the early Negro novel. There may be more of recent literary theory in *The Afro-American Novel and Its Tradition* than in *The Way of the New World*.

For feminists (or, indeed, nonfeminists), Barbara Christian, *Black Women Novelists: The Development of a Tradition, 1892–1976* (Westport, Conn., 1980), affords a deliberately particularized view of Afro-American fiction. It does give extended treatment to Harper's *Iola Leroy*. But its main purpose is to propound and defend a thesis which argues that such a tradition as black women novelists have managed to develop as their own is largely an exponential coefficient of the images of black women projected from the novels of black women novelists. Some of these images, like the image of the woman as lady, are by no means to be associated only with black fiction or black writers. Others of these images, like that rather familiar one of the black female as a loose woman, Christian is able, surely as the long-prevailing folklore about race in America would suggest, to use to very good advantage in the development of her thesis. A major conclusion of hers asserts a greater independence from white influence in their writing on the part of recent black women novelists than on the part of their black predecessors.

As analytic as *Black Women Novelists* is Jane Campbell, *Mythic Black Fiction: The Transformation of History* (Knoxville, 1986). This work reviews fourteen works of black fiction from *Clotel* to David Bradley's *The Chaneysville Incident*, published in 1981, and thus infuses with a substantial accumulation of evidence its debater's conclusion to the effect that the subjects of its study agree in a celebration of the efforts by American blacks to preserve their humanity in the very process, also, of acting as revisionist historians under thrall, even in their revisionism, to their dialectical dream of a better world to come. *Mythic*, nevertheless, should not be viewed here as a term out of place in its inclusion in the title of this book. To Campbell, whatever the tradition she hopes to be defining, the tradition she has in mind cannot be truly comprehended without an appreciation of the role played in its formation by the elements of myth organic to it through the agency of which a culture (obviously, here, the culture of black America) has sought to articulate its profoundest and most cherished conclusions about itself as well as to appeal to the jury of a sympathetically common humanity in any audience to which it may contrive to express itself. No less than *Mythic Black Fiction* a study of culture as well as of literature is Arlene Elder, *"The Hindered Hand": Cultural Implications of Early Afro-American Fiction* (Westport, Conn., 1978). The title of this work is, like the title of *Mythic Black Fiction*, not misleading. The mission of this work is, again like its counterpart in *Mythic Black Fiction*, the calculation of the impact on the first black fiction of a set of cultural forces which seem significantly responsible for the singularities discernible within that fiction.

A general assessment of the rhetorical strategies which have been developed or adopted by black Americans at least in part with some resort to the creative genius of the black folk is patently the result sought in Robert W. Mullen, *Black Communications* (Washington, D.C., 1982). Undoubtedly, however, no black rhetorician has provided, over a long span of years, a more conspicuous example of the successful use of rhetorical strategies among the black folk than the black folk preacher. Apparently that preacher as he was before the twentieth century is yet (and probably is never) to be recalled to life by scholars as precisely, through written remains of him, as any careful appraiser of the past might well wish. Yet this phenomenon of a vanished time does continue vividly to exist by word of mouth among the folk, as in the persistence of much that he supposedly once was in the pulpit utterances of the black folk preacher of today.

Scattered references to this former spokesman for and magistrate to the humble, this wraith of the long-since perished who has still not sunk into complete oblivion, in his authentic original setting of slavery and the antebellum South may readily be isolated in William H. Pipes, *Say Amen, Brother! Old-time*

Negro Preaching: A Study in American Frustration (New York, 1951). Pipes, as obviously he should be, is highly conscious of the close, anything but arbitrary connections between black folk preaching in our contemporary world and the black folk preaching which flourished within the world in which the spirituals were born and nurtured. Nevertheless, the bulk of *Say Amen, Brother!* is an exercise in field anthropology, a collection and an analysis, with the aid of modern methods and scholarship, of sermons delivered, during the 1940s in Macon County, Georgia, by black folk preachers to their congregations of black folk.

To some degree Bruce A. Rosenberg, *The Art of the American Folk Preacher* (New York, 1970), parallels *Say Amen, Brother!* Pipes, incidentally, is black, and Rosenberg is white. *The Art of the American Folk Preacher* establishes its base for clinical observation in congregations of folk Negroes who have left the South and migrated west, to California. Thus, of course, it associates itself with the outstanding single national event of American Negro history since slavery, the folk Negro's transfer of himself from the American South to the American North. No less, however, than *Say Amen, Brother!* does *The Art of the American Folk Preacher* specify the proper interrelations between the behavior in church of the black folk and their preachers which it monitors at first hand and legendary behavior of a similar kind which warrants belief in a tradition—indeed, a strong tradition, old and much repetitious of itself—of black folk preaching. The efforts to describe and dissect, as much as possible by techniques imported from the physical sciences, the sermons of black folk preachers, are considerably more elaborate in *The Art of the American Folk Preacher* than in *Say Amen, Brother!* Both books can be profitably used in acquiring knowledge about blacks, and especially about the black folk, as rhetoricians.

Distinctive qualities, whatever they may be, of Afro-American verbalized expression, along with explanations seeking to account for the nature of those qualities as well as for how and where those qualities became what they have been, obviously are not matters of concern to students of black rhetoric alone. The host of scholars who have pondered long and strenuously over Afro-American literature in various contexts which attempt to relate that literature cogently to art or society, or both, have published more of their own records of their experiments in this regard than can be conveniently all named and annotated in any one bibliography. Still, an intelligent winnowing from among such published records could hardly begin with better examples than with three works by the superbly skilled black critic Houston A. Baker, Jr., *Long Black Song* (Charlottesville, Va., 1972), *The Journey Back: Issues in Black Literature and Criticism* (Chicago, 1980), and *Blues, Ideology and Afro-American Literature* (Chicago, 1984), all of them attempts to do justice to the American Negro both in his uniqueness and in his complex and sometimes puzzling involvement with a large, complicated universe of which he is sometimes—yet not always—a congenial part.

Baker commands enormous respect as a black critic of black literature. For those interested in early black American literature, he can, incidentally, be of great immediate help through the close readings of early black writers—for instance, Phillis Wheatley, Jupiter Hammon, Gustavus Vassa, David Walker, and Frederick Douglass—to be found in his texts. He is also intensely conscious of the criticism by other black critics of black literature and should be consulted, if for no other reason, for his opinions of his colleagues. Reading Baker requires, more often than not, a rather sophisticated level of literacy. He is well schooled in such esoterica as semiotics and deconstruction and relies readily upon resorts, brief or extended, to their creeds, their bodies of knowledge, and their specialized vocabularies. Basically, however, with Baker, it is his polymath's acquaintance with black literature, his solidity as a humanist, and his inborn good sense which must be employed to judge him. And his eminence in the field of the criticism of black literature virtually mandates awareness of his work.

Similarly does the eminence of Henry Louis Gates, Jr., advise acquaintance with him. Gates is also black. He is some seven years younger than Baker. Whereas Baker studied for his degrees on both sides of the American continent, in the District of Columbia and in California, Gates, in a manner of speaking, duplicated this spanning of a great divide, but on the two sides of the Atlantic Ocean, specifically, at Yale and at Cambridge. Among his honors Gates counts a McArthur Fellowship. His interests in black literature have not been unlike those of Baker: the sturdy continuing tradition of black literature and the nature and sources of its claims to some distinctiveness; the criticism of black literature, especially by black critics; and the old, old question of the relationship of black-American literature to America, an obvious corollary, of course, of the conundrum of the relationship of American blacks to American whites.

Three titles associated with Gates may well be particularly pertinent here. They are Henry Louis Gates, Jr. (ed.), *"Race," Writing and Difference* (Chicago, 1986), Gates (ed.), *Black Literature and Literary Theory* (New York, 1984), and Gates, *Figures in Black: Words, Signs and the "Racial" Self* (New York, 1987). For students of early Afro-American literature, sections in *Figures in Black* on Phillis Wheatley, Frederick Douglass, and Harriet Wilson are decidedly worthy of perusal. Gates affects a healthy eclecticism which not only permits him to use, as through a wide-angled lens, the perspectives from the several schools of critics he exploits in his own work, but also renders him a mediating force between generations of black critics. He is, therefore, not a rebel bent only on condoning apostasies from old faiths he deems outworn or never valid. Rather, he promotes a consciousness of the criticism of black literature which tends towards a synthesis of the best insights of all black critics, whatever the generation of black critics to which they have belonged. Not for him should the baby and the bath ever be jointly expelled. Like Baker, however, he can often not be comfortably read by anyone ignorant of current literary theory.

Possibly at least one more work should be bracketed here with the just-cited works of Baker and Gates. That work is Dexter Fisher and Robert Stepto (eds.), *Afro-American Literature: The Reconstruction of Instruction* (New York, 1979), wherein, although Fisher and Stepto are both represented by essays written by themselves, other authors also contribute to the medley of essays constituting the book in its entirety. Even so, a unity of purpose and of ideological stance permits this book to achieve enough of a single voice in its treatment of the problem it addresses, the teaching of Afro-American literature, for it consistently to sound, not necessarily as if it advocates a repudiation of all the criticism of black literature before the 1960s, even that of black critics, but rather like an attempt to promote more use of the cumulative advances in scholarship applicable to Afro-American literature now (although formerly not) available for instruction about that literature. There is no lack of "blackness" in *Afro-American Literature: The Reconstruction of Instruction*. But it is not a "blackness" so intransigent as to preclude the championship of a universal human role for black literature.

In Afro-American literature, autobiography, in some form or other, is a very important genre. No small value, then, attaches itself to at least knowing what blacks have written autobiographically. That much, and more, may be learned from Rebecca Chambers Barton, *Witnesses for Freedom: Negro Americans in Autobiography* (New York, 1948), a work of criticism propounding a thesis (obviously announced in its title) as well as an adventure into literary history. In Stephen Butterfield, *Black Autobiography in America* (Amherst, Mass., 1974), exists another comprehensive treatment of black autobiography. In one of its dimensions, Butterfield's book is something of a census of black autobiographers. Its entire first section, in what surely constitutes enlightened policy, concentrates on slave narratives with particular reference to the themes and structures of such narratives.

The major concerns of Butterfield's work are, to a significant degree, subjected to further expert scrutiny in Sidonie Smith, *Where I'm Bound: Patterns of Slavery and Freedom in Black American Autobiography* (Westport, Conn., 1974), as is the interest in the slave narrative (which, after all, now may be encountered not merely in Butterfield but almost anywhere one cares to look in the professional scholarship on Afro-American literature of the moment). To receive additional evidence of the great strength of this interest, as well as to acquaint one's self with a work which, justifiably, has been highly praised by fellow scholars, one may turn (and fear few, if any, regrets) to William Andrews, *To Tell a Free Story: The First Century of Afro-American Autobiography, 1760–1865* (Urbana, Ill., 1986), which capitalizes both on its author's earnest and long commitment to his subject and on his ability to relate the slave narrative to the cultural and historical circumstances which may account for it and the manner of its development. Andrews does not malinger in any fashion over a treatment of individual autobiographies. A highly rewarding element of his work, however, is his presentation of a theory of evolution for the tradition of black autobiography which confers upon his work a firmly unifying central and summary statement of his conclusions which otherwise it might not have. Poststructuralism manifests itself at times in Andrews' text. Two bibliographies at its end distinguish between black autobiographies and black biographies.

A good argument can be made for the premise that the stage was set for all, or virtually all, of today's scholarly publication about the slave narrative by Charles H. Nichols, *Many Thousand Gone: The Ex-Slaves' Account of Their Bondage and Freedom* (Leiden, 1963), reprinted as a paperback by the Indiana University Press in 1969. Nichols is a black scholar who lived and taught overseas after World War II. He now teaches at Brown University. Scholarship though it is, *Many Thousand Gone* is also a somewhat delightful work of art. Rather than merely proceeding dutifully from one slave narrative to another, it follows the occurrence and reoccurrence of themes throughout many of the better-known of the slave narratives. Part Two, for example, dwells on the lessons to be learned about the slaves' sense of religion and the spiritual side of human existence from a study of slave narratives. Each of its parts, as a matter of fact, is concerned with a specified aspect of the collective consciousness of the American slave as represented by the utterances of individual slaves in the slave narratives. The total effect of *Many Thousand Gone*, however, is much more that of a good, enjoyable novel than of a dull monograph in the social sciences. Moreover, *Many Thousand Gone* must be considered not only a pioneering study about the slave narrative. There has been, for a period of years now, an increasing assertion of the categorical imperative that slaves should be heard about slavery and thus the wrong redressed which permitted a historiography in which virtually all the direct testimony describing slavery was taken from either slave owners or whites who consorted with them. So, *Many Thousand Gone* may also qualify as a pioneering effort in the redress of the wrong just described, the almost total absence from our picture of slavery of the slaves' thoughts about it. Nevertheless, it may not be amiss here to remark that pioneering on a significant scale in the study of the slave narrative can be traced at least as far back in the past as to an unpublished dissertation, submitted and approved at New York University in 1948, written by Marion W. Starling and entitled "The Black Slave Narrative: Its Place in American Literary History."

Comprehensive treatments of the slave narrative include Stanley Feldstein, *Once a Slave: The Slaves' View of Slavery* (New York, 1971), a corrective prescription, like *Many Thousand Gone*, to a unilateral perception of the antebellum South's peculiar institution, which, among other good things, lists in its bibliography over 125 slave narratives dating from 1704 to the 1940s (with the larger number of them dating from 1830 to 1860); Frances Smith Foster, *Witnessing Slavery: The Development of Ante-bellum Slave Narratives* (Westport, Conn., 1979), a truly useful examination of the slave narrative in terms largely

committed to analyzing aspects of the narrative on a level of summary generalization; and John Sekora and Darwin T. Turner (eds.), *The Art of the Slave
Narrative: Original Essays in Criticism and Theory* (Macomb, Ill., 1982), with an
impressive array of contributors, all of standing in the ranks of critics of the slave
narrative, a primary interest in the slave narrative as a form of art, and a bibliography, in its emphasis upon works of criticism, reflective of the primary interest of the book.

Far from exclusively an account of the slave narrative, but surely not to be
ignored as a work with comment on that narrative of value and importance, is
Robert Stepto, *From Behind the Veil: A Study of Afro-American Narrative* (Urbana, Ill., 1979). This book maintains that a valid understanding of Afro-
American narrative requires a recognition of the continuous presence within it
at a level of great significance of, in Stepto's language, a pregeneric myth. This
pregeneric myth, not at all incidentally, Stepto declares, serves, as a convenient
preservative force, the Afro-American's devotion to the quest for freedom and
literacy. *From Behind the Veil* is divided into two parts, designated "The Call"
and "The Response." It is in "The Call" that the slave narrative is considered
and categorized as either "eclectic," "integrated," "generic," or "authenticat-
ing." Deconstruction is decidedly an influence in Stepto's criticism.

Clearly only a step—a short one at that—is needed to pass from the slave
narrative to black folklore, or, for that matter, from black folklore to the
slave narrative. A quick—but not hasty in the derogatory sense—introduction
to Negro folklore may be obtained from the preface to Langston Hughes and
Arna W. Bontemps (eds.), *The Book of Negro Folklore* (New York, 1958). Speci-
mens of forms of Negro folklore covering a wide area of variation, not excluding
song, constitute the text of the book. An attitude toward Negroes in a mode of
thinking often no longer accepted as tolerable controls the selection and presentation of material in Newbell Niles Puckett (ed.), *Folk Beliefs of the Southern
Negro* (Chapel Hill, 1926). Puckett was a white Mississippian with scholarly
pretensions who must be credited in *Folk Beliefs of the Southern Negro* with at
least industry and curiosity. Furthermore, as is well known, stereotypes are never
completely fallacious. Nor is Puckett's research to be altogether disdained. Indeed, its reflection of its era may enhance its worth as it certainly can be conjectured to add a measure of interest to readings in it. The connection between
Afro-American folklore and African folklore may be made more apparent, and
specific, than might otherwise be the case by resort to Richard M. Dorson (ed.),
African Folklore (Bloomington, Ind., 1972). Dorson, incidentally, was white,
but altogether free of Puckett's problems in observing Negroes. Dorson, also,
was highly respected, as he should have been, in his field. Two studies which can
easily be complementary references to Dorson's *African Folklore* are Marion
Berghahn, *Images of Africa in Black American Literature* (Totowa, N.J., 1977),
and Warren L. d'Azvedo (ed.), *The Traditional Artist in African Societies* (Bloom-

ington, Ind., 1973). Robert C. Toll, *Blacking Up: The Minstrel Show in Nineteenth Century America* (New York, 1974), may well serve as a stimulus and aid in the further pursuit of ideas and knowledge about both the true self of the Negro folk and white perceptions of that self as exemplified in the thought patterns of a Puckett. For variety on the subject of black folklore, a variety which can only be more of a help than a harm, two of the essays in Gene Bluestein (ed.), *The Voice of the Folk: Folklore and American Literary Theory* (Amherst, Mass., 1972), discuss black cultural contributions to American music.

To speak of black folk and their music is, certainly for most students of American culture, to introduce a subject without some attention to which no appreciation of the Afro-American in any of his uses of the arts is complete. John Wesley Work, *Folk Song of the American Negro* (Nashville, 1907), represents a fairly early attempt (somewhat significantly by a black scholar) to survey and evaluate black folk music. Work, incidentally, was John Work II. His son, John Work III, also a musician and musicologist, like him worked long years at Fisk, continuing, all the while, to exemplify his father's interest in black folk song. With more of the fruits of the activity of researchers and collectors to draw upon than Work's *Folk Song,* Dena J. Epstein, *Sinful Tunes and Spirituals: Black Folk Music to the Civil War* (Urbana, Ill., 1977), does provide, in a goodly and reliable measure, an expansion of Work. Additionally, the title and organization of this work, as well as its content, emphasize the salient, readily observable fact that the black American folk have tended constantly to solace themselves in duress while simultaneously asserting the artfulness of their creative instincts by a resort to song, whether in the other-worldly accounts of the spirituals or in a lyricism reflective of their secular experience of life.

From two white scholars, practitioners of the social sciences at Chapel Hill in a manner no longer content to cling without serious deviation therefrom to the vicious portraits of Negroes prescribed by the traditions of the Old South, emanated the single volume, Howard W. Odum and Guy B. Johnson, *Negro Workaday Songs* (Chapel Hill, 1926), an effort, not only to acquire some documented evidence of the songs sung by southern Negroes as they performed the manual labor typically assigned them, but also to invest these songs with sociological significance. This work gains in quality from the breadth of interest and practice in anthropological enterprise common to Odum and Johnson in virtually any activity of theirs professionally. For a study of the traditions of song, instrumental music, and the dance developed in Africa and possibly, although not necessarily wholly, transmitted to America, there is Ashenafi Kebede, *Roots of Black Music: The Vocal, Instrumental, and Dance Heritage of Africa and Black America* (Englewood Cliffs, N.J., 1982), and in quest only for the West African origins of solely one form of black American folk song, Samuel Charters, *The Roots of the Blues: An African Search* (Boston, 1981). Anent the Negro spiritual, perhaps the most ambitious and, conceivably, most indispensable treatment resides in the quite large and heavily stored John Lovell, Jr., *Black Song: The Forge and the Flame* (New York, 1972). For years Lovell, a Negro, taught English, never music, at Howard University, where he found time not only to teach but also to publish and travel. Drama concerned him, for much of his career, as a specialty. *Black Song,* however, suffers from no lack of concentration upon the spiritual. It is, moreover, not only a big book many pages long. It is also comprehensive. And it is certainly a major study, if not the major study, of the Negro spiritual now extant. Even so, and for all of its relative brevity, the preface written by James Weldon Johnson for *The Books of American Negro Spirituals: Two Volumes in One* (New York, 1969), which he edited with his brother, J. Rosamond Johnson, remains too much a classic statement about the Negro spiritual to be ignored in a study of that spiritual.

A final category of works for this essay which can possibly aid the study of Afro-American literature includes those which focus on the black press in America. The earliest of such works, Irvine Garland Penn, *The Afro-American Press and Its Editors* (Springfield, Mass., 1891), among other offices it performs, immerses its reader in a resurrection of another age. Penn was a black leader of consequence—not great, yet still considerable—in his own time. Most contemporary students of the black press probably know of, and at least examine, Frederick G. Detweiler, *The Negro Press in the United States* (Chicago, 1922). Three rather recent studies may be combined to add increments of information and serve as appropriate supplements, particularly in the elimination of regrettable lacunae, to the works of Penn and Detweiler. These three works are Roland E. Wolseley, *The Black Press, U.S.A.* (Ames, Iowa, 1971), Penelope L. Bullock, *The Afro-American Periodical Press, 1838–1909* (Baton Rouge, 1981), and Walter C. Daniel, *Black Journals of the United States* (Westport, Conn., 1982). Wolseley's work devotes its second chapter explicitly to the beginnings of the black press. Both Bullock's work and Daniels' are careful and thorough. In Bullock, quick reference is exploited by sections designated as "Publication Data and Finding List," "Geography of the Periodicals," and "Chronology of the Periodicals."

Index